Histories of Labour

Histories of Labour

National and International Perspectives

Edited by
Joan Allen
Alan Campbell
John McIlroy

AAKAR

HISTORIES OF LABOUR: NATIONAL AND INTERNATIONAL PERSPECTIVES
Edited by Joan Allen, Alan Campbell and John McIlroy

Published in agreement with The Merlin Press Ltd., London for publication and sale only in the Indian Subcontinent (India, Pakistan, Bangladesh, Nepal, Maldives, Bhutan & Sri Lanka)

First Published in India 2011

ISBN 978-93-5002-128-6 (Hb)

Published by
AAKAR BOOKS
28 E Pocket IV, Mayur Vihar Phase I, Delhi 110 091
Phone : 011 2279 5505 Telefax : 011 2279 5641
info@aakarbooks.com; www.aakarbooks.com

Printed at
Mudrak, 30 A, Patparganj, Delhi 110 091

Contents

Contributors

Joan Allen is a Senior Lecturer in the School of Historical Studies at the University of Newcastle. She is the author of *Joseph Cowen and Popular Radicalism on Tyneside, 1829–1900* (2007) and editor, with Owen Ashton, of *Papers for the People: A Study of the Chartist Press* (2005). For many years she was Secretary of the Society for the Study of Labour History. She is currently an editor of *Labour History Review.*

Rana P. Behal is an Associate Professor in the Department of History, Deshbandhu College, University of Delhi. He is researching Assam tea plantation labour during colonial rule. He is the co-editor, with Marcel van der Linden, of *India's Labouring Poor: Historical Studies c.1600–c.2000* (2007). Rana is a founding member and Treasurer of the Association of Indian Labour Historians.

Alan Campbell is Honorary Senior Fellow and formerly Reader in Labour and Social History at the University of Liverpool. He is the author of the two-volume *The Scottish Miners, 1874–1939* (2000) and co-editor with John McIlroy and Nina Fishman of *The Post-War Compromise* (2nd edn, 2007) and *The High Tide of British Trade Unionism* (2nd edn, 2007). A long-standing member of the Executive Committee of the Society for the Study of Labour History, he is the Society's Chair.

Malcolm Chase is Professor of Social History at the University of Leeds. A former Chair of the Society for the Study of Labour History and editor of *Labour History Review*, his books include *Early Trade Unionism: Fraternity, Skill and the Politics of Labour* (2000) and *Chartism: A New History* (2007).

Elizabeth Faue is Professor of History at Wayne State University in Detroit, Michigan, USA. The author of *Community of Suffering and Struggle: Women, Men and the Labor Movement in Minneapolis, 1915–1945* (1991) and *Writing the Wrongs: Eva Valesh and the Rise of Labor Journalism* (2005), she is currently working on *Remembering Justice: Labor, the American Working Class, and the Uses of Memory*. She was co-ordinator of the North American Labor History Conference from 1991 to 2003.

Eric Hobsbawm taught until his retirement at Birkbeck College, University of London and subsequently at the New School for Social Research in New York. A founding member of the Society for the Study of Labour History, sometime Chair and long-time President, he is Britain's most eminent historian.

Chitra Joshi is an Associate Professor of History at the Department of History, Indraprastha College, University of Delhi. Her book *Lost Worlds: Indian Labour and its Forgotten Histories* (2003; 2nd edn, 2005) focuses on labour in North India during the late nineteenth and twentieth centuries. Chitra is a founding member of the Association of Indian Labour Historians and a member of its governing body.

Conor McCabe recently completed a PhD on railway workers in Ireland in the early twentieth century at the University of Ulster.

John McIlroy is Professor of Employment Relations at Middlesex University Business School. He was formerly Reader in Sociology at the University of Manchester and Professor of Industrial Relations at Keele University. He has published books on contemporary trade unionism and labour history, most recently John McIlroy, Alan Campbell and Keith Gildart (eds), *Industrial Politics and the 1926 Mining Lockout: The Struggle for Dignity* (2004; 2nd edn, 2009); and Gary Daniels and John McIlroy (eds), *Trade Unions in a Neoliberal World: British Trade Unions Under New Labour* (2009). He is Secretary of the Society for the Study of Labour History.

Takao Matsumura is Emeritus Professor of History at Keio University, Tokyo. He studied for his doctorate at the University of Warwick in the 1970s and taught at Keio until 2007. His publications include *The Labour Aristocracy: The Victorian Flint Glass Makers, 1850–80* (1983); *Japan: From Isolation to Occupation* (2001) with John Benson; and *The Judiciary and History: Unit 731 and Germ-warfare in the Courts* (2007).

Prabhu P. Mohapatra is Associate Professor of Modern Indian History at the Department of History, University of Delhi. His research interests include labour migration, informal work and labour law and regulation. He has published widely on these topics and with Marcel van der Linden co-edited a recent collection *Labour Matters* (2009). He is a founder member and currently Secretary of the Association of Indian Labour Historians, and involved with the Archives of Indian Labour.

Emmet O'Connor is a Senior Lecturer in History at Magee College, University of Ulster. He is a member of the Executive Committee of the Society for the Study of Labour History. His publications include *A Labour History of Ireland* (1992), *James Larkin* (2002) and *Reds and the Green: Ireland, Russia and the Communist Internationals, 1919–1943* (2004).

Bryan D. Palmer is the editor of *Labour/Le Travail* and the Canada Research Chair, Canadian Studies, Trent University. He has published a number of works in Canadian social and working-class history, among them a co-edited collection (with Joan Sangster), *Labouring Canada: Class, Gender, and Race in Canadian Working-Class History* (2008) and *Canada's 1960s: The Ironies of Identity in a Rebellious Era* (2009).

Greg Patmore is Professor of Business and Labour History and Pro-Dean in the Faculty of Economics and Business at The University of Sydney where he is Director of the Business and Labour History Group. He is editor of *Labour History* and President of the Australian Labour History Society. His major publications include Greg Patmore, *Australian Labour History* (1991), Greg Patmore and Martin Hearn (eds), *Working the Nation* (2001) and Greg Patmore (ed.), *Laying the Foundations of Industrial Justice* (2003).

Klaus Tenfelde trained as a miner and a policeman. Since 1995 he has been Professor of Social History and Social Movements at Ruhr-University Bochum, Director of the Institute for Social Movements and Chairman of the 'Stiftung Bibliothek des Ruhrgebiets'. He has published widely on German social and labour history, historical demography and the history of mining. He is currently working on a history of the Ruhr region.

Marcel van der Linden is Research Director at the International Institute of Social History and Professor of Social Movement History at the University of Amsterdam. Marcel's recent books include *Transnational Labour History: Explorations* (2003), *Western Marxism and the Soviet Union* (2007), and *Workers of the World: Essays toward a Global Labor History* (2008).

Preface

Looking Back Half a Century

Eric Hobsbawm

The birth of the Society for the Study of Labour History (SSLH) remains vividly in my memory, because it was responsible for ruining a stylish yellow sheepskin jacket I had recently bought. I wore it to travel from London to Leeds, to discuss the possible foundation of such a society. Like several other historical initiatives the idea of the society, though very much in the air, came from the collective of friends formed in the Communist Party Historians' Group. However, the Cold War was very much at its height in the 1950s in the intellectual and academic world as in the political and strategic, and apt to discriminate against any activity associated with members of the Communist Party (CP), as the troubles of the journal *Past & Present* had demonstrated. Since a commercial publisher, having commissioned me to write a book on the working class, had not long ago flatly refused to publish it on the grounds that it was 'too biased', it seemed advisable that a society of labour historians, however broadly based, should not be officially established or headed by characters like myself. It needed someone like Asa Briggs to put himself at its masthead. I had gone to Leeds to ask him. He agreed, but when I left him the black flakes of soot in the West Riding city atmosphere had settled on the white wool of my sheepskin. It was never the same again.

Asa Briggs was the obvious man to head a new labour history society, since he was, following the death of G.D.H. Cole, the most established academic historian with a record of work in this field and likely to be sympathetic to its objects. As John McIlroy explains in the first chapter in this book, he made the essential contribution to the society's actual foundation, though he did not play much of a part in it subsequently. Older survivors or sympathisers could no longer be expected to take an active part in the proceedings, although we tried to bring them in, notably R.H. Tawney who attended some early committee meetings at Birkbeck, an ancient and noble lion with a rucksack and ash on his trousers who, characteristically, refused our offer to provide him with a taxi. It may be that Lance Beales, notorious for his unwillingness to put pen to paper, also made an appearance, but quickly faded from sight. His lectures on labour history at the London School of Economics in the 1930s had influenced young historians of John Saville's generation there. Of the older generation only Margaret Cole, widow of G.D.H. and sister of Raymond Postgate (who had long put labour history behind him), took a consistent interest in the society. Royden Harrison, one of the most active of the founding members, thought she was instrumental in getting him elected as the official biographer of the Webbs, which unfortunately he was never able to complete. In effect, in the course of the 1950s British labour history had been taken over by the generation that reached maturity just before or during the war, and they were to conduct the affairs of the new Society.

They did so at the historical juncture when, for reasons that are not altogether clear, labour history suddenly acquired an identity and a place in the official institutions of education and learning. There had been very little space for it either in Britain or internationally, except as an adjunct to organizations of labour and the left like the Amsterdam International Institute of Social History (financed by an insurance company close to the Social Democratic Party), which devoted itself to saving archives in the Hitler years, and the initiatives of the leftwing (then CP) millionaire Giangiacomo Feltrinelli, who financed the journal *Movimento Operaio* (1947–55) and established a rival institute of labour and leftwing archives in 1949. Almost all such enterprises then concentrated on socialist or other leftwing organizations rather than working-class history in the broader sense. This is notably true of the postwar academic researches stimulated no doubt by the victory of the Labour Party in 1945, which produced an international crop of theses about the Fabian Society, Henry Pelling's exploration of the background to the foundation of the party, *Origins of the Labour Party* (1954), and several now forgotten American books like Stephen Graubard's *British Labour and the Russian Revolution* (1956), Richard Lyman's *The First Labour Government* (1957) and Philip Poirier's *The Advent of the Labour Party* (1958).

The actual organizations of the labour movement, other than the CP Historians' Group, seem to have contributed little to this research. Even within that group, the position of labour history was uncertain. An early attempt, inspired by Dona Torr, to launch systematic teaching of it in three volumes of documents ('History in the Making') edited respectively by Max

Morris, James B. Jefferys and myself, made no impact. For various reasons two of the authors were to drop out of labour history, and indeed out of active historical research. Later the group found it impossible to write an adequate History of the British Labour Movement requested by the CP, chiefly because the problems of writing realistically about the period since the foundation of the Party proved insoluble for the loyal members most of us were until 1956.

The change around 1960 was quite striking, though it had been anticipated by the relaunch of the Amsterdam Institute's *International Review of Social History* in 1956. The Feltrinelli Institute began to publish its *Annali* in 1958. In Austria, an association of labour historians, Verein für die Geschichte der Arbeiterbewegung, was born in 1959. In France *Le Mouvement Social*, child of the Institut Francais de l'Histoire Sociale (1948), began its current career under Jean Maitron in 1960. An International Commission for the History of Social Movements and Structures inspired by the great French social-economic historian Ernest Labrousse had existed since 1953, under the wing of the International Historical Congresses, and began to publish an ambitious, but at the time still primarily political, *Repertoire International* of sources for the study of nineteenth- and twentieth-century social movements in 1958. The SSLH was founded in the same year as the journal *Labor History* in the USA, a year before the (social-democratic) Friedrich Ebert Foundation began its *Archiv fuer Sozialgeschichte* and two years before *Labour History* was launched in Australia. The rise of labour history was thus by no means an isolated British phenomenon.

Nevertheless, in this country labour history was unlike other countries, for instance France where, to quote Gerard Noiriel, 'the working class has played a major role in politics, but was socially on the margin of society'. In Britain the nature and future of the working class and the labour movement were indeed central problems of British politics, especially on the left, but the industrial working class also had a uniquely strong and visible presence in national life and – through the mass media and football – culture.

Almost all the British labour historians in 1960 were self-educated in the subject, since official teaching had little place for it. There was no major university teacher like Ernest Labrousse in Paris, who fostered a school of socio-economic labour history (and gigantic doctoral dissertations) among the Sorbonne's researchers.

However, for many of the leading British practitioners 'labour history' was also only one dimension of their wider range of historical interests, whether in general history, social and economic history, or literature. Indeed, given the absence of the subject in university syllabuses, those in

British academic posts in the 1950s had to wear some other official hat, most usually as economic historians (Briggs, John Saville, Hobsbawm, Sidney Pollard). Probably most of these academics, though certainly not all, were the first in their families to have undergone a higher education. People in the small academic field of industrial relations (far smaller and less attractive to intellectuals than in the USA) were primarily occupied with practical problems, although the Oxford School with Hugh Clegg from the middle 1960s was to produce the first major history of British trade unions as a whole since the Webbs. Of its members Alan Fox was associated with the Society from the start.

Only in adult education was there much scope for actually teaching or studying the history of the labour movement, though generally in a traditional version. Adult and worker education probably provided the best home for aspiring young labour historians: E.P. Thompson, Henry Collins, J.F.C. Harrison and Royden Harrison. It also provided a home for a unique and vital British component of labour studies, the first generation of people born in the working class benefiting from both war and higher education, who documented and reflected upon their origins. In other countries there was no equivalent in the 1950s to writers like Raymond Williams, Richard Hoggart or the somewhat older Robert Roberts of *The Classic Slum.*

We may reasonably claim that the nation-wide collective of British labour historians played a particularly important part in the international evolution of the field, though in the 1950s British industrialization no longer attracted foreign observers as the pioneer and prototype of world industrialization and its social problems, and there was little interest in British working-class history as such outside the Commonwealth. At all events, after the foundation of the Society during the 1960s the impact of British labour history abroad rose steeply. This is very notable in France. 'The British model' (fostered by Michelle Perrot and Maitron) henceforth played a part in French labour history developments. *Le Mouvement Social* lost no time in keeping abreast of our Society, and a colloquium comparing the development of the two labour movements was soon held (1966) – characteristically in London. E.P. Thompson's *The Making of the English Working Class* enormously reinforced the British influence, long before that remarkable work was translated. Thompson was regarded as an indispensable key figure in the international round tables on social history of the *Maison des Sciences de l'Homme*, which were to meet in Paris and other European locations in the 1970s. I recall Clemens Heller, its chief, making a special day-trip from Paris to London to persuade him to join at a lunch he had pressed me to arrange.

What was our contribution? British labour history helped to widen the subject from the history of political events and organizations, via the study of actual working-class experience, theory and action, into a comprehensive history of the working classes in modern societies. This was not unintentional. At least some of the Society's founders, myself among them, were reluctant to see 'labour history' as a self-contained special field, and for this reason opposed the foundation of a full-scale periodical, publishing articles that should, we felt, find their place in the general history of Britain and the world. Hence the Society initially confined itself to a *Bulletin*, a working set of tools for researchers in the field rather than a journal devoted to publishing their work. In the long run this could not be maintained, but some of us still regret the increased ghettoization of specialized history, including labour history, in separate journals, however technically and professionally inevitable.

I suspect that what made British labour history influential, apart from the sheer size of its community of active practitioners and the high quality of some of the work produced, was its function as a catalyst of political rethinking on the British left. It was the product of an intellectual ferment unique in the old western world in the 1950s. Those who are old enough recall the heady mixture of debates rethinking Marxism and evolving socialist perspectives in successive waves of 'new lefts' which generated some of the most original and passionate contributions to social theory and labour history. Neither E.P. Thompson's *Making*, nor the last and most successful of Raph Samuel's initiatives, the 'History Workshop' movement, nor, for that matter my own *Primitive Rebels*, can be fully understood except as an attempt to find a way forward in left politics through historical reflection. And it was the passion behind these attempts which communicated itself to young intellectuals across the Channel and the Atlantic Ocean and, after the foundation of our Society, made British labour history for a time the most globally influential in its field.

Introduction

Histories of Labour: National and International Perspectives

John McIlroy, Alan Campbell and Joan Allen

Labour history is as old as the labour movement and two centuries on it is still going strong.[1] *Histories of Labour*, which documents the development of the subject in a variety of countries around the world, is published to commemorate the fiftieth anniversary of the formation of the Society for the Study of Labour History (SSLH), its organized expression in Britain.[2] It is simplistic to attribute the progress of any field of scholarship, its ebbs and flows, solely to the activities of associations dedicated to its well-being. A range of factors, from the influence of particular publications to developments in the academy and in politics and culture, have an effect.[3] Even brief consideration of the SSLH's initiatives, its conferences, seminars, publications and proselytisation since 1960, suggests that it is plausible to credit 'the oldest and arguably most important professional association promoting the study of social movements in Britain',[4] with some impact on the fortunes of the field over the last half century.

Those fortunes have been mixed. The two decades from 1960 witnessed the establishment and increasing prominence of labour history in the world of historical scholarship. They constituted in Britain what Eric Hobsbawm termed 'the golden age of labour history'.[5] There followed challenge, even, some felt, 'crisis'.[6] It is commonplace to view the subject in the first period as moving away from the 'old' labour history's preoccupation with the progress and the politics of the labour movement and institutional studies of the Labour Party and trade unions, which concentrated on leadership and policy, to focus more broadly on the working class. It is conventional to associate 'the golden age' with growing acceptance of labour history in universities and academic journals, as well as increased public awareness of the field. It was marked by the ascendancy of histories which turned away from studies of the leadership and the high politics of labour to critical assessments of the social forces moulding movements and their grassroots, to research which encompassed the experience of workers' lives beyond institutions and began to engage more fully with the experience of working-class women and with working-class culture. The field is depicted as relatively cohesive in those years: Marxism provided its directing theory and class its central organizing concept. In this discourse, decline from the 1980s was engendered by the collapse of the Marxist paradigm – the dissolution of the Soviet Union and the Eastern Bloc in 1989–92 is almost routinely invoked[7] – the emerging critique of class analysis in history and the social sciences, the gauntlet thrown down by the burgeoning of gender history and the challenge of 'the linguistic turn'.[8]

In some accounts new approaches to language and gender taught labour historians that class was substantially less important than they had once believed. It was now revealed to some practitioners as a discursive construct, its problematic existence disclosed by decoding the language of texts. Class consciousness and the politics of workers did not, as labour historians had apparently conceived, derive naturally and automatically from the economic and social structure. Nor had class constituted the exclusive, even predominant, sense of identity for workers through history. Gender, ethnicity, religion, craft, region, nation were all significant, sometimes equally significant, sometimes preponderant. Bereft of its simplistic verities, labour history went into decline.[9]

If labour history is to have a future, both its advocates and its critics need to properly comprehend its past. The element of truth in such accounts is undeniable; but it can be exaggerated. It is important to restore the nuances to conventional narratives. If we look more closely, matters were a little more complex. For example, a glance at the work of the Webbs on the one hand and the Hammonds on the other, often bracketed as the twin pillars of the 'old' labour history, confirms that both narrow organizational and broader social histories of the working class were present in embryo from the beginning. Moreover, the critical esteem in which their Marxist successors held the histories, if not the politics, of these Fabian socialists suggests the co-existence and cross-fertilization between different approaches which prevailed after 1960. In similar fashion, Hobsbawm valued the contribution that not only Douglas Cole but the new, institutional Oxford School of industrial relations was making to the history of trade unionism and the research of the emphatically empirical social scientist and Labour Party revisionist, Hugh Clegg.[10] His fellow Marxists, Royden Harrison and John Saville, commended the work of the anti-Communist, social democrat, Henry Pelling, on the Labour Party. Harrison's revision of the bibliography in Cole and Raymond Postgate's *The Common People* illustrated the ecumenism and pragmatism of British labour history.[11]

All of which tells us something about the Marxism which was indubitably integral to the labour historiography of 'the golden age'. It is necessary to specify and situate its nature and note that it was but one, albeit significant, strand in 'the new labour history', although the subject is often identified with it. Students will search this literature in vain for dogmatic explication of the laws of social development and dour adumbration of historical inevitability. One of us noted in a tribute to Saville that he consciously put aside the vulgar Marxism of his youth: 'He was a theoretical empiricist who worked in the archives and prioritized primary evidence.'[12] The critical concepts that Saville and other Marxist historians brought to bear in understanding and ordering that evidence included, as Edward Thompson put it: 'exploitation, class struggle, class determinism, ideology [...] concepts derived from and validated within a Marxist theoretical tradition'.[13] Within that framework, Marxist historians of labour were engaged, as Thompson explained, in an encounter with 'an evidence which is not infinitely malleable or subject to arbitrary manipulation [...] there is a real and significant sense in which the facts are "there", and that they are determining, even though the questions which may be proposed are various and will elucidate various replies'.[14] This 'empirical Marxism' provided common ground between Marxists and historians of different persuasions.

And there were differences between Marxists. Thompson's iconoclastic understanding of class turned on experience mediating between being and consciousness. In pronouncements varying over thirty years, he sometimes found it impossible to give theoretical priority to the 'economic' over the 'cultural'. His work stood as testimony to the openness of Marxist labour history, its creativity and vitality.[15] Hobsbawm, in contrast, maintained a more traditional Marxism in relation to class and the role that the base and superstructure played in historical development.[16] The Marxisms of labour historians were varied and eclectic. The work of Royden Harrison may be contrasted with that of Hobsbawm or John Foster, the work of Walter Kendall with that of James Hinton. In later years, Thompson found himself questioning whether the term 'Marxist' adequately described what he was about.[17] A range of labour historians held different views on structure and agency and culture and politics, and many other issues. As the writings of Harrison, Hobsbawm, Thompson, Pelling, Asa Briggs or Ross McKibbin suggest, class was important to labour historians, Marxist or otherwise. But the literature embraced more than one conception of class.[18]

Theory, values and evaluation, explicit or implicit, embedded or elaborated, are inevitable in the writing of history. Another of the SSLH's founders, J.F.C. Harrison, put matters simply:

> At some point the historian is required to transcend the perceptions of contemporaries, suggest a pattern of interconnectedness of events, and offer a tenable explanation. This pattern may be an elaborate and sophisticated theory of history, such as some version of Marxism, or it may be little more than an implicit belief that in the long run things get better [...] Most readers will find it acceptable to think about the history of the common people in terms of development and evolution [...] An alternative to some form of evolutionary theory is the idea of the people as an eternal presence.[19]

Marxisms have been important and the ways in which they have informed labour history have frequently proved fruitful. But the same applies, as Harrison suggests, to varieties of labourism and reformism, popular then and now. Labour history in Britain has always been theoretically and conceptually pluralist. From its birth it included a range of philosophies, approaches and methods. After 1960, political and institutional history continued to appear, indeed there was too much of it for the sensibilities of some contemporary social historians and later critics of labour history. Nor did new approaches entirely dispel antiquarianism and romanticism or the taste for description over explanation. What was perhaps more important in distinguishing the 'new' from the 'old' labour history was not so much the transcendence of institutionalism or the domination of Marxism as the switch in the site of its production. The Webbs, the Hammonds, Cole for some of his career, Postgate, Robin Page Arnot, never worked in universities – while Thompson's *William Morris* and *The Making* were written outside the walls. For better or for worse, their research and writing about the past formed a seamless part of their political activity. The new labour history brought in not only the workers beyond parties and unions, but also the universities. They brought in professional requirements, specialization, scholarly prestige and academic careers. The SSLH is illustrative of the point: unlike other societies in Ireland and, to some extent, Scotland, Wales and Australia, which recruited from the labour movement, by the 1980s it consisted predominantly of professional historians.[20]

This may help us to be a little less epistemological in explaining the difficulties labour history has encountered in Britain since the 1980s. The advent of neoliberalism, the disorientation of the left, changes in politics and economics, are relevant: labour was no longer at the centre of public policy, it was no longer a successful social actor. The collapse of the Eastern bloc had little to do with it.[21] Few labour historians in the 1980s subscribed to any totalized Marxist paradigm, still less one associated with the Soviet Union. Rather, in their practice some were judged guilty of 'capitulations to "empiricist ideology"'.[22] Nor is the emphasis that some place on the frailties of the conceptual anatomy of the field particularly convincing. It is difficult to agree that labour history in Britain from the 1960s to the 1980s was dependent on the simplistic theory of structural determination which some commentators insist it hinged on. Any serious excursion through the literature will demonstrate how few labour historians operated from that premise.[23]

Like the investigation of any branch of the discipline, close scrutiny of the historiography of labour will reveal elements of teleology and structural determinism. It will disclose Marxists struggling with determination and agency and work which is far from innocent of the complexities of mediations and reciprocities between structure, social experience, class and politics.[24] The labels applied by critics, who usually avoid detailed exegesis, do not do justice to the rich diversity of the subject.[25] Even Leninists accepted that politics did not develop naturally from economic and social conditions. Politics needed to be constructed through agitation, propaganda, political discourse, via the agency of human beings organized in a political party. This is not to diminish in the slightest the significance of economic and social structure as a starting point in understanding historical change. Analysis of the complicated, interactive relationships between structure and values, identity and action, how class is constructed and influences the actions of individuals, are indispensable to satisfactory explanations of political developments. The social-economic paradigm remains intensely relevant.[26] It is, however, to reject as myth the assertion that labour historians as a group, or labour history as a category, assumed that values, consciousness or politics were predetermined by structure.

The arrival on the agenda of theories of gender and language constituted an innovation of tremendous creative significance. Expanding our vision and methodology, it was welcome to all perceptive labour historians. A central truth in conventional accounts is that labour historians had neglected the importance of multiple identities in understanding, evoking and explaining the past. Awareness of the need to repair such neglect was widespread. The difficulties began with the consequent attempts to diminish class. In some of these accounts there was a failure to relate, order and prioritize identities in their historical context; others, employing a strong dash of presentism, accorded gender and divisions based on gender, primacy over class. For some, class became just one among a congeries of multiple, competing identities and for others an emphasis on gender or ethnicity dominated explanation.[27] Yet the evidence confirmed that class was the principal, although not the exclusive, instrument structuring experience in capitalist society. Class was the primary, but not the singular, prism through which most men and women in history had grasped the limits and possibilities of their lives.[28] Refusing essentialist theories of patriarchy or 'whiteness', most labour historians found no difficulty in integrating gender, ethnicity and other forms of oppression into thinking about the past which continued to see class as central. It rendered understanding history more difficult. It made writing it more complicated. In the end, it enriched it, although the promise of extensive work which fully incorporates gendered perspectives into class analysis remains to be fulfilled.

Similar, if more critical, points may be made about 'the linguistic turn'. Some labour historians found it stimulating. In this view it redirected attention to the important dimensions of language and subjectivity. It encouraged authorial self-consciousness and critical reflection about the way positivist history was constructed and composed by fallible human beings with a variety of values and viewpoints inescapably embodied in their creations. Its emphasis on the role that language played in linking structure and action, material conditions and consciousness, was sometimes perceived as illuminating.[29] Historians, some practitioners felt, should be initially sceptical about meta-narratives, imaginatively interpret evidence and be alert to the fragility of our retrieval of the past; scholars could learn from linguistic analysis and literary criticism, and the art and technique of story-telling. This, however, was part of the paraphernalia. It was already accepted by many historians, if arguably in need of restatement and refreshment.[30]

At the core of 'the linguistic turn' lay a relativism, a denial of objective knowledge and an assertion of the unknowability of the past corrosive of history. At its heart lay a linguistic determinism which rejected existing conceptions of class and the relevance of social and economic forces in explaining what happened in the past.[31] With the exception of Patrick Joyce, it is difficult to recall a single labour historian, at least in Britain, who was transformed by postmodernism or quit the field because of it.[32] Most historians and most labour historians questioned its philosophy; and, looking at the work labour historians have subsequently published, the majority failed to see how it could improve their practice.[33]

It is therefore rather difficult to see these challenges as contributing in fundamental fashion to a crisis in labour history, as distinct from a caricature of labour history. The subject's lack of a strong identity and institutional anchorage in universities by the 1980s is perhaps more pertinent to its problems.[34] Many labour historians came from economic or social or modern history or related fields, others taught in adult education before progressing to internal departments. They continued to hold appointments in those subjects and to identify themselves as such, rather than as labour historians. Labour history typically figured in the academy as a component of courses in economic or social history or other subjects. It was rarely taught as a subject in its own right. It never achieved the critical mass of staff and students necessary to embed itself as a distinct subject across higher education and repel encroachment.[35] When the academic world was transformed – partly through cultural changes as history from below diversified to take account of multiple forms of oppression but predominantly through political intervention – resistance was subdued. There was no centre to hold.

The impact of the policies of Conservative governments between 1979 and 1997 on universities, scholarly values and 'subversive subjects', changes in funding, (as well as career progression and early retirements), the demand for more fashionable courses, in a climate where labour in all its manifestations was unfashionable, secured a large degree of academic consent. The popularity of new approaches to history reinforced specialization. Interest in the labour movement had constituted a unifying factor. It declined with the movement. Labour history, always a limited coalition, fragmented; many of its adherents moved on. It was, and is, difficult to see this as primarily an internal, intellectual crisis of labour history.[36] Books and articles of quality continued to appear. The advent of Tony Blair and New Labour encouraged a new interest in labour politics and the announcement of a range of 'new' labour histories.[37] As departments of economic and social history were wound up, there was further fragmentation. Falls in the membership of the SSLH, the Economic History Society, the Social History Society as well as individual subscriptions to *History Workshop Journal*, suggested abatement of the historiographical revolution of the second half of the twentieth century or that many historians had lost the habit of association, aligned themselves with different trends in the discipline of history or turned their hand to ancillary fields.[38]

Reverses must be registered. The point we want to make, while eschewing complacency, is that they are serious but they are not intrinsic and therefore they are not terminal. The assertion that labour history in Britain faltered because it was little more than the property of a group of reductionist

Marxists who predicated unmediated connections between economics, class and politics, 'an intellectual cul de sac' which fell prey to 'political vanguardism', [39] is caricature not description. Labour history has always been a broad church. It has always been pluralist and it has always employed a plurality of Marxisms. It has, on the whole, been intellectually rigorous and resilient. The values it has demonstrated in the past remain indispensable to its revitalization and its future. What it has lacked since the 1980s has been a sense of identity. Too few scholars declare, 'I am a labour historian', rather than 'I am an economic historian', 'a historian of gender', 'a historian of industrial relations'. Too few speak out for labour history.

'The history of the common people', Hobsbawm wrote in 1988, 'no longer needs commercials.'[40] If it wishes to transcend antiquarianism, identity or heritage and 'do-it-yourself' history – none of which are without value and potential – if its purpose 'is not simply to discover the past but to *explain* it and in doing so to provide a link to the present',[41] it palpably does. Similar sentiments may be applied to other countries where the field has passed through transitions of various kinds and where historians of labour still look forward to a positive, if different, future.[42] It is in that spirit that this collection which surveys in some detail labour historiography around the world, discusses the literature, and addresses the work of labour historians, rather than stereotyping it to disregard it, is offered to readers.

A factor encouraging a guarded degree of optimism for the future is the enthusiasm for labour history which has developed in recent years outside the traditional strongholds of the field in Europe and North America. This has been accompanied by increasing attention to transnational labour history. The formation of the SSLH was part of an earlier wave of engagement with labour history across the globe. From its inauguration the Society built links with labour historians in Europe, North America, Australia, India and Japan.[43] A new wave of transnational history is presently emerging, particularly associated with the efforts of the International Institute of Social History in Amsterdam.[44] But national histories will, in all likelihood endure and transnational endeavour is only as strong as its national components permit. To facilitate ground clearing, stocktaking and learning from each other, the present volume assesses trends since 1960 in eight countries.

Other collections have looked at key issues in labour historiography such as class, gender and ethnicity and at moves towards transnationalism in theory and practice.[45] Jan Lucassen's *Global Labour History* contained essays on the history of labour movements in a number of countries as well as a number of papers on national historiographies.[46] *Histories of Labour* is the first text dedicated to historiography and related organizational developments. It surveys Britain, Ireland, the USA, Canada, Australia, Germany, India and Japan, and concludes with a plea for a global labour history. It is perforce incomplete. Latin America, North Africa and Russia have been discussed elsewhere.[47] A variety of reasons denied us contributions from France, South Africa and China. Despite these qualifications, we hope the book will prove useful to academics and students of history and related disciplines because of the authoritative but accessible introductions it provides to how things stand around the globe.

Contributors were charged with discussing the state of the historiography of labour in Britain and seven other countries. We asked them to concentrate on trends in the literature since 1960 and make brief reference to associations of labour historians. Given the provenance of the volume, three chapters are devoted to Britain. John McIlroy provides a snapshot of the formation and development of the SSLH. Joan Allen and Malcolm Chase assess the literature on labour in the nineteenth century published since 1960. Finally Alan Campbell and John McIlroy explore the historiography dealing with twentieth-century labour. These chapters focus in more detail on some of the developments touched on earlier in this introduction.

Ireland is examined in a chapter by Emmet O'Connor and Conor McCabe which begins with the trade union leader and socialist agitator, Jim Larkin, who also organized in Britain and America. It offers a number of contrasts with both these countries. Modern labour history started later in Ireland, during the 1970s. The Irish Labour History Society (ILHS), like the societies in Scotland and Wales but unlike the SSLH, forged close links with the trade unions and included working-class activists among its ranks. Together with its journal, *Saothar*, established in 1975, it remains buoyant. In a country where debate has recently centred on received and revisionist versions of the national narrative, the role of labour has constituted a subsidiary part of the historiographical agenda. Measured by the university curriculum and full-time posts in the field, labour history is relatively marginal. Yet this small country has produced a substantial literature, starting with the pioneering contributions in the 1970s and 1980s of John Boyle, Charles McCarthy and Arthur Mitchell. The historiography remains in an empirical mould. It is still skewed towards movements and leaders, trade unionism, working-class politics and auto/biography. Nonetheless, culture, religion, leisure, mentalities, gender and ethnicity are receiving attention and there is cross-fertilization with social scientists and, more recently, scholars of industrial relations.

American labour history has been different, in its size and sophistication and in its recent concerns. By the 1970s the new labour history, which attempted to transcend the emphasis on labour movements, industrialization and trade unionism pioneered by the 'Wisconsin School' of John R. Commons, Richard T. Ely and Selig Perlman, had consolidated its hold. Its influences embraced the American New Left, the social sciences and British Marxist historians such as Christopher Hill, Hobsbawm, Thompson and George Rudé. It was expanded by an abundance of gifted scholars, of whom Irving Bernstein, David Brody, Melvyn Dubofsky, Herbert Gutman and David Montgomery were only the most prominent. As Elizabeth Faue emphasises in her essay, the new labour history embodied not one but several approaches to writing the history of the American working class. For example, institutionalism was enriched rather than superseded.

Advance was embodied in the publication and popularity of the journals *Labor History*, *Radical History Review* and *International Labor and Working-Class History*. Conceptions of the working class were amplified by the growth of women's history and gender history, in which Alice Kessler-Harris and Joan Wallach Scott were influential, and histories of ethnicity and 'race' and racism, marked initially by interest in the work of W.E.B. Dubois and C.L.R. James. Nonetheless, the 1990s witnessed in America, as they did in Britain and Europe, heart searching about the health of labour history. There were anxieties about the continuing utility of class and its relation to gender, 'race' and ethnicity as competing categories of analysis, concerns about the implications of 'the linguistic turn' and worries about organizational as well as intellectual fragmentation in the absence of a national association. The latter gap was filled with the foundation of the Labor and Working-Class History Association in 1997. By the twenty-first century it was reasonable to conclude that the relationship between class, gender and ethnicity had enriched rather than impoverished the ability of historians to understand the working-class experience by providing an integrated, multi-dimensional tool. Work by, among others, Kessler-Harris, David Roediger and Jacquelyn Dowd Hall had reinforced the historiography and its heterogeneity. For Faue, the emergence of the Working-Class Studies Association and even the split in *Labor History* in 2004, which produced another new journal, promised progress through diversity.

The fortunes of American labour history since the 1960s constitute a reproach to those who see the contemporary state of scholarship as invariably related to the contemporary state of organized labour. Trade unionism in the USA has been in more or less sequential decline over the last fifty years. Canadian trade unions, in contrast, experienced a degree of renewal in the 1980s and 1990s. There have been similarities and differences in the way the field has unfolded in the United States and its northern neighbour. 'Canadian labour history', one British commentator remarked in the 1980s, 'deserves to be better known – and better regarded – than it is at present.'[48] Twenty-five years on, this has come to pass. As Bryan Palmer points out, Canadian labour historians have come to exercise influence on their country's historiographical mainstream and in the academic profession. In Canada, labour history did not need to emancipate itself from industrial relations and labour economics. It was nurtured by historians cast in the mould of the influential social-democratic scholar, Kenneth McNaught and personified by his students, David J. Bercuson and Irving Abella. If this generation was resistant to Marxism, the opposite went for the next generation. This group, in which Greg Kealey and Palmer were prominent, wrote cultural social histories centred on class struggle. They drew on the approaches of Thompson and Gutman and the New Left. In Quebec, the Francophone historiography was influenced by the methods of the *Annalistes* and Ernest Labrousse, and inclined towards institutional studies.

The Canadian Committee on Labour History and the journal, *Labour/Le Travail*, reflect the standing of labour history in Canada. In the 1980s and 1990s, research raised arguments about which kind of Marxism best explained social change, the limits of class analysis and the role of trade unionism. The literature developed to cover numerous aspects of the working-class experience. Women's history held strong appeal but its relation to the gender history associated with 'the linguistic turn' provoked debate. As in other countries, historians of labour are confronted with the dilemmas of diversification, academicization, identity and commitment. Labour history is written by scholars who would not call themselves labour historians. The integration of the subject into wider disciplines is cause for both congratulation and concern. It has implications for the future of a distinctive labour history in the academy but also, as Palmer stresses, for what labour history has to say to workers about their contemporary predicament.[49]

The field retains a strong presence in Australia. Since the 1960s, it has followed a similar path to that trodden in other countries in its own particular fashion. Inspirational and commemorative work, mixing history, legitimation and propaganda, gave way to professional histories, sometimes informed by the ideas of what Greg Patmore in his contribution terms 'the Old Left'. The work of academics, notably Robin Gollan and Eric Fry, inspired the creation of the Australian Society for the Study of Labour History (ASSLH) in 1961 – exactly one year after the establishment of its British counterpart. Its early years saw continued emphasis on political and institutional history. Developments in the 1970s again paralleled change elsewhere. Influenced by the Marxism of the post-1968 New Left, innovation in Britain and reaction against the older generation, younger historians, such as Terry Irving, Humphrey McQueen, Stuart Macintyre and Ann Curthoys, turned from studying organizations to studying class relations, workers' culture, women workers and racism. There was continuity: the older history still appeared, although the ASSLH journal, *Labour History*, reflected the popularity of new trends.

History from below influenced the way in which political and institutional history was written. Labour history showed itself receptive to a range of trends, from feminism to Harry Braverman and labour process theory, from studies of ethnicity in the Australian context to the influence of a recharged industrial relations. Rumours of the death of labour history have been more restricted than in other settings. In Australia, the field is characterized by a diverse historiography in which most aspects of the subject retain purchase. Histories of the labour movement remain resilient in the face of some decline in publications on gender, ethnicity and race and new interest in labour culture and anti-labour history. ASSLH conferences often reflect traditional agendas. In comparison with some other countries, the Society maintains close links with labour movement activists.

Germany's past is more chequered: the discontinuities in its history have influenced how history is conceived and written. In the German Democratic Republic from the 1950s to the 1980s, labour history dominated the broader discipline. Resources were devoted to the construction of teleological narratives of workers' movements which satisfied the agendas of a self-styled 'workers' state'. There were gains in knowledge. The price was often interpretive distortion which naturally favoured the Communists, their self-selected ancestors and the Soviet Union, privileged organization at the expense of the proletariat itself and attempted to wall-off students from historiographical innovations in the West.

In the Federal Republic, the new generation of historians after 1945 were often trained by those who had held university appointments during the National Socialist years. Younger scholars such as Gerhard Ritter and Helga Grebing made their mark in what was still very much 'the history of workers and workers' movements', with the emphasis on parties and unions. Neo-Weberian sociology, the *Annalistes* and Anglo-American historiography were increasingly important. From the 1970s the expansion of German universities was associated with the 'socio-historical turn'. There emerged what was, in comparison with some other countries, a social history of scope and sweep. One strand sought to locate the paths German labour had taken in the structural, systemic development of the economy, polity and society from the nineteenth century. Less unusual was subsequent engagement with the history of 'the everyday life of the common people' – which came to concentrate on the National Socialist era – and the appearance of gender history. In recent years, the compartmentalization of labour history common to other countries has become apparent. In the conclusion to his chapter, Klaus Tenfelde judges that a great deal of interest remains in the history of labour in Germany. However, changes in the composition, culture, politics and organization of the working class have ruptured the nexus between workers' movements and 'the history of workers and workers' movements'.

India has followed a different road, although again historiographical changes reflect to some degree developments elsewhere. The academic labour history of the 1950s, was, as in other countries, focused on institutions, sometimes insulated from economic and social change and even from the workers themselves. The continuing context included the twin teleologies of Marxism and modernization theory and the focus was on the organized, male, factory employee. The 1970s witnessed increased attention to peasant movements and rural protest. However, much research remained locked in the problematic of progress and transition on the Western or the Eastern model.

As Rana Behal, Chitra Joshi and Prabhu P. Mohapatra illustrate in their chapter, by the 1980s there was an attempt, influenced by Thompson and perhaps best represented by Dipesh Chakrabarty, a leading member of the Subaltern Studies collective, to eschew economic determinism and produce history from below. Historians refused master narratives based on the history of Europe and unilinear trajectories of change, and turned to explore culture in its own terms. Some claimed that the danger of a new cultural determinism lurked inside this 'post-colonial' approach. Others pointed to the danger of fixed conceptions of cultural reproduction. Such concerns sparked a variety of important studies by writers such as Raj Chandavarkar, Joshi, Janaki Nair and Dilip Simeon. This is the background to a revitalization of labour history as scholars have extended the emphasis away from the factory and plantation to the home and community, from men to women, from the employee to those working in the informal sector, the labouring poor and untypical forms of work and bondage. The formation of the Association of Indian Labour Historians in 1996 and its subsequent successful conferences promise a renewal of substance.

Japan escaped colonialism but not a form of fascism. Its labour history reflects the disruption experienced in Germany as well as the influence of modernization theory and Marxism found in India. Many of the themes in the historiography will find resonance in India, particularly Kazuo Okochi's rural migration theory, Masao Maruyama's conception of Japanese workers as 'atomized labour' and the developmental Marxism which examined the working class through the lens of Stalinist and Maoist conceptions of progress. The 'return to the peasant' in the sub-continent in the 1970s has parallels with the work of the people's historians in the Islands. An enduring preoccupation has been explaining why management-trade union relations took the form they did. As Takao Matsumura, McIlroy and Campbell suggest in their essay, subsequent innovation, the turn to social history, gender and the recuperation of racism reflected global changes. This pattern is also apparent in English language histories: recent work by the Australians Stephen Large and Joe Moore and the Canadian John Price combine history from below with political and sociological inflections. Integration of a range of approaches encased in social history has been the hallmark of the writings of the American historian, Andrew Gordon.

Japanese scholars have taken a persistent interest in the history of labour in other countries. A number of our contributors suggest that, in the face of the globalization of capital and labour, transnational approaches and a turn to global history are essential to the future vigour of our subject – and, it might be added, to the vitality of global labour. From Chile to China, Lima to Liverpool, workers are thinking and organizing internationally. In that context, Marcel van der Linden's essay constitutes an appropriate conclusion to the collection. The argument is that labour history needs to overcome aspects of its past rooted in Eurocentrism and methodological nationalism. A stimulus is provided by the recent surge of the subject and of organizational networks in 'the South', particularly in Africa, India and Latin America. In this narrative it is imperative to move towards a world history which is transnational in spirit and execution, which works against the national grain by inserting historical processes in their international context, by assessing interaction and by embedding comparison in research and writing about labour. Global history entails expanding our conceptions of labour, work, class and exploitation. It embraces not only the workplace but the household and the family and forms of informal and unfree labour as well as waged employment. In some cases it necessitates going beyond the conventional temporal boundaries which associate labour history with capitalism. Above all, it requires the transcendence of Eurocentric assumptions and methods.

This seems a good point with which to conclude the introduction and start the book. Reflecting on the defeats that European workers suffered during the nineteenth century and on his hopes for the twentieth century, Edward Thompson remarked: 'Causes which were lost in England might in Asia or Africa still be won.'[50] If that is to remain a possibility in the new century, in the face of innumerable obstacles, then labour historians have a contribution to make. In his popular celebration of labour's past dedicated to arming those fighting on the front lines of today and tomorrow, Paul Mason observes: 'If the new labour movement fails to thrive and the old one continues to decline, the least we can do is preserve the story of those who built the original.'[51] We can also help, at least a little, to recharge older movements and educate new ones by recuperating and illuminating the struggles, successes and failures of the past, in the new world as well as the old. Hopefully we can do this in work which like Thompson's is inspirational as well as scholarly, which privileges analysis, explanation and understanding but stimulates anger and action. Reading the following chapters, including those on Britain, has gone some way to refreshing our spirit. They have dispelled at least some of the doubts sounded at the beginning of this introduction. We hope they will have a similar impact on our readers.

Notes

1 The origins of labour history in Britain are usually associated with the work of Sidney and Beatrice Webb. It has recently been furnished with a longer pedigree stretching back to Thomas Ruggles' *The History of the Poor: Their Rights, Duties and the Laws Respecting Them*, 2 vols, 1793–4: see Jan Lucassen, 'Writing Global History, c.1800–1940: A Historiography of Concepts, Periods and Geographical Scope', in *Global Labour History: A State of the Art*, ed. idem (Bern: Peter Lang, 2006), pp. 39–90 (pp. 75–80).

2 The Society for the Study of Labour History (SSLH) has always been formally a British and informally an English society. Chapters in this book deal with developments in Britain rather than treating England, Scotland, Wales and Northern Ireland as distinct entities. A more fragmented approach, providing more detail, might have done greater justice to developments in Scotland and Wales – labour historians in Northern Ireland have usually been members of the Irish society – but would necessitate a longer text. Readers are referred for details to Rob Duncan, 'The Scottish Labour History Society: A Retrospect', in *Making History: Organizations of Labour Historians in Britain since 1960*, *Labour History Review* (*LHR*) Fiftieth Anniversary Supplement, April 2010, 115-23; Emmet O'Connor, 'The Irish Labour History Society: An Outline History', in ibid., 143-55; Deian Hopkin, 'Llafur: Labour History Society and People's Remembrancer, 1970–2009', in ibid., *125-42*.

3 John McIlroy, 'The Society for the Study of Labour History, 1956–1985: Its Origins and Its Heyday', in *Making History*, 17-110.

4 Stefan Berger, 'Introduction', *Mitteilungsblatt des Instituts für soziale*

Bewegungen, 27 (2002), 1–18 (p. 15).

5 Eric Hobsbawm, 'Preface', in idem, *Worlds of Labour: Further Studies in the History of Labour* (London: Weidenfeld and Nicolson, 1984), p. x.

6 David Howell, 'Editorial', *LHR*, 60, 1 (1995), 2.

7 See, for example, the reference to the doubts about the emancipatory potential of the labour movement harboured in the 1980s by 'a new generation of historians who had been disillusioned with the Stalinist dictatorships [...] the collapse of Communism had brought widespread assumptions of the imminent demise of labour history': Berger, 'Introduction', p. 5; and 'Labour does face a crisis both because of the collapse of Stalinist certainties [...] and because Tony Blair is challenging the whole history of what labour and the Labour Party is about': Keith Flett, 'Urgent Action Needed', *LHR*, 60, 3 (1995), 49; '[...] current perceptions of labour history in crisis [...] the collapse of "actual existing socialism" in the Soviet Union and Eastern Europe has already provided a trigger [...] Pessimism about the prospects of labour history has developed on the left': JLH and DM, 'The Labour History Prospect', ibid., 51.

8 Howell, 'Editorial', p. 2.

9 See Andrew August, 'Introduction', in idem, *The British Working Class, 1832–1940* (Harlow: Pearson Longman, 2007), pp. 1–6 (pp. 1–3).

10 Eric Hobsbawm, 'Trade Union Historiography', *Bulletin of the Society for the Study of Labour History* (*BSSLH*), 8 (1964), 31–36; idem, 'Trade Union History', *Economic History Review*, n.s., 20 (1967), 358–64 (p. 359).

11 John Saville, 'The Radical Left Expects the Past to Do Its Duty', *Times Higher Education Supplement*, 13 February 1976; Royden Harrison, 'Recommended Books', in G.D.H. Cole and Raymond Postgate, *The Common People, 1746–1946* (1st pub. 1938; London: Methuen, 1966), pp. 689–719.

12 John McIlroy, 'Obituary: John Saville, 1916–2009', *LHR*, 74 (2009), 330–38 (p. 332).

13 E.P. Thompson, *The Poverty of Theory and Other Essays* (London: Merlin Press, 1978), p. 14.

14 Ibid., p. 30.

15 See, for example, Harvey J. Kaye, *The British Marxist Historians: An Introductory Analysis* (Cambridge: Polity Press, 1984), pp. 172–215.

16 Ibid., pp. 153–56.

17 E.P. Thompson, 'Agenda for Radical History' (1st pub. 1995), in *The Essential E.P. Thompson*, ed. by Dorothy Thompson (New York: The New Press, 2001), p. 492.

18 And, as Neville Kirk has usefully reminded us, the 'mainstream' of the new labour history always had its critics: Neville Kirk, 'The Continued Relevance and Engagements of Class', *LHR*, 60, 3 (1995), 2–15 (p. 5).

19 J.F.C. Harrison, *The Common People: A History, From the Norman Conquest to the Present* (London: Fontana, 1984), p. 17.

20 See the references in n. 2 and Emmet O'Connor and Connor McCabe, 'Ireland', chapter 4, and Greg Patmore, 'Australia', chapter 7, in this volume, which refer to the closer relations that labour history societies in these countries developed with labour movement activists, many of whom became members. Of course,

different conditions pertained.

21 Cf. 'I do not know of a single western medievalist whose views it [the collapse of the Soviet Union] altered': Chris Wickham, 'Memories of Underdevelopment: What Has Marxism Done for Medieval History and What Can It Still Do?', in *Marxist History-Writing for the Twenty-First Century*, ed. by Chris Wickham (Oxford: Oxford University Press, 2007), p. 33. Substitute 'British labour historian' for 'western medievalist' and the sentiment applies equally to our subject.

22 Thompson, *Poverty*, p. 31.

23 David Howell, 'Reading Alastair Reid: A Future for Labour History?', in *Social Class and Marxism: Defences and Challenges*, ed. by Neville Kirk (Aldershot: Scolar Press, 1996), pp. 214–35.

24 See, for example, Ira Katznelson, 'Working-Class Formation: Constructing Cases and Comparisons', in *Working-Class Formation: Nineteenth-Century Patterns in Western Europe and the United States*, ed. by Ira Katznelson and Aristide R. Zolberg (Princeton: Princeton University Press, 1986), pp. 3–41; Neville Kirk, 'Decline and Fall, Resilience and Regeneration: A Review Essay on Social Class', *International Labor and Working-Class History*, 57 (2000), 88–102.

25 See McIlroy, 'Society', 101-110.

26 Richard Price, 'Surveying and Synthesizing Labour History', *BSSLH*, 56, 3 (1991), 37–39; idem, 'The Future of British Labour History', *International Review of Social History*, 36 (1991), 249–60.

27 See, for example, Sylvia Walby, *Patriarchy at Work: Patriarchal and Capitalist Relations in Employment* (Cambridge: Cambridge University Press, 1986); Sonya Rose, *Limited Livelihoods: Gender and Class in Nineteenth-Century England* (London: Routledge, 1992); Joan Scott, 'Gender: A Useful Category of Historical Analysis', *American Historical Review*, 91 (1986), 1053–75; idem, *Gender and the Politics of History* (New York: Columbia University Press, 1988); idem, 'The "Class" We Have Lost', *International Labor and Working-Class History*, 57 (2000), 69–75; and AHR Forum, 'Revisiting "Gender: A Useful Category of Historical Analysis"', *American Historical Review*, 113 (2008), 1344–1430.

28 Cf. the conclusion of a recent empirical survey: 'In the decades since 1940 broad changes in British society have transformed the experiences of working men and women in significant ways [...] Perhaps surprisingly, given these changes, class identity has proved resilient and remains central to how men and women understand themselves and society': August, *British Working Class*, p. 247. For discussion of these issues, see Price, 'The Future of British Labour History'; Henry Srebrnik, 'Class, Ethnicity and Gender Interwined: Jewish Women and the East London Rent Strikes, 1935–40', *Women's History Review*, 4 (1995), 283–99; the contributions in *Social Class and Marxism: Defences and Challenges*, ed. by Neville Kirk (Aldershot: Scolar Press, 1996); *Languages of Labour*, ed. by John Belchem and Neville Kirk (Aldershot: Ashgate, 1997), 'Introduction', pp. 1–8, and passim; Kirk, 'Decline and Fall'; Mike Savage, 'Class and Labour History', in *Class and Other Identities: Gender, Religion and Ethnicity in the*

Writing of European Labour History, ed. by Lex Heerma van Voss and Marcel van der Linden (Oxford: Berghahn, 2002), pp. 55–72; Alice Kessler-Harris, 'Two Labour Histories or One?', in ibid., pp. 133–49; John Belchem, 'Ethnicity and Labour History: With Special Reference to Irish Migration', in ibid., pp. 88–100.

29 John Belchem, 'Reconstructing Labour History', *LHR*, 62 (1997), 318–23.

30 One element in this was the influence of Raymond Williams and *Culture and Society* on the New Left historians, particularly Edward Thompson: see, for example, Dai Smith, *Raymond Williams: A Warrior's Tale* (Cardigan: Parthian, 2008), pp. 8–9, 308–9, 409–11, 422–23.

31 Mike Savage and Andrew Miles, *The Remaking of the British Working Class, 1840–1940* (London: Routledge, 1994), pp. 14–20.

32 Patrick Joyce, 'The End of Social History?', *Social History*, 20 (1995), 73–91.

33 Cf. Richard Price, 'Postmodernism as Theory and Practice', in Belchem and Kirk, *Languages of Labour*, pp. 12–43.

34 McIlroy, 'Society', 23-25, 90-98, details the position of labour history in the universities in the late 1950s and the early 1980s.

35 See McIlroy, 'Society', 90-98.

36 Cf. the comments that, in the context of Thatcherism, 'around 1980 in fact the fight drained out of the academy': Wickham, 'Memories of Underdevelopment', p. 33; and John Saville's reflection: 'The majority of British academics are technicians [... they] do not form part of an intelligentsia concerned with the wider cultural or political issues in the world [...]': John Saville, *Memoirs from the Left* (London: Merlin Press, 2003), p. 1.

37 Steven Fielding, '"New" Labour and the "New" Labour History', *Mitteilungsblatt des Instituts für soziale Bewegungen*, 27 (2002), 35–50 (pp. 46–49).

38 For SSLH membership, see John McIlroy, 'Organized Labour History in Britain: The Society for the Study of Labour History after Fifty Years', chapter 1 in this volume. The Social History Society has 370 members today compared with 700 two decades ago; *History Workshop Journal* has less than fifty individual subscribers. The fact that the labour history societies in Ireland, Scotland and Wales have to some extent bucked the trend, although their memberships have also declined, suggests it is not structurally determined.

39 Fielding, 'New Labour', passim.

40 Eric Hobsbawm, 'On History From Below' (1st pub. 1988), in idem, *On History* (London: Weidenfeld and Nicolson, 1997), p. 201.

41 Ibid., p. 214.

42 See, for example, *International Review of Social History*, 38 (1993), Supplement 1, 'The End of Labour History?'; Ira Katznelson, 'The "Bourgeois" Dimension: A Provocation About Institutions, Politics and the Future of Labor History', *International Labor and Working-Class History*, 46 (1994), 1–32; Marcel van der Linden and Jan Lucassen, *Prolegomena for a Global Labour History* (Amsterdam: IISG, 1999); Janaki Nair, 'Paradigm Lost: The Futures of Labour History', in Heerma van Voss and van der Linden, *Class and Other Identities*, pp. 150–59.

43 See McIlroy, 'Organized Labour History in Britain'.

44 Marcel van der Linden, *Global Labour History* (Amsterdam: IISG, 2006).
45 Heerma van Voss and van der Linden, *Class and Other Identities*; Marcel van der Linden, *Transnational Labour History: Explorations* (Aldershot: Ashgate, 2003); Marcel van der Linden, *Workers of the World: Essays toward a Global Labour History* (Leiden: Brill, 2008).
46 Lucassen, *Global Labour History*.
47 Frederick Cooper, 'African Labor History', in ibid., pp. 91–116; Zachary Lockman, 'Reflections on Labor and Working-Class History in the Middle East and North Africa', in ibid., pp. 117–46; Andrei Sokolov, 'The Drama of the Russian Working Class and New Perspectives for Labour History in Russia', in ibid., pp. 397–454; John D. French, 'The Latin American Labor Studies Boom', *International Review of Social History*, 45 (2000), 279–308.
48 John Benson, 'Canadian Labour History', *BSSLH*, 51, 1 (1986), 18–24 (p. 18).
49 See also Bryan D. Palmer, '*Fin de Siècle* Labour History in Canada and the United States: A Case for Tradition', in Lucassen, *Global Labour History*, pp. 195–226.
50 E.P. Thompson, *The Making of the English Working Class* (London: Gollancz, 1963), p. 13.
51 Paul Mason, *Live Working or Die Fighting: How the Working Class Went Global* (London: Harvill Secker, 2007), p. xiv.

1

Organized Labour History in Britain: The Society for the Study of Labour History After Fifty Years

John McIlroy

From the vantage point of 2010, it is difficult to recapture the very different world of the late 1950s, which constituted the context in which the Society for the Study of Labour History (SSLH) was born. The events of that period are easily recalled. Its structure of feeling, the ethos of its politics, the way history was organized, taught and written, how historians and their students felt about it, are harder to evoke. There was, among many of the Society's founders, a sense of change, an awareness that things were on the move. By 1959, when the creation of the Society was under discussion, there was a thaw in the Cold War, at least on the Home Front. The events of 1956 – Khrushchev's secret speech on Stalin, Hungary and Suez – promised 'the break up of the political Ice Age'.[1] They opened up new vistas for disillusioned sections of the left. Many had been disappointed by Labour's performance in office between 1945 and 1951 and its subsequent turn away from the left and Bevanism towards Gaitskellite revisionism. Others were now disenchanted with the Communist Party (CP). In high politics, the 1950s remained a right-wing decade, a fact emphasized by the Conservative Party's third successive electoral victory in 1959. On cinema screens *I'm All Right Jack* (1959) and *The Angry Silence* (1960) lampooned shop stewards. Yet the trade unions, stronger features of civil society and popular consciousness than they are today, remained dominated by a right wing loyal to Labour's revisionist leaders, despite significant change in the Transport Workers' Union. But by 1959 a New Left had crystallized. It cohered around the response to 1956, the emergence of CND, the resilience of inequality and the infirmities of the official movement, Labourist and Communist.[2]

The universities – a handful compared with today – substantially excluded the working class and recruited a tiny, privileged proportion of Britain's youth. Their conservative atmosphere, satirized in Kingsley Amis's *Lucky Jim*, was reflected in the mild McCarthyism which disqualified some members of the left from academic appointments, particularly in the early years of the decade.[3] On the whole, History departments were centres of common sense and moderation; the dominant philosophies were those of Isaiah Berlin, Sir Geoffrey Elton and Sir Lewis Namier. A downplaying of ideas, ideology and theory, and an assertion of objectivity which suited the Cold War climate, hegemonized mainstream historiography. There was a preference for high politics and political narrative as against long-term analysis and structural, social and economic explanation, a predilection for empiricism and the accumulation of facts rather than theorizing about them.[4]

There were countervailing tendencies. Economic and social history, T.S. Ashton, Mounia Postan and R.H. Tawney, had their place, although there were not, as there would be later, university departments dedicated to those fields. They rarely penetrated the mainstream. The appearance of *Past and Present* in 1952 and its involvement by 1959 of English non-Marxists such as Geoffrey Barraclough, Hugo Jones, Lawrence Stone and John Elliott, as well as representatives of the *Annales* school in France, illustrated the potential that radical social history possessed.[5] Its younger advocates chafed against the state of the world; or stoically endured it. The ice was cracking. After 1956 there was 'some unfreezing' of debate between historians and by the end of the decade there were other hopeful signs.[6] In 1960 E.H. Carr was composing his Trevelyan lectures which would detonate a small explosion in mainstream history.[7] The changing of the guard was symbolized, in different ways, by the passing of the pioneer of 'old' labour history, G.D.H. Cole, in the winter of 1959 and perhaps the most admired professional historian of the postwar period, Namier, in the summer of 1960. The emergence of the New Left, its critical stance on the labour movement and its accent on socialist humanism, the power of human agency and the centrality of cultural work gave some encouragement to history from below. On a wider front, the last years of the 1950s produced a small but increasing stream of academic literature dealing with diverse aspects of the history of labour.[8] John Saville retrospectively remarked: 'A more or less automatic reaction to the growing output of serious writing on the history of the British labour movement was the formation of a national society which would bring historians together for critical discussions.'[9]

I

The SSLH held its inaugural conference at Birkbeck College, London, on Friday, 6 May 1960.[10] The initiative came from a small and mixed group of scholars who wanted to develop labour history in the universities and popularize it beyond them. The idea had been in the air and the possibility had been discussed for some time. Part of the driving force of the early Society emanated from historians who had belonged to the CP before the ferment of 1956, many of whom were now active in the New Left. They included Henry Collins, Royden Harrison, Eric Hobsbawm (still a party member), Saville and Edward Thompson. Their experience and their mentors, particularly Dona Torr, 'taught us historical *passion* [...] She made us feel history on our pulses. History was not words on a page, not the goings-on of kings and prime ministers, not mere events. History was the sweat, blood, tears and triumphs of the common people, our people.'[11]

Such sentiments were shared by many on the left; they found favour with only a handful of academic historians. In an age when societies of historians were beginning to proliferate, historians of labour were looking for a home, a community and a pressure group which might advance their subject. The case for a broad association transcending the old CP group, rather than a narrower Marxist or socialist grouping, was canvassed and accepted by most of its members and former members. However, the inception of the project which produced our Society and its detailed planning must be credited to the social historian Asa Briggs, formerly Reader in Recent Social History at Oxford and at that time Professor of Modern History at the University of Leeds, and his colleague, J.F.C. Harrison, who served as Deputy Director of that university's department of adult education. They involved Royden Harrison, then teaching miners on day-release classes at the University of Sheffield extramural department, Saville, who was a senior lecturer in economic history at Hull, and Hobsbawm, who was preparing adult students for degrees at Birkbeck College, University of London. After further soundings, Briggs and Harrison convened the working group which met at Leeds in January 1960 to plan the inauguration. Sidney Pollard, a lecturer in economic history at Sheffield, Henry Pelling, at that time a Fellow of The Queen's College, Oxford, and Frank Bealey, a collaborator of Pelling, who taught politics at what would shortly become Keele University, also merit mention.[12]

Briggs was the doyen of the coming generation of social historians. His research was on the nineteenth century; it pioneered the local dimension and reflected his interest in labour. Working on the tail end of that century, Bealey and Pelling were studying the origins of the Labour Party; excavating the middle of it, Collins would shortly publish, together with another founding member, Chimen Abramsky, a volume on the First International, while Royden Harrison was researching the political role of the labour aristocracy; at the other end of the 1800s, and stretching further back into the previous century, Thompson, already known for his *William Morris*, was labouring on what would become *The Making of the English Working Class*. Saville did a bit of everything. Hobsbawm, who was becoming prominent by the end of the 1950s in the wake of his contributions to the controversy about living standards in the industrial revolution, his seminal essay on the labour aristocracy and his unusual, transnational *Primitive Rebels*, was likewise noted for an omnivorous intellectual appetite.[13]

The Society's influences were, as they would continue to be, catholic. Marxism, often of the New Left, anti-Stalinist variant, mingled with social democracy and left labourism; affiliation to different versions of economic and social history brushed shoulders with advocacy of varieties of institutional and political history. Moreover, Society activists taught a range of subjects beyond history: present, at the beginning, were industrial relations scholars, political scientists and sociologists. Adult education, and the freedom it offered to experiment, innovate and cross disciplinary lines, was particularly important: of the founders, Collins, the two Harrisons and Thompson worked in university departments of extramural studies while Briggs was president of the Workers' Educational Association (WEA). Amateur historians were represented by the formidable presence of Brian Pearce, later by the veteran engineering union activists Eddie Frow and Stanley Hutchins, and archivists and librarians by Willi Guttsman from the University of East Anglia and Irene Wagner and later Christine Coates, from the Labour Party and TUC respectively.[14]

In the Britain of 1960, history remained identified with practitioners such as Namier, Elton and, more popularly, A.J.P. Taylor.[15] Political and constitutional history still dominated the discipline, although E.H. Carr was already adumbrating some of the challenges of a new history which sought patterns in the past and attempted to explain their causes as well as their relevance to the present and the future. Published the following year, *What is History?* directed attention to the part that economic and social forces played in historical change. It suggested the need for historians to embrace the social sciences, as well as look beyond Europe, and it encouraged the minority of postwar historians who possessed an interest in social history, the working class and internationalism.[16]

In 1960 labour history meant the Webbs, the Hammonds, G.D.H. Cole and Raymond Postgate, as well as a wealth of fading endeavour around the adult education bodies, the National Council of Labour Colleges (NCLC) and the WEA. Labour History had developed outside the universities. It was marked to various degrees by sympathy with the labour movement and desire to celebrate its evolution and facilitate further progress, typically conceived in reformist, occasionally revolutionary terms, by providing it with an understanding of its past which would inspire and inform future advance. Teachers of labour history in adult classes, relatively free of the constraints of history departments, had the advantage, stressed by Thompson, of interacting with workers to the benefit of their scholarship. They had to negotiate the tensions between explaining the past in all its complexity and pedagogic pressures to smooth out its complications and ambiguities in order to cater for sometimes committed audiences. Indubitable achievement in NCLC and WEA-university extramural classes – faltering by the 1950s – has to be measured against a record which at times suggests occlusion of difficulty in heroic, black and white narratives, as well as an artificial cultivation of objectivity in some WEA work which, it has been argued, could debilitate judgement and constrain commitment.[17]

In the academy labour history was growing but remained marginal, although some of the Society's founders carried the influence of G.D.H. Cole in his last academic incarnation as Chichele Professor of Social and Political Theory at Oxford, and the lesser known but intellectually infectious Lance Beales, whose impact on future historians as a teacher at the London School of Economics, and Cambridge in wartime, exceeded his record of publications.[18] Special papers in labour history were offered at five universities while the subject formed a smaller component of teaching on a variety of broader courses in fourteen other higher education institutions. In comparison with some other areas of historical enterprise, particularly abroad, innovative technique and publications of quality remained lacking.[19]

The Society's purpose, in that faraway world of Khrushchev and Kennedy, Hugh Gaitskell and Frank Cousins, where television remained a novelty, men worked in factories and women laboured as housewives, where there was a colour bar for bus drivers in the Midlands, where professional footballers were paid a maximum of £20 a week and everybody knew the name of the world heavyweight champion, was to change all this. Its constitutional objectives were broad and straightforward: 'to encourage study, teaching and research in the field of labour history and to safeguard the preservation of labour archives'.[20] Stimulus came with the creation and ensuing resonance of key texts. The collection on Chartism edited by Briggs and published in 1959 was immensely influential. *Essays in Labour History,* which appeared in the year of the Society's formation, edited by Briggs and Saville with contributions from many of the founders, demonstrated the quality and range of current research. Uneven in the light of what was to come, often insightful sketches, these volumes suggested an agenda for change.[21] A fair wind came with the high sixties. From the middle years of that decade, there was a qualitative expansion of higher education; a more open, liberal and iconoclastic social and political atmosphere which continued into the 1970s; an explosive growth of trade unionism, industrial militancy, political radicalism and feminism; and, every bit as important, the agency of a relatively small number of energetic historians who took advantage of the new climate.[22]

By autumn 1960 the Society had 71 members. Membership increased annually. In spring 1967, the total figure had climbed from 538 the previous year to more than 700. By September 1972, there were 675 individual members with 203 subscriptions from libraries and 27 from trade unions and political bodies. In 1980 the total passed 1,000 members. The 1980s and 1990s, harder going, educationally and politically, provided a decidedly less receptive environment and membership gradually subsided to around the 650 mark. Yet even today the Society still enrols around 200 members with a further 150 subscriptions. Membership was and has always been diverse. It has encompassed a range of educational bodies and roles from postgraduate students to professors, from local historians to union officials. Financial crises, in 1968 and in 1980–2, were rare. They were weathered. A substantial element of stability was secured by careful husbandry after the decision, in which Saville played a key part, to seek charitable status in the early 1980s.[23]

The architects of the Society were deliberate in their designation. Economic history, Emmanuel Le Roy Ladurie's 'history without people', should embrace the study of workers: from that vantage point and despite improvements, the way it was typically taught in the academy was restrictive. Social history was too diffuse. As generally understood in Britain in the 1950s it referred to the history of customs, manners and everyday life. Popularly associated with Eileen Power and G.M. Trevelyan, it was sometimes coupled with economic history, glossing the latter's predominance. Some of the Society's founders would, as the 1960s developed, move like the *Annales* historians in France towards a conception of social history as a total approach to the past. Rejecting the terminology which might evoke either '*histoire totale*' or what would come to be sometimes disparagingly termed '*histoire obscure de tout le monde*', the founders consciously chose 'labour history'.[24] It represented their desire to place labour at the heart of historical enquiry, their conviction that the history of labour was important but neglected, and their affiliation to, and sometimes engagement with, organized labour. These were characteristics that they shared in different ways with the large majority of Society members.[25]

This left open the question of what approach was to be applied to labour history. Taking their cue from Cole, many of the SSLH's initiators believed that in the teaching and writing of history scholarly rigour could be combined with political commitment. The latter could spur the former but in relation to the existing historiography there existed a palpable need to deepen and extend scholarship. Pluralism was again conscious and calculated. Many of the founding cadre and probably a majority of the membership were advocates of history from below who were exponents of, or influenced by, various forms of Marxism, although they were far from eschewing 'history from above' or anathematizing institutional analysis, if it was good. To the chagrin of theorists such as Perry Anderson, they were, for the most part, empirical Marxists who insisted on work in the archives. They emphasized the need to transcend often celebratory organizational studies of labour movements by embedding institutional histories in their context, in class and capitalism. They aspired to go beyond the prevalent, often uncritical, attention to activists and leaders. They wanted to develop social history, to write the history of the common people, to reconstruct their everyday life, and to capture how they thought and felt as well as how they organized industrially and politically – without disdaining organization, or activists or underestimating the importance of leaders.[26] The degree to which they were able to achieve this and the extent to which, as the Society evolved, these aspirations were shared and prioritized by other Society members varied.

From its inception, the Society was open and ecumenical. It was a network and a forum not a school. Its purpose remained the exchange of ideas, the dissemination of research, research opportunities and new approaches and techniques embodied in research, in order to develop and popularize the field. Its major publication for three decades, the twice-yearly *Bulletin of the Society for the Study of Labour History*, was built around reviews, reports, debates and bibliography. It was launched, and its mission carefully guarded into the 1990s, as a unique 'tool of the trade' rather than a competitor to learned journals such as *Past and Present* and the *International Review of Social History*.[27] Originally motivated by understandable caution and scarcity of resources – the latter continued to play a constraining role – the preference for a *Bulletin*, rather than a journal, was also related to the conception that SSLH activists should begin to develop labour history through permeating the broader discipline of history. This would ensure that the significance of labour was properly recognized and its historiography gradually embedded in existing journals, degrees and departments, initially in those devoted to economic and social history. In this view, to attempt to launch a new, autonomous field was premature or, for a small minority, questionable on grounds of fragmentation.[28] In retrospect it may be thought that at some stage a journal would be perceived as helpful to any qualitative extension of interest in labour history.[29]

The Society's twice-yearly conferences, frequently attended in the 1970s and 1980s by around a hundred participants, covered – and continued to cover – almost every aspect of the developing field. They provided a platform for labour historians of all denominations. As reflected in recollection and confirmed by consultation of the *Bulletin*, the quality of reviews by and large exceeded that of academic journals today; the same went for the quality of writing; historical argument was, by current standards, robust, forensic, far-ranging, but rarely *ad hominem*. Properly regulated by authoritative officers and editors, it furthered the creation of an intellectual community.[30] The *Bulletin* also embodied members' interests in bibliography, historical periodicals and the location and preservation of records. An archives committee was established in the mid-1960s and Edward Thompson served on it for several years. There was recognition that the historian's vocation involved more than lecturing in the university or writing for an academic audience.

II

Perhaps inevitably, professionalization and the concerns of the universities won out over popularization and a public role. Scholarship, measured by the academy, predominated over wider dissemination and nurturing an audience beyond the profession. There was heart searching over how the Society could rehabilitate the teaching of labour history in the adult education classes from which many of its founders came, how it could reach out into the trade unions and later how it could influence funding opportunities for university postgraduates.[31] Little was achieved in any of these spheres but there were occasional public interventions.

In the 1970s the Society became involved in controversy over the withholding, weeding and destruction of documents by government departments prior to transfer to the national archives, particularly the 'recall' of police papers being reviewed for release under 'the thirty-year rule'. This culminated in questions in the House of Commons, discussions with cabinet ministers about the preservation of labour records and the publication in the *Bulletin* of police documents passed to its editor, Royden

Harrison, by a sympathetic source.[32] Unlike, for example, some of their West German counterparts, British labour historians possessed no formal affiliation with the Labour Party. But the Society took albeit a small part in its archival work and the successful negotiations which brought into being the National Museum of Labour History, first at Limehouse, London, and subsequently at Manchester.[33] That there were limits to what could be achieved in relation to the labour movement was illustrated by the Society's restricted role as advisor in a dispute between a member and the leaders of the Yorkshire Area of the National Union of Mineworkers over publication of an official history of the union.[34]

We were blessed with a relatively large repository of talented, active members and continuity in our leading officers. Suitably replenished, the founders presided over twenty years of progress.[35] In the immediate aftermath of the Society's creation, advance was embodied in a flow of multi-faceted contributions, different in their focus, approach, texture and technique. A few may be singled out: J.F.C. Harrison's novel integration of the development of adult education and the regional progress of the labour movement (1961); Pelling on the history of trade unions (1963); Clegg, Fox and Thompson's similarly institutionally-anchored examination of the formation of systems of industrial relations (1964); Hobsbawm's *Age of Revolution* (1962), *Industry and Empire* (1968) as well as the multi-facetted collection, *Labouring Men* (1964); Pollard's pioneering exploration of the emergence of modern management (1965); Royden Harrison's *Before the Socialists*, which carried forward the debate on the labour aristocrats, their origins, existence, ideas, influences and political strategies (1965); Peter Nettl's *magnum opus*, *Rosa Luxemburg* (1966); and the second volume of *Essays in Labour History* (1971).[36]

If Hobsbawm's work was broadest in scope and synthesis, and reached an audience beyond the confines of the universities, most influential in terms of its innovatory, totalizing approach, popular appeal and extraordinary impact around the world was Thompson's *Making of the English Working Class* (1963).[37] Taken together, these impressive texts suggested the extensive lineaments of the field and evoked the distinctive geology of different areas of the acreage coming under cultivation within it. They ignited an explosion of interest in British labour history beyond Britain. But the 'new labour history' was not without its critics. Questioning of the nature and uses of class, assertion of the essentially moderate, bread-and-butter concerns of workers and accentuation of the Liberal inheritance of the trade unions, featured in the 1960s as well as the 1980s.[38]

Intellectual advance was reflected in the inclusion of labour history to a greater degree than hitherto in university curricula as well as in enhanced public interest in the subject. This was recognized in Thompson's appointment in 1965 at the new University of Warwick where, from 1968, he headed a free-standing Centre for the Study of Social History and was succeeded from 1971 by Royden Harrison.[39] The establishment of an MA in Comparative Labour History at the Centre and the provision of doctoral opportunities attracted an array of talented students, from Britain and overseas. These initiatives produced a throughput of graduates who, in their turn, took up teaching appointments and strengthened earlier developments. The work of the Centre, and the freedom it initially enjoyed, stimulated scholarship and publication in a number of areas, notably the history of crime, law, leisure, sport and trade unionism, particularly, but far from exclusively, among craftworkers and miners. Its Masters degree in British and American labour history encouraged transnational and comparative thinking.

It was an era of generous state funding. Social Science Research Council (SSRC) studentships assisted the development of the Centre. Funds from the Leverhulme Trust facilitated the creation of the Modern Records Centre at Warwick (1973); it quickly became the most important repository of employer and trade union records. Leverhulme funding also enabled the publication of the monumental *Guide to British Labour Periodicals*.[40] The *Dictionary of Labour Biography* was very much the achievement of John Saville. Its conception and growth were nurtured by the Society and its members.[41]

Progress was uneven but in these years it was incontestable. By the 1980s labour history had matured. It had come in out of the cold and had permeated the mainstream of history. In Britain, the 1970s and early 1980s witnessed the high point of labour history and the achievement of much of what the Society's founders had hoped for in 1960. It was the turn to the social history of the working class that took the eye. There was an outpouring of research on most aspects of working-class life, on standards of living, on poverty, work, food, housing, credit, leisure, sport and migration.[42] But institutional and political histories continued to appear, sometimes demonstrating a greater grasp of context than had been displayed in the past, and so did studies of different groups of workers at different times, work which tracked in detail the distinctive ways in which they had organized and engaged with capital.[43]

The role of women changed and women's history became popular.[44] Traditional controversies about the immiserization or otherwise of workers during and after the industrial revolution and the existence or otherwise of a labour aristocracy and its role in explaining developments in the working class during the nineteenth and twentieth centuries, took on a new lease of life and an additional sophistication and attracted the impassioned interest of younger historians.[45] Teleology, narratives of assumed solidarity and organic unity and paradigms of proletarian progress were leavened by growing awareness of complexity, of fissures, fractures and difference in class, and the experience of class, constituted by gender, race and ethnicity as well as by exploitation. The intractabilities of structure, the state, the economic and political environment, and the relationship between agency and structure were increasingly perceived as a central issue for labour historians.

The achievement was real, although not without its problems. Social history, which momentarily promised to deliver the dream of a total history embracing labour history,[46] was already disclosing a deficit between ambition and its realization. Academic specialization, providing depth but sometimes militating against breadth and vision, continued its advance. The new social history, it was pointed out, neglected politics.[47] But it also neglected trade unions.[48] Conceptions of 'the forward march of labour' still informed much writing and on the whole, despite Carr's injunction in 1961 to transcend insularity, it remained circumscribed by British preoccupations. There was little systematic comparison with other countries, other varieties of capitalism or other labour movements.[49] Some still perceived a major purpose of labour history as 'producing the kind of history needed if the working class is to realise its historical mission in this country'.[50] Yet apart from questions of essentialism, pre-ordination and destiny, as well as the conflicts between the complexity necessary in the writing of good history and the simplification tempting although not inherent in its popularization, the public intellectual was a declining species. The gap between labour history and labour, between the engaged SSLH historian increasingly taken up with academic issues and the active citizen, had probably expanded since Cole's day.

There remained good grounds for satisfaction and an optimism which was succinctly expressed in Hobsbawm's judgement in the early 1980s:

> Labour history has been transformed since the 1950s [...] It is no longer true to say that 'there has been comparatively little work about the working classes (as distinct from labour organization and movements)'. On the contrary. Every aspect of the study of the working classes has flourished as never before, both in Britain and abroad. What is more to the point, it has produced a number of historical works of

major importance [...] The past twenty years have undoubtedly been a golden age for labour history.[51]

However, differences which impacted on organized labour history had already surfaced. On one flank, the Society leadership's insistence on professional standards and preoccupation with developing the subject in higher education had produced charges of 'institutionalization'. On this front, History Workshop emerged in the late 1960s (and the eponymous journal from 1976) and 'drew sustenance from the substantial outside support [of] the Society for the Study of Labour History'.[52] It advocated a radical, uncompromising people's history which proclaimed the centrality of experience and reconstructed experience; it insisted on the need to transcend the academy, the importance of worker historians, oral history and history as explicitly and proudly partisan, a significant weapon of the proletariat in the class struggle. It was increasingly dedicated to feminism.

On another flank, the Society's emphasis on labour, its traditions of openness, disputation, the identification of many of its leading lights with Marxism and the active commitment of many of the younger generation to organized labour, may have played some part in the formation, again in 1976, of the Social History Society. The new organization was committed to a greater degree of conventional academicization and extending its subject within the universities. From further afield, *International Labor and Working-Class History* – the title was suggestive of the new cachet of social history and the search for breadth – made its debut. That year also saw the appearance of the independent journal, *Social History*. It was influenced by Marxism and dedicated to the development of radical theory and its historiographical practice. In some quarters in Britain, the SSLH was viewed as too institutional, too academic, too oriented towards professional history and higher education. Others perceived it as too radical, too political and insufficiently 'institutionalized'.[53]

These differences should not be exaggerated. It could be argued that the three groupings, together with the Oral History Society, established between 1969 and 1973, were complementary; some historians retained membership of all four and some were active in more than one. But organizational innovation reflected and carried forward deeper changes in orientations to history, particularly the acceleration of interest in women's history and the application of new approaches to gender and later sexual orientation. Such trends found greater resonance in History Workshop than in the Society, although the latter was not unaffected.[54] There were historiographical difficulties. Debates which had lain at the heart of labour history, particularly in an era where militancy and insurgency 'from below', personified by powerful shop stewards, challenged the 'corporatism' of the leadership of the unions and the Labour Party, notably the arguments about the role of the labour aristocracy and the conflict between 'bureaucracy and rank and file', peaked and petered out.[55] There were problems of practice, politics and relevance. At an international gathering hosted by the Society at the University of Warwick, one participant inquired:

> Could labour historians explain what impact they had upon the working class and the building of a socialist movement. In the discussion that followed, answers were given which ranged from the entirely negative to expressions of faith and the assertion that since all experience enters into history what we do must have some impact.[56]

Such uncomfortable questions went hand in hand with reflection on the impasse of organized labour by the late 1970s and controversy informed by contemporary events about whether 'the forward march of labour' had been halted or, indeed, had ever constituted the reality many cherished.[57] Men and women make their own history. But, as we know from Marx and experience, and to our cost, not as they please. The political and cultural landscape in which labour history operated was darkening.

III

With the arrival of Margaret Thatcher in Downing Street, the golden age of labour history moved towards its terminus and history herself came under attack.[58] From the citadels of labour history's advance, from Warwick, Birkbeck and the London School of Economics, came disturbing news of hostile scrutiny and judgement of trends since the 1960s, not only in history but in the social sciences, particularly in sociology and industrial relations. There were reports of cuts in SSRC support for courses in social and labour history, budget reductions and mothballing of new appointments. As Thatcherism found its stride, there was, for the first time, talk of a crisis in labour history.[59]

The wider discipline of British history was also shifting ground. Some historians wanted to move away from radical social and economic explanations of historical change towards more conservative interpretations and return to the old securities of high politics. There seems in retrospect a fit between the gradual unfolding of revisionist Conservatism and the increasing popularity of the revisionist history that burgeoned from the 1970s onwards. Historians, of whom Conrad Russell was the most able, struck at the roots of social and socialist understandings of the English Civil War personified by Christopher Hill. Others, of whom J.C.D. Clark was the most prominent, questioned the reality of revolution and transformative social change in British history and concerned themselves with 'Breaking the Grip of the Social Sciences'.[60] Linda Colley, who would go on to become an ornament of the historical as well as the New Labour establishment, substituted for Thompson's portrait of the making of proletarian radicalism and the constitution of British trade unionism in the years around the French Revolution, an intriguing picture of the making of working-class nationalism and patriotism.[61]

Very different, but with its own conservative implications, was the turn to language and to critiques of class as the master concept in explaining historical change which gained momentum from the mid-1980s.[62] Some historians began to pit themselves against a determinism rarely found in actually existing labour history, in which politics flowed unproblematically from structural position. Rather, they asserted, with an insight hardly novel to either politicians or historians, the form politics took depended on a range of contingent factors and on the construction and mobilization of interests through language.[63] The postmodernists went further: class and gender, they insisted, were no more than ideological constructs.[64]

History was changing with the world. By the time Thompson died in 1993, the power of workers to make history and transform the world in their own image seemed to many a passing dream. The newly invincible agency of the ruling class carried all before it. In Britain, insurgent neoliberalism eroded the power of organized labour, precipitated the transformation of the Labour Party and contributed to the weakening of class consciousness and the resonance of socialist ideas. It remoulded the universities and consequently influenced the independence, consciousness and interests of many of their staff and students. Bureaucracy, control systems, measurement of staff output, the inspection and categorization of teaching and research blossomed and would culminate in the periodic research assessment exercises. Many of the Society's old hands were retiring from their posts and others were seeking fresh pastures. But replacements came forward. The Society's leadership in the 1980s and into the 1990s included 'second generation' labour historians often trained by and generally influenced by the founders, such as Logie Barrow, Alan Campbell, Ray Challinor, David Englander, John Field, John Halstead, Angela John, Henry Katz, Neville Kirk, Laurence Marlow, David Martin, Adrian Oldfield, Raphael Samuel, Stan Shipley, Margaret Walsh, Chris Wrigley and Eileen Yeo. However, there was less continuity in its office holders and talk of the crisis of labour history was accompanied by pronouncements of its terminal decline.[65]

Other historians took a more balanced position. Work of excellence, they maintained, was still appearing in the last years of the twentieth century. New studies of women, such as those from Jane Lewis and Barbara Taylor, stood out. There was a turn away from histories of women and towards histories of gender – to understand the world of women we needed to understand men and the construction of masculinity – although some of this work transcended the traditional realms of labour history, while much more of it emanated from outside rather than inside Britain.[66] The major home-grown contribution came from Catherine Hall. Her monograph written with the sociologist, Leonore Davidoff, focused on middle-class men and women; but it held lessons for working-class history.[67] The new attention to gender, 'race' and ethnicity, and the need to consider multiple identities and their role in consciousness, action and historical explanation, was an invaluable development. It expanded definitions of labour and enlarged historians' understanding of class and their conceptual armoury.

There were difficulties. Some writers seemed determined to generalize beyond what the evidence would bear, ironically a sometimes justified criticism of Marxist historians.[68] Others gave gender priority over class. In America, Joan Wallach Scott was instrumental in directing gender history towards poststructuralism. Sometimes the thrust was to displace, not extend, class analysis. Sonya Rose, who acknowledged Scott's influence, asserted the primacy of gendered practices in explaining workers' experience in nineteenth-century Britain.[69] There were, at last, significant incursions into comparative history. Notable here were Kirk's ambitious analysis of American and British labour over the two centuries to 1939 and Stefan Berger's monograph on social democracy in Britain and Germany.[70] There were new developments in intellectual history.[71] But change was inescapable and it was reflected in academic careers.

In his threnody of the triumphs and tribulations of social history and the troubled relations between politics and writing history since the 1960s, Geoff Eley offers Carolyn Steedman as representative of this later period. He singles her out to exemplify the innovations that have occurred since the 1960s and the growing influence of feminism in the 1980s and 1990s. As Eley notes, Steedman began her work in the slipstream of Thompsonian culturalism and her extramural journey – distinctive in new times – was comparable with that of Thompson in its relative isolation from the academic mainstream.[72] But her cultural preoccupations were very different. Despite a stint at the Centre for the Study of Social History at Warwick, Steedman, a feminist critic of Thompson, never identified herself as a labour historian and possessed few connections with organized labour history. This was a trajectory that she shared with others who had started out in the 1960s and 1970s under the wings of labour history but who had become distanced from it.

As we moved towards *fin de siècle*, decline was indubitable. It affected social history and History Workshop as well as the SSLH and labour history *per se*. The times were unpropitious. In comparison with the immediate postwar years labour history had enhanced its profile and executed a successful march into the institutions. So far as we can judge – the survey evidence is limited – the number of university courses in which labour history figured as a significant component increased after 1960. In the 1980s they diminished and, despite subsequent university expansion, decline continued. Nonetheless, the subject was embedded in the historiography and in mainstream courses, although specialist contributions remained dependent on a limited number of committed lecturers.[73]

In this context, criticism and consequent self-interrogation, defenders of the field emphasised, should be welcomed. Eras of creativity and advance are succeeded by periods of retrenchment, in historiography as well as history. Class analysis and the Marxist method remained indispensable tools. Their value to historians of labour had been dismissed; their redundancy, if properly and flexibly applied, had not been demonstrated. Significant insights could and should be gleaned from changes in class composition, from feminism and even postmodernism. Historical scholarship is inevitably, sometimes beneficially, influenced by the present state of the world. But historians have to exercise vigilance against ahistorical projection of current trends and moods onto a very different past. In the end they must retain a strong element of intellectual independence. They should not be followers of fashion or funding, of changes in political and economic regimes, of state approbation or disapproval of trade unionism, or the forward march or retreat of the labour movement.[74]

But some are. They moved into new fields. Labour history was diminished: change was reflected in critical appraisal. Some of it raised questions difficult to resolve in theory, but surely settled by achievement on the published page, such as the utility of Marxism in the writing of history.[75] Other commentators registered pertinent points, sometimes freighted by political as well as historiographical considerations, such as the repeated, sometimes rhetorical need to go beyond activists to study 'ordinary' workers. Discounting for presentism, labour history had indubitably neglected women and gender, minorities and ethnicity. The objection that the field remained overly concerned with working-class organizations at the expense of culture and community possessed some force. If we consider the literature in its entirety, the element of truth in these and similar aspersions was commonly amplified and the importance of institutions remains as unarguable as the need for social histories of the working class. Criticism of labour history's responsiveness, or lack of it, to new trends likewise varied from the perceptive to the blinkered. Adverse estimation was sometimes polemical and oblique: reductionism stood in for documented critique of the labour history of the 1960s and 1970s.[76] It was difficult not to concur with one educated estimate of:

> [...] the crude misinterpretations of some critics. Labour historians cannot be typecast as unreformed reductionists clinging limpet-like to a primitive Marxism. They have produced works of outstanding scholarship; they have often shown a sensitivity towards the complex relationship of theory and evidence that belies many indictments.[77]

What was unarguable was that the 1990s saw further historiographical and organizational fragmentation of what had never been an integrated field or, since the 1980s, an all-embracing Society. There was still a substantial amount of writing about the history of labour, some of it of high quality. Hardly any of it reached beyond the profession to educate a wider audience; much of it was enclosed and self-referential. Many of the factors which had animated the SSLH's founding fathers and helped to cohere a small intellectual community with a sense of common identity around the Society, had frayed. The decline of the labour movement and the influence of socialist ideas went hand-in-hand with a diminution in active political commitment among historians. The neoliberalization of the academy spurred further specialization, stimulated a passion for novelty and sometimes encouraged the pursuit of revisionism for the sake of it.

In comparison with the pioneers, fewer labour historians were possessed of a vision which encompassed general interest in the social history of the working class in the nineteenth and twentieth centuries, in the industrial revolution, in Chartism, the Labour Party, 'the great unrest', the general strike and the depression of the 1930s – as well as their own personal research concerns. Despite the popularity of history, fewer aspired to a public role. Television history, family history, heritage history, the historical detective novel, all possessed of tremendous educational potential all too often unrealized, flourished. In practice, popular history tended towards the private, towards nostalgia and narratives of nation building. It found little place for labour.[78] Within the academy, fewer conceived themselves as labour historians. In a world of niche markets, what they saw in the mirror was a historian of gender, sport, leisure, sexual orientation, the trade unions, the Labour Party or Communism. Fewer perceived the need to support an ecumenical society.

Nonetheless, we responded energetically through the 1990s to new times and new projects. In 1995, the historian of the ILP and the Labour Party, David Howell, urged the need for Society members to debate the by now well-known objections to labour history as still too institutionally based, Eurocentric, masculine, theoretically innocent, a Neanderthal in the brave new world of postmodernism and cultural history. His statement stimulated a number of responses from, among others, John Belchem, Malcolm Chase, Keith Flett, Steven Fielding, John Halstead, David Martin and John Saville.[79] The drift of the contributions was critically reflective but cautiously optimistic. The field retained vitality and was capable of progress which absorbed the best and rejected the worst of prevailing trends. The Society's May 1995 conference took up fundamental issues in contemporary controversy with papers from Hobsbawm, Kirk, Ali Rattansi and Eileen Yeo elaborating arguments about the continuing relevance of class, gender and class, and 'race', class and the state.[80] In Spring 1997, at a major conference of the Society in Manchester, we debated 'is there a future for labour history?' Six strands addressed recent research on work, class, culture, ethnicity, politics and postmodernism. Amongst a feast of controversy, the conference closed with papers from Patrick Joyce and James Vernon. Their insistence that not only engagement with, but acceptance of, postmodernism was inseparable from the future progress of our subject, provoked vigorous argument.[81] The report on these debates recorded:

> In recent years the subject has experienced a sharp and critical burst of activity [...] In academic circles the advent of postmodernism (itself shaped by wider political and social changes) has stimulated some acrimonious debates in the wake of, and often rechurning the still-contested concepts of gender and race. Within the Society [...] these developments have had an impact. As always, some have been eager to embrace new ideas while others have resisted or rejected the currents of change.[82]

After reviewing recent controversies it concluded: 'the subject is neither in crisis nor moribund [...] Labour history continues to be reformulated.'[83] Two contemporary collections on class and language edited by Belchem and Kirk put flesh on this verdict. Many of the essays defended the continuing salience of class while paying due regard to gender and ethnicity as fertile categories of historical analysis. The epistemology of postmodernism had to be rejected on philosophical grounds and in the face of the achievements of modern, positivist history. Some felt that linguistic approaches had their uses in terms of encouraging sensitivity to language, identities, style, scepticism and the eschewal of determinism: they could be applied, to take one example, to recuperate radical and socialist thinking while acknowledging the material influences on how it was formulated and understood.[84]

The end of the century saw evolutionary change in the Society. The *Bulletin* had developed gradually throughout its career, moving to thrice-yearly publication and adding documentary and bibliographical essays to its 'essays in review'. It had by 1990 metamorphosed into *Labour History Review* – half bulletin, half journal, for some, halfway house. Continuing pressure from libraries, which prioritized journals, and from academics confronting the increasing emphasis on research and its measurement, provided further stimuli to innovation. By the 1990s the SSLH remained a society of academics with few links with trade unionists or political activists. The absence of a journal was idiosyncratic: almost every other national labour history society had one. The constituency within the Society that had always favoured a journal was in the ascendant. Articles were now welcomed and in 1996 *Labour History Review* was relaunched as a conventional scholarly journal with an academic publisher.[85] Something was lost. It seemed, then and now, at least to the majority, a necessary and overdue compromise. One of the architects of the Society, still involved more than forty years on, remarked:

> I am myself modestly reassured at the state of the subject today in this country. The *Labour History Review*, for example, has become a most useful journal with a notable absence of the opaque jargon which disfigures so many social history journals [...] And I am encouraged by the intellectual calibre of enough of the published work in our field to feel confident of the future.[86]

John Saville's colleagues who gathered together to plan the Society in Leeds and London when Harold Macmillan was Prime Minister and Elvis was in the army would, we hope, be enthusiastic about the series 'Studies in Labour History', initiated by Chris Wrigley, in which twenty-eight volumes have been published since 1998. It covers very diverse subjects ranging from unemployed protest in France to Jewish workers and the labour movement, from minimum wage legislation to farm workers and patriotism. It includes several volumes on transnational history as well as five texts devoted to women's history. The inception of the series coincided with a spate of publications on the Labour Party. They were related to the advent of New Labour and the party's centenary and accompanied by the announcement of the arrival of 'the new, new labour history' and the 'new political labour history'. [87] Alas, these turned out to be little more than revamped versions of the old history of high politics.

Over the long haul, the historiographical progress is unquestionable. It may be gauged by comparing, to take one example, the work of the current chair, Alan Campbell, on miners with the state of the art in 1960; or to take another case, by placing the Society's first chair Asa Briggs's pioneering collection on Chartism alongside the text on the subject published by a recent chair, Malcolm Chase.[88] Continuity is reflected in our honorary office holders. Eric Hobsbawm remains president while Briggs, Ray Challinor, John Harrison, Dorothy Thompson (and John Saville until his recent death) serve as vice-presidents. A recent secretary, John Halstead, was for thirty years an editor of the *Bulletin* and the *Review*.[89]

We still attempt to project an integrated conception of labour history. We still seek to stimulate and sponsor scholarship across the field. We try to stand on the shoulders of the pioneers of both the old and the new labour history rather than regarding what they produced and the kind of history they envisioned as an intriguing historiographical remnant, even a historiographical cul-de-sac. If we eschew parochialism and turn to the future, the expansion of the working class and the transformation of labour across the globe seems to assure a vibrant future for historians of labour and organizations of labour history. The SSLH, we trust, will continue to make a contribution to that future in which the history of labour will take new and unforeseeable forms. We have had our reverses. As with all historiographical endeavour we have fallen short of our goals. Our achievements have been imperfect; overall, they have improved the state and quality of historical scholarship. We are still here and we have something to celebrate.

IV

Introducing the second volume of *Essays in Labour History* in 1971, Asa Briggs reflected: 'Since 1960 there has been something of an international boom in the study of labour history.'[90] Relating this to the development of the Society he observed: 'There are now parallel bodies in several other countries and joint sessions have been held with labour historians in France and the United States.'[91] Although it would go on to exercise an influence beyond Britain, the creation of the SSLH expressed wider trends. The

French journal that would later become *Le Mouvement Social*, had appeared as early as 1949. The foundation of the Austrian Society, Verein für der Geschichte de Arbeiterbewegung, preceded that of the SSLH by a year. In 1961 the Friedrich Ebert Foundation in West Germany commenced publication of its annual review, *Archiv für Sozialgeschichte*, which at that time featured extensive coverage of labour history. Despite a certain insularity and on the whole an enduring Eurocentrism, the Society always pursued international connections. From the beginning we had links with the Commission Internationale d'Histoire des Mouvements Sociaux; the International Institute of Social History in Amsterdam which had published the *International Review of Social History*, revamped as a journal in 1956, as a yearbook since 1936; a range of German historians, east and west; the Instituto Feltrinelli in Milan; with Russian historians; and with the group of American historians who brought out the first issue of *Labor History* sponsored by the Tamiment Institute in 1960.[92]

A welcome was extended to the creation of 'our sister Society' in Australia which published *Labour History* (Australia) from 1962. There were warm relations with the Canadian Committee for Labour History whose *Bulletin* subsequently became *Labour History/Histoire Ouvrière Canadienne*. In 1976 it was absorbed into *Labour/Le Travailleur*.[93] A fruitful dialogue was maintained with historians in Austria and in Japan, initiated via Chushichi Tsuzuki, the biographer of H.M. Hyndman.[94]

Nearer home, the Scottish Labour History Society, which superseded the Scottish Committee of the British Society, was launched in 1966 and its journal in 1969. It owed much to the animation of Ian MacDougall and W.H. Marwick, and later Hamish Fraser, Allan McLaren and Robert Duncan, among others. The Welsh Society was born in 1971 and its journal, *Llafur*, appeared a year later. Over the next two decades it was indebted to a talented group of young historians around Hywel Francis, Deian Hopkin, Dai Smith and later Neil Evans. Like its Scottish and Irish counterparts, the Welsh society successfully integrated itself with its national labour movement. The Irish Society was established in 1973. Since 1975 it has published the journal *Saothar* which unites historians north and south of the border. It benefitted in its early years from the indefatigable efforts of Fergus D'Arcy, Ken Hannigan and Francis Devine and later from the persistence of Emmet O'Connor and Therese Moriarty.[95] The flowering of regional groups in England should not be forgotten. The first were based in Leeds and Sheffield. The succeeding Yorkshire, Humberside and North Midlands group and the West Midlands, Sussex and North Staffordshire bodies did not endure beyond the 1980s. But labour historians in the north-west of

England continue to produce a lively journal while their counterparts in the north-east who published a *Bulletin* that grew into *North-East History* have remained equally active and vigorous.[96]

The Society's first major venture beyond these shores was a collaboration with the French Institute of Social History, the Anglo-French Colloquium on Trade Unions and Labour Movements, 1890–1914. This was inspired by Hobsbawm and convened at Birkbeck in April 1966. Chaired by Briggs and Jacques Droz from the Sorbonne, the conference discussed papers from, among others, Hobsbawm, François Bédarida, Jacques Juillard, Annie Kriegel, Henry Pelling, Michelle Perrot, Madeleine Robrieux and Rolande Trompé.[97] June 1968 saw the first of the Anglo-American colloquia with papers on an extended range of issues from, *inter alia*, Herbert Gutman, Royden Harrison, Helen Meller, Richard Morris, Maurice Neufeld, Henry Pelling, Stephan Thernstrom and Edward Thompson. It was repeated at Rutgers University in April 1973 when the speakers included James R. Green, Alice Kessler-Harris, Hobsbawm, Virginia Yans McLaughlin, David Montgomery, Gareth Stedman Jones and Thompson.[98]

The initial British-Dutch conference was held in Amsterdam in April 1977, jointly organized by Herman Diederiks and Henry Katz for the Society. It was a vibrant, two-day gathering addressed by speakers who included J.C. Blom, Ray Challinor, W.R. Garside, José Harris, C.J. van Laren, Sheila Lewenhak, G.J. Meijer, Erik Nijhoff, Robert Skidelsky, Theo van Tijn and Jay Winter. These biennial meetings became an integral part of the Society's activity. By the time of the eighth conference in Manchester in 1992 the meetings had become popular assemblies with up to thirty papers delivered and discussed. The last conference was held in 1994 but this experience laid the ground for the later, large-scale European Social Science History conferences with their popular Labour strand.[99] An impressive initiative came in 1980 when a three-day Commonwealth Labour History Conference met at Warwick and Lanchester Polytechnic, Coventry, in the autumn. There were 35 participants from Britain, 13 from Australia, 13 from Canada and 3 from New Zealand, with additional contributors from Germany, Ireland and the USA. The conference heard overviews of the progress of labour history in Australia, from Eric Fry and Susan Margery, in Canada, from Bryan Palmer, and in Britain, from Royden Harrison. Papers on a very extended range of subjects were read by, among others, Irving Abella, Philip Bagwell, Alan Clinton, David Frank, Jim Hagan, Greg Kealey, Sheila Lewenhak, John Lovell, Erik Olsen, Richard Price, Marika Sherwood, Jonathan Zeitlin and Noel Whiteside.[100]

International collaboration has remained a feature of the Society's activities with conferences at Rouen and the University of Ulster on transnational labour history in 2008 as we approached our Jubilee. The International Conference of Historians of the Labour Movement held annually at Linz in Austria was not a Society affair, although Royden Harrison was fond of remarking, with a degree of inflation, that it was Society policy that members should support it.[101] Many did so, and were initially bemused or disconcerted by the contention and diplomatic attempts to circumvent it between warring tribes of German historians conducted on neutral territory. Harrison was assiduous in seeking engagement with international organizations. Together with Irene Wagner he attended meetings of the International Association of Labour History Institutions which was formed in 1970. At one stage he was involved in an ambitious attempt to create a World Forum of Labour Historians involving the Amsterdam Institute, the Linz organizers, the Feltrinelli Institute, the Asociacion Mundial de Centros de Historia Obrera, Mexico City, the International Association and the Russian Commission for Multilateral Collaboration.[102]

Perhaps more directly productive was the flow of scholars from other countries into Britain and into the activities of the Society. Visiting academics at the Warwick centre who participated in our work included David Brody, Joe Conlin, Mel Dubofsky, Jim Green, Alice Kessler-Harris, John Laslett, Sally Miller, David Montgomery, James Weinstein and Paul Worthman. William Lazonick was Visiting Professor at Birkbeck and Gene Genovese at Cambridge, while a number of Japanese academics spent prolonged periods at Sheffield. Among students studying labour history at British universities in the 1970s, largely but not exclusively at Warwick, were Leon Fink, Douglas Hay, Michael Ignatieff, Peter Linebaugh, Robert Malcolmson, Takao Matsumura and Jonathan Zeitlin. To some extent at least, this reflected the influence of the Society's founding fathers. They always aspired to internationalism and they were travellers in every sense of the word. They maintained a variety of links with Australia (Briggs), Germany (Pollard), Japan (Royden Harrison) and the International Institute of Social History, Amsterdam (Saville). It was said of Thompson that he 'opened new ways of enquiring into the past in India and Latin America [...] He has influenced Chinese labour historians and inspired the feminist scholar of Arab texts, Fatima Mernissi.'[103] He lectured in Canada and the USA and maintained his family's links with India. His influence marked developments in labour history in all three countries. The same could be said for Hobsbawm who travelled and taught and inspired thousands across Europe, particularly Italy and France, and North and South America, notably in Brazil.[104]

The future will be different: 'For last year's words belong to last year's language / And next year's words await another voice.'[105] There can be little doubt that this direction – internationalism, transnationalism, organizational and historiographical – should constitute one important future route for labour history. Aspirations to globalization are imperative. As with aspirations to international trade unionism or international socialism they are, to a large extent, contingent on the vitality of the subject in nation states. Thriving national historiographies, encouraged by expanding networks of scholars looking outwards, provide an essential basis for fruitful international dialogue, cross-fertilization and progress towards the transcendence of national historiography.[106] Some concern about the long-term future of labour history, certainly organized labour history, in Britain today may be in order, at least if we measure its progress since the 1980s against the desire of some of its founders to create a new field. The second generation of modern labour historians is nearing retirement age. The presence of labour history in the universities and the labour movement, as represented by dedicated courses, is restricted. It has encountered greater success in attaining the more limited goal of penetrating the historiographical mainstream. Labour history has shaken up what Thompson termed 'history proper' without finding a proper place for itself in the academy.[107]

Nonetheless, *LHR* appears regularly and publishes work of scholarship on a wide range of issues. In its first five years from 1996 to 2000, 43 articles appeared. They covered conventional issues such as the Labour Party, trade unions, Chartism, Communism and particular groups of workers, as well as aspects of the history of labour in France, Italy and Nigeria. Only 10 articles, less than a quarter of the total, were concerned with the nineteenth century. Moreover, if we take these topics as a rough index of new trends, only 4 articles (9 per cent) dealt with women's history and gender issues, and all 4 were published in a special issue on 'Gender and Work'. In the following seven years to 2007, 80 articles appeared, of which 66 were devoted to the twentieth century and a mere 14 to the nineteenth century. Traditional staples of the field such as trade unions and the Labour Party continued to be well represented with a total of 20 articles, a quarter of the total. Moreover, 17 out of 80 (21 per cent) examined women's or gender history, compared with only 3 on racism and ethnicity; however, 6 of the 17 appeared in a special issue on masculinities. Neither has comparative and transnational research – another touchstone of the 'new' – featured particularly strongly in *LHR*, with 8 articles (10 per cent). With some exceptions, such as freemasonry or labour movement corruption, the journal tells a fairly conventional tale. The strong trend to the twentieth century is not wholly positive in terms of an integrated labour history. Moreover, historiographical and editorial discussion of new challenges has not always been reflected in the publication of substantive articles. However, since 2007 a new editorial team headed by Don MacRaild has taken things forward and there have been special issues on unemployed movements, Chartism and transnational labour history.

Beyond the journal, fragmentation is exhibited in the variety of contingents and the subjects they offer to 'the labour network stream' at the European Social Science History Conference. The language may evoke the tensions between the assurance that labour history has entered the mainstream and the maintenance of labour history as a distinct field of historical scholarship. Nonetheless, the extent of British representation pays testament to the continuing interest among young historians in a wide variety of labour history from Chartism to consumerism and household history, from urban proletariats to rural labour, from language, identity, biography and autobiography to local studies, migration and religion. A range of literatures from the traditional histories of working-class organization, labour markets and the role of the state, as well as more recent research on gender, ethnicity and sexuality, remain open to further development. Perennial problems pertaining to agency and structure and the links between class and more specific forms of oppression and identity demand further exploration, as they always will. Labour history and the networks to sustain it persist. History, the labour movement and society, whatever forms each may take as the century develops, will still need histories of labour. It is difficult to conceive of any robust history, effective workers' movement or good society which disregards labour history, the history of the potential, and the disfigurement, of work in all its forms, the analysis of exploitation and oppression and the struggles against them – although we have seen such disregard before and in the not too distant past.

In that context, there is much to be done. One-route recipes are unhelpful. The subject will always constitute a site of diversity and pluralism in content and approach. There will always be room for localized narratives, for micro-histories, for *Montaillou* as well as *La Mediterranée et le Monde*, for *Blood Feud* as well as *Framing the Early Middle Ages*, for *Landscape for a Good Woman* as well as *The Age of Extremes*. But *longue durée* history of transnational scope remains important and presently neglected in Britain. National historiographies work best when they look outwards, connect with the big picture, relate to the wider world, overlap with each other, embrace shared concerns. The old arguments of Braudel for interdisciplinary insights and the need to grasp changes in the whole before we can comprehend changes in the parts remain a compelling antidote to the isolationism, complacency and trivialization evident in some writing on British history.

We have few models for this in British labour history. In North America, Peter Linebaugh and Marcus Rediker's studies of the Atlantic world and Atlantic labour provide inspiring examples of scope; in very different ways and in different areas of the discipline we have the work of Catherine Hall and Chris Wickham.[108] We do have the example of Eric Hobsbawm. Only a few years before the creation of the SSLH, he remarked in declining a research assignment: 'I am not against Internationalism but my own academic interests are for local movements.'[109] In the ensuing years he did not neglect these interests. But he did expand them and went on to write four volumes which burgeoned into 'a history of the world in recent times'.[110] Labour historians start, naturally and beneficially, from history from below and from national preoccupations. It will not facilitate the future vigour of the subject in Britain if they remain 'caged' inside these concerns.[111] The SSLH was born into a world in which the most prestigious British historian of the day could exclude from the historical gaze 'the unrewarding gyrations of barbarous tribes in picturesque but irrelevant corners of the globe'.[112] It is time, more than time, to settle that account.

Notes

1 The phrase is Stuart Hall's: idem, 'The First New Left: Life and Times', in *Out of Apathy: Voices of the New Left 30 Years On*, ed. by Oxford University Socialist Discussion Group (London: Verso, 1989), p. 13. In Britain the term 'New Left' usually denotes the movement which developed in the aftermath of 1956, rather than, as elsewhere, the post-1968 generation.

2 See, for example, ibid. and Michael Kenny, *The First New Left: British Intellectuals After Stalin* (London: Lawrence and Wishart, 1995).

3 See, for example, Steve Parsons, 'British McCarthyism and the Intellectuals', in *Labour's Promised Land? Culture and Society in Labour Britain*, ed. by Jim Fyrth (London: Lawrence and Wishart, 1995), pp. 224–46. As late as 1963, Isaac Deutscher was denied appointment at Sussex University partly through the influence of Isaiah Berlin: Michael Ignatieff, *Isaiah Berlin: A Life* (London: Chatto and Windus, 1998), p. 235.

4 For a recent analysis, see Jim Obelkevich, 'New Developments in History in the 1950s and 1960s', *Contemporary British History*, 14 (2000), 125–42; idem, (ed.), 'Witness Seminar: New Developments in History in the 1950s and 1960s', ibid., 143–67. This is not intended to denigrate Namier's contribution as a student of structures and motivation or assimilate the different and changing approaches of establishment historians. For a personal recollection of the period, see Eric Hobsbawm, *Interesting Times: A Twentieth Century Life* (London: Allen Lane, 2002), passim, but particularly pp. 282–97. There seems to have been no great change since the 1930s when Hobsbawm found Cambridge history 'self-satisfied, insular, culturally provincial, deeply prejudiced': *The Times Higher Education*, 12 July 2002.

5 Negley Harte, 'The Economic History Society, 1926–2001', in *Living Economic and Social History*, ed. by Pat Hudson (Glasgow: Economic History Society, 2001), pp. 1–9; Christopher Hill, Rodney Hilton and Eric Hobsbawm, 'Past and Present: Origins and Early Years', *Past and Present*, 100 (1983), 3–14.

6 Gareth Stedman Jones, 'History: The Poverty of Empiricism', in *Ideology in Social Science: Readings in Critical Social Theory*, ed. by Robin Blackburn (London: Fontana, 1972), pp. 96–115 (p. 109).

7 E.H. Carr, *What is History?* (London: Macmillan, 1961).

8 On this see John McIlroy, 'The Society for the Study of Labour History, 1956–1985: Its Origins and Its Heyday', *Making History: Organizations of Labour Historians in Britain since 1960, Labour History Review* (*LHR*) Fiftieth Anniversary Supplement, April 2010, 17-110 (pp. 29-33).

9 John Saville, *Memoirs from the Left* (London: Merlin Press, 2003), p. 119.

10 *Bulletin of the Society for the Study of Labour History* (*BSSLH*), 1 (1960), 2.

11 George Thomson, Maurice Dobb, Christopher Hill and John Saville, 'Foreword' to *Democracy and the Labour Movement: Essays in Honour of Dona Torr*, ed. by John Saville (London: Lawrence and Wishart, 1954), p. 8. For the Communist historians, see Eric Hobsbawm, 'The Historians' Group of the Communist Party', in *Rebels and their Causes: Essays in Honour of A.L. Morton*, ed. by Maurice Cornforth (London: Lawrence and Wishart, 1978), pp. 21–48; Bill Schwartz, '"The People" in History: The Communist Party Historians' Group', in *Making Histories: Studies in Writing and* Politics, ed. by Centre for Contemporary Cultural Studies (London: Hutchinson, 1982); Harvey J. Kaye, *The British Marxist Historians: An Introductory Analysis* (Oxford: Polity Press, 1984).

12 I have written about the foundation of the Society and the historians involved in it at greater length in McIlroy, 'Society', pp. 23-44.

13 It should be stressed that apart from Briggs, Hobsbawm and Pelling, the founding cohort was, in academic terms, relatively junior and relatively unpublished. Their existing work included Asa Briggs, *The Age of Improvement, 1783–1867* (London: Longman, 1959); Frank Bealey and Henry Pelling, *Labour and Politics, 1900–1906* (London: Macmillan, 1958); Eric Hobsbawm, *Primitive Rebels: Studies of Archaic Forms of Social Movement in the Nineteenth and Twentieth Century* (Manchester: Manchester University Press, 1959); many of Hobsbawm's essays, written from 1949, were later published in Eric Hobsbawm, *Labouring Men: Studies in the History of Labour* (London: Weidenfeld and Nicolson, 1959); Henry Pelling, *The Origins of the Labour Party, 1880–1900* (London: Macmillan, 1954); Sidney Pollard, *A History of Labour in Sheffield* (Liverpool: Liverpool University Press, 1959); *Ernest Jones, Chartist: Selections from the Writings and Speeches*, ed. by John Saville (London: Lawrence and Wishart, 1952); idem, *Rural Depopulation in England and Wales, 1851–1951* (London: Routledge and Kegan Paul, 1957); E.P. Thompson, *William Morris: Romantic to Revolutionary* (London: Lawrence and Wishart, 1955). The other references are to Henry Collins and Chimen Abramsky, *Karl Marx and the British Labour Movement: Years of the First International* (London: Macmillan, 1965); and Royden Harrison, *Before the*

Socialists: Studies in Labour and Politics, 1861–1881 (London: Routledge Kegan Paul, 1965).

14 See John McIlroy, 'A Communist Historian in 1956: Brian Pearce and the Crisis of British Stalinism', *Revolutionary History*, 9, 3 (2006), 84–104. The major source for the Society's history remains the *BSSLH*, although there is a small archive at the Modern Records Centre, University of Warwick, and some relevant material in John Saville's papers at the Brynmor John Library, University of Hull. For a more detailed and extended discussion, see McIlroy, 'Society'.

15 See G.R. Elton, *The Practice of History* (1st pub. 1967; 2nd edn, Oxford: Basil Blackwell, 2002) and R.J. Evans, 'Afterword', ibid. (2nd edn), pp. 165–203.

16 Carr, *What is History? passim.*

17 See, for example, E.P. Thompson, *The Making of the English Working Class* (London: Gollancz, 1963), p. 14; Stuart Macintyre, *A Proletarian Science: Marxism in Britain, 1917–1933* (Cambridge: Cambridge University Press, 1980); John McIlroy, 'Independent Working-Class Education and Trade Union Education and Training', in Roger Fieldhouse and Associates, *A History of Modern Adult Education* (Leicester: National Institute of Adult Education, 1996), pp. 264–89; Roger Fieldhouse, 'The Ideology of English Adult Education Teaching, 1925–1950', *Studies in Adult Education*, 15, 1 (1983), 11–35; Jonathan Rose, *The Intellectual Life of the British Working Classes* (New Haven and London: Yale University Press, 2001), esp. ch. 8; and McIlroy, 'Society', 25-28.

18 See Asa Briggs's inaugural address, 'Open Questions of Labour History', *BSSLH*, 1 (1960), 2–3; McIlroy, 'Society', 23-44.

19 Ibid., 23-25.

20 Modern Records Centre, University of Warwick, SSLH Papers, MSS 207, 207/1, Foundation File, Constitution.

21 *Chartist Studies*, ed. by Asa Briggs (London: Macmillan, 1959); *Essays in Labour History: In Memory of G.D.H. Cole*, ed. by Asa Briggs and John Saville (London: Macmillan, 1960).

22 University departments, for example, at Birkbeck, Leeds and Sheffield, were generous in providing facilities for meetings and resources for editing the *Bulletin*.

23 *BSSLH*, 1 (1960), 31–3; *BSSLH*, 15 (1967), 12; *BSSLH*, 26 (1973), 2; *BSSLH*, 41 (1980), 2. Full membership lists featured in the *Bulletin* until 1968. Information from John Halstead and see, for example, 'Editorial', *BSSLH*, 44 (1982), 4.

24 See, for example, Eric Hobsbawm, 'From Social History to the History of Society' (1st pub. 1971) in idem, *On History* (London: Weidenfeld and Nicolson, 1997).

25 Cf. Hobsbawm, *Interesting Times*, p. 291; Saville, *Memoirs*, pp. 118–19.

26 E.J. Hobsbawm, 'Labour History and Ideology', *Journal of Social History*, 7 (1974), 371–81.

27 'Editorial', *BSSLH*, 37 (1978), 6; 'Editorial: Twenty Years On', *BSSLH*, 41 (1980), 2–5. Sixty-two issues of the *BSSLH* appeared in the twenty-nine years from 1960 to 1989. The first fifty issues were numbered consecutively.

From 1986 to 1989 the *Bulletin* was published in volumes which followed the earlier numbering, i.e. vols 51–54. Each volume included three issues of the publication. When *Labour History Review* was launched in 1990, the first issue was numbered vol. 55, no. 1, and it has continued with yearly volumes containing three parts or issues.

28 'Editorial', *BSSLH*, 4 (1962), 1; 'The Teaching of Labour History', ibid., 33.

29 I have discussed this matter, as well as the issue of professionalization, at greater length in McIlroy, 'Society', 50-53, 94-98.

30 Particular mention must be made in this regard of Royden Harrison when editing the *Bulletin* and Eric Hobsbawm and John Saville who were often trenchant but always educative when chairing conference sessions and who never made concessions to dumbing down as distinct from scholarly decorum.

31 See, for example, 'The Teaching of Labour History in Adult Classes', *BSSLH*, 6 (1963), 3–7; 'Editorial', *BSSLH*, 42 (1981), 2; 'Editorial', *BSSLH*, 43 (1987), 2.

32 See, for example, the editorials in *BSSLH*, 35 (1977), 2–5; *BSSLH*, 36 (1978), 2–3; *BSSLH*, 37 (1978), 2–4; Royden Harrison, 'New Light on the Police and the Hunger Marchers', *BSSLH*, 37 (1978), 17–49; *BSSLH*, 38 (1979), 2–4; 'Editorial', *BSSLH*, 39 (1979), 2–7.

33 'Editorial', *BSSLH*, 31 (1975), 3.

34 *BSSLH*, 35 (1977), 21–26; *BSSLH*, 36 (1978), 25–26.

35 The first officers were Briggs (chair), Hobsbawm (vice-chair), John Harrison (secretary), Frank Bealey (treasurer), Royden Harrison and Sidney Pollard (*Bulletin* editors). Henry Collins, from the Oxford Delegacy of Extra-Mural Studies, replaced John Harrison while the first executive elected in 1961 consisted of Chimen Abramsky, then a bookseller, later Professor of Hebrew Studies at University College, London; Stephen Coltham from Keele University, an authority on the mid-Victorian labour press; Alan Fox, trade union historian and industrial sociologist; and John Saville. By 1965 Pearce had succeeded Collins as secretary and the historian of the railway workers, Philip Bagwell, Henry Pelling and Edward Thompson sat on the executive. By 1968 Briggs had become the first president, Hobsbawm was chair and Bagwell had replaced Pearce. Younger members such as James Hinton and Eileen Yeo appeared on the executive and Thompson served on the archives committee with Guttsman and Wagner. Five years on and Pollard was president, John Harrison chair, Saville vice-chair and Grenda Horne, Bagwell's colleague at Regent Street Polytechnic, the secretary. John Halstead succeeded Pollard who spent eleven years as joint editor and Dorothy Thompson, Raphael Samuel, Walter Kendall and Hobsbawm were on the executive. Royden Harrison edited the *Bulletin* from 1960 until his retirement in 1982, remaining active thereafter. It is impossible, given the constraints of space, to provide a complete picture of the Society's office-holders throughout its history. These few details suggest its quality, diversity and continuity.

36 J.F.C. Harrison, *Learning and Living, 1790–1960: A Study in the History of the English Adult Education Movement* (London: Routledge Kegan Paul, 1961); Henry Pelling, *A History of British Trade Unionism* (Harmondsworth: Penguin,

1963); Hugh Clegg, Alan Fox and A. F. Thompson, *A History of British Trade Unions since 1889, vol. 1: 1889–1910* (Oxford: Clarendon Press, 1964); Eric Hobsbawm, *The Age of Revolution, 1789–1848* (London: Weidenfeld and Nicolson, 1962); idem, *Labouring Men*; Sidney Pollard, *The Genesis of Modern Management: A Study of the Industrial Revolution in Great Britain* (London: Edward Arnold, 1965); Harrison, *Before the Socialists*; J.P. Nettl, *Rosa Luxemburg*, 2 vols (Oxford: Oxford University Press, 1966); *Essays in Labour History, 1886–1923*, ed. by Asa Briggs and John Saville (London: Macmillan, 1971).

37 See n. 17.

38 See, for example, the criticisms discussed in Thompson, *Making*, (2nd edn, Harmondsworth: Penguin, 1968), pp. 916–39; and A.E. Musson, *British Trade Unions, 1800–1875* (London: Macmillan, 1972), passim.

39 Tony Mason and Jim Obelkevich, 'Labour History at the Centre for the Study of Social History, University of Warwick', *BSSLH*, 48 (1984), 22–23.

40 *The Warwick Guide to British Labour Periodicals, 1790–1970: A Checklist*, ed. by Royden Harrison, Gillian Woolven and Robert Duncan (Hassocks: Harvester, 1977).

41 The first volume appeared in 1972: *Dictionary of Labour Biography, vol. 1*, ed. by Joyce M. Bellamy and John Saville (London: Macmillan, 1972). The last volume in which Saville was involved, the tenth, was published in 2000. See Saville, *Memoirs*, pp. 135–37.

42 For example, John Burnett, *A Social History of Diet in England from 1815 to the Present Day* (London: Thomas Nelson, 1966); J.F.C. Harrison, *Robert Owen and the Owenites in Britain and America: The Quest for the New Moral World* (London: Routledge and Kegan Paul, 1969); Brian Inglis, *Poverty and the Industrial Revolution* (London: Hodder and Stoughton, 1971); John A. Garrard, *The English and Immigration, 1880–1910* (Oxford: Oxford University Press, 1971); P.H.J. Gosden, *Self Help: Voluntary Associations in the Nineteenth* Century (London: Batsford, 1973); E.H. Hunt, *Regional Wage Variations in Britain, 1850–1914* (Oxford: Oxford University Press, 1973); Robert W. Malcolmson, *Popular Recreation in English Society, 1700–1850* (Cambridge: Cambridge University Press, 1973); *The Standard of Living in Britain in the Industrial Revolution*, ed. by Arthur J. Taylor (London: Methuen, 1975); John Burnett, *A Social History of Housing, 1815–1970* (Newton Abbott: David and Charles, 1978); James Walvin, *Leisure and Society, 1830–1950* (London: Longmans, 1978); Patrick Joyce, *Work, Society and Politics: The Culture of the Factory in Victorian England* (Brighton: Harvester, 1980); Tony Mason, *Association Football and English Society, 1863–1915* (Brighton: Harvester, 1980); Melanie Tebbutt, *Making Ends Meet: Pawnbroking and Working-Class Credit* (Leicester: Leicester University Press, 1983).

43 For example, John Lovell, *Stevedores and Dockers: A Study of Trade Unionism in the Port of London, 1870–1914* (London: Macmillan, 1969); James Hinton, *The First Shop Stewards' Movement* (London: Allen and Unwin, 1973); John Foster, *Class Struggle and the Industrial Revolution: Early Industrial Capitalism in Three English Town* (London: Weidenfeld and Nicolson, 1974); W. Hamish

Fraser, *Trade Unions and Society: The Struggle for Acceptance, 1850–1880* (London: Allen and Unwin, 1974); Eric Taplin, *Liverpool Dockers and Seamen* (Hull: Hull University Press, 1974); Joseph L. White, *The Limits of Trade Union Militancy* (London: Greenwood Press, 1978); Alan Campbell, *The Lanarkshire Miners: A Social History of their Trade Unions, 1775–1874* (Edinburgh: John Donald, 1979); John Benson, *British Coalminers in the Nineteenth Century* (Dublin: Gill and Macmillan, 1980); Richard Price, *Masters, Unions and Men: Work Control in Building and the Rise of Labour, 1830–1914* (Cambridge: Cambridge University Press, 1980); Hywel Francis and Dai Smith, *The Fed: A History of the South Wales Miners in the Twentieth Century* (London: Lawrence and Wishart, 1980); David Howell, *British Workers and the Independent Labour Party, 1888–1906* (Manchester: Manchester University Press, 1983); H.A. Clegg, *A History of British Trade Unions since 1889, vol. 2: 1911–1933* (Oxford: Clarendon Press, 1985).

44 For example, Sheila Rowbotham, *Hidden from History: 300 Years of Women's Oppression and the Fight Against It* (London: Pluto, 1973); Therese M. McBride, *The Domestic Revolution: The Modernization of Household Service in England and France, 1820–1920* (London: Croom Helm, 1976); Sheila Lewenhak, *Women and Trade Unions: An Outline History of Women in the British Trade Union Movement* (London: Benn, 1977); Jill Liddington and Jill Norris, *One Hand Tied Behind Us: The Rise of the Women's Suffrage Movement* (London: Virago, 1978); Gail Braybon, *Women Workers and the First World War* (London: Barnes and Noble, 1981); Jane Lewis, *Women in England, 1870–1950* (Brighton: Wheatsheaf, 1984); *Unequal Opportunities: Women's Employment in England, 1800–1918*, ed. by Angela V. John (Oxford: Blackwell, 1986); Sylvia Walby, *Patriarchy at Work: Patriarchal and Capitalist Relations in Employment* (Cambridge: Polity Press, 1986).

45 For example, Taylor, *Standard of Living*; Eric Hobsbawm, 'The Labour Aristocracy in Nineteenth-Century Britain', in idem, *Labouring Men*, pp. 272–315; Foster, *Class Struggle and the Industrial Revolution*; Robert Gray, *The Labour Aristocracy in Victorian Edinburgh* (Oxford: Oxford University Press, 1976); Geoffrey Crossick, *An Artisan Elite in Victorian Society: Kentish London* (London: Croom Helm, 1978); D.S. Gadian, 'Class Consciousness in Oldham and other North-West Industrial Towns', *Historical Journal*, 21 (1978), 161–72; H.F. Moorhouse, 'The Marxist Theory of the Labour Aristocracy', *Social History*, 3 (1978), 61–82; 'Conference Report: The Labour Aristocracy: Twenty-Five Years After', *BSSLH*, 40 (1980), 6–11; Takao Matsumura, *The Labour Aristocracy Revisited: The Victorian Flint Glassmakers, 1850–1880* (Manchester: Manchester University Press, 1983); Gareth Stedman Jones, 'Class Struggle and the Industrial Revolution' (1st pub. 1975), in idem, *Languages of Class: Studies in English Working-Class History, 1832–1982* (Cambridge: Cambridge University Press, 1983), pp. 25–74; Eric Hobsbawm, *Worlds of Labour: Further Studies in the History of Labour* (London: Weidenfeld and Nicolson, 1984), pp. 227–51.

46 See n. 24.

47 Geoff Eley and Keith Nield, 'Why Does Social History Ignore Politics?', *Social*

History, 5 (1980), 249–71 (pp. 264–67).

48 See the remarks by Richard Hyman, 'Conference Report: The Labour Aristocracy: Twenty-Five Years After', p. 11.

49 Stefan Berger and Greg Patmore, 'Comparative Labour History in Britain and Australia', *Labour History* (Australia), 88 (2005), 9–24, makes the best of an uncompelling case for the standing of this genre in Britain.

50 John Foster, quoted in *BSSLH*, 42 (1987), 89.

51 Hobsbawm, *Worlds of Labour*, pp. ix–x. The internal quotation is from the introduction to Hobsbawm, *Labouring Men*, p. viii. The expansion of the subject was recorded in the bibliographies published annually in the *BSSLH* and in the impressive range of 4,000 books and articles collected in Harold Smith, *The British Labour Movement to 1970: A Bibliography* (London: Mansell Publishing, 1981).

52 Raphael Samuel, 'On the Methods of History Workshop: A Reply', *History Workshop Journal*, 9 (1980), 162–76 (p. 166). For the differences that some Society members maintained with Samuel's approach, see 'Twenty Years On', and the correspondence it provoked – for and against – in *BSSLH*, 42 (1981), 13–14, 16–18.

53 Conversations with Harrison and Halstead; 'Twenty Years On', p. 4; cf. 'The Social History Society was a straightforward professionalising initiative [...]'. Geoff Eley, *A Crooked Line: From Cultural History to the History of Society* (Ann Arbor: University of Michigan Press, 2008), p. 248, n. 1. *Social History* reflected the reach of academic Marxism and remained a forum for wide-ranging debate into the 1990s. For an alternative reading of the development of social history, see Miles Taylor, 'The Beginnings of Modern Social History', *History Workshop Journal*, 43 (1997), 155–76.

54 *British Feminist Thought: A Reader*, ed. by Terry Lovell (Oxford: Blackwell, 1990), pp. 21–27. Sheila Rowbotham, one of the most accomplished British feminist historians, was a long-standing participant in Society activity and the SSLH's first conference on women's history preceded that convened by History Workshop. However, many women historians welcomed the informality and orientations to activism of the Workshop: Sheila Rowbotham, *Threads Through Time: Writings on History and Autobiography* (London: Penguin, 1999), p. 19. In more recent times there was an ephemeral attempt to formalize parity between men and women on SSLH bodies and feminize *LHR*. At the time of writing, two out of four editors of the journal and six out of twelve members of the Editorial Advisory Board are women. The interest in gendered perspectives was demonstrated in the Special Issue of *LHR* on 'Gender and Work', *LHR*, 63, 1 (1998) and the collection in the Society's book series, *Working Out Gender: Perspectives from Labour History*, ed. by Margaret Walsh (Aldershot: Ashgate, 1999), which consisted of papers from a Society conference in 1998. Both were largely about women's history but a little later an issue of the journal was devoted to 'Working-Class Masculinities in Britain', *LHR*, 69, 2 (2004). For a critical stance, see Karen Hunt, 'Gender and British Labour History in the 1990s', *Mitteilungsblatt des Instituts für soziale Bewegungen*, 27 (2002), 185–200; for a corrective, see John McIlroy, Alan

Campbell, John Halstead and David Martin, 'Introduction: Fifty Years On', in *Making History*, 1-14 (pp. 5-6).

55 See, for example, 'The Labour Aristocracy Twenty-Five Years After'.

56 'The Commonwealth Labour History Conference, Coventry 2–4 September 1981', *BSSLH*, 44 (1982), 14.

57 Eric Hobsbawm, 'The Forward March of Labour Halted?' (1st pub. 1978), reprinted in *The Forward March of Labour Halted?*, ed. by Martin Jacques and Francis Mulhern (London: Verso, 1981), pp. 1–19.

58 'Editorial', *BSSLH*, 45 (1982), 2; *BSSLH*, 47 (1983), 2; Juliet Gardiner, *The History Debate* (London: Collins and Brown, 1990).

59 'Twenty Years On'; 'Editorial: The Long March of British Labour Historiography Halted? The Society in Crisis', *BSSLH*, 43 (1981), 2–3; editorials in *BSSLH*, 45 (1982), 2–3; *BSSLH*, 47 (1983), 2. See also the remarks in Alastair Reid, 'The Subject of Labour History', *LHR*, 55, 3 (1990), 5–6.

60 Conrad Russell, *The Origins of the English Civil War* (Oxford: Oxford University Press, 1973); idem, *The Causes of the English Civil War* (Oxford: Clarendon Press, 1990). The quotation is from the title of the first chapter of J.C.D. Clark, *Our Shadowed Present: Modernism, Postmodernism and History* (London: Atlantic Books, 2003). For recent discussion of these trends, see Ronald Hutton, 'Revisionism in Britain', in *Companion to Historiography*, ed. by Michael Bentley (London: Routledge, 1997), pp. 377–91; *History and Revolution: Refuting Revisionism*, ed. by Mike Haynes and Jim Wolfreys (London: Verso, 2007).

61 Linda Colley, *Britons: Forging the Nation, 1707–1837* (New Haven and London: Yale University Press, 1992); cf. E.P. Thompson, 'Which Britons?', in idem, *Persons and Polemics* (London: Merlin Press, 1994).

62 For the beginning of 'the linguistic turn', see Stedman Jones, *Languages of Class*, particularly pp. 16–24, 90–178, although this was different from what came after. *The Postmodern History Reader*, ed. by Keith Jenkins (London: Routledge, 1997) is a useful collection of articles from both enthusiasts and critics including social and labour historians. Richard J. Evans, *In Defence of History* (London: Granta Books, 1997) is a pugnacious but nuanced reiteration of the integrity of historical knowledge. More specifically, see Neville Kirk, 'Language, Ideas and Postmodernism', *Social History*, 19 (1994), 221–40.

63 See the perceptive comments on the followers of Gareth Stedman Jones in Susan Pederson, 'What is Political History Now?', in *What is History Now?*, ed. by David Carradine (Basingstoke: Palgrave Macmillan, 2002), pp. 36–56.

64 Patrick Joyce, *Visions of the People: Industrial England and the Question of Class, 1848–1914* (Cambridge: Cambridge University Press, 1991); idem, *Democratic Subjects: The Self and the Social in Nineteenth-Century England* (Cambridge: Cambridge University Press, 1994).

65 For a summary, see David Howell, 'Editorial', *Labour History Review* (*LHR*), 60, 1 (1995), 2. See also Marcel van der Linden, 'Editorial', *International Review of Social History*, 38 (1993), Supplement 1, 'The End of Labour History?', 163–73; and Ira Katznelson, 'The "Bourgeois" Dimension: A Provocation About Institutions, Politics and the Future of Labor History', *International Labor and*

Working-Class History, 46 (1994), 1–32 .

66 See, for example, Barbara Taylor, *Eve and the New Jerusalem* (London: Virago, 1983); Carolyn Steedman, *Landscape for a Good Woman: A Story of Two Lives* (London: Virago, 1986); *Labour and Love: Women's Experience of Home and Family, 1850–1940*, ed. by Jane Lewis (Oxford: Blackwell, 1986); Catherine Hall, *White, Male and Middle-Class: Explorations in Feminist History* (London: Routledge, 1988); Joan Wallach Scott, *Gender and the Politics of History* (New York: Columbia University Press, 1988); Sonya Rose, *Limited Livelihoods: Gender and Class in Nineteenth Century* England (Berkeley: University of California Press, 1992); Sally Alexander, *Becoming a Woman and other Essays in Nineteenth- and Twentieth-Century Feminist History* (London: Virago, 1994); Anna Clark, *The Struggle for the Breeches: Gender and the Making of the British Working Class* (Berkeley: University of California Press, 1995); Deborah Simonton, *A History of European Women's Work, 1700 to the Present* (London: Routledge, 1998); Katrina Honeyman, *Women, Gender and Industrialization, 1700–1870* (Basingstoke: Macmillan, 2000).

67 Leonore Davidoff and Catherine Hall, *Family Fortunes: Men and Women of the English Middle Class, 1750–1850* (London: Hutchinson, 1987). For different understandings of gender history, see Joan Wallach Scott, 'Gender: A Useful Category of Historical Analysis', *American Historical Review*, 91 (1986), 1053–75; and Catherine Hall, 'Politics, Post-Structuralism and Feminist History', *Gender and History*, 3 (1991), 204–10. For a criticism of Scott's version of gender history and a defence of women's history, see June Purvis, 'From "Women Worthies" to Poststructuralism? Debate and Controversy in Women's History in Britain', in *Women's History: Britain, 1850–1945*, ed. by June Purvis (London: Routledge, 1995), pp. 1–22 (pp. 12–15).

68 See the comments on Barbara Taylor's work in Angela Weir and Elizabeth Wilson, 'The British Women's Movement', *New Left Review*, 148 (1984), 85–88.

69 Walby, *Patriarchy*; Rose, *Limited Livelihoods*; idem, 'Gender and Labour History: The Nineteenth Century Legacy', *International Review of Social History*, 38 (1993), Supplement 1, 'The End of Labour History?', 145–62; Scott, 'Gender: A Useful Category'; idem, *Gender and the Politics of History*; idem, 'The "Class" We Have Lost', *International Labour and Working-Class History*, 57 (2000), 69–75; Bryan Palmer, *Descent into Discourse: The Reification of Language and the Writing of Social History* (Philadelphia: Temple University Press, 1990), pp. 78–86, 172–86.

70 Neville Kirk, *Labour and Society in Britain and the USA, vol. 1: Capitalism, Custom and Protest, 1750–1850; vol. 2: Challenge and Accommodation, 1850–1939* (Aldershot: Scolar Press, 1994); Stefan Berger, *The British Labour Party and the German Social Democrats, 1900–*1931 (Oxford: Clarendon Press, 1994). And see now Neville Kirk, *Comrades and Cousins: Globalization, Workers and Labour Movements in Britain, the USA and Australia from the 1880s to 1914* (London: Merlin Press, 2003).

71 Noel W. Thompson, *The People's Science: The Popular Political Economy of Exploitation and Crisis, 1816–34* (Cambridge: Cambridge University Press,

1984); Gregory Claeys, *Citizens and Saints: Politics and Anti-Politics in Early British Socialism* (Cambridge: Cambridge University Press, 1989).

72 Eley, *Crooked Line*, pp. 172–81.

73 See McIlroy, 'Society', 90-98; McIlroy et al., 'Introduction', 13-14.

74 See, particularly, John Saville, 'The "Crisis" in Labour History: A Further Comment', *LHR*, 61 (1996), 322–28. See also Howell, 'Editorial', and the contributions from Malcolm Chase, Steven Fielding and John Halstead, David Martin and Keith Flett in 'Debate: The Current and Future Position of Labour History', *LHR*, 60, 3 (1995), 46–53.

75 For a recent review of the arguments, see *Marxist History-Writing for the Twenty-First Century*, ed. by Chris Wickham (Oxford: Oxford University Press, 2007).

76 For a stimulating, albeit idiosyncratic, essay, see Harold Perkin, '"The Condescension of Posterity": The Recent Historiography of the English Working Class', *Social Science History*, 3 (1978), 87–101. For an important and provocative critique of the new labour history, arguing for a return to studying institutions, see Jonathan Zeitlin, 'From Labour History to the History of Industrial Relations', *Economic History Review*, n.s., 40 (1987), 159–84. For a political polemic, see Steven Fielding, '"New" Labour and the "New" Labour History', *Mitteilungsblatt des Instituts für soziale Bewegungen*, 27 (2002), 35–50. See also Hunt, 'Gender and Labour History'. There are a number of short comments by Alastair Reid. These are critically considered in David Howell, 'Reading Alastair Reid', in *Social Class and Marxism: Defences and Challenges*, ed. by Neville Kirk (Aldershot: Scolar Press, 1996), pp. 214–36. For insightful commentary on the wider state of labour history today, see the essays in *Class and Other Identities: Gender, Religion and Ethnicity in the Writing of European Labour History*, ed. by Lex Heerma van Voss and Marcel van der Linden (Oxford: Berghahn Books, 2002).

77 Howell, 'Editorial', p. 2.

78 On this, see John McIlroy and Gary Daniels, 'History Matters: Understanding the Future, the Present and the Past of Trade Unionism', in Trade Union Congress, *Union Futures* (London: Labour Research Department, 2007), pp. 5–14.

79 See n. 74.

80 *LHR*, 60, 3 (1995), 2–36.

81 The conference was reported in detail in 'Is There A Future for Labour History?', *LHR*, 62 (1997), 253–9. That issue also included John Belchem's contribution critically discussing postmodernist trends, 'Reconstructing Labour History', ibid., 318–23. Joyce's paper, 'Refabricating Labour History; or, From Labour History to the History of Labour', is in *LHR*, 62 (1997), 147–53. Despite the evidence of his earlier work, Joyce reflected: 'I have never considered myself a labour historian' (ibid., p. 147).

82 'Is There a Future for Labour History?', p. 253.

83 Ibid., p. 254.

84 Kirk, *Social Class and Marxism*; *Languages of Labour*, ed. by John Belchem and Neville Kirk (Aldershot: Ashgate, 1997). The latter volume, which brought

together papers from the Society's 1996 conference, was assessed as 'a salutary rebuttal of postmodernist academic imperialism': Noel Thompson, review, *LHR*, 64 (1999), 69. Attentiveness to language on the part of labour historians was, of course, far from novel: see Asa Briggs, 'The Language of "Class" in Early Nineteenth-Century England', in Briggs and Saville, *Essays in Labour History*, pp. 43–73.

85 'Editorial', *LHR*, 61 (1996), 1–3. Perhaps the argument should have centred less on the need for a journal, more on the kind of journal labour history societies should aspire to. *LHR* has made few concessions to the Society's purpose of popularizing history, at least beyond academics.

86 Saville, 'Crisis', p. 323. Between 1996 and the end of 2009, forty-two issues of *LHR* have been published, initially by Edinburgh University Press and then from 2002 by Maney Publishing. The Bulletin was regularly indexed and indices appeared in *LHR* until 2003. The most recent separate index is Victor F. Gilbert, *Cumulative Index to the Bulletin of the Society for the Study of Labour History, 1986–1989 and the Labour History Review, 1990–1995* (London: Society for the Study of Labour History, 1998).

87 Fielding, 'New Labour History', pp. 46–9.

88 Alan Campbell, *The Scottish Miners, 1874–1939, vol. 1: Industry, Work and Community; vol. 2: Trade Unions and Politics* (Aldershot: Ashgate, 2000); Malcolm Chase, *Chartism: A New History* (Manchester: Manchester University Press, 2007). The Merlin Press series on Chartism, edited by Owen Ashton, is also associated with the Society.

89 Since the 1990s the holders of the SSLH's main offices have been Chair: Ray Challinor, 1984–1994; Eileen Yeo, 1994–1997; Chris Wrigley, 1997–2001; John Halstead, 2001–2005; Malcolm Chase, 2005–2009; and Alan Campbell, 2009–; Secretary: John Belchem, 1990–1994; Joan Hugman (Allen), 1994–2007; John Halstead, 2007–2009; John McIlroy, 2009–. John Saville (1916–2009) died after this chapter was written.

90 Asa Briggs, 'Introduction', in Briggs and Saville, *Essays in Labour History, 1886–1923*, p. 1.

91 Ibid. For the history of labour history, see Marcel van der Linden and Lex Heerma van Voss, 'Introduction', in Heerma van Voss and van der Linden, *Class and Other Identities*, pp. 1–39. See also Marcel van der Linden, *Transnational Labour History* (Aldershot: Ashgate, 2003).

92 See, for example, *BSSLH*, 1 (1960), 4, 29; *BSSLH*, 2 (1961), 17–18.

93 *BSSLH*, 4 (1962), 64; *BSSLH*, 5 (1962), 41–2; *BSSLH*, 27 (1973), 4; *BSSLH*, 40 (1980), 2. The journal became the present *Labour/Le Travail* in 1983.

94 Information from John Halstead.

95 For the Scottish society see Robert Duncan, 'The Scottish Labour History Society: A Retrospect', in *Making History*, 113-23. For the Irish society, see Emmet O'Connor and Conor McCabe, 'Ireland', chapter 4 in this volume, and Emmet O'Connor, 'The Irish Labour History Society: An Outline History', in *Making History*, 143-55. For the Welsh society, see Deian Hopkin, 'Llafur: Labour History Society and People's Remembrancer, 1970–20', in ibid., 125-42.

96 Details of all the societies appeared regularly in the *Bulletin* until the 1980s.
97 *BSSLH*, 13 (1966), 13–21.
98 *BSSLH*, 17 (1968), 11–26; *BSSLH*, 27 (1973), 13–33.
99 *BSSLH*, 35 (1977), 19–20; *LHR*, 57, 1 (1992), 80. For publications from the conference, see, for example, *Industrial Conflict: Papers Presented to the Fourth Anglo-Dutch Conference in Labour History, Newcastle-upon-Tyne, 1984*, ed. by Lex Heerma van Voss and Herman Diederiks (Amsterdam: Stichting Beheer IISG, 1988); *Generations in Labour History: Papers Presented to the Sixth British Dutch Conference on Labour History*, ed. by Aad Blok, Dirk Damsma, Herman Diedericks and Lex Heerma van Voss (Amsterdam: Stichting Beheer IISG, 1989).
100 *BSSLH*, 42 (1981), 84–85; *BSSLH*, 44 (1982), 11–12. The limitations of the conference were announced in its subtitle, 'The Lands of White Settlement'.
101 Conversations with Royden Harrison.
102 See 'Editorial', *BSSLH*, 35 (1977), 5.
103 Sheila Rowbotham, 'The Informed Historian', *LHR*, 59, 1 (1994), 7.
104 For the international impact of British labour historians, see, for example, Saville, *Memoirs*, pp. 160–61, 170–73; *Visions of History*, ed. by Henry Abelove et al., interviews with Hobsbawm, Thompson and Rowbotham; E.P. Thompson, *Writing by Candlelight* (London: Merlin Press, 1980), pp. 135–48; E.P. Thompson, *Alien Homage: Edward Thompson and Rabindranath Tagore* (Delhi: Oxford University Press, 1993); Sumit Sarkar, *Writing Social History* (Delhi: Oxford University Press, 1997); Bryan Palmer, *E.P. Thompson: Objections and Oppositions* (London: Verso, 1994); Hobsbawm, *Interesting Times*, passim.
105 T.S. Eliot, 'Little Gidding'.
106 van der Linden, *Transnational Labour History*.
107 There have never been more than a handful of Professors or Readers in Labour History in British universities, and only then in recent years with the expansion of the professoriate. The number of courses dedicated to labour history, as distinct from courses in which aspects of the subject are taught, is also tiny.
108 Peter Linebaugh and Marcus Rediker, *The Many-Headed Hydra: Sailors, Slaves, Commoners and the Hidden History of the Revolutionary Atlantic* (London and New York: Verso, 2000); Marcus Rediker, *The Slave Ship: A Human History* (London: John Murray, 2007); Catherine Hall, *Civilizing Subjects: Metropole and Colony in the English Imagination, 1830–1867* (Oxford: Polity Press, 2002); idem, 'Marxism and its Others', in Wickham, *Marxist History-Writing*, pp. 112–39; Chris Wickham, *Framing the Early Middle Ages: Europe and the Mediterranean, 400–800* (Oxford: Oxford University Press, 2005). See also C.A. Bayley, *The Birth of the Modern World, 1780–1914* (Oxford: Oxford University Press, 2004).
109 University of Hull Archive, Brynmor John Library, Saville Papers, DJS/10, Hobsbawm to Saville, 24 March 1956.
110 Hobsbawm, *The Age of Revolution*; idem., *The Age of Capital, 1848–1875* (London: Weidenfeld and Nicolson, 1975); idem, *The Age of Empire, 1875–1914* (London: Weidenfeld and Nicolson, 1987); idem, *The Age of Extremes:*

The Short History of the Twentieth Century, 1914–1991 (London: Michael Joseph, 1995).

111 Cf. Wickham, *Framing*, p. 2.

112 Hugh Trevor-Roper, *The Rise of Christian Europe* (London: Thames and Hudson, 1965), p. 9, cited in Evans, *In Defence of History*, p. 178.

2

Britain: 1750–1900

Joan Allen and Malcolm Chase

Just as it is difficult to contemplate the history of the nineteenth century without reference to the pivotal economic transformations of the age – which even allowing for recent scholarly emphasis on the *longue durée* are still most readily characterized as an industrial *revolution* – so it is a commonplace that this period has been a particular stamping ground of successive generations of labour historians. As Richard Price observed, for a long time the nineteenth century was viewed as the 'moment when modern Britain was formed'.[1] Consensus as to its significance, however, has not manifested itself in a uniform approach and even those who saw themselves as working in the Marxist tradition invested their histories with their own nuanced readings and methodologies. Inevitably, twenty-first century labour historians view their task and the challenges that the complex history of the period poses differently to their counterparts writing just before and at the turn of the twentieth century.[2]

This chapter begins by offering a general appraisal of the state of labour history and the background of some of its practitioners around the time of the formation of the Society for the Study of Labour History (SSLH) in 1960.[3] An assessment will then be made of the major, overarching contribution to the field made by the key text of one of the founders, Edward Thompson's *The Making of the English Working Class*, which was published soon after the Society's formation. This is followed by an exploration of the debates surrounding the significance of Chartism and its legacy in the third quarter of the nineteenth century. The analysis then moves on to review the literature on two traditional themes in British labour historiography, the 'socialist revival' after 1880 and the history of trade unionism. The concluding section considers two recent developments, the elaboration of an intellectual history of labour movement ideologies and the contribution of postmodern approaches to the subject.

Nineteenth-century British labour historiography, c.1960

Early labour historians such as Sidney and Beatrice Webb, John and Barbara Hammond and G.D.H. Cole focused much of their attention on national studies. Their triumphalist approach was concerned with the commonality of the labouring experience and the collective battle against the forces of capitalism and an oppressive state. Between 1890 and *circa* 1960 (a new edition of Cole and Raymond Postgate's *The Common People, 1746–1946* appeared as late as 1968) their work celebrated the achievements of trade unions and other major working-class institutions.[4] While the role of the individual did not go unrecognized, they were primarily interested in identifying and documenting the leadership role of working-class heroes. Within this perspective, the rise of labour and the political and industrial maturity of British society were closely linked: the former was the predictable and unproblematic response to those changed conditions.

The labour historians of the first half of the century worked outside of the historical profession: neither the Webbs nor the Hammonds were academics, whilst Cole, *doyen* of the Labour Research Department, was 36 before he assumed a university post (as Oxford's Reader in Economics). In this respect the inception of the SSLH and the remarkable flurry of publications around the years of its formation, marked something of a departure. Three works particularly stand out: *Chartist Studies* (1959) edited by Asa Briggs; a second collection jointly edited by Briggs and John Saville, *Essays in Labour History* (1960); and, most obviously, Thompson's *The Making of the English Working Class* (1963).[5] Although the influence of Marxism would subsequently be widely cited as shaping the emergence of labour history at this time, other elements deserve no less emphasis. Yorkshire universities dominated the authorial affiliations, as did work in university adult education (or extramural studies as it was then generally known); and all three books deployed a finely nuanced understanding of locality and region which reflected and extended a rapidly developing area of English historical scholarship at this time.

The character of British labour history at this watershed can be discerned in the two edited collections. (Thompson contributed to *Essays in Labour History* and was originally to have written for *Chartist Studies* too.) Fully half the contents (based on page extents) of *Chartist Studies* and *Essays* was the work of lecturers from the universities of Hull, Leeds or Sheffield. Saville, co-editor of *Essays in Labour History*, taught economic and social history at Hull; two other contributors, Royden Harrison and Sidney Pollard, who would both go on to make seminal contributions to the development of labour history, taught at Sheffield. Thompson lectured in the Leeds department of extramural studies. A defining feature of extramural education, especially in Yorkshire, was a commitment to academic rigour, combined with a distinguished history of reaching out 'beyond the walls' to students in their own communities. Young labour historians would find themselves suddenly immersed in unfamiliar localities, amidst earnest students whose command of recent – and not-so-recent history – was often remarkable and compelling. 'One was conscious of being part of a tradition of adult education', Harrison has since written. Such an environment could not but have an enduring impact. Harrison was particularly influenced by one student, a woolpacker, who 'talked about Ernest Jones, the Halifax Chartist leader, as if he had died yesterday, instead of in 1869'.[6] Thompson dedicated *The Making* to Dorothy and Joseph Greenald, students from his Cleckheaton class who had been expelled from the local Labour Party for membership of the proscribed Yorkshire Federation of Peace Organisations. Royden Harrison dedicated his first book to the Derbyshire miners' leader 'Bert Wynn and all my friends and comrades in the coalfields of Derbyshire and Yorkshire'.[7]

Much labour history in this period was avowedly provincial: 'the national historian still tends to have a curiously distorted view of goings-on "in the provinces"', Thompson observed:

> Provincial leaders are commonly denied full historical citizenship [...] labour historians tend to fall into a double-vision; on the one hand, there are mass movements which grow blindly and spontaneously under economic and social pressures: on the other, the leaders and manipulators – the Places, the Chartist journalists, the Juntas and parliamentarians – who direct these elemental forces into political channels.

Thompson went on to argue that the 'superficial national approach is beginning to give way to a more mature school of local history'.[8] This development was significantly expedited by *Chartist Studies* and, to some extent, also by *Essays in Labour History* (through Thompson's account of the formation of the Independent Labour Party in West Yorkshire and Henry Collins's analysis of the English branches of the First International). Thompson's *Making* was similarly rooted in the Pennine uplands.

Of course, the remarkable flowering of labour history at the time that the

SSLH was founded was not *sui generis*. It reflected, as well as stimulating further, broader intellectual trends. 'Economic history is beginning to escape from the clutches of the economist', wrote the medievalist Herbert Hallam in 1958, 'the best economic historians are beginning to see the major factors in economic history which are not really economic at all.'[9] Michael Bentley has delineated the emergence of social history around this time, from a convergence of *Annaliste* influences, the increasing synthesis of economic, social and geographic elements and the earlier tradition of 'humanistic social commentary' epitomized by the Hammonds.[10]

To this should be added the earliest 'cultural turn' in historical studies of labour (a phenomenon that was to be of increasing importance from the 1980s) in the form of another path-breaking book from 1963, Louis James's *Fiction for the Working Man*. It, too, emanated from a Yorkshire university extramural department for James was a Hull staff-tutor in north Lincolnshire at the time. Although 'primarily the study of a *literature*' provided *for* working-class readers, James's inquisitiveness about reading habits 'closely unified by political and class feeling', together with his avowed intent to divest Dickens 'of the myth of a universal readership', constituted the foundation for literary scholarship's recovery of (and increasing respect for) working-class *writers*, a development closely linked with that of labour history.[11]

The Making of the English Working Class and its critics

In the words of the social-science historian, Charles Tilly, in 1963 'E.P. Thompson roared onto the terrain of class analysis like an invading army'.[12] Thompson's seminal study *The Making of the English Working Class* towered over the 1960s and demands specific attention. Extending to over 900 pages, the book was organized in three parts. The first traced plebeian political culture in the eighteenth century, culminating in the reception of Jacobin ideas in England in the 1790s; the second explored the experience of various groups of workers during the industrial revolution, both at work and in the community; the final section, taking up over half the text, recorded the growing 'working-class presence' in English politics, teasing out the underground networks and insurrectionary traditions that linked Jacobinism with Luddism, trade unionism, Owenism, cooperation and the radical agitations of the 1820s, to conclude that a new sense of class identity had been forged by the first Reform Act of 1832. Class, Thompson famously insisted on the first page of the book, could only be understood as a historical relationship. The enfranchisement of the middle classes in 1832 and the exclusion of the working class drew a line 'in social consciousness

[...] with the crudity of an indelible pencil'.[13]

Extraordinary though it was, in style, breadth and theoretical sophistication, the volume shared the circumstances of its production with other key labour history studies published around this time. This context helped secure a readership far beyond the academy, and its reception was assisted by the extent to which it chimed with other endeavours in the field. It may also help explain how and why British labour history, viewed as a field of academic endeavour, remained strikingly impervious to many of the criticisms meted out on the book. Thompson's claim that the working class shaped its own history was strongly rejected by Tom Nairn and Perry Anderson who accused him of, among other things, romanticism.[14] Instead, they insisted that the *ruling class* had primarily shaped working-class history. Thompson, confining his response to Nairn and Anderson to his separately published essay, 'The Peculiarities of the English', used the 'Postscript' to the second edition of *The Making* (1968) almost entirely to address matters of factual accuracy. The third edition (1980) limited its response to scholarship that had appeared since 1968, simply noting the work of five authors (and brushing aside two others).[15]

Nonetheless, he was disposed to address the criticism from some quarters that his *Making* was Anglo-centric, privileging English workers by suggesting that their class consciousness was more mature that that of the Scots, the Welsh or the Irish (the latter were referred to only in terms of their immigrant status). A 'note of apology' at the end of his 1963 preface claimed that any perceived neglect was 'not out of chauvinism but out of respect. It is because class is a cultural as well as an economic formation that I have been cautious as to generalising beyond English experience.' While he readily acknowledged that the Scots had been just as 'tormented', he stressed that their experiences were 'significantly different', not least because of the impact of Calvinism.[16] Such explanations seem to imply that culture can somehow be contained within geographical boundaries – a difficult premise to sustain given that wars and governmental convenience have determined the remarkable fluidity of the Welsh and Scottish borders.

Thompson's categories were, moreover, exclusively male and it is hardly surprising that feminist historians in Britain and overseas quarrelled with the absence of women in his account of class formation. As the women's movement gathered pace in the late 1960s, many British feminists were frustrated by the failure of the left to be more inclusive and this was given powerful expression when Sheila Rowbotham's groundbreaking text, *Hidden From History,* was published in 1973.[17] Carolyn Steedman observed in 1993 that Thompson's famous text 'was an active presence' in much of the work produced by feminist historians in the decades which followed.[18] Writing 'in the shadow of a labor history which silences them', historians such as Sally Alexander and Anna Davin, founding members of the editorial collective of *History Workshop Journal* (*HWJ*), nevertheless set out with broadly similar objectives.[19] They, too, were eager to write a 'history from below', for they were convinced that 'it is the relationships like that between the two worlds, between the sexual division of labour and class struggle, home and work, or the private sector and the public, the social relationships between men and women, which form the substance of feminist history, and will enrich socialist history'.[20]

Feminist historians and writers certainly enriched the field though, in the main, it was the relaxed ethos of the History Workshop collective rather than the ranks of labour history that enabled them to find their voice. Their voice was so strong that *HWJ* formally acknowledged the importance of feminist history by adding the term to its title in Spring 1982.[21] The question of female class consciousness, moreover, was to prove more elusive than Alexander and Davin expected, at least in terms of working women. As the writers of both feminist history and women's history became ever more caught up in an exploration of the gendered separation of spheres,[22] this gradually produced some important work on middle-class identity, most notably Davidoff and Hall's *Family Fortunes,* but little headway had been made on working-class identity.[23] In 1993, Steedman was at pains to point out that progress lay within their grasp: if middle-class women 'were *formed*' by their class relationship with their servants, then the same might be held true for working women. Until the latter decades of the nineteenth century, when women increasingly looked elsewhere for work, a large percentage of the female population spent a period of their working lives in some form of domestic service. This, Steedman argued, was a relationship historians urgently needed 'to get the measure of: its antagonisms, its space for the most exquisite torture, its painful and dreadful silences; one of the places where class consciousness was formed'.[24]

Clearly, feminist perspectives on the nineteenth century have critically informed key areas of labour history: in the work of Jutta Schwartzkopf, Dorothy Thompson, Anna Clark and Eileen Yeo on Chartism and in that of Jill Liddington and June Purvis on women's suffrage.[25] Yet is noticeable that much work on the latter clusters (perhaps necessarily so) around the turn of the century.[26] On the other hand, scholarship on working women's lives (by, for example, Sonya Rose, Katrina Honeyman, Sheila Blackburn, Maggie Walsh, Deborah Simonton and Pamela Horn) has made substantial progress in rectifying the gender deficit in nineteenth-century labour history.[27] Domestic service, however, remains a curious hiatus, given that this was by a considerable distance the greatest source of waged employment for females throughout our period. 'Thompson's thesis concerning class and class formation has been scrutinised, adjusted, altered, moved back and forward in time, and gendered', Steedman has recently observed, 'but servants are no more part of the story than they were when it was first written.'[28]

The other conspicuous weakness of *The Making* was its treatment of agricultural labourers. Though not ignored completely, and updated for the second edition, even Thompson himself cheerfully conceded that his 'chapter on "The Field Labourers" [...] still remains inadequate to its theme'.[29] The publication in 1969 of a classic study of labour protest by Eric Hobsbawm and George Rudé, *Captain Swing*, which explored the extent and meaning of widespread rural protest in 1830 as well as the identities of the insurgents, went some way towards retrieving the situation. However, like the labour history of women, it was from within History Workshop that agricultural labour history received its earliest authoritative treatment.[30]

Wherein, then, did the originality of *The Making* lie? Much more than the other works we have discussed so far, it was concerned with the cultural and social environment (religious, family, community, recreational) within which labouring lives were lived. One of the great strengths of Thompson's work lay in his innovative analysis of popular culture. This offered labour historians a new direction – a more fruitful field of endeavour which was organically connected with the work then being produced by Rudé, a member of the Communist Party (CP), on the dynamics of crowd activity and mentalities.[31] Thompson, Rudé and younger scholars like Raphael Samuel, who would later co-found the History Workshop movement, sought to raise the visibility of the common man's involvement in political protest and excavate what motivated them. As Thompson most famously expressed it, they set about 'rescuing the poor stockinger, the Luddite cropper [...] from the enormous condescension of posterity'.[32]

Chartism and beyond

Thompson's *Making* culminated on the cusp of Chartism's emergence and would be widely read as providing essential context to understanding the causation and nature of the movement. It had, indeed, a profound influence upon the historiography of Chartism and it is a moot point whether this influence was all to the good. First, Thompson's bravura performance left those who contemplated writing about the Chartist period with the sense that his was an impossibly hard act to follow. For a time its impact was so great that a much needed, large-scale labour history was effectively stalled. A sequel from Thompson's own hand was widely anticipated. 'Why has the author gone back in time to write the pre-history of the English working class', a founding editor of *HWJ* lamented: '[d]id any other readers, like me, look forward to volumes 2 and 3 on the Chartist movement and "10 Hours"?'[33] In the two decades after *The Making*, the only history which claimed to appraise Chartism in its entirety was written from a perspective profoundly antagonistic to the movement (and, even more-perplexingly, without recourse to archival material of any kind).[34]

Instead, the localizing trend initiated by *Chartist Studies* was powerfully reinforced. Of the approximately 140 local studies (published and unpublished) of Chartism, only a dozen appeared before *Chartist Studies.* The latter itself contained 6 more; 15 further local studies appeared in the 1960s, 44 in the 1970s, and 48 in the 1980s, slowing to a mere 13 since 1990.[35] In part, this phenomenon was driven by the material circumstances of higher education from the 1960s, as an expanding number of institutions and professional historians turned out growing numbers of students who needed dissertation topics at undergraduate, masters' and doctoral levels. The *Chartist Studies* volume was in itself inspirational, but there has never been a parallel explosion of local studies of other key episodes in labour history.[36] However, it can be suggested that something else was happening here. 'There are not many points in modern British history at which the historian can profitably speculate whether a revolutionary situation might have developed but did not', J.F.C. Harrison observed, adding that Chartism seemed to pose the threat of the barricades on at least two occasions (the winter of 1839 and spring and summer of 1848).[37] What also stimulated the flood of local studies of Chartism was a form of revolutionary antiquarianism – historiography as a form of comradeship with the past, and the writing of history almost as consolation for failure.

One of the consequences of this local studies boom was to firmly evict the London Working Men's Association's leader, William Lovett, from a place of eminence in the Chartist pantheon. The thinly disguised Fabian agenda of early, national histories of Chartism had found in Lovett an exemplary labour leader – working-class, self-taught and patient. As the Parliamentary Labour Party lost much of its 1945 General Election shine, it was inevitable that labour historians (even those who had never affiliated to the CP) should review critically the merits of gradualism.[38] References to Feargus O'Connor outnumber Lovett by a ratio of more than two to one in *Chartist Studies.* Though a crude indicator, this reflects the inevitable consequences of disaggregating the narrative of Chartism; Lovett's authority was imperfect even in London: elsewhere, and especially in northern industrial centres, Chartism and O' Connorism were close to synonymous.

From the 1970s there was a further force at work on the historiography of Chartism that likewise privileged O'Connor over the movement's other leaders. A generation of historians active in – or at least schooled against the background of – the campaigns for nuclear disarmament, black civil rights in the USA and opposition to the Vietnam War, were disposed to view favourably the politics of direct action; they were also much less insistent upon the importance of conventional party organization, preferring instead to see class consciousness and working-class associational culture as the vehicles that drove Chartism forward. This generation was less overt in proclaiming its political sympathies, in the way that pre-war historians of Chartism had done. But the flags were clearly planted for those who wanted to see them. One reviewer saw a forest of them in Dorothy Thompson's *The Chartists* (1984) and accused her of writing 'O'Connor hagiography'.[39] The preliminary pages of John Belchem's biography of O'Connor's avowed role model, Henry Hunt, commenced by quoting from the song written by the black American soul singer, Sam Cooke, 'A Change is Gonna Come'. And James Epstein's biography of O'Connor, *The Lion of Freedom*, concludes that the Chartists 'fought with a resilience perhaps best captured in O'Connor's words, "and No Surrender"'.[40]

The final point to be made about the historiography of Chartism up to the early 1980s is that it largely evaded the thorny question of why Chartism failed. The challenge posed by the Land Plan to class-based interpretations of Chartism was ducked.[41] Epstein's biography of O'Connor closed not with his death (1855), nor even in 1848, but in 1842. Not until Dorothy Thompson's groundbreaking study in 1984 did any labour historian attempt to explain why Chartism failed and provide a concerted survey (albeit of only ten pages) of its consequences.[42] The broader historiographical landscape was also decisively shifting. Dorothy Thompson had had a significant hand in this as convenor, in 1977–78, of two colloquia on Chartism. The resultant volume avowedly sought to move the field beyond *Chartist Studies*.[43] Although it included local studies, the collection was most notable for opening out new areas of investigation: the movement's Irish dimension, the collapse of the mass platform after 1848, the practice of democracy within the movement itself, and 'the language of Chartism'. The latter, expanded by its author Gareth Stedman Jones the following year as 'Rethinking Chartism', became a seminal chapter in the historiography not just of Chartism but of labour and society generally.[44]

'Rethinking' had five important consequences. First, its publication crossed with both Dorothy Thompson's *The Chartists* and with David Goodway's *London Chartism: 1838–1848.*[45] This had the unfortunate result that the two most authoritative histories of the movement to appear in the twentieth century seemed to have no reply to the arguments Jones deployed. Second, the latter advanced a powerful case that the plethora of local studies had atomized understanding of Chartism, obscuring both the movement's strengths and weaknesses. A profound shift in the trajectory of studies of the movement followed. While there was limited direct engagement with Jones's views from specialists on Chartism, local studies fell from favour.[46] This is evident in the important series of volumes published since the late 1990s by Merlin Press. This largely eschews locally based research in favour of 'niche', biographical and thematic studies.[47] Local research, when included, has taken the form of substantial longitudinal studies that achieve a depth of contextualization (and engagement with the key issues of continuity and change in labour politics) unmatched in the earlier tradition initiated by the Briggs volume.[48]

Thirdly, though the Merlin series has very much kept Chartism alive as a field of historical study, it has sometimes been marked by a certain introspection that compounded the relative silence which met 'Rethinking' from Chartist specialists and other labour historians alike. A tradition of scholarship rooted in empiricism within a generalized Marxisant framework – and shared with labour history as a whole – was ill-equipped to respond to the post-Marxist and continental-inflected 'linguistic turn'. In several respects this new social history can be viewed as pacesetting, open to new theories and perspectives. And it was left to an Australian scholar to provide the most engaged and effective response to Jones from a specifically Chartist historiographical perspective.[49]

The fourth consequence of 'Rethinking', and particularly of its call for greater attentiveness to the textual remnants of Chartism, led naturally to considerable emphasis being placed upon the literature of the movement. As we have already indicated, this was not in itself a novelty, nor was it unwelcome; but this more recent iteration has promoted a somewhat exaggerated deference to Chartism's literary lions. Ernest Jones has been the most obvious beneficiary, with the reprinting of a substantial amount of his literary work and a major biographical study, *Ernest Jones: Chartism and the Romance of Politics, 1819–69*, its title signalling an argument that more significance lay in the interplay of late romanticism and mass politics, than it did in the contribution of Karl Marx to the British labour movement.[50] At the same time, the Britain of Rupert Murdoch showed increasing interest in George Reynolds, whose reputation as a significant Chartist rests far more upon sensational journalism and titillating fiction than upon any political acumen (his effective contribution to Chartism being confined to 1848–50).[51]

The most profound consequence of 'Rethinking', however, was its seemingly authoritative dismissal of class consciousness as having any explanatory traction for the history of early Victorian Britain. Stedman Jones deftly avoided the interpretative chasm left by *The Making* (noted above) by questioning the notion that there was ever a class-conscious labour movement in the first place. This was achieved by a detailed examination of 'the language of Chartism', through which Stedman Jones confronted the apparent exceptionalism of Chartism (a feature endorsed – explicitly or tacitly – by all historians of the movement since the nineteenth century). Chartism certainly appears exceptional, as the one epic and truly national mass agitation for electoral reform in modern Britain. It is questionable if even the early twentieth-century movement for women's suffrage approached Chartism in extent or potency. As Jones himself pointed out (though he was widely misinterpreted as arguing the opposite): 'Chartism could not have been a movement except of the working class, for the discontents which the movement addressed were overwhelmingly, if not exclusively, those of wage earners, and the solidarities upon which the movement counted were those between wage earners.'[52]

However, in analysing Chartism in relation to class and the languages by which class is understood, 'Rethinking' focused almost exclusively upon one linguistic trope, 'old corruption', thereby underplaying the potency that class analyses brought to the ideology of the movement, especially from 1842 onwards. An appropriate and necessary part of historical analysis of the years from *circa* 1830 turns on working people's growing awareness of their distinctive situation and common sense of political purpose. This is not to surrender to a metaphysical concept of class, in which 'the working class' becomes almost an historical actor in its own right, seemingly capable of independent thought and action. Nor is it to suggest that class consciousness was uniform across all occupations and localities. But it is surely beyond dispute that Chartism was a national movement of unprecedented scope, intellectual reach, cultural vitality and political ambition. Reiteration of the traditional radical rhetoric of 'old corruption' could not alone engender those qualities.

Of course, a common understanding of themselves 'as labourers [...] opposed to the interests of the other classes of society', was not all that Chartists thought they had in common.[53] They articulated other 'ways of seeing' their situation: as the politically excluded, as unwilling subjects of a corrupt state and its venal administrators, as true patriots and as 'the People'. And the means through and by which this repertoire was articulated were not restricted to print alone. 'Rethinking' caused much confusion by seemingly suggesting that it was. This implication was compounded by the relatively narrow range of contemporary references that the essay cited. Fewer than 15 per cent of its citations of historical material relate to the years after 1839, while significantly more than half of the remainder pre-date Chartism.

More critically, 'Rethinking Chartism' was read as privileging print over other forms of communication – speech, ritual, iconography – and as down-playing (or perhaps even denying) the existence of reality beyond language. There was always an element of caricature about this reading, while Stedman Jones has himself qualified the extent to which his seminal essay shares Derrida's conviction that 'there is nothing outside the text'.[54] Even if research into Chartism is confined to printed text alone, it is clear that its language drew heavily on the vocabulary and conceptual apparatus of class. This was a movement deeply rooted in a shared conviction among wage-earners that their economic and political interests starkly contrasted with those of the rest of society. Too often, however, its history has been written as if this is *all* that is needed to explain Chartism. Plainly it is not and this largely explains the enduring influence of 'Rethinking'.

Only in the last few years has this particular gauntlet begun to be seized. Whereas in the past there was a notable tendency to shy away from the idea that the movement exhibited a plurality of motives, was sprawling and untidy – disorderly rather than uniform – the most recent histories have evinced a greater willingness to examine the movement's intrinsic complexity. For example, Robert Hall's *Voices of the People* exposed the internal divisions which inflected relations between working men and the way that post-Chartist affiliations could be shaped by personal ambitions as much as political consensus.[55] On a more sustained level, the full-length narrative afforded by Malcolm Chase's *Chartism: A New History* has taken this progressive agenda forward, exploiting biographical case studies as well as a wealth of primary data to demonstrate the sheer diversity of a movement and re-evaluate the importance of its social aspects as well as its more-obvious political dimensions.[56]

Caesuras and continuities

A further development in our understanding of Chartism concerns the legacy of the movement and its long-term significance, 'ever present to the progressive mind' as the Durham miners' leader and Lib-Lab MP,

John Wilson, put it in 1910.[57] In most quarters, and particularly the most influential sections of the labour history fraternity, the case for political continuity was scarcely contemplated as a possibility let alone a tenable hypothesis until the early 1990s. Labour historians such as Anderson, Hobsbawm and Thompson were at pains to explain that the lack of revolutionary zeal in Britain in the twentieth century lay not in the failings of the Labour Party or the trade unions but in the past. Not only were the turbulent class relations which epitomized the Chartist decades held to have been profoundly transformed during the 'mid-century equipoise' but the debacle of Kennington Common was heralded as the absolute demise of radicalism.

This focus on a caesura between 1848 and the 1880s, for so long espoused by historians on the left, ultimately facilitated the construction of a more heroic socialist initiative in the closing decades of the nineteenth century. For Hobsbawm these doldrum years of labourism and compromise, 'unlike either what went before or what came after', stood in stark contrast to the politics of conflict precipitated by the resurgence of economic crisis.[58] The era of the 'Great Depression' was marked by the rise of a confident and more open trade unionism and labour with a capital 'L', as a generation of workers untouched by Chartism carved out their own democratic agenda without the supportive framework of an older tradition.

Much of this analysis turned upon widespread adherence to the labour aristocracy thesis which identified an aspirational, skilled stratum of the working class who benefited most from the up-turn in the economy at the mid-century. The labour aristocracy were held to espouse the ideals of self-help and bourgeois respectability and, as spokesmen, mediated capitalist industrial practices to a workforce robbed of effective, articulate leadership. The labour aristocracy thesis loomed large in the writings of leading labour historians in the postwar period, especially in the 1970s and 1980s.

The idea that the labour aristocracy had sought its own advancement at the expense of other workers was not new. Engels's original hostile assessment in the preface to his classic text was somewhat ameliorated in the writings of the Webbs in the 1890s, only to be challenged by Cole in the mid-1930s.[59] But it was in the postwar years that the debate truly took off, at a time when leading Marxists were disillusioned with the performance and collaborationist inclinations of the Labour Party. Hobsbawm published a seminal essay in 1954 (reproduced a decade later as a chapter in his influential collection, *Labouring Men*) which drew up a typology of the labour aristocrat based on six criteria, among which the level and regularity of earnings was deemed the most important.[60]

Some historians agreed with his assessment that the labour aristocracy comprised about 10 per cent of the working classes between 1840 and 1890 but empiricists like Henry Pelling and A.E. Musson raised fundamental objections. According to Pelling, the evidence did not support the existence of a distinctly separate labour elite marked by acquiescent political behaviour: the concept did 'more harm than good to historical truth'.[61] Musson insisted that since 'trade societies had almost *always* been composed of "labour aristocrats"' [emphasis in original], the notion could not explain any alleged shift in mid-century, a claim he considered to be 'grossly exaggerated'.[62] Royden Harrison's study *Before the Socialists,* which aimed to rehabilitate the labour aristocracy by demonstrating that their collaborative activities delivered real benefits to other workers, in many ways foreshadowed the controversy which took off in the 1970s when John Foster produced his work on three industrial towns between 1820 and 1850.[63]

Foster's study focused primarily on Oldham. There he discerned a revolutionary consciousness among a labour elite emerging by the 1830s which was later checked by the growth of piecework and pacemaking in the town's principal industries: engineering, cotton spinning and coal mining. Foster's controversial analytical framework, which drew significant inspiration from Leninism, certainly heated up the debate and generated several critical responses, in the Society's *Bulletin* and more fully elsewhere, for example, in *New Left Review, Radical History Review* and *Social History.*[64] Gareth Stedman Jones questioned whether there had been any revolutionary consciousness in Oldham before the 1840s; he argued that Foster's timeframe was too early and quarrelled with his identification of the checkweighman in mining as a labour aristocrat.[65] A younger generation of historians, writing with the grain of Gramscian Marxism, were eager to explore the concept in terms of cultural hegemony. Geoffrey Crossick's work on London and Robert Gray's on Edinburgh set out to counter Foster's model by demonstrating that the labour aristocracy sought respectability through patterns of collective not individual self-help.[66]

A debate that at times was ill-tempered and wrong-headed nevertheless took our knowledge of the world of work and its detailed organization forward, enabled a richer appreciation of the connection between work-based fraternity and work-related associational life as well as qualitatively enhancing labour historiography's engagement with the sociology of the nineteenth-century working class. It also raised anew questions about working-class consciousness and the moment when the working class was 'made'.[67] Discussion of the labour aristocracy resonated and intersected with related contemporary debates on working-class consciousness. There were echoes of the Thompson-Anderson/Nairn dispute in the controversy over the degree to which the working class was 'incorporated' into bourgeois society and its values.[68] This was followed by debate concerning the extent to which working-class acquiescence was primarily rooted in changes in the workplace or accommodation to authority relations in the community.[69]

While these debates were reaching a peak in the early 1980s, some labour historians were more engaged in challenging Stedman Jones's insistence that radicalism was redundant by 1848. Kate Tiller's work on Chartism in Halifax in the 1850s was an important early contribution, demonstrating the resilience and vitality of radical traditions in this Yorkshire town, as was Bill Lancaster's study of working-class politics in Leicester during the second half of the century.[70] Both authors were pragmatic and registered the pace of change as well as continuity, but the distinguishing feature of their studies was the extent to which an earlier, indigenous political tradition retained its hold on the people. Margot Finn's work, *After Chartism*, further raised the tenor of the discussion by considering the way that the cause of European republicanism energized English radicals during the third quarter of the nineteenth century.[71]

A conference at Cambridge in 1989 eventually produced the volume of essays edited by Eugenio Biagini and Alastair Reid which developed such arguments. They set out to demonstrate that there was a 'substantial continuity in popular radicalism throughout the nineteenth and into the twentieth century' which rendered redundant the search for a labour aristocracy to explain a caesura.[72] The geographical and chronological reach of the contributions gave substance to the editors' claims that there was a radical dimension to Gladstonian liberalism as well as 'radical liberal elements' in early Labour Party activism.[73] Their exposition was seen as helpful in some quarters, particularly among those who remained unconvinced by the idea of an absolute disjuncture between the politics of Chartism and that of the early socialists.

This trail-blazing agenda subsequently energized new work, particularly by postmodernist scholars subscribing to a consensus rather than a conflict model of mid-century politics. For them, the mid-century was epitomized by the happy convergence of a post-Chartist respectable radicalism and the reconfiguration of popular Liberalism that was beginning to establish itself as a force in British political life. What is at issue here then is not the question of whether radicalism still had a voice and a constituency after 1848 but rather the extent to which labour historians can accept the Radical/Liberal alliance as an 'untroubled unity'.[74] Antony Taylor, for example, presents a strong case that London does not readily conform to this model but instead should be seen as 'a site of conflict' in which the 'fault line' between local radicals and the reform agenda of the Liberals was all too apparent.[75]

Yet the idea of an 'absolute' rupture was something of a straw man. The third quarter of the century was marked by overlapping continuities and disruptions, and the extent and importance of each was an obvious issue for debate among historians. The very title of Royden Harrison's work *Before the Socialists* was interpreted by Biagini and Reid as evidence of its author's teleological intent. Yet Harrison, who asserted the explanatory power of the labour aristocracy and assumed a 'massive transformation' in the labour movement in the two decades after 1861, had nonetheless warned his readers that while the 'temptation to over-draw the contrast [had] proved irresistible to many historians [...] the current reaction against this practice has over-compensated for the earlier emphasis on discontinuity'.[76] Accentuating continuities or alternatively watersheds depended to some extent on what one was interested in. Whereas historians such as Musson emphasised lack of change in the organizational forms of trade unionism in the third quarter against the Webbs's portrayal of a 'New Model', Harrison identified a changed spirit, an altered relationship between unions and the wider labour movement.[77]

A socialist revival?

Whatever the debates regarding continuities or caesuras in the mid-nineteenth century, the 1880s have traditionally been perceived as a major turning point, marking 'the revival of socialism' and foreshadowing the emergence of the Labour Party by the turn of the century.[78] Surveying labour historiography in 1958, John Saville welcomed Thompson's first major work, *William Morris*, published three years earlier, which he judged 'the most important piece of writing in this field since the war', and Henry Pelling's *Origins of the Labour Party*, which had appeared in 1954.[79] But Saville pointed to the lack of a proper account of the Social Democratic Federation (SDF) and its leader, H.M. Hyndman, as well as any considered assessment of the Fabians. Notwithstanding Thompson's self-criticism in a second edition of *Morris* that he had been guilty of 'hectoring political moralisms', 'Stalinist pieties' and 'vulgarities' in some polemical passages, the book remains a landmark in the historiography of the early socialist movement, far more than a simple 'life', and is still the most extended account of Morris's Socialist League.[80] Pelling's *Origins* continues to be a standard text after more than five decades.

The gaps noted by Saville for the 1880s have largely been filled. The distinguished Japanese scholar, Chushichi Tsuzuki, provided biographies of Hyndman, which served as a counterpoint to Thompson's *Morris*, and Eleanor Marx, which added further to our knowledge of the Socialist League.[81] The Socialist League had disintegrated as anarchists assumed a dominant position. The 'lost history' of the revolutionary libertarian strand of British socialism was ably excavated by John Quail and David Goodway.[82] Martin Crick's institutional history of the SDF depicted a more fragmented and diverse body than that derived from an earlier focus on its leadership, although why its membership remained concentrated in London and certain parts of Lancashire requires further analysis.[83] Henry Collins's early account of the SDF's Marxism as dogmatic and hostile to trade unionism was significantly qualified by Graham Johnson's exposition of the organization's theories and political ideology which demonstrated more pragmatic attempts to apply Marxism to British conditions.[84] We also have a more specialized account of the SDF's attitude to 'the woman question' and a detailed and nuanced analysis of democratic ideas and the labour movement in the period.[85]

In contrast, the third component of the socialist revival, the Fabian Society, has been largely neglected since the appearance of the general histories published in the 1960s.[86] Hobsbawm's brief but suggestive analysis in *Labouring Men* insisted it was an accidental rather than integral element in the socialist movement. He identified the Fabians with a 'new social stratum', the salaried professional and administrative cadre of modern capitalism, whose elitist and gradualist socialism was an intellectual response to 'the breakdown of mid-Victorian certainties'.[87] Their most prolific leading activists, the Webbs, have been the subject of meticulous biographical treatment and Paul Thompson's still valuable study of labour politics in the metropolis reflects the careful empirical approach of his mentor, Henry Pelling.[88] The movement as a whole may be ripe for further investigation and re-evaluation in the age of New Labour and neoliberalism.

Other research has demonstrated further linkages between mid-century radicalism and the socialist revival. Stan Shipley's evocation of the club culture of London's radical artisans in the 1870s, with their disputatious discussions of Marxism, Owenism, the Paris Commune and the theories of Bronterre O'Brien, portrayed an environment in which a socialist movement emerged in the 1880s. Mark Bevir persuasively demonstrated the influence of O'Brienites in the early SDF and its forerunner, the Democratic Federation.[89] More fundamentally, Jon Lawrence has emphasised the longevity of radicalism throughout the nineteenth century and its continuing influence on the emergent socialist movement. Lawrence challenged on grounds of its crudity the three-stage periodization, apparent in both liberal and, particularly, Marxist historiography from the 1930s. The tendency was to depict the decades between 1850 and 1880, between the militancy of Chartism and the Socialist Revival, as atypically quiescent. Instead, he suggested how, in the 1880s and 1890s, competing socialisms drew on elements of the radical tradition.[90]

The extent and depth of the socialist revival of the 1880s should not be overstated. Paul Watmough's estimates of early SDF membership suggested an organization with rarely more than 3,000 members, often much less; the Socialist League and the Fabians each enrolled less than 1,000.[91] The Independent Labour Party (ILP), established in 1893, enjoyed greater support, but its reach, too, was restricted. In his major study of the movement, David Howell traced its local roots, its areas of trade union strength and weakness, and its geographical concentration in Lancashire, Yorkshire and Scotland, with isolated outposts such as Leicester.[92]

The culture of the early socialist movement was masterfully recovered in Stephen Yeo's extended essay on 'the religion of socialism'. Yeo evoked the quasi-religious character – crusades, conversions, rituals, labour churches, scriptural language – of self-contained socialist organizations. His conclusion that engagement with electoral politics from the mid-1890s undermined this culture was contested by some who perceived its greater longevity.[93] Chris Waters, however, has explored the obstacles to 'making socialists' which this sectarian internal life, with its hostility to new forms of commercial leisure, created.[94] From different perspectives, other studies of popular culture also identified barriers to socialist advance: Stedman Jones portrayed a London working class which sought consolation in the passive escapism of the music hall; Ross McKibbin not only delineated the structural and ideological tendencies which militated against the implantation of Marxism in Britain but also the rich associational culture created by working men, which competed with socialist activities.[95]

Trade union histories and the turn from institutional labour history

Debates around the formation and function of the labour aristocracy and the continuity (or otherwise) of radical labour politics in the second half of the nineteenth century, typified both the intellectual vitality of the work of labour historians in the twentieth century and their willingness to work over a broad canvas. In many ways the starkest contrast between labour history after 1960, compared to what had gone before, was its relative indifference to institutional narratives. The earlier part of the twentieth century had seen numerous institutional histories; but newly emerging labour history professionals largely rejected the time-honoured medium: J.F.C. Harrison, for example, was for a time the official historian of the Post Office Engineering Union, but happily relinquished the contract to concentrate on Robert Owen and the Owenites.[96] Not only could an institutional history all too easily tend to hagiography and teleology, a field that accentuated class and the growth of working-class consciousness was ever impatient with the sectionalism that was an innate feature of almost all trade union histories. As a result, histories of individual trade unions since 1960 were often written by non-historians, sometimes representing the author's only foray into labour history.[97]

Discussing the literature in 1964, Hobsbawm noted the haphazard coverage, chronological unevenness and distortions which the patchwork of individual histories produced. While he judged that the advances of trade union history had been more impressive than the deficiencies, he warned of the dangers of specialization and urged integration of the labour movement into the wider history of the working class.[98]

Hobsbawn had pioneered such an approach in a series of overlapping essays in *Labouring Men* on trends in trade unionism, which in their broad scope and ambition to discern structural patterns were in stark contrast to antiquarian, institutional accounts of individual societies. In particular, he focused on the 'New Unionism' after 1889.[99] For Hobsbawm, New Unionism's explosive novelty lay in new strategies and forms of organization, a more radical political stance and the recruitment of previously unorganized groups of workers. Subsequent scholars refined or contested these characterizations. Hugh Clegg and his colleagues were reluctant to credit the extent of socialist influence whereas Hobsbawm insisted on the numerical presence of socialists among the new unions' officers.[100] Richard Price located New Unionism in a restructuring of the labour process.[101] Derek Matthews has challenged a number of these propositions, notably the role of socialists, yet his re-assessment provides support for elements of Hobsbawm's original analysis in its identification of the operation of the unskilled labour market and the availability of blacklegs as the key explanatory variable of New Unionism and its survival.[102]

With regard to the eighteenth century, Thompson expressed impatience with what he called (in a paper to the SSLH Anglo-American colloquium in 1968) 'the Webbian walling off of trade unionism proper from guild traditions'.[103] It was to be some time before a concerted attempt to deconstruct 'the Webbian walling off' was made, though much material for this was generated through the collective endeavours of researchers at the Centre for the Study of Social History, established at Warwick University by Thompson when he left Yorkshire in 1965, as the gestation of the essays that comprise Thompson's later book, *Customs in Common*, attests.[104] However, it was John Rule, a first generation postgraduate at the Centre (working initially on Cornish miners and Chartism) who effectively broke the ground in the early 1980s, first with a book, *The Experience of Labour in Eighteenth-century Industry*, and then with an edited collection on the years between 1750 and 1850, derived from a SSLH conference marking the 150th anniversary of 'the Tolpuddle Martyrs' in 1984.[105] Together with Rodney Dobson's study of the 'prehistory of labour relations', these reinforced the Warwick Centre's powerful intervention during the 1970s into the historiography of eighteenth-century England.[106]

Much subsequent eighteenth-century labour history was associated directly or indirectly with what might be reasonably termed 'the Thompson school'.[107] Its defining features might be summarized as an impressive depth of empirical research, entwined with a passionate humanism – not necessarily Marxist but broadly accepting, as Thompson himself argued in a seminal article, that labouring people were not 'confined within the fraternal loyalties and the "vertical" consciousness of particular trades', and thus that wider solidarities and '"horizontal" consciousness of class' was possible.[108] Yet Rule's influential work on craftsmen revealed a profound sense among artisans of possessing a property in skill and a consequent cleavage in labouring identities between 'skilled' and 'unskilled', underlining that 'the Thompson school' has never been doctrinaire but, rather, distinguished by a broad structure of humane historical engagement.[109]

By the late 1990s, when the SSLH launched a book series reassessing broad themes in labour history, the inclusion of a volume surveying the evolution of trade unionist *mentalités* from the seventeenth to the mid-nineteenth century was seen as entirely appropriate.[110] Yet in a series of 28 titles, this volume was one of only four offering coverage of eighteenth-century Britain.[111] The initial promise of 'the Thompson school' was hardly sustained beyond the early 1990s, mainly because economic history became increasingly absorbed in the demand, as opposed to the supply, side of the experience of industrialization. The resulting emphasis upon cultures of consumption discomforted labour historians, naturally predisposed to perceive workers as producers, not consumers.[112] It is too soon to predict whether the recent reassertion of the supply side's driving role (in tandem with 'a high wage economy') in industrialization will be either sustained, or stimulate further labour histories of the long eighteenth century.[113]

However, in labour history's original, nineteenth-century heartland, the influence of Royden Harrison (who followed Thompson as director of the Warwick Centre in 1971) helped ensure an enduring vitality. The Centre's large postgraduate community and an academic staff which included such talented labour historians as James Hinton, Tony Mason, Fred Reid and Jay Winter, was annually replenished by visiting American professors who transplanted the latest developments in the 'new social history' from the United States. The Warwick Centre nurtured a generation of scholars who, in the following decade, produced a nineteenth-century labour history which contextualized trade union organization by combining reconstruction of working-class communities with a then-fashionable focus on the labour process. Harrison's punctilious scholarship somewhat constrained his own published output;[114] but he was a generous and productive editor and supervisor, as a range of influential books attest.[115]

This tradition of scholarship consolidated an approach to labour history of which Hobsbawm was a notable pioneer, seeking wider perspectives than that of conventional institutional histories, instead focusing on broader thematic issues in labour history or on longitudinal studies of particular occupational groups. But whereas Hobsbawm's strengths were either the essay (exemplified in his 1964 collection *Labouring Men*) or the panoptic synthesis,[116] monographs have dominated subsequent work on the social history of labour in nineteenth-century Britain: for example, the politics of production in the workshop sector and in coalmining, the evolution of industrial wage bargaining, and the legal context within which trade unions operated.[117]

New trends in the 1980s and 1990s

Whereas Thompson's impact on eighteenth-century labour history had been manifest, the influences upon nineteenth-century studies, as the works just cited attest, were far more diffuse – testimony also to the 'mainstreaming' of labour history in many history departments from the late 1970s. Two further strands stand out: the infusion of a history of ideas approach into labour history; and engagement with postmodernist concepts.

The University of Cambridge, particularly a circle of scholars associated with Stedman Jones, has been closely associated with the first of these strands. His own first book, *Outcast London*, emerged from the convergence of initial research in nineteenth-century liberal thought and political commitment to the New Left, precisely at the time *The Making* was being debated.[118] At least in retrospect, Anderson's much-contested essay, 'Origins of the Present Crisis', can be seen as defining a great deal of the territory that a more intellectualized labour history subsequently explored. As Stedman Jones reflected:

> The focus of attention was shifted away from the historical reconstruction of popular struggles and the elaboration of Marxian propositions about the history of English capitalism towards the allegedly conformist and compliant theoretical traditions of the English intelligentsia and what was argued to be its part consequence, the absence of a mass party possessing revolutionary ambition.[119]

One legacy of this trajectory has been the wide deployment of the techniques of intellectual history to illuminate the evolution and apparently distinctive character of British radical thought. The approach of an earlier Cambridge-educated historian, J.F.C. Harrison, to Owenism was a notable precursor here.[120] However, a younger generation, closely associated with Stedman Jones, now dominate this field.[121]

Not everyone evinced the same willingness to intellectualize labour history or to engage with the debate about postmodernism whose reverberations were beginning to be felt across the disciplinary divide from the mid-1980s onwards. For labour historians, in particular, the attack on the traditional history of class and class formation was considered to be a step too far and something amounting to a standoff ensued.[122] But ignoring the important questions that were being raised, however unpalatable to labour history sensitivities, was simply not an option. As noted above, the lively exchanges precipitated by Jones's 'Rethinking Chartism' polemic were ultimately productive because they generated light as well as heat. Undoubtedly, Patrick Joyce's 1991 study, *Visions of the People*, and his *Democratic Subjects* published three years later, were profoundly unsettling, for they called into question the received wisdom (described by Joyce as 'dead weight') of when the working class was made. The former work pushed the timeframe beyond the end of the nineteenth century to 1914.[123] However, some critics pointed to Joyce's deployment of a straw man, an ideal conception of class constructed on a reductionist base, which, when it could not be discerned in the discourse of working people, was therefore held not to exist; others pointed to discrepancies between the empirical core of *Visions of the People* and Joyce's proclaimed intent, suggesting that Joyce's documentation of 'the people' was also an exposition of working-class identities, a possibility Joyce himself had entertained in his conclusion.[124]

Joyce gathered around him a small but influential group of like-minded theorists, notably James Vernon, who rejected a realist epistemology and held that non-class identities were just as important, if not more so, than those based on class.[125] In a landmark journal article in 1995, Joyce warned that if historians continued to shun participation in the academic discourse around concepts of postmodernity they ran the risk of allowing the intellectual agenda to be 'set in their absence'.[126] Yet few labour historians have fully embraced the postmodern agenda. Its most positive outcome has perhaps been a renewed attention to the use of language, an increased sensitivity to the dangers of reductionist analyses and an enhanced appreciation of the tentativeness and fragility inherent in historical interpretation. Jon Lawrence – described by one trenchant critic of Joyce and Vernon as 'the welcome face of post-structuralism'[127] – endeavoured to eschew reductionism but retain an appreciation of material factors in his analysis of popular politics in Wolverhampton. Rejecting assumptions that political affiliation necessarily reflected class positions, Lawrence emphasized how local politicians had to construct communities of support and the language they deployed to do so in engaging with the concerns of their constituents; thus popular Toryism after 1885 was based on opposition to non-conformist attempts to regulate working-class leisure.[128]

Conclusion

It is striking that British labour history, while frequently a highly theorized and contested field of academic endeavour, has seldom been unmindful of the moral imperatives that so powerfully motivated the labour historians with whose work this chapter began. For all its reputation as a foundational text for Anglophone postmodern history, Joyce's *Visions of the People* offered an essentially empirical account of Victorian and Edwardian working people, the freshness of which derived as much from its author's generous vision of what constituted historically significant behaviour by waged workers and their families, as it did from his resolute determination not to resort to the conceptual apparatus of class. 'I wanted still to write a grand, traditional narrative', Joyce has since explained, 'and sought, uneasily, to find the subject for that narrative in "the people".'[129] That admission was made in a later book constituted from a comparative biography of John Bright and Edwin Waugh, and a meditation upon the nature of biography as a discursive historiographical strategy. None would readily claim the mill-owning Liberal statesman for labour history; but the life of Edwin Waugh, born in a Rochdale cellar, an errand boy, printer and autodidact, encompasses several of the tropes of labour history.

There has always been a tension between histories of labour that privilege reconstruction (that is, description) over theorized analysis. The current revival of narrative and of biography as discursive strategies by specialists in nineteenth-century labour history perhaps reflects a post-postmodernist suspicion of theory.[130] However, biography has been central to the development of British labour history, almost from the beginning of the years surveyed in this chapter. Those who would wish to retain class as a category tool would concur with E.P. Thompson that it (class) is a relationship and not a thing. The contexts and arenas (workplaces, communities, families, the public and the private, the commercial, the contractual and the intimate) in which those relationships are worked out remains the central ground for labour history.

Notes

This chapter has emerged from wide-ranging discussions with a number of colleagues and our students; we are especially grateful to Alan Campbell and John McIlroy for their advice and support.

1 Richard Price, *British Society, 1680–1880: Dynamism, Containment, Change* (Cambridge: Cambridge University Press, 1999), p. 2.

2 The following account of the historiography is necessarily selective. For overviews, see E.H. Hunt, *British Labour History, 1815–1914* (London: Weidenfeld and Nicolson, 1981); Mike Savage and Andrew Miles, *The Remaking of the British Working Class, 1840–1940* (London: Routledge, 1994); Royden Harrison, 'Introduction to the Second Edition', in idem, *Before the Socialists: Studies in Labour and Politics, 1861–1881* (1st pub. 1965; Aldershot: Gregg Revivals, 1994), pp. xv–lviii; John E. Archer, *Social Unrest and Popular Protest in England, 1780–1840* (Cambridge: Cambridge University Press, 2000); Donald M. MacRaild and David E. Martin, *Labour in British Society, 1830–1914* (Basingstoke: Macmillan, 2000). The latter contains a useful bibliographical essay. See also the annual bibliographies contained in *Labour History Review* (*LHR*).

3 For more on this, see John McIlroy, 'Organized Labour History in Britain: The Society for the Study of Labour History after Fifty Years', chapter 1 in this volume, and idem, 'The Society for the Study of Labour History, 1956–1985: Its Origins and its Heyday', *Making History: Organizations of Labour Historians in Britain since 1960, Labour History Review* (*LHR*) Fiftieth Anniversary Supplement, April 2010, 17-110.

4 G.D.H. Cole and Raymond Postgate, *The Common People, 1746–1946* (1st pub. 1938; London: Methuen, 1968).

5 *Chartist Studies*, ed. by Asa Briggs (London: Macmillan, 1959); *Essays in Labour History: In Memory of G.D.H. Cole*, ed. by Asa Briggs and John Saville (London: Macmillan, 1960); E.P. Thompson, *The Making of the English Working Class* (London: Gollancz, 1963).

6 J.F.C. Harrison, *Scholarship Boy: A Personal History of the Mid-Twentieth Century* (London: Rivers Oram, 1995), pp. 127, 175.

7 David Goodway, 'E. P. Thompson and the Making of the English Working Class', in *Beyond the Walls: 50 Years of Adult and Continuing Education at the*

University of Leeds, 1946–1996, ed. by Richard K.S. Taylor (Leeds: University of Leeds, 1996), pp. 133–43 (pp. 138–9); Royden Harrison, *Before the Socialists: Studies in Labour and Politics, 1861–1881* (London: Routledge and Kegan Paul, 1965), p. v.

8 E.P. Thompson, 'Homage to Tom Maguire', in Briggs and Saville, *Essays in Labour History*, pp. 276–316 (pp. 276–77).

9 Quoted in Michael Bentley, *Modernizing England's Past: English Historiography in the Age of Modernism, 1870–1970* (Cambridge: Cambridge University Press, 2005), pp. 132–33.

10 Ibid.

11 Louis James's *Fiction for the Working Man: A Study of the Literature Produced for the Working Classes in Early Victorian Urban England* (Oxford: Oxford University Press, 1963), pp. xv and xvi. Scholarship on nineteenth-century working-class writers is too extensive to be reviewed here: salient texts include Brian Maidment, *The Poorhouse Fugitives: Self-taught Poets in Victorian Britain* (Manchester: Carcanet, 1987); Ian Haywood, *Working-Class Fiction: From Chartism to Trainspotting* (Plymouth: Northcote House, 1997); Anne Janowitz, *Lyric and Labour in the Romantic Tradition* (Cambridge: Cambridge University Press, 1998); Mike Sanders, *The Poetry of Chartism: Aesthetics, Politics, History* (Cambridge: Cambridge University Press, 2009).

12 Thompson, *Making*; Charles Tilly, 'Softcore Solipsism', *Labour/Le Travail*, 34 (1994), 259–68 (p. 259).

13 Thompson, *Making*, p. 903.

14 Perry Anderson, 'Origins of the Present Crisis', *New Left Review*, 23 (1964), 26–53; Tom Nairn, 'The British Political Elite', ibid., 19–25.

15 E.P. Thompson, 'The Peculiarities of the English', *Socialist Register 1965*, ed. by Ralph Miliband and John Saville (London: Merlin Press, 1965), pp. 311–62; Thompson, *Making* (3rd edn, London: Gollancz, 1980), p. 14. The five were Iorwerth Prothero, *Artisans and Politics in Early Nineteenth-Century London: John Gast and his Times* (Folkestone: Dawson, 1979); J.F.C. Harrison, *The Second Coming : Popular Millenarianism, 1780–1850* (London: Routledge and Kegan Paul, 1979); Patricia Hollis, *The Pauper Press* (Oxford: Oxford University Press, 1970); Joel H. Wiener, *The War of the Unstamped : The Movement to Repeal the British Newspaper Tax, 1830–1836* (New York: Cornell University Press, 1969); Albert Goodwin, *The Friends of Liberty* (London: Hutchinson, 1979). Thompson dismissed Duncan Bythell, *The Handloom Weavers* (Cambridge: Cambridge University Press, 1969) and 'several works on the Luddite movement' by Malcolm Thomis.

16 Thompson, *Making*, pp.13–14

17 Sheila Rowbotham, *Hidden From History: 300 Years of Women's Oppression and the Fight Against It* (London: Pluto Press, 1973).

18 Carolyn Steedman, 'The Price of Experience: Women and the Making of the English Working Class', *Radical History Review*, 59 (1994), 108–119 (p. 110).

19 Ibid.

20 Sally Alexander and Anna Davin, 'Feminist History', *History Workshop Journal*, 1 (1976), 4–6 (p. 4). For a wider discussion, see also June Purvis,

'From "Women Worthies" to Postructuralism? Debate and Controversy in Women's History in Britain', in *Women's History: Britain 1850–1945*, ed. by June Purvis (London: Routledge, 1995), pp. 1–22.

21 *History Workshop Journal: A Journal of Socialist and Feminist History*, 13 (1982), Editorial, 'History Workshop and Feminism' (no pagination).

22 For example, see Anna Clark, *The Struggle for the Breeches: Gender and the Making of the British Working Class* (London: Rivers Oram, 1995); Barbara Taylor, *Eve and the New Jerusalem: Socialism and Feminism in the Nineteenth Century* (London: Virago, 1983).

23 Leonore Davidoff and Catherine Hall, *Family Fortunes: Men and Women of the English Middle Class, 1780–1950* (London: Hutchinson, 1987).

24 Steedman, 'Price of Experience', 117.

25 Jutta Schwartzkopf, *Women in the Chartist Movement* (Basingstoke: Macmillan, 1991); Dorothy Thompson, *The Chartists: Popular Politics in the Industrial Revolution* (New York: Pantheon Books, 1984); *Radical Femininity: Women's Self Representation in the Public Sphere*, ed. by Eileen Janes Yeo (Manchester: Manchester University Press, 1998); *Our Mothers' Land: Chapters in Welsh Women's History 1830–1939*, ed. by Angela V. John (Cardiff: University of Wales Press, 1991); Jill Liddington and Jill Norris, *One Hand Tied Behind Us: The Rise of the Women's Suffrage Movement* (London: Virago, 1978).

26 Despite a promising title, L.E.N. Mayhall, *The Militant Suffrage Movement: Citizenship and Resistance, 1860–1930* (Oxford: Oxford University Press, 2003), is no exception to this generalization. But see Helen Rogers, *Authority, Authorship and the Radical Tradition in Nineteenth-Century England* (Aldershot: Ashgate, 2003); *Women in British Politics, 1760–1860: The Power of the Petticoat*, ed. by Kathryn Gleadle and Sarah Richardson (London: Palgrave, 2000).

27 Pamela Horn, *The Rise and Fall of the Victorian Servant* (Dublin: Gill and Macmillan, 1975); Sonya Rose, *Limited Livelihoods: Gender and Class in Nineteenth-Century England* (Berkeley: University of California Press, 1992); Deborah Simonton, *A History of European Women's Work: From 1700 to the Present* (London: Routledge, 1998); Margaret Walsh, *Working Out Gender: Perspectives from Labour History* (Aldershot: Ashgate, 1999); Katrina Honeyman, *Women, Gender and Industrialisation in England, 1700–1870* (Basingstoke: Macmillan, 2000); Sheila Blackburn, *A Fair Day's Wage for a Fair Day's Work? Sweated Labour and the Origins of Minimum Wage Legislation in Britain* (Aldershot: Ashgate, 2007).

28 Carolyn Steedman, *Master and Servant: Love and Labour in the English Industrial Age* (Cambridge: Cambridge University Press, 2007) p. 22. Steedman's study goes some way towards addressing the hiatus.

29 Thompson, *Making*, p. 916.

30 Eric Hobsbawm and George Rudé, *Captain Swing* (London: Lawrence and Wishart, 1969); *Village Life and Labour*, ed. by Raphael Samuel (London: Routledge and Kegan Paul, 1975); Alun Howkins, *Whitsun in 19th-Century Oxfordshire* (Oxford: History Workshop, 1974); Alun Howkins, *Poor Labouring Men: Rural Radicalism in Norfolk, 1872–1923* (London: Routledge

and Kegan Paul, 1985). See more recently, *Class, Conflict and Protest in the English Countryside, 1700–1880*, ed. by Mick Reed and Roger Wells (London: Cass, 1990); and Barry Reay, *Rural Englands: Labouring Lives in Nineteenth-Century England* (Basingstoke: Palgrave, 2004).

31 George Rudé, *The Crowd in the French Revolution* (Westport: Greenwood Press, 1959); idem, *The Crowd in History: A Study of Popular Disturbances in France and England* (New York: Wiley, 1964).

32 Thompson, *Making*, p. 12.

33 Tim Mason, 'Letter to the Editor: The Making of the English Working Class', *History Workshop Journal*, 7 (1979), 224.

34 J.T. Ward, *Chartism* (London: Batsford, 1973). To a significant extent Ward's deficiencies were remedied by the appearance of D.J.V. Jones, *Chartism and the Chartists* (London: Allen Lane, 1975). However, this volume appeared, at the publisher's insistence, bereft of any references (letter from the author to Malcolm Chase, 16 October 1984).

35 Figures based on J.F.C. Harrison and Dorothy Thompson, *Bibliography of the Chartist Movement* (Hassocks: Harvester, 1978) and Owen Ashton et al., *The Chartist Movement: A New Annotated Bibliography* (London: Mansell, 1995), plus subsequent annual bibliographies in *LHR*.

36 The general strike of 1926 would seem to lend itself to local historical treatment. Yet the excellent bibliography prepared by John McIlroy and others for its eightieth anniversary identifies only seventy-two local studies: see 'The General Strike and Mining Lockout of 1926: A Select Bibliography', *Historical Studies in Industrial Relations* 21 (2006), 183–206 (pp. 188–91).

37 J.F.C. Harrison, *Early Victorian Britain, 1832–51* (London: Fontana, 1979), pp. 185–86.

38 The argument here is elaborated in more detail in Malcolm Chase, 'The "Prehistory" of Labour History', forthcoming.

39 Norman McCord, 'Adding a Touch of Class', *History*, 70 (1985), 410–19 (p. 411).

40 John Belchem, *'Orator' Hunt: Henry Hunt and English Working-Class Radicalism* (Oxford: Oxford University Press, 1985), p. v; James Epstein, *The Lion of Freedom: Feargus O'Connor and the Chartist Movement, 1832–42* (London: Croom Helm, 1982), p. 315.

41 On this historiography see Malcolm Chase, '"We Wish Only To Work for Ourselves": The Chartist Land Plan', in *Living and Learning: Essays in Honour of J.F.C. Harrison*, ed. by Malcolm Chase and Ian Dyck (Aldershot: Scolar Press, 1996), pp. 133–48 (pp. 133–34).

42 Thompson, *The Chartists*, pp. 330–39.

43 *The Chartist Experience: Studies in Working-Class Radicalism and Culture, 1830–60*, ed. by James Epstein and Dorothy Thompson (London: Macmillan, 1982).

44 Gareth Stedman Jones, 'Rethinking Chartism', in idem, *Languages of Class: Studies in English Working-Class History, 1832–1982* (Cambridge: Cambridge University Press, 1982), pp. 90–178.

45 David Goodway, *London Chartism, 1838–1848* (Cambridge: Cambridge

University Press, 1982).

46 The principal exceptions were reviews by Dorothy Thompson and James Epstein, in respectively *Bulletin of the Society for the Study of Labour History* (*BSSLH*), 52,1 (1987), 54–57, and *International Labor and Working-Class History* 28 (1985), 69–78; Paul Pickering, 'Class Without Words: Symbolic Communication in the Chartist Movement', *Past and Present*, 112 (1986), 144–62; Miles Taylor, 'Rethinking the Chartists: Searching for Synthesis in the Historiography of Chartism', *Historical Journal*, 39 (1996), 479–95.

47 See especially *The Chartist Legacy*, ed. by Owen Ashton, Robert Fyson and Stephen Roberts (London: Merlin Press, 1999); *Papers for the People: A Study of the Chartist Press*, ed. by Joan Allen and Owen Ashton (London: Merlin Press, 2005); Keith Flett, *Chartism after 1848: The Working Class and the Politics of Radical Education* (Monmouth: Merlin Press, 2006); Paul Pickering, *Feargus O'Connor: A Political Life* (Monmouth: Merlin Press, 2008).

48 Joan Allen, *Joseph Cowen and Popular Radicalism on Tyneside, 1829–1900* (Monmouth: Merlin Press, 2007); Robert G. Hall, *Voices for the People: Democracy and Chartist Political Identity, 1830–1870* (Monmouth: Merlin Press, 2007).

49 Pickering, 'Class without Words'.

50 Ian Heywood, *Chartist Fiction, vol. 2: Ernest Jones, Woman's Wrongs* (Aldershot: Ashgate. 2001); Miles Taylor, *Ernest Jones, Chartism and the Romance of Politics, 1819–69* (Oxford: Oxford University Press, 2003).

51 *G.W.M. Reynolds: Nineteenth-Century Fiction, Politics, and the Press*, ed. by Anne Humpherys and Louis James (Aldershot: Ashgate, 2008).

52 Jones, 'Rethinking Chartism', p. 95.

53 This quotation is taken from the Liberal MP John Roebuck, *Trades' Unions: Their Advantages to the Working Classes* (London: John Longley, 1834), p. 5.

54 See his '*Postface*' to the French translation of 'Rethinking Chartism' in *Revue d'histoire moderne et contemporaine*, 54 (2007), 63–68.

55 Hall, *Voices for the People*, p. 140.

56 Malcolm Chase, *Chartism: A New History* (Manchester: Manchester University Press, 2007).

57 John Wilson, *Memories of a Labour Leader: The Autobiography of John Wilson, J. P., M.P.* (London: T.F. Unwin, 1910), p. 30.

58 Eric Hobsbawm, *Worlds of Labour: Further Studies in the History of Labour* (London, Weidenfeld and Nicolson, 1984), p. 182. See also the Introduction to his earlier work, Eric Hobsbawm, *The Age of Capital 1848–1875* (London: Weidenfeld and Nicolson, 1962), pp. 1–5.

59 Friedrich Engels, *The Condition of the Working Class in England*, (1st pub. 1845; Harmondsworth: Penguin, 1987), Preface to the English Edition, p. 42; Sidney and Beatrice Webb, *The History of Trade Unionism* (London: Longmans, Green, 1894); G.D.H. Cole, 'Some Notes on British Trade Unionism in the Third Quarter of the Nineteenth Century', *International Review of Social History*, 2 (1937), 1–27.

60 Eric Hobsbawm, 'The Labour Aristocracy in Nineteenth-Century Britain', in *Democracy and the Labour Movement: Essays in Honour of Dona Torr*, ed. by

John Saville (London: Lawrence and Wishart, 1954), pp. 201–39, reprinted in idem, *Labouring Men: Studies in the History of Labour* (London: Weidenfeld and Nicholson, 1964), pp. 272–315.

61 Henry Pelling, *Popular Politics and Society in Late Victorian Britain* (London: Macmillan, 1968), pp. 37–61 (p. 61).

62 A.E. Musson, *British Trade Unions, 1800–1875* (Basingstoke: Macmillan, 1972), pp. 49–56 (p. 50, original emphasis); idem, 'Class Struggle and the Labour Aristocracy, 1830–1860', *Social History*, 3 (1976), 335–56.

63 Harrison, *Before the Socialists*; John Foster, *Class Struggle and the Industrial Revolution: Early Industrial Capitalism in Three English Towns* (London: Weidenfeld and Nicolson, 1974).

64 See Michael A. Shepherd. 'The Origins and Incidence of the Term "Labour Aristocracy"', *BSSLH*, 37 (1978), 51–67, and the ensuing correspondence on the topic from David McNulty, *BBSLH*, 38 (1979), 19; Joseph Melling, *BLLSH*, 39 (1979), 16–22; John Baxter, *BSSLH*, 40 (1980), 13–16, and Shepherd's rejoinder, ibid., 16–18. The Society's 1979 conference, 'The Labour Aristocracy Twenty-Five Years After', was addressed by several protagonists including Eric Hobsbawm, Keith McLelland, Bert Moorhouse and John Field. The short report perhaps fails to convey the extent to which the SSLH and its members were exercised by the issue: see *BSSLH*, 40 (Spring 1980), 6–11. See also Gareth Stedman Jones, 'Class Struggle in the Industrial Revolution' (1st pub. 1975), in idem, *Languages of Class*, pp. 25–75; John Field, 'British Historians and the Concept of the Labor Aristocracy', *Radical History Review*, 19 (1978–79), 61–85; H.F. Moorhouse, 'The Marxist Theory of the Labour Aristocracy', *Social History*, 3 (1978), 61–82.

65 Stedman Jones, 'Class Struggle in the Industrial Revolution'; see also D.S. Gadian, 'Class Consciousness in Oldham and other North-West Industrial Towns', *Historical Journal*, 21 (1978), 161–72.

66 Geoffrey Crossick, *An Artisan Elite in Victorian Society: Kentish London, 1840–1880* (London: Croom Helm, 1978); Robert Gray, *The Aristocracy of Labour in Victorian Edinburgh* (Oxford: Clarendon Press, 1976).

67 For overviews of the debate see Field, 'British Historians'; Robert Gray, *The Aristocracy of Labour in Nineteenth-Century Britain, c.1850–1900* (London: Macmillan, 1981).

68 H.F. Moorhouse, 'The Political Incorporation of the British Working Class', *Sociology*, 7 (1973), 341–59; Robert Q. Gray, 'The Political Incorporation of the Working Class', *Sociology*, 9 (1975), 101–104; H.F. Moorhouse: 'On the Political Incorporation of the British Working Class: A Reply to Gray', *Sociology*, 9 (1975), 105–110.

69 Richard Price, 'The Labour Process and Labour History', *Social History*, 8 (1983), 57–75; Patrick Joyce, 'Labour, Capital and Compromise: A Response to Richard Price', *Social History*, 9 (1984), 67–76; Richard Price, 'Conflict and Cooperation: A Reply to Patrick Joyce', *Social History*, 9 (1984), 217–24; Patrick Joyce, 'Languages of Reciprocity and Conflict: A Further Response to Richard Price', *Social History*, 9 (1984), 225–31. Both these historians had produced major and influential monographs which illustrated their differing

conceptions of working-class political attitudes and behaviour: Richard Price, *Masters, Unions and Men: Work Control in Building and the Rise of Labour, 1830–1914* (Cambridge: Cambridge University Press, 1980); Patrick Joyce, *Work, Society and Politics: The Culture of the Factory in Later Victorian England* (Brighton: Harvester, 1980).

70 Kate Tiller, 'Late Chartism: Halifax 1847–58', in Epstein and Thompson, *Chartist Experience*, pp. 311–44; Bill Lancaster, *Radicalism, Co-operation and Socialism: Leicester Working-Class Politics 1860–1906* (Leicester: Leicester University Press, 1987).

71 Margot Finn, *After Chartism: Class and Nation in English Radical Politics 1848–1874* (Cambridge: Cambridge University Press, 1993).

72 *Currents of Radicalism: Popular Radicalism, Organized Labour and Party Politics in Britain 1850–1914*, ed. by Eugenio F. Biagini and Alastair J. Reid (Cambridge: Cambridge University Press, 1991), pp. 1, 4.

73 Ibid., p. 1.

74 Antony Taylor, 'Post-Chartism: Metropolitan Perspectives on the Chartist Movement in Decline 1848–80', in *London Politics, 1760–1914*, ed. by Matthew Cragoe and Antony Taylor (London: Palgrave, 2005), pp. 75–96 (p. 75).

75 Ibid., p. 76. See also, John Belchem, *Popular Radicalism in Nineteenth Century Britain* (Basingstoke: Macmillan, 1996) pp. 129–131; Allen, *Joseph Cowen*, p. 104.

76 Harrison, *Before the Socialists*, pp. 4–5.

77 Ibid., p. 15; cf. Musson, *Trade Unions*, pp. 51–55. See also Royden Harrison's 'Afterword' to the 'Introduction to the Second Edition' of his *Before the Socialists* (2nd edn, 1994), pp. liv–lviii.

78 For such conventional periodization, see, for example, Paul Adelman, *The Rise of the Labour Party, 1880–1945* (Harlow: Longman, 1972); Keith Laybourn, *The Rise of Socialism in Britain, c.1881–1951* (Stroud: Sutton, 1997).

79 John Saville, 'Labour Movement Historiography', *Universities and Left Review*, 3 (1958), 73–77 (p. 74); E.P. Thompson, *William Morris: Romantic to Revolutionary* (London: Lawrence and Wishart, 1955); Henry Pelling, *Origins of the Labour Party, 1880–1900* (London: Macmillan, 1954).

80 E.P. Thompson, 'Postscript: 1976', in idem, *William Morris: Romantic to Revolutionary* (New York: Pantheon, 1976), p. 769.

81 Chushichi Tsuzuki, *H.M. Hyndman and British Socialism* (Oxford: Oxford University Press, 1961); idem, *The Life of Eleanor Marx, 1855–1898* (Oxford: Oxford University Press, 1967).

82 John Quail, *The Slow Burning Fuse: The Lost History of British Anarchism* (St Albans: Granada Publishing, 1978). See also Hermia Oliver, *The International Anarchist Movement in Late Victorian London* (Beckenham: Croom Helm, 1983); and David Goodway, *Anarchist Seeds Beneath the Snow: Left-Libertarian Thought and British Writers from William Morris to Colin Ward* (Liverpool: Liverpool University Press, 2006).

83 Martin Crick, *The History of the Social-Democratic Federation* (Keele: Ryburn Publishing, 1994); see also Jeffrey Hill, 'Requiem for a Party? Writing the History of Social-Democracy', *LHR*, 61 (1996), 102–109.

84 Henry Collins, 'The Marxism of the Social Democratic Federation', in *Essays in Labour History, vol. 2: 1886–1923*, ed. by Asa Briggs and John Saville (London: Macmillan, 1971), pp. 47–69; Graham Johnson, *Social Democratic Politics in Britain, 1881–1911* (Lewiston, Queenston and Lampeter: Edwin Mellon Press, 2002).

85 Karen Hunt, *Equivocal Feminists: The Social Democratic Federation and the Woman Question, 1884–1911* (Cambridge: Cambridge University Press, 1996); Logie Barrow and Ian Bullock, *Democratic Ideas and the British Labour Movement, 1880–1914* (Cambridge: Cambridge University Press, 1996).

86 Margaret Cole, *The Story of Fabian Socialism* (London: Heinemann, 1963); A.M. McBriar, *Fabian Socialism and English Politics, 1884–1918* (Cambridge: Cambridge University Press, 1966).

87 Eric Hobsbawm, 'The Fabians Reconsidered', in idem, *Labouring Men*, pp. 250–71 (p. 266).

88 Royden J. Harrison, *The Life and Times of Sidney and Beatrice Webb, 1858–1905: The Formative Years* (Basingstoke: Macmillan, 2000); Paul Thompson, *Socialists, Liberals and Labour: The Struggle for London, 1885–1914* (London: Routledge and Kegan Paul, 1967).

89 Stan Shipley, *Club Life and Socialism in Mid-Victorian London* (Oxford: History Workshop Pamphlet No. 5, 1971); Mark Bevir, 'The British Social Democratic Federation, 1880–1885: From O'Brienism to Marxism', *International Review of Social History*, 36 (1992), 207–29.

90 Jon Lawrence, 'Popular Radicalism and the Socialist Revival in Britain', *Journal of British Studies*, 31 (1992), 163–86.

91 Paul Watmough, 'The Membership of the Social Democratic Federation, 1885–1902', *BSSLH*, 34 (1977), 35–40; Thompson, *Morris*, p. 414; Hobsbawm, 'Fabians', p. 268.

92 David Howell, *British Workers and the Independent Labour Party, 1888–1906* (Manchester: Manchester University Press, 1983); Lancaster, *Radicalism*. See also *The Centennial History of the Independent Labour Party*, ed. by David James, Tony Jowitt and Keith Laybourn (Halifax: Ryburn Academic Publishing, 1992).

93 Stephen Yeo, 'A New Life: The Religion of Socialism in Britain, 1883–1896', *History Workshop Journal*, 4 (1977), 5–56; cf. Laybourn, *Socialism*, pp. 19–20.

94 Chris Waters, *British Socialists and the Politics of Popular Culture, 1884–1914* (Manchester: Manchester University Press, 1990).

95 Gareth Stedman Jones, 'Working-Class Culture and Working-Class Politics in London: Notes on the Remaking of a Working Class, 1870–1900', *Journal of Social History*, 7 (1974), 460–508, reprinted in idem, *Languages of Class*, pp. 179–238; Ross McKibbin, 'Why was there No Marxism in Britain?', *English Historical Review*, 99 (1984), 297–331; and idem, 'Work and Hobbies in Britain, 1880–1950', in *The Working Class in Modern British Society: Essays in Honour of Henry Pelling*, ed. by Jay M. Winter (Cambridge: Cambridge University Press, 1983), pp. 127–46: both essays are reprinted in Ross McKibbin, *The Ideologies of Class: Social Relations in Britain, 1880–1950* (Oxford: Oxford University Press, 1990), pp. 1–41, 139–66.

96 'John Harrison: An Appreciation', in *Living and Learning*, p. 5; J.F.C. Harrison, *Robert Owen and the Owenites in Britain and America: The Search for the New Moral World* (London: Routledge and Kegan Paul, 1969).

97 For example Richard Gurnham, *200 Years – A History of the Trade Union Movement in the Hosiery and Knitwear Industry, 1776–1976: The History of the National Union of Hosiery and Knitwear Workers, Its Evolution, and Its Predecessors* (Leicester: National Union of Hosiery and Knitwear Workers, 1976); Ken Coates and Tony Topham, *The History of the Transport and General Workers' Union, vol. 1: The Making of the Transport and General Workers' Union: The Emergence of the Labour Movement 1870–1922*, (Oxford: Blackwell, 1991), see Part 1: '1870–1911: From Forerunners to Federation'; Carolyn Baylies, *The History of the Yorkshire Miners, 1881–1918* (London: Routledge and Kegan Paul, 1993). Exceptions to this generalization include two notable products of the early 1960s, J.E. Williams, *The Derbyshire Miners: A Study in Industrial and Social History* (London: Allen and Unwin, 1962) and Philip S. Bagwell, *The Railwaymen: The History of the National Union of Railwaymen* (London: Allen and Unwin, 1963), and, a little later, John Lovell, *Stevedores and Dockers: A Study of Trade Unionism in the Port of London, 1870–1914* (London: Macmillan, 1969).

98 E.J. Hobsbawm, 'Trade Union Historiography', *BSSLH*, 8 (1964), 31–36.

99 E.J. Hobsbawm, 'British Gas-workers, 1873–1914', in idem, *Labouring Men*, pp. 158–78; idem, 'General Labour Unions in Britain, 1889–1914', in ibid., 179–203; idem, 'National Unions on the Waterside', in ibid., 204–30. See also idem, 'The "New Unionism" Reconsidered', in *The Development of Trade Unionism in Great Britain and Germany, 1880–1914*, ed. by Wolfgang J. Mommsen and Hans-Gerhard Husung (London: Allen and Unwin, 1985), pp. 13–31.

100 Hugh Clegg, Alan Fox and A. F. Thompson, *A History of British Trade Unions since 1889, vol. I: 1889–1910* (Oxford: Oxford University Press, 1964); see also E.J. Hobsbawm, 'Trade Union History', *Economic History Review*, n.s., 20 (1967), 358–64, which is a review of the volume by Clegg and his colleagues.

101 Richard Price, 'The New Unions and the Labour Process', in Mommsen and Husung, *Development of Trade Unionism*, pp. 133–49.

102 Derek Matthews, '1889 and All That: New Views on the New Unionism', *International Review of Social History*, 36 (1991), 24–58.

103 Conference Report, *BSSLH*, 17 (1968), 20.

104 E.P. Thompson, *Customs in Common* (London: Merlin, 1991), pp. ix–xii.

105 John Rule, *The Experience of Labour in Eighteenth-Century Industry* (London: Croom Helm, 1981); *British Trade Unionism 1750–1850: The Formative Years*, ed. by John Rule (London: Longman, 1988).

106 C.R. Dobson, *Masters and Journeymen: A Prehistory of Industrial Relations, 1717–1800* (London: Croom Helm, 1980); Douglas Hay et al., *Albion's Fatal Tree : Crime and Society in Eighteenth-Century England* (London: Allen Lane, 1975); E.P. Thompson, *Whigs and Hunters : The Origin of the Black Act* (London: Allen Lane, 1975).

107 For example, Roger Wells, *Insurrection: The British Experience, 1795–1803*

(Gloucester: Sutton, 1983); Malcolm Chase, *The People's Farm: English Radical Agrarianism, 1775–1840* (Oxford: Oxford University Press, 1988); Adrian Randall, *Before the Luddites: Custom, Community and Machinery in the English Woollen Industry, 1776–1809* (Cambridge: Cambridge University Press, 1991); Janette Neeson, *Commoners: Common Right, Enclosure and Social Change in England, 1700–1820* (Cambridge: Cambridge University Press, 1993); *Crime, Protest and Popular Politics in Southern England, 1740–1850*, ed. by John Rule and Roger A.E. Wells (London: Hambledon Continuum, 1997). For a useful overview of this literature which summarizes key debates, see Archer, *Social Unrest.*

108 E.P. Thompson: 'Patrician Society, Plebeian Culture', *Journal of Social History*, 7 (1974), 382–405 (pp. 396–97).

109 John Rule, 'The Property of Skill in the Period of Manufacture', in *The Historical Meanings of Work*, ed. by Patrick Joyce (Cambridge: Cambridge University Press, 1987); cf. Rule's authorship of Thompson's entry in the *Oxford Dictionary of National Biography* and editorship, with Robert Malcolmson, of *Protest and Survival, the Historical Experience: Essays for E.P. Thompson* (London: Merlin, 1993).

110 Malcolm Chase, *Early Trade Unionism: Fraternity, Skill and the Politics of Labour* (Aldershot: Ashgate, 2000).

111 The others are *The Invisible Woman: Aspects of Women's Work in 18th Century Britain*, ed. by Isabelle Baudino, Jacques Carré and Cecile Révauger (Aldershot: Ashgate, 2005); Janet Greenlees, *Female Labour Power: Women Workers' Influence on Business Practices in the British and American Cotton Industries, 1780–1860* (Aldershot: Ashgate, 2007); Katrina Honeyman, *Child Workers in England, 1780–1820* (Aldershot: Ashgate 2007).

112 See, for example, Maxine Berg, *Luxury and Pleasure in Eighteenth-Century Britain* (Oxford: Oxford University Press, 2005).

113 See Robert C. Allen, *The British Industrial Revolution in Global Perspective* (Cambridge: Cambridge University Press, 2009).

114 Aside from *Before the Socialists*, Harrison's only single-authored, book-length work was *The Life and Times of Sydney and Beatrice Webb.* See John McIlroy and John Halstead, 'A Very Different Historian: Royden Harrison, Radical Academics and Suppressed Alternatives', *Historical Studies in Industrial Relations*, 15 (2003), 113–43.

115 Notably, *Independent Collier: The Coal Miner as Archetypal Proletarian Reconsidered*, ed. by Royden Harrison (Hassocks: Harvester, 1978); Alan Campbell, *The Lanarkshire Miners: A Social History of their Trade Unions, 1775–1874;* (Edinburgh, Donald, 1979); R. Merfyn Jones, *The North Wales Quarrymen, 1874–1922* (Cardiff: University of Wales Press, 1983); Takao Matsumura, *The Labour Aristocracy Revisited: The Victorian Flint Glassmakers, 1850–1880* (Manchester: Manchester University Press, 1983); *Divisions of Labour: Skilled Workers and Technological Change in Nineteenth-Century England*, ed. by Royden Harrison and Jonathan Zeitlin (Brighton: Harvester, 1985); Lancaster, *Radicalism.*

116 See, for example, Hobsbawm's essays in *Labouring Men* and *Worlds of Labour*;

cf. idem, *The Age of Revolution, 1789–1848* (London: Weidenfeld and Nicolson, 1962) and idem, *Age of Capital.*

117 Clive Behagg, *Politics and Production in the Early Nineteenth Century* (London: Routledge, 1990), Roy A. Church et al., *The History of the British Coal Industry. vol. 3, 1830–1913: Victorian Pre-Eminence* (Oxford: Oxford University Press, 1986); James Jaffe, *The Struggle For Market Power: Industrial Relations in the British Coal Industry, 1800–1840* (Cambridge: Cambridge University Press, 1991) and idem, *Striking a Bargain: Work and Industrial Relations in England, 1815–1865* (Manchester: Manchester University Press, 2000); John V. Orth, *Combination and Conspiracy: A Legal History of Trade Unionism, 1721–1906* (Oxford: Oxford University Press, 1991); Mark Curthoys, *Governments, Labour and the Law in Mid-Victorian Britain: The Trade Union Legislation of the 1870s* (Oxford: Oxford University Press, 2004).

118 Gareth Stedman Jones, *Outcast London: A Study in the Relationship between Classes in Victorian Society* (Oxford: Oxford University Press, 1971).

119 Gareth Stedman Jones, preface to the 1984 edition of *Outcast London* (New York: Pantheon Books, 1984), pp. xiii–xiv.

120 Harrison, *Robert Owen and the Owenites.*

121 See, for example, Gareth Stedman Jones, 'Languages of Class', his editorial introduction and notes to *Karl Marx and Friederich Engels, The Communist Manifesto* (London: Penguin, 2002) and idem, *An End to Poverty? A Historical Debate* (London: Profile, 2004); Gregory Claeys, *Machinery, Money and the Millennium: From Moral Economy to Socialism, 1815–60* (Cambridge: Polity, 1987) and idem, *Citizens and Saints: Politics and Anti-Politics in Early British Socialism* (Cambridge: Cambridge University Press, 1989); Noel W. Thompson, *The People's Science: The Popular Political Economy of Exploitation and Crisis, 1816–34* (Cambridge: Cambridge University Press, 1984); David Stack, *Nature and Artifice: The Life and Thought of Thomas Hodgskin, 1787–1869* (Ipswich: Boydell and Brewer, 1998).

122 For a critical response to postmodernism by one British labour historian, see Neville Kirk, 'History, Language, Ideas and Postmodernism: A Materialist View', *Social History,* 19 (1994), 221–40.

123 Patrick Joyce, *Visions of the People: Industrial England and the Question of Class, 1848–1914* (Cambridge: Cambridge University Press, 1991), p. 1; idem, *Democratic Subjects: The Self and the Subject in Nineteenth-Century England* (Cambridge: Cambridge University Press, 1994).

124 John Belchem, 'A Language of Classlessness', *LHR,* 57, 2 (1992), 43–45; Tilly, 'Softcore Solipsism'; Joyce, *Visions of the People,* pp. 329–43.

125 Most notably, James Vernon, 'Who's Afraid of the "Linguistic Turn"? Social History and Its Discontents', *Social History,* 19 (1994), 81–97, and idem, *Politics and the People: A Study in English Political Culture, c.1815–1867* (Cambridge: Cambridge University Press, 1993).

126 Patrick Joyce, 'The End of Social History', *Social History,* 20 (1995), 73–91.

127 Michael Bentley, 'Victorian Politics and the Linguistic Turn', *Historical Journal,* 42 (1999), 883–902 (p. 899).

128 Jon Lawrence, *Speaking for the People: Party, Language and Popular Politics in*

England, 1867–1914 (Cambridge: Cambridge University Press, 1998).

129 Joyce, *Democratic Subjects*, p. 11.

130 Allen, *Joseph Cowen*; Chase, *Chartism*; Rohan McWilliam, *The Tichborne Claimant: A Victorian Sensation* (London: Hambledon Continuum, 2007); Paul Pickering, *Feargus O'Connor: A Political Life* (Monmouth: Merlin, 2008); Taylor, *Ernest Jones*; Jill Liddington, *Rebel Girls: Their Fight for the Vote* (London: Virago 2007); John Shepherd, *George Lansbury: At the Heart of Old Labour* (Oxford: Oxford University Press, 2002); Craig Nelson, *Thomas Paine: Enlightenment, Revolution, and the Birth of Modern Nations* (London: Viking, 2006); Tristram Hunt, *The Frock-Coated Communist: The Revolutionary Life of Friedrich Engels* (London: Allen Lane, 2009).

3

Britain: The Twentieth Century

Alan Campbell and John McIlroy

In 1960, labour history in Britain stopped at 1914. In the scholarly literature and in university teaching the twentieth century received only minor attention. Surveying the historiography in 1958, John Saville indicated significant silences: substantial gaps in our knowledge of the interwar working class, a lack of studies of the Independent Labour Party (ILP), little about the Communist Party (CP) – there were, of course, many more such absences.[1] Some disregarded such work because it entailed not only practical but political problems.[2] In terms of methodology and approach, no distinction was made between the years before or after 1900, although archival difficulties were acknowledged. The formation of the Society for the Study of Labour History (SSLH) in 1960 is often viewed as a landmark in the development of the 'new labour history' but there were different views of what this entailed.[3] One of the SSLH's founders, Eric Hobsbawm, aspired to fuse the history of labour organizations with the social history of the working class, but he also reached out to world history. Less ambitiously, Saville urged the need to blend economic, political and diplomatic history and address not only labour but also capital.[4] The SSLH's first chair, Asa Briggs, enunciated the bones of an agenda at the Society's founding conference in May 1960:

> [The] study of the working class 'situation' taken in terms of health, leisure, etc. Social history in the fullest sense, including politics, but not tied exclusively to politics; studies which focus attention on class relations, the impact of other classes and class organizations on the workers; and a strictly economic history of labour. There is also a need for studies of leadership, rank and file relations in labour organizations, and for a closer examination of 'militancy' and 'commitment'.[5]

Most of his listeners would have gone along with that; but uniformity of response should not be assumed. Hobsbawm wished to transcend the 'old' labour history, 'the narrative history of labour movements' pioneered by the Webbs and G.D.H. Cole, while Edward Thompson was soon to provide major stimulus to the 'new social history' with *The Making of the English Working Class.* But not all productive members of the infant SSLH – Hugh Clegg and Henry Pelling spring immediately to mind – were devotees of history from below or eager to abandon institutional or economic histories.[6] The Society was pluralist, a forum rather than a school. Not all members considered themselves Marxists or social historians.[7] Briggs's comments suggest at most a shared line of march that recognized the aspirational virtue of an integrative agenda combining traditional histories of labour organizations and elites with a revived, more rigorous address of the condition of the common people. This chapter explores the historiography of British labour in the twentieth century published after 1960 and discusses how these varied approaches were applied in practice. In accordance with the nature of labour history fifty years ago, it looks first at the literature on trade unions and industrial relations, then political organizations and finally at the historiography of the working class conceived more broadly.[8]

Trade unions, industrial relations and the state

In 1960 labour history was often identified with the history of trade unions and collective bargaining. That area represented a meeting place for labour historians and industrial relations scholars, some of whom were active in the early SSLH. Institutional studies of individual unions, rather than their members, were a staple of the historiography. They were often commissioned and this restricted critical approaches; some disclosed a strong streak of antiquarianism, others verged on hagiography. Some account was taken of economic and political contexts but examination of the institutional workings of the organization, its existential struggles and its *progress*, despite setbacks, predominated. Dependence on head-office records, the goodwill of full-time officials and the opinions of interested survivors produced a generally top-down, sometimes partisan, concentration on leaders and policies.[9]

There were salutary exceptions. Analysing the unions in cotton textiles over two centuries in 1963, the industrial relations academic, H.A. Turner, extrapolated from their experience and distinguished between 'open' and 'closed' patterns of growth and decline. His categories of 'exclusive democracies' of craftsmen, 'aristocracies' dominated by skilled groups, and 'popular bossdoms' in the general unions of the unskilled workers, related internal organization to environment. His case studies developed an analytical framework of wider application.[10] A decade later, another industrial relations scholar, Richard Hyman, drew important theoretical implications about how unions operated from his account of the Workers' Union. He used his history of developments between 1898 and 1929 as a basis from which to explore classic themes in the sociology of organizations: displacement of radical goals; espousal of business unionism due to institutional needs; a democratic constitution succumbing to oligarchy, although some disjuncture remained between Hyman's analytic narrative and his theoretical apparatus.[11]

Union histories continued to be written, often by industrial relations experts. Few explicitly applied these insights. There was, however, greater attention to context, internal conflicts and the influence of technology in work which included but went beyond institutional history to explore the characteristics of particular groups of workers and how they affected specific forms of collectivism.[12] The challenge of comprehending diverse contexts and capturing local and national experience that confronted the genre was highlighted by the first volume of the official history of the Transport and General Workers' Union (TGWU): it ran to 900 pages before it reached the union's foundation in 1922. Nonetheless, Ken Coates and Tony Topham successfully interrogated a wealth of national and union records, supplemented by existing accounts of the TGWU's forerunners and reinforced by seminars involving academics and union veterans. Focused on organizational issues, the book did not ignore the wider labour movement or its politics. Its scope was testimony to the scale of Ernest Bevin's achievement in constructing a centralized organization that accommodated occupational diversity.[13] An alternative, less successful, approach was attempted for a much smaller union, the Fire-fighters: chapters contributed by historians were combined with activists' memoirs.[14]

By the 1980s, emphasis on the social history of labour had produced beneficial results. A comparison of W.R. Garside's *Durham Miners*, a traditional work by an economic historian, with Hywel Francis and Dai Smith's analysis of the 'Fed' in South Wales a decade later illustrates this shift. The latter drew on oral sources to recuperate the role of union activists in their communities and to map changes in culture as well as the strategies key actors employed after the defeat of 1926. In the 1990s, the sociologists Huw Beynon and Terry Austrin developed a more comprehensive analysis of work, community, class, culture and politics centred on the Durham Miners' Association which illuminated the nature of 'labourism'.[15]

At their most basic, individual studies constituted building blocks for broader work. The first edition of Pelling's *History* appeared in 1963, the initial volume of Clegg's trilogy detailing the growth of trade unions from 1889 to 1951, the following year. Both pursued an institutional approach and both displayed an inclination towards consensual industrial relations. There was sound sense in Hobsbawm's contemporary evaluations of the former as 'modest but useful', the latter as 'indispensable', despite its resolute empiricism, insistence on particularism and neglect of 'the mental world' of trade unionists.[16] There were ambitious attempts to integrate histories of trade unionism into overviews aimed at replacing Cole's history of the working-class movement published in 1948. These, too, reflected their author's political predilections: Kenneth Brown emphasized 'bread-and-butter' issues and reformist labourism while James Hinton depicted tensions between organized labour's defensive concerns in capitalist society and its potential for socialist advance.[17]

Traditional histories of trade unionism were gender-blind; practitioners of women's history redressed matters. Sheila Rowbotham's seminal 1973 survey of feminism and socialism from early capitalism to the 1930s contained preliminary studies of women's trade union organization in the First World War and women's participation in unemployed movements during the interwar years. Further work appeared by the end of the decade, which analyzed women's political struggles and explained their lower levels of unionization by resort to domestic responsibilities or gender antagonism.[18] These accounts added a vital dimension to androcentric narratives; they remained conventionally focused on organization.

Other scholars integrated examination of industrial conflict and the role of workplace activists into analysis of trade unionism. In contrast to Branko Pribicevic's institutional account of the shop stewards' movement between 1910 and 1922, Hinton developed debates about the labour aristocracy and employed social history to recreate the mentality of the skilled engineer. He insisted that war-time tensions between craft conservatism and militancy directed against state control produced a kernel of potential radicalism: syndicalist shop stewards perceived embryonic soviets in the workers' committees established in major munitions centres.[19] The fiftieth anniversary of the 1926 general strike prompted renewed research at national and, particularly, local level, which superseded the journalistic accounts written in the 1950s; only recently has extended documentation and analysis of the mining lockout been published.[20] Richard Croucher analyzed relations between engineering workers, shop stewards, union leaders and the state in the very different context of the Second World War, when Communist activists first fomented then suppressed militancy. In the Cold War, the CP again attempted to amplify industrial unrest. Government responses have been sketched but the role that Communists played in key unions merits greater exploration.[21]

Treatment of industrial disputes at aggregate level was initiated by K.G.J.C. Knowles, who explored the character, causes and consequences of strikes before 1947. James Durcan and his colleagues extended this classic study for the postwar decades. They traced patterns of conflict nationally and in strike-prone industries, highlighted the influence of government on these trends and urged procedural reform. These were statistical studies by industrial relations scholars within restricted timeframes. James Cronin more ambitiously explored strike waves from 1890 until the 1970s. His methodologically sophisticated analysis developed a model that linked qualitative shifts in the character and incidence of strikes to phases of economic growth, mediated through consciousness and organization. Cronin contested notions of conflict as dysfunctional, depicted strikes as 'creative acts of an offensive kind', and challenged accounts of labour's gradual integration into British society.[22] His application of statistical methods such as regression analysis reminds us that labour history in the 1970s drew on innovative quantitative techniques, not only novel qualitative sources. Such studies became unfashionable with the decline of union membership, shop stewards and strikes: their continuing utility was suggested by an analysis of mining disputes that demonstrated, albeit in a depopulated fashion which neglected the role of activists, their highly uneven distribution in that strike-prone industry.[23]

Ben Roberts' determinedly institutional and moderate history of Britain's trade union centre, the Trades Union Congress (TUC), appeared in 1958. Subsequent accounts followed a similar approach, although more imaginative study of that organization from 1926 focused upon its general secretaries and their relations with government. The TUC was represented in the localities by trades councils, federations of union branches. Alan Clinton's study remains the only analysis of their activities. Using their records and the local labour press, it traced the growing influence of these bodies after 1914. However, its radical sympathies regarding their potential for working-class power in 1926 contrasted with their limited ambitions in practice and, by the 1930s, their growing subordination to the TUC. Their activities after 1940 still await address.[24]

The TUC's operations during the Cold War have attracted particular attention. Anthony Carew's valuable history of the Marshall Plan's impact on labour and the consequent split in the World Federation of Trade Unions (WFTU) concentrated on the period after 1947 and the anti-

Russian role that the TUC took in collaboration with the Foreign Office. Stressing the TUC's corporatism and sympathetic to the Communists in the continuing debates over the provenance of the Cold War, Peter Weiler located problems in the TUC's subservience to a social-democratic state still marked by imperialism and colonialism. The TUC's anti-Communism was depicted as a Cold War over-reaction, corrosive of international workers' unity. Perhaps more satisfactorily, Denis McShane inserted the breach between East and West into the sustained Russian opposition to socialism and the long-term antagonism between democratic socialists and official Communists, which stretched back to 1921 and was not removed by the wartime alliance with Russia. Marshall aid, the creation of the Cominform, the Czechoslovak coup, detonated these tensions. In the WFTU, the role of autonomous international trade secretariats and their dedication to independent trade unionism proved an important factor in splitting the organization.[25]

Briggs's advocacy of the study of capital, employers and managers was implemented only gradually as historians of labour too often ceded the field to business historians.[26] Nevertheless, Clegg's history of trade unions was also a history of employers' federations and collective bargaining. A three-volume series on the history of British industrial relations, sometimes rather formally conceived, added useful case studies.[27] The publication of Harry Braverman's *Labor and Monopoly Capital* in Britain in 1974 stimulated widespread interest in the labour process. Richard Price mounted the most ambitious attempt to reinterpret labour history in light of this vogue.[28] Convinced that post-Thompsonian scholars had too narrowly focused on cultures of everyday life, he provided a grand narrative of economic and political transitions, exploring the linkages between relations of production and political developments. If the former were not 'primary', such connections, he insisted, could be discerned. Price transcended the fragmented nature of many labour process studies. His concentration on workplace relations at the expense of sources of solidarity such as community, ensured that he only partially fulfilled his totalizing aspirations.

Research on employer behaviour published in the 1980s and 1990s further undermined notions of a monolithic capitalist class with unitary interests which was evident in some Marxist writing, notably Braverman's work. Steven Tolliday and Jonathan Zeitlin shifted the emphasis towards the diversity of employers' attitudes to collective association and the range of choices they made in the management of labour, while Howard Gospel highlighted the significance of product and labour markets in shaping managerial strategies. Other historians contributed to our understanding of the ways in which 'employers' displayed internal stratification rather than homogeneity: the analyses of the bourgeoisie on Clydeside by Joseph Melling and Ronnie Johnston constituted insightful examples.[29]

Growing interest in studying the state characterized labour history in the 1970s, a period when, from the viewpoint of labour, the extended state reached its zenith. Keith Middlemas cogently and influentially expounded his theory of 'corporate bias', which elevated the TUC and employers' organizations from pressure groups into 'governing institutions', to help explain social stability after 1926.[30] His book stimulated interest in how the state worked; yet it is questionable whether these bodies were capable of exerting significant control over their constituents or if threats to social order in Britain required elaborate explanation in comparison with countervailing factors such as rising living standards. There were less ambitious accounts of contingency planning and policing industrial conflict: Roger Geary portrayed overly unilinear abandonment of violence during disputes; Jane Morgan and Barbara Weinberger delineated the evolution of police organization, Home Office policy and local powers.[31]

By the mid-1980s, in tandem with the new post-labour mood, revisionist historians were countering these approaches. Alastair Reid and Iain McLean questioned the nature of wartime militancy and debunked 'the legend of Red Clydeside' and its impact on support for Labour, endeavours disputed by John Foster and others.[32] Reid was associated with Zeitlin's attempt to revise pluralist and Marxist conceptions of the state's role in industrial relations, postulating that it prioritized its own autonomous interests, which might sometimes be better served by collaborating with workers against management.[33] Zeitlin's wider project aimed to divert labour history from its post-1960 course through redefining it as the history of industrial relations. He challenged what he perceived as prevalent assumptions attributing revolutionary potential to workers at the point of production and inherent accommodation to capital to union leaders; instead, he urged attention to factional processes within unions.

The importance of institutions in terms of constructing, articulating and defending class identities probably required re-emphasis in the face of a developing, diffuse and sometimes depoliticized social history. But Zeitlin's strategy would have narrowed labour history's expanded horizons, as his blunt caricature of a diverse historiography as 'rank-and-fileist' demonstrated.[34] Against this neo-institutionalism, other historians advocated a broader vision of *industrial politics*, engaging with the social and economic contexts of industrial relations, but with politics from above and below at its core. They located politics inside the institutions of labour, employers and the state but also in workplaces and communities. They advocated consideration of the political values of leaders, activists and workers and their role in mobilizing support.[35]

The relative absence of biographical studies of union leaders and activists was partially repaired after 1960. Alan Bullock's magisterial *Ernest Bevin* remains a landmark, a life but also the times of the British labour movement before 1939. Vic Allen's pioneering exploration of Arthur Deakin may be favourably contrasted with journalistic treatment of Frank Cousins, two of Bevin's successors as TGWU general secretary; nonetheless, each text provided insights into the politics and governance of the largest 'popular bossdom'.[36] The 'Lives of the Left' series, published in the 1980s and edited by David Howell, contained some trade union subjects, notably a thoughtful rehabilitation of the charismatic miners' tribune, A.J. Cook. There remains a dearth of scholarly studies of postwar leaders. Given their political significance, biographies of Hugh Scanlon of the Engineers, Jack Jones of the TGWU, and Arthur Scargill and Michael McGahey, leaders of the National Union of Mineworkers during the strike of 1984–5, could ensure a further means to re-assess postwar industrial politics.[37]

Reid's one-volume history of trade unionism, which appeared in the new century, attempted, in the context of twenty years of general trade union retreat, to readjust traditional narratives of progress: there was no reference whatsoever to the Webbs' work. Yet Reid privileged continuity between the twentieth-century labour movement and the Liberalism, responsibility and respectability of the emergent craft unionism of the nineteenth century over change, instability and insurgence. Accommodationist aspects were amplified at the expense of complementary instances and periods of resistance and turbulence. Militant tendencies were perceived as untypical. Reid's classification of workers as 'assembly', 'process' or 'general' with corresponding 'craft', 'seniority' and 'federal' unions was empirically flawed and less analytically useful than conventional categorization. Textual segregation of each group imposed fragmentation at the expense of the solidarity expressed in particular incidents and periods.[38] Chris Howell's analysis of the state's role in industrial relations contested traditional emphases on voluntarism and stressed its interventionist character during three phases: collective *laisser-faire*, 1890–1940; decentralization, 1940–79; and decollectivization from 1979. The collapse of British trade unions under Thatcherism was convincingly attributed to the inability of a movement nurtured under corporate sponsorship to withstand the radical turn to a hostile state.[39]

Labour historians have only occasionally engaged with twentieth-century labour law, although it is an important and distinctive aspect of British industrial relations. In 1960 Saville published a ground-breaking account of the background to the Taff Vale decision that rendered unions liable for damages when taking industrial action. He followed it three decades later with a study of the 1906 Trade Disputes Act, which overturned that judgement. In the intervening period there were specialist articles but no extended study of the politics and impact of labour law in the twentieth century by a labour historian.[40] Matters have improved, but there is still no comprehensive historical account of the Trades Disputes Act 1927, Order 1305 or the employment legislation of the 1970s and 1980s.[41]

In 1962, Hobsbawm looked towards creative cross-fertilization between labour historians and industrial relations scholars.[42] It did not happen. Industrial relations developed as a specialized, largely history-free field fundamentally concerned with policy in the present. So, in a different fashion, did political science. Both neglected the history of trade unions and, increasingly, so did historians of labour. The literature on unions, employers' federations, collective bargaining and industrial militancy concentrated largely on organizational issues. This produced a fragmented, relatively impoverished historiography. Despite the best efforts of Turner and Hyman there was little theoretical exploration, little historical sociology and little excavation of the culture of what Raymond Williams considered were, together with the Labour Party, British labour's major cultural achievements. By the 1990s, with the decline of organized labour, there was more interest in the politics of the party than the behaviour of the unions.

Political organizations

The historiography of the Labour Party was a growing component of labour history in 1960, testifying to the still prevalent focus on the labour movement. Cole's insider knowledge and mastery of detail made for effective treatment of developments between 1914 and 1945 in his *History of the Labour Party*. Aspiring to tell 'the complete story' from the party's emergence as a national force during the First World War to majority government at the end of the Second, Cole combined dense narrative with partisan commentary: for example, emphasizing the 'outstanding part' played by the 'vanities' of Ramsay MacDonald and Philip Snowden in 'the sorry story' of 1931. Culminating in Labour's 1945 electoral landslide, his text devoted relatively little attention to Labour's less auspicious experiences of minority government. It was both history and celebration of Labour's forward march.[43] Pelling's *Short History*, published in 1961, acknowledged its debt to Cole. A more modest, more balanced effort, it briskly surveyed the party's development over the twentieth century. Numerous editions testify to its utility as an empirical primer. Recent versions, extending the chronology and co-authored with Reid, more contentiously reflect on socialism's unpopularity and Liberalism's resilience, affirmed for some in the emergence of New Labour.[44]

Ralph Miliband's *Parliamentary Socialism* was very different. Covering Labour's first six decades, its central theme was what it posed as a pivotal conflict between aspirations to humanely administer capitalism or construct socialism. Miliband identified the 'sickness of Labourism' with its leaders' commitment to parliamentary reform and nationalism which obstructed the development and mobilization of a socialist constituency and radical social change. Published as the debates on Gaitskellite revisionism climaxed, this was less a work of historical enquiry into the possibilities and constraints the party had confronted, not least the reformist, economistic character of Britain's working class and labour movement, than a political argument. It implicitly urged transformation of the party given the weakness of socialist purpose disclosed by its past.[45]

Labour's early history and pre-history had been quarried before 1960. The archival research of Pelling and Frank Bealey established the essential components in the party's advent. These pioneering narratives stressed the role of socialists in creating the Labour Representation Committee in 1900 and highlighted trade union influence thereafter; they recognized geographical and religious divisions shaping electoral support as well as the significance of high politics during secret negotiations with the Liberals. Roy Gregory's psephological examination of Labour's implantation or rejection in the coalfields identified 'front runners', 'slow starters' and 'laggards' to underline the unevenness of Labour's support before 1914.[46]

David Howell's study of the ILP was more ambitious. Utilizing local union, political and press records, he analysed the diversity of the party's industrial and regional bases, as well as where it failed to establish roots, before examining policies and activities at national and local levels. In contrast to accounts depicting Labour's electoral growth as a union reflex to Taff Vale and the outcome of electoral agreement with the Liberals, Howell highlighted links between workers' lived experience and their socialist politics; he demonstrated the ILP's importance within early Labour's grassroots as activists constructed a national organization from 'a tangled web of local opportunities, constraints and responses'.[47]

Debate developed about whether Labour's emergence and accession to government by 1924 were the 'inevitable' outcomes of social and economic change. Historians of the Liberal Party emphasized that organization's vitality before 1914, claiming that only its wartime divisions created political space for Labour after 1918. In contrast, Ross McKibbin's analysis of the Labour Party's national, regional and local organization based on extensive reading of internal correspondence, National Executive minutes and the press, argued that Labour's identification with the unions, and union identification with the working class, would have ensured success *ante bellum*, but for the restrictions of the pre-1918 franchise. Local studies buttressed his conclusions. Royden Harrison contributed an important essay on the significance of the War Emergency National Workers' Committee in keeping Labour's divisions in check, in contrast to Liberal ruptures over the war.[48] In the mould of Peter Clarke's earlier approach, Duncan Tanner's monograph on constituency politics before 1918 pointed to electoral and political fragmentation rather than uniform social change. It echoed Liberal historians, concluding that Labour had not consolidated its class base by 1914, that it was strongest where the Liberals were weak, and consequently a 'progressive alliance' between Liberals and Labour remained viable. Critics put forward competing interpretations on the basis of evidence drawn from local party records, election results and the press, noting, for example, the pre-war support for Labour in Liberal strongholds in West Yorkshire, Leicester and Durham.[49]

Controversy also embraced Labour's commitment to common ownership in 1918. For Jay Winter, the experience of wartime collectivism was paramount in projecting Webbian socialism. McKibbin argued that Clause 4 represented 'a sop to the professional bourgeoisie' from non-socialist trade unionists. Harrison's characterization of collective ownership as a shared 'rallying point' around which different interests and ideologies could coalesce, remains the most satisfactory resolution of these conflicting views.[50]

The historiography of Labour's experience in office represents a sub-genre that commenced with R.W. Lyman's volume on the 1924 Labour administration.[51] The following year Reginald Bassett, an erstwhile supporter of Ramsay MacDonald, presented a controversial account of the 1931 crisis sympathetic to the government. Robert Skidelsky's valuable monograph on MacDonald's second term appeared almost a decade later.[52] Its argument, that there existed greater scope for radical solutions to unemployment than government conservatism allowed, was challenged by McKibbin's adumbration of economic, political and intellectual obstacles, including the structural features of the British economy, the nature of the British state and the absence of viable reflationary policies elsewhere.[53] Neil Riddell's broader examination, which covered now familiar ground, reinforced pessimistic conclusions. If we accept David Marquand's convincing depiction of MacDonald as a talented political strategist in his monumental biography, Skidelsky's interpretation may be further qualified.[54]

Such analyses were based on traditional sources for research into elite politics, such as personal papers and government archives (although Skidelsky's achievement was the more impressive for completion before reduction of the 50-year rule governing release of cabinet papers). More recently, Howell explored party culture during the 'MacDonald years', drawing on an extensive range of documents including diaries, memoirs, union minutes, party records and correspondence, Hansard and the press. The book was not institutional history in the conventional sense. Elaboration of the particularities of major unions preceded examination of other identities: in the ILP, among former Liberals, by women and around anti-Communism. It was satisfyingly peopled and complexity was emphasized. It constituted a significant addition to political-cultural history. This came at a price: eschewal of narrative and conclusions; no overall argument was sustained nor were existing analyses of 1931 redefined. On the whole, the culture is the message: embedded codes of union solidarity and party loyalty render the crisis 'understandable and highly probable'.[55]

Stephen Brooke's text on the party during the Second World War turned on high politics, but the nature of Labour's growing support after 1940 remains contentious. Richard Sibley's innovative use of opinion polls demonstrated Labour's lead was established between February 1940 and June 1943; greater precision is impossible given the tantalizing absence of data.[56] Using party records, government reports and Mass Observation surveys, a group including Steven Fielding and Nick Tiratsoo attempted to overturn traditional notions of this 'shift to the left' in public mood after 1940. Dubbed 'the Apathy School' by their most trenchant critic, they postulated widespread cynicism and political *ennui*.[57] This intervention helpfully prompted re-appraisal of simplistic notions of radicalization. Yet the authors' un-modulated pursuit of their case underestimated the complexity of relations between activists and their constituencies as well as the fluidity of popular feeling: arguably it founders on the unprecedented participation rates in the 1950 and 1951 elections and the solidification and resilience of Labour's working-class support.

The 1945–51 governments have been regarded as the apotheosis of Labour's active commitment to social reform. Critics emphasized their limited ambitions. Such complaints tend to overestimate the political forces that were available to be mustered for radical change and minimize structural constraint. Revisionist studies have, in contrast, stressed the impediments to reform.[58] Fuelled by the release of Cabinet papers, the Labour governments of 1964–70 have now been subjected to similar analysis and some rehabilitation. Given the centrality of the trade union 'problem' for the Wilson administrations, treatment of the unions is curiously muted in comparison with studies of Labour published earlier in the century.[59] With the Blair and Brown governments in power, the last decade has produced a plethora of work by journalists and political scientists on New Labour, which defined itself by maintaining Thatcherism's embrace of the market, rejection of regulation, continuing privatization and marginalization of the unions. Simplified polemics asserted beyond the evidence the continuity between 'New' and 'Old' Labour, although they encountered correction. Cronin provided more nuanced analysis, situating the phenomenon within assessments of the Wilson and Callaghan governments.[60]

Political biography has flourished. All of Labour's leaders have been the subject of multiple studies; even the best do not always avoid a critical empathy which can tilt towards identification.[61] Factional opposition has also been well researched, although extended study of the National Left Wing Movement of the 1920s is lacking. Ben Pimlott's critical analysis of unsuccessful attempts by Labour leftwingers to establish united and popular fronts and alienation of the majority through their Communist associations, remains a starting point for the 1930s. It has been supplemented by Paul Corthorn's organizational account of the non-Communist left, particularly the Socialist League, which emphasizes how Russophilia became more ambivalent, even hostile, towards Stalinism following the purges.

The limitations of the left under the Attlee governments were skilfully dissected by Jonathan Schneer. Bevanism marked the high point of rank-and-file mobilization within the party, when individual membership briefly topped one million. In a sometimes overlooked but stimulating text, Mark Jenkins corrected misconceptions that Bevanites lacked working-class roots or union influence, concluding that the movement's Achilles heel was failure to comprehend the character of the Kremlin in the postwar world. Eric Shaw ably demonstrated how Labour's apparatus maintained control of dissent until the 1970s while entrism by the Trotskyist Militant Tendency revived disciplinarianism in the 1980s.[62]

The historical significance of trade unions as the central pillar of the party, and, until the late 1960s, a protective bulwark for the leadership, has long been acknowledged. For the postwar years such research was largely undertaken by political scientists, although Martin Harrison's pioneering scrutiny of union-party links was superseded by Clegg's analysis of unions and the Atlee governments.[63] Leo Panitch situated enduring tensions between Labour's leadership and unions over incomes policy within the party's contradictory functions: representing working-class interests and integrating that class into the national polity. Growing industrial militancy from the 1960s highlighted the limits of neo-corporatism and prompted a turn towards coercive measures by the 1970 Conservative government. Valuable for its exposition of union-party relations, its Milibandian perspective generated pessimistic conclusions on possibilities for socialist 'remobilization'.[64]

The political scientist Lewis Minkin's outstanding studies tell historians much about the texture of the union-party relationship. *The Contentious Alliance* combined overview of relations until the 1970s; a detailed dissection of left-led attempts at constitutional reform and the re-consolidation of leadership authority; and evaluation of union contributions to policymaking and mobilization. Minkin sought to explain what many leftwing commentators had found surprising: union leaders' self-willed subordination to the political leadership. Its central explanatory axis turned on a deciphering and elaboration of the unwritten codes governing transactions between Labour's political and industrial wings, at their most effective in the 1950s when wages policy was less contentious.[65]

The expansion of women's history from the 1970s opened new doors. Christine Collette examined the independent Women's Labour League before its dissolution into 'the Men's Party' in 1918. Pamela Graves documented the interwar years, when absorption of working-class women into local Labour activities distanced them from middle-class feminists.[66] Mechanistic assumptions correlating union membership and growing electoral success in this period were qualified by Mike Savage, who pointed to their divergent trends. In an exemplary account of Preston, he identified varieties of 'practical' politics by which working-class families attempted to reduce economic insecurity: 'mutualist' provision of services; 'economistic' struggles by unions; and 'statist' measures. Savage's monograph and subsequent essays traced the displacement of economistic union influence within the local Labour Party by neighbourhood-based women's sections seeking amelioration of hardship through the local state.[67] We now have a multitude of studies of Labour in other regions, cities and constituencies; they often lack Savage's rigour. The best have contextualized local parties in their communities, although a recent collection, while demonstrating the diversity of grassroots activities, smacks of antiquarianism.[68]

The literature on the ILP remains uneven and disjointed. Robert Dowse merely sketched developments. Howell's monumental study ends in 1906. The centennial collection contained thematic and regional essays, though with a Yorkshire bias, that affirmed the significance of the organization within the Labour Party. The most comprehensive local study examined Clydeside, where activists successfully bridged workplace grievances and community concerns. The party's fortunes following disaffiliation from Labour in 1932 await full analysis. Gidon Cohen's re-evaluation of prospects for a non-Communist left outside the Labour Party was handicapped by an institutional focus and neglect of relevant material in the archives documenting the CP's sustained attempts to undermine its rival.[69]

The CP became the most significant organization beyond Labour; its membership was small, its failure to challenge Labour's hegemony almost total. Accepting its reach in the unions and amongst intellectuals, the literature devoted to it reflects the political and romantic predilections of some historians and the willingness of others to exploit newly accessible archives.[70] The first academic analyses were critical, political and institutional. Pelling demonstrated the party's sustained subservience to Moscow. Walter Kendall portrayed an alien body animated by 'Russian gold'. His counterfactual hypothesis that an unsubsidised and autonomous native left would otherwise have flourished was questionable; his findings on funding were reinforced by subsequent archival revelations.[71] This literature initiated an ongoing controversy: the degree to which the CP's subordination to Russia's rulers permits it to be characterized as a 'normal' British party, incarnating the militancy of British workers.

With the collapse of the party the emphasis shifted to social history and work which sometimes disclosed admiration for its politics but more often diminished politics and sidelined the centrality of the Soviet Union in order to commend Communists as activists embedded in unions, communities and popular protest. The CP's own apologetic narratives were academicized. There were historiographical costs: artificial portrayal of a two-tier party with economistic militants at its base and only its elite, differentially and rarely emphatically, tainted by Stalinism. The danger of writing histories of Communists with the official Communism left out was exemplified by revisionist work that exaggerated the Britishness of the CP's policies.[72]

Membership of Trotskyist, Maoist and anarchist organizations was even smaller. Histories of these marginal movements, often written by activists, can demonstrate the dangers of identification and antiquarianism; they can also demonstrate scholarly standards not matched by some academics. Their disregarded pasts, which did not wholly escape the influence of Stalinism, do not merit the condescension of posterity any more than when Thompson wrote: justifiable in itself, address of failed alternatives tells us something about history's winners; peripheral movements provided a distinctive critique of labourism and official Communism that exerted wider influence; their cadres at times could mobilize local support; and they could serve as training grounds for militants in the wider labour movement.[73]

The historiography of working-class political organization has developed impressively since 1960. It has reflected not only political change but also the balkanization of history and the history of labour which continued through the last decades of the twentieth century. Research on the Labour Party has produced a body of work immensely richer than that of fifty years ago. But it has become a relatively specialist, deradicalized, less critical genre. There are historians who write exclusively about Labour and present their subject in isolation from other aspects of labour history, even trade unions. Some seem to believe that labour history *is* the history of the Labour Party.[74]

Parochialism is only occasionally relieved by any significant comparative dimension. On the whole, the history of twentieth-century labour has remained 'our island story'. Stefan Berger's 1994 study of British Labour and German Social Democracy was an exception. Innovative in its comparative method, it challenged stereotypes of national peculiarities through a 'diachronic' analysis of their differing trajectories. Its substantive conclusions were achieved at the cost of exaggerating similarities and downplaying real differences in state policy in Britain and Germany, as well as significant contrasts in culture and ideology between the two labour movements. In the trade union field Kendall's pioneering outline, published in the 1970s, has not been qualitatively developed. A collection of essays on trade unionism in Britain and Germany before 1914 contained important national contributions but made little explicit comparison. Roger Fagge's aspiration to write a comparative study of politics and trade unionism in West Virginia and South Wales lapsed into a juxtaposition of parallel narratives to conclude that miners in each coalfield 'inhabited very different social and cultural worlds'.[75] Neville Kirk mounted the most ambitious project, drawing on extensive reading of secondary literature to provide a wide-ranging analysis of the labour movements in Britain and the United States between 1750 and 1939. His central concerns were to explicate the making and remaking of class in each society and contest notions of the trajectory of American labour as 'exceptional'. While acknowledging multiple sources of social division, Kirk's insightful analysis demonstrated the enduring if uneven importance of class; but its greater significance in Britain served only to qualify the 'exceptionalism' thesis.[76]

The literature of Labour is presently dominated by more approbatory, revisionist interpretations whose coherence should not be exaggerated. At least two tendencies can be detected. Tanner's criticism of class-based explanations of Labour's rise as 'social determinism' represents one trend, reminiscent of the features of traditional 'high politics' in its emphasis on the 'primacy' of politics. Symptomatically, his co-edited centennial history contained a chapter on gender but not class.[77] This scepticism contrasts with McKibbin's deterministic deployment of class to explain political phenomena. Fielding adopts McKibbin as totemic of a 'new' labour history, perhaps unsurprisingly, since Fielding and his colleagues arguably reduce Labour politics in the 1940s to apathetic workers. This sits uneasily with McKibbin's insistence on a 'radical', 'permanent', 'movement to the left among the working classes' during the Second World War.[78]

The late 1970s and 1980s witnessed a turn from political histories to social histories in which politics sometimes got lost. This has sometimes been true of work on Communism. But there have also been studies of particular groups of workers, unions, localities, gender, where social history also dissolves the bigger picture. We are presented with what are essentially micro-histories – depoliticized but also de-socialized in any expanded sense of the 'social' – which, unlike the classics of that genre, fail to illuminate macro-issues.

The social history of the working class

The desirability of a shift from largely institutional and political histories of labour movements towards social histories of labour was a key motif of the new labour history of the 1960s. If in Thompsonian form this foregrounded culture and class formation, shared experience generating collective agency, expansion of the historical sociology of the working class highlighted fissures of skill, region, gender, religion and ethnicity. There were parallels between historiographical developments and the move away from the radicalism of the 1960s to the neoliberalism of the 1980s. One observer noted: 'in the first phase of labour history the customs and traditions of labouring men were shown to be sources of revolt. In the second phase, other aspects of working-class culture and community become the sources of passivity.'[79]

It took time for these tendencies to disclose themselves in research into twentieth-century labour. From the mid-1970s, contributions to the History Workshop Series exemplified strengths and weaknesses. The opening volume proclaimed the necessity of rediscovering 'the real life experience of people themselves'. Accounts of extractive industries detailed working practices, with unions appearing only in shadow, whereas treatment of farm labourers centred on radicalism and unions. Oral history was championed. A text based on interviews with trawlermen explored contradictory aspects of mutual dependence at work with isolation in small crews; it successfully integrated local studies of industrial conflict, gender relations and community. Gerry White's reconstruction of the informal economies of London's slum dwellers and their culture – egalitarian, individualistic, class-antagonistic, patriotic in turn – shed light on groups ignored by organized labour and traditional labour history. More controversially, given its unelaborated methodology, the reminiscences of East End gangster Arthur Harding, employed to terrorize pickets in 1926, provided insights into the criminal *demi-monde.*[80]

Through vigorous excavation of particular trades and localities, diet, housing, leisure and credit and much else, such work extended the parameters and the methods of labour history.[81] But the drift of social history was indicated by Standish Meacham's overview of English working-class life. It was pioneering in its integration of women at home and at work, neighbourhood and childhood, as well as husbands and fathers. Although inspired by Thompson and Hobsbawm, ultimately it represented a variant of Trevelyan-style social history with the politics left out.[82] Characteristically, it was Hobsbawm who initiated debate about the nature of working-class culture in a duo of boldly drawn overviews. He identified the emergence of a relatively homogeneous, labourist, trade unionist, 'modern' working class between 1870 and 1914, rooted in industrial concentration, residential segregation and enhanced leisure, saturated with class consciousness. Typified by cloth caps, football, fish and chips and holidays in Blackpool, it shared 'a profound sense of the separateness of manual labour, an unformulated but powerful moral code based on solidarity, "fairness", mutual aid and cooperation [...]'.[83] Hobsbawm was not referring to an activist elite but to the class as a whole, which increasingly identified with Labour.

His depiction of 'a single, fairly standard pattern of working-class life' came under challenge as social historians disaggregated such unitary notions.[84] McKibbin's equally broad-brush contribution portrayed a sectionalized class enjoying a rich associational culture and displaying reformist politics rooted in 'Lib-Labism'.[85] Thereafter, the diversity of workers' industrial and social experiences was documented. Against theories of progressive deskilling, revisionist historians indicated skilled workers' ability to resist these tendencies in industries such as engineering, shipbuilding and printing, where managers were portrayed as ineffectual.[86] Women's historians contributed well-upholstered accounts of daily lives in the public and private spheres of waged work and domestic labour. Elizabeth Roberts' oral history of Lancashire women evoked the drudgery of married life and the achievements of household management through which respectability was maintained. Carl Chinn disputed middle-class stereotypes of the urban poor by uncovering a hidden matriarchy in Birmingham that was independent and creative in survival techniques. In a broader, more explicit challenge to Hobsbawm, Paul Johnson scrutinized the institutions of thrift and credit to which working-class families resorted in making ends meet. In contrast to the world of work, the sphere of consumption was depicted as 'intensely personal', with the working class 'decomposed into many strata' characterized by 'interpersonal competition'. The cooperative movement, for Hobsbawm an index of growing class consciousness, was largely concerned with 'self'.[87]

Whereas Hobsbawm pointed to commercialized popular recreation fostering commonality, Andrew Davies' oral history of Manchester and Salford claimed that the unemployed were excluded from such pursuits, which were in many cases segregated by gender. Fielding, too, focused on Manchester to reveal the enduring ethnic and religious identities of working-class Catholics of Irish descent and their qualified adherence to Labour. In an uneven overview of working-class culture – which paid inadequate attention to the impact of two world wars – Joanna Bourke judged solidaristic, working-class communities 'retrospective constructions'; she portrayed localities united only by instrumental assistance and riven by interpersonal tensions.[88]

John Benson's interim stocktaking, which did not neglect the labour movement, concluded: 'working people continued to be divided in very many ways'; the view that they constituted a 'homogeneous mass' was unsustainable.[89] Trevor Griffiths's monograph on his deliberately pluralized Lancashire 'working classes' epitomized this trend. In a detailed comparison of miners and cotton workers in Bolton and Wigan, Griffiths illustrated the exacerbation of skill differentials, the significance of families spreading economic risk through occupational diversity, the importance of thrift. In a study ending in 1930, the emphasis was on continuity, not 'remaking'. Mutuality and extended bonds of solidarity were displaced by the nuclear family, 'the moral and material centre of working-class life'; neighbourliness was a 'pragmatic response to financial necessity'; 'unions articulated the views of minorities'; labour markets were more important than labour processes; class was 'more often than not, subordinated to other sources of identity' by 'privatized' workers.[90]

These accounts were extremely useful in expanding our knowledge of 'the working-class situation', particularly that of the northern working class, which provided much of the evidence underpinning Hobsbawm's argument. Yet there were elements of a straw man in some critiques of Hobsbawm. The supple and sagacious exponent of the labour aristocracy thesis was only too aware of status divisions: nonetheless, he was in search of a determining judgement and insisted that the class had become 'bound together in a community of fate irrespective of its internal differences'.[91] There is still much to be said for this view, even if it must be rendered more specifically and more conditionally. Where Hobsbawm's conclusions were certainly questionable, like those of Thompson for an earlier period, was in their categorical timeframe, his insistence that 'the traditional working class' had been 'made' by 1914.

Researchers highlighted regional variations in working-class experience during the interwar years, particularly differences between the 'depressed areas' reliant on coal, steel, shipbuilding and textiles, such as South Wales, Lancashire, the North-East and Western Scotland, and the more prosperous Midlands and the South-East, where new industries such as car manufacture and electrical engineering expanded. Miriam Glucksmann's innovative integration of class and gender in her engrossing analysis of women factory workers in London can be contrasted with Griffiths's evocation of 'traditional proletarian' life, while Savage compared weak trade unionism in the boom town of Slough with Preston's well-rooted labour movement.[92] There is an extensive literature debating the impact of unemployment on living standards which also highlights the rarity of labour historians' engagement with the work of historical demographers, and case studies of localities which could be extended with profit.[93] The unemployed were not without sources of resistance, for example, in the form of the National Unemployed Workers' Movement. But it, too, displayed significant regional disparities in the distribution and activity of its membership.[94]

Cronin offered a longer chronology than Hobsbawm, in an often overlooked but as yet unsurpassed synthesis where two world wars and the interwar depression held significant impact. The years from 1945 to 1951 constituted a unique moment when working-class identity, heralded in 1926, homogenized and found corresponding, albeit temporary, political expression in the governments of Attlee, Morrison, Bevin and Bevan. Support for this trajectory comes from three directions. First, work. Revisionist arguments drew on research in a narrow range of industries before 1920. The conclusion that by 1950 new work regimes had emerged involving intensification of labour, fragmentation of skill and more bureaucratic managerialism is persuasive.[95] Second, Savage and Andrew Miles's fertile study of class formation demonstrated demographic consolidation by 1914 with firmer boundaries between the working and middle classes and declining internal differentiation within the working class, coupled with greater homogeneity in labour markets and urban spaces, by the inter-war years. Denying any monolithic social formation, these writers insisted on 'the unprecedented social and political presence' of the working class in British society in the first three decades of the twentieth century and pertinently counselled against projecting contemporary scepticism regarding the salience of class on to the historical record. Finally, the detailed analysis of class and class relations provided by McKibbin, hardly an ideological ally of Cronin or Hobsbawm, depicted a 'profoundly work-centred' male working-class culture, adduced evidence of 'intense class consciousness' during the interwar years, and documented 'an obvious lurch to the left in working-class opinion' during the Second World War.[96]

Yet just as sociologists began discovering this recently forged 'traditional working class' in the 1950s,[97] its homogeneity and political loyalties were seen to unravel. Again Hobsbawm stimulated controversy. Influenced by the events of the 1970s, he suggested that labour's 'forward march' had halted by the early 1950s as the 'common style of proletarian life' became fractured by changes in the composition of the working class, resultant decline in Labour's vote and resort to sectional militancy.[98] This provocative and influential essay was open to criticism for its assumptions of unilinear advance until the 1940s and after that increasing social fragmentation and industrial and political retreat, neglect of countervailing episodes of solidarity and exaggeration of the unarguable links between social structure and class politics; he has acknowledged some of these points. If Hobsbawm was prescient in his attention to the shifting character of working-class structure and culture, it is arguably overly deterministic and short-term for an exponent of the *longue durée* to explain the prolonged crisis that afflicted the British labour movement after 1979 primarily by reference to the postwar decades.[99]

With the exception of Cronin, whose *Labour in British Society* constituted a sophisticated engagement with Hobsbawm's prognoses, labour historians have neglected postwar working-class culture. Recent forays have been superficial: for example, Lawrence Black's survey of political culture after 1950 argued that leftwing activists' hostility to aspects of affluence rendered them remote from the electorate. It largely ignored trade unions – the instruments whereby activists secured the fruits of affluence for their members – and concentration on left organizations failed to explore wider class culture. Fielding's more sustained effort to relate Labour's policies in the 1960s to social change merits similar judgement.[100]

If labour historians' concern to explore the culture and consciousness of labour was the initial dynamo in the revival of social history, expansion and diffusion of the latter into specialisms and sub-fields created consequences unforeseen by the SSLH's founders. Far from attaining the *desideratum* of an integrated 'history of society', social history developed a specialized and often apolitical life of its own, sometimes absorbing the energies of former labour historians and students who might have undertaken research into labour, and increasingly rejecting the validity of class as a central, organizing concept.

The picture remains uneven. Synergy between labour historians and social historians of medicine has expanded our knowledge of the neglected topic of occupational health.[101] Recent research in the social and cultural history of identities continues to tell us something of 'the working-class situation', if only tangentially. Matt Houlbrook's mapping of *Queer London*, for example, was as sensitive to class as to the other social attributes of his protagonists and innovatively inserted queer identity into notions of working-class masculinity.[102] Frank Mort's analysis of striptease in the capital contains intriguing but undeveloped accounts of the employment regimes under which the artistes laboured.[103] Broader interpretations of national identity situated class divisions alongside other sources of social differentiation. Sonya Rose's ambitious deconstruction of the myths of national unity during the Second World War explored cultural tensions around class, gender and ethnicity which contested any uniform notion of British citizenship. However, the labour movement and industrial conflict – highly relevant to considerations of equality of sacrifice and class antagonism – were decentred in an account which failed to transcend existing literature on these matters.[104]

The growing gap between the divergent trajectories followed by labour history and social history in Britain can be demonstrated by surveying the recent contents of the two British journals dedicated to social history. *Social History* was established in 1976 with an editorial team not unsympathetic to labour history – its founding statement acknowledged the contribution to the field of 'masterpieces' by Hobsbawm and Thompson. But its animators were concerned to develop theoretically informed analyses of social processes. Labour history featured regularly in its pages during the following decades. However, only 5 articles out of the 149 published between 1999 and 2008 fit within a broad definition of twentieth-century British working-class history.[105] Perusal of *Cultural and Social History*, launched by the Social History Society in 2004, reveals a similar situation: only 3 articles out of 95 published to date meet this criterion.[106]

Looking back, looking forward

This survey is far from comprehensive; yet the writing reviewed in it testifies to a prodigious output and expanding horizons since 1960. The general judgement of one leading historian is convincing:

> The contribution of labour history to the broadening of historical enquiry is easy to underestimate [...] no labouring population anywhere in the world has been so intensively studied as that of Britain [...] While traditional labour history has excavated to quite unprecedented depths the personnel and character of labour organizations and trade unions, there has also been an impressive range of case studies of particular groups, industries and localities.[107]

Absences remain. For example, it is doubtful if Asa Briggs's reference in 1960 to the need for research on the impact of capitalist organization on workers has been adequately redeemed by rigorous, extensive studies of employers and management. The ambition of labour historians to integrate political and trade union history with the social history of the working class has been fulfilled in only limited fashion. Nonetheless, in the years after 1960 the new labour history tilled uncultivated areas using new methods. Change may be gauged by comparing, say, the histories of Labour written by Bassett and Lyman in the 1950s with the analytical work of Savage on Labour in the localities written in the 1980s and 1990s and, further, Howell's cultural history of MacDonald's party composed in the new century. A similar sense of development may be gained by reading Garside's history of the Durham miners – itself an advance on Robin Page Arnot's earlier work in terms of its more analytical and contextualized approach to institutional and political issues – with Beynon and Austrin's political and social history published in the 1990s. Most obvious was the trend to social history, vestigial in 1960. In testimony to never ending changes in historiography, that too has now abated and throughout the last five decades a wide range of organizational and political histories of labour have continued to be published.

Talk of a paradigm shift is somewhat stultified by awareness that, from the 1960s to the 1980s, while change was real, diversity endured, albeit diversity linked and leavened by the limited sense of community and shared ethos that the ascendancy of the SSLH imparted to those working in the field. Historians of different historiographical and political denominations congregated and contended in the catholic fora of the Society. There was never anything like adherence to one gospel and, since the 1980s, organizational flaking has gone hand-in-hand with a greater degree of differentiation, sometimes insulation, between distinctive historiographical trends. The fragmentation of labour history has reflected political changes and their impact on the academy. In an age where the labour movement in Britain has been decisively debilitated, some practitioners actively disdain the designation 'labour historian' as outmoded. In the early twenty-first century, labour history in Britain is a tenuous and divided field. In theory it is united by a focus on labour. In practice many define themselves and their histories in terms of party, movement, class, culture or specific academic sub-specialisms.[108]

From the 1990s there was concern that labour history in Britain was in crisis: 'institutionally based, Eurocentric, prioritizing the experience of male workers, theoretically naïve and verging on and sometimes collapsing into antiquarianism'.[109] Such indictments contained a significant element of truth. But labour history was far from the only historical field where empiricism or antiquarianism was present; institutional histories are not necessarily inferior to social or cultural histories. Studies of local labour movements demonstrated the possibility of transcending narrow approaches to produce social histories of politics and trade unionism which fulfilled, however imperfectly, the integrative aspirations of some of the SSLH's founders. Many focused on occupational communities, permitting wide-ranging analyses in which waged labour was merely one component and gender and ethnicity were not neglected.[110]

The popularity of the history of women, and to a lesser degree gender history and 'race' and ethnic history, has expanded and enriched the history of labour and the working class, although the best work has excavated nineteenth-century Britain.[111] The continued salience of class has been demonstrated and re-demonstrated. Recent research rejects the essentialist currents swirling around histories of male patriarchy or white racism evident in cruder versions of women's and black history and employs more sophisticated frameworks. Selina Todd's pioneering study of young women workers examines her subjects in the contexts of employment, the family economy, leisure and the labour movement; she explicitly rejected the 'multiplicity of competing social identities' approach in favour of 'a sensitive reappraisal of gender and generational relations within the class structure'.[112] While ethnicity has not been ignored in twentieth-century labour historiography, relations between white workers and ethnic minorities in Britain are often portrayed as inherently conflictual. Laura Tabili's more nuanced analysis 'situates Black colonized workers inside rather than outside British class formation'.[113]

Such work affirms the continuing relevance of the agendas of the new labour history, sympathetically and suitably revised and updated. A variety of prescriptions for future development, including greater attention to language, institutions, gender and household, ethnicity, consumption, the law, and local, comparative and transnational studies, can all be sensibly endorsed, provided a dash of restraint and realism is added to some of the rhetoric.[114] Transnational history has remained a neglected area, although we should not overlook Hobsbawm's multi-volume 'history of the world', analyzing economic, social and political developments since 1789 which culminated in 1994 with the acclaimed *Age of Extremes*.[115] We should remember, however, that without rigorous method and the distillation and deployment of intensive and extensive original research, transnational histories can collapse into mechanical juxtaposition of sometimes flawed secondary accounts and facile conclusions. On the home front, the history of trade unionism, once prominent, is relatively unfashionable and perhaps in consequence social histories of organized labour constitute a deficit. Labour biography continues to flourish as a sub-genre, though even the best examples retain a traditional 'life and times' approach. Collective biography and prosopography offers one route to bridge the duality of structure and agency and to explore the micro-impact of macro-level social processes.[116]

If a major achievement of British labour historiography has been to reconstruct 'total histories' of labouring communities, treatment of the urban working class in the twentieth century remains restricted. John Belchem has provided us with an accomplished, integrated history of the Liverpool Irish. Glasgow and its hinterland is well-trodden territory, at least until the 1930s; Birmingham, Manchester and Leeds and a host of smaller towns demand further exploration.[117] Such studies would enable syntheses and comparisons: English and Welsh historiography would be enriched by multi-dimensional texts such as William Knox's *Industrial Nation*. That volume's terminus in the 1990s suggests, too, the need for labour history to encompass class relations under Thatcherism. The Freedom of Information Act has undermined the slow-moving wall of the 'thirty-year rule'. In the twenty-fifth anniversary of the 1985 miners' defeat, the time is ripe for fully historicized accounts of the retreats, accommodations and resistances of the neoliberal years.

Debates on the future of labour historiography have had at their core contested relationships between structure and agency, the social and the political, the dialectic between diversity and unity, class, gender and ethnicity, connections between the national and the global, and issues about the meaning and direction of history and the role the working class has played in it. While teleological and essentialist tendencies have been present, they have increasingly been discarded, while 'forward march' narratives of proletarian progress have been probed and re-specified. Yet a mistaken, pervasive, usually unreferenced, straw man continues to be deployed to suggest that labour historians remain handicapped by commitment to labour and hamstrung by assumptions about a 'unitary' working class and the direct translation of attitudes from class position to politics.

The reality is that most labour historians are as ready as their colleagues to detect and control Whig approaches, liberal or Marxist. Most remain as dedicated as their counterparts in other branches of history to the comprehension and embodiment in their work of complexity, contradiction and contingency. Most are committed to eschewing crude versions of determinism and critically addressing linkages, however complicated, changing, bi-directional, perhaps in the end unresolvable, between the economic, social and political spheres.[118] For one revisionist current almost completely absent from research on *twentieth-century* British labour, influential only on style and scepticism, has been 'the linguistic turn'. Both old 'new' labour historians and recent revisionists, despite their ideological, interpretive and methodological differences, share a realist epistemology. The spirit that animated the creation of the SSLH in 1960 helped turn attention to new subjects and new approaches. Historians will continue to innovate and contribute valuable work if they continue to explore and integrate the sometimes elusive mediations between workers, economy and society which lie, and will continue to lie, at the heart of the history of labour.

Notes

1 John Saville, 'Labour Movement Historiography', *Universities and Left Review* (*ULR*), 3 (1958), 73–77.

2 Hobsbawm reflected that to write about events post-1917 risked denunciation by the CP 'as a political heretic': Eric Hobsbawm, *Interesting Times: A Twentieth-Century Life* (London: Allen Lane, 2002), p. 291.

3 John McIlroy, 'The Society for the Study of Labour History, 1956–1985: Its Origins and Heyday', *Making History: Organizations of Labour Historians in Britain since 1960, Labour History Review* (*LHR*) Fiftieth Anniversary Supplement, April 2010, 17-110.

4 Eric Hobsbawm, 'Commitment and Working Class History', *ULR*, 6 (1959), 71–72; Saville, 'Labour Movement', 73–74.

5 Asa Briggs, 'Open Questions of Labour History', *Bulletin of the Society for the Study of Labour History* (*BSSLH*), 1 (Autumn 1960), 2–3.

6 E.J. Hobsbawm, *Labouring Men: Studies in the History of Labour* (London: Weidenfeld and Nicolson, 1964), p. vii; E.P. Thompson, *The Making of the*

English Working Class (London: Gollancz, 1963).

7 McIlroy, 'Society', 20-21, 34-40.

8 Lack of space precludes attention to the cooperative movement, but see particularly Peter Gurney, *Co-operative Culture and the Politics of Consumption in England, 1870–1930* (Manchester: Manchester University Press, 1996); and for a survey of the literature, see Chris Wrigley, 'The Co-operative Movement', in *Mitteilungsblatt des Instituts für soziale Bewegungungen*, 27 (2002), 103–116.

9 Eric Hobsbawm, 'Trade Union Historiography', *BSSLH*, 8 (1964), 31–36. Robin Page Arnot, *The Miners: Years of Struggle* (London: Allen and Unwin, 1955). As Hobsbawm noted, there were improvements after 1945; see, for example, James B. Jefferys, *The Story of the Engineers, 1800–1945* (London: Lawrence and Wishart, 1945) and J.E. Williams, *The Derbyshire Miners: A Study in Industrial and Social History* (London: Allen and Unwin, 1962).

10 H.A. Turner, *Trade Union Growth, Structure and Policy: A Comparative Study of the Cotton Unions* (London: Allen and Unwin, 1962).

11 Richard Hyman, *The Workers' Union* (Oxford: Clarendon Press, 1971).

12 For example, John Lovell, *Stevedores and Dockers: A Study of Trade Unionism in the Port of London, 1870–1914* (London: Macmillan, 1969); Eric Taplin, *The Dockers' Union: A Study of the National Union of Dock Labourers, 1889–1922* (Leicester: Leicester University Press, 1986); John Lloyd, *Light and Liberty: The History of the EETPU* (London: Weidenfeld and Nicolson, 1990).

13 Ken Coates and Tony Topham, *The History of the Transport and General Workers' Union, vol. 1: The Making of the Transport and General Workers' Union* (Oxford: Basil Blackwell, 1991). No further volumes have been published.

14 *Forged in Fire: The History of the Fire Brigades Union*, ed. by Victor Bailey (London: Lawrence and Wishart, 1992).

15 W.R. Garside, *The Durham Miners, 1919–1960* (London: Allen and Unwin, 1971); Hywel Francis and David Smith, *The Fed: A History of the South Wales Miners' Federation in the Twentieth Century* (London: Lawrence and Wishart, 1980); Huw Beynon and Terry Austrin, *Masters and Servants: Class and Patronage in the Making of a Labour Organization: The Durham Miners and the English Political Tradition* (London: Rivers Oram Press, 1994).

16 Henry Pelling, *A History of British Trade Unionism* (London: Macmillan, 1963); Hugh A. Clegg, Alan Fox and A.F. Thompson, *A History of British Trade Unions since 1889, vol. 1: 1889–1910* (Oxford: Clarendon Press, 1964). The second and third volumes, by Clegg alone, appeared in 1985 and 1994; Hobsbawm, 'Historiography', p. 31; E.J. Hobsbawm, 'Trade Union History', *Economic History Review*, n.s., (*EcHR*), 20 (1967), 358–64 (p. 359).

17 G.D.H. Cole, *A Short History of the British Working-Class Movement, 1789–1947* (1st pub. 1948; London: Allen and Unwin, 1960); Kenneth D. Brown, *The English Labour Movement, 1700–1951* (Dublin: Gill and Macmillan, 1982); James Hinton, *Labour and Socialism: A History of the British Labour Movement, 1867–1974* (Brighton: Wheatsheaf, 1983).

18 Sheila Rowbotham, *Hidden from History: 300 Years of Women's Oppression and the Fight Against It* (London: Pluto Press, 1973); Sheila Lewenhak,

Women and Trade Unions: An Outline History of Women in the British Trade Union Movement (London: Benn, 1977); Jill Liddington and Jill Norris, *One Hand Tied Behind Us: The Rise of the Women's Suffrage Movement* (London: Virago, 1978); Sarah Boston, *Women Workers and the Trade Union Movement* (London: Davies-Poynter, 1980).

19 Branko Pribicevic, *The Shop Stewards' Movement and Workers' Control, 1910–1922* (Oxford: Blackwell, 1959); James Hinton, *The First Shop Stewards' Movement* (London: Allen and Unwin, 1973).

20 John McIlroy, 'Memory, Commemoration and History – 1926 in 2006', *Historical Studies in Industrial Relations* (*HSIR*), 21 (2006), 65–108; John McIlroy, Alan Campbell, Quentin Outram and Keith Laybourn, 'The General Strike and Mining Lockout of 1926: A Select Bibliography', ibid., 183–206; *The 1926 Mining Lockout and Industrial Politics: The Struggle for Dignity*, ed. by John McIlroy, Alan Campbell and Keith Gildart (1st pub. 2004; Cardiff: University of Wales Press, 2009).

21 Richard Croucher, *Engineers at War, 1939–1945* (London: Merlin Press, 1982); see also James Hinton, *Shop-Floor Citizens: Engineering Democracy in 1940s Britain* (Aldershot: Edward Elgar, 1994); Justin Davis Smith, *The Attlee and Churchill Administrations and Industrial Unrest, 1945–55* (London: Pinter, 1990).

22 K.G.J.C. Knowles, *Strikes: A Study in Industrial Conflict, with Special Reference to British Experience between 1911 and 1947* (Oxford: Basil Blackwell, 1952); J.W. Durcan, W.E.J. McCarthy and G.P. Redman, *Strikes in Post-War Britain: A Study of Stoppages of Work due to Industrial Disputes, 1946–73* (London: Allen and Unwin, 1983); James Cronin, *Industrial Conflict in Modern Britain* (London: Croom Helm, 1979), p. 9.

23 Roy Church and Quentin Outram, *Strikes and Solidarity: Coalfield Conflict in Britain, 1889–1966* (Cambridge: Cambridge University Press, 1998).

24 Ben C. Roberts, *The Trades Union Congress, 1868–1921* (London: Allen and Unwin, 1958); John Lovell and B.C. Roberts, *A Short History of the TUC* (London: Macmillan, 1968); Ross M. Martin, *TUC: The Growth of a Pressure Group, 1968–1978* (Oxford: Clarendon Press, 1980); Robert Taylor, *The TUC: From the General Strike to New Unionism* (Basingstoke: Palgrave, 2000); Alan Clinton, *The Trade Union Rank and File: Trades Councils in Britain, 1900–1940* (Manchester: Manchester University Press, 1977).

25 Anthony Carew, *Labour Under the Marshall Plan: The Politics of Productivity and the Marketing of Management Science* (Manchester: Manchester University Press, 1987); Peter Weiler, *British Labour and the Cold War* (Stanford: Stanford University Press, 1988); Denis McShane, *International Labour and the Origins of the Cold War* (Oxford: Clarendon Press, 1992).

26 Asa Briggs, 'Trade Union History and Labour History', *Business History*, 8 (1966), 39–47 (p. 40); e.g. *Employers and Labour in the English Textile Industries, 1850*–1939, ed. by J.A. Jowett and Arthur McIvor (London: Routledge, 1988).

27 *A History of British Industrial Relations, 1875–1914*, ed. by C.J. Wrigley (Brighton: Harvester, 1982); the second and third volumes, published in 1986 and 1996, covered 1914–39 and 1939–79 respectively.

28 Richard Price, *Labour in British Society* (London: Croom Helm, 1986).

29 *The Power to Manage? Employers and Industrial Relations in Comparative Historical Perspective*, ed. by Steven Tolliday and Jonathan Zeitlin (London: Routledge, 1991); Howard Gospel, *Markets, Firms and the Management of Labour in Modern Britain* (Cambridge: Cambridge University Press, 1991); Joseph Melling, 'Scottish Industrialists and the Changing Character of Class Relations in the Clyde Region, c.1880–1918', in *Capital and Class in Scotland*, ed. by Tony Dickson (Edinburgh: John Donald, 1982), pp. 61–142; Ronald Johnston, *Clydeside Capital: A Social History of Employers, 1870–1920* (East Linton: Tuckwell Press, 2000); see also Quentin Outram, 'Class Warriors: The Coalowners', in McIlroy, Campbell and Gildart, *Industrial Politics and the 1926 Mining Lockout*, pp. 107–36.

30 Keith Middlemas, *Politics in Industrial Society: The Experience of the British System since 1911* (London: Deutsch, 1979).

31 Roger Geary, *Policing Industrial Disputes, 1893–1985* (London: Methuen, 1986); Jane Morgan, *Conflict and Order: The Police and Labour Disputes in England and Wales, 1900–1939* (Oxford: Clarendon Press, 1987); Barbara Weinberger, *Policing Strikes in Britain, 1906–1926* (Oxford: Berg, 1991).

32 For this literature, see Terry Brotherstone, 'Does Red Clydeside Really Matter Any More?' in *Militant Workers: Labour and Class Conflict on the Clyde*, ed. by Robert Duncan and Arthur McIvor (Edinburgh: John Donald, 1992), pp. 52–80.

33 *Shop-Floor Bargaining and the State: Historical and Comparative Perspectives*, ed. by Steven Tolliday and Jonathan Zeitlin (Cambridge: Cambridge University Press, 1985). For a more prosaic, pluralist account, see Rodney Lowe, *Adjusting to Democracy: The Role of the Ministry of Labour in British Politics, 1916–1939* (Oxford: Clarendon Press, 1986).

34 Jonathan Zeitlin, 'From Labour History to the History of Industrial Relations', *EcHR*, 40 (1987), 159–84; idem, '"Rank and Fileism" in British Labour History: A Critique', *International Review of Social History* (*IRSH*), 34 (1989), 42–61, and the responses in that issue by Price and Cronin.

35 *British Trade Unions and Industrial Politics: The Post-War Compromise*, 1945–1964, ed. by Alan Campbell, Nina Fishman and John McIlroy (Aldershot: Ashgate, 1999); *British Trade Unions and Industrial Politics: The High Tide of Trade Unionism, 1964–1979*, ed. by John McIlroy, Nina Fishman and Alan Campbell (Aldershot: Ashgate, 1999); John McIlroy, 'Reflections on British Trade Unions and Industrial Politics', in *The High Tide of British Trade Unionism: Trade Unions and Industrial Politics, 1964–79*, ed. by John McIlroy, Nina Fishman and Alan Campbell (Monmouth: Merlin Press, 2007), pp. xv–xlii (pp. xxvi–xxx) .

36 Alan Bullock, *The Life and Times of Ernest Bevin, vol. 1: Trade Union Leader, 1881–1940* (London: Heinemann, 1960); V.L. Allen, *Trade Union Leadership: Based on a Study of Arthur Deakin* (London: Longmans Green, 1957); Geoffrey Goodman, *The Awkward Warrior: Frank Cousins: His Life and Times* (London: Davis Poynter, 1979).

37 Paul Davies, *A.J. Cook* (Manchester: Manchester University Press, 1987). There

are hostile, impressionistic biographies of Scargill contributed by engaged journalists.

38 Alastair J. Reid, *United We Stand: A History of Britain's Trade Unions* (London: Allen Lane, 2004). See also Keith Laybourn, *A History of British Trade Unionism, c.1770–1990* (Stroud: Sutton, 1992); W. Hamish Fraser, *A History of British Trade Unionism, 1770–1998* (Basingstoke: Macmillan, 1998).

39 Chris Howell, *Trade Unions and the State: The Construction of Industrial Relations Institutions in Great Britain, 1890–2000* (Princeton: Princeton University Press, 2005). See also Simon Deakin and Frank Williamson, *The Law of the Labour Market: Industrialization, Employment and Legal Evolution* (Oxford: Oxford University Press, 2005).

40 John Saville, 'Trade Unions and Free Labour: The Background to the Taff Vale Decision', in *Essays in Labour History: In Honour of G.D.H. Cole*, ed. by Asa Briggs and John Saville (London: Macmillan, 1960), pp. 317–50; idem, 'The Trades Disputes Act of 1906', *HSIR*, 1 (1996), 11–45. See, for example, Henry Pelling, 'The Politics of the Osborne Judgement', *Historical Journal*, 25 (September 1982), 889–909; Michael J. Klarman, 'Osborne: A Judgement Gone Too Far?', *English Historical Review*, 103 (1988), 21–39.

41 See, for example, John McIlroy and Alan Campbell, 'Beyond Betteshanger: Order 1305 in the Scottish Coalfields during the Second World War', parts 1 and 2, *HSIR*, 15 (2003), 27–72, and *HSIR*, 16 (2003), 39–80; the essays collected in *The Right to Strike: From the Trade Disputes Act 1906 to a Trade Union Freedom Bill 2006*, ed. by K.D. Ewing (Liverpool: Institute of Employment Rights, 2006); Sheila Blackburn, *A Fair Day's Wage for a Fair Day's Work? Sweated Labour and the Origins of Minimum Wage Legislation in Britain* (Aldershot: Ashgate, 2007).

42 Hobsbawm, 'Trade Union Historiography', pp. 33–34.

43 G.D.H. Cole, *A History of the Labour Party from 1914* (London: Routledge and Kegan Paul [RKP], 1948), pp. 257–8. Historians have only recently attempted to re-survey the party during this period; see Matthew Worley, *Labour Inside the Gate: A History of the British Labour Party between the Wars* (London: I.B. Tauris, 2005), largely a work of secondary synthesis.

44 Henry Pelling, *A Short History of the Labour Party* (1st pub. 1961; London: Macmillan, 2005). For a more detailed account, see Andrew Thorpe, *A History of the British Labour Party* (1st pub. 1997; Basingstoke: Palgrave, 2008).

45 Ralph Miliband, *Parliamentary Socialism: A Study in the Politics of Labour* (London: Allen and Unwin, 1961). Miliband's approach was adopted by others, for example, David Coates, *The Labour Party and the Struggle for Socialism* (Cambridge: Cambridge University Press, 1975).

46 Henry Pelling, *The Origins of the Labour Party, 1880–1900* (London: Macmillan, 1954); Frank Bealey and Henry Pelling, *Labour and Politics, 1900–1906: A History of the Labour Representation Committee* (London: Macmillan, 1958); Roy Gregory, *The Miners and British Politics, 1906–1914* (Oxford: Clarendon Press, 1968).

47 David Howell, *British Workers and the Independent Labour Party, 1888–1906* (Manchester: Manchester University Press, 1983), p. 389.

48 Ross McKibbin, *The Evolution of the Labour Party, 1910–1924* (Oxford: Oxford University Press, 1974); Keith Laybourn and Jack Reynolds, *Liberalism and the Rise of Labour, 1890–1914* (London: Croom Helm, 1984); Royden Harrison, 'The War Emergency National Workers' Committee, 1914–1920', in *Essays in Labour History, 1886–1923*, ed. by Asa Briggs and John Saville (London: Macmillan, 1971), pp. 211–59.

49 Peter F. Clarke, *Lancashire and the New Liberalism* (Cambridge: Cambridge University Press, 1971); Duncan Tanner, *Political Change and the Labour Party, 1900–1918* (Cambridge: Cambridge University Press, 1990); Keith Laybourn, 'The Rise of Labour and the Decline of Liberalism: The State of the Debate', *History*, 80, 289 (1995), 207–26.

50 Jay M. Winter, *Socialism and the Challenge of War: Ideas and Politics in Britain, 1912–1918* (London: RKP, 1974); McKibbin, *Evolution*, p. 97; Harrison, 'The War Emergency National Workers' Committee, 1914–1920', p. 259.

51 R. W. Lyman, *The First Labour Government* (London: Chapman and Hall, 1957); see now John Shepherd and Keith Laybourn, *Britain's First Labour Government* (Basingstoke: Palgrave, 2006).

52 Reginald Bassett, *Nineteen Thirty-One: Political Crisis* (London: Macmillan, 1958); Robert Skidelsky, *Politicians and the Slump: The Labour Government of 1929–1931* (London: Macmillan, 1967); see also Andrew Thorpe, *The British General Election of 1931* (Oxford: Clarendon Press, 1991).

53 Ross McKibbin, 'The Economic Policy of the Second Labour Government, 1929–1931', *Past and Present* (*P&P*), 65 (1975), 95–123.

54 Neil Riddell, *Labour in Crisis: The Second Labour Government, 1929–1931* (Manchester: Manchester University Press, 1999). David Marquand, *Ramsay MacDonald* (London: Cape, 1977).

55 David Howell, *MacDonald's Party: Labour Identities and Crisis, 1922–31* (Oxford: Oxford University Press, 2002), p. 415.

56 Stephen Brooke, *Labour's War: The Labour Party during the Second World War* (Oxford: Clarendon Press, 1992); Richard Sibley, 'The Swing to Labour during the Second World War: When and Why?', *LHR*, 55, 1 (1990), 23–34.

57 Steven Fielding, Peter Thompson and Nick Tiratsoo, *'England Arise!' The Labour Party and Popular Politics in 1940s Britain* (Manchester: Manchester University Press, 1995); James Hinton, '1945 and the Apathy School', *History Workshop Journal*, 43 (1997), 266–73.

58 Kenneth O. Morgan, *Labour in Power, 1945–51* (Oxford: Clarendon Press, 1984); David Howell, *British Social Democracy: A Study in Development and Decay* (London: Croom Helm, 1976); David Rubinstein, 'Socialism and the Labour Party: the Labour Left and Domestic Policy, 1945–50', in *Ideology and the Labour Movement*, ed. by David E. Martin and David Rubinstein (London: Croom Helm, 1979); *The Attlee Years*, ed. by Nick Tiratsoo (London: Pinter, 1991).

59 Steven Fielding, *The Labour Governments, 1964–70, vol. 1: Labour and Cultural Change* (Manchester: Manchester University Press, 2003); Jim Tomlinson, *The Labour Governments, 1964–70, vol. 2: Economic Policy* (Manchester: Manchester University Press, 2003); cf. Leo Panitch, *Social Democracy*

and Industrial Militancy: The Labour Party and Incomes Policy, 1945–1974 (Cambridge: Cambridge University Press, 1976).

60 Steven Fielding, *The Labour Party: Continuity and Change in the Making of New Labour* (Basingstoke: Palgrave Macmillan, 2003); Richard Toye, '"The Smallest Party in History"? New Labour in Historical Perspective', *LHR*, 69 (2004), 83–103; McIlroy, 'Reflections', p. xxix; James E. Cronin, *New Labour's Pasts: The Labour Party and its Discontents* (Harlow: Pearson Longman, 2004). And see now *Trade Unions in a Neoliberal World: British Trade Unions Under New Labour*, ed. by Gary Daniels and John McIlroy (London: Routledge, 2009).

61 For example, Marquand, *MacDonald*; Kenneth O. Morgan, *Callaghan: A Life* (Oxford: Oxford University Press, 1997); John Shepherd, *George Lansbury: At The Heart of Old Labour* (Oxford: Oxford University Press, 2002). See also Michael Foot, *Aneurin Bevan: A Biography, vol. 1: 1897–1945* (London: MacGibbon and Kee, 1962); idem, *Aneurin Bevan: A Biography, vol. 2: 1945–1960* (London: Davis-Poynter, 1973); John Campbell, *Nye Bevan and the Mirage of British Socialism* (London: Weidenfeld and Nicolson, 1987). For an exemplary biography of a leading woman, see Patricia Hollis, *Jennie Lee: A Life* (Oxford: Oxford University Press, 1997).

62 Ben Pimlott, *Labour and the Left in the 1930s* (Cambridge: Cambridge University Press, 1977); Paul Corthorn, *In the Shadow of the Dictators: The British Left in the 1930s* (London: Tauris, 2006); Jonathan Schneer, *Labour's Conscience: The Labour Left, 1945–51* (London: Unwin Hyman, 1988); Mark Jenkins, *Bevanism: Labour's High Tide* (Nottingham: Spokesman, 1979); Eric Shaw, *Discipline and Discord in the Labour Party: The Politics of Managerial Control in the Labour Party, 1951–87* (Manchester: Manchester University Press, 1988).

63 Martin Harrison, *Trade Unions and the Labour Party since 1945* (London: Allen and Unwin, 1960); Hugh A. Clegg, *A History of British Trade Unions since 1889, Vol. 3: 1934–1951* (Oxford, Clarendon Press, 1994), pp. 293–409.

64 Panitch, *Social Democracy*.

65 Lewis Minkin, *The Contentious Alliance: Trade Unions and the Labour Party* (Edinburgh: Edinburgh University Press, 1991); see also idem, *The Labour Party Conference* (London: Allen and Unwin, 1978).

66 Christine Collette, *For Labour and for Women: The Women's Labour League, 1906–1918* (Manchester: Manchester University Press, 1989), p. 140; Pamela M. Graves, *Labour Women: Women in British Working-Class Politics, 1918–1939* (Cambridge: Cambridge University Press, 1994).

67 Michael Savage, *The Dynamics of Working-Class Politics: The Labour Movement in Preston, 1880–1940* (Cambridge: Cambridge University Press, 1987); idem, 'Urban Politics and the Rise of the Labour Party, 1918–39', in *State, Private Life and Political Choice*, ed. by Lynn Jamieson and Helen Corr (Basingstoke: Macmillan, 1990), pp. 204–23.

68 For example, Sam Davies, *Liverpool Labour: Social and Political Influences on the Development of the Labour Party in Liverpool, 1900–1939* (Keele: Keele University Press, 1996); Declan McHugh, *Labour in the City: The Development*

of the Labour Party in Manchester, 1918–1931 (Manchester: Manchester University Press, 2006); *Labour's Grass Roots: Essays on the Activities of Local Labour Parties and Members, 1918–45*, ed. by Matthew Worley (Aldershot: Ashgate, 2005).

69 Robert E. Dowse, *Left in the Centre: The Independent Labour Party, 1893–1940* (London: Longmans, 1966); *The Centennial History of the Independent Labour Party*, ed. by David James, Tony Jowett and Keith Laybourn (Halifax: Ryburn Press, 1992); *The ILP on Clydeside, 1893–1932: From Foundation to Disintegration*, ed. by Alan McKinlay and Robert J. Morris (Manchester: Manchester University Press, 1991); Gidon Cohen, *The Failure of a Dream: The Independent Labour Party from Disaffiliation to World War II* (London: Tauris, 2007).

70 See John McIlroy and Alan Campbell, 'Histories of the British Communist Party: A User's Guide', *LHR*, 68 (2003), 33–59.

71 Henry Pelling, *The British Communist Party: A Historical Profile* (London: Adam and Charles Black, 1958); Walter Kendall, *The Revolutionary Movement in Britain, 1900–1921: The Origins of British Communism* (London: Weidenfeld and Nicolson, 1969).

72 See McIlroy and Campbell, 'Histories'; Kevin Morgan, *Against Fascism and War: Ruptures and Continuities in British Communist Politics, 1935–1941* (Manchester: Manchester University Press); Nina Fishman, *The British Communist Party and the Trade Unions, 1933–1945* (Aldershot: Ashgate, 1995); Andrew Thorpe, *The British Communist Party and Moscow, 1920–1943* (Manchester: Manchester University Press, 2000); Matthew Worley, *Class Against Class: The Communist Party in Britain between the Wars* (London: Tauris, 2002).

73 For example, Reg Groves, *The Balham Group: How British Trotskyism Began* (London: Pluto Press, 1974); John Callaghan, *British Trotskyism* (Oxford: Basil Blackwell, 1984); Sam Bornstein and Al Richardson, *Against the Stream: A History of the Trotskyist Movement in Britain, 1924–38* (1st pub. 1986; Monmouth: Merlin Press, 2007); idem, *War and the International: A History of the Trotskyist Movement in Britain, 1937–1949* (1st pub. 1986; Monmouth: Merlin Press, 2007); Mark Shipway, *Anti-Parliamentary Communism: The Movement for Workers' Councils in Britain, 1917–45* (London: Macmillan, 1988); John McIlroy, '"Always Outnumbered, Always Outgunned": The Trotskyists and the Trade Unions', in McIlroy, Fishman and Campbell, *High Tide*, pp. 259–96. And see various issues of the journal *Revolutionary History*.

74 For example, the Labour History Group and its journal *Labour History*. See also Steven Fielding, 'British Communism: Interesting But Irrelevant?', *LHR*, 60, 2 (1995), 120–23.

75 Stefan Berger, *The British Labour Party and the German Social Democrats, 1900–1931* (Oxford: Clarendon Press, 1994); Walter Kendall, *The Labour Movement in Europe* (London: Allen Lane, 1975); *The Development of Trade Unionism in Great Britain and Germany, 1880–1914*, ed. by Wolfgang J. Mommsen and Hans-Gerhard Husung (London: Allen and Unwin, 1985); Roger Fagge, *Power, Culture and Conflict in the Coalfields: West Virginia and South Wales,*

1900–1922 (Manchester: Manchester University Press, 1996), p. 262.

76 Neville Kirk, *Labour and Society in Britain and the USA, vol. 1: Capitalism, Custom and Protest, 1750–1850; vol. 2: Challenge and Accommodation, 1850–1939* (Aldershot: Scolar Press, 1994).

77 Susan Pedersen, 'What is Political History Now?', in *What is History Now?*, ed. by David Cannadine (Basingstoke: Palgrave, 2002), pp. 38, 42; Tanner, *Political Change*, 11–12, 420, 441; *Labour's First Century*, ed. by Duncan Tanner, Pat Thane and Nick Tiratsoo (Cambridge: Cambridge University Press, 2000).

78 Ross McKibbin, 'Why Was There No Marxism in Britain', *English Historical Review*, 99 (1984), 297–331; idem, *Classes and Cultures: England, 1918–1951* (Oxford: Oxford University Press, 1998), pp. vi, 532; Steven Fielding, '"New Labour" and the "New" Labour History', *Mitteilungsblatt des Instituts für soziale Bewungungen*, 27 (2002), 35–50 (pp. 46–47).

79 Jay Winter, 'Introduction: Labour History and Labour Historians', in *The Working Class in Modern British History: Essays in Honour of Henry Pelling*, ed. by Jay Winter (Cambridge: Cambridge University Press, 1983), pp. vii–xii (p. viii).

80 *Village Life and Labour*, ed. by Raphael Samuel (London: RKP, 1975), p. xiii; *Miners, Quarrymen and Saltworkers*, ed. by Raphael Samuel (London: RKP, 1977); Alun Howkins, *Poor Labouring Men: Rural Radicalism in Norfolk, 1872–1923* (London: RKP, 1985); Paul Thompson with Tony Wailey and Trevor Lummis, *Living the Fishing* (London: RKP, 1983); Jerry White, *The Worst Street in North London: Campbell Bunk, Islington between the Wars* (London: RKP, 1986); Raphael Samuel, *East End Underworld: Chapters in the Life of Arthur Harding* (London: RKP, 1981).

81 See, for example, John Burnett, *Plenty and Want: A Social History of Diet in England from 1815 to the Present Day* (London: Nelson, 1966); idem, *A Social History of Housing, 1815–1970* (Newton Abbott: David and Charles, 1978); Frank McKenna, *The Railway Workers, 1840–1970* (London: Faber, 1980); Stephen Humphries, *Hooligans or Rebels: An Oral History of Working-Class Childhood and Youth, 1889–1939* (Oxford: Blackwell, 1981); *Leisure in Britain, 1780–1939*, ed. by John K. Walton and James Walvin (Manchester: Manchester University Press, 1983); Stephen G. Jones, *Workers at Play: A Social and Economic History of Leisure, 1918–1939* (London: RKP, 1986); *Sport and the Working Class in Modern Britain*, ed. by Richard Holt (Manchester: Manchester University Press, 1990); John K. Walton, *Fish and Chips and the British Working Class, 1870–1940* (Leicester: Leicester University Press, 1992).

82 Standish Meacham, *A Life Apart: The English Working Class, 1890–1914* (London: Thames and Hudson, 1977). Cf. Geoff Eley and Keith Nield, 'Why Does Social History Ignore Politics?', *Social History*, 5 (1980), 249–71.

83 Eric Hobsbawm, *Worlds of Labour: Further Studies in the History of Labour* (London: Weidenfeld and Nicolson, 1984), chs 10 and 11, originally written 1979 and 1981 (p. 191).

84 Ibid., p. 204.

85 McKibbin, 'Marxism'.

86 For an overview, see Arthur J. McIvor, *A History of Work in Britain, 1880–1950*

(Basingstoke: Palgrave, 2001).

87 Elizabeth Roberts, *A Woman's Place: An Oral History of Working-Class Women, 1890–1940* (Oxford: Blackwell, 1984); Carl Chinn, *They Worked All their Lives: Women of the Urban Poor in England, 1880–1939* (Manchester: Manchester University Press, 1988); Paul Johnston, *Saving and Spending: The Working-Class Economy in Britain, 1870–1939* (Oxford: Clarendon Press, 1985), pp. 9, 231, 232

88 Andrew Davies, *Leisure, Gender and Poverty: Working-Class Culture in Salford and Manchester, 1900–1939* (Buckingham: Open University Press, 1992); Steven Fielding, *Class and Ethnicity: Irish Catholics in England, 1880–1939* (Buckingham: Open University Press, 1993); Joanna Bourke, *Working-Class Cultures in Britain, 1890–1960* (London: Routledge, 1994), esp. ch. 5 (p. 169).

89 John Benson, *The Working Class in Britain, 1850–1939* (Harlow: Longman, 1989), p. 207.

90 Trevor Griffiths, *The Lancashire Working Classes, c.1880–1930* (Oxford: Clarendon Press, 2001), pp. 264, 327, 8, 321, 331.

91 Hobsbawm, *Worlds*, p. 207.

92 Miriam Glucksmann, *Women Assemble: Women Workers and the New Industries in Inter-War Britain* (London: Routledge, 1990); Savage, 'Urban Politics'.

93 For overviews of this debate, see Stephen Constantine, *Unemployment in Britain Between the Wars* (Harlow: Longmans, 1980); Charles Webster, 'Healthy or Hungry Thirties', *History Workshop Journal*, 13 (1982), 110–29; Bernard Harris, *The Origins of the British Welfare State: Social Welfare in England and Wales, 1800–1945* (Basingstoke: Palgrave, 2004), pp. 197–218; and see the comments in Jay Winter, 'Unemployment, Nutrition and Infant Mortality in Britain, 1920–1950', in Winter, *The Working Class in Modern British History*; Kate Nicholas, *The Social Effects of Unemployment on Teeside, 1919–39* (Manchester: Manchester University Press, 1986); Merseyside Socialist Research Group, *Genuinely Seeking Work: Mass Unemployment on Merseyside in the 1930s* (Liverpool: Liver Press, 1992).

94 Richard Croucher, *We Refuse to Starve in Silence: A History of the National Unemployed Workers' Movement, 1920–1946* (London: Lawrence and Wishart, 1987); see also the 'Special Issue on the History of Unemployed Movements', *LHR*, 73 (2008).

95 McIvor, *Work*; W.W. Knox, *Industrial Nation: Work, Culture and Society in Scotland, 1800–Present* (Edinburgh: Edinburgh University Press, 1999).

96 James Cronin, *Labour and Society in Britain, 1918–1979* (London: Batsford, 1984), esp. ch. 8; Mike Savage and Andrew Miles, *The Remaking of the British Working Class, 1840–1940* (London: Routledge, 1994), p. 90; McKibbin, *Classes*, pp. 161, 529, 531.

97 Norman Dennis, Fernando Henriques and Cliff Slaughter, *Coal is Our Life: An Analysis of a Yorkshire Mining Community* (London: Eyre and Spottiswoode, 1956); Michael Young and Peter Wilmott, *Family and Kinship in East London* (London: Routledge, 1957).

98 Eric Hobsbawm, 'The Forward March of Labour Halted?' (1st pub. 1978), reprinted in *The Forward March of Labour Halted?*, ed. by Martin Jacques and

Francis Mulhern (London: Verso, 1981), pp. 1–19.

99 Alan Campbell, Nina Fishman and John McIlroy, 'The Post-War Compromise: Mapping Industrial Politics, 1945–64', in Campbell, Fishman and McIlroy, *British Trade Unions*, pp. 88–101; Eric Hobsbawm, 'Afterword', in ibid., pp. 312–13; McIlroy, 'Reflections', pp. xxiii–xxvi.

100 Cronin, *Labour*, pp. 1–15; Lawrence Black, *The Political Culture of the Left in Affluent Britain, 1951–1964: Old Labour, New Britain* (Basingstoke: Palgrave, 2002); Fielding, *Labour Governments.*

101 For example, Arthur McIvor and Ronnie Johnston, *Miners' Lung: A History of Dust Disease in British Coal Mining* (Aldershot: Ashgate, 2007), which draws extensively on oral sources.

102 Matt Houlbrook, *Queer London: Perils and Pleasures in the Sexual Metropolis, 1918–1957* (Chicago: Chicago University Press, 2005).

103 Frank Mort, 'Striptease: The Erotic Female Body and Live Sexual Entertainment in Mid-Twentieth Century London', *Social History*, 32 (2007), 27–53 (pp. 47–48).

104 Sonya Rose, *Which People's War? National Identity and Citizenship in Wartime Britain, 1939–1945* (Oxford: Oxford University Press, 2003). Robert Mackay's *Half the Battle: Civilian Morale in Britain during the Second World War* (Manchester: Manchester University Press, 2002), argues for greater recognition of national unity but similarly says nothing new on the condition of labour in wartime.

105 Julie-Marie Strange, '"She Cried a Very Little": Death, Grief and Mourning in Working-Class Culture, c.1880–1914', *Social History*, 27 (2002), 143–61; Peter Ackers and Jonathan Payne, 'Before the Storm: The Experience of Nationalization and the Prospects for Industrial Relations Partnership in the British Coal Industry, 1947–1972: Rethinking the Militant Narrative', ibid., 184–209; Neville Kirk, 'The Conditions of Royal Rule: Australian and British Socialist and Labour Attitudes to the Monarchy, 1901–11', *Social History*, 30 (2005), 64–88; Peter Shapely, 'Tenants Arise! Consumerism, Tenants and the Challenge to Council Authority in Manchester, 1968–92', *Social History*, 31 (2006), 60–78; Pamela Dale, Janet Greenlees and Joseph Melling, 'The Kiss of Death or a Flight of Fancy? Workers' Health and the Campaign to Regulate Shuttle Kissing in the British Cotton Industry, c.1900–52', *Social History*, 32 (2007), 54–75.

106 Daniel Weinbren, 'Beneath the All-Seeing Eye: Fraternal Order and Friendly Societies' Banners in Nineteenth- and Twentieth-Century Britain', *Cultural and Social History*, 3 (2006), 167–91; Martin Johnes, 'Pigeon Racing and Working-Class Culture in Britain, c.1870–1950', *Cultural and Social History*, 4 (2007), 361–83; Andrew Davies, 'The Scottish Chicago? From "Hooligans" to "Gangsters" in Inter-War Glasgow', *Cultural and Social History*, 4 (2007), 511–27.

107 John Stevenson, 'Social History', in *Modern British History: A Guide to Study and Research*, ed. by L.J. Butler and Anthony Gorst (London: Tauris, 1997), p. 209.

108 For further discussion of some of these issues see McIlroy, 'The Society', 101-110.

109 D.H. [David Howell], 'Editorial', *LHR*, 60, 1 (1995), 2.

110 For example, Savage, *Preston*; Richard Whipp, *Patterns of Labour: Work and Social Change in the Pottery Industry* (London: Routledge, 1990); Chris Williams, *Democratic Rhondda: Politics and Society, 1885–1951* (Cardiff: University of Wales Press, 1996).

111 The literature on the twentieth century is still often locked in a women's history problematic, documenting women's work and struggles and experiences; see for example, Gail Braybon, *Women Workers and the First World War* (London: Barnes and Noble, 1981); Jane Lewis, *Women in England, 1870–1950* (Brighton: Wheatsheaf, 1984); *Unequal Opportunities: Women's Employment in England, 1800–1918*, ed. by Angela V. John (Oxford: Blackwell, 1986); Sandra Holton, *Feminism and Democracy: Women's Suffrage and Reform Politics in Britain, 1900–1918* (Cambridge: Cambridge University Press, 1986); *Women's History: Britain, 1850–1945*, ed. by June Purvis (London: UCL Press, 1995); Penny Summerfield, *Reconstructing Women's Wartime Lives: Discourse and Subjectivity in Oral Histories of the Second World* War (Manchester: Manchester University Press, 1998); *Women in Twentieth-Century Britain*, ed. by Ina Zweiniger-Bargielowska (Harlow: Longman, 2001); Gerry Holloway, *Women and Work in Britain since 1840* (London: Routledge, 2005); Jill Liddington, *Rebel Girls: Their Fight for the Vote* (London: Virago 2007). For an attempt at a more integrative approach, see Henry Srebrnik, 'Class, Ethnicity and Gender Interwined: Jewish Women and the East London Rent Strikes, 1935–40', *Women's History Review*, 4 (1995), 283–99.

112 Selina Todd, *Young Women, Work and the Family in England, 1918–1950* (Oxford; Oxford University Press, 2005), p. 226. For a critique of essentialist conceptions of patriarchy, see Sylvia Walby, *Patriarchy at Work: Patriarchal and Capitalist Relations in Employment* (London: Polity Press, 1986).

113 *Race and Labour in Twentieth-Century Britain*, ed. by Kenneth Lunn (London: Frank Cass, 1985); Laura Tabili, *'We Ask For British Justice': Workers and Racial Difference in Late Imperial Britain* (Ithaca: Cornell University Press, 1994), p. 14.

114 For example, Richard Price, 'The Future of British Labour History', *IRSH*, 34 (1991), 249–60; *Class and Other Identities: Gender, Religion and Ethnicity in the Writing of European Labour History*, ed. by Lex Heerma van Voss and Marcel van der Linden (New York and Oxford: Berghahn Books, 2002).

115 Eric Hobsbawm, *The Age of Revolution: Europe, 1789–1848* (London: Weidenfeld and Nicolson, 1962); idem, *The Age of Capital, 1848–1875* (London: Weidenfeld and Nicolson, 1975); idem, *The Age of Empire, 1875–1914* (London: Weidenfeld and Nicolson, 1987); idem, *The Age of Extremes: The Short Twentieth Century, 1914–1991* (London: Michael Joseph, 1994).

116 For example, Bill Williamson, *Class, Culture and Community: A Biographical Study of Social Change in Mining* (London: Routledge, 1982); John McIlroy, 'The Establishment of Intellectual Orthodoxy and the Stalinization of British Communism, 1928–1933', *P&P*, 192 (2006), 187–230.

117 John Belchem, *Irish, Catholic and Scouse: The History of the Liverpool Irish, 1800–1939* (Liverpool: Liverpool University Press, 2007). Coventry is atypically

well researched: *Life and Labour in a 20th Century City: The Experience of Coventry*, ed. by Bill Lancaster and Tony Mason (Coventry: Cryfield Press, 1986); Nick Tiratsoo, *Reconstruction, Affluence and Labour Politics: Coventry, 1945–60* (London: Routledge, 1990).

118 Price, 'Future', p. 255. Even Tanner allows that: 'Popular perceptions [...] were influenced by political factors *as well as* 'objective' social realities' [emphasis added]: Tanner, *Political Change*, p. 13.

4

Ireland

Emmet O'Connor and Conor McCabe

Ireland can be puzzling for labour historians. In *A Lost Left* published in 1985, David Howell remarked on the curiosity of having a mainline railway terminus in a 'Western European' capital named after a Marxist.[1] Had he been writing a few years later, he might have deleted 'Western'. Nor, since 1991, can there be many principal streets in European capitals with an imposing statue of a Communist chief. Yet Big Jim Larkin, once a candidate-member of the Executive Committee of the Communist International, delegate to the Moscow Soviet for the Moscow International Communist Tailoring Factory, battalion commander in the Red Army and leader of Irish Communism in the 1920s, stands proudly atop a plinth in O'Connell Street. Paul Mason's clarion call for a labour history organic to struggle, *Live Working or Die Fighting*, begins and ends with Larkin. 'Today', Mason enthuses, 'the arms of his statue spread out above the main thoroughfare of Dublin, its fingers forked like black lightning. His story is part of a national legend and needs no retelling.'[2] And this in a country where the Labour Party has averaged 11 per cent of the vote since 1922, and which did not produce a labour history society until 1973 or see a general history of labour penned by an Irish academic until 1977. Of course, Dublin's Connolly Station is a tribute to James Connolly's role in the Easter Rising, and Larkin is remembered as a trade unionist, his Communist connections largely forgotten.

The interaction of Labour and nationalism, the contrast between a vibrant trade unionism and a sinewy trade union memory as well as the weakness of other aspects of Labour culture are among the great enigmas of Irish labour history.[3] They have ensured that the historiography has reflected European trends in an uneven way. Trade unionists wove the first workers' portraits of Irish history – a common theme was the prosperity of Erin before her enforced union with Great Britain in 1800 – and they paraded them on their banners from the 1830s onwards.[4] The first wave of written labour history at the turn of the century found resonance in Ireland in a radical pamphleteering tradition. The outstanding example is Connolly's work, especially his still-studied *Labour in Irish History*.[5] It was a measure of the importance of Labour in the age of Connolly and Larkin that the period saw the publication of two contemporary histories, one on the 1913 lockout and the other on the Citizen Army, as well as the first attempt at a survey of Irish labour's past.[6]

The second wave of labour history, in which the subject acquired the institutional backing of trade unions or political parties, had a slight impact on a movement distanced from the continental European concern with the creation of research institutes, libraries, museums, and archives. Some false dawns during the great age of agitation initiated by Larkin in 1907 yielded to the *dorchadas*, the dark night of that catastrophic year of 1923, when the era of heroic struggle crashed into economic slump, and shattered in industrial defeat amid a welter of internecine rancour. The wounds festered until the 1950s and no one emerged from the fractiousness with any great credit. In these circumstances it suited union leaders to remember Larkin in 1913, and Connolly and 1916, and draw a veil over subsequent events. The field was not entirely fallow, indeed three sources produced a modest harvest.

First, there were trade union publications. The Irish Transport and General Workers' Union (ITGWU) was unique among unions in aspiring to embody and broadcast a view of Irish history, based on its identification with Connolly, its own role in the re-birth of the Irish Labour movement and the struggle for independence, and its self-designated destiny as the 'One Big Union'. Between 1948 and 1951 the ITGWU issued a trilogy of Connolly's writings under the titles, *Socialism and Nationalism*, *Labour and Easter Week*, and *The Workers' Republic*, a bold initiative in the intensely anti-communist climate of the time.[7] With a jealous regard for its heroic adolescence and its contemporary legitimacy, the ITGWU also burnished its guiding myths through defences of its confrontations with Larkin and other unions, and souvenirs of its early history. But even the mighty 'One Big Union' was timorous about the post-1923 period. Its long-time leader William O'Brien refused to take his memoirs beyond that year, although he did not retire as ITGWU general secretary until 1946.[8] All in all, the way trade unions managed their past had the effect of confirming a public perception that anything of labour's past worth remembrance began with Larkin and ended with Connolly. Certainly some workers were alive to their own union's history; but there was no agreed general narrative in the public sphere.

Secondly, there were political and semi-popular publications. Connolly's approach to history, with its emphasis on anti-imperialism rather than labour organization, informed a corpus of Marxist – mainly Communist – and left-republican histories, ranging from slim pamphlets to fuller treatments. Through the Connolly Association and the indefatigable Desmond Greaves, the current attracted contributions from British Marxists like Tommy Jackson and Peter Berresford Ellis. The most prolific of semi-popular authors was R.M. Fox, who produced a stream of work in the Connolly genre.[9] If some of these publications went beyond 1916, the accent on Connolly reinforced the myth of labour history culminating in the Easter Rising.

Finally, there were academic publications. But apart from a handful of articles and postgraduate dissertations, professional historians in Ireland showed a near absolute disinterest in the subject. Academic input was confined to intermittent studies from scholars based in Britain, the United States, Canada and Germany. These were distinguished by a concern simply to chart what they regarded as *terra incognita* and explore what they conceived as the defining conundrum of Irish Labour, its wilful embrace of a suffocating relationship with nationalism.[10] They possessed little popular impact. Before the 1970s, the third wave, the 'new labour history', based in many countries on the universities and associations of labour historians, and rooted in conceptions of social history and history from below that recovered the past not only of labour movements but of workers themselves, affected Ireland at first faintly and from afar. There remained vast blank spots on the canvas, especially in respect of events before 1890 and after 1923. And excepting the interminable national question, there was little debate on questions of the past of Irish labour.

The emergence of the new labour history

The radicalism of the late 1960s generated mounting curiosity about the absence of labour from Irish history, at least on the left. Initially, this found expression in renewed interest in Connolly, prompted by the fiftieth anniversary celebrations of the Easter Rising, and the centenary of Connolly's birth in 1968. Three selected editions of his writing and a major biography appeared between 1967 and 1973.[11] A countervailing influence was the new labour history in Britain. Its development accelerated after the creation of the British Society for the Study of Labour History in 1960, and it would prove to have the more formative impact on the future.[12] When the Irish Labour History Society (ILHS) was founded in 1973,[13] there existed two broad conceptions of the subject. The first, well-worn by the Connolly school, understood the working class as the vanguard of the still uncompleted national struggle against imperialism, and considered labour primarily in relation to that dynamic. The second believed that labour history should be about labour and nothing more. The ILHS gravitated towards the second conception. Radical history was felt to be endemically biased. Much of it indeed was poor in quality, and jaded in its endless re-working of the Connolly theme. As Ireland was becoming predominantly urban and industrial, popular historical interest was widening from issues of nation-building to questions of class formation and economic and social development. The great lacuna in the canon of the Connolly school was its neglect of labour organization – Connolly himself ended *Labour in Irish History* at the dawn of modern trade unionism – and organization was the central fascination of the new generation of researchers.

Moreover, with the rise of resurgent republicanism in Northern Ireland, Connolly's politics no longer enjoyed an unquestioned dominance on the left, and a number of those who formed the constituency of the ILHS were attracted to labour history as post-nationalist terrain. The English example was attractive, too, in developing a form of history that was scholarly and implicitly, rather than explicitly, *engagé*, and apparently successful in winning approval from both academics and activists. Thus, many felt that Irish labour history should be linked organically with the labour movement, but by means of scholarship rather than agitation. It would deal primarily with labour and satisfy the intellectual palate of an industrial, secular, and (in the eyes of some at least) post-national society. This approach was not to everyone's taste: in 1978 some Connollyites founded the Dublin History Workshop, as a forum dedicated to Irish language publication, focused on people's rather than labour history, and more politically committed.[14] The Workshop convened a few conferences and issued a short-lived journal *Irish History Workshop: Saotharlann Staire Éireann* before fading away in the early 1980s. Unlike the ILHS, it lacked the ballast of institutional support from trade unions.

The stimulus to the formation of the ILHS was not the development of the historiography but the preservation of trade union records. Over the Society's history, the four pillars of ILHS membership have been archivists and curators, union officials and other Labour apparatchiks, academics and students, and political sympathisers. The Society is unusual in being, overwhelmingly, a non-academic fraternity, with stronger links to the unions and the left – chiefly the Labour Party – than to the universities.

Arguably, this has been essential to its survival and broadened its public impact. It has also led the Society to devote its resources, increasingly, to the maintenance of archives rather than the promotion of scholarship. Nonetheless, the Society's annual journal, *Saothar* [*Labour*], which first appeared in 1975, together with its newsletters and occasional publications, have been extremely important in giving an identity to labour history and encouraging interest in it. There was no concern in the ILHS to produce an academic journal, but equally it was accepted – with surprisingly little contention – that *Saothar* needed to meet scholarly standards if the subject was to be taken seriously. The journal's stamina and quality have come as a pleasant surprise to the Society. By 2006, *Saothar* had run to thirty-one volumes, almost 4,000 pages, and two million words.

While the new labour historians are, for the most part, university graduates, there are very few full-time labour historians in Ireland. Academic neglect has been something of a hobby-horse in *Saothar* editorials. In defence of the academy, Joe Lee has pleaded that until the 1970s Irish universities were under-financed, and small history departments had little time for research or specialized teaching.[15] Since then faculties have expanded, new fields of enquiry have been established – including some in the labour-related areas of social and economic history, emigration studies, women's studies, and industrial relations. Yet there is still not a single person employed as a labour historian in any college or research centre in Ireland. It should be added that some academics have been supportive of the ILHS and helped out whenever called upon, while a number write on labour topics occasionally. Postgraduate dissertations on labour are no longer a rarity. Taught courses at undergraduate and postgraduate level have been introduced, at some point or other, in most universities. However, because of labour's limited inclusion in mainstream historiography, the public history of labour retains a fragmented quality, confined to a few outstanding personalities, or dramatic episodes like the 1913 lockout or Irish involvement in the Spanish Civil War.

Ideology and methodology in the new labour history

Labour historiography commonly evolves through four stages: identification, exploration, overview and inclusion. The new labour history began in the 1970s with two surveys which offered a point of departure: Arthur Mitchell's *Labour in Irish Politics, 1890–1930* and Charles McCarthy's *Trade Unions in Ireland, 1894–1960*.[16] Both of these texts were novel in that they provided scholarly accounts of the political and trade union leadership respectively. McCarthy's book is rich in its probing of mentalities; it is limited because it is written 'from above', Dublin-centred and narrow in its definition of labour. Digging deeper and wider, historians have become more conscious of workers as well as leaders, rural as well as urban workers, women as well as men, and the provinces as well as Dublin. Subsequent excavation of the past has sought to push the frontiers backwards and forwards from the Connolly-Larkin era.

Nonetheless, rigorous overviews remain underdeveloped. John Boyle's *The Irish Labor Movement in the Nineteenth Century* was a major contribution to exploration of key events and issues; but it was weaker as an overview. It was essentially a series of small monographs, while methodologically it was of the old school, and remained sternly fixed on labour organization.[17] Fergus D'Arcy and Ken Hannigan's *Workers in Union* was a series of documents, with commentaries, dating from 1199 to 1959. The one general new labour history published to date remains Emmet O'Connor's *A Labour History of Ireland, 1824–1960.* It has been supplemented by Fintan Lane and Donal Ó Drisceoil's *Politics and the Irish Working Class, 1830–1945*, the first collection of academic essays on labour history.[18] Writing labour history that is inclusive of general history has yet to be attempted.

Reflecting their provenance in Irish academe, most of our new labour historians have ignored the issue of ideology and pursued 'value-free' history. In practice, their thinking has been strongly shaped by liberal idealism and modernization theory. The influence of the former is evident in the importance some historians attached to superstructural factors – especially personalities and ideas like religion and nationalism – rather than material forces, in determining labour behaviour. Modernization theory understands the slow progress of Labour as a consequence of Ireland's late industrialization and the enduring power of those three villains of socialist demonology, the priest, the peasant and the patriot.

A related trait of early writing in the genre was Anglo-centrism. In the absence of an empirically grounded overview, authors made assumptions, *faute de mieux*, about the course of history which were derived from the British experience. They sought Irish equivalents of British Labour's mythical 'forward march', or invested analogous institutions, like the Irish Trades Union Congress (ITUC), with the degree of importance in Ireland which their namesakes possessed in Britain. In 1980, for example, no one thought it odd that the ILHS convened its biggest ever conference under the title 'The Making of the Irish Working Class', though, in contrast to Britain, nineteenth-century capitalism led to de-industrialization and the 'unmaking' of the working class.[19] The explanatory value of liberal idealism and modernization theory has been challenged in O'Connor's neo-Connollyite *A Labour History of Ireland* but both are ubiquitous in the fourteen essays in Lane and Ó'Drisceoil's collection, *Politics and the Irish Working Class.*

Marxist analysis, often polemical and associated chiefly with controversy on the national question, especially about Connolly and Northern Ireland, was an animated feature of debate in socialist history circles in the 1970s and 1980s. Critics of Connolly's republicanism made much of their Marxism as a means of validating their revisionism; these polemics had little impact on other fields of labour historiography.[20] Ultimately, the debate was about nationalism and the North, and did little to advance Marxism or historiography. Writing in the Connolly tradition continues to appear, some of it more scholarly, but more of it agitational, rehearsing the same old themes. A distinctive, Northern perspective is offered in the polemical and semi-popular work of Andrew Boyd.[21] In Ireland the 'cultural turn' was most evident in literary criticism, where the Field Day Collective did much to generate a discourse on perceptions of the Irish condition as either postmodern or postcolonial. But with some exceptions, such as David Lloyd's *Irish Times*, the warring protagonists have not looked to labour history for material.[22]

In terms of method, the majority of academic scholarship remains doggedly empirical: it is guided by a traditional emphasis on documents, and focused on structures and leaders or movements. The emergence of what some might see as a fourth wave of labour history, distinguished by a rejection of teleology, a desire to restore from the shadows women's history, gender, sexual orientations, ethnicity and identities, is discernible but it has yet to have a major impact on Ireland. At the same time, topics like culture, religion, social life and leisure, mentalities and values, are beginning to receive some attention. If most work in these areas has been undertaken by social historians, sociologists, or anthropologists, can labour historians be far behind?

Publications: progress and perspectives

The literature since the 1970s will be reviewed in relation to the three largest categories of writing: trade unionism, politics and auto/biography. We also survey work on more marginal topics, including rural labour, migrants and emigrants, local movements and women. Irish labour in the diaspora, a topic which features regularly in *Saothar* and its bibliographies, which appeared annually until 2003, would require a separate essay. To date, the subject has been examined within its various overseas contexts, rather than from a transnational perspective. As yet, transnational studies have been limited to certain phases of republican history, notably Fenianism. Critical discussion of the historiography is likewise an undeveloped genre. Though a common feature of conference papers, the first such survey did not appear until 1995, and it has since been joined by only two others.[23]

Trade unionism

Studies of organized workers continue to form the staple of labour history, and publications fall into three periods; before, during and after the pivotal 1889–1923 era. It was a measure of the political importance of the trades before 1848 that interest in the guilds and early craft unions had already generated a small corpus of academic research before the 1970s.[24] The 1970s and 1980s were a particularly fruitful period for the reconstruction of the Indian summer of early craft unionism, which ran from 1824 to 1848, with controversies emerging on workers' politics. D'Arcy stressed the conservatism of the Dublin trades in their support for Daniel O'Connell's Repeal campaign rather than Chartism, while Jacqueline Hill emphasized the tenacity of Orangeism among the Dublin Protestant working class. By contrast, Bernard Reaney argued for the existence of significant rank-and-file sympathy with Chartism, and Takashi Koseki demonstrated that the trades swung to the left in 1847–48.[25] Remarkably, the 1848 rising is still seen simply as another in the chain of nationalist revolts in Ireland, and it has been left to English historians like Dorothy Thompson to uncover the connections between Young Irelanders and Chartists. Christine Kinealy's work promises a fresh emphasis on radicalism in the rising.[26] The immediate post-Famine decades remain a trough in historiography as they had been in history. Monographs on this period have concentrated on agricultural labour and trade unionism in Belfast (see below), and Boyle's volume remains the definitive text on urban labour and radical politics between 1825 and 1906.

During the 1980s, attention began to shift towards the action-packed age of agitation from 1889 to 1923. These years have become the best researched in the annals of Irish labour, and interpretations are becoming steadily more refined. McCarthy thought the new unionism hardly existed in Ireland. Boyle treated it as similar to new unionism in Britain. Shane McAteer has shown that it enjoyed more uncritical support from artisans than its British counterpart.[27] Emmet Larkin had lionized his namesake in an impressive biography in 1967, and Dermot Keogh's *The Rise of the Irish Working Class: The Dublin Trade Union Movement and the Labour Leadership, 1890–1914* sought to diminish the legend by stressing the role of moderate, 'second string' leaders at Larkin's expense. But Big Jim's reputation, for these years at least, is growing with age.[28]

Once understood as a mentality within the ITGWU, Larkinism has been re-defined as a method of agitation embraced by large sections of unskilled workers. A very readable illustration is John Gray's *City in Revolt: James Larkin and the Belfast Dock Strike of 1907*, which was re-issued by the Services, Industrial, Professional, and Technical Union (SIPTU), successor to the ITGWU, to mark the centenary of the strike.[29] Not until 2000 did a definitive history appear of Ireland's most famous industrial dispute, in the form of Padraig Yeates's *Lockout: Dublin 1913*. The overall pattern of Larkinite unrest is also beginning to receive attention in studies like John Newsinger's *Rebel City*.[30] The conventional wisdom that militancy disappeared with the departure of Larkin to the United States in 1914 and the death of Connolly in 1916 was challenged in O'Connor's *Syndicalism in Ireland, 1917–23*.[31] The syndicalist era was the one period in modern trade union history where the rank and file thrust themselves into the foreground, through various forms of direct action, including sabotage, soviets and sympathetic strikes. Yet precisely because of the absence of high-profile leaders, interest in these 'red flag times' remains sluggish.[32]

From 1923 onwards, the dynamics of industrial struggle were made more complex by a variety of factors such as the intensification of inter-union divisions; the formation of Fianna Fáil; the emergence of the state in union politics after the party came to power for the first time in 1932; and subsequent attempts at statutory reform of industrial relations. The standard account of unions after 1923 remains that of McCarthy; yet almost 500 of the 588 pages of his *Trade Unions in Ireland* are devoted to the period from 1930 to 1960. However, it has been supplemented by monographs on labour-state relations, by Kieran Allen's *Fianna Fáil and Irish Labour*, and by the emergence of a rich industrial relations literature.[33] Studies in Irish industrial relations were few and far between before the late 1980s. However, the reconfiguration of wage bargaining in national 'social partnership' pacts from 1987 constituted an obvious stimulus. Industrial relations scholarship in Ireland is wary of Marxism, and of class as a valuable instrument of explanation, and tends to treat labour history, perfunctorily, as an introductory background. It has, nonetheless, helped focus attention on the post-1923 years.[34] Its benign view of social partnership has been challenged by a few dissenting voices from the disciplines of sociology and anthropology, in particular Allen, Colin Coulter and Steve Coleman.[35]

There has been a gratifying increase in the output of official trade union histories, and it is also heartening that the phenomenon reflects the close connections between unions and the ILHS. Only two unions, the Irish

Bakers, Confectioners and Allied Workers, and the Irish National Teachers' Organization, had commissioned histories before 1970, although the ITGWU and the Workers' Union of Ireland had sponsored more specific publications.[36] Beginning with volume one of the ITGWU's history in 1982, the list has now extended to thirteen unions, in addition to trades councils in Dublin and Waterford, the Irish Congress of Trade Unions and the People's College.[37] Other Labour bodies, including trades councils in Belfast, Derry and Wexford, have supported more limited efforts. Impending mergers or special anniversaries and bigger bank balances are often the stimulants to commemorative histories. Unfortunately, the prevailing concern is to compile a chronicle of organization, and commissions usually go to amenable colleagues with a bit of time on their hands. And while articles and dissertations on unions are common, unofficial histories are not.[38]

Politics

Politics constitutes the second major focus of publications. A scattering of pamphlets in the Connolly tradition almost monopolized writing on the political left before 1970. The situation is now much improved. But it is a mirror opposite of the literature on trade unions, in the sense that there are very few official histories. Research has concentrated on the period after 1890. Socialist groups had a slight and intermittent presence up to that point and the absence of a 'pure' radical tradition partly explains the neglect of labour's lively involvement with nationalism. Boyle's *The Irish Labor Movement* virtually ignored labour-nationalism, while D'Arcy was dismissive of trade union backing for O'Connell. Radical, as distinct from labour, historians have been less sceptical. Jim Smyth's *Men of No Property* and Newsinger's work on the Fenians argued for the radical strain in, and rational basis to, working-class participation in the United Irish and Fenian movements.[39] The intermittent work on labour politics in the late eighteenth and nineteenth centuries continues to dwell on connections with the salient national movements. But occasional attention is now being given to class-based organizations like the Chartists and the International Working Men's Association, while the various micro-factions that comprised socialism BC (Before Connolly) are treated definitively in Lane's *The Origins of Modern Irish Socialism.*[40]

Connolly remains a watershed, a point of departure and a touchstone of many of the main debates on labour history, centrally the relationship between socialism and nationalism. Connollyology grows apace. About 200 books, articles, pamphlets, and dissertations on Connolly were available in 1980. Today the tally stands at around 350. The latest affirmation of his relevance to contemporary politics is Eoin Ó Broin's *Sinn Féin and the Politics of Left Republicanism*.[41] At the same time, scholarship is moving beyond the controversies about Connolly to attend to leftwing political parties. In addition to Connolly's own Irish Socialist Republican Party, which finally attracted a comprehensive monograph in 2005, full-length accounts now exist of Sinn Féin, the Communist Party of Ireland (CPI), the Labour Party, the Northern Ireland Labour Party (NILP), the Social Democratic and Labour Party and Clann na Poblachta.[42]

There are also studies of syndicalism, socialist republicanism and Communism.[43] Socialist republicanism has engaged scholarly interest because of its intersection with the ever-contentious topic of nationalism, and was the subject of high profile assaults in the late 1980s and 1990s from Henry Patterson and Richard English, who insisted on the inherent incompatibility of the two creeds.[44] Research on Communism received a boost, in Ireland as elsewhere, from the opening of the Comintern archives after the collapse of the Soviet Union.[45] One aspect which has generated substantial popular attention is the Connolly Column – a blanket term for Irish International Brigaders. Michael O'Riordan's *Connolly Column*, in effect a CPI history, was produced in East Germany in 1979, for want of an amenable publisher in Ireland. Since 1984, fourteen memorials have been erected to men of the Connolly Column and there has been a steady stream of publications on the Irish in the Spanish Civil War.[46]

Two obvious areas of neglect are Trotskyism – which appeared in Ireland in the late 1930s and again in a variety of factions from the 1960s[47] – and the elephant in the room, social democracy, or whatever it is that motivates the Labour Party. The party was the subject of a political science monograph in 1981 and a comprehensive history in 2007, which is finely textured but tentative in analysis.[48] A less obvious field, overlooked for want of coherence and definition, is what might be called radical community activism. After Ireland became predominantly urban and industrial in the 1970s, a succession of small, far-left groups – the Socialist Labour Party, the Democratic Socialist Party, the Workers' Party and the Socialist Party – managed to win toe-holds of parliamentary representation, chiefly through intense clientelism in socially deprived districts. How certain communities were persuaded to vote outside the political consensus, and the growth of working-class community initiatives on problems ranging from tax reform to drug dealing, warrant scrutiny. The stifling assumption that national political parties and their leaders stand almost alone in affecting social and political discourse has kept Irish historiography, pencil in hand, at election counts and out of the community centres. Most labour historians remain fixated with the so-called 'bigger' picture, with high politics and the national question.

Writing on the North may be placed under the rubric of 'politics', as almost all work on the Six Counties is informed by the political divide. Socialist histories of the North were especially topical in the late 1970s and 1980s, with Michael Farrell and Eamon McCann arguing for the irreformable nature of the 'sectarian Northern statelet', and Paul Bew, Peter Gibbon and Henry Patterson, as well as Austen Morgan and Bob Purdie, challenging the validity of Connollyite theses.[49] Only in recent years has empirical research caught up with the debate, and now that we have a better understanding of the Northern Labour movement, the public is not so interested. The first phase of empirical work focused on the pre-partition years and the problem of working-class support for Unionism. Patterson's *Class Conflict and Sectarianism: The Protestant Working Class and the Belfast Labour Movement, 1868–1920* and Morgan's *Labour and Partition: The Belfast Working Class, 1905–23* were particularly influential.[50]

Subsequent work has tended to address Labour politics in Northern Ireland. Most historians take a sympathetic view of Labourites as well-meaning progressives who battled vainly against the dark forces of sectarianism. They differ as to whether the reformist enterprise had any hope of success. In *The Politics of Frustration: Harry Midgley and the Failure of Labour in Northern Ireland*, and in other work, Graham Walker has argued that only the extension of the British party system to the North could have ruptured sectarian solidarities.[51] In contrast, Christopher Norton, Terry Cradden and Aaron Edwards have contended that the NILP could have achieved greater success had it not been ambushed by extremists. Edwards's *The Northern Ireland Labour Party* is the first complete history of the NILP and, alas, an apologia. A.C. Hepburn's update of Rumpf's *Nationalism and Socialism in Twentieth Century Ireland* is a rare, balanced introduction to the NILP.[52]

Trade unionism is less well covered, indeed it has been strangely neglected in socialist debate on the North. Boyd Black has written on the structure of the labour force and on industrial relations, while Cradden's informative *Trade Unionism, Socialism and Partition* is restricted to the years from 1939 to 1953. Fortunately, a few articles have been appearing on the post-1969 years. Black and Cradden uphold the view of unions as effective in neutralizing sectarianism within their sphere of operations, whereas Andrew Boyd and Bill Rolston are critical of their failure to combat sectarianism and address discrimination.[53] How a united, secular trade union movement has managed to function in a confessional society among the very people most divided by sectarianism is a fundamental question which suggests a wide agenda for future research. So, too, does the assertion that the efficient secret, and the secret inefficacy, of trade unionism in Northern Ireland lies in mass non-active participation in the unions.

Auto/biography

Four lives of Connolly, three of Constance Markievicz, two of Larkin, and one each of Michael Davitt and Louie Bennett, had been published before 1970, together with biographies of William Thompson, Feargus O'Connor and Bronterre O'Brien, books which were as unknown in Ireland as their subjects.[54] Unusually, Radio Éireann broadcast and published a useful series of Thomas Davis lectures on 'leaders and workers' in 1966, which extended the inventory to John Doherty, Fintan Lalor and William Walker.[55] Nonetheless, Irish leaders of the early British Labour movement continue to be neglected in Ireland. Of the 'big four', only Thompson has started to receive his due, having acquired iconic status for socialists and feminists in his native Cork. Doherty enjoyed some ephemeral acclaim in Donegal at the turn of the century.[56] The indifference to 'the great Feargus' and the intellectually greater Bronterre is odd.[57] Otherwise, the genre is in good health. Connolly's ideas, of course, have come under severe and extensive scrutiny. His personal life is harder to fault – Morgan's *Political Biography* is the most hostile – and continues to fascinate, with the most comprehensive biography being published in 2005.[58] Plans are afoot, too, for a 'bio-pic'.

By contrast, there was little on Larkin that was both substantial and scholarly – and much that was not – at least until the 1990s. O'Connor's exposé opened a new set of controversies on Larkin's post-lockout career and received some outraged reviews.[59] The focus is gradually extending beyond the 'twin towers' to embrace lesser mortals. Apart from Davitt, the lens is fixed mainly on twentieth-century people.[60] Contemporary, journalistic biographies of politicians have included the most electorally successful of Labour Party leaders, Dick Spring.[61]

There is now an awareness of labour biography as a field full of potential. Since 1990 the ILHS has published twelve booklets in its *Studies in Irish Labour History* series, most on second echelon union leaders, *Saothar* has included a 'Labour lives' feature in each issue since 1999, and the ILHS Galway branch convened a 'Socialist Lives' conference in 2009, with papers on twenty-five individuals.[62] In 1998, Cork University Press embarked on an ambitious, sixteen-volume project under the title *Radical Irish Lives*. Regrettably, financial difficulties forced its discontinuation after volume three, as well as the shelving of a planned *Dictionary of Irish Labour Biography*.[63] The genre remains limited by its excessively personal focus.

Few studies connect their subject adequately to his or her context and interrogate their record in the light of the forces at their disposal or the options that were open to them. In consequence, such work has little to say on the concept of leadership or about power relations within the Labour movement, and contributes little to the wider debate on the trajectory of Labour. An up-beat approach, identifying with and presenting the subject in the best way possible, seems *de rigeur*.

Political autobiography, a suspect indulgence in Ireland's austere, conformist society from the post 1916–21 generation to the 1980s, is no longer regarded as egregious and a handful of Labour politicians have published memoirs. Appropriately, the trend was pioneered by the maverick Noel Browne.[64] Other than O'Brien, the fashion has yet to extend to trade unionists, at any level. Symptomatically, Matt Merrigan, the senior Irish officer of the Amalgamated Transport and General Workers' Union, published an unrevealing, unofficial union history rather than a memoir on his retirement.[65] The Labour movement is conspicuously absent in working-class autobiography, and not since Seán O'Casey has anyone tried to present a microcosm of working-class life.[66]

On the margins

McCarthy's observation, in 1977, that: 'An understanding of the Irish trade union movement is an understanding of two cities, Dublin and Belfast', encapsulated a mentality that is happily *passé*.[67] Rural workers scarcely featured in labour history up to the 1980s. The opening agenda was set by social histories of Whiteboyism, a generic name for agrarian movements, with M.R. Beames's, *Peasants and Power: The Whiteboy Movements and Their Control in Pre-Famine Ireland* and Samuel Clark and James Donnelly's collection, *Irish Peasants: Violence and Political Unrest, 1780–1914*, being the cream of the crop.[68] In more limited contributions, labour historians, notably Pádraig and Fintan Lane, have since focused on the post-Famine era, and been concerned chiefly with attempts to introduce trade unionism in agriculture and mobilize labourers in politics, demographic decline, hiring fairs, and social conditions – especially housing.[69]

The inclusion of agricultural workers in labour history has been of importance in broadening the parameters of the subject beyond conventional trade unionism, and in introducing an alternative politics. Through their Land and Labour Associations, farm workers maintained until 1918 the alliance with nationalism spurned by urban labour in the 1890s. The success of the Land and Labour Associations in securing legislative change contrasts with the dismal record of the ITUC in achieving social reform and raises a tantalizing, and neglected, counterfactual. However, Fintan Lane is sceptical about the benefits secured by agricultural workers from their support for the nationalists.[70] A related group of workers were migrants and seasonal workers, who have been somewhat overshadowed by the more common category of emigrants.[71] And while emigration is a well developed field of scholarship, the literature has had a tenuous connection with labour. The link will be strengthened by the recently established Irish Oral History Archive, which will record the stories of those who left for Britain during and after the Second World War. Still in its tentative stages, it promises to create a unique documentation of a central experience in the history of Irish working life.

Local studies have sprouted and some have blossomed. Most have taken the form of restricted histories of incidents, personalities or the local response to salient national events. General accounts have so far been confined to Cork, Waterford, Galway and the west, and the crucible that was Belfast between 1880 and 1921.[72] Belfast was obviously different, but so too, in more subtle ways, was the provincial experience in the south and west, where the working class was usually dispersed across a wide range of small-scale employments. As John Cunningham noted, over 50 per cent of Irish workers were entered under the 'miscellaneous' category of British labour statistics in the early twentieth century, and the British paradigm is an inadequate prism through which to view the Irish working class.[73] Agricultural labourers are no longer, to use that cliché of the 1980s, 'the forgotten men of Irish history'.

That invidious honour might be passed to other rural and small town operatives – such as dairymaids, creamery hands, roadmen, shopboys, draymen – who have been incorporated into labour history only in periods, like the syndicalist years, when they joined unions in large numbers. In their anthropology of Thomastown, a small centre of the sort not conventionally associated with Labour or class consciousness, Marilyn Silverman and P.H. Gulliver found a rural industrial proletariat of millers, brewers, tanners, maltsters and self-employed artisans, and cultural ideas and political and economic organizations about which Irish historiography was silent. 'Clearly, Irish historians', they wrote, 'had constructed their own very partial version of society.'[74] Silverman's subsequent volume on Thomastown, *An Irish Working Class*, challenged labour historians to find ways of routinely including these invisible people.[75]

In conclusion, a comparison with the historiography of women's history is instructive. Women's history is of relatively recent vintage. Margaret MacCurtain and Donnacha Ó Corráin's *Women in Irish Society*, which appeared at the end of the 1970s and covered topics such as family, politics, the Church, work and trade unionism, is often cited as the starting point of academic publication in the field.[76] Monographs on women and the republican movement, the Irish Women Workers' Union and the suffragists followed in the 1980s.[77] The late 1980s saw a shift away from leader-led studies towards research on work and life in areas such as family and home, religious orders, domestic service, prostitution, factory work and the medical professions. More recently, women's history has focused more on the inter-relationships between gender, power and society.[78] Class and class relations in housework, suffragism and philanthropy have featured strongly in work by Joanna Bourke, Caitriona Clear, Mona Hearn and Cliona Murphy.[79] Maria Luddy's work on prostitution is an exploration of a part of Irish history which is all too often ignored: the stories of the destitute, the marginalized and the outcast.[80] It is also an exploration of power and authority in Ireland.

Clear's study of nuns and their working lives focuses on an aspect of labour which is generally overlooked by labour historians. Nuns worked as educators, nurses and social workers. However, the religious nature of their role and the relative seclusion of their situation, as well as that of priests, brothers and missionaries, mean that their impact and experiences remain fertile ground for research and discussion. Mary Cullen has noted the difficulty in uncovering the voices of working-class women, as distinct from the details of their lives. But much is being done in the sphere of memory and oral history, and critical attention is being devoted to questions of silence and silencing, remembering and forgetting.[81] Whilst feminists might justifiably protest their continuing marginality, women's history has been more successful in finding a niche within the academy, and the fruits are evident in a more rapidly diversifying and a more conceptually challenging scholarship.

Future directions

The 1970s constituted a turning point for Irish labour history. The decade saw Ireland catch the third wave of the new labour history. Within that paradigm, progress has been steady, if not spectacular. The challenges ahead relate to reach and quality. A primary objective of labour historians must be to sustain and deepen the relevance of the subject to the general public. In this respect, Ireland is reasonably well placed. Chiefly through the ILHS and *Saothar*, the field has acquired public recognition and developed strong links with the Labour movement. Its standing was little affected by the 'fall of the wall' and the ebb tide of the 1990s; partly because one cannot lose what one never had, but also because it had established organic foundations. Consolidating this rootedness is vital. The second challenge is to connect Irish historiography with the fourth wave. Indeed, one could argue that recently labour history has embarked on a fifth wave, characterized by an ambition to integrate labour with kindred studies, in gender, race and culture; and by a greater emphasis on transnational comparison, and on labour as a globalized concept. What hope is there for Ireland in this endeavour without a critical mass of full-time labour historians? Progress in theory will continue to be slow and patchy within the rubric of the traditional historiography. On the other hand, the emergence of new fields in Irish industrial relations, sociology, gender and culture studies, and anthropology offers exciting possibilities for the kind of interdisciplinary work which could plug Irish labour history into the forefront of new thinking and see it make a quantum leap from the third to the fifth wave.

Notes

1 David Howell, *A Lost Left: Three Studies in Socialism and Nationalism* (Manchester: Manchester University Press, 1986), p. 17.

2 Paul Mason, *Live Working or Die Fighting: How the Working Class Went Global* (London: Harvill Secker, 2007), p. xv.

3 'Labour' in this chapter refers to trade union organizations and socialist parties, and 'labour' to all waged labour.

4 See Belinda Loftus, *Marching Workers: An Exhibition of Irish Trade Union Banners and Regalia* (Belfast: Arts Council of Ireland, 1978); and Fergus D'Arcy and Ken Hannigan, *Workers in Union: Documents and Commentaries on the History of Irish Labour* (Dublin: National Archives, 1988).

5 James Connolly, *Labour in Irish History* (Dublin: Maunsel, 1910). Since 1974, the Cork Workers' Club, Historical Reprints Series, has published some twenty pamphlets in this tradition.

6 Arnold Wright, *Disturbed Dublin: The Story of the Great Strike of 1913–14 with a Description of the Industries of the Irish Capital* (London: Longmans, Green, 1914); P. Ó Cathasaigh [Seán O'Casey], *The Story of the Irish Citizen Army* (Dublin: Maunsel, 1919); W.P. Ryan, *The Irish Labour Movement, From the 'Twenties to Our Own Day* (Dublin: The Talbot Press, 1919).

7 *Socialism and Nationalism: A Selection from the Writings of James Connolly*, with an introduction and notes by Desmond Ryan (Dublin: Three Candles, 1948); *Labour and Easter Week: A Selection from the Writings of James Connolly*, ed. by Desmond Ryan (Dublin: Three Candles, 1949); *The Workers' Republic: A Selection from the Writings of James Connolly*, ed. by Desmond Ryan (Dublin: Three Candles, 1951).

8 ITGWU, *The Attempt to Smash the Irish Transport and General Workers' Union* (Dublin: ITGWU, 1924); *P.T. Daly's Libel Suit* (Dublin: ITGWU, 1925); *Thomas Johnson's Libel Suit* (Dublin: ITGWU, 1925); *Some Pages from*

Union History: The Facts Concerning Larkin's Departure to America (Dublin: ITGWU, 1927); *Three Men and Three Days: A Fight for Irish Trade Unionism* (Dublin: ITGWU, 1934); *Fifty Years of Liberty Hall: The Golden Jubilee of the Irish Transport and General Workers' Union, 1909–1959* (Dublin: ITGWU, 1959); *The Planting of a Seed: An Account of the Founding of the ITGWU and the Role it Played in the Period up to the Rising in 1916* (Dublin: ITGWU, 1966); William O'Brien, *Forth the Banners Go: Reminiscences of William O'Brien as Told to Edward MacLysaght* (Dublin: Three Candles, 1969).

9 C. Desmond Greaves, *The Life and Times of James Connolly* (London: Lawrence and Wishart, 1961); T.A. Jackson, *Ireland Her Own: An Outline History of the Irish Struggle for National Freedom and Independence* (London: Cobbett Press, 1946); Peter Berresford Ellis, *A History of the Irish Working Class* (London: Gollancz, 1972); R.M. Fox's major publications were *Marx, Engels, and Lenin on the Irish Revolution* (London: Modern Books, 1932); *Rebel Irishwomen* (Dublin: Talbot Press, 1935); *Smoky Crusade: An Autobiography* (London: Hogarth Press, 1937); *Green Banners: The Story of the Irish Struggle* (London: Secker and Warburg, 1938); *The History of the Irish Citizen Army* (Dublin: J. Duffy, 1943); *Labour in the National Struggle* (Dublin: Propaganda Dept. of the Labour Party, 1945); *James Connolly: The Forerunner* (Tralee: The Kerryman, 1946); *Years of Freedom: The Story of Ireland 1921–48* (Cork: Trumpet Books, 1948); *Jim Larkin: The Rise of the Underman* (London: Lawrence and Wishart, 1957); and *Louie Bennett: Her Life and Times* (Dublin: Talbot Press, 1958).

10 The leading examples were J. Dunsmore Clarkson, *Labour and Nationalism in Ireland* (New York: Columbia University Press, 1925); Emil Strauss, *Irish Nationalism and British Democracy* (London: Methuen, 1951); and Erich Rumpf, 'Nationalizmus und Sozialismus in Irland', unpublished PhD thesis, University of Heidelberg, 1959.

11 Samuel Levenson, *James Connolly: A Biography* (London: Martin Brian and O'Keefe, 1973); see also Owen Dudley Edwards, *The Mind of an Activist: James Connolly* (Dublin: Gill and Macmillan, 1971).

12 See John McIlroy, 'Organized Labour History in Britain: The Society for the Study of Labour History after Fifty Years', chapter 1 in this volume, and idem, 'The Society for the Study of Labour History, 1956–1985: Its Origins and its Heyday', *Making History: Organizations of Labour Historians in Britain since 1960, Labour History Review* (*LHR*) Fiftieth Anniversary Supplement, April 2010, 17-110.

13 See Emmet O'Connor, 'The Irish Labour History Society: An Outline History', in *Making History*, 143-55.

14 *Irish History Workshop/Saotharlann Staire Éireann*, 'Saotharlann staire: réamhrá', 1 (1981), 1–2.

15 J.J. Lee, '*Saothar* and Its Contribution to Irish Historical Studies', in *An Index to Saothar and Other ILHS Publications, 1973–2000*, comp. by Francis Devine (Dublin: ILHS, 2000), pp. 9–11.

16 Arthur Mitchell, *Labour in Irish Politics, 1890–1930: The Irish Labour Movement in an Age of Revolution* (Dublin: Irish University Press, 1974); Charles McCarthy, *Trade Unions in Ireland, 1894–1960* (Dublin: Institute of

Public Administration, 1977).

17 John W. Boyle, *The Irish Labor Movement in the Nineteenth Century* (Washington, DC: Catholic University of America, 1988).

18 Emmet O'Connor, *A Labour History of Ireland, 1824–1960* (Dublin: Gill and Macmillan, 1992); *Politics and the Irish Working Class, 1830–1945*, ed. by Fintan Lane and Donal Ó Drisceoil (Basingstoke: Palgrave Macmillan, 1992).

19 The conference included 450 participants from twenty-five countries.

20 For a review of the debate and leftwing perspectives on Northern Ireland, see Terry Cradden, *Trade Unionism, Socialism, and Partition: The Labour Movement in Northern Ireland, 1939–1953* (Belfast: December Publications, 1993), pp. 1–22.

21 Andrew Boyd, *The Rise of the Irish Trade Unions, 1729–1970* (Dublin: Anvil Books, 1972); updated as *The Rise of the Irish Trade Unions* (Dublin: Anvil Books, 1985); and idem, *Have the Trade Unions Failed the North?* (Cork: Mercier Press, 1984).

22 David Lloyd, *Irish Times: Temporalities of Modernity* (Dublin: Field Day, 2008).

23 Emmet O'Connor, 'A Historiography of Irish Labour', *Labour History Review*, 60, 1 (1995), 21–34; idem, 'Ireland', *Labour/Le Travail*, 50 (2002), 243–48; Fintan Lane, 'Envisaging Labour History: Some Reflections on Irish Historiography and the Working Class', in *Essays in Irish Labour History: A Festschrift for Elizabeth and John W. Boyle*, ed. by Francis Devine, Fintan Lane and Niamh Puirséil (Dublin: Irish Academic Press, 2008), pp. 9–25.

24 J.J. Webb, *The Guilds of Dublin* (Dublin: Three Candles, 1929); Séamus Pender, 'The Guilds of Waterford, 1650–1700, parts I–V', *Journal of the Cork Historical and Archaeological Society*, (1953–7), 58–62; Rachel O'Higgins, 'Ireland and Chartism: A Study of the Influence of Irishmen and the Irish Question on the Chartist Movement', unpublished PhD thesis, Trinity College, Dublin, 1959; Fergus A. D'Arcy, 'Skilled Tradesmen in Dublin, 1800–50: A Study of Their Opinions, Activities, and Organizations', unpublished MA dissertation, University College, Dublin, 1968.

25 Fergus A. D'Arcy, 'The Artisans of Dublin and Daniel O'Connell, 1830–47', *Irish Historical Studies*, 66 (1970), 221–43; 'The National Trades' Political Union and Daniel O'Connell, 1830–1848', *Éire-Ireland*, 17, 3 (1982), 7–16; Jacqueline Hill, 'The Protestant Response to Repeal: the Case of the Dublin Working Class', in *Ireland under the Union: Varieties of Tension*, ed. by F.S.L. Lyons and R.A.J. Hawkins (Oxford: Oxford University Press, 1980); idem, 'Artisans, Sectarianism, and Politics in Dublin, 1829–48', *Saothar*, 7 (1981), 12–27; Bernard Reaney, 'Irish Chartists in Britain and Ireland: Rescuing the Rank and File', *Saothar*, 10 (1984), 94–103; Takashi Koseki, 'Patrick O'Higgins and Irish Chartism', Hosei University Ireland-Japan Papers, vol. 2 (Hosei, n.d.); idem, 'Dublin Confederate Clubs and the Repeal Movement' (Hosei, 1992). See also Mel Doyle, 'The Development of Industrial Organizations Among Skilled Artisans in Ireland, 1780–1838', unpublished MPhil thesis, University of Southampton, 1973; and Brian Henry, 'Combinations, the Law, and Industrial Violence in Late Eighteenth Century Dublin', *Saothar*, 18

(1993), 19–33. See also Michael Huggins, 'Democracy or Nationalism? The Problems of the Chartist Press in Ireland', in *Papers for the People: A Study of the Chartist Press*, ed. by Joan Allen and Owen R. Ashton (London: Merlin Press, 2005), pp. 129–45.

26 Dorothy Thompson, 'Ireland and the Irish in English Radicalism before 1850', in *The Chartist Experience: Studies in Working Class Radicalism and Culture, 1830–60*, ed. by James Epstein and Dorothy Thompson (London: Macmillan, 1982), pp. 120–152; Christine Kinealy, '"Brethren in Bondage": Chartists, O'Connellites, Young Irelanders and the 1848 Uprising', in Lane and Ó Drisceoil, *Politics and the Irish Working Class*, pp. 87–112. Kinealy is also completing a biography of Thomas Francis Meagher.

27 Shane McAteer, 'New Unionism in Derry, 1889–91: A Demonstration of its Inclusive Nature', *Saothar*, 16 (1991), 11–22.

28 Emmet Larkin, *James Larkin, 1876–1947: Irish Labour Leader* (London: Routledge and Kegan Paul, 1965); Dermot Keogh, *The Rise of the Irish Working Class: The Dublin Trade Union Movement and the Labour Leadership, 1890–1914* (Belfast: Appletree Press, 1982).

29 John Gray, *City in Revolt: James Larkin and the Belfast Dock Strike of 1907* (Belfast: Blackstaff Press, 1985; 2nd edn, Dublin: SIPTU, 2007).

30 Pádraig Yeates, *Lockout: Dublin 1913* (Dublin: Gill and Macmillan, 2000); John Newsinger, *Rebel City: Larkin, Connolly and the Dublin Labour Movement* (London: Merlin Press, 2004); see also Emmet O'Connor, 'What Caused the 1913 Lockout? Industrial Relations in Ireland, 1907–13', *Historical Studies in Industrial Relations*, 19 (2005), 101–21.

31 Emmet O'Connor, *Syndicalism in Ireland, 1917–23* (Cork: Cork University Press, 1988).

32 See especially David Fitzpatrick, 'Strikes in Ireland, 1914–21', *Saothar*, 6 (1980), 26–39; D.R. O'Connor Lysaght, 'The Munster Soviet Creameries', *Saotharlann Staire Eireann*, 1, (1981), 36–49; Liam Cahill, *Forgotten Revolution, The Limerick Soviet, 1919: A Threat to British Power in Ireland* (Dublin: The O'Brien Press, 1990).

33 Finbarr Joseph O´Shea, 'Government and Trade Unions in Ireland, 1939–46: the Formation of Labour Legislation', unpublished MA dissertation, University College Cork, 1988; Kieran Allen, *Fianna Fáil and Irish Labour: 1926 to the Present* (London: Pluto Press, 1997).

34 The current standard works are *Irish Industrial Relations in Practice*, ed. by Thomas V. Murphy and William K. Roche (2nd edn, Dublin: Oak Tree Press, 1997); and Joseph Wallace, Patrick Gunningle and Gerard McMahon, *Industrial Relations in Ireland: Theory and Practice* (1st pub. 1995; Dublin: Gill and Macmillan, 2004).

35 Kieran Allen, *The Celtic Tiger: The Myth of Social Partnership in Ireland* (Manchester: Manchester University Press, 2000); Colin Coulter and Steve Coleman, *The End of Irish History? Critical Reflections on the Celtic Tiger* (Manchester: Manchester University Press, 2003).

36 John Swift, *History of the Dublin Bakers and Others* (Dublin: Irish Bakers', Confectioners' and Alllied Workers' Union, 1948); T.J. O'Connell, *100 Years*

of Progress: The Story of the Irish National Teachers' Organization (Dublin: Irish National Teachers' Organization, 1968); *Workers' Union of Ireland, 1913: Jim Larkin and the Dublin Lockout* (Dublin: Workers' Union of Ireland, 1964). For the ITGWU, see above.

37 C. Desmond Greaves, *The Irish Transport and General Workers' Union: The Formative Years, 1909–1923* (Dublin: Gill and Macmillan, 1982); Seán Redmond, *The Irish Municipal Employees' Trade Union, 1883–1983* (Dublin: Irish Municipal Employees' Trade Union, 1983, John Coolahan, *The ASTI and Post-Primary Education in Ireland, 1909–1984* (Dublin: Cumann na Meánmhúinteoirí, Éire, 1984); Mary Jones, *These Obstreperous Lassies: The History of the Irish Women Workers' Union* (Dublin: Gill and Macmillan, 1988); John Campbell, *A Loosely Shackled Fellowship: The History of Comhaltas Cána* (Dublin: PSEU, 1989); Garry Sweeney, *In Public Service: A History of the Public Service Executive Union, 1890–1990* (Dublin: PSEU, 1990); John Campbell, *An Association to Declare: A History of the Preventive Staff Association* (Dublin: PSEU, 1996): James Murphy, *The Bartenders' Association of Ireland: A History* (Dublin: Bartenders' Association, 1997); Martin Maguire, *Servants to the People: A History of the Local Government and Public Services Union, 1900–1992* (Dublin: Institute of Public Administration, 1998); *Teachers' Union: The TUI and its Forerunners, 1899–1994*, ed. by John Logan (Dublin: A. and A. Farmer, 1999); Charles Callan, *Painters in Union: The Irish National Painters' and Decorators' Trade Union and its Forerunners* (Dublin: Watchword, 2008); Séamus Cody, John O'Dowd, and Peter Rigney, *The Parliament of Labour: 100 Years of Dublin Council of Trade Unions* (Dublin: Dublin Council of Trade Unions, 1986); Jim Cooke, *Technical Education and the Foundation of the Dublin United Trades Council* (Dublin, Teachers' Union of Ireland, 1987); Emmet O'Connor, *A Labour History of Waterford* (Waterford: Waterford Council of Trade Unions, 1989); *Trade Union Century*, ed. by Donal Nevin (Cork: Mercier Press, 1994); Ruaidhri Roberts, *The Story of the People's College* (Dublin: The O'Brien Press, 1986).

38 An exception is Matt Merrigan, *Eagle or Cuckoo? The Story of the ATGWU in Ireland* (Dublin: Matmer Publications, 1999). Paul Starrett, 'The ITGWU, 1909–23', unpublished PhD thesis, University of Ulster, 1985, and Conor McCabe, 'The Amalgamated Society of Railway Servants and the National Union of Railwaymen in Ireland, 1911–23', unpublished PhD thesis, University of Ulster, 2006, are among the very few doctoral theses directly on individual unions, though MA dissertations are common, as are PhDs on trade unionism more generally.

39 Jim Smyth, *The Men of No Property: Irish Radicals and Popular Politics in the Late Eighteenth Century* (Dublin: Gill and Macmillan, 1992). For a debate on the character of Fenianism, see John Newsinger, 'Fenianism Revisited: Pastime or Revolutionary Movement?', and R.V. Comerford's riposte, 'Comprehending the Fenians', in *Saothar*, 17 (1992), 46–56; see also John Newsinger, 'Old Chartists, Fenians, and New Socialists', *Éire-Ireland*, 2 (1982), 19–45.

40 Seán Daly, *Ireland and the First International* (Cork: Tower Books, 1984); Fintan Lane, *The Origins of Modern Irish Socialism, 1881–1896* (Cork: Cork

University Press, 1997).

41 Eoin Ó Broin, *Sinn Féin and the Politics of Left Republicanism* (London: Pluto Press, 2009). For the most recent bibliography, see Donal Nevin, *James Connolly: A Full Life* (Dublin: Gill and Macmillan, 2005).

42 David Lynch, *Radical Politics in Modern Ireland: The Irish Socialist Republican Party, 1896–1904* (Dublin: Irish Academic Press, 2005); Brian Feeney, *Sinn Féin: A Hundred Turbulent Years* (Dublin: O'Brien Press, 2002); Ian McAllister, *The Northern Ireland Social Democratic and Labour Party: Political Opposition in a Divided Society* (London: Macmillan, 1977); Gerard Murray, *John Hume and the SDLP: Impact and Survival in Northern Ireland* (Dublin: Irish Academic Press, 1998); Eithne MacDermott, *Clann na Poblachta* (Cork: Cork University Press, 1998).

43 O'Connor, *Syndicalism in Ireland*; Henry Patterson, *The Politics of Illusion: Republicanism and Socialism in Modern Ireland* (London: Hutchinson Radius, 1989); Richard English, *Radicals and the Republic: Socialist Republicanism in the Irish Free State, 1925–37* (Oxford: Clarendon Press, 1994); Mike Millotte, *Communism in Modern Ireland: The Pursuit of the Workers' Republic since 1916* (Dublin: Gill and Macmillan, 1984); Emmet O'Connor, *Reds and the Green: Ireland, Russia, and the Communist Internationals, 1919–43* (Dublin, UCD Press, 2004). The CPI's own *Outline History* (Dublin: CPI, 1979) is little more than a collection of sketches.

44 Patterson, *The Politics of Illusion;* English, *Radicals and the Republic.*

45 For the impact of the Comintern papers, compare Millotte, *Communism in Modern Ireland,* with O'Connor, *Reds and the Green.*

46 Michael O'Riordan, *Connolly Column: The Story of the Irishmen Who Fought in the Ranks of the International Brigades in the National-Revolutionary War of the Spanish People, 1936–1939* (1st pub. 1979; Pontypool: Warren and Pell, 2005), pp. 2–3. On the politics and literature of commemoration of the Connolly Column, see Emmet O'Connor, 'Identity and Self-representation in Irish Communism: the Connolly Column and the Spanish Civil War', *Socialist History,* 34 (2009), 36–51.

47 But see Ciarán Crossey and James Monaghan, 'The Origins of Trotskyism in Ireland', *Revolutionary History,* 2/3 (1996), 4–57; and D.R. O'Connor Lysaght, *Early History of Irish Trotskyism* (Dublin: the author, 1982).

48 Michael Gallagher, *The Irish Labour Party in Transition, 1957–81* (Manchester: Manchester University Press, 1982); Niamh Puirséil, *The Irish Labour Party, 1922–73* (Dublin: UCD Press, 2007).

49 Michael Farrell, *Northern Ireland: The Orange State* (London: Pluto Press, 1980); Éamonn McCann, *War and an Irish Town* (Harmondsworth: Penguin Books, 1974); Paul Bew, Peter Gibbon and Henry Patterson, *The State in Northern Ireland, 1921–72* (Manchester: Manchester University Press, 1979); Paul Bew and Henry Patterson, *The British State and the Ulster Crisis* (London: Verso Books, 1985); *Ireland: Divided Nation, Divided Class,* ed. by Austen Morgan and Bob Purdie (London: Inklinks, 1980).

50 Henry Patterson, *Class Conflict and Sectarianism: The Protestant Working Class and the Belfast Labour Movement, 1868–1920* (Belfast: Blackstaff Press, 1980);

Austen Morgan, *Labour and Partition: The Belfast Working Class, 1905–23* (London: Pluto Press, 1991).

51 Graham Walker, *The Politics of Frustration: Harry Midgley and the Failure of Labour in Northern Ireland* (Manchester: Manchester University Press, 1985); and idem, 'The Northern Ireland Labour Party, 1924–1945', in Lane and Ó Drisceoil, *Politics and the Irish Working Class*, pp. 229–45.

52 Christopher Norton, 'The Left in Northern Ireland, 1921–32'; *Labour History Review*, 60, 1 (1995), 3–20; and idem, 'The Irish Labour Party in Northern Ireland, 1949–58', *Saothar*, 21 (1996), 47–59; Aaron Edwards, *The Northern Ireland Labour Party* (Manchester: Manchester University Press, 2009); E. Rumpf and A.C. Hepburn, *Nationalism and Socialism in 20th Century Ireland* (Liverpool: Liverpool University Press, 1977), was based on a dissertation by Rumpf and updated by Hepburn. See also Emmet O'Connor, 'Labour and the Left', in *Northern Ireland Politics*, ed. by Arthur Aughey and Duncan Morrow (London: Longman, 1996), pp. 48–55; Henry Patterson, 'The Decline of the Collaborators: The Ulster Unionist Labour Association and Post-War Unionist Politics', in Devine, Lane and Puirséil, *Essays in Irish Labour History*, pp. 238–53.

53 Boyd Black, 'Reassessing Irish Industrial Relations and Labour History: The North-East of Ireland up to 1921', *Historical Studies in Industrial Relations*, 14 (2002), 45–85; Boyd Black, 'Industrial Relations', in *The Northern Ireland Economy: A Comparative Study in the Economic Development of a Peripheral Region*, ed. by R.I.D. Harris, C.W. Jefferson and J.E. Spencer (London: Longman, 1990), 207–33; Terry Cradden and Andrew Erridge, 'Employers and Trade Unions in the Development of Public Policy in Northern Ireland', in *Public Policy in Northern Ireland: Adoption or Adaptation*, ed. by M.E.H. Connolly and S. Loughlin (Belfast: Policy Research Institute, 1990), pp. 99–123; Terry Cradden, 'The Trade Union Movement in Northern Ireland', in Nevin, *Trade Union Century*, pp. 66–84; Terry Cradden, *Trade Unionism, Socialism, and Partition* (Belfast: December Press, 1993); Boyd, *Have the Trade Unions Failed the North?*; Bill Rolston, 'The Limits of Trade Unionism', in Liam O'Dowd, Bill Rolston and Mike Tomlinson, *Northern Ireland: Between Civil Rights and Civil War* (London: CSE Books, 1980), pp. 68–94. See also, Andrew Finlay, 'Sectarianism in the Workplace: The Case of the Derry Shirt Industry, 1868–1968', *Irish Journal of Sociology*, 3 (1993), 79–93; and Don Anderson, *14 May Days: The Inside Story of the Loyalist Strike* (Dublin: Gill and Macmillan, 1994).

54 Desmond Ryan, *James Connolly: His Life, Work and Writings* (Dublin: Talbot Press, 1924); Nora Connolly O'Brien, *James Connolly: Portrait of a Rebel Father* (Dublin: Four Masters, 1935); Fox, *James Connolly*; Greaves, *The Life and Times of James Connolly*; Seán Ó Faoláin, *Constance Markievicz: or, the Average Revolutionary* (London: Cape, 1934); Anne Marreco, *The Rebel Countess* (London: Weidenfeld and Nicolson, 1963); Jacqueline Van Voris, *Constance de Markievicz in the Cause of Ireland* (Boston: University of Massachusetts, 1967); Fox, *Jim Larkin* ; Larkin, *James Larkin*; Francis Sheehy Skeffington, *Michael Davitt: Revolutionary Agitator and Labour Leader* (London: T.F. Urwin, 1908);

Fox, *Louie Bennett*; R.K.P. Pankhurst, *William Thompson (1775–1833): Pioneer Socialist*, (1st pub. 1954; London: Pluto Press, 1991); Donald Read and Eric Glasgow, *Feargus O'Connor: Irishman and Chartist* (London: Edward Arnold, 1961); Alfred Plummer, *Bronterre: A Political Biography of Bronterre O'Brien, 1804–1864* (Toronto: University of Toronto Press, 1971).

55 *Leaders and Workers*, ed. by J.W. Boyle (Cork: Mercier Press, 1966).

56 Doherty was recognized in his native Buncrana with a memorial in 2000 and a pamphlet *John Doherty: Voice of the People* (Buncrana: SIPTU, 2002). The leading biography is R.G. Kirby and A.E. Musson, *The Voice of the People: John Doherty, 1798–1854, Trade Unionist Radical and Factory Reformer* (Manchester: Manchester University Press, 1975).

57 But see the work of the Australian scholar, Paul A. Pickering, *Feargus O'Connor* (Monmouth: Merlin Press, 2008).

58 Austen Morgan, *James Connolly: A Political Biography* (Manchester: Manchester University Press, 1988); Nevin, *James Connolly*.

59 Emmet O'Connor, *James Larkin* (Cork: Cork University Press, 2002); *James Larkin: Lion of the Fold*, ed. by Donal Nevin (Dublin: Gill and Macmillan, 1997), while uneven in quality, is a great compendium and includes a valuable bibliography of some 500 books and articles referring to Larkin.

60 The most recent study, Laurence Marley, *Michael Davitt: Freelance Radical and Frondeur* (Dublin: Four Courts Press, 2007), gives greater attention to his labour politics. Fintan Lane, *In Search of Thomas Sheahan: Radical Politics in Cork, 1824–1836* (Dublin: Irish Academic Press, 2001) is a rare account of a minor nineteenth-century figure. J. Antony Gaughan, *Thomas Johnson* (Dublin: Kingdom Books, 1980); Andro Linklater, *An Unhusbanded Life: Charlotte Despard, Suffragette, Socialist, and Sinn Féiner* (London: Hutchinson, 1980); John P. Swift, *John Swift: An Irish Dissident* (Dublin: Gill and Macmillan, 1991); Charlie McGuire, *Roddy Connolly and the Struggle for Socialism in Ireland* (Cork: Cork University Press, 2008); Thomas J. Morrissey, *William O'Brien, 1881–1968: Socialist, Republican, Dáil Deputy, Editor and Trade Union Leader* (Dublin: Four Courts Press, 2007).

61 Tim Ryan, *Dick Spring: A Safe Pair of Hands* (Dublin: Blackwater Press, 1993).

62 The *Studies in Irish Labour* Series includes Anthony Coughlan, *C. Desmond Greaves, 1913–1988: An Obituary Essay* (Dublin: ILHS, 1991); Manus O'Riordan, *The Voice of a Thinking Intelligent Movement: James Larkin Junior and the Ideological Modernisation of Irish Trade Unionism* (Dublin: ILHS, 1995); Francis Devine, *Acting for the Actors: Dermot Doolan and the Organisation of Irish Actors and Performing Artists* (Dublin: ILHS, 1997); Helga Woggan, *Silent Radical – Winifred Carney, 1887–1943: A Reconstruction of Her Biography* (Dublin: ILHS, 2000); Bill McCamley, *The Third James: James Fearon, 1874–1924: An Unsung Hero of Our Struggle* (Dublin: ILHS, 2000); Anton McCabe and Francis Devine, *The Stormy Petrel of the Transport Workers: Peadar O'Donnell, Trade Unionist, 1917–1920* (Dublin: ILHS, 2000); Francis Devine, *Navigating a Lone Channel: Stephen McGonagle, Trade Unionism and Labour Politics in Derry* (Dublin: ILHS, 2000); Helga Woggan, *Ellen Grimley (Nellie Gordan) –*

Reminiscences of her Work with James Connolly in Belfast (Dublin: ILHS, 2000); Francis Devine, *Understanding Social Justice: Paddy Cardiff and the Discipline of Trade Unionism* (Dublin, ILHS, 2002); Joseph Deasy, *Fiery Cross: The Story of Jim Larkin* (Dublin, ILHS, 2004); Francis Devine, *An Eccentric Chemistry: Michael Moynihan and Labour in Kerry, 1917–2001* (Dublin, ILHS, 2004); Francis Devine and Manus O'Riordan, *James Connolly, Liberty Hall and the 1916 Rising* (Dublin, ILHS, 2006); Francis Devine and Norman Croke, *James Connolly Labour College, 1919–1921* (Dublin: ILHS, 2007).

63 The subjects of the published volumes were Louie Bennett, Peadar O'Donnell and James Larkin.

64 Noel Browne, *Against the Tide* (Dublin: Gill and Macmillan, 1986); Paddy Devlin, *Straight Left: An Autobiography* (Belfast: Blackstaff Press, 1993); Barry Desmond, *Finally and in Conclusion: A Political Memoir* (Dublin: New Island, 2000); Ruairi Quinn, *Straight Left: A Journey in Politics* (Dublin: Hodder Headline Ireland, 2005).

65 Merrigan, *Eagle or Cuckoo?*; 'Socialist Trade Unionist: Matt Merrigan's Political Formation', *Saothar*, 12 (1987), 94–106, an interview with Merrigan by Francis Devine, was subsequently circulated privately as a 'memoir'.

66 Michael MacGowan, *The Hard Road to Klondike* (London: Routledge and Kegan Paul, 1973); *A Life in Linenopolis: the Memoirs of William Topping, Belfast Damask Weaver, 1903–56*, ed. by Emmet O'Connor and Trevor Parkhill (Belfast: Ulster Historical Foundation, 1992); Liam O'Donnell, *The Days of the Servant Boy* (Cork: Mercier Press, 1997); Lily O'Connor, *Can Lily O'Shea Come Out to Play?* (Dingle: Brandon, 2000); Bill Cullen, *It's a Long Way From Penny Apples* (Dublin: Mercier Press, 2001); *Loyalism and Labour in Belfast: The Autobiography of Robert McElborough, 1884–1952*, ed. by Emmet O'Connor and Trevor Parkhill (Cork: Cork University Press, 2002); *Founded on Fear: Letterfrack Industrial School, War and Exile*, ed. by Peter Tyrrell and Diarmuid Whelan (Dublin: Irish Academic Press, 2006).

67 McCarthy, *Trade Unions in Ireland*, p. 1.

68 M.R. Beames, *Peasants and Power: The Whiteboy Movements and Their Control in Pre-Famine Ireland* (Brighton: Palgrave Macmillan, 1983); *Irish Peasants: Violence and Political Unrest, 1780–1914*, ed. by Samuel Clark and James S. Donnelly, Jr (Manchester: Manchester University Press, 1983).

69 P.L.R. Horn, 'The National Agricultural Labourers Union in Ireland, 1873–9', *Irish Historical Studies*, 67 (March 1971), 340–52; Padraig G. Lane, 'The Agricultural Labourers in Ireland, 1850–1914', unpublished PhD thesis, University College Cork, 1980; Emmet O'Connor, 'Agrarian Unrest and the Labour Movement in Co. Waterford, 1917–23', *Saothar*, 6 (1980), 40–48; David Fitzpatrick, 'The Disappearance of the Irish Agricultural Labourer, 1841–1912', *Irish Economic and Social History*, 7 (1980), 66–92; John W. Boyle, 'A Marginal Figure: The Irish Rural Labourer', in Clark and Donnelly, *Irish Peasants*, pp. 311–38; Frederick H.A. Aalen, 'The Rehousing of Rural Labourers in Ireland under the Labourers (Ireland) Acts, 1883–1919', *Journal of Historical Geography*, 12 (1986), 287–306; Dan Bradley, *Farm Labourers: Irish Struggle, 1900–1976* (Belfast: Athol Books, 1988); E. Margaret Grawford,

'Diet and the Labouring Classes in the Nineteenth Century', *Saothar*, 15 (1990), 87–96; Fintan Lane, 'Rural Labourers, Social Change and Politics in Late Nineteenth-Century Ireland', in Lane and Ó Drisceoil, *Politics and the Irish Working Class*, pp. 113–39; Michael O'Hanlon, *Hiring Fairs and Farm Workers in North-West Ireland* (Derry: Guildhall Press, 1992); May Blair, *Hiring Fairs and Market Places* (Belfast: Appletree Press, 2007).

70 Lane, 'Rural Labourers'.

71 The best known migrants are the 'tattie-hokers', who went to Scotland, picking potatoes. See Anne O'Dowd, *Spalpeens and Tattie Hokers: History and Folklore of the Irish Migratory Agricultural Worker in Ireland and Britain* (Dublin: Irish Academic Press, 1991). On emigrants, see L. Lees, 'Mid-Victorian Migration and the Irish Family Economy', *Victorian Studies*, 20 (1976), 25–43; H.R. Diner, *Erin's Daughters in America: Irish Immigrant Women in the Nineteenth Century* (Baltimore: Johns Hopkins Press, 1983); *The Irish in Britain, 1815–1939*, ed. by Roger Swift and Sheridan Gilley (London: Pinter Press, 1989); *The Irish World Wide, History, Heritage, Identity, vol. 4: Irish Women and Irish Migration*, ed. by Patrick O'Sullivan (London: Leicester University Press, 1995); Roger Cooter, *When Paddy Met Geordie: The Irish in County Durham and Newcastle, 1840–1880* (Sunderland: University of Sunderland Press, 2005); John Belchem, *Irish, Catholic and Scouse: The History of the Liverpool-Irish, 1800–1939* (Liverpool: Liverpool University Press, 2007). For recent discussion of this area, see the symposium, 'Perspectives on the Irish Diaspora', *Irish Economic and Social History*, 33 (2006), 35–58.

72 Maura Cronin, *Country, Class or Craft? The Politicization of the Skilled Artisan in Nineteenth-Century Cork* (Cork: Cork University Press, 1994); O'Connor, *Labour History of Waterford*; John Cunningham, *Labour in the West of Ireland: Working Life and Struggle 1890–1914* (Belfast: Athol Books, 1995); and idem, *'A Town Tormented By the Sea': Galway, 1790–1914* (Dublin: Geography Publications, 2004). For Belfast, see above.

73 Cunningham, *Labour in the West of Ireland*, p. 178.

74 Marilyn Silverman and P.H. Gulliver, 'Historical Anthropology and the Ethnographic Tradition: A Personal, Historical and Intellectual Account', in *Approaching the Past: Historical Anthropology Through Irish Case Studies*, ed. by Marilyn Silverman and P.H. Gulliver (New York: Columbia University Press, 1992), p. 8.

75 Marilyn Silverman, *An Irish Working Class: Explorations in Political Economy and Hegemony, 1800–1950* (Toronto: University of Toronto Press, 2001).

76 *Women in Irish Society: The Historical Dimension*, ed. by Margaret MacCurtain and Donnacha Ó Corráin (Dublin: Women's Press, 1978). We are obliged to Caitríona Clear and Mary Clancy for comments on this paragraph. Neither is to blame for the content.

77 Margaret Ward, *Unmanageable Revolutionaries: Women and Irish Nationalism* (London, Pluto Press, 1983); Rosemary Cullen Owens, *Smashing Times: A History of the Irish Women's Suffrage Movement, 1889–1922* (Dublin: Attic Press, 1984); Jones, *These Obstreperous Lassies*; Clíona Murphy, *The Women's Suffrage Movement and Irish Society in the Early Twentieth Century*

(Philadelphia: Temple University Press, 1989).

78 Mary O'Dowd and Phil Kilroy, 'Thoughts on Gender History', in *Gender and Power in Irish History*, ed. by Maryann Gialanella Valiulis (Dublin: Irish Academic Press, 2009), pp. 9–18 (p. 12).

79 Joanna Bourke, *Husbandry to Housewifery: Women, Economic Change and Housework in Ireland, 1890–1914* (Oxford: Clarendon Press,1993); Caitríona Clear, *Nuns in Nineteenth-Century Ireland* (Dublin: Gill and Macmillan, 1987); idem, *Women of the House: Women's Household Work in Ireland, 1922–1961* (Dublin: Irish Academic Press, 2000); Mona Hearn, *Below Stairs: Domestic Service Remembered in Dublin and Beyond, 1880–1922* (Dublin: Lilliput Press, 1993); *Women Surviving: Studies in Irish Women's History in the 19th and 20th Centuries*, ed. by Maria Luddy and Clíona Murphy (Dublin: Poolbeg Press, 1989).

80 Maria Luddy, *Prostitution and Irish Society* (Cambridge: Cambridge University Press, 2007).

81 Mary Cullen, 'The Potential of Gender History', in Gialanella Valiulis, *Gender and Power*, pp. 19–31.

5

The United States of America

Elizabeth Faue

The year 2010 marks the fiftieth anniversary of the British Society for the Study of Labour History (SSLH). It also marks the fiftieth anniversary of the flagship journal of the field in the United States, *Labor History*. The intertwining of British and American social science, especially in social and labor history, is not news to most scholars. Scholarly exchange of ideas about class and labor, in both a national and a comparative framework, has contributed enormously to the development of the subject. More specifically, partisans of the 'new labor history', nearly fifty years old itself, recognize the pivotal role of E.P. Thompson's *The Making of the English Working Class* and the work of other British historians such as Eric Hobsbawm, Christopher Hill, and George Rudé, in transforming the historiography of labor in the United States.

Such nods aside, American labor history as it is practised today draws upon a diverse set of influences, including institutional labor economics, sociological theory and anthropological method, New Left social movements, the work of W.E.B. DuBois and C.L.R. James, feminist theory and the residual romanticism of Popular Front culture.[1] In this way labor history in the United States has become a scholarly endeavour of such hybrid design that it does not permit of easy synthesis, as early essays on the new labor history attest.[2] In fact, the new labor history has not produced a parallel either to the landmark *History of Labor in the United States*, co-authored by labor economist John R. Commons and his students, or to Selig Perlman's *Theory of the Labor Movement*, which elegantly theorized the distinctive character of the American labor movement.[3] Apart from the American Social History Project, which produced the survey, *Who Built America?*,[4] labor and working-class historians have focused instead on responding to and arguing with the work of Commons, Perlman and their Marxist counterpart, Philip S. Foner, about the character of the American working class, its labor movement and its political consciousness. This argument is fundamentally about how class identity and experience manifest themselves in a working class divided by race, ethnicity, religion, region and, at its most basic level, gender.[5]

Unlike the earlier labor economists, however, the practitioners of the new labor and working-class history have viewed differences among workers less as disruptive of class experience than as intrinsic to its fundamental expression.[6] Guarding against a Whiggish view of history as primarily national, labor historians have probed the local – whether in workplaces, occupations, communities, or families. Through hundreds of community and occupational studies, collective and individual biographies, accounts of working-class protests and social movements, analyses of labor and immigration laws, and explorations of working-class subcultures, our imagination of labor has become deeper and more complex but reveals the same understanding of class pluralism as turn-of-the-century labor economics. We have broadened our concept of who the workers are, extended our vision and understanding of the organizations they created and refined the measures of success for their strivings; but ultimately we endorse the view of American workers as a contentious and divided lot.

Read differently, the multiple voices and perspectives of labor history represent an attempt to capture the effects of slavery, immigration and male dominance on the working classes and the labor movements in the United States as well as diverse responses to capitalism in a global industrial (and later post-industrial) economy. Each generation of labor scholars has generated new language and forged new tools to understand the complex origins and trajectories of working-class experience, even as the intellectual origins and experience of labor historians themselves have changed. Beyond their political and intellectual differences, however, labor historians have demonstrated a common scholarly and political engagement with the broad-based working class. The field's pluralism has been reflected in the range of organizations, conferences and journals that give expression to the diverse labor and working-class past.

The origins of labor history in the United States

As an academic or an amateur field of study, labor history in the United States originated in the 1880s, when a handful of intellectuals – both of the working classes and of the rising professional class – became interested in the contemporary labor question. Industrialization and the growing class conflict of the Gilded Age and Progressive Era stirred the imagination and the conscience of social reformers, social scientists and social activists alike. The Wisconsin School of labor history, sometimes known as the Commons School, or 'the old labor history', had its origins in the intellectual and political ferment of that period. The prolific scholarship of Commons and his students, and their brand of labor economics and labor history, dominated the field and gave rise to the post-World War II emergence of industrial relations and its subsequent sequestering in industrial and labor relations schools.[7]

Among the earliest contributors to the field of labor history was Richard T. Ely, a political economist and progressive reformer. Ely helped to create the school of economics, political science and history at the University of Wisconsin, one of the top four economics departments in the nation. He was also a founder of the institutionalist school of labor economics, later known as the Wisconsin or Commons School, after Ely's younger colleague. The rooting of labor history in economics departments and later, after World War II, in industrial relations schools, cast the field as distinct from, and often peripheral to, the emerging discipline of history, which was national in scope and separate from the disciplines of economics, political science, sociology and anthropology. Although labor history and national history were, in their origins, multi- and interdisciplinary in approach and method, they were consolidated as distinct fields by the 1950s.

The Wisconsin School's contributions to labor history were, by any measure, vast. By the turn of the century, Ely had hired Commons to head a documentary editing project on the history of American industrial society. Funded by the American Bureau of Industrial Research and the Carnegie Foundation, this massive history was eventually published as the work of five authors in ten volumes in 1910–1911. Commons and his students later wrote a multi-volume history of labor in the United States as a broad synthesis that began with the American Revolution and ended, appropriately, before the New Deal dawned. This history, broad in scope and rooted in rigorous primary research, was published in two stages. Volumes 1 and 2, which were published in 1918, presented a narrative of labor history from colonial times through 1915; the second tranche of volumes covered working conditions and labor legislation, and completed the narrative history of the labor movement to 1932.

Commons was the major figure in the evolving School. His studies of institutional economics and labor problems, from administration to immigration and assimilation, marked him as one of the foremost scholars of the Progressive Era. He and his students also played an integral part in influencing the reformist social legislation of the day. Policy-makers as well as scholars, their work aided the design, creation and planning of workers' compensation, labor law, unemployment insurance and public pensions. Their political engagement expressed the centrality of the labor question to the politics of the twentieth-century United States as well as their own preferences for strong trade unions and state solutions to social problems. Commons and his outstanding students, who included Edwin Witte, Don Lesochier and Selig Perlman, transformed the way labor and its past was understood, not only in the academy but also in wider society. As expressions of the accent the field placed on the basic conservatism of American workers, Perlman's *Theory of the Labor Movement* and *History of Trade Unionism* encapsulated the past of workers not as a social history but as a history of institutions and the quest for political legitimacy. It also marginalized the experience of workers outside the confines of labor unionism.

The success of the Commons School in both labor economics and labor history was an expression of the growing strength of the labor movement in the United States. One of the last great practitioners of labor history in that tradition, Philip Taft, taught a series of students most of whom were tied to the labor movement institutionally and participated in the growing field of union-sponsored labor education. However, the revitalization of industrial unionism during the Great Depression and the tremendous gains made during World War II gave rise to specialized fields of labor law and industrial relations, even as labor economics and labor history were moved into new schools of industrial and labor relations in the 1940s and 1950s. As only one expression of this trend, the journal *Industrial and Labor Relations Review* was founded in 1947.

At the same time, the isolation of labor history within industrial relations meant that the history of workers and labor movements was marginal to the national story, even as labor economics, whether with a historical bent or not, increasingly became a peripheral interest in economics departments. At the apogee of institutionalism, labor historians and labor economists began to lose ground in scholarly organizations and publications. Aided and abetted by anti-communism, an increasingly anti-union political culture and a Cold War scholarly bias against understandings of class, labor historians were silenced outside the halls of industrial relations schools and labor union conventions.

Reviving labor history

With the merger of the American Federation of Labor and the Congress of Industrial Organizations in 1956 as the AFL-CIO, some labor unionists, librarians and historians became aware that public knowledge and memory of labor's past, especially of the epic struggles of the early twentieth century, was evaporating. A small group of labor scholars and enthusiasts met in 1958 to discuss the preservation of labor union documents and labor movement history. At the Tamiment Institute and the New York Public Library, Cornell School of Industrial and Labor Relations, Michigan State University and Wayne State University (which established the Walter P. Reuther Archives of Labor and Urban Affairs that year), scholars, archivists and librarians conducted surveys of national and local unions to find out how their documents – and the past that they illuminated – were being preserved. As the international unions had moved their offices to Washington, D.C., in the 1950s, they had destroyed or packed away in warehouses what archivists and historians understood to be the raw materials of their history. Preserving these records, and finding new outlets for the publication of labor history, became a pressing concern of those interested in the public memory and academic scholarship. The effort of preserving these documents sparked interest in the writing of labor history.

Like the British SSLH, the organizations, forums and organs of labor history in the United States began to emerge in the mid- to late 1950s. In 1959, the newly formed coalition of labor librarians, scholars and activists, was able to persuade the AFL-CIO to pass a resolution on the preservation of union records. Following on this effort, the group, under the leadership of Columbia University historian, Richard B. Morris, founded the journal, *Labor History*, which will also celebrate its fiftieth anniversary in 2010. Begun as an academic response to the disappearance of J.B.S. Hardman's *Labor and the Nation*, *Labor History* became the flagship journal of the field.[8] The first editorial board of the journal embraced a wide range of scholars. They included the colonial historian Richard Morris, the sociologist Daniel Bell, the labor economist Walter Galenson, the historians Philip Taft and Maurice Neufeld, and Brendon Sexton of the United Auto Workers. Headed by editor Norman Jacobs and associate editor John Hall, the editorial group recruited a range of talented authors who were concerned not simply with the meat-and-potatoes narrative of institutional labor history but also dealt with the need for better archival sources and repositories, addressed major social and political issues, and – as the journal and the subject evolved – incorporated new areas and approaches in labor history.[9]

The journal's first editors, Norman Jacobs and Milton Cantor (who headed *Labor History* from 1964 to 1974), proved themselves able to capitalize both on the institutional strength of the labor movement in the United States (then representing over 30 per cent of all wage-earners) and on the emerging intellectual trends of interdisciplinarity and comparative study. Moreover, in the first few years of the journal, the call for history 'from the bottom up', shorthand for the revival of social and social science history, shaped the journal's contents. While its founding was made possible by the vibrancy and sheer economic vitality of the labor movement, by the 1960s labor history had outgrown its origins in labor economics. Moreover, labor historians began to tap new sources and document working-class experiences outside the confines of industrial and labor relations. Over the course of the next fifty years, labor history in the United States reinvented itself.

Class and community, workplace, and the 'new institutionalism'

While *Labor History* was established at the height of the labor movement's power in the United States, historians of the working class also responded to contemporary social movements for their inspiration and subject matter. In particular, the Civil Rights movement, the anti-war movement, and Women's Liberation, along with rank-and-file worker revolts and union reform efforts in labor strongholds like Detroit, Michigan, Lordstown, Ohio and the coalfields of Appalachia, provided the context for a different approach to labor and working-class history. Commencing as a challenge to conventional thinking about American foreign relations and the Cold War, students of the New Left began to re-examine the formation of the welfare state and the role of ordinary men and women in shaping American politics from the American Revolution to the New Deal.[10] Challenges to national labor unions like the autoworkers, mine workers and teamsters not only sparked activism but attracted scholarly observers and allies. Despite hostility toward 'Big Labor' and the institutional labor movement expressed in the student movement and in the work of its mentors, such as C. Wright Mills, there were many who believed that worker resistance was not only about bread-and-butter issues or union membership. As the lingering anti-communism of the 1950s began to fade, labor historians, and many other academics, explored anew the history of working-class protest and resistance.[11]

Drawing upon a range of theoretical and political perspectives, the new labor history pursued three separate approaches to studying the working class. The first of these emphasized class in its social and cultural expression and its location in physical communities and subcultures; the second re-emphasized the workplace as the engine of class consciousness and explored work culture and rituals as well as informal worker resistance and formal worker organization; and the third revisited labor and political history in order to examine how workers encountered the law, entered the political process and engaged in collective action and union negotiations. All three approaches were steps removed from the purely institutional studies of the 1950s, but the third approach sought to reinvigorate the old labor history and to integrate it with the new.[12]

The class and community school emphasized local and community studies, where it was possible to trace out through thick description and cultural interpretation the emergence of working-class culture and worker protest. Moving away from the institutional realm of the union and the formal workplace, studies of working-class communities explored issues such as social mobility, occupational structure, cultural differences and the life cycles of workers in industrial society. Influenced by new work on immigration and urban history, community studies in labor history expanded to include twentieth-century cities and cultures of skilled trades and ordinary workers, in ways that employed 'new social history' methodologies in order to ask and answer questions about class formation and class politics.[13]

A central figure in this development, Herbert Gutman, served as associate editor on *Labor History* for more than a decade, and he began publishing his ground-breaking work on Gilded Age labor in the first few years of the journal. Gutman's focus on local and community studies of workers fundamentally changed how people imagined and wrote about the working-class past, as he emphasized the importance of immigrant subcultures, work customs and neighbourhoods in working-class struggles and in everyday resistance. In its accomplished exploration of the lives of miners in Braidwood, Illinois, and mill workers in Paterson, New Jersey, as well as African-American workers in slavery and after emancipation, Gutman's work stood in iconoclastic contrast to earlier visions of a largely undifferentiated and quiescent working class in the United States and significantly furthered understanding of its social conflicts and cultural continuities.[14]

Following the lead of the British labor historians Thompson and Hobsbawm, Gutman consciously addressed how the origins and development of the American working class were both more diverse and more continually disrupted than their nineteenth-century British counterparts. While his interpretation found resonance with the Wisconsin School on the exceptional character of the American labor movement, Gutman argued that American working-class formation was frequently disturbed but also renewed as each successive generation of immigrants, coming from agrarian and artisanal economies, encountered industrialization. Immigrants were simultaneously introduced to new forms of wage labor and subjected to novel, often onerous industrial discipline. Gutman published his most important collection of essays, *Work, Culture and Society*, in 1978, but he continued his research and writing, both as a sole author and in collaboration with fellow historian Ira Berlin, in tracing out the diverse origins of the American working class and how it expressed collective action and identity. In the later years of his career, Gutman sought to extend the analysis of the immigrant origins of the urban working class to the nineteenth-century South and to connect together his work on African-American communities and families with a broader understanding of working-class culture.[15]

The second touchstone of the new labor history was the workplace, where workers faced automation and new forms of management as well as the growing hostility of corporations towards union labor. David Montgomery, whose work is often invoked as the exemplar of this school, focused his sights on changing technology, workers' responses and their engagement with the state. Trained as a political and intellectual historian, his first book, *Beyond Equality*, concentrated primarily on how Radical Republicans had incorporated issues of class inequality into their political views in the years after the Civil War. There, as in later work, Montgomery probed ideological and political differences among workers. During a sojourn at the University of Warwick, Montgomery began researching the early nineteenth century, in particular the cultural dimensions of workers' lives, religious beliefs, working-class forms of protest and pre-industrial cities.[16]

By the 1970s, influenced by the shop stewards' movement in Britain, Montgomery shifted his research to the late nineteenth and early twentieth centuries. In essays analyzing work culture and occupational identity, he provided the template for subsequent studies of what he came to call 'workers' control'. Exploring how workers negotiated the conditions of their work and compensation, especially with the introduction of scientific management and state regulation, Montgomery wrote *Workers' Control in America*.[17] Known not only as a historian but also as a mentor of more than fifty labor historians, Montgomery put his imprint on the field through this work of synthesis, *The Fall of the House of Labor*. The book centred on the workplace experiences of class, even as it drew some of its findings from studies of working-class communities and the immigrant working classes.[18] Montgomery's attention to workers' control and customary work practices inspired a generation of studies rooted in work cultures. Although he focused on the power of skilled workers, later working-class historians drew upon his modelling of workplace resistance to explore how cigar makers, electrical workers, casual laborers, shop girls and hatters formed similar workplace bonds around the rituals of work and the habits of resistance, even in mass-production factories. The work cultures of railroad and canal workers, miners and waitresses served to mould everyday work and shape worker protest.[19]

The third school of labor history may be defined around the questions involving workers, the trade union movement and the state. Those who published in the early years of *Labor History* were caught between the new labor history's stress on grassroots social history and their own training and predilections, which increasingly connected them to questions about labor law, uses of power within the institutional labor movement and workers' engagement in the political process. Although these neo-institutional labor historians revisited the major themes of the Wisconsin School, they also brought new perspectives, including theories about the state and political culture to their investigations. Among the leading practitioners was Irving Bernstein, who wrote a trilogy of books on labor unionism in the 1920s and 1930s that shaped much of the subsequent historiography of the labor movement during the New Deal. Beginning with *The Lean Years*, Bernstein documented the political, legal and cultural changes that made possible both the repression of the American labor movement after World War I and its rebirth in *The Turbulent Years* of the Great Depression. While this work centred on the institutional and political expressions of worker and union power, Bernstein tried to capture not only what was happening to the trade unions and the labor market but also to reconstruct the role of workers in the evolution of American political and economic life. Concentrating on grassroots political changes, Bernstein's careful recuperation of the rise of industrial unionism in the CIO set the stage for the re-emergence of a recharged institutional labor history in the 1990s.[20]

Two other historians contributed significantly to the revival of questions about labor and the state. In their early explorations of Progressive-Era labor, David Brody and Melvyn Dubofsky worked against the grain of the old labor history while they laid the foundations of a new institutional understanding of labor. In his work on steel workers and the steel strike of 1919, for example, Brody provided new models for the study of non-union workers, focusing not only on union accounts and strikes but utilizing a range of sources to explore steelworkers' lives in the workplace and community. He investigated the division of labor within the factory and how differences among workers created the basis for both stability and conflict. Brody's early, powerful works led back to institutional labor history and in particular the engagement of the labor movement with political parties and the state. His later essays explored how labor organizations and protests changed over time, taking advantage of structural opportunities but also limited by bureaucratic organization and form.[21]

In a similar vein, Dubofsky, whose most cited work is his massive study of the Industrial Workers of the World (IWW), *We Shall Be All*, returned to consideration of questions about labor organizations and the state. *We Shall Be All* was in itself an unprecedented achievement. Taking issue with historiographical and political traditions that viewed the IWW as radical, of foreign origin and marginal, Dubofsky demonstrated how the Wobblies emerged from western labor radicalism to challenge employers across a wide range of issues, industries and communities. Among the first to use extensive local sources on the union, Dubofsky set in motion a revival of studies both of American syndicalism and labor in the Progressive Era more broadly. His subsequent work on labor and the state also fostered research on the cataclysmic changes in government labor relations in the twentieth century.[22]

Focus on a few of the individuals involved does not do justice to the vast number of labor historians in the United States who have contributed to our knowledge of the working-class past in intellectual ways but also as documentary and journal editors, reviewers and essayists, conference organizers, teachers and advisors, organizers and officers, and also as labor activists. Many academic labor historians have worked with community activists in recording oral interviews with workers and labor leaders, in helping to preserve historical sites and organize museum exhibits, in teaching labor and worker education classes, and writing newspaper columns and popular accounts of working-class lives and struggles. The historiographical essays cited give only a glancing look at the rich scholarship produced in the past fifty years as a generous contribution to understanding not only the history of workers and the labor movement but towards properly comprehending the United States national history as well.

Institutionalizing labor history: proliferating publishing outlets

Labor History maintained its status as the only journal in the field for over a decade. By the late 1960s, there was a need for more publication outlets and, moreover, a sense that *Labor History* was drawn from too narrow a design. When Dan Leab became editor in 1974 under the direction of editorial board head, Sidney Fine, the journal dedicated most of its attentions to neo-institutional studies of the labor movement. Simultaneously, there was a push to expand beyond the boundaries of the journal into mainstream historical debates. Both politically and methodologically, *Labor History* had remained dedicated to classic narratives of strikes, unions and legal and political struggles. Over time, its editors published fewer articles that incorporated methods and theories from other disciplines.

What is more important is that the new emphasis on historical research in the social sciences had given rise to an identifiable workers and industrialization network of the Social Science History Association (SSHA), an interdisciplinary association established in 1974. The labor network provided a forum for comparative studies of the working classes that employed quantitative historical methods and social science theories. The group included historical sociologists, economists, anthropologists and geographers as well as historians, and it addressed what it considered to be the central questions about the emergence, development, and effects of industrial capitalism.[23]

Fundamentally, the new labor history was less rooted in its 1950s rebirth as an academic field than in the new social history. Its practitioners focused less on unionized labor and trade unions or even on working-class radicalism and more on the history of ordinary workers, most of whom were neither trade union members nor radicals. Drawing largely on studies of urban immigration, historians such as Stephen Thernstrom and Charles Stephenson utilized new sources beyond labor newspapers and union records – manuscript census records, city directories and other documents of working-class social and cultural life. A major preoccupation of these studies was with the diverse ways ordinary men and women adapted to or resisted assimilation within American culture; so, too, was an interest in social mobility within and across generations, and geographical persistence over time within communities. These questions had derived from the literature on immigration, but they also touched upon a central issue of concern to both the Wisconsin School and the new labor history, namely whether workers had access to social mobility in the United States and how opportunity or lack thereof may have shaped political consciousness and identity. Thernstrom's careful reconstruction of workers' lives, including their patterns of home-ownership and community persistence, suggested how limited intergenerational social mobility acted as a drag on class consciousness, a finding in accord with the conclusions of the Wisconsin School. At the same time, the high rate of geographical mobility, lack of community persistence and relatively high internal migration also shaped class experience in the United States, as Charles Stephenson argued.[24]

Anthropological theory and method mattered, too, as the reconstruction of daily life, and of working-class culture through religious beliefs, ethnic association and folklore yielded valuable insights into the consciousness and identity of working-class men and women. *Social Science History* dedicated a special issue to 'The Skilled Worker and Working-Class Protest', edited by Michael Hanagan and Stephenson.[25] The issue, and subsequent SSHA conferences throughout the 1980s, revealed a vital engagement among labor and working-class historians that crossed disciplinary and national lines. The SSHA's Workers and Industrialization network also established a new bulletin for European historians of labor, *European Labor and Working-Class Historians' Newsletter*, and, within a few years, a journal, *International Labor and Working-Class History*. The latter debuted in 1976 and flourished under the editorship of Montgomery and later historians and historical sociologists Louise Tilly, Hanagan and Ira Katznelson, attracting a readership worldwide.

Further, the influence of New Left politics and social movements on academic history helped bring into being other journals. Under the editorship of Paul Buhle, *Radical America* was heavily influenced by C.L.R. James and arguments about worker self-activity; the journal published some of the most important early work in radical working-class history. *Socialist Revolution* (later *Socialist Review*), and the Mid-Atlantic Radical Historians' Organization's (MARHO) *Radical History Review*, similarly connected left theory and analysis with broadly defined radical history. They successfully combined attention to the history of the working classes internationally with the history of gender, sexuality, poverty and imperialism.[26]

The rising tide of labor history conferences

The growing number of journals was mirrored by a parallel development in conferences devoted to labor and working-class history. The Southern Labor Studies Conference (SLSC) began as the first of its kind in 1966. It was originally organized at a Southern Historical Association meeting, where labor and working-class historians met and formed their own group, the Association of Southern Labor Historians. Although it disbanded after a few years, the association prompted Merl E. Reed and Gary M. Fink of Georgia State University to establish a biennial conference to continue the effort to promote labor history regionally by 1972. In collaboration with Southern Labor Archives, the Southern Labor History (later Labor Studies) Conference had its first meeting in Atlanta in 1976. The conference rotated among different institutions until at the 2004 meeting in Birmingham, Alabama, the SLSC program committee initiated an effort to create a new, more permanent association. In 2007, the group created the Southern Labor Studies Association, affiliated with the national association of labor historians, the Labor and Working-Class History Association (LAWCHA).[27]

The SSHA's workers and industrialization network seemed too specialized and distant from immediate political concerns and divorced from the labor movement-inspired labor studies. In that spirit, the South West Labor History (later Labor Studies) Association was founded in 1974. It had its first meeting the following year under the auspices of the University of the Pacific and the directorship of the historian Sally Miller.[28] The South West Labor Studies Conference (SWLSC) drew heavily upon labor activists and educators in addition to labor historians, and its participants were often engaged in grassroots collection of interviews and documents along with union organizing campaigns in the active arena of the American Southwest. While remaining a fairly small conference, SWLSC was and is able to engage its participants in contemporary labor struggles. In 2009 the SWLSC held its thirty-fifth annual meeting.

In the Midwest, labor historians organized around a national labor history conference. In 1978, faculty at Wayne State University (the historians Stanley Shapiro, Robert Zieger and Christopher H. Johnson, and archivist Philip Mason), organized the first North American Labor History Conference (NALHC). Wayne State was uniquely situated to host the conference. Home of the Walter P. Reuther Library and Archives of Labor and Urban Affairs, the repository of records of some of the most important labor unions in the twentieth century, including the United Auto Workers, the Industrial Workers of the World, the United Farm Workers and the Service Employees International Union, the university had hired a strong core of social and labor historians. At the first NALHC conference, some of the leading scholars of labor and the working class in the United States and Europe, including Alexander Saxton, Montgomery, Louise Tilly, William Sewell, Joan Scott and John Merriam, participated in wide-ranging discussions of working-class politics and labor organization. Over the next few years, the History department at Wayne and the Reuther Library dedicated new resources toward the nation's first and only annual labor history conference, rotating the position of conference coordinator among faculty throughout the 1980s. Its participants included not only labor historians but labor activists, union leaders, public historians and policy-makers.[29]

Despite the vigour of its original meetings, when Robert Zieger left the faculty at Wayne, the conference lost some of its momentum. Like regional labor studies conferences, it shrank to a smaller, predominantly regional core of participants. Because Detroit was the Motor City and home to the United Auto Workers, conference programs tended to centre on the crisis of labor in mass production industry. At the same time, the field of labor history continued to prosper. Every year, *Labor History* listed hundreds of articles, dissertations and books treating the broad history of workers in the United States, in institutional histories as well as community and cultural studies. The failure of labor history as a field to create a new synthesis sparked new debates about the role class analysis should play and controversies as to whether the diverse character of the American working class could sustain either a unified labor movement or a unitary narrative in labor history. Moreover, there were others who believed that class as a category of analysis, and labor history as a subject, had lost ground in contemporary scholarship.

In 1984, a small, invitation-only conference addressed the state of labor history, its new directions and the problem of synthesis in the field. For many, the volume, *Perspectives in Labor History*, published in 1989, signified the imminent decline of labor history's scholarly influence.[30] Pluralism and diversity in the American working class led, some believed, only to the fragmentation of labor's story. While this criticism failed to acknowledge the breadth of recent scholarship and the critical inclusion of race and gender into the vocabulary and concerns of labor historians, the absence of an organizational centre and a national forum became major targets of historians' discontent. The volume's authors strove to piece together the burgeoning scholarship on the antebellum working classes, labor and the state, and the role of class consciousness and culture, but there was little agreement among them about how that narrative would look. Further, conference participants began to ask whether labor history and labor studies were losing their hold within higher education, even as the field continued to grow at a phenomenal rate. Especially troubling for some was the continued marginalization of gender and race in labor history.

Political and intellectual developments brought these questions to the surface. The ascendancy of cultural analysis and critical race theory, the continued expansion of women's and gender studies, and the decline of the labor movement in both numbers and influence, brought a shift not only in scholarly interests but also in priorities. Moreover, twenty years of scholarship in labor history had only underlined the crucial role of fragmentation and diversity among workers in the United States. Other critics of labor history wondered whether class consciousness was a sufficient vehicle for understanding the breadth of American working-class experience. While African-American history and women's history developed their own narratives, most accounts of working-class community and protest remained remarkably white and male and, surprisingly, focused on native-born or northern European immigrant workers. Critics suggested that the new labor history seemed particularly segmented and segregated from developments in immigrant, ethnic and religious history, from African-American, Latino and Asian-American history, and the history of women and gender.[31] While *Labor History* provided an occasional forum for the growing scholarship on labor, gender and race, the field continued to face challenges both in terms of integrating these categories and in how gender (both as the study of women and of masculinity and femininity), race (as the study not only of racial difference but of the meanings of whiteness), and other salient categories (increasingly, as the century ended, religion and sexuality) were marginalized in the main narrative of labor history.[32]

Where gender and labor history intersect, there has been an increasingly prolific literature that dates back to before the new labor history and which continues to extend the boundaries of the field. There are two central tendencies in the literature. The first, best captured by the work of Joan Scott, explores the meanings of gender in labor and working-class life and in class politics. Scott's own research focused on the French and European workers' movements and on women's work throughout continental Europe. However, her book, *Gender and the Politics of History*, best known for its postmodernist challenge to historical scholarship, directed much of its critique at the assumptions of the new social history and working-class history in particular. Probing the languages of labor and how they framed working-class struggle, Scott's work constituted a model for how to understand the politics of class. Her influence, demonstrated most vividly in the resonance of the collection, *Work Engendered: Toward a New History of American Labor*, and more broadly in the turn to masculinity studies, provoked strong opposition to 'the linguistic turn' and also helped some labor historians to rethink their suppositions about class in history.[33]

A second facet of scholarship on gender in labor history scrutinized the relationship of women workers to the economy and the state. In this arena, Alice Kessler-Harris took the lead in documenting how women workers were integrated into the labor force as well as the labor movement, and how state policy, both in protective labor legislation and as a part of social entitlements, set the conditions for a gendered citizenship. Kessler-Harris's early essays on women labor activists in the garment trades and on women's labor activism in the Progressive period were followed by what has now become the standard narrative, *Out to Work*, and her recent book, *In Pursuit of Equality*.[34] Throughout her career, Kessler-Harris has provided a template for how to integrate the rich documentation of women's industrial lives with the social and cultural questions of class and gender politics. She has been able to unite concerns about the household and community with explorations of the workplace, union and polity. In these ways, she stood as a model not only for women's labor historians but for all those who sought to bring together the varying historical dimensions of workers' lives.

The scholarship on race and labor has had a similar effect on labor and working-class history, in that labor historians have been adept at examining how race discrimination and racial inequality shaped the labor market and the labor movement on the one hand, and how, on the other hand, race has shaped class identity and experience. Inspired both by the Civil Rights movement but also by the expansion of African-American studies, labor historians have shown how racial identity influences working-class consciousness and action, both from within minority workers' communities and within the white community itself. Extensive research on black, Chicano and Asian workers has made the history of the working classes in the United States more complex, even as it has raised questions about the possibilities for racial cooperation and the limitations of racial conflict.[35]

National organizations for labor and working-class scholars

By 1990, the contradiction between a vibrant sub-field of labor history and its lack of an adequate institutional home provided the context for a new revival. Wayne State University hired its first labor historian in five years in 1991, when it brought me, Elizabeth Faue, to teach labor history and to take over as coordinator and chair of the NALHC. I had, it might be said, no mandate from an organization; what I had, however, was a vehicle for bringing together labor and working-class historians and union leaders and activists at a series of conferences addressing the major problems and concerns of labor in the United States. My first conference in 1991 was on 'Men, Women and Labor', a theme that encapsulated my own research. Labor historians Kessler-Harris, Leon Fink and Earl Lewis presented papers outlining the challenges of incorporating gender into labor history at a plenary session with nearly 200 people in attendance.[36] In subsequent years, we addressed the state, citizenship, international and comparative labor history, workers and the city,[37] class and politics, and labor, migration and the global economy. The thematic approach, and an organizing philosophy learned at SSHA which privileged an inclusive program and self-organization and initiative, attracted some of the best labor historians, from graduate students to distinguished professors, to our doors.

The success of the NALHC built on the vast network of labor scholars and activists in the United States. While the institutional support remained critical for the continued vitality of the field, the possibilities for expansion were limited to the annual conference structure. Regional labor studies conferences notwithstanding, labor history lacked a centre and an organizational presence, something which other sub-fields in American history had. By the late 1990s, there were enough labor and working-class historians to make such a national organization possible.

In 1997, the NALHC provided the institutional context for the founding of LAWCHA. Prompted by a request from Kessler-Harris and Fink, the NALHC program committee organized a plenary session and workshops to discuss the need for an organization and create basic guidelines. John Bukowczyk and Roger Horowitz worked out a constitution and bylaws for the nascent organization. Tom Klug played a central role in establishing the organization and continues to serve as treasurer. Elected co-chairs Faue and Julie Greene headed the organization in its first year; they were later elected to terms on the board of directors.[38]

The first president was Jacquelyn Dowd Hall of the University of North Carolina; she was succeeded by Joe William Trotter, Jr, of Carnegie Mellon University, James R. Green of the University of Massachusetts-Boston, and Michael Honey of the University of Washington-Tacoma. Each has shifted the centre of LAWCHA geographically and institutionally, as the organization has expanded its resources and advanced its political engagement and institutional reach. For the first seven years, LAWCHA conducted its annual meeting at the NALHC; beginning in 2005, however, the board of directors elected to shift to an annual meeting, which they would rotate among conferences.

Working from a distinctly different base, scholars interested in the revival of class analysis across a wide range of disciplines formed the Working-Class Studies Association (WCSA) in the 1990s. Capturing some of the same initial impulses as the new labor history of the 1970s, and inspired by British cultural studies, Working-Class Studies surfaced as an academic sub-field in the early 1990s. John Russo and Sherry Lee Linkon helped to establish the Center for Working-Class Studies at Youngstown University, the first of its kind, in 1995. Russo and Linkon had been involved in the movement to resist plant closures in the declining steel industry. Together they, and other scholars such as the geographer Don Mitchell, the economist Michael Zweig, the historians Peter Rachleff and David Roediger, the political scientist Dorian Warren, and the labor studies scholars Kitty Krupat and Renny Christopher, organized regional conferences on working-class studies and laid the groundwork for the field. Importantly, much of the impetus for working-class studies came not primarily from labor historians but from working-class scholars, activists and artists inspired by the failing fortunes of the labor movement and extensive plant closures. Deindustrialization became the backdrop to a reconsideration of what class meant and means in contemporary America.[39]

In 1996, Linkon, Russo, Janet Zandy and others organized a session on working-class studies at the NALHC in Detroit. In 2003, their organizing call brought together scholars from a wide range of fields to create the WCSA at the yearly conference in Youngstown. Social scientists and humanists, including labor historians and public historians of labor and the working classes, sought to give the study of class, and the working class in general, greater visibility but also to uniquely focus an engaged scholarship on the problems of working-class men and women in the United States. Working-class studies as a whole was dominated by literary scholars and sociologists, with only nominal attention at first to labor and working-class history. Today, working-class studies continues to flourish. The WCSA holds an annual conference, 'How Class Works', in addition to the Youngstown conference, and there are several centres for working-class studies across the United States.

A collection, *New Working-Class Studies*, edited by Russo and Linkon, provides an overview of the field. It contains papers on how working-class studies has fared, which include essays on labor and working-class history as part of the new field of study. The authors direct their attention to the same issues as framed early labor history. They seek to explore the cultural and political meanings of class from an inter- and multi-disciplinary perspective. The volume thus combines historical research on workers and the labor movement with oral histories of contemporary workers, and perspectives on the economic, cultural, and geographic bases of class experience and identity. Central to these concerns was the engagement of working-class studies scholars within working-class communities. Race has played a central part in working-class studies from the beginning; so too has gender as it has shaped working-class experience and politics, whether in the realm of labor activism or in the production of culture and education. The mandate for working-class studies, much as it was for the early years of the new labor history, was to create a field 'from the bottom up', democratically inclusive in subject matter and with a pedagogical vision that was broad and capacious.[40]

Labor history in the United States today

The proliferation of labor history institutions that commenced in the late 1970s was echoed early in the twenty-first century. *Labor History*'s editor for over a decade, Daniel J. Leab, resigned in 2000, and Leon Fink, of the University of Illinois-Chicago, took over as chief editor. During 2002 and

2003, the editorial group brought a new energy to the journal and published provocative essays linking labor history scholarship to the contemporary labor movement and new information technology.[41] Seeking to move the journal further from its moorings, and establish a new scholarly base for labor history, the editorial board left the publisher and established a new journal, *Labor: Studies in Working-Class History in the Americas*, which published its first number in 2004. Its mission was further political engagement, new scholarly vigour and a geographical expansion in subject matter, so that *Labor* now encompasses Latin American and Canadian history.

Labor History found a new editor in Craig Phelan, of the University of Kingston (UK), and the US editor, the economist Gerald Friedman, of the University of Massachusetts. The renovated *Labor History* seeks to return the field to its industrial relations roots, insisting as well on international and 'ecumenical' perspectives on labor history and labor studies. At the same time, MARHO's *Radical History Review* remains an outlet for research by labor historians, although it draws upon the broad range of radical history. *International Labor and Working-Class History* is now in its thirty-third year. It continues to rely on the familiar terrain of comparative social science history, with a much stronger theoretical basis and international coverage. Still published only twice annually, it fosters a rich dialogue on the issues confronting labor scholars in the United States.

Since the founding of the LAWCHA, labor history conferences in the United States have proliferated and at the same time helped to decentralize the field. For the years between 1991 and 2003, the NALHC served as the major annual labor history conference in the United States, drawing between 225 and 250 participants (both domestic and international) at its peak. Over 2,000 labor historians have presented their work at Wayne State University in Detroit, on programs that were thematically focused and inclusive of scholars and activists across the political, social and professional spectrum. While NALHC continues to present strong labor history programs, the increasing number of competing venues has trimmed its once vigorous numbers. Southwest Labor History Conference and the Pacific Northwest Labor Studies Conference have seen similar decline, while the Southern Labor Studies Conference has reorganized itself into a regional affiliate of LAWCHA, a development spurred by LAWCHA's annual meeting being held in 2007 at a labor history conference at Duke University.

In real ways, LAWCHA's policy over the past four years of moving its annual meeting from one venue to the next has ensured that regional labor history conferences have benefited from the occasional presence and limited resources of the national organization, but each conference finds it more difficult to recruit participants. The SSHA, whose workers and industrialization network provided the earliest impetus for the new labor history, has declined in terms of the number of panels and participants in its labor network. These limiting factors have been exacerbated by the economic climate in higher education, where travel funds have been cut or eliminated and conference costs escalated.

Membership of LAWCHA has grown to over 550, and its dues-paying members receive a subscription to *Labor: Studies in Working-Class History in the Americas*, as part of their membership. The organization has been able to consolidate resources with its oversight of the Herbert Gutman Distinguished Dissertation Award in Labor and Working-Class History, originally part of the University of Illinois Working Class in America series; it further coordinates the Philip Taft book award in Labor History, a longstanding prize given by Cornell University. Bringing these resources under the umbrella of LAWCHA has given structure to the informal networks of labor historians in the United States.

There are areas of concern. The shifting interests and resources of labor historians and institutions of higher education are embattled in a fragile economy. With the founding of LAWCHA, labor historians had hoped to stabilize the position and ensure the continued growth of their field. Recent reports from the academic job market, however, show a decline in the number of positions, as colleges and universities are faced with hiring freezes. Appointments in labor history have not been plentiful since the 1970s: few universities now hire in the field, preferring to combine labor history with other sub-fields in social and political history. The diminishing power of the labor movement, even under a labor-friendly government, has further stripped resources and suppressed the visibility of labor history as a field.

Despite these setbacks, labor and working-class history in the United States has benefited from the prolific scholarship and imaginative rethinking of the relationship between class and wider historical questions about gender, race, ethnicity, power and culture. Indeed, labor and working-class history has been most productive and exciting when it asks questions at the intersection of disciplines and methods. As the review of the literature shows, labor historians have benefited from engagement with scholarship on the state and labor relations, pushed beyond the realms of work and production into issues of consumption, culture and leisure. Because both immigrants and migrants have played a vital role in the development of the American workforce and working-class organization, ethnicity and race have become major sources of contention and cooperation for working-class struggle. Understanding region, religion, popular culture, gender norms and family practices has not only enriched the reconstruction of the ordinary lives of working men and women but also explained their patterns and expressions of class protest and identity.

To use one stunning example, *Like a Family*, a study of cotton mill workers, explored the broad set of issues that have come to characterize labor and working-class history since the 1980s as well as a specific regional context. Drawing on a base of rich oral histories of Piedmont industrialization, the book explored cotton mill workers' lives inside and outside the factory, in the mill villages and also in households, churches and social networks that they created, on back roads and also in courtrooms. As a co-authored work, *Like a Family* capitalized on the strengths of the field as a whole and can be seen as a template for how collective research makes possible a methodological breadth and interpretive creativity that few individually authored studies can employ.[42]

Among labor historians, there remain doubts about the ability of even such finely crafted labor history to change the way that national history is written and taught in America. Still, major scholars in the field continue to train students, and those students have broadened the boundaries of labor history. Currently, there is a growing interest in personal narratives and the formation of class identity. The revival of labor and working-class biographies, new studies exploring working-class religion and ritual, and issues of sexuality and gender identity, have added to our understanding of the subjective dimensions of class consciousness and how intimate relations shape class conflict and politics.[43]

US labor historians also have moved beyond national borders into an interest in transnational and global labor history, as the movement of labor and capital continues to evolve and transform what constitutes work, in what context it is performed, who constitutes the working classes, and under what conditions they labor. Observing recent trends in the globalization of labor, labor historians also have had the opportunity to re-examine the past and discover similar forces at work throughout American history. What is different about globalization in a twenty-first century world, and how diversity both characterizes and limits working-class protest against globalization, is on the agenda for the future.[44]

Today, labor historians are among the most visible and published scholars of American history. They have led national historical organizations and hold positions in prestigious research universities. Their subject, the history of workers and working-class organization in the United States, has bridged the divide between national history and the history of labor, fulfilling in many ways the vision of the founders of the journal, *Labor History*. Beyond these professional advances, however, the labor history that has emerged over the past five decades is not only incorporated in the national narrative; it has expanded to assimilate other experiences into labor's story. Indeed, labor and working-class history in the United States is a product not simply of historians interested in working-class experience but of historians who understand that there is no class experience that is not also an experience of race and gender, ethnicity and religion, region and community. Acknowledging that diverse and different experiences of being working class are at the core of labor history, the field today looks considerably different than it did when John R. Commons led seminars in labor economics at the University of Wisconsin.

Notes

1 There are a dizzying number of historiographical accounts of the origins of the new labor history, many of them cited below. This essay argues for multiple origins and influences at play. The background for much of contemporary labor and working-class history in the United States, however, remains the Popular Front image of workers, best articulated and explored in Michael Denning, *The Cultural Front: The Laboring of American Culture in the Twentieth Century* (New York: Verso, 1996). Two significant works that have influenced contemporary labor history are W.E.B. DuBois, *Black Reconstruction* (New York: Russell and Russell, 1935), from which current literature on labor and whiteness studies can be traced, and C.L.R. James, *Black Jacobins: Toussaint L'Ouverture and the San Domingo Revolution* (1st pub.1938; New York: Vintage Books, 1963), who, in his reconstruction of the Haitian Revolution, provided a model for labor historians interested in worker self-organization. See David Roediger, '"Labor in White Skin": Race and U.S. Working-Class History', in *Reshaping the U.S. Left*, ed. by Mike Davis and Michael Sprinker (London: Verso, 1988), pp. 287–307; and Francille Rusan Wilson, *The Segregated Scholars: Black Social Scientists and the Creation of Black Labor Studies, 1890–1950* (Charlottesville: University of Virginia Press, 2006), which provide insights into the diverse origins of labor history and allied studies.

2 By the early 1970s, the New Labor History, both as embedded in, and as distinct from, the new social history, had emerged as a recognizable subfield. Early assessments include Paul Faler, 'Working-Class Historiography', *Radical America*, 3 (1969), 56–68; Thomas A. Krueger, 'American Labor Historiography, Old and New', *Journal of Social History*, 4 (1971), 277–85; Robert Zieger, 'Workers and Scholars: Recent Trends in American Labor Historiography', *Labor History*, 13 (1972), 245–66. It was Zieger who, with foresight, predicted that synthesis would elude labor historians and, we might add, bedevil them as well. See also A.A.M. van der Linden, *A Revolt Against*

Liberalism: American Radical Historians, 1959–1976 (Amsterdam: Rodopi, 1996), pp. 133–51, for the New Left influences on the new labor history.

3 John R. Commons, David J. Saposs, Helen L. Sumner, E.B. Mittelman, H.E. Hoagland, John B. Andrews, Selig Perlman, Don D. Lescohier, Elizabeth Brandeis and Philip Taft, *History of the Labor Movement in the United States*, 4 vols, (New York: Macmillan, 1918–1935); John R. Commons, Ulrich B. Phillips, Eugene A. Gilmore, Helen L. Sumner and John B. Andrews, *A Documentary History of the American Industrial Society*, 10 vols, (Cleveland: A.H. Clark, 1910–11); Selig Perlman, *A History of the Labor Movement in the United States* (New York: Macmillan, 1923); idem, *A Theory of the Labor Movement* (New York: Macmillan, 1928); see also Philip Taft, 'A Rereading of Selig Perlman's "A Theory of the Labor Movement"', *Industrial and Labor Relations Review*, 4 (1950), 70–77. Taft, often recognized as the heir to the Wisconsin School, published a series of narrative histories on the American Federation of Labor and other international unions. See the special issue on Taft, *Labor History*, 19, 1 (1978).

4 American Social History Project, *Who Built America? Working People and the Nation's Economy, Politics, Culture and Society*, 2 vols (New York: Pantheon, 1989, 1992).

5 Philip S. Foner, *A History of the Labor Movement in the United States*, 10 vols (New York: International Publishers, 1947–1994), was his unfinished project (The tenth volume ends before the rise of the CIO). Foner authored over one hundred books on the labor movement, some of which treat later labor movements. For an assessment, see Melvyn Dubofsky, 'Give Us That Old Time Labor History: Philip S. Foner and the American Worker', *Labor History*, 26 (1985), 118–37.

6 Indeed, contemporary labor activists and scholars' understanding of the underlying fragmentation and differentiation of the working classes in the United States is intimately connected with the history of the labor movement, its limitations and its possibilities for survival in the twenty-first century. See David Roediger's thoughtful essay, 'What If Labor Were Not White and Male? Recentering Working-Class History and Reconstructing the Debates on Unions and Race', *International Labor and Working-Class History*, 51 (1997), 72–95.

7 For studies of the Wisconsin School, see Maurice Isserman, '"God Bless Our American Institutions": The Labor History of John R. Commons', *Labor History*, 17 (1976), 309–28; Leon Fink, '"Intellectuals" versus "Workers": Academic Requirements and the Creation of Labor History', *American Historical Review*, 96 (1991), 395–421; idem, *Progressive Intellectuals and the Dilemmas of Democratic Commitment* (Cambridge, MA: Harvard University Press, 1997), pp. 52–79; Bruce Kaufman, 'John R. Commons and the Wisconsin School on Industrial Relations Strategy and Policy', *Industrial and Labor Relations* Review, 57 (2003), 3–30; idem, 'Industrial Relations and Labor Institutionalism: A Century of Boom and Bust', *Labor History*, 47 (2006), 295–318; Malcolm Rutherford, 'Wisconsin Institutionalism: John R. Commons and His Students', *Labor History*, 47 (2006), 161–88. To place these developments

in context, see Ellen Fitzpatrick, *History's Memory: Writing America's Past, 1880–1980* (Cambridge, MA: Harvard University Press, 2002).

8 For a brief account of the journal's origins, see Richard B. Morris, 'Preface', *The Labor History Reader*, ed. by Daniel J. Leab, (Urbana: University of Illinois Press, 1985), pp. xiii–xvi; David Brody and Herbert Gutman, 'Introduction', in ibid., pp. xvii–xx; see also *Labor History*, 1, 1 (1960); Daniel J. Leab, 'Labor History: Past, Present, and Future', *Labor History*, 42 (2001), 325–6; Zieger, 'Workers and Scholars'.

9 *Labor History*, 1, 1 (1960). For a somewhat disingenuous account of the 'founding' of the new labor history, see Melvyn Dubofsky, *Hard Work: The Making of Labor History* (Urbana: University of Illinois Press, 2007), pp. 5–40.

10 Writing history 'from the bottom up' became the slogan of the new social history and especially the history of workers. See, for example, Jesse Lemisch, 'Jack Tar in the Streets: Merchant Seamen in the Politics of the American Revolution', *William and Mary Quarterly*, 21 (1968), 371–417; *Rank and File: Personal Histories of Working-Class Organizers*, ed. by Alice and Staughton Lynd (Boston: Beacon Press, 1973).

11 Historians often point to the Civil Rights movement and the New Left as sources for the new labor history, but rank-and-file worker movements played a significant role in recasting the view of labor's past. A recent study is Sheila Cohen, 'The 1968–1974 Labor Upsurge in Britain and America: A Critical History and a Look at What Might Have Been', *Labor History*, 49 (2008), 395–418; see also Stanley Aronowitz, *False Promises: The Shaping of American Working-Class Consciousness* (New York: MacGraw Hill, 1973); Dan Georgakas and Marvin Surkin, *Detroit, I Do Mind Dying: A Study in Urban Revolution* (New York: St. Martin's, 1975); Dan La Botz, *Rank-and-File Rebellion: Teamsters for a Democratic Union* (London and New York: Verso, 1990); Philip W. Nyden, *Steelworkers Rank and File: The Political Economy of a Union Reform Movement* (New York: Bergin and Garvey, 1984); Glenn Perusek and Kent Worcester, *Trade Union Politics: American Unions and Economic Change, 1960s–1990s* (Atlantic Highlands: Humanities Press, 1995). On the sometimes ambivalent relationship of the New Left to the labor movement of the time, see Peter B. Levy, *The New Left and Labor in the 1960s* (Urbana: University of Illinois Press, 1994), especially pp. 108–66.

12 Important accounts of the new labor history include David Brody, 'The Old Labor History and the New: In Search of an American Working Class', *Labor History*, 17 (1976), 485–509; idem, 'Reconciling the Old Labor History and the New', *Pacific Historical Review*, 62 (1993), 1–18; David Montgomery, 'To Study the People: The American Working Class', *Labor History*, 21 (1980), 485–512. For calls to return to union-centred history, see Howard Kimeldorf, 'Bringing the Unions Back In (or Why We Need a New Old Labor History)', *Labor History*, 32 (1991), 91–103, and comments and response, 104-129; Ira Katznelson, 'The "Bourgeois" Dimension: A Provocation about Institutions, Politics, and the Future of Labor History', *International Labor and Working-Class History*, 46 (1994), 7–32.

13 There are too many studies to be listed here. Representative examples for the nineteenth century would include Alan Dawley, *Class and Community: The Industrial Revolution in Lynn, Massachusetts* (Cambridge, MA: Harvard University Press, 1976); Daniel Walkowitz, *Worker City, Company Town: Iron and Cotton Workers' Protest in Cohoes, New York, 1855–1885* (Urbana: University of Illinois Press, 1978); Thomas Dublin, *Women at Work: The Transformation of Work and Community in Lowell, Massachusetts, 1826–1860* (New York: Columbia University Press, 1979); Bruce Laurie, *The Working People of Philadelphia, 1800–1850* (Philadelphia: Temple University Press, 1980); Sean Wilentz, *Chants Democratic: New York City and the Rise of the American Working Class* (New York: Oxford University Press, 1984); Peter Rachleff, *Black Labor in the South* (Philadelphia: Temple University Press, 1984); Leon Fink, *Workingmen's Democracy: The Knights of Labor and American Politics* (Urbana: University of Illinois Press, 1985); Steven J. Ross, *Workers on the Edge: Work, Leisure and Politics in Industrializing Cincinnati, 1788–1890* (New York: Cambridge University Press, 1985); Christine Stansell, *City of Women: Sex and Class in New York City, 1790–1860* (New York: Knopf, 1986); on the twentieth century, John T. Cumbler, *Working-Class Community in Industrial America: Work, Leisure and Struggle in Two Industrial Cities, 1880–1930* (Westport: Greenwood Press, 1979); David Corbin, *Life, Work and Rebellion in the Coal Fields* (Urbana: University of Illinois Press, 1981); James R. Barrett, *Work and Community in the Jungle: Chicago's Packinghouse Workers, 1894*–1922 (Urbana: University of Illinois Press, 1987); Gary Gerstle, *Working-Class Americanism: The Politics of Labor in a Textile City, 1914–1960* (Cambridge: Cambridge University Press, 1989); Lizabeth Cohen, *Making a New Deal: Industrial Workers in Chicago, 1919–1939* (Cambridge: Cambridge University Press, 1990); Elizabeth Faue, *Community of Suffering and Struggle: Men, Women, and the Labor Movement in Minneapolis, 1915–1945* (Chapel Hill: University of North Carolina Press, 1991); Ardis Cameron, *Radicals of the Worst Sort: Laboring Women in Lawrence, Massachusetts, 1860–1912* (Urbana: University of Illinois Press, 1993); Mary Murphy, *Mining Cultures: Men, Women, and Leisure in Butte,1914–1941* (Urbana: University of Illinois Press, 1997); Elizabeth Jameson, *All That Glitters: Class, Conflict, and Community in Cripple Creek* (Urbana: University of Illinois Press, 1998); Laurie Mercier, *Anaconda: Labor, Community and Culture in a Montana Smelter City* (Urbana: University of Illinois Press, 2001); Frank Tobias Higbie, *Indispensable Outcasts: Hobo Workers and Community in the American Midwest, 1880–1930* (Urbana: University of Illinois Press, 2003); Randi Storch, *Red Chicago: American Communism at its Grassroots, 1928–1935* (Urbana: University of Illinois Press, 2008).

14 Herbert G. Gutman, *The Black Family in Slavery and Freedom* (New York: Random House, 1976); idem, *Work, Culture and Society in Industrializing America* (New York: Random House, 1976); idem, *Power and Culture: Essays on the American Working Class*, ed. by Ira Berlin (New York: Pantheon, 1987).

15 David Montgomery, 'Gutman's Nineteenth Century America', *Labor History*,

19 (1978), 416–29; special issue on Herbert G. Gutman, *Labor History*, 29, 3 (1988), ed. by David Brody; Melvyn Dubofsky, 'If All the World Were Paterson: Herbert Gutman, the American Working Class, and the Future of Labor History', in Dubofsky, *Hard Work*, pp. 220–34. For an extension of Gutman's argument about class formation and development that foregrounds worker agency, see James R. Barrett, 'Americanization from the Bottom Up: Immigration and the Remaking of the Working Class in the United States, 1880–1930', *Journal of American History*, 79 (1992), 996–1020.

16 David Montgomery, *Beyond Equality: Labor and the Radical Republicans, 1862–1872* (New York: Knopf, 1967); idem, 'Working Classes of the Pre-industrial City', *Labor History*, 9 (1968), 3–22; idem, 'The Shuttle and the Cross: Weavers and Artisans in the Kensington Riots of 1844', *Journal of Social History*, 5 (1972), 411–39.

17 David Montgomery, *Workers' Control in America: Studies in the History of Work, Technology, and Labor Struggles* (Cambridge: Cambridge University Press, 1979), a compilation of his essays on this theme. For a study with similar methods, see Bruno Ramirez, *When Workers Fight: The Politics of Industrial Relations in the Progressive Era, 1898–1916* (Westport: Greenwood Press, 1978).

18 David Montgomery, *The Fall of the House of Labor: The Workplace, The State and American Labor Activism, 1865–1925* (Cambridge: Cambridge University Press, 1987). For his influence on what some have called 'the Pittsburgh School', see Alan Dawley, 'The Worker's Brain under the Historian's Cap', *Radical History Review*, 40 (1988), 101–114; James Barrett, 'Class Act: David Montgomery, The "Pittsburgh School", and Working-Class Historiography', presented at the North American Labor History Conference, October 2002, paper in the author's possession; idem, 'Class Act: An Interview with David Montgomery', *Labor: Studies in Working-Class History in the Americas*, 1 (2004), 23–54. Among his students, Julie Greene, *Pure and Simple Politics: The American Federation of Labor and Political Activism, 1881–1917* (Cambridge: Cambridge University Press, 1998), follows most closely the early political thrust of Montgomery's work. See also Eric Arnesen, *Waterfront Workers of New Orleans: Race, Class and Politics, 1863–1923* (New York: Oxford University Press, 1991); Dana Frank, *Purchasing Power: Consumer Organizing, Gender and the Seattle Labor Movement, 1919–1929* (Cambridge: Cambridge University Press, 1994), both of which approach their subjects through the door of workplace-based political organization.

19 Representative studies include Walter Licht, *Working for the Railroad: The Organization of Work in the Nineteenth Century* (Princeton: Princeton University Press, 1983); Ronald Schatz, *Electrical Workers: A History of Labor at General Electric and Westinghouse, 1923–1960* (Urbana: University of Illinois Press, 1983); Mark McColloch, *White Collar Workers in Transition: The Boom Years, 1940–1970* (Westport: Greenwood Press, 1983); David Bensman, *The Practice of Solidarity: American Hat Finishers in the Nineteenth Century* (Urbana: University of Illinois Press, 1985); Susan Porter Benson, *Counter Cultures: Saleswomen, Managers and Customers in American Department Stores,*

1890–1940 (Urbana: University of Illinois Press, 1986); Patricia Cooper, *Once a Cigar Maker: Men, Women and Work Culture in American Cigar Factories, 1900–1919* (Urbana: University of Illinois Press, 1987); Shelton Stromquist, *A Generation of Boomers: The Pattern of Railroad Conflict in Nineteenth Century America* (Urbana: University of Illinois Press, 1993); Peter Way, *Common Labor: Workers and the Digging of North American Canals, 1780–1860* (Cambridge: Cambridge University Press, 1993); Gunther Peck, *Reinventing Free Labor: Padrones and Immigrant Workers in the American West, 1880–1930* (Cambridge: Cambridge University Press, 2000). Recent work on masculinity has revived this aspect of labor history; see, for example, Steve Meyer, 'Work, Play and Power: Masculine Culture on the Automotive Shop Floor, 1930–1960', in *Boys and Their Toys? Masculinity, Technology, and Class in America*, ed. by Roger Horowitz, (New York: Routledge, 2001), pp. 33–53; Nancy Quam-Wickham, 'Rereading Man's Conquest of Nature: Skill, Myths, and the Historical Reconstruction of Masculinity in Western Extractive Industries', in Horowitz, *Boys and Their Toys?*, pp. 91–110.

20 Irving Bernstein, *The Lean Years: A History of the American Worker, 1920–1933* (Boston: Houghton Mifflin, 1960); idem, *The Turbulent Years: A History of the American Worker, 1933–1941* (Boston: Houghton Mifflin, 1969); idem, *A Caring Society: The New Deal, the Worker and the Great Depression* (Boston: Houghton Mifflin, 1985); 'Irving Bernstein's Labor History: A Symposium', *Labor History*, 37 (1995–1996), 75–110. The work of Sidney Fine is in a similar vein. See, for example, Sidney Fine, *Sit-Down: The General Motors Strike of 1936–1937* (Ann Arbor: University of Michigan Press, 1969).

21 David Brody, *Steelworkers in America: The Non-Union Era* (Cambridge, MA: Harvard University Press, 1960); idem, *Labor in Crisis: The Steel Strike of 1919* (Philadelphia: Lippincott, 1965); idem, *Workers in Industrial America: Essays on the Twentieth Century Struggle* (New York: Oxford University Press, 1981), are only a few of his works. For Brody's influence, see, for example, Michael Kazin, *Barons of Labor: The San Francisco Building Trades and Union Power in the Progressive Era* (Urbana: University of Illinois Press, 1987); Bruce Nelson, *Workers on the Waterfront: Seamen, Longshoremen, and Unionism in the 1930s* (Urbana: University of Illinois Press, 1989); Marjorie Murphy, *Blackboard Unions: The AFT and the NEA* (Ithaca: Cornell University Press, 1991); Dorothy Sue Cobble, *Dishing It Out: Waitresses and Their Unions in the Twentieth Century* (Urbana: University of Illinois Press, 1992); Joshua Freeman, *Working-Class New York: Life and Labor since 1945* (New York: Metropolitan Books, 2000). Nelson Lichtenstein's work similarly can be described as part of the neo-institutional school of labor history: see Nelson Lichtenstein, *Labor's War at Home* (Cambridge: Cambridge University Press, 1982); idem, *The Most Dangerous Man in Detroit: Walter Reuther and the Fate of American Labor* (New York: Basic Books, 1995); idem, *The State of the Union: A Century of American Labor* (Princeton: Princeton University Press, 2002); Kevin Boyle, *The UAW and the Heyday of American Liberalism, 1945–1968* (Ithaca: Cornell University Press, 1998) is cut from similar cloth. For alternative neo-institutional approaches, see Christopher L. Tomlins, *The*

State and the Unions: Labor Relations, Law and the Organized Labor Movement in America, 1880–1960 (Cambridge: Cambridge University Press, 1985); Richard A. Greenwald, *The Triangle Fire, the Protocols of Peace, and Industrial Democracy in Progressive Era New York* (Philadelphia: Temple University Press, 2005).

22 See Melvyn Dubofsky, *We Shall Be All: A History of the Industrial Workers of the World* (Chicago: Quadrangle Books, 1969); idem, *The State and Labor in Modern America* (Chapel Hill: University of North Carolina Press, 1994). Important heirs to this approach are Colin J. Davis, *Power at Odds: The 1922 National Railroad Shopmen's Strike* (Urbana: University of Illinois Press, 1997), and Joseph A. McCartin, *Labor's Great War: The Struggle for Industrial Democracy and the Origins of Modern American Labor Relations, 1912–1921* (Chapel Hill: University of North Carolina Press, 1998).

23 *Social Science History* 1, 1 (1976), republished the association's constitution.

24 The most important text is Stephen Thernstom, *Poverty and Progress: Social Mobility in the Nineteenth Century* (Cambridge, MA: Harvard University Press, 1964); see also Clyde and Sally Griffen, *Natives and Newcomers: The Ordering of Opportunity in Nineteenth Century Poughkeepsie* (Cambridge, MA: Harvard University Press, 1978); Charles Stephenson, '"There's Plenty Waiting at the Gates": Mobility, Opportunity, and the American Worker', in *Life and Labor: Dimensions of American Working-Class History*, ed. by Charles Stephenson and Robert Asher (Albany: SUNY Press, 1986), pp. 72–91; Ileen A. De Vault, *Sons and Daughters of Labor: Class and Clerical Work in Turn-of-the-Century Pittsburgh* (Ithaca: Cornell University Press, 1990). For a critique, see James A. Henretta, 'The Study of Social Mobility: Ideological Assumptions and Conceptual Bias', as reprinted in Leab, *The Labor History Reader*, pp. 28–41.

25 *Social Science History*, 4, 1 (1980), which includes David Montgomery's essay on strikes in nineteenth century America. The article critiques Edward Shorter and Charles Tilly, *Strikes in France, 1830–1968* (Cambridge: Cambridge University Press, 1974), one sign of the engagement of American labor historians with the growing literature on European industrialization and worker protest.

26 *Radical America* began publishing in 1967; in 1983, James R. Green edited a collection of its essays on working-class history entitled, *Workers' Struggles, Past and Present: A Radical America Reader* (Philadelphia: Temple University Press, 1983). *Radical History Review* started publication in 1975, as a continuation of the *MARHO Newsletter*. The book-length account of the origins and influence of the Radical Historians is van der Linden, *Revolt Against Liberalism*, esp. pp. 133–50.

27 See the association's website: http://southernlaborstudies.org/Site/About.html. For LAWCHA, see below.

28 Announcement, *Labor History* 15 (1974), 315; see Sally M. Miller, 'On Involving Labor in Labor Studies', *Newsletter, European Labor and Working-Class History*, 8 (1975), 13–15. Miller noted that labor historians would eventually found a national association, perhaps, she said optimistically, after two or three annual meetings, as an effort to connect the regional labor studies

groups with state labor history societies.

29 Christopher H. Johnson, Robert Zieger and Elizabeth Faue, 'Twenty-Fifth Anniversary Meeting of the North American Labor History Conference', *Labor, War and Imperialism*, Twentieth-Fifty Annual NALHC Program, October 16–18, 2003. The current NALHC website has digital copies of the first thirty conference programs: http://nalhc.wayne.edu/NALHC/30_Years.html. *International Labor and Working-Class History* sporadically published conference reports. See, for example, Michael Hanagan, 'Second Annual North American Labor History Conference', *International Labor and Working-Class History*, 19 (1981), 57.

30 *Perspectives in American Labor History: The Problem of Synthesis*, ed. by J. Carroll Moody and Alice Kessler-Harris (DeKalb: Northern Illinois University Press, 1989).

31 For the critical literature, see Robin Kelley, '"We Are Not What We Seem": Rethinking Black Working-Class Opposition in the Jim Crow South', *Journal of American History*, 80 (1993), 75–112; Alice Kessler-Harris, 'Treating the Male as Other: Re-defining the Parameters of Labor History', *Labor History*, 34 (1993), 190–204; David Roediger, 'Race and the Working-Class Past in the United States: Multiple Identities and the Future of Labor History', in *International Review of Social History*, 38 (1993), Supplement 1, 'The End of Labour History?', 127–43; Herbert Hill, 'The Problem of Race in Labor History', *Reviews in American History*, 24 (1996), 180–208; Eric Arnesen, 'Up from Exclusion: Black and White Workers, Race and the State of Labor History', *Reviews in American History*, 26 (1998), 146–74; Elizabeth Faue, 'Reproducing the Class Struggle: Class, Gender and Social Reproduction in U.S. Labor History', *Mitteilungsblatt des Instituts für soziale Bewegungen*, 25 (2001), 47–66; idem, 'Gender, Class, and History', in *New Working-Class Studies*, ed. by John Russo and Sherry Lee Linkon (Ithaca: Cornell University Press, 2005), pp. 19–31.

32 *Labor History*, 10, 3 (1969), published a special issue on the Black worker; *Labor History*, 17, 1 (1976) was a special issue devoted to women and work, and later reprinted as *Class, Sex and the Woman Worker*, ed. by Milton Cantor and Bruce Laurie (Westport: Greenwood, 1978); *Labor History*, 34, 2–3 (1993), was a special issue on gender and labor history, edited by Elizabeth Faue; *Labor History*, 35, 4 (1994), was a special issue on race and labor, edited by Joe William Trotter, Jr. Other journals have followed suit in showcasing these aspects of labor and working-class history. See the recent special issue, 'Working-Class Subjectivities and Sexualities', *International Labor and Working-Class History*, 69 (2006); and the forum on 'The Body at Work: How Useful a Historical Concept?', *Labor: Studies in Working-Class History in the Americas*, 4 (2007), 23–64.

33 Joan Wallach Scott, *Gender and the Politics of History* (New York: Columbia University Press, 1988); *Work Engendered: Toward a New Labor History*, ed. by Ava Baron (Ithaca: Cornell University Press, 1991); Nan Enstad, *Ladies of Labor, Girls of Adventure: Working Women, Popular Culture, and Labor Politics at the Turn of the Century* (New York: Columbia University Press, 1999), and

Daniel E. Bender, *Sweated Work, Weak Bodies: Anti-Sweatshop Campaigns and Languages of Labor* (New Brunswick: Rutgers University Press, 2004) use gender analysis in similar ways. See also Bryan Palmer's critique, *Descent into Discourse: The Reification of Language and the Writing of Social History* (Philadelphia: Temple University Press, 1990), esp. pp. 48–144.

34 Among her works, see Alice Kessler-Harris, *Out to Work: A History of Wage-Earning Women in the United States* (New York: Oxford University Press, 1982); idem, *In Pursuit of Equity: Women, Men, and the Quest for Economic Citizenship in Twentieth Century America* (New York: Oxford University Press, 2002); idem, *Gendering Labor History* (Urbana: University of Illinois Press, 2007). Kessler-Harris was not alone in exploring the issues of gender discrimination in the labor movement. See James Kenneally, 'Women in Trade Unions, 1870–1920', *Labor History*, 14 (1973), 45–55; Nancy Gabin, 'Women Workers and the UAW in the Post-World War II Period', *Labor History*, 21 (1979–1980), 373–98; Ruth Milkman, 'Organizing the Sexual Division of Labor: Historical Perspectives on Women's Work and the American Labor Movement', *Socialist Review*, 49 (1980), 95–150; Ann Schofield, 'Rebel Girls and Union Maids: The Woman Question in the Journals of the AFL and the IWW', *Feminist Studies*, 9 (1983), 335–58; Sharon Hartman Strom, 'Challenging "Woman's Place": Feminism, the Left and Industrial Unionism in the 1930s', *Feminist Studies*, 9 (1983), 359–86. See also Nancy Gabin, *Feminism in the Labor Movement: Women and the United Autoworkers, 1935–1975* (Ithaca: Cornell University Press, 1990); Nancy Maclean, 'The Hidden History of Affirmative Action: Working Women's Organizations in Workplace Struggles in the 1970s and the Gender of Class', *Feminist Studies*, 25 (1999), 43–78; Dennis Deslippe, *Rights, Not Roses: Unions and the Rise of Working-Class Feminism, 1945–1960* (Urbana: University of Illinois Press, 2000); Dorothy Sue Cobble, *The Other Women's Movement: Workplace Justice and Social Rights in Modern America* (Princeton: Princeton University Press, 2005).

35 The classic text is W.E.B. DuBois, *Black Recontruction in America* (New York: Harcourt, Brace, 1935), almost wholly ignored at the time of its publication but rediscovered in the 1970s as both the new labor history and African-American history came to the fore. More recently, DuBois's construction of the white worker has spurred whiteness studies and in particular the work of David Roediger: see his *The Wages of Whiteness: Race and the Making of the American Working Class* (London: Verso, 1991); idem, *The Abolition of Whiteness: Essays on Race, Politics, and Working-Class History* (London: Verso, 1994); Neil Foley, *The White Scourge: Mexicans, Blacks, and Poor Whites in Texas Cotton Culture* (Berkeley: University of California Press, 1997). There have been prolific studies of African-American, Mexican-American, and Asian-American workers. A representative sample includes Vicki L. Ruiz, *Cannery Women, Cannery Lives: Mexican Women, Unionization, and the California Food Processing Industry, 1930–1950* (Albuquerque: University of New Mexico Press, 1987); Joe W. Trotter, Jr, *Coal, Class and Color: Blacks in Southern West Virginia, 1915–1932* (Urbana: University of Illinois, 1990); Robin Kelley, *Hammer and Hoe: Alabama Communists During the Great Depression* (Chapel

Hill: University of North Carolina Press, 1990); Michael K. Honey, *Southern Workers and Civil Rights: Organizing Memphis Workers* (Urbana: University of Illinois Press, 1993); Chris Friday, *Organizing Asian-American Labor: The Pacific Coast Canned-Salmon Industry, 1870–1942* (Philadelphia: Temple University Press, 1995); Tera Hunter, *'To Joy My Freedom': Southern Black Women's Lives and Labors after the Civil War* (Cambridge, MA: Harvard University Press, 1997); Rick Halpern, *Down on the Killing Floor: Black and White Workers in Chicago's Packinghouses, 1904–1954* (Urbana: University of Illinois Press, 1997); Daniel Letwin, *The Challenge of Interracial Unionism: Alabama Coal Miners, 1878–1921* (Chapel Hill: University of North Carolina Press, 1998); Kimberly Philips, *Alabama North: African-American Migrants, Community, and Working-Class Activism in Cleveland, 1915–1945* (Urbana: University of Illinois Press, 2000); Peter Cole, *Wobblies on the Waterfront: Interracial Unionism in Progressive-Era Philadelphia* (Urbana: University of Illinois Press, 2002); Dorothy B. Fujita-Rony, *American Workers, Colonial Power: Philippine Seattle and the Transpacific Northwest, 1919–1941* (Berkeley: University of California Press, 2002); Eric Arnesen, *Brotherhoods of Color: Black Railroad Workers and the Struggle for Equality* (Cambridge, MA: Harvard University Press, 2002); Robert Korstad, *Civil Rights Unionism: Tobacco Workers and the Struggle for Democracy in the Twentieth Century South* (Chapel Hill: University of North Carolina Press, 2003); William P. Jones, *The Tribe of Black Ulysses: African American Lumber Workers in the Jim Crow South* (Urbana: University of Illinois Press, 2005); Zaragosa Vargas, *Labor Rights are Civil Rights: Mexican American Workers in Twentieth Century America* (Princeton: Princeton University Press, 2007); David M. Lewis-Coleman, *Race Against Liberalism: Black Workers and the UAW in Detroit* (Urbana: University of Illinois Press, 2008).

36 The plenary papers and a selection of others were published as a special issue on gender and labor history, *Labor History*, 34, 2–3 (1993).

37 Selected papers were published in a special issue, 'The Working Classes and the Urban Public Sphere', *Social Science History*, 24,1 (2000).

38 Nineteenth Annual North American Labor History Conference, *Workers and the City* conference program, October 23–25, 1997; James R. Barrett, 'National Association for Working-Class History', *International Labor and Working-Class History*, 53 (1998), 191–94. See also LAWCHA's website: http://www.lawcha.org/index.php

39 Kitty Krupat, Sherry Linkon, Dorian Warren and Michael Zweig to 'Dear Colleagues', letter, July 2, 2004; Sherry Linkon to Elizabeth Faue, email, June 7, 2004; 'Working-Class Studies Association – Planning Notes', [2004]; all in the author's possession; *Working-Class Notes*, 7, 2 (2004), documents the original organizing meeting in April 2004.

40 Elizabeth Faue, 'Gender, Class and History', David Roediger, '"More than Two Things": The State of the Art of Labor History', and Kimberley L. Phillips, '"All I Wanted Was a Steady Job": The State and African American Workers', in Russo and Linkon, *New Working-Class Studies*, pp. 19–53. These essays directly address labor history as part of Working-Class Studies.

Another important source, however, is folklore studies. A recent study of Archie Green, an important folklorist and labor historian, comes the closest to a full-length examination: Sean Burns, 'Vernacular Strut: The Intellectual and Activist Legacy of Archie Green', unpublished PhD thesis, University of California-Santa Cruz, 2008; see also Kieran Taylor, Interview, 'Shipwrights and Salmonbellies: How Archie Green Discovered Laborlore', *Labor: Studies in Working-Class History in the Americas*, 4 (2007), 33–58. The work of George Lipsitz on popular music and film provides another angle on working-class culture and experience pertinent to labor history.

41 One indication of the changing times was Thomas Dublin, 'Labor History on the World Wide Web: Thoughts of Jumping onto a Moving Express Train', *Labor History*, 43 (2002), 69–79, updating an earlier article, John H. Summers, 'The Future of Labor's Past: American Labor History on the World Wide Web', *Labor History*, 40 (1999), 69–79.

42 Jacquelyn Dowd Hall, James Leloudis, Robert Korstad, Mary Murphy, Lu Ann Jones and Christopher P. Daly, *Like a Family: The Cotton Mill Workers' World* (Chapel Hill: University of North Carolina Press, 1987). For a study with similar strengths, see Korstad, *Civil Rights Unionism.*

43 Recent labor biographies include Paula F. Pfeffer, *A. Philip Randolph: Pioneer of the Civil Rights Movement* (Baton Rouge: Louisiana State University Press, 1990); James R. Barrett, *William Z. Foster and the Tragedy of American Communism* (Urbana: University of Illinois Press, 1999); Yvette Richards, *Maida Springer: Pan Africanist and International Labor Leader* (Pittsburgh: University of Pittsburgh Press, 2000); Elizabeth Faue, *Writing the Wrongs: Eva Valesh and the Rise of Labor Journalism* (Ithaca: Cornell University Press, 2002). On the new subjective dimension, see Kathleen Brown and Elizabeth Faue, 'Social Bonds, Sexual Politics, and Political Community on the U.S. Left, 1920s-1940s', *Left History*, 7 (Spring 2000), 9–45; idem, 'Revolutionary Desire: Redefining the Politics of Sexuality of American Radicals, 1919–1945', in *Sexual Borderlands: Constructing an American Sexual Past*, ed. by Kathleen Kennedy and Sharon Ullman (Columbus: Ohio State University Press, 2003), pp. 273–302; Elizabeth Faue, 'Retooling the Class Factory: United States Labour after Marx, Montgomery and Postmodernism', *Labour History*, 82 (2002), 109–19; James R. Barrett, 'Was the Personal Political? Reading the Autobiography of American Communism', *International Review of Social History*, 53 (2008), 395–423. Joshua Greenberg, *Advocating the Man: Masculinity, Organized Labor, and the Household in New York, 1800–1840* (New York: Columbia University Press, 2008) employs these dimensions in ways that enrich our earlier understanding of the antebellum working class.

44 Recent studies include Jefferson R. Cowie, *Capital Moves: RCA's Seventy-Year Quest for Cheap Labor* (New York: New Press, 2000); David Pellow and Lisa Park, *Silicon Valley of Dreams: Environmental Justice, Immigrant Workers, and the High-Tech Global Economy* (New York: NYU Press, 2002); Leon Fink, *The Maya of Morganton: Work and Community in the Nuevo New South* (Urbana: University of Illinois Press, 2007); Aviva Chomsky, *Linked Labor Histories: New England, Colombia, and the Making of a Global Working Class* (Durham: Duke University Press, 2008).

6

Canada

Bryan D. Palmer

The writing of Canadian labour history has always unfolded at the interface of national specificity and international currents of influence, be they in the realm of analysis or activism. Yet an assessment of Canadian working-class history's rise and reconfiguration also highlights some 'peculiarities of the Canadians'. First, Canada is a big country, but its academic culture is decidedly small. This means that debates within Canadian labour history can be, and have easily become, quite sharp and, even, personalized. Second, with a weak communist tradition but a strong social democratic presence, a scholarly field such as labour history tended to concentrate attention on contentious differences within the left, especially as these were evident, initially, in social history's rise and, subsequently, in cultural history's later challenges. Third, for these and other reasons, working-class history in Canada has arguably had a much greater influence on more general historiographic debates and trends than in other countries, where study of workers' pasts may well be more insulated from the hegemonic mainstream. Fourth, and finally, labour historians have played an important role in the upper reaches of the academic profession in Canada, perhaps more so than in any other country. All things considered, labour history in Canada has led a charmed life. And yet it is both relatively young and not without something of a tumultuous past.

The past as prologue

Until the modern labour historiography of Canada emerged out of the ferment of the 1960s, professional historians played second fiddle to a band of economists, political scientists, and even specialists in English Literature in writing on the country's workers and their labour movement.[1] Paralleling these academic developments were radical and Communist commentaries, but such writing was hardly influential, especially in comparison with other English-speaking settings.[2] By the 1960s, Communist publications that addressed the history of class formation in Canada and the development of the trade union movement included Charles Lipton's *Trade Union Movement of Canada, 1827–1959* (1966) and Stanley Ryerson's *Unequal Union: Confederation and the Roots of Conflict in the Canadas, 1815–1873* (1968). An autodidactic dissident Communist, Jack Scott, expelled from the Communist Party of Canada (CPC) in 1962, also produced a series of labour history studies in the 1960s and early 1970s. He opened one study with the declaration that: 'Historians – with a few honourable exceptions – take virtually no note of the existence of workers in society.'[3]

Lipton, Ryerson and Scott resonated with an emerging contingent of New Left-influenced students in the 1960s, to be sure.[4] As a mid-1960s historiographic article in the *Canadian Historical Review* by Stanley Mealing indicated, however, mainstream historians were by no means convinced that 'the concept of social class' was highly relevant to understanding national identity and the country's history.[5] Canada lacked anything comparable to the influence of the Hammonds, the Webbs and G.D.H. Cole in England, where the Fabian and moderate socialist analytic stream ran historically deep, with specific currents having a pronounced impact on disciplines and fields such as economics, history and political thought. Nothing comparable to the American Wisconsin School, associated with the substantial researches of John R. Commons, Richard T. Ely and Selig Perlman existed north of the forty-ninth parallel. Liberal individualism on the one hand, and patrician sensibilities, on the other, incarcerated most Canadian historians in an academic aesthetics that shunned approaching the nation and its past in class ways as troublingly base. '[T]he study of the common, or common-place man,' wrote Arthur R.M. Lower in 1929, 'if overdone, would no doubt make for common-place history.'[6]

Kenneth McNaught presented a similar barrier to new approaches to labour within the small 'left' of academic historiography. McNaught, a committed social democrat associated with the Co-operative Commonwealth Federation (CCF), had been schooled in the late-1940s variants of contemporary 'culture wars'. This education was a battleground that pitted moderate socialists of the parliamentary road against the nefarious 'reds', who threatened to bore from within essential democratic institutions, in the process contaminating if not destroying them. So small were the concentric circles of Canadian labour studies in this period that McNaught would leave his mark indelibly on what would come to be a post-1960s rupture of two intimately forged research cohorts. They began to create modern working-class history in the aftermath of what was arguably the country's most tumultuous decade.[7]

The layered 1960s: modern labour historiography and its divergent camps

One significant difference separating the historiography of Canadian workers from that of research and writing in other national contexts was that Canadian labour history gave rise to two roughly identifiable orientations to the study of class in English Canada in a relatively short time frame. In French Canada, a distinct labour historiography also appeared in the same period. These metaphorical 'generations' of scholarship were marked by decidedly different impulses and engagements, but all emerged from the cauldron of the 1960s.[8]

The first English Canadian contingent, which entered PhD programmes mostly in the early-to-mid-1960s, was largely untouched by Marxism and was either liberal or 'liberal in a hurry' (moderately social democratic). Arguably the most significant of its authors – David J. Bercuson and Irving Martin Abella – were trained at the University of Toronto by McNaught. The conception of the working class that animated this loose grouping was one of institution, episodic conflict, material inequality, the forward march of labour as enshrined in the realization of trade union entitlements such as collective bargaining, and an accent on labour politics that privileged the social democratic/labourist traditions. Framed very much within a national discourse, the scholarship of this cohort set new standards of professionalism in the writing of Canadian labour history.[9]

This initial production of modern labour history was recognizable in the moderation of its analytic directions as well as in its focus on the more modern period. Bercuson's history of the Winnipeg General Strike, for instance, concluded by stressing the 'futility and tragedy of massive confrontation combined with hysteria and intransigence', casting a plague on both the Houses of the militant labour left and the state ideologues and agencies of repression.[10] Abella's discussion of the Canadian Congress of Industrial Organizations (CIO) unions, the CCF and the CPC, acknowledged the often heavy-handed tactics adopted to drive the reds from the unions, pointing out that the expulsion of the left wing served the workers' movement poorly. Nonetheless, in Abella's view, the main story of the CIO in Canada was the achievement of 'an industrial union movement', albeit one dominated from without, not by Communists but by Americans.[11]

All of this was most emphatically a twentieth-century story. It was not uncommon for historians to suggest, as did Abella in an edited collection on major Canadian strikes, that: 'Labour's trauma started in Winnipeg in 1919. Until then its horizons had seemed unclouded and propitious.'[12] The struggle to achieve working-class rights was thus telescoped into a frame where state-labour relations dominated and victories were won in terms of trade union development, the achievement of collective bargaining rights, and political advances registered in the rise of parties willing to promote the cause of 'ordinary Canadians'. Studies of poverty in the industrial city and immigrant radicals complicated this Whiggish narrative somewhat, but most Canadian labour history was increasingly understandable against the backdrop of socialism's so-called early-to-mid 1940s 'golden age', when the CCF achieved electoral breakthroughs.[13]

One early figure who problematized this emerging, respectable face of labour history was Michael S. Cross. Cross studied the nineteenth century rather than the twentieth (in which he also had an interest), and was more concerned with the history of riot and raucous confrontation than he was in hitching the cart of workers' revolt to the wagon of social democracy.[14] In his exploration of the timber workers' social and ethnocultural conflict, articulated in a pioneering discussion of the Ottawa Valley Shiners' Wars of the 1830s, Cross addressed class less as an institution and more as a messy historical happening.[15] Cross thus linked metaphorical arms, not only with his generational colleagues who championed implicitly the study of the respectable faces of labour history, but also with a second loose grouping of social historians whose connections to the 1960s were more activist than accidental.

For members of this new contingent, their experience was often one of engagement with politics to the left of the now renamed social democratic successor to the CCF, the New Democratic Party (NDP). Never the tightly knit, coherent collectivity that some imagined it to be, members of this soon to be misnamed 'school' of 'new labour history' gravitated to one another, not so much out of an understanding of what they were *for* as on the basis of a shared appreciation of what they were *against.*[16] There was relatively common agreement that the history of class formation, rather than conventional accounts of the trade union and the political party, was what working-class history was all about. This was not to say, of course, that institutions and politics were unimportant, only that they were *part of* a larger process. In general, much of the initial research and writing of this cohort addressed the years from 1860 to 1930. Many of these emerging historians of the working class went to graduate schools in the United States, where they were educated in the break from the consensus historiography of Richard Hofstadter and other prominent figures of the 1950s. Others studied at Warwick University in England in the mid-to-late 1970s. All read widely in the international literature that was, from the mid-1960s onwards, making working-class history an exciting field, alive with new ideas and fresh perspectives.

E.P. Thompson's *The Making of the English Working Class* (1963) was, for many, an inspiring text, while others found in the circulation of Herbert G. Gutman's unpublished articles of the late 1960s a *samizdat*-like body of writing that opened new interpretive possibilities about ways to write about workers and their presence within and influence on civil society. Theory animated this new research agenda, perhaps as it never had before in the writing of Canadian history. Marx was read, of course, but so too were anthropologists like Claude Lévi-Strauss; subterranean thinkers such as Antonio Gramsci and Georg Lukács; commentators on the culture of everyday life, from George Lefebvre to Raymond Williams; and young New Leftists from both sides of the Atlantic: the sociologist C. Wright Mills, the feminist historian Sheila Rowbotham, and the impressively wide-ranging editor of the *New Left Review*, Perry Anderson.[17]

By the time that the first major statements of this loose historiographic approach appeared in the late 1970s and early 1980s, it was apparent that the now contentious field of labour history had in some ways rocked historians of Canada out of a complacent somnolence. My own *A Culture in Conflict: Skilled Workers and Industrial Capitalism in Hamilton, Ontario, 1860–1914* (1979), Gregory S. Kealey's *Toronto Workers Respond to Industrial Capitalism, 1867–1892* (1980), and our jointly-authored *Dreaming of What Might Be: The Knights of Labor in Ontario, 1880–1900* (1982), were all either nominated for major academic prizes or won such awards. Fair-minded commentators such as Ramsay Cook assessed such studies as significant breakthroughs.[18] Others were less generous. Bercuson, for instance, took aim at *Dreaming of What Might Be* and characterized it as 'pretentious, problematic, and tedious [...] a Sunday sermon [...] dry, boring, and devoid of any feeling for the workers'.[19]

Debates may well have been, in the words of the country's foremost historiographic commentator, Carl Berger, 'captious, intemperate, and confusing'. They also revealed the analytic fault lines that could run through *all* historical interpretation, whatever the claims to objectivity, however different the attachment to divergent understandings of political engagement. And Berger was generous in his acknowledgement that writing influenced by Thompson's 'humanistic Marxism' had 'recovered copious and scarcely suspected details on social life in the Victorian period [... helping] move to the centre of attention the social conflict that accompanied the arrival of industrial society, [... according] a place to ideas and attitudes in history that belied the commonplace image of Marxist scholarship as materialistic [...]'. Referring to the importance of quantitative methods and their significance within methodological debates in the 1970s, Berger also added, in a comparison that contrasted the approaches of Michael Katz and his highly funded and team-researched social history of stratification and inequality in Hamilton, Ontario, with the social histories of workers' struggle, that writing on late nineteenth-century class formation 'contributed far more to the ultimate clarification of class – and class in history – than the statisticians of social mobility'.[20]

At the pinnacle of the national historical culture, the *Canadian Historical Review*, edited in 1981 by Bercuson and J.L. Granatstein, commissioned a lead article on writing about labour and the left by the doyen of a patrician, social democratic approach to working-class studies, Kenneth McNaught. McNaught suggested that 'those young researchers who have been lovingly adapting E.P. Thompson to the mines, production lines, and even the countryside of Canada's past' needed to get back to appreciating how much the 'smart union leadership' of the 1930s and 1940s (which had extracted concessions from the employers, beaten back the reds and negotiated a place in the state-orchestrated system of post-World War II industrial pluralism) needed study and emulation. The goal of that sophisticated layer of union builders, McNaught stressed in the last line of his essay, 'was not to defend an Archie Bunker-charivari culture, but, rather, to liberate those who had been entrapped by the economic-cultural constraints imposed by political capitalists'. The *CHR* promptly awarded McNaught's essay, commissioned by partisans and itself a highly partisan statement, the journal's annual prize as the best article published in its pages.[21]

Years later, J.L. Granatstein, increasingly a spokesman for the view that Canadian historiography had overspecialized to the point of trivializing the country's past as the study of insignificant servant girls when there were important Prime Ministers to write about and momentous events such as wars and elections to commemorate, would conclude that 'the struggle for the past' began in Canada in labour history. 'The old-style institutional labour historians were either driven out of the field or left the field to seek new areas to work in', Granatstein wrote in 1998, adding: 'The Marxists had complete control of the labour history field, including the journals and the students, and they maintain it still, notwithstanding the discrediting of Marxism everywhere in the world. The universities, sheltered from the real world, continue to protect their Marxists.'[22] This was Canada's 'end of history'.[23]

Francophone historians of Quebec's working class were, for the most part, uninvolved in these historiographic controversies, nor was their work all that much referred to in the debates. This reflected the undeniable reality of Canada's 'two solitudes', which historians of the country struggled to bridge. To be sure, there was evidence of conceptual convergence. One of Kealey's first forays into the social history of nineteenth-century workers was an abridged edition of the critically important workers' testimony before the first Canadian Royal Commission investigating the conditions of labour and capital in the decade of Knights of Labor upheaval, the 1880s. This subject also captivated the attentions of Quebec's leading sociological commentator on class formation in this period, Fernand Harvey.[24] Abella's counterpart among francophone historians was the prolific Jacques Rouillard, who charted the nationalist course of Quebec's institutional labour history over the course of the twentieth century.[25] In both French and English Canada, the early 1970s preface to a spate of new histories was important bibliographic work.[26]

Yet the historiography of Quebec workers had indeed developed differently than had the study of labour in English Canada. Quebec historians, in general, looked more to interpretive trends associated with France, where the *Annales* School was prominent,[27] than they did to the British Marxists, such as Thompson, Christopher Hill and Eric Hobsbawm, or American social historians of working-class life such as Gutman or David Montgomery.[28] Working-class history in Quebec had long borne the imprint of Laval University's Jean Hamelin. His 1950s sojourn at the École Pratique des Hautes Études in Paris had schooled Hamelin in the unique structuralist blend of the materialism of Marxism and an *Annaliste* concern with the *longue durée*, especially as it was manifested in the economic conditions of the *menu peuple*. It was in many ways this intellectual interface that animated the work of Ernest Labrousse who, in turn, decidedly influenced both Hamelin and his most precocious collaborator, Fernand Ouellet. Ouellet would not so much be concerned with *labour* and *workers* as he was with a class analysis that did not sidestep Quebec's limitations. He was himself somewhat disappointed that the social history of Quebec's workers seemed routinized in institutional studies of trade unions and accounts of labour politics, most of which were firmly situated within conventional understandings of *la question nationale*.[29]

The Labroussian accent on long-term trends in the economic formation of society, in which particular points of demarcation were delineated as *conjonctures*, would factor in Quebec labour history's early attempts to address strike trends and patterns of class formation.[30] However much twentieth-century studies in Quebec tended to highlight the peculiarities of leadership and organization associated with the province's Catholic unions,[31] there was nevertheless significantly more attention paid to the pre-industrial capitalist era in Quebec than in English Canada, although maritime labour and early nineteenth-century poverty had been sensitively explored by Judith Fingard.[32] Stimulating studies of early artisans and apprenticeship resulted in publications founded upon the different kinds of documents relating to contracted craft training that proliferated because of French Canada's legal system and the importance of notarial records. They revealed an economic history premised on something other than the staples trade in fur pelts, fish and timber that had long been regarded as central to the ostensibly dominant mercantile order.[33] As the insightful work of Joanne Burgess suggested, the young cohort of working-class historians emerging in French Canada concentrated their interests on issues of labour recruitment processes and trade training.[34]

Ironic interlude: labour history's Canadian institutional formation

Trends in working-class history thus diverged within English Canada, just as the nature of the first sustained waves of labour scholarship in Quebec and the rest of the country seemed differentiated.[35] In spite of heated debates, which focused on institutional versus social accents in the writing of history, this was also a period in which the formal apparatus of a labour history *society* was established and consolidated. Marxists and non-Marxists, social democrats and dissident communist oppositionists, anglophone and francophone, westerners, easterners, and those in the Ontario 'centre' – all collaborated and worked together to establish the Committee on Canadian Labour History (CCLH). Historians such as Robert Babcock, whose research was decidedly institutional, worked closely and productively with younger, more socially and culturally attuned, colleagues.[36] On occasion this coming together was expressed in textbooks, as in the documentary collections on workers in the nineteenth and twentieth centuries edited by Cross, on the one hand, and Abella and David Millar, on the other.[37]

A subsection of the Canadian Historical Association (CHA), the CCLH's initial meeting took place at Winnipeg in June 1970. Shortly thereafter, the CCLH produced a biannual, bilingual newsletter/bulletin. Discussions ensued about establishing a formal journal of Canadian labour studies. Founded as an annual in 1976 under the editorship of Kealey and James D. Thwaites, *Labour/Le Travailleur* was launched as the official journal of the CHA-affiliated CCLH. Its membership was constituted through subscription to the annual publication and it met once a year during the meeting times of various Canadian academic discipline associations in an annual late May/early June gathering. Published yearly from 1976 to 1980, *Labour/Le Travailleur* would soon be edited solely by Kealey. Incorporating a range of material in its pages, the journal soon supplanted the *Bulletin*, which was allowed to lapse. Becoming a biannual in 1980, and changing its name to *Labour/Le Travail* in 1983 in order to transcend the gender-specific nature of its original title, the journal and the CCLH (renamed the Canadian Committee on Labour History in 1991 in order to incorporate broad, transnational interests) came, by the mid-1980s, to symbolize the coming of age of working-class history in Canada. CCLH President Irving Abella proclaimed with enthusiasm in 1982: 'Canadian labour history has finally arrived!'[38]

That arrival had been the product of scholarship contributed by varying camps. The mainstays of the early CCLH Executive were Abella and Kealey, representatives of divergent analytic streams in Canada's developing field of working-class history. If Kealey provided much of the energy and enterprise in the founding of the journal, its editorial board was always reflective of the breadth of the contentious field. Debates and discussions of what to publish and how to do it were often heated, and disagreements were many, but there was never, in my recollection, a point where the project itself was felt to be either compromised, or on the brink of some destructive implosion.

Stabilization and diversity: fin-de-siècle triumphs and testings

A measure of labour history's consolidation was the explosion of graduate theses written in the field in the late 1970s. Whereas in 1966 the Canadian Historical Association's *Register of Post-Graduate Dissertations in Progress in History and Related Disciplines* recorded a total of nine MA and PhD theses in the field, a decade later the comparable figure was a whopping ninety-nine.[39]

Labour had become one of those 'limited identities' much discussed as vanguard topics of consideration in the late 1960s.[40] In barely a decade and a half such subjects managed to find an institutional niche in professional historical circles, where journals, conferences and societies proliferated on the periphery of a still fairly traditional historiographic mainstream. But that periphery was encroaching upon the centres of conventional historical interpretation, where research tended to concentrate on orthodox political history and narratives of national development. Topics once considered marginal were becoming increasingly difficult to ignore, and now encompassed women's history, robust studies of regionalism's significance on the national canvas, consideration of ethnicity and, unmistakably, the study of class. Moreover, it was in these years that Canadian working-class history consolidated transnational connections, cultivating ties with other societies dedicated to the study of labour history, engaging in dialogue over comparative studies of workers in Canada, the United Kingdom, Wales and Australia.[41]

To complicate matters, however, the last two decades of the twentieth century would be marked by new developments that constantly reconfigured the nature of the historiography of Canadian workers in this period. In what follows immediately below I address the significance of the changing *personnel* involved in the writing of labour history in the 1980s and beyond.

First, an older contingent of once influential figures began to vacate the field in the late 1970s, moving away from labour studies to take up research and writing in such areas as military history (Bercuson, Terry Copp and, to some extent, Desmond Morton, who had always oscillated between histories of the military, the labour movement and social democratic politics) or ethnicity (Abella). Second, as the playing field of labour history in Canada seemed to be levelled in ways that left Kealey and Palmer standing firm in their interpretive direction, a new research agenda surfaced. It differentiated itself from the institutional-political orientation of the McNaught-Bercuson-Abella approach at the same time as it voiced growing concerns with the ostensible 'romanticism' of their original critics. To some extent this was merely the articulation of analytic differences that had long existed within a broad contingent of historians which happened to encompass a variety of individuals, all of whom were charting new directions, many of them highly cognizant of fissiparous relations and contentious understandings of what constituted a politics of the left.

At issue, again, was the vantage point of twentieth-century/nineteenth-century difference, which, in particular, posed the 'crisis of the craftsman' in ways that suggested a divergent politics of understanding. Looked at from the perspective of the 1880s, framed within a research vision that addressed the period from 1860 to 1914, a number of skilled workers often seemed to be on the cutting edge of class mobilization, robust architects of resilient mechanisms of shopfloor structures of workers' control and leading spokesmen in bodies like the Knights of Labor, which, for all of its limitations, struggled to promote the politics of labour reform as had no other working-class organization of the nineteenth century. Peering backward at this experience, analysing it in terms of skill dilution and the workplace transformations associated with the early twentieth-century Second Industrial Revolution, as well as awareness of the programmatic clarifications of revolutionary politics in the years 1917 to 1925, conditioned a different perspective. Craig Heron thus accented 'the ambivalence of artisanal culture' and the persistent 'defence of craft privilege' that the British historian James Hinton had labelled 'the clinging dross of exclusivism'.[42] Wayne Roberts tried to bridge this chronological and political chasm, suggesting that sectors of the skilled straddled the traditions of the past and the tendencies of the future, harbouring consciousnesses of craft distinctiveness as well as the politics of revolution, but his subtle appreciations of complexity tended to be lost in the hardening view that one was either *for* or *against* the craftsman.[43]

An orientation stressing the possible significance of aristocratic divisions within the working class dovetailed nicely with research increasingly attentive to the labour process, work segmentation and the fragmentation of labour in the twentieth century.[44] Canadian studies animated by such concerns brought much of the scholarship together in an engagement with and refinement of the arguments of Harry Braverman, whose 1974 *Labor and Monopoly Capital* had unleashed a plethora of studies and productive debates in the United States, Canada and the UK. This labour process literature both highlighted generalized alignments in the study of Canadian workers as well as subtle but emerging interpretive fissures.[45]

Of these fissures the most significant was, as it had been in the early McNaught-Bercuson-led charge against the supposed Thompsonians, the issue of culture. But the debate now leaned left, relying not on atheoretical and rhetorical labelling of ostensible class-ordered cultural autonomies, as it had in the Bercuson and McNaught critiques, but on a revived Marxist attachment to base-superstructure distinctions, an insistence on the rigours of political economy and a refusal to concede anything to the 'dogmas of culture'. Ian McKay led the offensive against what he dismissed as a culturalist 'retrospective anthropology'. Along the way, McKay deplored the theoretical cost of accommodating what he presented as the indiscriminate conceptual meanderings of Raymond Williams. In McKay's words, these had 'allowed social historians to indulge in retrospective cheerleading for progressive ideas', enabling 'them to forget that "emergent" socialist values did not, in fact, "emerge" and win the acceptance of the majority'. With Thompson's *The Poverty of Theory* (1978) fresh in his mind, McKay railed against Thompson's capacity to reel out culture after culture, concluding that conceptually 'culture' was little more than a non-explanatory buzz-word designating whatever happened to engage academic interest. 'Rather than making this inability to explain a merit in itself,' McKay argued, 'we should envisage the creation of logico-historical models by which this realm of consciousness may be made the object of scientific discourse [...] We close the logical and political circles only by a return to the concrete: to the determinate abstractions of *Capital* and to a logical political practice.'[46]

This was heady stuff, but it did not quite manage to capture the historiographic moment. For the most part, the differentiations that emerged in the 1980s played themselves out less at the level of advancing Canadian labour history through recourse to more rigorous scientific Marxist analysis, which was what McKay was attempting to encourage. Rather, more mundane separations ensued. Bercuson's attempt to understate the voice of Canadian working-class revolutionaries by downplaying the subjective, conscious adherence to anti-capitalist ideas and affiliations in the era of the Winnipeg General Strike, explained the labour revolt of these years in deterministic terms, placing interpretive accent on the environment of the western industrial frontier. This approach was challenged decisively in Kealey's pan-Canadian account of the 1919 labour revolt. Most labour historians, by the late 1980s, accepted Kealey's claims that the upheaval of the post-World War I years had been national, as opposed to regional. But the developing scholarship tended to accent more 'labourist', ballot-box orientations and, with considerable subtlety and sophistication, drew a picture of the rising of the workers that concentrated less on Kealey's outline of general and sympathetic strikes as rooted in a new adherence to revolutionary program than it did in elaborating the cracks in the walls of working-class solidarity.[47]

Increasingly under fire was Kealey and Palmer's suggestion that the 1880s had been a significant moment of class mobilization, in which the Noble and Holy Order of the Knights of Labor had played a major and, certain limitations aside, laudatory role.[48] An entire volume was produced to, in some ways, offset what was felt to be the metropolitan focus on labour in Toronto and Hamilton – Ontario's pre-eminent industrial cities – that Paul Craven associated with the Thompsonian-influenced historiography emerging out of the 'debate between institutional labour historians and the New Left'. Not surprisingly, the essays in this volume highlighted the importance of paternalism, religion and other cross-class components of plebeian life, stressed the linkages of home and work, and detailed the limitations of craft organization.[49] Echoes of the McNaught-Bercuson position reverberated in this criticism. Those earlier attacks rebounded more forcefully in a polemical shot fired across the Kealey-Palmer bow by a left-nationalist political economist, Daniel Drache, in a 1984 *Studies in Political Economy* article. Drache downplayed industrial-capitalist development in Canada, drawing on Harold Innis's fixation on the resource economy's reliance on a series of staples: fish, fur, timber, wheat and, later in the twentieth century, oil and gas. He depicted craft unions as little more than vehicles of working-class colonialism constituting a reactionary élite, and insisted that Canadian labour had been historically mired in its internal fragmentations.[50]

By the 1990s and into the first decade of the twenty-first century, there were those who sought to define themselves against what they considered a problematic reading of the nineteenth-century working-class past. Concentrated at York University, these critics tended to understate class tensions, conflicts and struggles, and instead focused on experiences of a cross-class character. Thus, Lynne Marks's account of working-class life in Victorian Ontario used the small town as a prism through which to envision workers' place in society. She argued that class, as an analytic category, had been 'privileged' to the point that it had become unduly 'fundamental'. If this approach had the potential to interpretively moderate some of the analytics of enthusiasm characteristic of earlier writing, and to develop the historiography by addressing areas long understudied in class ways, such as religion, Marks too often relied on misrepresentation of the actual positions she was at pains to overturn and read too much into evidence that was at best ambiguous and thin.[51]

A contemporary of Marks, Robert B. Kristofferson, later challenged what he referred to as 'the dispossession model' of 'the proletarianization of the craftsworker', associated in Canada with Kealey and Palmer. Kristofferson researched assiduously in records that allowed him to produce a statement on how, in Hamilton, Ontario, the mid-century years witnessed the march of Marx's 'really revolutionizing path to industrial capitalism', craft capital transforming itself into industrial capital. Yet he also ignored evidence and interpretive issues inconvenient to his argument. Important, quantitatively-derived perspectives on inequality marshalled by Michael Katz and his associates were awkwardly sidestepped. So, too, were fundamental issues of periodization, in which the class-struggle perspectives of work addressing peak labour mobilizations in the 1880s offers a diametrically different chronology from Kristofferson's, which was generated out of the 1850s and 1860s. The result was a book that unnecessarily understated the complexities and meanings of the first stages of class struggle in Canada. As a perceptive review by Douglas McCalla in the *American Historical Review* has recently noted, Kristofferson too readily caricatures positions in the scholarly literature that he is critiquing. My own book, *A Culture in Conflict*, is held up by McCalla as a 'particular target' that is mishandled in a variety of ways. Most readers of Kristofferson's book will rightly wonder what the point is in battling over this old ground, misrepresenting a book published almost thirty years ago, when something new and fresh could have emerged out of his research.[52]

From other quarters, the graduate seminars of the 1980s yielded different results. An eclectic mix of graduate students at Queen's University in the 1980s and 1990s tackled a diversity of research subjects. Peter S. McInnis took up the challenge of McNaught, Morton and others to develop a sophisticated reconsideration of the reconstruction of Canadian society in the aftermath of World War II, when labour militancy, the emergence of the welfare state and strategies of incorporation evident in certain government and business circles, culminated in a postwar compromise that set the stage for future decades of class relations.[53] Stimulating studies of nineteenth- and early-twentieth-century sexuality, in which readings of violence against women, familial disorder, and male same-sex relations were framed within analyses attentive to the importance of a class-divided society, were produced by Karen Dubinsky, Steven Maynard, and Annalee [Golz] Lepp.[54] In one of the more creative readings of the history of dispossession associated with the great depression, Todd McCallum drew on Paul Lafargue's *The Right to be Lazy* and the critical practice of the hobo to reframe analysis of the human meaning of capitalist 'unemployment'.[55] At the interface of the history of workers, the history of ideas and the mobilizations of the left, Peter Campbell charted a discussion of strands of Canadian Marxism from 1900 to 1940 that separated themselves out from the dominant, and bifurcated, party allegiances of social democracy and communism.[56]

Equally eclectic were the researches of graduate students emanating from Memorial University in the same period. Much of this work understandably addressed a political economy of material constraint and marginalization, yielding impressive new perspectives on the resource sector (especially the fishery), the colonial condition, and the last province to enter into Confederation, Newfoundland only joining Canada in 1949.[57] Undoubtedly the most influential of this revisionist work has been that of Sean Cadigan. His articles, critiques and books include a recent synthetic statement on the history of Newfoundland from prehistoric times to the present. Cadigan argues a case for seeing the history of one of Canada's most unique regions as a struggle against environmental odds that have been even further loaded against the masses of Newfoundlanders by the undeniable class inequalities of specific political and economic formations.[58] Miriam Wright's *A Fishery for Modern Times* (2001) added a gender dimension to this kind of rewriting of Newfoundland history and the book was complemented by a growing body of feminist Atlantic Canada writing.[59]

Other graduate students of these years made significant interventions into vital issues of national and international significance. Mark Leier was among the first wave of this cohort. Arguably he is its most prolific player, producing studies that historicized appreciation of the making of the trade union bureaucracy, as well as an imaginative and pedagogically inspired text on the case of a notable and intricately complicated West Coast labour spy, Robert Gosden.[60] Among the second wave, Andrew Parnaby looked at the dock workers of the West Coast and, in the process, aligned labour history and aboriginal history, outlining an encounter of 'Indians at work' that had first been broached seriously decades earlier by the maverick anthropologist, Rolf Knight.[61] Important studies on Canadian Communism appeared at the end of the 1990s, realizing the promise of scholars such as David Frank and John Manley.[62]

Working-class history's developing level of sophistication registered in the quantity of articles published in *Labour/Le Travail*, as well as the publication program and ongoing annual workshops of the CCLH. By 2000 the Committee had published almost twenty volumes, most of them oral biographies and memoirs, as well as eight volumes of the Royal Canadian Mounted Police Security Bulletins.[63] In addition, the CCLH had organized a Secretary of State-sponsored 1983–1984 lecture series on labour history at four Canadian universities, publishing a selection of the popularly-pitched talks in *Lectures in Canadian Labour and Working-Class History* (1985) and also making available six of the videotaped lectures. By the 1990s, its annual workshop brought together trade union activists and labour studies academics in day-long events which drew audiences of 100 participants and more. Three 'surveys' of labour history were published over the course of the 1980s, and by the 1990s all had been reprinted in revised editions. A 1999 publication of the CCLH, *The Woman Worker, 1926–1929*, edited by Margaret Hobbs and Joan Sangster, gathered together articles from the official newspaper of the CPC-affiliated Canadian Federation of Women's Labor Leagues. These articles provide commentary from the late 1920s on women and wage work, protective legislation, social reform, war and peace, women and the sex trade, family, domestic labour, and birth control. The volume suggested how central women had become to the project of labour history.[64]

Paradigm shift I: women's history reconfigures the labouring subject

In Canada women's history and working-class history emerged in tandem. The institutional consolidation of these fields, with their societies, professional networks, and journals overlapped. Women were present on the editorial board of *Labour/Le Travailleur* from its inception, but it would be wrong to discount the extent to which the journal's making as a durable project and its original intellectual content were largely male enterprises. By 1990, however, fully eight of the fifteen-member editorial *équipe* responsible for *Labour/Le Travail* were women (the comparable figure for the United States journal, *Labor History*, was *two*). Morton's content analysis of *Labour/Le Travail* from 1976 to 1999 confirms the significance of this shift. In the 1970s 2 articles addressed gender issues; by the 1980s that number had climbed to 12; and over the course of the 1990s fully 26 articles could be placed in the gender category, making women's and gender issues the single most prominent subject written about among studies of industrial relations, strikes, unions, working lives, ethnicity and politics. Looking back on these years, Sangster later commented:

> Labour history generally welcomed feminist research exploring gender and class. Though *some* (usually, but not always, male) practitioners saw class as definitive, gender a critical additive, they were always willing to contest this issue with those of us who disagreed. If tensions were there, between class and gender, feminism and socialism, debating 'who was on top', in which theory, and why, they were not necessarily negative: they could be productive.[65]

Research on labouring women often addressed the seemingly perennial question, asked most forcefully in the United States by Alice Kessler-Harris, of what barriers existed in Canada to women working for wages and joining the trade union movement.[66] The answers varied from the cultural to the structural.[67] Interpretive developments of the 1970s and 1980s produced writing that, in its unambiguous and often rigorous debate over socialist-feminist labour studies and Marxist conceptualizations, catapulted Canadian scholarship into a critically important exchange of views on the meaning and significance of reproductive labour.[68] As feminism transformed political economy, countless studies began to address women's work – in the present as well as in the past – in new and rigorous ways.[69] This helped stamp the Canadian women's movement of this period with a radical, socialist-feminist edge and a working-class content that situated it to the left of many of its international counterparts.[70]

Bettina Bradbury charted a new course of appreciation of working-class families, her quantitatively-derived discussions of Victorian Montreal emphasizing the complexity of the labouring poor's domestic economy and the significant contributions made to it by the unpaid labour of women and children. In establishing definitively the precarious nature of the working-class household, she established the gendered nature of everyday lives bifurcated by public/private and productive/reproductive social constructions.[71] Feminist historians of the organized left provided a range of studies that demonstrated the extent to which orthodox parties of communism and social democracy had understated women's oppression at the same time as they had nurtured a vocal contingent of female organizers, writers and activists who insisted on bringing the women's question into the politics of revolution and reform.[72] Histories of specific occupational sectors or unions in which women's work predominated and leftist politics proved influential, such as the garment trades or the United Electrical, Radio, and Machine Workers' Union, might well produce discussions of the organized left *and* workplace-familial relations.[73] Increasingly, moreover, such research emphasized the reciprocities of gender, ethnicity and occupation. Immigrant women laboured at various jobs, both waged and unwaged, and in a myriad of ways they exposed how fragile were supposedly entrenched adherences to the middle-class ideal of domesticity.[74] Indeed, two books that situated their subjects in different ways in the world of the 1920s and 1930s native-born Canadian women revealed that the domestic ideal for working-class women of *any* ethnic background was more fiction and faith than fact.[75]

Increasingly the study of women was subsumed within a *theoretical* insistence on studying gender as a system of social organization demarcating the sexes, a project that dovetailed with the emergence of critical thinking at the *fin-de-siècle.* As Canadian historians gravitated to gender as, in Joan Scott's words, 'a useful category of historical analysis', they were also drawn into the complex swirl of conceptualization associated with the rise of postmodernism and discourse analysis.[76]

Paradigm shift, II: labour history and 'the linguistic turn'

What I will designate (largely because it is the most eclectic and open-ended of terminologies) 'the linguistic turn' shifted historians' perspectives on meaning. Against the ostensible determinative fix of social history's loose association with materialism in general and Marxism in particular, in which the *structures* of political economy established boundaries within which human agency unfolded, 'the linguistic turn' instead suggested the need to complicate analysis by recognizing that all language, including that of individual authors, has shaped both understandings of events and the nature of interpretation in the past and subsequent 'readings' and 'representations' of such happenings. That this intellectual movement into new understandings of more discursive appreciations of determination and causality took place at the same time that the Soviet Union imploded, and that complex debates about the 'end of history' were reconfiguring not only the liberal, mainstream 'centre' but also the left, was, of course, noteworthy. In Canada the context was complicated further by an intensification of reaction against the entire *oeuvre* of social history as certain well-placed, mainstream historians attacked labour, women's and regional historians for narrowing Canadian history to a trivializing focus on the insignificant and ignoring the grandeur of the politics of nation building. The result was a popular front-like unity of all progressives against 'the Granatsteinian enemy'. In a supreme irony, this was constructed with a rhetorical flourish that papered over quite significant differences among the ranks of seemingly like-minded advocates of an undifferentiated social history.[77]

Gendered labour histories became the site where 'the linguistic turn' played itself out most clearly within Canadian historical writing. Over the course of the 1990s gender histories attentive to class subjects abounded and included studies of nursing, agricultural labour, skill and labour reform, working girls and networks of urban leisure, and politics in the automobile industry.[78] Collections of essays on 'gendered pasts' contained, of course, much that did not touch down on working-class history, but in most cases such texts – whether they brought together previously unpublished contributions or reprinted articles – featured labouring lives prominently.[79]

Joy Parr's *The Gender of Breadwinners: Women, Men, and Change in Two Industrial Towns, 1880-1950* (1990) was arguably one of the more influential of a host of 1990s writings. Suggesting that past interpretations of labouring life had been incarcerated in constrained interpretive failure to simultaneously explore the ways in which class *and* gender ordered being, Parr provided Canadian historians with an admonition that would orchestrate much scholarship for the next decade and a half:

> The challenge now plainly is to think beyond this history of dualisms and its accompanying assertion of an ahistorical hierarchy of oppressions. We need to problematize and unmake the chain of binary oppositions – masculine/feminine, market/non-market, public/private, waged/non-waged – and rethink the categoricalism that cantonizes gender, class, race, ethnicity, and nationality, so as to see past the conceptual signage, which has illuminated the previously invisible but now threatens to obstruct our view of the living space beyond.

Oddly enough, the important empirical findings of Parr's study relating to labour recruitment, work processes and the gendered nature of labour-capital relations and class conflict, often seemed to emerge against the grain of the book's insistence on the need to transcend binary oppositions. Indeed, Parr's organizing framework *was* just such a powerful dualism, dependant as it was on the contrasting outlines of work in an ostensible 'men's town' of furniture production and in a 'women's town' of knitting mills. Theoretical strictures aside, gender's significance usually overshadowed class in Parr's interpretive history.[80]

Different in tone and orientation was Sangster's volume of Peterborough-based studies of working women in a manufacturing town. Sangster eschewed the more grandiose promises of postmodernism and settled instead for an exploration of gender *at work*, concentrating her conceptualization at the conjuncture, rather than the disjuncture, of Marxism, feminism and productive suggestions of 'the linguistic turn'. The result was a book that looked primarily at women's experience, concentrating on how working women were socialized into their gender and class roles; how they adapted to the gendered division of labour in the home and in the waged workplace; and how they managed, over time, to straddle the fence of accommodation and resistance, embracing understandings of respectability and trade union principles, being mothers and militants. Sangster's studies thus convey a sense of gender difference and class solidarity that is attentive to what is distinctive in women's experience as well as what crosses the boundaries of masculine and feminine in a generalized framing of the relations of labour and capital.[81]

Sangster's approach led to her refusal of the tendency, evident in positions articulated by some gender historians, that women's history was *passé* and that only the study of an all-encompassing gender order, constitutive of the normative identities of masculine and feminine, could unlock the meaning of the past.[82] Revealingly, one young historian, Steve Penfold, perhaps licenced by the climate of dismissal that was becoming commonplace, was brought to task by Sangster for stating bluntly that:

> Until recently, paying attention to gender meant nothing more than discussing women. But under the influence of postmodern theorists, historians (even those who would reject much of postmodern philosophy) have begun to advance a more complex understanding of gender which focuses on the interplay of ideals of femininity and masculinity.[83]

Sangster's understandable rejoinder – 'a revealing pejorative comment, as if this was *nothing*' – was replied to by Penfold. He claimed that his statement had been directed at 'the intellectual posture of gender-blind labour historians'.[84] This seemingly inconsequential exchange captured a certain development of the 1990s in which gender history, 'the linguistic turn' and working-class history could, in the hands of particular practitioners, separate. The more sharply and polemically 'the linguistic turn' was taken, the more likely it was that past writing in the field of working-class history would be misrepresented and caricatured.[85] Small wonder that one working-class historian posed the question 'w[h]ither class' in the writing on his region's history.[86]

Nonetheless, labour history in Canada has not died, and 'the linguistic turn', while certainly influential, has perhaps slowed of late. On the one hand, its insights have been absorbed, while an earlier aggressive challenge to a materialist social history of class has softened.[87] On the other, attentiveness to language and the social constructions so evident in the past has prodded historians to rethink a range of important dimensions of working-class experience, including its gendered and racialized nature. Indeed, 'the linguistic turn' has been foundational in stimulating new studies of racialized otherness that are central to understanding class formation. Many of them springboard off from concerns with gender, and *Labour/Le Travail* has often been an original forum in which research has been showcased before developing into a monograph.[88]

If working-class history in Canada has not yet quite achieved the totalizing articulation of the interlocking hierarchies of class, ethnicity, race and gender called for by Ruth Frager in 1999, then it has travelled a considerable distance in the right direction.[89] Ethnicity, class and gender coalesce, for instance, in the many edited collections on immigrants, transnational diasporas and state policy emanating from the ongoing research and collaborative study of Franca Iacovetta.[90] A reader, designed for use in labour history courses, and first published in 1992, reflected this advance, reprinting a plethora of articles that addressed the nature and meaning of workers' lives in Canada, especially in terms of how class, race, and gender intersected.[91]

Labour history at the current conjuncture

A variety of monographs suggest Canadian labour history's diversity in the twenty-first century. Steven High's *Industrial Sunset: The Making of North America's Rust Belt, 1969–1984* (2003) uses a cross-border comparison of de-industrialization in Canada and the United States to outline the continuing relevance of combining working-class history and political economy. This peculiarly Canadian marriage has spawned considerable comment on the 'revolution from above' which has reconfigured contemporary industrial relations. Leo Panitch's and Donald Swartz's many editions of what is now titled *From Consent to Coercion: The Assault on Trade Union Freedoms* (2003) is arguably the most stimulating, politically effective and widely read of a number of important studies.[92] Equally important, Canadian political economy and gendered labour studies have recast the analytic stage on which working-class histories of struggle and resistance are rethought in light of the importance of fundamental structures such as state power and policy, family and economy.[93] Legal scholars, in turn, have situated labour's history in relation to changes in the law.[94]

The most recent course-designed reader, Palmer and Sangster's *Labouring Canada: Class, Gender, and Race in Canadian Working-Class History* (2008), gathers together twenty-eight articles that introduce students to class formation from early colonization and aboriginal dispossession to the state of the unions in an epoch of neoliberal assault and working-class retrenchment. Gender and race receive considerable coverage, as do state policies, household economies, and class struggles and their advocates. In but one indication of how the field has expanded its inclusiveness, there is an important discussion of sex work, reprinting Becki L. Ross's critical reflections on exotic dancing, 'Bumping and Grinding on the Line: Making Nudity Pay', which originally appeared in a special 'millennium edition' of *Labour/Le Travail*.[95]

Labour history in Canada, then, has long left behind a debate over whether its focus would be institutions and politics or the social life and cultural experience of working people. On one level this debate was always more of a *political* disagreement than it was a discussion of the substance and content of actual research and study, as subsequent commentary defending industrial legality as an unambiguous advance would make abundantly clear.[96] And this political divide remains, surviving in often complicated ways, even as new work addressing 'the cultural' is now seemingly much in vogue.[97] Those of us who, decades ago, suggested that there was a need to attend to the cultural realm (which did not, of course, imply that other realms were insignificant and not worthy of study) did so because we conceived of culture as something of a web of 'connective tissues of an ambiguous realm of everyday life that bridged the chasm separating class as a silent structure and class as a potential force for revolutionary change'. Such 'tissues were never, however, simply one-way threads tying class place to the realization of class consciousness; more often than not they wrapped themselves around class experience in ways that produced web-like mazes in which little was direct and obvious'.[98] Labour history, in this understanding of the moment of a particular birth in the 1970s, was indeed about grappling with class as an agent of social transformation. Those who charted this analytic path 'self-identified' as 'working-class historians', and in so doing consciously separated themselves from those who, while they wrote labour history, named themselves differently and would soon be drawn to other fields.

The political and economic conjuncture in which modern Canadian labour history was formed, however, differs markedly from the current conjuncture. Intellectually, 1970s scholarship was forged in the crucible of the 1960s, and it rested, as had that decade, on New Left visions and a boundless sense of the possibility of dissidence. Today's moment can barely remember such a time, coming after decades of coerced left retreats and material assault on working-class well-being on the one hand, and, on the other, waves of academic fashion that have called into question class-based politics. Marxism had become, by the early 1970s, a viable answer for many New Leftists who discovered, as their movements wound down or fractured into factions, much to appreciate and emulate in an older left's programmatic grasp of the traditions associated not only with Marx and Engels but with Lenin and Trotsky. The turn to class was, in Canada as elsewhere, a logical political and intellectual move. In 2009, no such grasp is easily within reach. A new generation of progressive scholars turns to proliferating identities, discursive practices and a less singular subject. Someone like Ian McKay, whose original studies of the 1970s and 1980s addressed workers, has now turned to the history of the Canadian left enlightenment, which he is at pains to claim is not about 'a death-defying mastery of Marx's *Capital*, or defeating rivals in theoretical and political combat in the ritualized dialectical duels for which Marxist men have long been famous'. Well, no, to be sure, no reasonable human being would want to be associated with *that*! Instead, what McKay suggests is needed is a 'life commitment to shared conversations and collective acts that hasten the day of a more generous democracy'. And in this conversation, 'Canadian leftism cannot be seen as the passive reflection of the working class', just as, of course, it cannot write the workers off entirely either. Class matters in the current conjuncture, but the project of our times, the making not of working-class power but of 'a more generous democracy', cannot be reduced to proletarian initiative.[99]

Leaving aside the politics of such strictures, with which it is possible to both agree to some extent and disagree in other ways, my point in concluding this discussion of the historiography of Canadian workers is that this positioning serves as a useful suggestion about the actual environment in which labour history now exists. The surroundings of our time are stimulating, productive and have generated important and fresh perspectives on the lives of Canada's labouring men, women and children. But new studies that are doing this are not, for the most part, framed as labour history. Class matters in this writing, but *not* centrally so. The material social histories of class formation and struggle of the 1970s and 1980s are long separated from the gendered, classed and raced, largely cultural histories that have begun to appear in the post-2005 years.[100] There are very few, if any, 'new' working-class historians in Canada precisely because it is rare indeed for graduate students to name themselves 'labour historians'. To the extent that 'labour' is appended consciously to new scholars' identities, they tend to come from disciplines such as sociology, political economy and, most emphatically, labour studies, spheres that are welcoming to but different from working-class *history*.

Of course this is *precisely* the kind of interdisciplinary crossing of conceptual and investigative borders that takes working-class history in new directions and enlivens the field. *Labour/Le Travail*, which has always been something of a bell-wether of working-class history in Canada, is now very much an illustration of this process. The articles that appear in its pages are seldom easily and narrowly categorized as 'labour history', although there are, inevitably, specific pieces of this kind. But for the most part, the journal is now what might be designated a 'cross-over' publication. Many of the articles that make their way through our peer review process and into print, do so as examinations of working-class life that conjoin labour being a *class* with a host of other considerations, among them gender, race, region, age, sexual orientation, etc. This is to the good. And yet it should also raise concerns. Because if 'labour history' is advanced by its integration into larger analyses of social, cultural, political, and economic life, so too is it the case that when a subject cannot sustain its name, it is in danger of losing itself among those many other subjects that have no shyness about proclaiming *their* identity.

In this sense labour history needs to perhaps revitalize itself, not in some defensive posture of asserting its claims against other subjects and identities, but in stepping up a sense of the contributions it can make, and what it is that is uniquely significant about the working-class past and its legacies. We need the history of the working class now more than ever. Given the challenges that workers as a class face at the close of the twenty-first century's first decade, its institutions, traditions and well-being threatened by a capitalist crisis *not* of its making but most emphatically dire in its consequences for labouring people, it is arguably the case that *class politics from below* need reviving in the face of the onslaught of destructive *class politics from above.*

Just as those class politics from below will never be reinvigorated without an appreciation of the ways in which working-class life and struggle involves dimensions of experience beyond the wage and the workplace, so too is the history of labour's combativity and defence of its material circumstances centrally important in charting a new politics of resistance. Such a politics, to be sure, demands much more than a nuanced and radical sense of the past; but such understanding has its own small role to play in mobilizing a future.

Notes

1 For detailed accounts of this early writing, see Gregory S. Kealey, 'Writing About Labour', and idem, 'H.C. Pentland and Working-Class Studies', *Workers in Canadian History* (Toronto: University of Toronto Press, 1995), pp. 3–47; idem, 'Looking Backward: Reflections on the Study of Class in Canada', *The History and Social Science Teacher*, 16 (1981), 213–22.

2 Note for comparative purposes Terry Irving and Allen Seager, 'Labour and Politics in Canada and Australia: Towards a Comparative Approach to Developments to 1960', *Labour/Le Travail*, 38 (1996), 239–77; Eric Hobsbawm, 'The Historians' Group of the Communist Party', in *Rebels and Their Causes: Essays in Honour of A.L. Morton*, ed. by Maurice Cornforth (London: Lawrence and Wishart, 1978), pp. 21–48; James R. Barrett, 'Class Act: An Interview with David Montgomery', *Labor: Studies in Working-Class History of the Americas*, 1 (2004), 23–54.

3 For discussion of Communist labour history, see Gregory S. Kealey, 'Stanley Bréhaut Ryerson: Canadian Revolutionary Intellectual', and idem, 'Stanley Bréhaut Ryerson: Marxist Historian', *Studies in Political Economy*, 9 (1982), 103–71. Jack Scott's writings are discussed in *A Communist Life: Jack Scott and the Canadian Workers' Movement, 1927–1985*, ed. by Bryan D. Palmer (St. John's, Newfoundland: Committee on Canadian Labour History, 1989); and Scott is quoted from Jack Scott, *Sweat and Struggle: Working Class Struggles in Canada, Volume I: 1789-1899* (Vancouver: New Star, 1974), p. 1.

4 See, for instance, *Capitalism and the National Question in Canada*, ed. by Gary Teeple (Toronto: University of Toronto Press, 1972).

5 S.R. Mealing, 'The Concept of Social Class and the Interpretation of Canadian History', *Canadian Historical Review*, 46 (1965), 201–18 (pp. 217–18).

6 A.R.M. Lower, 'Some Neglected Aspects of Canadian History', Canadian Historical Association, *Report* (1929), 66.

7 Kenneth McNaught, *A Prophet in Politics: A Biography of J.S. Woodsworth* (Toronto: University of Toronto Press, 1959); idem, *Conscience and History: A Memoir* (Toronto: University of Toronto Press, 1999).

8 Bryan D. Palmer, 'Working-Class Canada: Recent Historical Writing', *Queen's Quarterly*, 86 (1979/1980), 594–616.

9 Irving Martin Abella, *Nationalism, Communism, and Canadian Labour: The CIO, the Communist Party, and the Canadian Congress of Labour, 1935–*

1956 (Toronto: University of Toronto Press, 1973); David Jay Bercuson, *Confrontation at Winnipeg: Labour, Industrial Relations, and the General Strike* (Kingston and Montreal: McGill-Queen's University Press, 1974); David Jay Bercuson and Kenneth McNaught, *The Winnipeg General Strike: 1919* (Toronto: Longman, 1974); A.R. McCormack, *Reformers, Rebels, and Revolutionaries: The Western Canadian Radical Movement, 1899–1919* (Toronto: University of Toronto Press, 1977).

10 Bercuson, *Confrontation at Winnipeg*, p. 175. Cf. *Winnipeg, 1919: The Strikers' Own History of the Winnipeg General Strike*, ed. by Norman Penner (Toronto: James Lewis and Samuel, 1973).

11 Abella, *Nationalism, Communism, and Canadian Labour*, esp. pp. 1, 222.

12 *On Strike: Six Key Labour Struggles in Canada, 1919–1949*, ed. by Irving Abella (Toronto: James Lorimer, 1975), p. xii.

13 Terry Copp, *The Condition of the Working Class in Montreal, 1897–1929* (Toronto: McClelland and Stewart, 1974); Michael J. Piva, *The Condition of the Working Class in Toronto, 1900–1921* (Ottawa: University of Ottawa Press, 1979); Donald Avery, *'Dangerous Foreigners': European Immigrant Workers and Labour Radicalism in Canada, 1896–1932* (Toronto: McClelland and Stewart, 1979).

14 See *The Decline and Fall of a Good Idea: CCF-NDP Manifestoes, 1932–1969*, ed. by Michael S. Cross (Toronto: New Hogtown Press, 1974).

15 Michael S. Cross, 'The Shiners' War: Social Violence in the Ottawa Valley in the 1930s', *Canadian Historical Review*, 44 (1973), 1–26.

16 H. V. Nelles, 'Creighton's Seminar', *Canadian Forum* (September 1980), 6; Desmond Morton, 'Some Millennial Reflections on the State of Canadian Labour History', *Labour/Le Travail*, 46 (2000), 11–36, refers to working-class historians as 'one of the most homogeneous and influential groups in the disparate crowd of Canadian historians' (p. 21).

17 Note, for comparative purposes, Gareth Stedman Jones, 'History and Theory: An English Story', *Historeian: A Review of the Past and Other Stories*, 3 (2001), 103–24.

18 Bryan D. Palmer, *A Culture in Conflict: Skilled Workers and Industrial Capitalism in Hamilton, Ontario, 1860–1914* (Kingston and Montreal: McGill-Queen's University Press, 1979); Gregory S. Kealey, *Toronto Workers Respond to Industrial Capitalism, 1867–1892* (Toronto: University of Toronto Press, 1980); Gregory S. Kealey and Bryan D. Palmer, *Dreaming of What Might Be: The Knights of Labor in Ontario, 1880–1900* (New York: Cambridge University Press, 1982). These works had been preceded by surveys of archival holdings and an early collection of essays: *Primary Sources in Canadian Working Class History, 1860–1930*, ed. by Russell Hann, Gregory S. Kealey, Linda Kealey and Peter Warrian (Kitchener: Dumont Press, 1973); *Essays in Canadian Working Class* History, ed. by Gregory S. Kealey and Peter Warrian (Toronto: McClelland and Stewart, 1976). Shortly after the appearance of the major monographs on Hamilton and Toronto I published an overview of Canadian working-class history: Bryan D. Palmer, *Working-Class Experience: The Rise and Reconstitution of Canadian Labour, 1800–1980* (Toronto: Butterworth's,

1983). Ramsay Cook was among the most generous of mainstream, liberal commentators on this writing: see Ramsay Cook, 'The Making of Canadian Working-Class History', *Historical Reflections*, 10 (1983), 127–42.

19 David J. Bercuson, review of *Dreaming of What Might Be* in *Business History Review*, 57 (1983), 589–91.

20 Carl Berger, *The Writing of Canadian History* (Toronto: University of Toronto Press, 1986), pp. 306–7. For the important work of Katz and his colleagues, see Michael Katz, *The People of Hamilton, Canada West: Family and Class in a Mid-Nineteenth Century City* (Cambridge, MA: Harvard University Press, 1976); Michael Katz, Michael Doucet, and Mark Stern, *The Social Organization of Early Industrial Capitalism* (Cambridge, MA: Harvard University Press, 1983).

21 Kenneth McNaught, 'E.P. Thompson vs. Harold Logan: Writing about Labour and the Left in the 1970s', *Canadian Historical Review*, 42 (1981), 141–68. Lest those unfamiliar with Canadian historical writing be perplexed with a reference to Archie Bunker-charivari culture, I had just published an article in *Labour/Le Travail* on the ritual of charivari, relating it to class formation and its varied tensions and antagonisms. See Bryan D. Palmer, 'Discordant Music: Charivaris and Whitecapping in Nineteenth-Century North America', *Labour/Le Travailleur*, 3 (1978), 5–62. See also Desmond Morton, 'E.P. Thompson dans les arpents de neige: les historiens Canadiens-Anglais et la classe ourvière', *Revue d'Histoire de l'Amérique français*, 37 (1983), 165–84.

22 J.L. Granatstein, *Who Killed Canadian History?* (Toronto: Harper Collins, 1998), pp. 60–61. Marxist labour historians also attracted the attention of the Royal Canadian Mounted Police, which received reports from a spy. See Gregory S. Kealey, 'The Empire Strikes Back: The Nineteenth-Century Origins of the Canadian Secret Service', *Journal of the Canadian Historical Association*, 10 (1999), 3–18.

23 Francis Fukuyama, *The End of History and the Last Man* (New York: Free Press, 1992). Insightful commentary appeared in Perry Anderson, 'The Ends of History', in idem, *A Zone of Engagement* (New York and London: Verso, 1992), pp. 279–375.

24 See *Canada Investigates Industrialism: The Royal Commission on the Relations of Labor and Capital, 1889*, ed. by Greg Kealey (Toronto: University of Toronto Press, 1973); Fernand Harvey, *Révolution industrielle et travailleurs: une enquêsur les rapports entre le capital et le travail au Québec à la fin du 19e siècle* (Montréal: Boréal Express, 1978). An early gendered reading is Susan Mann Trofimenkoff, 'One Hundred and One Muffled Voices: Canada's Industrial Women of the 1880s', *Atlantis*, 3 (1977), 67–82.

25 See Jacques Rouillard, *Les travailleurs du cotton au Québec* (Montréal: Les presses de l'Université du Québec, 1974); idem, *Les Syndicats nationaux au Québec de 1900 à 1930* (Montréal: Les presses de l'Université Laval, 1979); idem, *Histoire de la CSN, 1921–1981* (Montréal: Boréal Express, 1981).

26 Hann et al., *Primary Sources in Canadian Working-Class History*; André E. LeBlanc and James D. Thwaites, *Le Monde Ourvier au Québec: bibliographie retrospective* (Montréal: Les presses de l'Université du Québec, 1973).

27 Note particularly Alfred Dubuc, 'L'influence de l'école des "Annales" au Québec', Unpublished mimeograph, Département d'histoire, Université du Québec à Montréal, 1978; Fernand Harvey, 'L'histoire des travailleurs québécois: les variations de la conjuncture et de l'historiographie', in *Le movement ouvrier au Québec,* ed. by Fernand Harvey (Montréal: Boréal Express, 1979), pp. 9–43.

28 Contrast the accent on North American traditions and the British Marxists evident in Russell Hann and Gregory S. Kealey, 'Documenting Working-Class History: North American Traditions and New Approaches', *Archivaria,* 4 (1977), 92–114, and the discussion of theory and 'the state of the question' in Noël Belanger et al., *Les Travailleurs Québecois, 1851–1896* (Montréal: Les presses de l'Université du Québec, 1975).

29 Fernand Ouellet, 'La modernization de l'historiographie et l'emergence d l'histoire sociale', *Recherches Sociographiques,* 26 (1985), 11–83. On institutions and ideas as the subject of work of the late 1960s and early 1970s see Louis-Marie Tremblay, *Évolution de la philosophie du syndicalisme au Québec, 1940–1965* (Ottawa: Éditions de l'Université d'Ottawa, 1968); Jacques Dofny et Paul Bernard, *Le syndicalisme au Québec: structure et movement* (Ottawa: Bureau do Conseil Privé, 1968); Louis-Marie Tremblay, *Le syndicalisme québécois: idéologies de la C.S.N. et de la F.T.Q., 1940–1970* (Montréal: Les presses de l'Université de Montréal, 1972); Jean Hamelin et Fernand Harvey, *Les Travailleurs Québecois, 1941–1971* (Québec: Institut superieur des sciences humaines, Université Laval, 1976).

30 Jean Hamelin, Paul Larocque, and Jacques Rouillard, *Répertoire des grèves dans la province de Québec au XIXe siècle* (Montréal: Lespresses de l'École des Hautes Études Commerciales, 1970); Noel Belanger, Jacques Bernier, Judith Burt, Fernand Harvey, Jean-Guy Lalande, Paul Larocque et Jacques Rouillard, sous la direction de Jean Hamelin et al., *Les Travailleurs Québécois, 1851–1896* (Montréal: Presses de l'Université du Québec, 1975).

31 Aside from Rouillard's important work, see, for suggestive statements from union activists, J. Francoeur, J.-P. Lefebvre, P. Vadeboncoeur and J.-L. Roux, *En grève! L'histoire de la C.S.N. et des luttles menées par ses militants de 1937 à 1963* (Montréal: Les Éditions du Jour, 1963); Alfred Charpentier, *Cinquante ans d'action ouvrière: les memoirs d'Alfred Charpentier* (Québec: Les Presses de l'Université Laval, 1971).

32 The opening statements of this research would be Judith Fingard, 'The Winter's Tale: Contours of Poverty in British North America, 1815–1860', Canadian Historical Association, *Annual Papers* (1974), 65–94; and idem, 'The Decline of the Sailor as a Ship Labourer in 19th Century Timber Ports', *Labour/ Le Travailleur,* 2 (1977), 35–53. But see also idem, *Jack in Port: Sailortowns of Eastern Canada* (Toronto: University of Toronto Press, 1982), critiqued in Richard Rice, 'Sailortown: Theory and Method in Ordinary People's History', *Acadiensis,* 13 (1983), 154–67.

33 Consider, for instance, the number of relatively early articles and studies that addressed the pre-1850 years, among them: Hélène Espeset, Jean-Pierre Hardy et David-Thiery Ruddel, 'Le monde dur travail au Québec au XVIIe et au XIXe

siècles: historiographie et état de la question', *Revue d'histoire de l'Amérique français*, 25 (1972), 499–539; Peter Moogk, 'Apprenticeship Indentures: A Key to Artisan Life in New France', Canadian Historical Association, *Annual Report* (1971), 65–83; Jean-Pierre Hardy and David-Thiery Ruddel, *Les apprentis artisans à Québe, 1660–1825* (Montréal: Les presses de l'Université du Québec, 1977); Robert Tremblay, 'La formation matérialle de la classe ouvrière à Montréal entre 1790 et 1830', *Revue d'histoire de l'Amérique français*, 33 (1979), 301–35. Note on the early economy, Louise Dechêne, *Habitants and Merchants in Seventeenth-Century Montreal* (Kingston and Montreal: McGill-Queen's University Press, 1992).

34 Compare Gregory S. Kealey, 'Artisans Respond to Industrialism: Shoemakers, Shoe Factories, and the Knights of St. Crispin in Toronto', Canadian Historical Association, *Historical Papers* (1973), 137–57; idem, 'The 'Honest Workingman' and Workers' Control: The Experience of Toronto Skilled Workers', *Labour/ Le Travailleur*, 1 (1976), 32–68; Joanne Burgess, 'L'industrie de la chaussure à Montréal (1840–1870): Le passage de l'artisanal à la fabrique', *Revue d'histoire de l'Amérique français*, 31 (1977), 187–210.

35 Joanne Burgess, 'Exploring the Limited Identities of Canadian Labour: Recent Trends in English Canada and Quebec', *International Journal of Canadian Studies*, 1–2 (1990), 149–73; Ronald Rudin, *Making History in Twentieth-Century Quebec* (Toronto: University of Toronto Press, 1997), pp. 193–4.

36 See Robert H. Babcock, *Gompers in Canada: A Study in American Continentalism before the First World War* (Toronto: University of Toronto Press, 1974).

37 *The Workingman in the Nineteenth Century*, ed. by Michael S. Cross (Toronto: Oxford University Press, 1974) and *The Canadian Worker in the Twentieth Century*, ed. by Irving M. Abella and David Millar (Toronto: Oxford University Press, 1978).

38 Irving M. Abella, 'Labour and Working-Class History', in *A Readers' Guide to Canadian History, Vol. 2: Confederation to the Present*, ed. by J.L. Granatstein and Paul Stevens (Toronto: University of Toronto Press, 1982), pp. 114–36 (p. 114).

39 Morton, 'Millennial Reflections', p. 36.

40 Ramsay Cook, 'Canadian Centennial Cerebrations', *International Journal*, 31 (1967), 663; J.M.S. Careless, '"Limited Identities" in Canada', *Canadian Historical Review*, 40 (1969), 1–10.

41 The first such jointly sponsored endeavour was the September 1981 Commonwealth Labour History Conference at Warwick University, involving scholars from Australia, Canada and the United Kingdom. Later conferences resulted in publications. See *Class, Community, and the Labour Movement: Wales and Canada, 1850–1930*, ed. by Deian R. Hopkin and Gregory S. Kealey (No Place: Llafur/CCLH, 1989); *Canadian and Australian Labour History: Towards a Comparative Perspective*, ed. by Gregory S. Kealey and Greg Patmore (St. John's, Newfoundland: CCLH, 1990); and *Labour/Le Travail*, 38 (1996), also issued as *Labour History*, 71 (1996).

42 Craig Heron, 'The Crisis of the Craftsman: Hamilton's Metal Workers in the Early Twentieth Century', *Labour/Le Travailleur*, 6 (1980), 7–49 (esp. p. 72,

quoting Hinton).

43 Wayne Roberts, 'Artisans, Aristocrats, and Handymen: Politics and Unionism Among Toronto Skilled Building Trades Workers, 1896–1914', *Labour/Le Travailleur*, 1 (1976), 92–121; Roberts, 'Toronto Metal Workers and the Second Industrial Revolution, 1896–1914', *Labour/Le Travailleur*, 6 (1980), 49–72.

44 Ian McKay, 'Capital and Labour in the Halifax Baking and Confectionary Industry in the Last Half of the Nineteenth Century', *Labour/Le Travailleur*, 3 (1978), 61–108.

45 Among many writings see, for instance, *On the Job: Confronting the Labour Process in Canada* ed. by Craig Heron and Robert Storey (Kingston and Montreal: McGill-Queen's University Press, 1986); Ian Radforth, *Bush Workers and Bosses: Logging in Northern Ontario, 1900–1980* (Toronto: University of Toronto Press, 1987); Craig Heron, *Working in Steel: The Early Years in Canada, 1883–1935* (Toronto; McClelland and Stewart, 1988).

46 Ian McKay, 'The Three Faces of Canadian Labour History', *History Workshop*, 24 (1987), 172–79; idem, 'Historians, Anthropology, and the Concept of Culture', *Labour/Le Travailleur*, 8/9 (1981–1982), 185–241 (esp. pp. 185-186, 216, 223, 225, 240–41). Contrast these early 1980s reflections on Williams with McKay's more recent efforts to present an overarching history of emergent socialist thought in Canada. See, for instance, Ian McKay, *Rebels, Reds, Radicals: Rethinking Canada's Left History* (Toronto: Between the Lines, 2005), in which Marx is presented as 'a dynamic and changing cultural code' (p. 15), and Ian McKay, *Reasoning Otherwise: Leftists and the People's Enlightenment in Canada, 1890–1920* (Toronto: Between the Lines, 2008).

47 David Jay Bercuson, 'Labour Radicalism and the Western Industrial Frontier, 1897–1919', *Canadian Historical Review*, 48 (1977), 154–75; and his historiographic afterword in the reprint of Bercuson's *Confrontation at Winnipeg: Labour, Industrial Relations, and the General Strike* (Kingston and Montreal: McGill-Queen's University Press, 1990), pp. 196–205. For Kealey's rejoinder see: '1919: The Canadian Labour Revolt', *Labour/Le Travail*, 13 (1984), 11–44. Other writing of a slightly different accent includes Craig Heron, 'Labourism and the Canadian Working Class', *Labour/Le Travail*, 13 (1984), 45–76; James Naylor, *The New Democracy: Challenging the Social Order in Industrial Ontario, 1914–1925* (Toronto: University of Toronto Press, 1991); *The Workers' Revolt in Canada, 1917–1925*, ed. by Craig Heron (Toronto: University of Toronto Press, 1998).

48 An early challenge focused on the quantitative evidence relating to Knights of Labor local assemblies. See Michael Piva, 'The Bonds of Unity: A Comment', and Gregory S. Kealey and Bryan D. Palmer, 'The Bonds of Unity: Some Further Reflections', *Histoire Sociale/Social History*, 31 (1983), 169–89. Piva was responding to Bryan D. Palmer and Gregory S. Kealey, 'The Bonds of Unity: The Knights of Labor in Ontario, 1880–1900', *Histoire Sociale/Social History*, 28 (1981), 369–411.

49 *Labouring Lives: Work and Workers in Nineteenth-Century* Ontario, ed. by Paul Craven (Toronto: University of Toronto Press, 1995).

50 Drache's article and my rejoinder appear in *Canadian Labour History: Selected Readings*, ed. by David J. Bercuson and David Bright (Toronto: Copp, Clark, Longman, 1984), pp. 6–75.

51 Lynne Marks, *Revivals and Roller Rinks: Religion, Leisure, and Identity in Late-Nineteenth-Century Small-Town Ontario* (Toronto: University of Toronto Press, 1996). I raised a number of issues about evidence and interpretation in Marks's writings in Bryan D. Palmer, 'Historiographic Hassles: Class and Gender, Evidence and Interpretation', *Histoire Sociale/Social History*, 33 (2000), 105–44, which was responded to by Marks, 'Heroes and Hallelujahs – Labour History and the Social History of Religion in English Canada: A Response to Bryan Palmer', *Histoire Sociale/Social History*, 34 (2001), 169–86.

52 Robert B. Kristofferson, *Craft Capitalism: Craftworkers and Early Industrialization in Hamilton, Ontario, 1840–1872* (Toronto: University of Toronto Press, 2007), esp. pp. 8–9, 246, 202, 15–16, 112; Douglas McCalla review in *American Historical Review*, 113 (2008), 1513–14.

53 Peter S. McInnis, *Harnessing Labour Confrontation: Shaping the Postwar Settlement in Canada, 1943–1950* (Toronto: University of Toronto Press, 2002).

54 Among a number of studies, see Karen Dubinsky, *Improper Advances: Rape and Heterosexual Conflict in Ontario, 1880–1929* (Chicago: University of Chicago Press, 1993); Steven Maynard, '"Horrible Temptations": Sex, Men, and Working-Class Male Youth in Urban Ontario, 1890–1935', *Canadian Historical Review*, 78 (1997), 191–235; idem, 'Through a Hole in the Lavatory Wall: Homosexual Subcultures, Police Surveillance, and the Dialectics of Discovery, 1890–1930', *Journal of the History of Sexuality*, 5 (1994), 207–42; Annalee Golz, 'Family Matters: The Canadian Family and the State in the Postwar Period', *Left History*, 1 (1993), 9–50.

55 Todd McCallum, 'The Reverend and the Tramp, Vancouver, 1931: Andrew Roddan's *God in the Jungles*', *BC Studies*, 147 (2005), 51–88; idem, 'The Great Depression's First History? The Vancouver Archives of Major J.S. Matthews and the Writing of Hobo History', *Canadian Historical Review*, 87 (March 2006), 79–107; idem, 'Vancouver Through the Eyes of a Hobo: Experience, Identity, and Value in the Writing of Canada's Depression-Era Tramps', *Labour/Le Travail*, 59 (2007), 43–68.

56 J. Peter Campbell, *Canadian Marxists and the Search for a Third Way* (Kingston and Montreal: McGill-Queen's University Press, 1999).

57 For the scope of much of this work see *Labour and Working-Class History in Atlantic Canada: A Reader*, ed. by David Frank and Gregory S. Kealey (St. John's, Newfoundland: Institute of Social and Economic Research, 1995).

58 Among many possible statements, see especially Sean T. Cadigan, *Hope and Deception in Conception Bay: Merchant-Settler Relations in Newfoundland, 1785–1855* (Toronto: University of Toronto Press, 1995); idem, 'Battle Harbour in Transition: Merchants, Fishermen, and the State in the Struggle for Relief in a Labrador Fishing Community during the 1930s', *Labour/Le Travail.* 26 (1990), 125–50; idem, *Newfoundland and Labrador: A History* (Toronto: University of Toronto Press, 2009).

59 Miriam Wright, *A Fishery for Modern Times: The State and the Industrialization of the Newfoundland Fishery, 1934–1968* (Toronto: Oxford University Press, 2001); Marilyn Porter, '"She Was Skipper of the Shore Crew": Notes on the Sexual Division of Labour in Newfoundland', *Labour/Le Travail,* 15 (1985), 105–23; Barbara Neis, 'From "Shipped Girls" to "Brides of the State": The Transition from Familial to Social Patriarchy in the Newfoundland Fishing Industry', *Canadian Journal of Regional Science,* 16 (1993), 185–202.

60 Mark Leier, *Red Flags and Red Tape: The Making of a Labour Bureaucracy* (Toronto: University of Toronto Press, 1995); idem, *Rebel Life: The Life and Times of Robert Gosden – Revolutionary, Mystic, Labour Spy* (Vancouver: New Star Books, 1999).

61 Andrew Parnaby, *Citizen Docker: Making a New Deal on the Vancouver Waterfront, 1919–1939* (Toronto: University of Toronto Press, 2008); Rolf Knight, *Indians at Work: An Informal History of Native Indian Labour in British Columbia, 1858–1930* (Vancouver: New Star Books, 1978); Steven High, 'Native Wage Labour and Independent Production during the "Era of Irrelevance"', *Labour/Le Travail,* 37 (1996), 243–64.

62 David Frank, *J.B. McLachlan: A Biography – The Story of a Legendary Labour Leader and the Cape Breton Coal Miners* (Toronto: James Lorimer, 1999); John Manley, 'Preaching the Red Stuff: J.B. McLachlan , Communism, and the Cape Breton Coal Miners, 1922–1935', and David Frank and John Manley, 'The Sad March to the Right: J.B. McLachlan's Resignation from the Communist Party of Canada, 1936', both in *Labour/Le Travail.* 30 (1992), 65–134; John Manley, 'Moscow Rules? "Red" Unionism and "Class Against Class" in Britain, Canada, and the United States', *Labour/Le Travail,* 56 (2005), 9–50.

63 For background to the interest in state security issues, see Gregory S. Kealey, 'State Repression of Labour and the Left in Canada, 1914–1920: The Impact of the First World War', *Canadian Historical Review,* 73 (1992), 281–314.

64 *Lectures in Canadian Labour and Working-Class History,* ed. by W.J.C. Cherwinski and Gregory S. Kealey (St. John's, Newfoundland: CCLH, 1985); *The Woman Worker, 1926–1929,* ed. by Margaret Hobbs and Joan Sangster (St. John's, Newfoundland: CCLH, 1999). The three surveys of Canadian labour history offered readers highly different accounts and analytic accents, and here I cite their 1990s issues: Desmond Morton, *Working People: An Illustrated History of the Canadian Labour Movement* (Toronto: Summerhill Press, 1990); Bryan D. Palmer, *Working-Class Experience: Rethinking the History of Canadian Labour, 1800–1991* (Toronto: McClelland and Stewart, 1992); Craig Heron, *The Canadian Labour Movement: A Short History* (Toronto: Lorimer, 1996).

65 Joan Sangster, 'Feminism and the Making of Canadian Working-Class History: Exploring the Past, Present, and Future', *Labour/Le Travail,* 46 (2000), 125–65 (pp. 139–40, 146); Morton, 'Millennial Reflections', p. 35.

66 Alice Kessler-Harris, 'Where Are the Organized Women Workers?', *Feminist Studies,* 3 (1975), 92–110. Much of the research and writing of this period addressed women's waged work on the one hand, and middle-class women's reform movements on the other. See *A Not Unreasonable Claim: Women and Reform in Canada, 1880s to 1920s* ed. by Linda Kealey (Toronto: Women's

Press, 1979); *Travaillueses et feminists: les femmes dans la société québécois*, ed. by Marie Lavigne and Yolande Pinard (Montréal: Boreal Express, 1983); *Union Sisters: Women in the Labour Movement*, ed. by Linda Briskin and Linda Yanz (Toronto: Women's Press, 1983).

67 Wayne Roberts and Alice Klein, 'Besieged Innocence: The "Problem" and Problems of Working Women, Toronto, 1896–1914', in *Women at Work: Ontario, 1880–1930*, ed. by Janice Acton et al. (Toronto: Canadian Women's Educational Press, 1974), pp. 211–60, strikes a structural note of explanation as opposed to the 'ideological' and 'cultural' analysis evident in other essays in the same edited collection. See also Wayne Roberts, *Honest Womanhood: Feminism, Femininity and Class Consciousness among Toronto Working Women, 1893–1914* (Toronto: New Hogtown Press, 1976).

68 *Hidden in the Household: Women's Domestic Labour Under Capitalism*, ed. by Bonnie Fox (Toronto: Women's Educational Press, 1980); Meg Luxton, *More Than a Labour of Love: Three Generations of Women's Work in the Home* (Toronto: Canadian Women's Educational Press, 1980); *The Politics of Diversity: Feminism, Nationalism, and Marxism*, ed. by Michèle Barrett and Roberta Hamilton (London: Verso, 1986); Wally Seccombe, *A Millennium of Change: Feudalism and Capitalism in Northwestern Europe* (London: Verso, 1992); idem, *Weathering the Storm: Working-Class Families from the Industrial Revolution to the Fertility Decline* (London: Verso, 1994).

69 See *Feminism and Political Economy: Women's Work, Women's Struggles*, ed. by Heather Jon Maroney and Meg Luxton (Toronto: Methuen, 1987).

70 See Meg Luxton, 'Feminism as a Class Act: Working-Class Feminism and the Women's Movement in Canada', *Labour/Le Travail*, 48 (2001), 63–88; Heather Jon Maroney, 'Feminism at Work', *New Left Review*, 141 (1983), 51–71.

71 Bettina Bradbury, *Working Families: Age, Gender, and Daily Survival in Industrializing Montreal* (Toronto: McClelland and Stewart, 1993). See also Peter A. Baskerville and Eric W. Sager, *Unwilling Idlers: the Urban Unemployed and Their Families in Late Victorian Canada* (Toronto: University of Toronto Press, 1998).

72 Joan Sangster, *Dreams of Equality: Women on the Canadian Left, 1920–1960* (Toronto: McClelland and Stewart, 1989); Janice Newton, *The Feminist Challenge to the Canadian Left, 1900–1918* (Montreal and Kingston: McGill-Queen's University Press, 1995); Linda Kealey, *Enlisting Women for the Cause: Women, Labour and the Left in Canada, 1890–1920* (Toronto: University of Toronto Press, 1998); Andrée Levesque, *Virage à gauche interdit: les communists, les socialistes, and leur enemies au Québec* (Montréal: Boréal Express, 1984); idem, *Scènes de la Vie en Rouge: L'époque de Jeanne Corbin, 1906–1944* (Montréal: Boréal Express, 1999).

73 Ruth Frager, *Sweatshop Strife: Class, Ethnicity, and Gender in the Jewish Labour Movement of Toronto, 1900–1939* (Toronto: University of Toronto Press, 1992); Mercedes Steedman, *Angels of the Workplace: Women and the Construction of Gender Relations in the Canadian Clothing Industry, 1900–1940* (Toronto: McClelland and Stewart, 1998); Julie Guard, 'Fair Play or Fair Pay: Gender Relations, Class Consciousness, and Union Solidarity in the Canadian

UE', *Labour/Le Travail*, 37 (1996), 149–77.

74 Varpu Lindström Best, *Defiant Sisters: A Social History of Finnish Immigrant Women in Canada, 1890–1930* (Toronto: Multicultural History Society of Ontario, 1988); Franca Iacovetta, *Such Hardworking People: Italian Immigrants in Postwar Toronto* (Montreal and Kingston: McGill-Queen's University Press, 1992).

75 Veronica Strong-Boag, *The New Day Recalled: The Lives of Girls and Women in English Canada, 1919–1939* (Toronto: Copp Clark, 1988); Suzanne Morton, *Ideal Surroundings: Domestic Life in a Working-Class Suburb in the 1920s* (Toronto: University of Toronto Press, 1995).

76 Joan Scott, 'Gender: A Useful Category of Historical Analysis', *American Historical Review*, 91 (1986), 1053–75. For the impact of Scott's article see the 2008 forum, 'Revisiting "Gender: A Useful Category of Historical Analysis"', *American Historical Review*, 113 (2008), 1344–1430.

77 A major statement of mainstream animosity was Michael Bliss, 'Privatizing the Mind: The Sundering of Canadian History, the Sundering of Canada', *Journal of Canadian Studies*, 26 (Winter 1991–1992), 5–17; and for a drawing together of some of his previous thoughts, Granatstein, *Who Killed Canadian History?* The most sustained response appeared in A.B. McKillop, 'Who Killed Canadian History? A View from the Trenches', *Canadian Historical Review*, 80 (1999), 269–99. I offered a complicating rejoinder to McKillop in Bryan D. Palmer, 'Of Silences and Trenches: A Dissident View of Granatstein's Meaning', *Canadian Historical Review*, 80 (1999), 676–86.

78 Kathryn McPherson, *Bedside Matters: The Transformation of Canadian Nursing, 1900–1990* (Toronto: Oxford University Press, 1996); Cecilia Danysk, *Hired Hands: Labour and the Development of Prairie Agriculture, 1880–1930* (Toronto: McClelland and Stewart, 1995); Cristina Burr, *Spreading the Light: Work and Labour Reform in Late Nineteenth-Century Toronto* (Toronto: University of Toronto Press, 1999); Carolyn Strange, *Toronto's Girl Problem: The Perils and Pleasures of the City, 1880–1930* (Toronto: University of Toronto Press, 1995); Pamela Sugiman, *Labour's Dilemma: The Gender Politics of Automobile Workers in Canada, 1937–1979* (Montreal and Kingston: McGill-Queen's University Press, 1994).

79 *Gender and History in Canada*, ed. by Joy Parr and Mark Rosenfeld (Toronto: Copp Clark, 1996); *Gendered Pasts: Historical Essays in Femininity and Maculinity in Canada*, ed. by Kathryn McPherson, Cecilia Morgan, and Nancy M. Forestell (Toronto: Oxford University Press, 1999).

80 Joy Parr, *The Gender of Breadwinners: Women, Men, and Change in Two Industrial Towns, 1880–1950* (Toronto: University of Toronto Press, 1990), esp. pp. 11, 8, 119; idem, 'Gender History and Historical Practice', *Canadian Historical Review*, 76 (1995), 354–76.

81 Joan Sangster, *Earning Respect: The Lives of Working Women in Small Town Ontario, 1920–1960* (Toronto: University of Toronto Press, 1995); idem, '"We No Longer Respect the Law": The Tilco Strike, Labour Injunctions, and the State', *Labour/Le Travail*, 53 (2004), 47–88.

82 Joan Sangster, 'Beyond Dichotomies: Re-Assessing Gender History and

Women's History in Canada', *Left History*, 3 (1995), 109–121. This article was replied to in force by two teams of two historians, with Sangster responding in *Left History*, 3–4 (1995–1996), 205–48.

83 Steven Penfold, '"Have You No Manhood in You?": Gender and Class in the Cape Breton Coal Towns, 1920–1926', *Acadiensis*, 23 (1994), 21–44 (p. 23).

84 Steven Penfold to *Left History* editors and Joan Sangster, 'Reconsidering Dichotomies', *Left History*, 3–4 (1995–1996), 238, 241.

85 Note the particularly personalized and often wrong-headed commentary in Mariana Valverde, 'Some Remarks on the Rise and Fall of Discourse Analysis', *Histoire Sociale/Social History*, 33 (2000), 59–77 (esp. pp. 64–65).

86 Mark Leier, 'W[h]ither Class: Regionalism, Class, and the Writing of BC History', with responses by Palmer, Strong-Boag, and Robert A.J. Macdonald, and a rejoinder by Leier, *BC Studies*, 111 (1996), 61–98.

87 This is how I read a trend in contemporary historiographic reflection. Note, for instance, William H. Sewell, *Logics of History: Social Theory and Social Transformation* (Chicago: University of Chicago Press, 2005); Geoff Eley and Keith Nield, *The Future of Class in History: What's Left of the Social?* (Ann Arbor: University of Michigan Press, 2007).

88 Alicia Muszynski, *Cheap Wage Labour: Race and Gender in the Fisheries of British Columbia* (Montreal and Kingston: McGill-Queen's University Press, 1996); Gillian Creese, *Contracting Masculinity: Gender, Class, and Race in a White Collar Union, 1944–1994* (Toronto: Oxford University Press, 1999); Julie Guard, 'Authenticity on the Line: Women Workers, Native "Scabs", and the Multi-Ethnic Politics of Identity in a Left-Led Strike in Cold War Canada', *Journal of Women's History*, 15 (2004), 117–40.

89 Ruth Frager, 'Labour History and the Interlocking Hierarchies of Class, Ethnicity, and Gender: A Canadian Perspective', *International Review of Social History*, 44 (1999), 217–47.

90 *Women, Gender, and Transnational Lives: Italian Workers of the World*, ed. by Donna Gabaccia and Franca Iacovetta (Toronto: University of Toronto Press, 2002); Franca Iacovetta, *Gatekeepers: Reshaping Immigrant Lives in Cold War Canada* (Toronto: Between the Lines, 2006).

91 *Canadian Working-Class History: Selected Readings*, ed. by Ian Radforth and Laurel Sefton (Toronto: Canadian Scholars' Press, 1992).

92 Leo Panitch and Donald Swartz. *From Consent to Coercion: The Assault on Trade Union Freedoms* (Toronto: Garamond Press, 2003) has gone through many printings and revisions, and is now in its third edition. Its origins lie in an article published in *Labour/Le Travail*, 13 (1984), 133–157. See also Yonatan Reshef and Sandra Rastin, *Unions in the Time of Revolution: Government Restructuring in Alberta and Ontario* (Toronto: University of Toronto Press, 2003).

93 See especially Meg Luxton and June Corman, *Getting by in Hard Times: Gendered Labour at Home and on the Job* (Toronto: University of Toronto Press, 2001); Ann Porter, *Gendered States: Women, Unemployment Insurance and the Political Economy of the Welfare State in Canada, 1945–1997* (Toronto: University of Toronto Press, 2003).

94 Judy Fudge and Eric Tucker, *Labour Before the Law: The Regulation of Workers' Collective Action in Canada, 1900–1948* (Toronto: Oxford University Press, 2001).

95 *Labouring Canada: Class, Gender, and Race in Canadian Working-Class History*, ed. by Bryan D. Palmer and Joan Sangster (Toronto: Oxford University Press, 2008); Becki L. Ross, 'Bumping and Grinding on the Line: Making Nudity Pay', *Labour/Le Travail*, 46 (2000), 221–50.

96 See, for instance, the arguments of Laurel Sefton MacDowell, *Renegade Lawyer: The Life of J.L. Cohen* (Toronto: University of Toronto Press, 2001), p. 295.

97 Contrast contemporary treatment of the 'cultural' aspects of working-class life with studies of the late 1970s and 1980s. See, for instance, Craig Heron, *Booze: A Distilled History* (Toronto: Between the Lines, 2003); and Craig Heron and Steve Penfold, *The Workers' Festival: A History of Labour Day in Canada* (Toronto: University of Toronto Press, 2006).

98 Palmer, *Working-Class Experience* (1992), pp. 11–28 (pp. 13, 20).

99 McKay, *Rebels, Reds, Radicals*, pp. 47–48.

100 Magdalena Fahrni, *Household Politics: Montreal Families and Post-War Reconstruction* (Toronto: University of Toronto Press, 2005); Jarrett Rudy, *The Freedom to Smoke: Tobacco Consumption and Identity* (Montreal and Kingston: McGill-Queen's University Press, 2005); Christopher Dummitt, *The Manly Modern: Masculinity in Postwar Canada* (Vancouver: UBC Press, 2007).

7

Australia

Greg Patmore

This chapter examines the development of the study of labour history in Australia. It looks at its origins and the influence on its emergence of what is sometimes termed in Australia the 'Old Left'. It moves on to assess the impact of the 'New Left' on labour history during the 1960s and 1970s. It then discusses how the field fared in the 1980s and early 1990s as it embraced social history and operated in the context of the longest period of Labor federal government in Australian history. The final section of the chapter scrutinizes how labour history survived the Howard years from 1997 to 2007 and beyond.

The origins of Australian labour history

The genesis of labour history in Australia was linked to the growing strength of the Australian labour movement before 1914. In 1891, over 20 per cent of the New South Wales (NSW) workforce was organized in trade unions; by 1914, 45 per cent of Australian workers were union members. In the early 1890s, trade unionists established Labor Parties which formed governments at the federal level and in several states by the outbreak of the First World War. Labour's success in Australia attracted the interest of many overseas commentators, including Sidney and Beatrice Webb and Lenin.[1]

Some participants in the Australian labour movement believed it to be their duty to document these events for others. Following a visit to the US, John Norton, a labour journalist, adapted *The History of Capital and Labour in all Lands and Ages* from a US publication for Australian readers in 1888, the centenary of white settlement in Australia. The book reviewed not only the history of labour in Australia, but also developments internationally since antiquity. In addition to Australian chapters written by local trade unionists, there was a section on the history of US labour written by Terence Powderly, the then Grand Master Workman of the US Knights of Labor.[2] In the introduction to this volume of over 900 pages, Norton argued 'that the discovery and settlement of America and Australia are the two most important events of modern times. Christopher Columbus and James Cook were the saviours of society.' He claimed that while the 'sympathies and interests' of the US and Australia were similar, 'Australia was pre-eminently a labour state.' Norton celebrated Australian democracy and labour's role in building and preserving it. This link between nationalism, democracy and the labour movement remained a theme in Australian labour history.[3]

William Murphy, who contributed chapters on Tasmania and Victoria to *The History of Capital and Labour* and was a former Secretary of the Melbourne Trades Hall Council, subsequently published the *History of the Eight Hours Movement.* This two-volume work, which appeared in 1896 and 1900, reviewed the eight-hour movement in Australia and overseas. Murphy argued that Australian workers were the first to establish the eight-hour day. He attacked British authors such as James Edward Thorold Rogers and Sidney Webb for 'the continued repetition' of a 'fallacy' that the eight-hour system operated in medieval England. He claimed that in the US or the 'land of the Great Republic', capital had gained the assistance of the state in suppressing the movement towards the eight-hour day. Murphy also blamed the ethnic divisions within US labour for the failure to achieve the eight-hour day. The different nationalities in some major US unions were more concerned with resolving the 'congested ethics of continental socialism' than achieving shorter hours.[4]

Two other prominent 'activist' labour historians were George Black and William Guthrie Spence. Black was one of the first Labor Party parliamentarians in the NSW Legislative Assembly in 1891 and a Minister in the Holman NSW Labor Government. He wrote several pamphlet histories of the Labor Party prior to state elections for propaganda purposes. Black completed an official history of the Labor Party of NSW in 1915 and a multi-part pamphlet history in the late 1920s. Spence was the foundation president of the Amalgamated Shearers' Union, the foundation secretary of the Australian Workers' Union (AWU) and a federal Labor parliamentarian.[5] He wrote *Australia's Awakening* (1909) and *The History of the A.W.U.* (1911). Spence argued that the 1890 maritime strike was the turning point in Australian labour history because Australian unions adopted political means to achieve reforms and better conditions. He believed that unionism freed the bush worker from tyranny and extended the 'feeling of mateship'.[6]

Prior to the First World War, labour history found no place in Australian universities. British tradition dominated academic history, which was perceived as a positive science composed of facts. Once historians had collected the empirically verifiable facts, it was their duty to judge them. They could not study class or modes of production as these concepts were not empirically verifiable. British historians also adopted a 'whig view' of history, as the study of great men and the beneficial development of the English constitution – Britain's gift to the world. They argued that theories of humanity had to be drawn from great men rather than 'dwarfs and cripples'. These views were not seriously questioned until the 1960s.[7]

Australian university history departments hardly taught any Australian history, preferring to study the superior 'centres of civilization in Britain and Europe'. This was partly challenged when Ernest Scott became Professor of History at the University of Melbourne in 1914. He encouraged students to examine Australian sources. The establishment of archives, such as the Mitchell Library, and the publication of *Historical Records of Australia* facilitated this interest. These studies focused on exploration and settlement rather than labour history.[8]

The First World War shook the optimism of the early activist historians. Workers criticized Labor governments for failing to control prices and eroding civil liberties. This conflict culminated in the split over conscription and the defection of the pro-conscriptionists to more conservative parties. The split and the Russian Revolution increased the influence of radical groups such as the Industrial Workers of the World (IWW), the One Big Union, and later the Communist Party (CP). They argued that the Labor Party and trade union officials had sold out working-class interests.[9]

One source of labour history that reflected these divisions was the Workers' Educational Association (WEA). The WEA came to Australia from Britain just prior to the First World War. It aimed to combine the resources of the universities and the labour movement in order to promote worker education. At each participating university a Director of Tutorial Classes supervised worker education. Prominent WEA activists believed that the labour movement had played an important role in Australian history, but argued that labour should use its power 'responsibly' and curb militancy. These liberal views led to tension with trade unionists. Further, Meredith Atkinson, the English-born first Director of Tutorial Classes at the University of Sydney, angered unionists by supporting conscription.[10]

Despite these problems, WEA activists researched and published labour history. Garnet Portus, Director of Tutorial Classes and an economic history lecturer at the University of Sydney, contributed an article on the history of trade unionism to a collection of essays edited by Atkinson and published in 1920. He challenged the radicals and argued that the Australian labour movement was not doctrinaire socialist, but Fabian or reformist. Portus claimed that middle-class reformers had made the advent and power of the Labor Party possible. He warned radicals that neglect of the middle class would imperil the Labor Party. Less forthright were Leila Thomas and James Sutcliffe. Thomas, the WEA lecturer at the University of Sydney, completed the first known postgraduate thesis on Australian labour history in 1919. She examined the history of the labour movement in Sydney from 1788 to 1848. Sutcliffe, an English-born statistician with the Commonwealth Bureau of Census and Statistics and WEA teacher, published a joint paper in 1915 with Gerald Lightfoot, a colleague at the Bureau, on the history of Australian trade unionism. The paper provided a narrative history, which attributed the success of Australian trade unionism to arbitration, the Labor Party and 'effective organisation and discipline'. It also constituted the basis for Sutcliffe's book in 1921 on the history of Australian trade unionism.[11]

In contrast to the WEA labour historians, Vere Gordon Childe was sympathetic to the radical critique of Australian labour. He was a Sydney and Oxford University graduate, anti-conscription activist and private secretary to a NSW Labor Party leader. In *How Labour Governs* (1923) he argued that the objective of the labour movement should be the end of workers' enslavement under capitalism. He agreed with labour historians that the Australian labour movement had achieved a degree of 'formal perfection' and 'triumph' unequalled anywhere in the world. However, labour parliamentarians had failed to achieve the objective, not only as a result of 'selfish and cowardly' opportunism, but because their program in office had disillusioned and disorganized the workers. He also saw 1890 as the turning point in Australian labour history because of the labour movement's decision to take political action. Unlike the WEA labour historians, he even argued that trade union history before this turning point was not worthy of any 'special attention'. Childe believed that another turning point occurred with the arrival of the IWW from the United States in 1907. He claimed that although it neglected 'constructive plans for the future', the IWW played an important role in shifting the trade unions and the Labor Party to the left, particularly by its agitation for industrial unionism. Childe held that Australia would make the transition to socialism when a 'real' Labor government moved beyond 'threadbare' Labor Party Fabianism by coordinating its program of nationalization and defence of workers' conditions with the struggles of industrial unionists for self-management. Not surprisingly, labour historians sympathetic to parliamentarianism (or 'politicalism' as Childe called it) were not impressed with Childe's volume. Black claimed it was a book of 'blunders' and 'balderdash'. Childe left Australia and became a leading archaeologist in the United Kingdom.[12]

Meanwhile, in London, Timothy Augustine Coghlan, NSW Agent-General and former NSW Government Statistician, completed his four-volume *Labour and Industry in Australia* in 1918. He discussed the history of labour in Australia from white settlement in 1788 to federation in 1901, drawing upon his vast repository of statistics and other data. His work was detached from the contemporary debates over the labour movement in Australia. Coghlan's focus was wider than the conventional Australian pre-occupation with labour institutions. He examined the impact of wages, prices, land settlement, immigration and public works upon workers' lives. His broad-ranging social history foreshadowed the later criticisms of the narrowness of Australian labour history.[13]

The 'Old Left' 1930–1970

Following Childe's book, little Australian labour history was written until the rise of the 'Old Left', which included Brian Fitzpatrick, Russel Ward, Robin Gollan and Ian Turner. Their common background was the economic suffering of the 1930s depression and the growth of the CP. The Labor Party's failure to protect Australian workers during the depression and the CP's Popular Front policy in the late 1930s helped the Communists gain ground among workers and intellectuals. Although the party's credibility was tested by its initial opposition to the Second World War, its support for the war effort following the German invasion of the Soviet Union consolidated its growth. By the end of the Second World War, its membership exceeded 20,000. Communist influence declined with the Cold War and many intellectuals left the party following Khrushchev's denunciation of Stalin and the Soviet suppression of the Hungarian uprising in 1956.[14]

The Old Left historians generally saw Marxism not only as an ideology, but also as a methodology. On the whole, they endorsed the view that socialism would inevitably replace capitalism. But some Old Left labour historians were not Marxists. Brian Fitzpatrick did not join the CP and found Marxism 'neither a means of prediction nor a guarantee of revolution'.[15] Other notable labour historians of this period such as Bede Nairn and Russel Ward were labour supporters but not Marxists. The Old Left were nationalists – asserting Australia's cultural, economic and political independence. The weakening of Australia's links with Britain during the Second World War and the postwar struggle against colonialism encouraged their nationalism.[16]

Two of the earliest Old Left historians, Fitzpatrick and Lloyd Ross, studied at the University of Melbourne in the mid-1920s, when Ernest Scott was championing Australian history. Both were interested in leftwing politics and foundation members of the University Labor Club in 1925. Ross was a WEA lecturer and secretary of the NSW Branch of the Australian Railways Union from 1935 to 1943. He was a member of the CP during the late 1930s, but left the party in 1940 over its war policy. Ross's sympathetic biography of the socialist William Lane (1935) attacked the Labor Party for subordinating socialism to beliefs such as nationalism and individual advancement. He contended that Lane would be a hero when labour transformed Australia into a socialist society.[17]

Fitzpatrick was more significant. He was unable to obtain a full-time academic position, relying on journalism and occasional university grants. He wrote two major economic histories – *British Imperialism and Australia, 1788–1833* (1939) and *The British Empire in Australia, 1834–1939* (1941). His other major general works are *The Australian People* (1946) and *The Australian Commonwealth* (1956). He argued that economic developments underlay politics and challenged historians who presented the imperial relationship between Britain and Australia as advantageous; British capital exploited Australia for its advantage. Fitzpatrick claimed that the Australian labour movement tried to challenge British capital and achieve a more egalitarian society. Thus imperial and class relations merged. In these studies, Fitzpatrick doubted the success of legislative reform and expressed concern at the corruption of ideals and erosion of civil liberties.[18]

Fitzpatrick's most direct contribution to Australian labour history was his *A Short History of the Australian Labour Movement* (1940). He drew upon and simplified material from his two major economic histories to compose this text for soldiers. Fitzpatrick conceived the history of the Australian people as a struggle between the organized rich and the organized poor. Labour was the force for change, while Non-Labour opposed the 'advancement of society'. Fitzpatrick saw 1890 as the crucial date in Australian history, when the 'progressive' phase of capitalism ended and an alliance arose between the capitalists and the state against workers. Later critics cited this book and ignored Fitzpatrick's major publications in order to attack labour history.[19]

CP activists and educators relied upon Fitzpatrick's research to write crude Marxist interpretations of Australian labour history. They argued that the foundation of the CP was the most significant event in the history of the Australian labour movement. Utilizing Lenin's critique, Communists claimed that the Australian Labor Party and trade union officials were liberal bourgeois reformers, divorced from socialism. The CP was Lenin's 'Socialist Labour Party', which would lead Australian workers along the inevitable path towards the overthrow of capitalism.[20]

Fitzpatrick's work also influenced a small but growing band of academic labour historians in the 1950s and 1960s. The Chifley and Menzies Federal Governments considerably expanded Australian universities. They founded the Australian National University (ANU) at Canberra, where the Research School of Social Sciences provided a favourable climate for postgraduate research into Australian labour history. This new wave of labour historians came from tertiary training programmes for returned soldiers and high school teaching.[21]

One of the ANU postgraduate scholars was Russel Ward. He had served in the Second World War and was a schoolteacher. His book, *The Australian Legend* (1958), tried to trace the source of the myth of the typical Australian – the practical, egalitarian and hospitable man. He focused on the bush tradition of 'mateship', which he claimed assisted the formation of the Amalgamated Shearers' Union and permeated the trade union movement. From the trade unions it spread widely through Australian society. Ward believed that mateship explained why Australians were more tolerant of socialist and collectivist ideas than Americans. His exploration of a distinctive Australian legend was another example of the Old Left's nationalist sentiment.[22]

Robin Gollan had served in the Royal Australian Air Force during the Second World War and won an ANU scholarship to the London School of Economics where he completed his doctorate. His thesis was published as *Radical and Working Class Politics* (1960). Gollan defended the assumption that Australia had achieved major political and social advances during the second half of the nineteenth century. He argued that the Labor Party was the descendant of the progressive, nineteenth-century movements for democracy, land reform and the eight-hour day. These movements and the Labor Party shared the aim of making life tolerable for the majority. Labour was a force for change and a key to understanding Australian history.[23]

Gollan and other labour historians established the Australian Society for the Study of Labour History (ASSLH) in May 1961. British labour historians had formed the Society for the Study of Labour History (SSLH) in 1960 and the visit to Australia of its inaugural chair, Asa Briggs, encouraged the Australians to form their own society. Australia's political and intellectual environment also assisted the foundation of the Society. The conservative ascendancy in Australian postwar politics heightened the need for historians to assist the labour movement by examining the 'lessons of history' and highlighting the positive contribution of labour to Australian society. Further, the decline of the CPs in both Australia and Britain had resulted in the disarray of the left. The weakening of ideological divisions also encouraged dialogue between Marxist and non-Marxist labour historians. While the use of 'labour' rather than 'labor' in the name of the Society reflected a preference for the English rather than the US spelling, there was also a desire to avoid the new Society being viewed as an 'offshoot' or 'adjunct' of the Australian Labor Party. The ASSLH provided a focal point for labour historians and drew in political scientists and industrial relations practitioners.[24] As Gollan later noted: 'the Labour History Society was a kind of popular front, politically and intellectually'.[25] The Society was based at the ANU. One significant difference with the SSLH was the decision taken by the ASSLH to publish a refereed scholarly journal rather than a bulletin, with conference reports, research reports and book reviews. The first issue of its journal, later to be known as *Labour History*, appeared in January 1962. The founders of the Society were concerned with establishing the academic credentials of labour history in the hostile Cold War climate. This led to a bias in the ASSLH membership towards academics and accusations by some in the labour movement that historians were not writing for them but for 'career advancement'.[26]

In the first issue of the journal, Gollan, the inaugural president of the ASSLH, reviewed the state of labour history in Australia. He expressed anxiety at its narrow limits – the emphasis on biography and political history. However, he noted that there was still work to be done even here. For example, there were no suitable biographies of trade union leaders. Gollan called for a broader approach that included the social history of the working class, class relations, the history of popular culture, the history of ideas and histories of major trade unions. Since Coghlan, there had been few attempts to write a broad labour history. Ward's *The Australian Legend* had examined popular culture, while Eric Fry, another major early activist in the ASSLH, had completed a superb doctoral thesis at the ANU in 1956 on the Australian urban working class in the 1880s.[27]

In 1963 Gollan furthered his earlier call for more trade union history by producing *The Coalminers of New South Wales*. While his study focused on the history of the miners' union from 1860 to 1960, his nineteenth-century chapters went beyond this and presented an analysis of class relations in the coal industry. Gollan drew upon the records at the Australian Agricultural Company, the leading coal mining enterprise, to show how the union promoted employer mobilisation and organisation. However, his broad analysis did not extend to a close examination of workers' lives at home and in the community.[28]

Two years later, Ian Turner published his *Industrial Labour and Politics* from a doctoral thesis completed at the ANU. Turner had been an active member of the Melbourne University Labor Club and a member of the CP until 1958. His study examined the relationship between trade unions and politics in Eastern Australia from 1900 to 1921, when the Australian Labor Party adopted the objective of socialization of industry. Turner argued that labour history was a new kind of history because it focused on the 'masses rather than elites as the moving forces in the historical process'.[29] He took a more optimistic view of the labour movement than Childe. Turner claimed that there were more forces at work within the labour movement than any other social institution which helped ensure that the leadership did not manipulate the rank and file. He believed that 'the labour movement is the institutional method by which the masses transform themselves from passive to active elements in society, from weights to be pushed around to social levers in their own right'.[30]

Other labour historians also concentrated on narrow labour history – political parties, trade unions and labour biography. Ken Buckley contributed a history of the Amalgamated Society of Engineers, while Jim Hagan completed a history of the printers' unions. Les Louis examined relations between trade unions and political parties in Victoria during the 1930s depression. Leslie Crisp, Laurie Fitzhardinge and Patrick O'Farrell published biographies of the labour leaders Ben Chifley, William Morris Hughes and Harry Holland respectively. Political scientists wrote histories of the CP and Labor Party. The sole example of a broader labour history was Peter Macarthy's doctoral thesis on working-class living standards in Sydney and Melbourne from 1890 to 1920.[31]

There were several reasons why the narrower approach dominated labour history. First, specialization, whether it be in economic, military or labour history, was embedded in Australian history. Narrow labour history, with its emphasis on trade unions and political parties, fitted the theme. Second, doctoral theses were the source of many publications. Supervisors required their students to write 100,000 words on safe topics. Trade unions and political parties had distinct beginnings, clear themes of growth and survival, and easily contrived conclusions. Third, the growth of trade union archives, especially at what is now known as the Noel Butlin Archives Centre at the ANU, provided students with accessible empirical data. Finally, some of the 1960s labour historians came from working-class backgrounds and were interested in tracing their class origins.[32]

Both inside and outside universities there were critics of labour history. The Cold War and the fear of Communism made many labour historians easy targets for criticism and even political discrimination – the University of NSW denied Russel Ward a lectureship on political grounds. Critics included Manning Clark and Peter Coleman – later a Liberal politician. In 1956, Manning Clark attacked the view that Australia was the political and social laboratory of the world in the second half of the nineteenth century. He believed this view ignored the period before the gold rushes, over-emphasized the extent of political democracy after the gold rushes and lost sight of the importance of squatters and the urban bourgeoisie before 1890. Manning Clark criticized Childe and Fitzpatrick for providing an illusion of the Labor Party as pure and untainted in the 1890s, which made their histories read rather like the stories of 'fallen women'.[33] In 1962, Coleman argued that labour history had produced an Australian version of 'whig history' – an uncritical view of progress and an obsession 'with the creative role of the Labor movement and a denial of the contribution of the middle classes, the churches, the universities and non-radical reformist and liberal movements'.[34] These criticisms were based on Fitzpatrick's *A Short History of the Australian Labour Movement* rather than his more substantial works in which Fitzpatrick qualified his views of the labour movement and progress.[35]

The 'New Left' and social history 1970–1981

The 'New Left' also challenged the 'Old Left' labour historians. The background to its emergence and development included the protests over Australia's involvement in Vietnam, the demands for the civil and land rights of Aborigines, and the growth of the women's liberation movement in the late 1960s and early 1970s. Tertiary students were involved in these movements and they attacked Australian universities for failing to develop courses that dealt with power, imperialism, race and gender. The radical ideas of Louis Althusser, the French Marxist philosopher, the Italian thinker Antonio Gramsci and others influenced the dissidents, and journals such as *Arena* and *Intervention* became the focal point for their critique of Australian society. Four British historians especially influenced the New Left critique of Australian labour history – Edward Thompson, Eric Hobsbawm, E.H. Carr and Gareth Stedman Jones.[36] In Britain, the influence of these historians was apparent on the founders of *Social History*, which appeared in 1976. The inaugural editorial of this journal proclaimed that social history was not another specialized area such as labour history, but constituted 'a new kind of history'. It urged that the essential task of history was to explain 'the total social process' and analyse 'the whole range of forces promoting change and transformation, stability and continuity in past societies'.[37] Social historians were also concerned with the use of 'explicit theories and detailed models in the arduous task of constructing a history of societies'.[38] Australian New Left historians included Humphrey McQueen, Stuart Macintyre and Terry Irving. They criticized the Old Left for failing to define concepts such as class, ignoring issues such as racism and failing to develop an alternative historical methodology.[39]

In Australia Terry Irving was an early critic of Old Left labour history. He trained in history at the University of Sydney and later transferred to the department of government there. During the late 1960s he taught at the Free University, which Sydney radicals established as an alternative to conservative university courses. At a symposium on Australian labour history in 1967 he criticized Ian Turner and others for failing to define class and initiated the New Left argument that wage-earners in nineteenth-century NSW did not constitute a class. Three years later, Irving and Baiba Berzins argued that the Old Left tradition had retarded the analysis of revolutionary change in Australia. They claimed that the Old Left adopted the earlier 'radical' view that Australians during the nineteenth century had established a 'new country' that avoided Europe's class-based and class-divided society. The Old Left therefore accepted the existing structure of Australian society and believed that progress would inevitably lead to socialism.[40] Irving and Berzins called upon socialists 'to recognise that there is a middle-class hegemony which has imprisoned the left'.[41]

Humphrey McQueen's *A New Britannia* (1970) was the first major history publication from the New Left. McQueen cited with approval Carr's critique of the positive methodology of British history and Stedman Jones's call for socialist historians not to retreat to the 'safe pastures of labour history'. He agreed with Thompson's rejection of the 'base determines superstructure' model of Marxism. McQueen emphasized ideology, drawing upon Gramsci's concept of 'hegemony' and György Lukács's notion of 'false consciousness'. He accepted the conservative argument that the Old Left portrayed the labour movement as a tale of decline – 'a once radical people corrupted by their own victories'. Like Irving, McQueen criticized the Old Left for accepting the 'radical' view of democracy in nineteenth-century Australia rather than demolishing it. McQueen argued that the 'legend' was 'anti-radical and counter-revolutionary', debasing contemporary struggles. He dismissed the 1890s as a turning point, insisting that the Labor Party embodied the traditional petit-bourgeois values of Australian workers – 'acquisitive competition' and 'gross materialism'. The labour movement's socialism was not a novelty, since government intervention had been necessary in colonial society. McQueen disagreed with Fitzpatrick's view that Australia was a victim of British capitalism. Australia was rather a frontier of white capitalism on the edge of Asia. Nationalists wanted a stronger British Empire to defend them from Asian invasion. Their nationalism incorporated racism. Both the Old and the New Left criticized McQueen's book for over-emphasizing the class collaboration of the labour movement, excluding evidence of conflict and ignoring women and aborigines. Generally the critics agreed that McQueen's main contribution was to highlight the role of racism in Australian nationalism and 'mateship'.[42]

While McQueen highlighted the neglect of racism in Australian labour historiography, feminists emphasized the absence of women. Ward's 'mateship' did not include women and Turner's *Industrial Labour and Politics* excluded important groups of women workers because they did not form 'significant' trade unions.[43] Against the background of the worldwide women's movement in the early 1970s and the New Left critique of labour history, feminists began to challenge the male domination of Australian history. In an influential article in *Arena* in 1970, Ann Curthoys argued for a 'history of women' that went further than merely restoring women to the pages of history books. Curthoys contended that a new approach must analyse why historians had been preoccupied with public life and why men had dominated public life. Important issues to be considered included the impact of industrialization and Christianity on women.[44] Curthoys's call for a 'history of women' was assisted by a favourable political climate between December 1972 and November 1975. The progressive Whitlam Federal Labor Government raised community awareness of the status of women in Australian society through supporting equal pay cases before the Commonwealth Conciliation and Arbitration Commission and provided financial assistance for women's refuges and health centres. Whitlam established a Women's Section in his own department and appointed a feminist as his chief adviser on women's issues. During International Women's Year in 1975, the government provided hundreds of thousands of dollars for research into women's issues. Against this background a number of important books were published on women's history in 1975 and 1976. They included Anne Summers's *Damned Whores and God's Police*, Miriam Dixson's *The Real Matilda*, Beverly Kingston's *My Wife, My Daughter and Poor Mary Ann* and Edna Ryan and Anne Conlon's *Gentle Invaders*. In combination with other contributions, they broadened the focus of Australian labour history and raised the issue of class and gender.[45]

The New Left was also concerned with the neglect of class relations. In 1972 Stuart Macintyre asserted that the history of labour alone was inadequate to understand the totality – historians had to focus on class relations. John Rickard's *Class and Politics* (1976) and Raewyn Connell and Terry Irving's *Class Structure in Australian History* (1981) did shift the focus of Australian labour history away from one class – labour. Rickard examined NSW, Victoria and the Commonwealth from 1890 to 1910. He accepted Thompson's view that class arises out of the relationship between capital and labour. Rickard also took a broad view of class consciousness, noting that it embraced 'some sort of consciousness of an identity of interest [...]'. He discussed labour, compulsory arbitration and employers' organizations. However, Rickard's use of concepts such as class and class consciousness was imprecise. He drew upon both Karl Marx and Max Weber, using their different ideas when it suited him and ignoring their inconsistencies. Connell, like Irving, had taught at the Free University and moved from history to another discipline – sociology. The first chapter of their book dealt exclusively with the concept of class. They adopted the Thompsonian view of class with its emphasis upon the historical creation of class relationships. However, they did not believe that a high degree of class consciousness was a necessary condition for the creation of a class. Their historical analysis focused on the development of the capitalist mode of production in Australia from 1788 to 1975 and emphasized hegemony – 'a situation of cultural dominance held by one class in society as a whole'. While reviewers took issue with the book for neglecting women, aborigines, working-class agitators and capitalist accumulation, it constituted the most ambitious attempt by the New Left to combine theoretical concepts with historical narrative.[46]

The New Left and the development of social history also influenced the editorial committee of *Labour History*. Special issues appeared: 'Women at Work' (1975) and 'Who are Our Enemies? Racism and the Working Class in Australia' (1978). The range of articles widened to include convict protest, nineteenth-century feminism, the political consciousness of the unemployed and juvenile delinquency. In May 1981 the journal adopted the subtitle, 'A Journal of Labour and Social History'.[47] However, John Merritt, the editor, noted that, 'We have no intention [...] of simply jumping on a social history bandwagon [...] Nor do we intend to abandon the older style labour history, which always has covered far more than labor parties and unions.'[48] Merritt was to later note that there was also a pragmatic concern with keeping younger scholars interested in the ASSLH, with the establishment of feminist history journals and even talk at the ANU of a journal of social history.[49]

The 'older style' labour history continued to appear during this period. There were biographies of Labor Party leaders such as Tom Ryan, Jack Lang, James Scullin, John Curtin and Arthur Calwell. Labour historians completed more histories of unions, the Labor Party and radical political groups. Bede Nairn's *Civilising Capitalism* (1973) examined the labour movement in NSW from 1870 to 1900. He adopted a pluralist perspective, arguing that organized labour tamed the worst aspects of capitalism, but did not support the revolutionary overthrow of it. Hagan's *The History of the A.C.T.U.* (1981) explored the Australian principle of 'labourism' – a strong trade union movement, a parliamentary Labor Party, a protective tariff, a 'White Australia' and compulsory arbitration. Ian Turner wrote an introductory text on the history of Australian trade unionism (1976) and Dennis Murphy, a Queensland history academic, encouraged local labour activists to publish autobiographies and union histories.[50]

New Left and social historians failed to fundamentally alter the views of many labour historians during the 1970s, particularly the non-Marxist supporters of labour such as Nairn, who retained a strong belief in the progressive role of the labour movement in Australian history and remained sceptical about the analytical value of class.[51] Labour historians criticized the New Left and social historians for not understanding the political and intellectual context of the Old Left. The Old Left had challenged another one-class view of history – the conviction that elites alone were worthy of study – and several were victimized for their beliefs in the anti-Communist hysteria of the 1950s and early 1960s. The lack of a sophisticated Marxist analysis in Australia during the 1950s explained the failure of Fitzpatrick, Gollan and others to develop theoretical constructs such as class. Labour historians noted that Gollan did call for the broadening of labour history in 1961 and that he and his colleagues understood the complexity and importance of class relations. There was criticism of the assumption that the history of totalities was more important than their constituent parts. Labour historians claimed that New Left and social history books, articles and theses failed to meet expectations. They maintained that social historians were 'antiquarian' and unable to apply social theory borrowed from sociology and anthropology to history.[52] As Merritt noted in the May 1981 *Labour History* editorial, 'it is one thing to counsel perfection, another to achieve it'.[53]

Labour history, 1981–1996

After the publication of Merritt's *Labour History* editorial in May 1981 the percentage of articles in the journal dealing with the traditional fare of Australian labour history – the Labor Party, the CP, trade unions, strikes and radical movements – declined over the next fifteen years. From May 1981 to November 1996, only 39 per cent of the 242 articles concentrated on these traditional concerns. Stephen Garton has estimated that in the 1960s and 1970s this figure was 79 and 65 per cent respectively.[54]

While there was a decline in the coverage of traditional topics by *Labour History*, many books continued to focus on labour parties, radical movements and trade unions during this period. These included histories of the Australian Railways Union, the Australian Workers' Union, the Australian Bank Employees' Union and the Clothing and Allied Trades' Union. Histories of the Labor Party at the federal and state levels were also completed. Peter Love, in *Labour and the Money Power* (1984), examined labour populism in his analysis of the development of a theory of capitalist finance by the Australian labour movement – the 'Money Power'. Labour biographies continued to be important; for example Macintyre's *Militant: The Life and Times of Paddy Troy* (1984) and Nairn's *The Big Fella: Jack Lang and the Australian Labor Party 1891–1949* (1986). Frank Farrell's *International Socialism and Australian Labour* (1981) and Verity Burgmann's *'In Our Time': Socialism and the Rise of Labour, 1885–1905* (1985) broadened the analysis of the left.[55]

The critiques of the 1960s and 1970s concerning theory and history from below did impact on some institutional labour histories. One example was Ray Markey's *The Making of the Labor Party in New South Wales 1880–1900* (1988). The title of Markey's book reflected the New Left influence of Thompson. Markey linked the origins of the NSW Labor Party to the production process, economy and society. He criticized both 'traditional' and New Left labour historians for focusing on leaders rather than the relationship between leaders and their constituents. Markey defined the working class as an objective category – 'those men and women who possessed nothing but labour, which they sold for a price on the market'. He also identified an 'intermediate social strata' – semi-independent men on the land, miners and white-collar workers – who belonged to neither the working class nor the ruling class during his period of analysis. Markey argued that the importance of this intermediate group and the dream of independence for 'small men' gave rise to the ideological phenomenon of 'populism' – the dominant force in the Labor Party by 1900.[56]

On the whole institutional historians failed to explore directly theoretical debates concerning labour institutions – government, structure and growth. Where these issues are discussed in the literature, they remain marginal to charting the chronological development of the organization. An important exception to this was again Markey, who dealt explicitly with the concepts of new unionism, labour aristocracy and trade union democracy. Sometimes these problems reflected the constraints associated with writing official histories. Many are written in a context of limited time and financial resources, with a client institution expecting the historian to cover a major portion of Australian history.[57]

Despite these problems the continued publication of institutional labour history reflects the relative resilience of the Australian labour movement. As in most other OECD countries, trade union density declined during this period, falling from 49.5 per cent of the Australian workforce in 1982 to 31.1 per cent by 1996. However, in contrast to the industrial wing of the labour movement, the Labor Party held federal government for the longest period in its history from 1983 to 1996 and held government in every state for varying periods. Thus Australian unions operating through the Australian Council of Trade Unions, the sole national trade union centre, exercised unprecedented influence based on several versions of an Accord originally concluded with the Federal Labor Party in 1983. Institutional histories continued to constitute an important link between labour historians and the labour movement.[58]

While *Labour History*'s coverage of labour institutions and strikes declined from 1981 to 1996, its examination of issues raised by the feminists, the New Left and social historians increased. Articles on gender grew from 2 per cent in the 1960s to 15 per cent and there was another special issue of *Labour History* devoted to women and work in November 1991. Articles on race and racism rose from 3 per cent in the 1960s to 12 per cent in this period. One specific focus in this broad category was Aboriginal history, with a special issue of *Labour History* in November 1995 devoted to Aboriginal workers. Articles drawn from social history, but not related to work, constituted 15 per cent of the articles. There were also contributions on convicts, occupational health, culture and the role of the state.[59]

The New Left and social history have also influenced numerous texts written by labour historians. The Sydney Labour History Group's *What Rough Beast?* (1982) examined how the state has tried to ensure social order and dealt with challenges such as the Industrial Workers of the World. Kay Saunders's *Workers in Bondage* (1982) examined Melanesian indentured labour, while Henry Reynolds's *The Other Side of the Frontier* (1982), *Frontier* (1987) and *Law of the Land* (1987) provided fresh insights into the conquest of Aboriginal Australia.[60] A large number of books on gender appeared. Katrina Alford's *Production or Reproduction?* (1984) challenged the neglect of women before 1850 in Australian economic history. Stephen Nicholas's edited readings, *Convict Workers* (1988), provided a controversial re-interpretation of convict labour. Oral history provided the scope to reinforce history from below and bridged the gap between activists and academics. Important examples of the use of oral history were Wendy Lowenstein's *Weevils in the Flour* (1978) and *Under the Hook* (1982), a study of the great depression and an examination of the lives of Melbourne waterside workers, and John Shields's *All Our Labours* (1992), a collection of essays exploring twentieth-century Sydney workplaces.[61]

There were four other important publications. Janet McCalman's *Struggletown* (1984) was a community history of the Melbourne working-class suburb of Richmond from 1900 to 1965. She examined childhood, domestic life, housing, religion, work and local Labor politics. Ken Buckley and Ted Wheelwright's *No Paradise for Workers* (1988) combined Old Left Marxism with New Left concerns such as sexism and racism to present a social and economic history of white Australia prior to 1914. The authors questioned the view that Australia was a workers' paradise before that date, highlighting the casual and seasonal nature of most work, inferior housing and the neglect of public health.[62] Verity Burgmann and Jenny Lee's four-volume edited collection, *A People's History of Australia since 1788* (1988), constituted a critical challenge to the celebratory bicentennial histories of Australia. They asserted 'that we can only understand Australian history by analysing the lives of the oppressed'.[63] Their volumes included essays on aborigines, women, immigrants, popular culture, homosexuality and work. Terry Irving's edited volume, *Challenges to Labour History* (1994), confronted the continued reluctance of Australian labour historians to engage in explicitly theoretical debates. The essays dealt with issues such as Marxism, postmodernism, community, racism and gender and asserted Australian labour history's continued intellectual relevance.[64]

During this period, academics in university departments of industrial relations developed a growing influence in Australian labour historiography. Industrial relations and labour history shared common interests in regard to trade unions and the regulation of work. In Australia, industrial relations involves multi-disciplinary analysis, drawing upon economics, history, law and sociology. Labour history courses were part of industrial relations programmes. As industrial relations departments expanded in this period, they also employed labour historians who had been trained in history departments. The two main academic industrial relations journals, *Labour and Industry* and *The Journal of Industrial Relations*, published labour history. While there had been emphasis on prescriptive policy making, industrial relations scholars were increasingly interested in theoretical issues and even developing a radical political economy of industrial relations. Industrial relations academics were to further strengthen the interests of Australian labour history in areas such as the history of the state, particularly compulsory arbitration, employers' associations, the labour process and comparative labour history.[65]

Compulsory arbitration established minimum wages and conditions and aided unions through award provisions that gave preference to unionists in promotion and retention under certain conditions. During the 1980s attacks by de-regulationists on the arbitration system provided the background for a re-assessment of its genesis and early impact by labour historians and others supportive of the system. The most comprehensive discussion of compulsory arbitration was in a collection of essays edited by Stuart Macintyre and Richard Mitchell. The contributions were written by scholars drawn from industrial relations, history, law and economic history. The issues examined were: the origins of compulsory arbitration; who supported it; the effects; and theoretical perspectives, highlighting Marxism, liberalism, corporatism, feminism and labour process theory. One interesting finding was the crucial role that liberal lawyers played in developing the idea of compulsory arbitration and assisting the passage of the appropriate legislation. There are also case studies of three industries – building, road transport and retailing – which gave the reader a good overview of the before and after effects of compulsory arbitration in specific contexts.[66]

Labour process theory, popularized by Harry Braverman's *Labor and Monopoly Capital* (1974) and subsequent modifications of Braverman's thesis by writers such as Richard Edwards and Michael Burawoy, influenced Australian labour history. Approximately 7 per cent of the articles published in *Labour History* during this period focused on the labour process. As elsewhere, the rediscovery of the labour process allowed labour historians to explore the workplace and closely scrutinize management's labour practices. Labour process analysis also permitted Australian labour historians to gain further insights into gender relations, compulsory arbitration and unorganised workers.[67] Rae Frances, in an innovative article in *Labour History* in 1986, combined feminism with labour process theory, criticizing Braverman for being male-orientated and ignoring the ways in which patriarchal values undermined workers' resistance to changes in the labour process.[68]

Examinations of the Australian labour process pursued a variety of themes. While Chris Nyland indicated that scientific management played an important role in justifying a reduction of working hours after the First World War, Peter Cochrane argued that the Second World and the postwar labour shortages encouraged its dispersion throughout industry. Chris Wright highlighted the importance of management consultants in introducing scientific management and personnel practices after World War II. Braverman's emphasis on deskilling has triggered debates over the meaning of skill. John Shields, in a study of apprenticeship and craft work in nineteenth-century NSW, challenged the applicability of Braverman's deskilling thesis to Australia during that period. In contrast, Frances argued that deskilling was a major tendency in the clothing, boot and printing industries in Victoria from 1880 to 1939. However, Frances distinguished between 'specialisation' and 'fragmentation'. The former occurs where a worker with a general expertise has to perform a narrower range of tasks. The latter refers to a task that was formerly part of a unified whole and requires no knowledge of the total process to perform. 'Fragmentation' may involve reskilling as workers are required to learn new machines and operate them at high speeds. Labour historians indicated that state intervention through compulsory arbitration and wages boards had ambiguous consequences for the labour process. Several studies also focused on the attempts by US managers in Australia to introduce 'overseas best practices' in rifle manufacture and steel. There was also a major debate between Wright and Lucy Taksa over the significance of scientific management in Australia.[69] The labour process studies culminated in a major publication by Wright in 1995 which examined the history of Australian labour management practices and emphasized the significance of employers in understanding the labour experience both in the workplace and in the broader realm of industrial relations.[70]

There was also growing interest in comparative labour history. Labour historians from industrial relations backgrounds were influenced by comparative industrial relations research which increased the scope for explanation at a national level by examining similar and dissimilar industrial relations regimes. There had been few comparative labour history papers in *Labour History* and more broadly only a handful of studies took a comparative approach. In 1984 Brian Kennedy, for example, engaged in micro-comparative labour history in his study of the mining towns of Johannesburg and Broken Hill between 1885 and 1925. Australian labour historians have also participated in a number of international conferences and projects of a comparative nature. Eric Fry edited a collection of essays on Australian and New Zealand labour history. However, the comparative analysis was undertaken by the editor of the volume rather than the contributors.[71] A subsequent conference of Australia and Canadian labour historians in 1988 faced similar problems. While over thirty papers were presented at the conference and six subsequently published in an edited volume, only two papers drew direct comparisons. They examined railway labour and state intervention in industrial disputes.[72]

Comparative labour history reached its peak in the November 1996 *Labour History*, which was published as a joint issue with the Canadian *Labour/Le Travail*. This issue explicitly challenged the previous neglect of a comparative approach to labour history in the journal. It provided Australian-Canadian comparisons jointly authored by national experts whose close co-operation ensured the emergence of genuine comparative perspectives. The collection included work on trade unions and labour-in-politics, the traditional institutional foundations of labour history. There were also contributions that reflected a shift in both Australian and Canadian labour history towards social history. There were papers on culture, gender, state welfare and the labour process. This project served as a model and inspiration for later comparative labour history projects involving Australian labour historians. There were a number of findings in the volume on Australia and Canada that provided fresh insights into Australian labour history. Frances, Linda Kealey and Joan Sangster noted that Australian wages tribunals and compulsory arbitration provided Australian women with improved wages and a 'floor of protection' not available to Canadian women. Mark Bray and Jacques Rouillard suggested that the growth of mass unions in Australia and the Australian unions' political strategies led to a more sympathetic state that allowed Australian unions to prosper relative to Canadian unions before the 1940s.[73]

While labour history continued to expand, there were some concerns about its future. Burgmann argued that the rise of new social movements such as feminism and the relative decline of the labour movement made labour history irrelevant and boosted social history. Others such as Frances and Bruce Scates pointed out that rather than labour history being supplanted by social history, it had absorbed it and survived.[74] Labour history's traditionally critical perspective of Australian society, particularly its sympathy for the disadvantaged and emphasis on social equity, had been enhanced by social history rather than weakened by it. As the editorial policy of *Labour History* noted in May 1992: 'The history of labour, the classic social movement, has much to offer the new social movements. In turn labour history can learn from feminism and environmentalism.'[75]

Labour history in Australia: the Howard years and beyond

The concerns that Verity Burgmann raised about the future of the labour movement were heightened during the period of the Howard conservative federal government from 1996 to 2007, which through legislation such as *Work Choices* eroded the special legally protected place of unions in Australia.

Trade union density fell from 30.3 per cent of the labour force in 1997 to only 18.9 per cent in 2007. Australian universities came under pressure financially and the political climate was less favourable to more progressive scholarship. Industrial relations departments, an important source of labour history, were absorbed into larger departments of management, business and organizational studies. Exercises such the Research Quality Framework (RQF) placed greater pressure on academic labour historians to justify their scholarship and defend *Labour History*. Even within this climate the Labor Party continued to do well at the state level and, by the time of the defeat of the Howard federal Conservative government in November 2007, it had held government in every Australian state and territory. The ASSLH also joined a successful campaign to prevent the closure of the Noel Butlin Archives at the Australian National University in 1997. Even with the election of the Rudd federal Labor government these pressures continue. The repeal of *Work Choices* has not meant the full restoration of the special legal protection for Australian unions and the RQF has been replaced by a similar exercise, Excellence in Research for Australia (ERA).[76]

Compared to the previous period, there was a further slight decline in articles in *Labour History* dealing with traditional issues such as trade unions and political parties, with 34 per cent of the 228 articles dealing with these concerns. Some labour historians attempted to link their research directly to broader concerns about declining trade union membership. The issue of organizing new members, which is a major priority for an Australian trade union movement, has traditionally been marginal in charting the history of trade unions. The November 2002 issue featured a special thematic section on the history of union organizing with an introduction by Greg Combet, then secretary of the ACTU, highlighting the continued links between labour historians and the labour movement. There was also a decline in some of the topics that were associated with the rise of the New Left. Social history articles not relating to work, that dealt with issues such as health, death and marriage, dramatically declined compared to the previous period, from 15 per cent to 2 per cent. There was also a dramatic drop in the number of articles on gender – to 5 per cent. Articles on race and ethnicity also fell from 12 per cent to 8 per cent, with half of these articles on aboriginal history.

There was a significant growth in the articles concerned with the role of the state (11 per cent), particularly compulsory arbitration. This reflected broader pre-occupations with the dismantling of compulsory arbitration during this period, with a special thematic section of *Labour History* in November 2007 devoted to the centenary of the Harvester Judgement, when the Commonwealth Arbitration established a basic wage for male workers. There was growing interest in occupational health and safety (4 per cent), volunteer labour (4 per cent), consumption (3 per cent), particularly cooperatives, and local labour history (6 per cent). These categorizations can have broader implications. Local labour history provides insights into the local organization of workers into trade unions and political parties, giving answers to broader questions such as why unions form peak councils. Under the themes of volunteer labour and local labour history, labour historians have expanded our understanding of the historical experiences of women in Australia.[77]

Three developments in *Labour History* during this period relate to cultural history, anti-labour history and the continued expansion of the journal's focus beyond Australia. Articles dealing with cultural issues grew from 2 per cent in the previous period to 10 per cent. The term 'culture' has attracted fierce debates as to its meaning and historical importance.[78] As Curthoys noted in November 1994, cultural studies is a 'field of study, with particular interests in images, representations and modes of narration'.[79] The various expressions of 'labour culture' include music, working men's clubs, museums, banners, gambling, theatre, sports grounds and posters.[80] Curthoys emphasised that cultural history enhanced labour history by providing further insights into the 'less powerful people' and providing an 'active voice for those who did not leave direct records'.[81] *Labour History* published two separate thematic sections relating to culture. The first in November 2000 included contributions on rugby league, performance poetry and union banners. The link between labour culture and labour mobilization, a traditional concern of labour historians, is highlighted by Taksa in her study of the Eveleigh railway workshops in Sydney. The second thematic section in November 2003 examined the role of Australian museums and galleries in interpreting working life and culture. The issue highlighted the contested terrain of heritage preservation and management. There have been other examples. Nick Dyrenfurth and Marian Quartly in their contribution to the May 2007 issue of *Labour History* looked at the classic labour representation of the capitalist class – the 'Fat Man'. Labour intellectuals used the image of the villainous 'Fat Man' in cartoons to mobilize workers to defend 'the People' against the excesses of capitalism.[82]

Anti-labour history highlights a major problem underlying the field. How can you talk about labour in isolation from capital? Without understanding employers and conservative political groups, it is difficult to provide a clear analysis of trade union and left political parties' strategy and tactics. Labour historians from the Old and the New Left, such as Gollan, Rickard, Connell and Irving incorporated capital in their research. Labour process studies also encouraged labour historians to focus on employers. Anti-labour history, which provided 6 per cent of the articles in this period, has been strongly influenced by the work of labour historian Andrew Moore, who had undertaken major studies of the fascist New Guard during the interwar period and the Right in Australia.[83] Moore edited a thematic section of the November 2005 issue of *Labour History* which examined topics such as the New Guard and Pauline Hanson's One Nation.

In the pages of *Labour History*, Australian labour historians continued to extend their focus beyond Australia. Following on the Australian-Canadian model, *Labour History* published the results of similar comparative labour history projects with the UK (May 2005) and with New Zealand (November 2008). In the November 1998 issue of *Labour History* there was a series of articles that looked at the links between Australia and Ireland that arose from the 1798 Rebellion in Ireland. There have been articles on the history of labour movements in Asian countries such as Hong Kong, Vietnam and South Korea. Other contributions have included comparisons of the British and Australian Labour Parties and the influence of liberalism on Australian and US labour leaders in the late nineteenth century. The growing internationalization of *Labour History* was recognized in an editorial in May 2004, which explicitly welcomed articles from other countries and regions on labour and social history, while maintaining a primary focus on Australasia.[84]

There are other outlets for publication associated with the ASSLH. The successful Australian-Canadian Labour History Conference in Sydney in 1988 set a precedent for the ASSLH to hold biennial conferences. The first of these was in Melbourne in 1991. The branch of the Society in the particular locality runs the conferences with logistical and financial support provided by the federal society. At the Wollongong Conference in October 1999 there were fifty-five papers. While there has been a decline in traditional fare such as labour parties and trade unions in *Labour History*, 47 per cent of papers related to these matters. Other significant categories included gender (11 per cent), racism (9 per cent) and local labour history (5 per cent). Similar trends can be seen at the conference held at the University of Melbourne in July 2007, where sixty-one papers were presented. Almost two-thirds of the papers (64 per cent) related to traditional issues such as the Labor Party, the CP and trade unions. There were papers relating to women (8 per cent), but there were no papers relating to issues such as racism. The only other significant area was a range of papers on the role of the state (10 per cent) dealing with questions such as compulsory arbitration, particularly reflecting concerns about the attacks on arbitration and the rise of *Work Choices*.[85]

Why is there a greater interest in the traditional fare of Australian labour history at the Society conferences rather than in *Labour History*? As noted before, the branches of the Society organize the conferences. The branches tend to be run by non-academics and have close links to local labour movement and labour activists. While the journal attracts professional academics seeking the kudos of a refereed article in a university-based publication, the conferences have a wider range of participants drawn from academics and non-academics. There are more direct concerns with the challenges of declining union membership and the issues of political activism. Unions and community groups provide sponsorship, further broadening the base of the conferences. The conferences strengthen the study of labour history in Australia by ensuring a wider audience beyond the university.[86]

Several branches produce their own publications that also broaden the appeal of labour history. In 1982 there was only one branch in Melbourne and now there are seven. Their memberships vary anywhere between 10 and 160. The Sydney branch publication, *Hummer*, particularly contains articles on labour activists, sometimes autobiographical. Authors include secondary school teachers such as Rowan Cahill and Tony Laffin. Laffin, for example, has published pioneering work in the Hunter Valley on the impact of Christian socialists and friendly societies on the mainstream labour movement. Other branches with regular publications are Illawarra, Melbourne and Perth. The branches also run their own conferences bringing together academics and activists.[87]

The publishing of books by Australian labour historians remains a vigorous area of intellectual endeavour. Institutional labour histories remain important and reflect the continued significance of the labour movement in Australian society. Recent years have seen the appearance of significant histories of the NSW Builders Labourers' Federation, with its pioneering 'green bans' in support of environmental issues, and the CP. In 2003, Bobbie Oliver completed a major history of the ALP and the Trades and Labour Council in Western Australia. Autobiographical and biographical studies of Labor Party and trade union leaders also remain an important focus of book publication in Australian labour history. The trend to go beyond institutional labour history continues with labour historians focusing on community, gender, race, the workplace and the state.[88] In his re-examination of Australia in the 1890s in *New Australia* (1997), Scates hoped to create a more 'open and contingent history' by blending institutional labour history with a history of labour written from below. He incorporates the 'squabbling' of local Labor Party branches, the aspirations of the unions' rank-and-file members and middle-class intellectuals. He combines gender with class and pursues the notion of citizenship.[89] Mary Anne Jebb's excellent study of the relationship between Aboriginal pastoral workers and their European employers in the Kimberley region of Western Australia synthesized Aboriginal history and labour history. Labour historians were involved in projects writing the centennial histories of the federal and NSW compulsory arbitration systems and providing insights into the federation of the Australian colonies in 1901. Eric Eklund, Jim Hagan, Michael Hogan and others explored the labour movement and politics at the community and regional level.[90]

Conclusion

Labour movement activists laid the foundations of Australian labour history by writing celebratory histories of trade unions and the Labor Party in the last decades of the nineteenth century. In the first decade of the twenty-first century, Australian labour history is no longer merely a celebratory history of the Australian labour movement, but is an important area of intellectual endeavour. Its ranks have expanded beyond historians to include political scientists, sociologists and industrial relations academics. Australian labour history, by adopting a critical perspective towards Australian society, sympathizes with the disadvantaged. At its best, Australian labour historiography provides a dynamic conceptual framework for understanding the relationship between capital and labour. As the interest in union organizing indicated, Australian labour historians are also willing to examine the historical dimension of contemporary issues and debates. Labour historians are currently involved in projects that look at the anti-union strategies of employers, labour and the environment, and the relationship between social democratic governments and business. Overall, there has been a growth in the level of labour history publications in Australia through *Labour History*, books, conference proceedings and branch publications. While there are differences between the focus of *Labour History* and other vehicles for publication, all enrich labour history in Australia and provide it with an appeal which resonates beyond the universities.

Notes

1 Greg Patmore, *Australian Labour History* (Melbourne: Longman Cheshire, 1991), p. 1.
2 *The History of Capital and Labour in all Lands and Ages: Their Past Condition, Present Relations and Outlook for the Future*, ed. by John Norton (Sydney: Oceanic Publishing Co., 1888); Greg Patmore, 'Australian Labor Historiography: The Influence of the US', *Labor History*, 37 (1996), 520–34 (pp. 526–7).
3 Norton, *History of Capital and Labour*, pp. v–ix.
4 William Murphy, *History of the Eight Hours Movement*, 2 vols (Melbourne: J.T. Picken, 1896, 1900), vol. 1, pp. 1–10, vol. 2, pp. 3–4, 39.
5 Patmore, *Australian Labour History*, p. 2.
6 William Guthrie Spence, *Australia's Awakening: Thirty Years in the Life of an Australian Agitator* (Sydney: Worker Trustees, 1909), pp. 18, 53; William Guthrie Spence, *History of the AWU* (Sydney: Worker Trustees, 1911).
7 Patmore, *Australian Labour History*, p. 2.
8 Ibid.
9 Ibid.
10 Ibid., pp. 2–3.
11 Ibid., p. 3; Greg Patmore, 'James Thomas Sutcliffe (1876–1938)', in *A Biographical Dictionary of Australian and New Zealand Economists*, ed. by John King (Cheltenham: Edward Elgar, 2007), pp. 269–70.
12 George Black, *A History of the NSW Labor Party from its Conception until 1917*, 12 parts (Sydney: George A. Jones, 1926–27), part 2, p. 9; Vere Gordon Childe, *How Labour Governs: A Study of Workers' Representation in Australia* (1st pub. 1923; Melbourne: Melbourne University Press, 1964); Terence Irving, 'New Light on How Labour Governs: Rediscovered Political Writings by V. Gordon Childe', *Politics*, 23 (1988), 70–77.
13 T. A. Coghlan, *Labour and Industry in Australia: From the First Settlement in 1788 to the Establishment of the Commonwealth in 1901*, 4 vols (London: Oxford University Press, 1918); Patmore, *Australian Labour History*, p. 4.
14 Andrew Wells, 'The Old Left Intelligentsia 1930 to 1960', in *Intellectual Movements and Australian Society*, ed. by Brian Head and James Walter (Melbourne: Oxford University Press, 1988), pp. 214–34 (pp. 220, 222–23).
15 Don Watson, *Brian Fitzpatrick: A Radical Life* (Sydney: Hale and Iremonger, 1979), p. 171.
16 John Merritt, 'Labour History', in *New History: Studying Australia Today*, ed. by Graeme Osborne and William Mandle (Sydney: George Allen and Unwin, 1982), pp. 113–41 (pp. 116–17); Lucy Taksa, 'What's in a Name? Labouring Antipodean History in Oceania', in *Global Labour History: A State of the Art*, ed. by Jan Lucassen (Bern: Peter Lang, 2006), pp. 335–71 (p. 353).
17 Frank Farrell, 'Labour History in Australia', *International Labour and Working-Class History*, 21 (1982), 1–17 (pp. 9–10); Lloyd Ross, *William Lane and the Australian Labor Movement* (Sydney: Author, 1935), pp. 356–58, 366.
18 Patmore, *Australian Labour History*, p. 5.

19 Brian Fitzpatrick, *A Short History of the Australian Labour Movement* (Melbourne: Rawson's Bookshop, 1940), pp. 9, 15.

20 Ernest Campbell, *History of the Australian Labor Movement: A Marxist Interpretation* (Sydney: Current Book Distributors, 1945); Lance Sharkey, *An Outline History of the Australian Communist Party* (Sydney: Australian Communist Party, 1944).

21 Patmore, *Australian Labour History*, pp. 5–6.

22 Rob Pascoe, *The Manufacture of Australian History* (Melbourne: Oxford University Press, 1979), pp. 50–53; Russel Ward, *The Australian Legend* (Melbourne: Oxford University Press, 1966, 2nd edn), pp. 1–2, 212–17.

23 Robin Gollan, *Radical and Working Class Politics: A Study of Eastern Australia 1850–1910* (Melbourne: Melbourne University Press, 1960).

24 Robin Gollan, 'Australian Labour History', in *Canadian and Australian Labour History: Towards a Comparative Perspective*, ed. by Gregory Kealey and Greg Patmore (Brisbane: Australian-Canadian Studies, 1990), pp. 5–19 (pp. 7–9); Merritt, 'Labour History', p. 118; Greg Patmore, 'The Right Wing Won't Write – Labour History in 1962', *Labour History*, 82 (2002), vii–ix (p. vii).

25 Gollan, 'Australian Labour History', p. 8.

26 John Merritt, 'R.A. Gollan, E.C. Fry, and the Canberra Years of the Australian Society for the Study of Labour History', *Labour History*, 94 (2008), 17–23 (p. 20).

27 Robin Gollan, 'Labour History', *Bulletin of the Australian Society for the Study of Labour History*, 1 (1962), 3–5; Merritt, 'Labour History', pp. 119–20.

28 Robin Gollan, *The Coal Miners of New South Wales: A History of the Union, 1860–1960* (Melbourne: Melbourne University Press, 1963); Raewyn Connell, *Ruling Class, Ruling Culture: Studies of Conflict, Power and Hegemony in Australian Life* (Cambridge: Cambridge University Press, 1977), pp. 13–14; Pascoe, *The Manufacture of Australian History*, p. 54.

29 Ian Turner, *Industrial Labour and Politics: The Dynamics of the Labour Movement in Eastern Australia, 1900–1921* (Canberra: ANU Press, 1965), p. xvii.

30 Ibid.

31 Merritt, 'Labour History', p. 120.

32 Gollan, 'Australian Labour History', p. 9; Merritt, 'Labour History', p. 121.

33 Patmore, *Australian Labour History*, p. 8.

34 Peter Coleman, 'Introduction: The New Australia', in *Australian Civilization*, ed. by P. Coleman (Melbourne: F.W. Cheshire, 1962), pp. 1–11 (p. 6).

35 Merritt, 'Labour History', p. 123.

36 Patmore, *Australian Labour History*, pp. 8–10.

37 Editorial, *Social History*, 1 (1976), 1–3 (p. 1).

38 Ibid.

39 Merritt, 'Labour History', pp. 123–24; Wells, 'The Old Left Intelligensia', pp. 228–29.

40 Terry Irving and Baiba Berzins, 'History and the New Left: Beyond Radicalism', in *The Australian New Left: Critical Essays and Strategy*, ed. by Richard Gordon (Melbourne: Heinemann, 1970), pp. 66–94; Pascoe, *The Manufacture of*

Australian History, p. 66; 'Symposium: What is Labour History?', *Labour History*, 12 (1967), 60–81.

41 Irving and Berzins, 'History and the New Left', p. 93.

42 Humphrey McQueen, *A New Britannia: An Argument Concerning the Social Origins of Australian Radicalism and Nationalism* (Ringwood: Penguin, 1970); Patmore, *Australian Labour History*, p. 11.

43 Eric Fry, 'The Writing of Labour History in Australia', in *Common Cause: Essays in Australian and New Zealand Labour History*, ed. by Eric Fry (Wellington: Allen and Unwin/Port Nicholson Press, 1986), pp. 139–55 (pp. 150–51); Turner, *Industrial Labour and Politics*, p. 3.

44 Ann Curthoys, 'Historiography and Women's Liberation', *Arena*, 22 (1970), 35–40.

45 Ann Curthoys, Susan Eade and Peter Spearritt, *Women at Work* (Canberra: Australian Society for the Study of Labour History, 1975); Miriam Dixson, *The Real Matilda: Women and Identity in Australia 1788–1975* (Ringwood: Penguin, 1976); Beverley Kingston, *My Wife, My Daughter and Poor Mary Ann: Women and Work in Australia* (Melbourne: Nelson, 1975); Edna Ryan and Anne Conlon, *Gentle Invaders: Australian Women at Work 1788–1974* (Melbourne: Nelson, 1975); Anne Summers, *Damned Whores and God's Police: The Colonization of Women in Australia* (Ringwood: Penguin, 1975).

46 Stuart Macintyre, 'Radical History and Bourgeois Hegemony', *Intervention*, 2 (1972), 47–73; idem, 'The Making of the Australian Working Class: An Historiographical Survey', *Historical Studies*, 18 (1978), 233–53 (pp. 243–45); Raewyn Connell and Terry Irving, *Class Structure in Australian History: Documents, Narratives and Arguments* (Melbourne: Longman Cheshire, 1980); Patmore, *Australian Labour History*, p. 12; John Rickard, *Class and Politics: New South Wales, Victoria and the Early Commonwealth, 1890–1910* (Canberra: Australian National University Press, 1976), p. 2.

47 Merritt, 'Labour History', p. 138.

48 John Merritt, 'Editorial', *Labour History*, 40 (1981), v–vi.

49 Merritt, 'R.A. Gollan', p. 21.

50 Jim Hagan, *The History of the ACTU* (Melbourne: Longman Cheshire, 1981); Bede Nairn, *Civilising Capitalism: The Labor Movement in New South Wales, 1870–1900* (Canberra: Australian National University Press, 1973).

51 Frank Bongiorno, 'Nairn, (Noel) Bede (1917–)', in *The Oxford Companion to Australian History*, ed. by Graeme Davison, John Hirst and Stuart Macintyre (Melbourne: Oxford University Press, 1998), p. 452.

52 Patmore, *Australian Labour History*, p. 13.

53 Merritt, 'Editorial', p. v.

54 Stephen Garton, 'What Have We Done? Labour History, Social History, Cultural History', in *Challenges to Labour History*, ed. by Terry Irving (Sydney: University of New South Wales Press, 1994), pp. 42–74 (p. 47).

55 Margo Beasley, *The Missos: A History of the Federated Miscellaneous Workers' Union* (Sydney: Allen and Unwin, 1996); idem, *Wharfies: The History of the Waterside Workers' Federation* (Sydney: Halstead Press, 1996); Mark Hearn and Harry Knowles, *One Big Union: A History of the Australian Workers'*

Union 1886–1994 (Cambridge: Cambridge University Press, 1996); Peter Love, *Labour and the Money Power: Australian Labour Populism* (Melbourne: Melbourne University Press, 1984); Greg Patmore, 'Australian Labor History', *International Labor and Working-Class History*, 46 (1994), 161–71 (pp. 161–65).

56 Raymond Markey, *The Making of the Labor Party in New South Wales 1880–1900* (Sydney: The University of New South Wales Press, 1988).

57 Patmore, 'Australian Labor History', pp. 161–62.

58 Ibid., p. 166; David Peetz, *Unions in a Contrary World: The Picture of the Australian Trade Union Movement* (Cambridge: Cambridge University Press, 1998), p. 6.

59 Garton, 'What Have We Done?', p. 54; Patmore, 'Australian Labor History', p. 166.

60 Henry Reynolds, *The Other Side of the Frontier: An Interpretation of the Aboriginal Response to the Invasion and Settlement of Australia* (Ringwood: Penguin, 1982); Henry Reynolds, *Frontier: Aborigines, Settlers and Land* (Sydney: Allen and Unwin, 1987); Henry Reynolds, *The Law of the Land* (Ringwood: Penguin, 1987); Kay Saunders, *Workers in Bondage: The Origins and Bases of Unfree Labour in Queensland 1824–1916* (St. Lucia: University of Queensland Press, 1982).

61 Katrina Alford, *Production or Reproduction? An Economic History of Women in Australia, 1788–1850* (Melbourne: Oxford University Press, 1984); Wendy Lowenstein, *Weevils in the Flour: An Oral Record of the 1930s Depression in Australia* (Melbourne: Hyland House, 1978); Wendy Lowenstein and Tom Hills, *Under the Hook: Melbourne Waterside Workers Remember Working Lives and Class War, 1900–1980* (Melbourne: Melbourne Bookworkers, 1982); *Convict Workers: Reinterpreting Australia's Past*, ed. by Stephen Nicholas (Cambridge: Cambridge University Press, 1988); *All Our Labours: Oral Histories of Working Life in Twentieth Century Sydney*, ed. by John Shields (Sydney: The University of New South Wales Press, 1992).

62 Patmore, *Australian Labour History*, p. 15.

63 *A Most Valuable Acquisition: A People's History of Australia Since 1788*, ed. by Verity Burgmann and Jennifer Lee (Melbourne: McPhee Gribble/Penguin, 1988), p. xii.

64 Irving, *Challenges to Labour History*.

65 Patmore, *Australian Labour History*, pp. 16–17.

66 *Foundations of Arbitration: The Origins and Effects of State Compulsory Arbitration 1890–1914*, ed. by Stuart Macintyre and Richard Mitchell (Melbourne: Oxford University Press, 1989).

67 Patmore, 'Australian Labor Historiography', p. 531.

68 Raelene Frances, 'No More Amazons: Gender and Work Process in the Victorian Clothing Trades, 1890–1939', *Labour History*, 50 (1986), 95–112.

69 For discussion of these texts, see Patmore, 'Australian Labor Historiography', pp. 532–33.

70 Christopher Wright, *The Management of Labour: A History of Australian Employers* (Melbourne: Oxford University Press, 1995).

71 Eric Fry, *Common Cause: Essays in Australian and New Zealand Labour History* (Wellington: Allen and Unwin, 1986); Brian Kennedy, *Silver, Sin and Sixpenny Ale: A Social History of Broken Hill, 1883–1921* (Melbourne: Melbourne University Press, 1978).

72 *Canadian and Australian Labour History: Towards a Comparative Perspective*, ed. by Gregory Kealey and Greg Patmore (Brisbane: Australian-Canadian Studies, 1990).

73 Ibid. See also Stefan Berger and Greg Patmore, 'Comparative Labour History in Britain and Australia', *Labour History*, 88 (2005), 9–24 (p. 18).

74 Bongiorno, 'Nairn (Noel) Bede', pp. 369–71; Verity Burgmann, 'The Strange Death of Labour History', in *Bede Nairn and Labor History*, ed. by NSW Branch of the Australian Labor Party (Sydney: Pluto Press, 1991), pp. 69–81; Rae Frances and Bruce Scates, 'Is Labour History Dead?', *Australian Historical Studies*, 100 (1993), 470–81.

75 *Labour History*, 62 (1992), inside back cover.

76 Greg Patmore, 'A Voice for Whom? Employee Representation and Labour Legislation in Australia', *The University of New South Wales Law Journal*, 29 (2006), 8–21; Australian Social Trends, 2008 http://www.abs.gov.au/AUSSTATS/abs@.nsf/Lookup/4102.0Chapter7202008 accessed 20 January 2009.

77 Greg Patmore, 'Working Lives in Regional Australia: Labour History and Local History', *Labour History*, 78 (2000), 1–6.

78 Grant Michelson, 'Labour History and Culture', *Labour History*, 79 (2000), 1–10.

79 Ann Curthoys, 'Labour History and Cultural Studies', *Labour History*, 67 (1994), 12–22 (p. 20).

80 Michelson, 'Labour History and Culture', p. 4.

81 Curthoys, 'Labour History and Cultural Studies', p. 21.

82 Nick Dyrenfurth and Marian Quartly, '"Fat Man v. The People": Labour Intellectuals and the Making of Oppositional Identities, 1890–1901', *Labour History*, 92 (2007), 31–56; Lucy Taksa, 'Pumping the Life-Blood into Politics and Place: Labour Culture and the Eveleigh Railway Workshops', *Labour History*, 79 (2000), 11–34.

83 Andrew Moore, *The Right Road? A History of Right-wing Politics in Australia* (Melbourne: Oxford University Press, 1995); idem, *The Secret Army and the Premier* (Sydney: University of New South Wales Press, 1989).

84 Robin Archer, 'American Liberalism and Labour Politics: Labour Leaders and Liberty Language in Late Nineteenth Century Australia and the United States', *Labour History*, 92 (2007), 1–16; Leighton James and Ray Markey, 'Class and Labour: The British Labour Party and the Australian Labor Party Compared', *Labour History*, 90 (2006), 23–42; Greg Patmore, 'Australia', *Labour/Le Travail*, 50 (2002), 255–60; Greg Patmore, 'Editorial', *Labour History*, 86 (2004), p. v.

85 *Labour Traditions: Papers from the Tenth National Labour History Conference, Held at the University of Melbourne. 4–6 July, 2007*, ed. by Julie Kimber, Peter Love and Phillip Deery (Melbourne: ASSLH, 2007); Patmore, 'Australia', 259–60.

86 Patmore, 'Australia', p. 260.

87 Ibid.

88 Bobbie Oliver, *Unity is Strength: A History of the ALP and the Trades and Labor Council in Western Australia, 1899–1999* (Perth: Australian Public Intellectual Network, 2003); Patmore, 'Australia', p. 260.

89 Bruce Scates, *A New Australia: Citizenship, Radicalism and the First Republic* (Cambridge: Cambridge University Press, 1997), pp. 8–10.

90 Erik Eklund, *Steel Town: The Making and Breaking of Port Kembla* (Melbourne: Melbourne University Press, 2002); *A History of Work and Community in Wollongong*, ed. by Jim Hagan and Henry Lee (Sydney: Halstead Press, 2001); Michael Hogan, *Local Labor: A History of the Labor Party in Glebe 1891–20 3* (Sydney: Federation Press, 2004); *The New Province for Law and Order: 100 Years of Australian Conciliation and Arbitration*, ed. by Joe Issac and Stuart Macintyre (Cambridge: Cambridge University Press: 2004); Patmore, 'Australia', p. 260; *Laying the Foundations of Industrial Justice: The Presidents of the Industrial Relations Commission of NSW 1902–1998*, ed by Greg Patmore (Sydney: Federation Press, 2003); Mary Anne Jebb, *Blood, Sweat and Welfare: A History of White Bosses and Aboriginal Pastoral Workers* (Perth: University of Western Australia Press, 2002).

8

Germany

Klaus Tenfelde

To grasp the continuities and ruptures in German historiography generally, and the historiography of workers and labour movements in German-speaking countries in the postwar period in particular, we have to look back as far as the early twentieth century, and even beyond, to consider Imperial Germany. For there is no other country in Europe and America where political changes of comparable magnitude have occurred, and where such changes have had such a comparatively enduring influence on the fundamental tendencies of historiography. It was primarily in Germany that modern historicism developed in the early nineteenth century as the core method of historical research. This left clear biases in our national historiography, and this occurred even before national unity was achieved with the founding of the German Empire in 1871. Already at this point extensive research was being conducted on economic history, and to a lesser extent on social history. However, such research fell outside the domain of historical seminars; it was carried out almost exclusively as part of the extensive discipline of national economics. In the great debates about how to interpret national history before 1914, and even in the brief years of the Weimar Republic from 1918 to 1933, social history was discussed at best by way of exception and almost always in passing.

This neglect applied even more to the history of the workers, the *homines novi* of the industrial age, and – in the homeland of Karl Marx and Friedrich Engels – it applied even more to the history of workers' movements. These movements were prohibited, oppressed, and persecuted by the state continuously until 1918 – the high point of this repression occurring under Bismarck's Laws against Socialists (*Sozialistengesetz*, 1878–1890). It was precisely this socio-political isolation which rendered the socialist labour movement in Germany before 1914 extraordinarily strong and which made it the leading component of the Second International. Despite its strength and significance, the labour movement could not become the object of academic historiography because, despite the high international ranking of this discipline, its protagonists remained almost exclusively attached to political and national conceptions of history. In 1904, when Hermann Oncken, a young historian of the new generation, published – in his capacity as university lecturer – a biography of Ferdinand Lassalle, the founder of the German Social Democrats, it caused a sensation amongst his contemporaries.[1] Detailed scientific analysis of the history of social movements, particularly labour movements, was taboo. So indeed was the analysis of the social consequences of industrialization, and this disapproval continued into the Weimar Republic. Such analysis was, for obvious reasons, even less possible during the National Socialist dictatorship.

Even during the postwar period, professorial chairs in German universities were occupied, at least at first, by academics who had been formed and received their scholarly training during the German Empire. This situation only began to change in West Germany in the 1960s, whereas in the German Democratic Republic (GDR) at this time, the history of workers' movements – although not the history of workers, strikes and living conditions amongst different strata of the working classes as a whole – was already being cultivated very intensively and in a typically one-dimensional way. All this does not mean that a well-developed historiography of labour movements did not exist already – only that it was not produced by academics but almost exclusively by those who took an interest in history from within the labour movement's own organizations.[2]

For the early German labour leaders were notable historians in many respects. This was certainly true of Marx and Engels. It was the case with party leaders such as Wilhelm Liebknecht and August Bebel, and it was also true of party intellectuals such as Eduard Bernstein and Karl Kautsky. It was true above all of Franz Mehring, who had originally written a critique of social democracy, but who then published in 1893 the *History of German Social Democracy* which ran to several editions. Mehring's book demonstrated great sympathy for the movement's founder Lassalle and it placed clear emphasis on the history of the party's programme and organizations.[3] It was also Mehring and Liebknecht who, in a very early polemical assault on 'bourgeois' historiography, endeavoured to produce a comprehensive interpretation of Prussian-German history written from a social democratic perspective (although not necessarily on a Marxist basis). Partly inspired by this work, and partly of its own accord, an impressive body of historical literature developed by 1914, written by workers' leaders and in particular by trade union leaders in order to record the histories of their respective movements.

During its first great flowering, in the years between the end of the anti-socialist law and the beginning of the First World War (1890–1914), the German labour movement created its own historical culture. By now it had become the leading force within the Second International, as well as a model which exerted a great deal of influence on labour movements in smaller European countries. And it had become deeply rooted amongst the working classes of the German Empire, thanks to the emergence of a dense network of local associations and a profusion of cultural associations. Precisely because of this it had to write its own history, *nolens volens.* As examples one can cite two brilliant works which, in their competing origins, reflected the situation of the German trade unions. In 1908 Heinrich Imbusch, editor for the Association of Christian Miners, published a comprehensive study of the coal miners' movement from a Catholic perspective (later, in the Weimar Republic, he was to become undisputed leader of the Christian trade unions). His colleague and rival Otto Hue, editor for the social-democratic Federation of German Miners, followed the Imbusch book with *The Miners,* an exhaustive account of their history in two volumes.[4]

Even today, these two works remain required reading for all scholars concerned with the history of early labour movements in Germany, because trade union archives were almost completely destroyed or ransacked after the National Socialists seized power in 1933. Much the same happened to numerous local and regional records of socialist movements, whilst the Social Democratic Party's (SPD) own famous archive, which contained the manuscripts and papers of Marx and Engels amongst others, was smuggled out of the country with extreme difficulty after 1933. It was then sold in Amsterdam by the exiled leaders of the SPD because they had to raise money. There it formed the initial core collection of what is today the extensive archive of the International Institute of Social History, and it remains indispensable for researchers working on Marx, Engels and the history of the German SPD.

This 'interrupted' transmission of primary sources made the new beginning of German labour history which took place in the 1960s even more problematic: apart from union and party publications and other printed records, the only other documents available in state and regional archives consisted almost exclusively of official government records, and above all of police reports. These sources are extremely abundant because of the neurotically anti-socialist character of Prussian state surveillance;

precisely because of this, these sources need to be used with caution. Police officers on surveillance duty tended to produce biased reports, and as for reports by spies, such as the police reports on the pub scene in Hamburg published by Richard Evans, these should invariably be interpreted with restraint.[5] It is not only problems of transmission which have hindered the development of an empirically well-founded and analytically skilled labour history in Germany. In the final analysis, the divide between a nationally oriented, bourgeois, professional academic historiography, which refused to study the lower classes, and the historiography of the labour movements, reproduced precisely the political class divide in society and the ideological tensions which were to lead to 'the age of extremes' in the twentieth century.

It is self-evident that the writing of history by workers' leaders was intended to legitimise the interests of the party or workers' movement: for them, history was an instrument in the class struggle. Nothing could illustrate this more clearly than the differences between the two works on the miners by Imbusch and Hue mentioned above. One could say that the self-authored historiography of the workers' movements was ideological in a double sense: it oriented itself in a society which enclosed it and yet excluded it, and it developed historical legitimations which seemed capable of facilitating the labour movement's objective, namely to establish a different society, perhaps a socialist society and in any case a democratic republic. At the same time, historiography emanating from within the labour movement was forced into polemical arguments against competing positions held by others within the labour camp and not only socialists of different persuasions. The Christian trade union movement, with the Centre Party as its political spearhead, achieved considerable political importance within the German Empire. The weight of such traditions continued to be felt until well after 1945.

New beginnings in the Cold War

An independent 'labour history' – the nearest German equivalent is '*Arbeiter- und Arbeiterbewegungsgeschichte*' ('History of Workers and Workers' Movements') – only developed, and then very hesitantly, in the first two decades after 1945. There were numerous reasons for this. The end of the dictatorship did not automatically lead to a rapid renewal of the science of history. A major obstacle to such renewal was the fact that it was the most critical thinkers who had been forced to leave the country after 1933.[6] Among them were Hans Rosenberg (1904–1988) and Eckart Kehr (1902–1933), whose works helped to found the new social historical way of thinking in the 1960s, even though they were partly written before 1933. Other critical émigrés included Arthur Rosenberg (1889–1943) and Franz Borkenau (1900–1957), both of whom devoted their attention to the labour movement very early on. Ernst Engelberg (b. 1909) and Jürgen Kuczynski (1904–1997) played a considerable role in establishing historiography in the GDR; in doing so they helped to sketch out a very narrow picture of the history of the German labour movement. Other émigrés such as Hajo Holborn (1902–1969) remained attached to their critical liberal values or, like the returnee from exile Hans Rothfels (1891–1976), regarded themselves as belonging to the conservative school of old German national historiography.

The most important positions in the universities continued to be occupied by individuals who had often completed their studies during the German Empire, and who had been connected with the National Socialist regime, in several cases in a direct way. The de-nazification process often left them undisturbed, or brought only fleeting restrictions to their academic careers. Only a handful proved to be truly untainted by any connection to the regime, such as Gerhard Ritter (1888–1967), who played a decisive role in the reconstruction of the historical sciences; in doing so he tended to reinforce traditional interpretations. Without doubt a few historians had learned to revise their opinions. Hans Herzfeld (1892–1982), for example, had emerged from World War I as a highly decorated young officer. In 1928 he wrote a thoroughly nationalist book on German social democracy during the war. In it he blamed the Socialists for the collapse of the 'home front', an interpretation entirely in accordance with the 'stab in the back' legend (*Dolchstoßlegende*). As a 'quarter Jew' he barely survived the Nazi Holocaust. His teaching activity at the Free University in Berlin after 1945 influenced some of the representatives of reform who, like Gerhard A. Ritter (b. 1929), devoted themselves to labour movement history very early on and who helped to found a new historiography within this field.

The latter is also true, in a different way, of Theodor Schieder (1908–1984) and Werner Conze (1910–1986). During their time as academics in Königsberg they had lent their intellectual support to National Socialist pillage and population programmes in Eastern Europe. Details of this activity have only surfaced since 1998, when a big debate on this subject took place among German historians at the annual historians' conference in Frankfurt. Based in Cologne and Heidelberg, Schieder and Conze trained some of the most important historians among the generation of reformers, including Hans-Ulrich Wehler (b. 1931). Together with Jürgen Kocka (b. 1941, a student of Gerhard A. Ritter), Wehler went on to found a centre for the study of history as a critical social science at the new University of Bielefeld, and also founded the journal *Geschichte und Gesellschaft* (*History and Society*) which broke new ground in this field. Conze became, at least at first, the most influential figure in the field of social history. He played a decisive role in promoting amongst his students the study of the history of workers, trade union movements and political workers' movements.

It is evident that changes in perspective in the academic sphere are always connected with important generational transitions. To this extent the expansion of German universities and the growth of their academic personnel which took place at the beginning of the 1970s not only caused the influx of a new generational cohort. It was also combined with new intellectual orientations. This shift was accompanied and underpinned by certain social developments. Under Konrad Adenauer, society in the Federal Republic had focused on reconstruction, and had remained essentially conservative and largely uninterested in the history of reformist and revolutionary movements in Germany. Above all, however, it was the political mentality of the Federal Republic in the Cold War which favoured this adherence to traditional attitudes, an adherence which was moreover reinforced in many ways by the legacy of the Nazi regime. The creation of the GDR produced another Germany, one which claimed to be revolutionary, even if it was, in reality, a satellite state. The economic and political rise of the Soviet Union and the victory over Hitler had made the prospect of a global transition to socialism seem more likely than ever before. That which many had imagined and anticipated for such a long time, namely the political rise of the new working classes to a position of global leadership, appeared to be a real possibility. Legitimised by the historical experiences and political objectives of the working class, the leaders of the Soviet occupation zone and subsequently the GDR did their utmost to force these objectives through.

Because of this, the history of workers' movements became the chief branch of history within the GDR and the subject of numerous new projects. These initiatives extended from programmes researching the local and regional history of workers' movements all the way to vast new editions of source material and comprehensive synthetic accounts in which a leading historical role was ascribed to the Communist workers' movement. There was no shortage of misinterpretation and even falsification of history; virtues were made of stylisation and omission, as can easily be demonstrated in the case of the historiography of the German Revolution of 1918–20. This approach to the writing of history was impoverished, though important achievements in factual knowledge cannot be denied. It was particularly resistant to new interpretations from the West and to new methodological approaches. But these new interpretations felt themselves to be challenged and so, indirectly rather than directly, they adopted impulses from this form of historiography which understood itself to be Marxist.

Much more significant for the reorientation of the entire discipline of history in West Germany since the 1960s have been other influences and developments. For perhaps a decade, the history of workers and workers' movements did indeed exert decisive influence on this reorientation, and this emphasis invited direct comparison with developments in historical thinking in the GDR. I have already mentioned the generational transition occurring amongst historians in the West. From it, a number of individuals emerged who, for the first time without major setbacks, were able to forge academic careers for themselves based upon their research on the history of labour movements. Gerhard A. Ritter obtained his doctorate as early as 1953 under the supervision of Herzfeld with a groundbreaking study of trade unions and Social Democrats in the 1890s. It was published in 1959 and even today it is still considered to be the standard reference work on the rise of the labour movement after the annulment of the Law against Socialists.[7] Erich Matthias's studies of Karl Kautsky were similarly influential, particularly in terms of clarifying the ideological positions within the early social democratic movement.[8]

Helga Grebing (b. 1930) took a career path which is characteristic of the postwar complications of Germany's divided history: she trained to be a saleswoman, at the same time attending the workers' and peasants' faculty of the Humboldt University, a typical means of promotion for the lower classes in the early GDR, and from there she took up the academic study of history. Developments in the GDR caused her to move to West Berlin. There she gained her doctorate under Herzfeld as early as 1952 with a study of the Centre Party and Catholic workers in the Weimar Republic. In 1972 she took up a full Professorship in Göttingen, and in 1988 she moved to the Ruhr University in Bochum in order to become the Director of the Institute for Research on the History of European Workers' Movements, today the Institute for Social Movements. Throughout her entire academic career Grebing has published extensively on the history of German workers' movements and she has also written the most widely read complete history of the subject, which has run to numerous editions; alongside this, her other main research interest has always been twentieth-century currents within the history of ideas.[9]

These examples demonstrate that a new historiography of the German labour movement was well under way, quite independently of the developments in the GDR, when in the late 1960s a younger generation of students became committed to dedicating themselves to this field of inquiry. Alongside the expansion of the university system following the educational reforms, which culminated in the founding of important new universities, the most significant impulses came from general socio-political developments. The grand coalition in federal politics, and then the coalition between the SPD and the Liberals under Willy Brandt provoked widespread interest in the history of the Social Democrats, now the leading party of the Federal Republic, while the student movements of the years 1968–72 also referred to the traditions of the labour movement. It was not uncommon for young socialist academics to turn to the local and regional history of workers' movements as part of a personal quest for tradition; many of them gained their doctorates through these studies, and soon they belonged to the group of academic lecturers who were to cultivate this field of research for a long period of time.

Within a short time the research and publication infrastructures of this new field of research became well developed. After the Friedrich Ebert Stiftung was established permanently in Bonn with taxpayers' money as a political foundation for social democracy, the *Archiv für Sozialgeschichte* (*Archive for Social History*) appeared from 1961 as a scientific organ for historical research. Its first editor was Georg Eckert (1912–1974), the director of the Institute for International Textbook Research in Braunschweig. The choice of title was far-sighted, but the first volumes of the yearbook mainly featured studies of the early organizational history of social democracy. The *Internationale wissenschaftliche Korrespondenz zur Geschichte der deutschen Arbeiterbewegung* (*International Scientific Correspondence on German Labour Movement History*) considered itself to be more of a review, and was rightly esteemed for a long period. It began to document research work as early as 1964 in association with the Historical Commission in Berlin, and was edited for many years by Henryk Skrzypczak (b. 1926). Both journals regarded themselves as rising to the challenge represented by *Beiträge zur Geschichte der Arbeiterbewegung* (*Contributions to the History of the Labour Movement*), which had appeared in East Berlin since 1959 in the wake of the dogmatization of the humanities in the GDR. In this respect, the official GDR *History of the German Labour Movement*, which appeared as a collective work in two volumes in 1966, represented a particular challenge. This proliferation of different periodicals conveys the conflict of interpretations which had flared up between the GDR view of history and the West German historiography of the labour movement.

Early on it became apparent that the decisive factor in this interpretive struggle would be the amount of resources available to each side. Thus the

Friedrich Ebert Stiftung quickly produced extensive bibliographies in order to mark out the field of research, although it did not exert direct influence on the content of these volumes.[10] High points of this interpretive competition occurred at the 'Linz Conference', the International Conference of Labour Movement Historians, which was renowned during the Cold War; it took place annually in Linz from 1964 onwards under the control of Austrian historians. Highly conflicting interpretations from East and West often collided there on 'neutral soil' until well into the 1980s. This conference only gained a distinct social history profile very slowly.

The socio-historical turn and the 'Sonderweg' ('special path')

The rise of West German 'labour history' converged with the rise of social history as a field of study and as a perspective within the historical sciences. In the GDR this convergence was not fulfilled; on the contrary, the 'party line' was characterized by defensive reactions towards such a differentiating and relativizing mode of research.[11] Scholars deliberately shielded themselves from Western ideas; whereas in the Federal Republic, the impact of Conze, Wehler, Kocka and others ensured that a lively engagement began with the new currents of thought.[12] Conze was one of the first to adopt the new approaches of the *Annales* School around Marc Bloc, Lucien Febvre and Fernand Braudel. Wehler and Kocka were more interested in developments in Anglo-American historiography, and, together with the sociologist M. Rainer Lepsius (b. 1928) and Wolfgang Mommsen (1930–2004), they saw to it that there was a reflective rediscovery of the work of Max Weber (1864–1920), certainly the most important and influential German sociologist of the early twentieth century.

In a volume dedicated to the fiftieth anniversary of organized labour history in Britain, some reference to the influence of British historians is in order. It was the work of Eric Hobsbawm, who, of course, possessed a background in Austria and Germany, above all his collection of essays, *Labouring Men* (1964) which was read in West Germany at first, as well as his *Primitive Rebels* (1959). Among other British authors who had a significant, positive reception, and whose work was partly translated into German, were E.P. Thompson and Raymond Williams. This reception showed itself in independent studies of the English labour movement by German historians.[13] Correlatively, a lively interest in German history in general and the German labour movement in particular, developed in the 1970s among a new generation of British historians. Young doctoral students such as John Breuilly, Dick Geary, Richard Evans, David Blackbourn, Geoff Eley and Ian Kershaw among others, carried out research in German archives, as did numerous American doctoral students, often supervised by German émigrés. Working in Britain and America, these historians established their own research culture in which to discuss and evaluate German history. A high point here was the debate about the German *Sonderweg* or 'special path', which was started in 1980 by David Blackbourn and Geoff Eley, who strongly criticized the Bielefeld school of social historiography which was blossoming at the time.[14]

In the nineteenth and early twentieth centuries, conservative nationalist historiographers had interpreted the geopolitical situation of Germany standing embattled between Tsarist Russia and the French 'enemy' in terms of a German *Sonderweg*. This concept implied that it was not only legitimate but also essential for the German Empire to assume a leadership role in Europe and the world. However, in the postwar period, and in the aftermath of the monstrous National Socialist dictatorship and its impact internationally, a central interpretive question seemed unavoidable: which long-term defective development had given rise to National Socialism? In order to answer this question it seemed necessary to have extensive recourse to nineteenth-century history.

Beginning with the undemocratic reforms 'from above' in Prussia in response to the Napoleonic occupation and the belated but extraordinarily rapid and successful industrialization, and continuing with the failure of the 'bourgeois' revolutions of 1848–49 and consequently the strange 'hermaphroditic' form of Prussian constitutionalism in the German Empire, and reaching its first climax in Germany's leading role in the outbreak of the First World War, an interpretive context seemed to emerge which centred explanation predominantly on domestic factors. According to this view, it was structural and systematic developments within German politics which had led with a certain inevitability to the catastrophe of 1933. Characteristic features of this interpretation included the notion of a 'weak middle class' which was unable to achieve its liberal and democratic objectives of 1848–49.[15] And the notion of a labour movement which was unable to share in political power until 1918 and which, precisely because of this, reshaped itself in a revolutionary manner due to its adoption of Marxism – the Erfurt Conference of 1891 was seen as a high point in this respect – and grew extraordinarily rapidly in numerical terms. The German labour movement thus became a refuge for the remaining democratic forces.

A first touchstone for this debate in the 1960s, in other contexts, was the famous Fischer controversy. It erupted over Fritz Fischer's (1904–1999) new interpretation of the responsibility of the German Empire for the outbreak of the First World War, first published in 1961.[16] This thesis, together with the research of a new generation of historians which followed it, strongly influenced the prevailing view of political history. In general, historical thinking became more liberal in West Germany. During this period, and with the significant involvement of non-German historians, new research into the rise of National Socialism ranked equally with new research into the history of the socialist labour movement, which was the only major political force which did not support the Enabling Act in March 1933, and which, particularly in its Communist wing, was the victim of a political ban which was enforced with unprecedented brutality. Because of this, for example, the attitude of the independent trade unions in 1933, during the months of the National Socialists' seizure of power, became a test case. Towards the end of the 1960s, the policies of the majority social democratic leadership during the revolution of 1918–20, influenced by the contemporary notion of a 'third way' between reform and socialization which was popular at the time, were keenly debated. It was a sign of the mature condition of democracy in the Federal Republic when, in the wake of the student movement and the social-democratic-liberal coalition since 1969, models of democracy based on workers' councils found sympathy with the New Left. The reasons for the parliamentary Social Democrats' decision to approve the war budget on 4 August 1914 were also vigorously discussed, often understandably with direct reference to Fischer's arguments.[17]

Blackbourn and Eley called the new, critical interpretation of the German *Sonderweg* into question at a time when a broad current of research with a socio-historical orientation was already well established. Previously in the Federal Republic, and again in competition with corresponding research schemes in the GDR, studies of the local and regional history of the political labour movement had appeared, mainly focused on its organization and policies. Moreover, it was not coincidental that many young historians at this time were deeply interested in the ideological debates within the social democratic movement following the Erfurt programme of 1891 which culminated in the debate about revisionism stimulated by the arguments of Eduard Bernstein. The new socio-historical studies which increasingly followed were, however, very differently structured: their authors were primarily interested in the creation and development of the modern industrial workforce from the middle of the nineteenth century onwards. The temporal focus of interest here was clearly on the period well before 1914.[18] The goal of these investigations was often, although not always, to achieve a more precise understanding of the processes through which trade unions and political labour movements were initially constituted.

On the whole, these processes were studied on the basis of factory and business history, or within the framework of regional history or trade history. It must be conceded that these studies involved an unspoken determinism: they were expected to lead to an overarching interpretation. Cultural knowledge and mentalities were often left out of the picture; for example, it was rare that anyone made the effort to study the presence and significance of religion among the lower classes and the workers. On the plus side, though, these researchers focused attention for the first time on the lower classes. They thereby added a social dimension to German industrial history; until then it had been predominantly oriented in terms of economics. Moreover, it was now possible to categorize these insights, as may be quickly shown by the following comparative key questions: Why, in contrast to England, did social democratic parties come into being distinctly earlier than trade unions in most continental countries and above all in Germany? Why did trade union movements in Germany, France, the Netherlands and in some other countries fragment into different factional federations? How do we explain different models of protest and strike action? This meant that attention was focused mainly on England, but also partly on France, and further studies into non-German workforces and labour movements were produced.[19] Towards the end of the 1970s, the West German historiography of workers and labour movements was unmistakeably in full bloom. University seminars on these subjects were packed out and, with the support of the Friedrich Ebert Stiftung, work began upon an extensive, multi-volume overarching analysis of the entire field under the editorship of Gerhard A. Ritter; even now this multi-volume edition is far from complete.[20]

The debate about Germany's *Sonderweg* within European history still remains unresolved. Blackbourn and Eley had inquired, if the term '*Sonderweg*' had to be used at all, whether it was not more applicable to the English path to industrialization and modernity; however, it was still possible to cite reasons why the term was appropriate in the case of Germany. Apparently clear characteristics could be adduced here to support the terminology, in particular the roles of the bureaucracy and the military, the tradition of reform from above, the late achievement of national unity and the political role of outmoded elites. Above all though, the great challenge remained, which was to provide an adequate explanation for the developments which led to National Socialism, Hitler's dictatorship and the horrors of the Holocaust. After the Fischer controversy and the debate about the German *Sonderweg*, further arguments between historians, which were also simultaneously conducted in the feature sections of national newspapers, have essentially all been connected with this same problematic.

The same approach continues to apply after the German reunification of 1989–90, even if since then there is now an additional 'syndrome' of German history which requires interpretation, namely the dictatorship in the GDR.

Differentiation between socio-historical fields of research

From its beginning, the new social history, and with it the history of workers and workers' movements, 'labour history', cast its spell on other disciplines. Indeed, under its influence these disciplines changed in calibre. This can be illustrated by traditional folklore's development into modern ethnology, by the strong shifting tendencies in sociology towards analyses of stratification, class formation and social inequality, or even by pointing to the new socio-historical perspectives in literary history. And even today it remains an open question whether social history should be practised as a structural history or whether it should in essence be a history of social organizations such as families, cities, economic sectors and professions, businesses and companies, and above all social strata and classes. Another question which has proved just as controversial is whether social history, and thus 'labour history' too, is a field of research alongside economic, political or diplomatic history, deserving the same rights as those other fields – or whether it is a way of viewing all history, a perspective which offers deep insights into the development of modern societies since the social upheavals of industrialization.

In this process of questioning, the fields of inquiry have been continually expanded and have gained a certain autonomy from each other. This did not occur without controversies which were violent at the time. Thanks to the reception of the works of, say, Sven Lindquist, Clifford Geertz or Carlo Ginzburg, as well as the efforts of the History Workshop in England, so-called 'everyday history' experienced a major upturn in Germany.[21] This involved more than establishing the direction the historiography should take. It characterized a type of historiography, one which also became attractive for lay people, and involved history workshops and local history initiatives, a new approach which to a great extent necessitated the search for the past of people by 'ordinary' people in their own places.

Favoured by political developments – new social movements and particularly the Green Party entered the political scene – a broad historical current emerged which focused upon the world of the 'common people'. This entailed what Gert Zang has termed 'an unceasing approach to the individual'.[22] It has had a tremendously enlivening effect upon museum culture in Germany and it has also helped to preserve historic monuments; modern museums of industry such as in the Ruhr area, in Nuremberg and above all in Hamburg, where a Museum of Work was opened, were created as a result of these changes.

Ultimately, everyday history had little theoretical ambition. Indeed, the interest in it expressed a form of weariness with a historiography focused on large structural developments, one which seemed to have very little interest in people themselves. According to some critics, a type of historiography had developed in which there was no longer any room for human beings, 'a social history with the people left out'. Such criticisms were directed in particular against the new research produced by a highly quantitative social historiography, which, having adopted the ideas of the 'new urban history', had focused on the history of social protests, migrations or on research into collective biographies. In the field of labour history, it was Alf Lüdtke (b. 1943) in particular who directed attention back to the lives and sufferings of the people themselves, considering working life in terms of the fates of individuals.[23] Such everyday histories no longer expressed much interest in the social protests which were still a focal point of socio-historical research in the 1970s;[24] and they had even less to say about trade union movements or the history of social democracy. 'Give history back to the people' was the emphatic slogan. At this time, oral history was widely used, particularly in order to research 'everyday life under National Socialism'.[25]

Other important fields of research showed a comparable tendency to compartmentalize themselves and to become independent enclaves. This could be seen in the cases of modern urban history, family history and business history. For around two decades now, migrations in and out of Germany, particularly during the postwar period, have been intensively researched, thanks in part to the founding of a dedicated research institute in Osnabrück.[26]

If one of the aims of labour history, no matter what its theoretical orientation, was to work out the process of class formation and its political consequences, then this line of inquiry was increasingly pushed into the background. Social structures viewed in their totality hardly seemed interesting any more. Instead many historians focused their attention on those associations which, excluding class formation in German social history, were particularly effective in terms of social significance: these associations were termed 'milieus'. Hugely influential in this respect was an essay by Lepsius on 'The party system and social structure' in German history.[27] Lepsius explained why some associations became politically effective in terms of the creation of 'social moral milieus', in which dominant social connections and relationships were formed and in which moral values could be articulated. His chief example was the Catholic milieu, which was suppressed by Bismarck in the *Kulturkampf* (cultural struggle) after the founding of the German Empire and which because of this had developed its own trade unions and its own political party, the Centre Party, which cut across class distinctions.

The socialist labour movement with its affiliated free trade unions and the numerous organizations of workers' cultural movements constituted a further example. Like the Catholics in the *Kulturkampf*, it had suffered oppression under the Law against Socialists of 1878–1890, and precisely because of this had, after the end of legal persecution by the state, been able to develop successfully and sustain a powerful connection with the working classes. More than the other milieus (the conservative agrarian, the progressive liberal and the national liberal milieus), Lepsius argued that it was the Catholic and social-democratic milieus and the values which they expressed which had a formative influence on political attitudes and on processes of party formation. This has been proved emphatically, for example, by voting patterns during the Weimar Republic: voting patterns for Catholic and leftwing parties remained astonishingly stable throughout the crisis years and even continued in West Germany after 1945. Only in the later postwar period, from the 1960s, did researchers note the rapidly accelerating erosion of these milieus and fragmentation, which was linked to diverse processes, including secularization, individualization, mobilization and commercialization. This will be discussed below in the context of the currently revived debate about the end of the labour movement.

The compartmentalization of social historiography has made it unrecognizable as a unified field; this has occurred entirely under the influence of the so-called 'turn' (in German the English term is now also used) within recent historiography. For instance, 'thick description' was followed by 'iconic' or rather 'pictorial' or 'spatial' description, and above all by the 'cultural turn', which is only now showing signs of abating. As for the new gender history, after initially producing a few important publications it soon left women workers and issues of female participation in labour movements by the wayside. It sought instead to achieve a much more extensive interpretive goal, namely the creation of a comprehensive 'genderizing history'. In actual fact, women played hardly any role in the German trade union movement and only a small role within social democracy. Moreover, the great female protagonists of the labour movement, Rosa Luxemburg, for instance, or Clara Zetkin, were evidently unsuitable to serve as vehicles for a genderized history of the entire labour movement.[28]

It was above all two social historians who produced comprehensive pictures of German social history based upon the interpretation of historical structures, which were undisturbed by the various fashionable new directions that ebbed and flowed in modern historiography: in his five-volume *History of German Society*, Hans Ulrich Wehler maintained his procedure, one which was deeply influenced by Max Weber, expounded a modified version of the German *Sonderweg* thesis, and insisted on analysing class formation and the development of social inequality, the study of which he has always held to be the 'royal road' of social history.[29] And Hartmut Kaelble has successfully brought the special features of German history into new focus, thanks to his comparative structural investigations into European social history, particularly in the twentieth century.[30]

Focal points of research

After approximately half a century of often strenuous research into workers' history and labour movement history in both the GDR and West Germany, tens of thousands of essays and books on this theme have been published. A chronologically ordered attempt to provide at least a preliminary overview of this field must start with the 'Constitutional phase of the German labour movement', which extended from the Vormärz period in the 1840s, via the revolution of 1848–49, into the 1860s.

Studies on this topic, including many noteworthy publications, appeared in the 1960s and were therefore characterized by new socio-historical perspectives to a lesser degree. However, they shed light on the combined activity of diverse forces during the period of illegality and the revolutionary period, in which the Workers' Alliance (*Arbeiterverbrüderung*) and the Communist League sought early on to exert influence in very different ways.[31] For decades, the latter was the central focus of labour movement research in the GDR, where an extensive collection of documents relating to early workers' organizations was gathered.[32] It is a characteristic of German historiography in general that significant collections of documents are published, and this approach applies to labour movement history as well. Until well into the 1990s, the International Institute for Social History in Amsterdam, a key archive for German labour history, has participated in these efforts. It has published important correspondence from its collections, including, of course, editions of the *Nachlass*, which were originally published in Moscow and in East Berlin (*Works of Marx and Engels*), and work still continues on the *Collected Works of Marx and Engels*.

There has been wider participation in this edition of primary sources, notably by the Israeli historian Shlomo Na'aman. He also deserves credit for having published the first great biography of Lassalle.[33] Moreover, very detailed studies have been published on the question of the continuity of workers' organizations during the 1850s as well as on the complicated issue of the formation of the trade unions in the decade before the foundation of the German Empire.[34] This research led to the fundamental insight that the 'beginning' of the German labour movement should not be dated from the founding of the German General Workers' Association (*Allgemeiner Deutscher Arbeiterverein*) by Lassalle, an event that is still celebrated today by Social Democrats. Instead, it should be dated from 1848–49, when the first workers' organizations were formed which possessed some claim to national representation.

The chronological focus of socio-historical research into factory history and business history (already described above) was principally the period 'after the founding of the German Empire in 1870–71', which corresponded to Germany's rise to the status of an industrial nation.[35] Researchers have naturally devoted particular attention to the twelve years of oppression under the Law against Socialists; on this subject there have been numerous local and regional studies, but overarching summaries have also been produced. There has been a wealth of publications on the trade union movement and the workers' movement after Bismarck's fall in 1890. One of the achievements of this research was to differentiate between the influential political and ideological currents within the social democratic movement, i.e. between reformism (Georg von Vollmar), revisionism (Eduard Bernstein) and centrism (Karl Kautsky). Important collections of sources were published, for example on the history of the social democratic parliamentary party, and of course the achievements of outstanding labour leaders, most notably August Bebel, received special emphasis, particularly in the GDR.[36] Biographical research tended at first to be an exception, however, because of the prevailing influence of structural social history. The fact that this gap has been filled since the 1990s, thanks to the publication of a series of very detailed biographies, indicates a return to more traditional methods and 'old fashioned' means of formulating questions.[37]

It is understandable that the decision by the Social Democrats and the free trade unions to make a truce with the authorities when the First World War broke out has been debated for decades, sometimes heatedly. This 'War and Revolutionary Phase 1914–1920' is regarded as a turning point – and simultaneously as the period in which the split within the labour movement, which fundamentally weakened Weimar democracy from the very beginning, occurred. Interpretations of this split have often been shaped by the political standpoints of the authors rather than by careful, balanced analysis, and this is still true today. Socio-historical research on this period soon gained strong support thanks to Jürgen Kocka's and Gerald D. Feldman's analyses of 'Class Society in Wartime'.[38] Virtually at the same time, bitter controversies surfaced about such issues as the development of the trade unions, particularly during the revolutionary period, the policies of the Council of People's Representatives and the founding of the German Communist Party (KPD) in the course of the movement of revolutionary workers' councils. For this period too, extensive volumes of sources have been published, for example relating to the revolutionary workers' councils. In addition, a multi-volume series documenting twentieth-century trade union history begins with an important volume focusing on 1914. Once again, the research interests of GDR historians were focused mainly on the history of the KPD, while in the Federal Republic Hermann Weber (b. 1928) published a groundbreaking study of the 'Stalinization' of the KPD which has remained to this day the standard work in the field.[39]

Many of the new socio-historical trends came together for a time in research on the history of 'Workers in the period of National Socialist dictatorship'. Research on the KPD's resistance to Hitler was produced almost exclusively in the GDR, until the publication of essays and, especially, documentation on social policy in the Third Reich by the British social historian Timothy Mason (1940–1990).[40] After that, studies appeared which concentrated on particular sectors of industry and on different aspects of workers' lives. The major research project carried out by the Institute of Contemporary History (*Institut für Zeitgeschichte*) in Munich on 'Bavaria in the National Socialist period' completely redefined our conception of resistance. Numerous, often local and regional, publications and exhibitions on 'Resistance and Persecution in the Third Reich' revealed increasing public interest in this period of recent history. As a field of research it was occupied above all by the many history workshops which emerged, and often showed a marked preference for using oral traditions.[41]

As usual, the emphasis was on the attitudes and behaviour of the 'common people'. But there was also extensive research on resistance by Social Democrats and trade unionists, as well as on the effectiveness of the activities of the exiled party and trade union leaders based in Prague, Paris, Britain, the USA and in the Scandinavian countries. This area of study received a further major boost in the 1990s, when the debate about compensation for inmates of forced labour camps created a stir. Widespread public interest in this topic developed, so that town councils, big businesses, churches and other major institutions felt called upon to commission their own independent research in order to shed light on their own respective involvements with the brutal practices of forced labour.[42] In this way research became particularly focused on the way work was organized under the National Socialists, and the results of these investigations also acted as an important stimulus leading to a renewal of business history.

This limited overview makes it clear that by now the socio-historical challenges of the 1960s and 1970s appear to have been largely integrated into German labour history. However, this new synthesis does not mean that detailed studies of political developments have become superfluous. The once bitter debate about the social democratic reception of Marxism has almost completely faded away; and the disputes about the Communist League and the development of the First and Second International, arguments which were conducted over a period of decades at the above-mentioned Linz Conference, are no longer heard. Much the same holds true for issues concerning the development of social democracy, trade unions and the KPD, including its leftwing splinter groups during the period of the Weimar Republic. It is hard to avoid the conclusion that a very substantial role must be ascribed to the Cold War, and subsequently its termination, in shaping the controversies and points of research focus within the field of German labour history.

The end of the labour movement – the end of the historiography of labour movements?

One is tempted to ascribe to the German and European *Wende* of 1989–90 (the reunification of Germany and the collapse of Communism) a fundamental (and negative) influence on historical interest in labour movements. Those who incline towards this view should remember that there has already been a debate about 'the end of the labour movement' which took place in the 1980s in Germany.[43] This debate did not attract particular attention and it was in some respects absurd. It was absurd to the extent that it was based upon interpretations which denied that trade unions were important in the context of everyday politics and competing interests. Such interpretations often claimed to be 'post-industrial' and placed key emphasis on the transition of the SPD from a party representing working-class interests to a modern mainstream party appealing to all classes. This was indeed a fundamental change. Moreover, the postwar 'decades of European social democracy', which saw a rise of the social state that was very remarkable at least in comparison with the USA, appeared to be at an end with the onset of the 'Kohl era', when Helmut Kohl was the Federal Chancellor from 1982 to 1998. The economic and political models which previously characterized the system had indubitably shifted in favour of monetarist economic policy; economic growth rates were considerably lower; and cuts in social spending seemed to be inevitable. In reality, the policies of the Kohl government were hardly less Keynesian than those of its social-democratic predecessor: to take one example, the social state was even extended with the introduction of nursing care insurance.

It seems that there are deeper reasons for the decreasing research interest in the labour movement. Some of these may be outlined as follows.[44] Starting in the 1960s, German society, which previously had always been described as a 'society of workers' by writers from Ernst Jünger to Hanna Arendt,[45] experienced fundamental structural changes. As well as the rise of the service sector, the most significant innovation was the decline in formerly crucial sectors of industry such as the textile industry and the coal and steel industries. As a consequence, entire cultures of working life and familiar groups of workers have disappeared into the history books; the decline of industry in the Ruhr area is a classic example of this. Class formation and working life hardly perform the same functions of social integration which typified German society well into the postwar period,[46] and which typified society in the GDR even longer – until 1990 – because of the controlled economic policy and outmoded ideological structure which prevailed there. Types of occupation in the service sector have become extraordinarily diverse. The majority of workers in the service sector are women, and trade union activity and recruitment is very difficult to organize in both the public and private service sectors.

Just as important is the fact that the social state, in what is often called the 'Rhenish capitalism' of the Federal Republic of Germany, has to a great extent guaranteed secure livelihoods and living wages, and ensured protection against work-related risks. Formal wage labour no longer occupies such a huge proportion as it once did of people's daily, weekly and yearly lives, or indeed of time across their life-span. Technical progress has reduced the physical exertion once linked with work, and where manual labour continues to persist, such occupations usually function as a way into the labour market for migrant workers. The influx of migrant workers into Germany since the late 1950s, first from the South of Europe, and then, particularly, from Turkey, created new lower strata within the previously dominant class of skilled workers. These changes produced novel, often precarious forms of cultural orientation for migrant milieus which are often more or less self-sufficient. In contrast, traditional industrial working-class milieus, whether Catholic or social democratic, have been eroded almost beyond recognition. This has been a creeping process and it is not entirely complete today. Yet it has transformed and corroded the prized institutions of organized working-class culture, its countless sporting, leisure and cultural associations. It is not even necessary to discuss secularization, commercialization, mobilization and other factors in order to understand why the formerly strong link between workers, voters and social democracy – a connection which was once particularly strong in Germany – has become much looser, while the party itself has for a considerable period been energetically courting other electoral constituencies.

It is perceptions of these fundamental shifts which, more than the end of the Cold War, have reduced interest in researching the history of the labour movement in Germany. These developments corresponded to changing currents within the discipline of historiography itself: for example, the emergence of new cultural and constructivist forms of interpretation. Yet considerable interest in labour history endures. The major periodicals mentioned above continue to be published. New and different approaches have been applied, such as analyses beyond the national frame: the history of leftwing elites in Europe, and transnational history as a history of political relations, comparative ideologies and political aims.[47] We shall have to await the empirical fruits of a renewed global history of work, reaching beyond the – by and large limited – national perspectives achieved during the blossoming of structural social history. The compartmentalization of knowledge is progressing: but as each new field is explored, it also produces important results for labour history.

But the formerly firm connection between labour history and the history of labour movements has now been broken. The most obvious sign of this is that since the 1990s a new interest in labour history has clearly manifested itself.[48] This interest has been fed not least by the perception that, due to the process of globalization, broad sections of wage labour which were formerly rooted in particular locations have been (so to say) 'exported'. Because of this, it now seems advisable to adopt global and transnational perspectives and methodologies in order to research labour history to its best advantage.[49]

Notes

I wish to thank Ernest Schonfield for his careful translation of this chapter.

1 Hermann Oncken, *Lassalle: eine politische Biographie* (Stuttgart: Frommans, 1904); abbreviated edition, idem, *Lassalle: Zwischen Marx und Bismarck*, ed. by Felix Hirsch (Stuttgart: Kohlhammer, 1966).

2 For this section, see *Bibliographie zur Geschichte der deutschen Arbeiterschaft und Arbeiterbewegungen 1863 bis 1914: Berichtszeitraum 1945–1975*, ed. by Klaus Tenfelde and Gerhard A. Ritter (Bonn: Neue Gesellschaft, 1981),

Introduction, pp. 37–141.

3 Franz Mehring, *Geschichte der deutschen Sozialdemokratie,* 2 vols (Stuttgart: Dietz, 1893, published in a book series entitled *Die Geschichte des Sozialismus in Einzeldarstellungen*; second revised edition, 4 vols (1903–04); see Franz Mehring, *Gesammelte Schriften*, ed. by Thomas Höhle et al., 15 vols (vols 1 and 2, Berlin-GDR: Dietz, 1960–67).

4 Heinrich Imbusch, *Arbeitsverhältnis und Arbeiterorganisationen im deutschen Bergbau: Eine geschichtliche Darstellung*, 1908 (reprint Bonn and Berlin: J.H.W. Dietz Nachf., 1980); Otto Hue, *Die Bergarbeiter: Historische Darstellung der Bergarbeiter-Verhältnisse von der ältesten bis in die neueste Zeit*, 2 vols, 1910–1912 (reprinted, Berlin and Bonn: J.H.W. Dietz Nachf., 1981). As with many of their colleagues, both these writers published numerous articles and abbreviated versions of their studies, not least for popular use.

5 *Kneipengespräche im Kaiserreich: Die Stimmungsberichte der Hamburger Politischen Polizei 1892–1914*, ed. by Richard J. Evans (Reinbek bei Hamburg: Rowohlt, 1989).

6 See *Deutsche Historiker im Exil (1933–1945): Ausgewählte Studien*, ed. by Mario Kessler (Berlin: Metropol Friedrich Veitl-Verlag, 2005); Jens Adamski, *Ärzte des sozialen Lebens: Die Sozialforschungsstelle Dortmund 1946–1969* (Essen: Klartext, 2009).

7 Gerhard A. Ritter, *Die Arbeiterbewegung im Wilhelminischen Reich: Die Sozialdemokratische Partei Deutschlands und die Freien Gewerkschaften 1890–1900* (2nd edn, Berlin: Colloquium, 1963); see also Gerhard A. Ritter and Klaus Tenfelde, 'Der Durchbruch der Freien Gewerkschaften Deutschlands zur Massenbewegung im letzten Viertel des 19. Jahrhunderts', in Gerhard A. Ritter, *Arbeiterbewegung, Parteien und Parlamentarismus: Aufsätze zur deutschen Sozial- und Verfassungsgeschichte des 19. und 20. Jahrhunderts* (Göttingen: Vandenhoeck and Ruprecht, 1976), pp. 55–101.

8 See especially Erich Matthias, 'Kautsky und der Kautskyanismus: Die Funktion der Ideologie in der deutschen Sozialdemokratie vor dem ersten Weltkrieg', in *Marxismusstudien 2. Folge*, ed. by Iring Fetscher (Tübingen: Mohr, 1957), pp. 151–91.

9 Helga Grebing, *Geschichte der deutschen Arbeiterbewegung: Von der Revolution 1848 bis ins 21. Jahrhundert* (Berlin: Vorwärts Buch, 2007); *Geschichte der sozialen Ideen in Deutschland. Sozialismus – Katholische Soziallehre – Protestantische Sozialethik: Ein Handbuch*, ed. by Helga Grebing, (1st pub. 2000; Wiesbaden: Verlag für Sozialwissenschaften, 2005).

10 For books and articles on the subject published between 1945 and 1975, see *Bibliographie zur Geschichte der deutschen Arbeiterbewegung, sozialistischen und kommunistischen Bewegung von den Anfängen bis 1863*, ed. by Dieter Dowe (3rd edn, Bonn-Bad Godesberg: Neue Gesellschaft, 1981); for 1863–1914 see above, n. 2; *Bibliographie zur Geschichte der deutschen Arbeiterbewegung 1914–1945*, ed. by Kurt Klotzbach (2nd edn, Bonn-Bad Godesberg: Neue Gesellschaft, 1976); *SPD, KPD/DKP, DGB in den Westzonen und in der Bundesrepublik Deutschland 1945–1973*, ed. by Klaus Günther and Kurt Thomas Schmitz (2nd edn, Bonn-Bad Godesberg: Neue Gesellschaft, 1980). Since 1976, the Friedrich

Ebert Stiftung has published a yearly bibliography accessible via the Internet.

11 This statement is based on discussions with several GDR historians, mostly during the Linz conferences, for instance with Dieter Fricke who was one of the leading representatives of the profession in the East. As an exceptional case, Jürgen Kuczynski (1904–1997), who published (partially with co-authors) the 40-volume *Geschichte der Lage der Arbeiter unter dem Kapitalismus*, enjoyed far-reaching liberties in the GDR. A certain social historical insight into the features of proletarian existence was made possible under the umbrella of ethnological studies (*Volkskunde*) and in studies of agrarian feudalism in East Prussia. As an important exception to the compulsory orthodox mainstream of labour *movement* history, Hartmut Zwahr's research on the Leipzig proletariat in the nineteenth century, based on the godfather registers, was immediately perceived as significant in West German historiography: *Zur Konstituierung des Proletariats als Klasse: Strukturuntersuchung über das Leipziger Proletariat während der industriellen Revolution* (1st pub. 1978; Munich: C.H. Beck Verlag, 1981).

12 See Jürgen Kocka, *Sozialgeschichte. Begriff-Entwicklung-Probleme* (1st pub. 1977; Göttingen: Vandenhoeck and Ruprecht, 1986); *Sozialgeschichte in Deutschland: Entwicklungen und Perspektiven im internationalen Zusammenhang*, 4 vols, ed. by Wolfgang Schieder and Volker Sellin (Göttingen: Vandenhoeck and Ruprecht, 1986–1987); *Europäische Sozialgeschichte: Festschrift für Wolfgang Schieder*, ed. by Cristof Dipper et al. (Berlin: Duncker and Humblot, 2000). A starting point of the discussion was *Moderne Deutsche Sozialgeschichte*, ed. by Hans-Ulrich Wehler (Cologne: Kiepenheuer and Witsch, 1966).

13 Largely following Thompson: Michael Vester, *Die Entstehung des Proletariats als Lernprozess* (Frankfurt: Europäische Verlagsanstalt, 1970); for a comparative perspective, see Christiane Eisenberg, *Deutsche und englische Gewerkschaften: Entstehung und frühe Entwicklung bis 1878 im Vergleich* (Göttingen: Vandenhoeck and Ruprecht, 1986).

14 David Blackbourn and Geoff Eley, *Mythen deutscher Geschichtsschreibung: Die gescheiterte bürgerliche Revolution von 1848* (Frankfurt: Ullstein, 1980); idem, *The Peculiarities of German History* (New York: Oxford University Press, 1984).

15 The hypothesis of a 'weak middle class' in Germany played a decisive role in the introduction of a 'special research area' (*Sonderforschungsbereich*, SFB) of the German Research Association at the University of Bielefeld. Between 1985 and 1997, forty junior researchers investigated the history of the middle classes in Germany (and also in comparative perspective) since the late Middle Ages. In the light of the results, the *Sonderweg* hypothesis was decisively modified. Thanks to an engagement with the works of Pierre Bourdieu and Michel Foucault, the SFB also introduced revised socio-cultural methods into German social history. See for instance, *Wege zur Geschichte des Bürgertums*, ed. by Klaus Tenfelde and Hans-Ulrich Wehler (Göttingen: Vandenhoeck and Ruprecht, 1994); *Sozial- und Kulturgeschichte des Bürgertums: Eine Bilanz*, ed. by Peter Lundgreen (Göttingen: Vandenhoeck and Ruprecht, 2000).

16 Fritz Fischer, *Griff nach der Weltmacht: Die Kriegszielpolitik des kaiserlichen Deutschlands 1914/1918* (Düsseldorf: Droste, 1961). There have been numerous reprints; the text appeared in English translation as idem, *Germany's Aims in the First World War* (New York: W.W. Norton, 2007). For a comprehensive recent interpretation, see Christoph Cornelißen, *Gerhard Ritter: Geschichtswissenschaft und Politik im 20. Jahrhundert* (Düsseldorf: Droste, 2001).

17 To mention just the most important contributions to this question: Susanne Miller, *Burgfrieden und Klassenkampf: Die deutsche Sozialdemokratie im Ersten Weltkrieg* (Düsseldorf: Droste, 1978); Dieter Groh, *Negative Integration und revolutionärer Attentismus: Die deutsche Sozialdemokratie am Vorabend des Ersten Weltkrieges* (Frankfurt: Ullstein, 1974).

18 See Klaus Tenfelde, 'Wege zur Sozialgeschichte der Arbeiterschaft und Arbeiterbewegung: Regional- und lokal-geschichtliche Forschungen (1945–1975) zur deutschen Arbeiterbewegung bis 1914', in *Die moderne deutsche Geschichte in der internationalen Forschung 1945 bis 1975*, ed. by Hans-Ulrich Wehler (Göttingen: Vandenhoeck and Ruprecht 1978), pp.197–255; idem, 'Neue Forschungen zur Geschichte der Arbeiterschaft', *Archiv für Sozialgeschichte*, 20 (1980), 593–615; see also *Arbeiter und Arbeiterbewegung im Vergleich. Berichte zur internationalen historischen Forschung*, ed. by Klaus Tenfelde (Munich: Oldenbourg, 1986).

19 See, for example, Friedhelm Boll, *Arbeitskämpfe und Gewerkschaften in Deutschland, England und Frankreich: ihre Entwicklung vom 19. zum 20. Jahrhundert* (Bonn: J.H.W. Dietz Nachf., 1992); and Eisenberg, *Deutsche und englische Gewerkschaften.* A detailed interest in English and British history is on display in Willibald Steinmetz, *Das Sagbare und das Machbare: Zum Wandel politischer Handlungsspielräume – England 1780–1867* (Stuttgart: Klett-Cotta, 1993); see also *Private Law and Social Inequality in the Industrial Age: Comparing Legal Cultures in Britain, France, Germany, and the United States*, ed. by Willibald Steinmetz (Oxford: Oxford University Press, 2000).

20 Heinrich A. Winkler: *Arbeiter und Arbeiterbewegung in der Weimarer Republik 1918–1933*, 3 vols (Bonn-Bad Godesberg: J.H.W. Dietz Nachf., 1984–1987), Jürgen Kocka, *Weder Stand noch Klasse – Unterschichten um 1800* (Bonn-Bad Godesberg: J.H.W. Dietz Nachf., 1990); idem, *Arbeitsverhältnisse und Arbeiterexistenzen — Grundlagen der Klassenbildung im 19. Jahrhundert* (Bonn-Bad Godesberg: J.H.W. Dietz Nachf., 1990); Gerhard A. Ritter and Klaus Tenfelde, *Arbeiter im Deutschen Kaiserreich 1871–1914* (Bonn-Bad Godesberg: J.H.W. Dietz Nachf., 1992); Michael Schneider, *Unterm Hakenkreuz: Arbeiter und Arbeiterbewegung 1933 bis 1939* (Bonn-Bad Godesberg: J.H.W. Dietz Nachf., 1999); see also Kurt Klotzbach, *Der Weg zur Staatspartei: Programmatik, praktische Politik und Organisation der deutschen Sozialdemokratie 1945–1965* (Bonn-Bad Godesberg: J.H.W. Dietz Nachf., 1982).

21 Sven Lindqvist, *Grabe wo du stehst: Handbuch zur Erforschung der eigenen Geschichte* (Bonn: Verlag J.H.W. Dietz Nachf., 1989); Clifford Geertz, *Dichte Beschreibung: Beiträge zum Verstehen kultureller Systeme* (1st pub. 1983; Frankfurt: Suhrkamp, 2003); Carlo Ginzburg, *Der Käse und die Würmer:*

Die Welt eines Müllers um 1600 (Frankfurt: Syndikat, 1979); Alf Lüdtke, *Alltagsgeschichte* (Frankfurt: Campus, 1989); Klaus Tenfelde, 'Schwierigkeiten mit dem Alltag', *Geschichte und Gesellschaft*, 10 (1984), 376–94.

22 Gert Zang, *Die unaufhaltsame Annäherung an das Einzelne: Reflexionen über den theoretischen und praktischen Nutzen der Regional- und Alltagsgeschichte* (Konstanz: Arbeitskreis für Regionalgeschichte, 1985).

23 Alf Lüdtke, *Eigen-Sinn. Fabrikalltag: Arbeitererfahrungen und Politik vom Kaiserreich bis in den Faschismus* (Hamburg: Ergebnisse, 1993).

24 See, among other work, *Sozialer Protest: Studien zu traditioneller Resistenz und kollektiver Gewalt in Deutschland vom Vormärz bis zur Reichsgründung*, ed. by Heinrich Volkmann and Jürgen Bergmann (Opladen: Westdeutscher Verlag, 1984).

25 The most important contributions can be found in *Lebenserfahrung und kollektives Gedächtnis: Die Praxis des 'Oral History'*, ed. by Lutz Niethammer (Frankfurt: Syndikat, 1980); *Lebensgeschichte und Sozialkultur im Ruhrgebiet 1930–1960*, 3 vols, ed. by Lutz Niethammer (Bonn: J.H.W. Dietz Nachf., 1983–1985).

26 See *Enzyklopädie Migration in Europa vom 17. Jahrhundert bis zur Gegenwart*, ed. by Klaus J. Bade, Pieter C. Emmer, Leo Lucassen and Jochen Oltmer (Paderborn: Wilhelm Fink, 2008).

27 M. Rainer Lepsius, 'Parteiensystem und Sozialstruktur', in idem, *Demokratie in Deutschland: Ausgewählte Aufsätze* (1st pub. 1966; Göttingen: Vandenhoeck and Ruprecht, 1993), pp. 25–50. For what follows, see Klaus Tenfelde, 'Historische Milieus: Erblichkeit und Konkurrenz', in *Nation und Gesellschaft in Deutschland: Historische Essays (Festschrift für Hans-Ulrich Wehler)*, ed. by Manfred Hettling and Paul Nolte (Munich: C.H. Beck, 1996), pp. 247–68; Wilhelm Damberg, *Abschied vom Milieu? Katholizismus im Bistum Münster und in den Niederlanden 1945–1980* (Paderborn: Schöningh, 1997); see also idem, 'Formation of Christian Working-Class Organizations in Belgium, Germany, Italy and the Netherlands (1840s–1920s)', in *Between Cross and Class: Comparative Histories of Christian Labour in Europe 1840–2000*, ed. by Lex Heerma van Voss, Patrick Pasture and Jan De Maeyer (Bern, Berlin, Brussels: Peter Lang, 2005), pp. 49–80.

28 See, for example, Stefan Bajohr, *Die Hälfte der Fabrik: Geschichte der Frauenarbeit in Deutschland 1914 bis* 1945 (1st pub. 1979; Marburg: Verlag Arbeiterbewegung und Gesellschaftswissenschaft, 1984); Richard J. Evans, *Sozialdemokratie und Frauenemanzipation im Deutschen Kaiserreich* (Berlin and Bonn: J.H.W. Dietz Nachf., 1979); Tânia Puschnerat, *Clara Zetkin: Bürgerlichkeit und Marxismus* (Essen: Klartext Verlag, 2003). On female workers during the First World War see, for example, Ute Daniel, *Arbeiterfrauen in der Kriegsgesellschaft 1914–1918: Beruf, Familie und Politik im Ersten Weltkrieg* (Göttingen: Vandenhoeck and Ruprecht, 1989), English version: idem, *The War from Within: German Working-Class Women in the First World War* (Oxford: Berg, 1997).

29 Hans-Ulrich Wehler, *Deutsche Gesellschaftsgeschichte*, 5 vols (Munich: C.H. Beck, 1987–2008).

30 Hartmut Kaelble, *Sozialgeschichte Europas: 1945 bis zur Gegenwart* (Munich:

C.H. Beck, 2007).

31 Wolfgang Schieder, *Anfänge der deutschen Arbeiterbewegung: Die Auslandsvereine im Jahrzehnt nach der Julirevolution von 1830* (Stuttgart: Klett, 1963); Frolinde Balser, *Social-Demokratie 1848–1863: Die erste deutsche Arbeiterorganisation 'Allgemeine deutsche Arbeiterverbrüderung' nach der Revolution*, 2 vols (Stuttgart: Klett, 1962).

32 *Bund der Kommunisten 1836–1852*, ed. by Martin Hundt (Berlin: Akademie Verlag, 1988). In what follows, space permits only a few of the major publications to be mentioned.

33 Shlomo Na'aman, *Lassalle* (Hanover: Verlag für Literatur und Zeitgeschehen, 1970).

34 Toni Offermann, *Arbeiterbewegung und liberales Bürgertum in Deutschland 1850–1863* (Bonn: Neue Gesellschaft, 1979); Ulrich Engelhardt, '*Nur vereinigt sind wir stark': Die Anfänge der deutschen Gewerkschaftsbewegung 1862/63 bis 1869/70*, 2 vols (Stuttgart: Klett, 1977).

35 See, for example, Willy Albrecht, *Fachverein – Berufsgewerkschaft – Zentralverband: Organisationsprobleme der deutschen Gewerkschaften 1870–1890* (Bonn: Neue Gesellschaft, 1982); Vernon L. Lidtke, *The Outlawed Party: Social Democracy in Germany, 1878–1890* (Princeton: Princeton University Press, 1966); *Geschichte der deutschen Gewerkschaften von den Anfängen bis 1945*, ed. by Ulrich Borsdorf (Köln: Bund Verlag, 1984); Michael Schneider, *Die christlichen Gewerkschaften* (Bonn: J.H.W. Dietz, 1982); Dirk H. Müller, *Versammlungsdemokratie und Arbeiterdelegierte in der deutschen Gewerkschaftsbewegung vor 1918* (Berlin: Colloquium, 1987); Hans-Josef Steinberg, *Sozialismus und deutsche Sozialdemokratie* (Hannover: Verlag für Literatur und Zeitgeschehen, 1967); Helga Grebing, *Der Revisionismus: Von Bernstein bis zum Prager Frühling* (Munich: C.H. Beck Verlag, 1987); see also ns 7, 8 and 17, above.

36 August Bebel, *Ausgewählte Schriften*, 10 vols (East Berlin: Dietz, since 1978; and Munich, Saur). The edition was completed after reunification.

37 See, for example, Jürgen Mittag, *Wilhelm Keil, 1870–1968: Sozialdemokratischer Parlamentarier zwischen Kaiserreich und Bundesrepublik* (Düsseldorf: Droste, 2001); Ursula Reuter, *Paul Singer (1844–1911): Eine politische Biographie* (Düsseldorf: Droste, 2004).

38 Jürgen Kocka, *Klassengesellschaft im Krieg. Deutsche Sozialgeschichte 1914–1918* (Göttingen: Vandenhoeck and Ruprecht, 1973); Gerald D. Feldman, *Army, Industry, and Labor in Germany, 1914–1918*, (Princeton: Princeton University Press, 1966).

39 Hermann Weber, *Die Wandlung des deutschen Kommunismus: Die Stalinisierung der KPD in der Weimarer Republik*, 2 vols (Frankfurt: Europäische Verlagsantalt, 1969); see also Klaus-Michael Mallmann, *Kommunisten in der Weimarer Republik: Sozialgeschichte einer revolutionären Bewegung* (Darmstadt: Wissenschaftliche Buchgesellschaft, 1996).

40 Timothy Mason, *Arbeiterklasse und Volksgemeinschaft: Dokumente und Materialien zur deutschen Arbeiterpolitik, 1936–39* (Opladen: Westdeutscher Verlag, 1975).

41 See above n. 25. As examples, see *Hochlarmarker Lesebuch: Kohle war nicht alles. 100 Jahre Ruhrgebietsgeschichte*, ed. by Hochlarmarker Geschichts-Arbeitskreis; (Oberhausen: Asso Verlag, 1981); and Michael Zimmermann, *Schachtanlage und Zechenkolonie: Leben, Arbeit und Politik in einer Zechensiedlung 1880 bis 1980* (Essen: Klartext Verlag, 1987). Most important is Rüdiger Hachtmann, *Industriearbeit im 'Dritten Reich': Untersuchungen zu den Lohn- und Arbeitsbedingungen 1933–1945* (Göttingen: Vandenhoeck and Ruprecht, 1986). See also Ian Kershaw, *Popular Opinion and Political Dissent in the Third Reich: Bavaria, 1933–45* (Oxford: Clarendon Press, 1983).

42 To provide just one example: *Zwangsarbeit im Bergwerk: Der Arbeitseinsatz im Kohlenbergbau des Deutschen Reiches und der besetzten Gebiete im Ersten und Zweiten Weltkrieg: vol. 1, Forschungen; vol. 2, Dokumente*, ed. by Klaus Tenfelde and Hans-Christoph Seidel (Essen: Klartext Verlag 2005). The research project was initiated by the Ruhr mining company.

43 See, for example, *Das Ende der Arbeiterbewegung in Deutschland? Ein Diskussionsband zum 60. Geburtstag von Theo Pirker*, ed. by Rolf Ebbighausen et al. (Opladen: Westdeutscher Verlag, 1984); Frank Deppe, *Ende oder Zukunft der Arbeiterbewegung – Gewerkschaftspolitik nach der Wende: Eine kritische Bestandsaufnahme* (Cologne: Pahl-Rugenstein, 1984). For recently published articles on the history of work and workers in the GDR and in the Eastern European postwar societies, see *Arbeiter in der SBZ-DDR*, ed. by Peter Hübner and Klaus Tenfelde (Essen: Klartext Verlag, 1999); *Arbeiter im Staatssozialismus*, ed. by Peter Hübner, Christoph Kleßmann and Klaus Tenfelde (Cologne: Böhlau, 2005).

44 For examples of careful interpretation, see Peter Brandt, 'Die Arbeiterbewegung des 19. und 20. Jahrhunderts. Entwicklung – Wirkung – Perspektive', in idem, *Soziale Bewegung und politische Emanzipation: Studien zur Geschichte der Arbeiterbewegung und des Sozialismus* (Bonn: Neue Gesellschaft, 2008) pp. 457–72; Jürgen Kocka, 'New Trends in Labour Movement Historiography: A German Perspective', in *Class and Other Identities: Gender, Religion, and Ethnicity in the Writing of European Labour History*, ed. by Lex Heerma van Voss and Marcel van der Linden (Oxford: Berghahn, 2002), pp. 42–54. See also Klaus Tenfelde, 'Europäische Arbeiterbewegungen im 20. Jahrhundert', in *Demokratischer Sozialismus in Europa seit dem Zweiten Weltkrieg*, ed. by Dieter Dowe (Bonn: Friedrich-Ebert-Stiftung, 2001) pp. 9–40.

45 Ernst Jünger, *Der Arbeiter. Herrschaft und Gestalt*, 1932, in idem, *Gesammelte Werke, vol. 6: Essays II* (Stuttgart: Klett-Cotta, no date); Hannah Arendt, *Vita activa oder vom tätigen Leben*, 1958–59 (Munich and Zurich: Piper, 2006).

46 See Andreas Wirsching, 'Konsum statt Arbeit? Zum Wandel von Indiviudalität in der modernen Massengesellschaft', *Vierteljahreshefte für Zeitgeschichte*, 57 (2009), 171–99.

47 See Thomas Kroll, *Kommunistische Intellektuelle in Westeuropa: Frankreich, Österreich, Italien und Großbritannien im Vergleich (1945–1956)*, (Köln: Böhlau, 2007); Joachim Schröder, *Internationalismus nach dem Krieg: Die Beziehungen zwischen deutschen und französischen Kommunisten 1918–1923* (Essen: Klartext Verlag, 2008).

48 See Richard Biernacki, *The Fabrication of Labor: Germany and Britain, 1640–1914* (Berkeley: University of California Press, 1995); *Die Rolle der Arbeit in verschiedenen Epochen und Kulturen*, ed. by Manfred Bierwisch (Berlin: Akademie, 2003); *Unfreie Arbeit: Ökonomische und kulturgeschichtliche Perspektiven*, ed. by M. Erdem Kabadayi and Tobias Reichardt (Hildesheim: Georg Olms, 2007); *Geschichte und Zukunft der Arbeit*, ed. by Jürgen Kocka and Claus Offe (Frankfurt: Campus, 2000).

49 Marcel van der Linden, *Workers of the World: Essays toward a Global Labor History* (Leiden: Brill, 2008).

9

India

Rana P. Behal, Chitra Joshi and Prabhu P. Mohapatra

Recent years have witnessed a renewed scholarly interest in historical studies of labour in India and other parts of the world. This revival is distinctive both in terms of its location and also in its central concerns. It has emerged from the countries of 'the South' and its preoccupations are not confined to the traditional working class alone. Apart from the study of the industrial workforce, labour history has been enriched by scholarly attention to migratory, mobile labour, to the lives of artisans, women and peasant migrants, and to plantations in the colonial world. Earlier, the major emphasis of labour history was on the core countries such as the USA, Canada, Western Europe and Japan. Now there has been a shift of focus to nation states on the peripheries of world capitalism.

The reversal of location and the broadening of the scope of labour history provide a basis for innovative global comparisons. The earlier Eurocentric labour history often possessed an implicit comparison: development in the West was the model for the future of the periphery and the rest of the world was to be measured against the West. At the heart of classical labour history stood the figure of the free, male wage-worker, labouring in the modern factory and a member of a trade union. However, it is increasingly evident that this figure – if he ever existed – was in a minority, even in the industrialized West. With the expansion of processes of informalization and the increasing feminization of the workforce, assumptions about the centrality of the male, unionized worker are no longer tenable. The same processes have also thrown into question the privileging of formal employer-employee relationships. As the dualities of free-unfree labour, wage-work, non-wage work, formal and informal labour, blur, labour historians have to take into account the multiplicity of relationships, locations and temporalities that underpin forms of labour and within which the individual worker is embedded.

These issues are being increasingly raised and discussed by historians in many parts of the world including South Asia. The resurgence of scholarly interest in South Asian labour history, as Sumit Sarkar pointed out in a recent critical review of Indian labour historiography, 'is not a revival in the sense of a mere return to old interests and approaches. It has been accompanied by intense debates, auto-critiques, the exploration of new themes, dimensions, methods.'[1]

In this essay we will attempt to relate the renewal of labour studies to the changing landscapes of labour in India. We will seek to understand why in the years after independence there was an intellectual interest in labour policy and how in recent years there has been a revitalization of labour history. We will argue that this revival of interest can be sustained only by understanding the dominant optic that has framed labour history, foregrounding certain issues and occluding others. To do so we need to begin with a reflection on the changing traditions of Indian labour history.[2]

Bringing labour into the public domain

The earliest writings on issues of labour in the colonial context appeared from the mid-nineteenth century onwards in India with the development of modern industrial and infrastructural activities in the form of textile and jute factories, iron ore, gold and coal mining, tea, coffee and rubber plantations and construction of roads and railways. Two distinctly opposed approaches can be discerned in the official and nationalist writings on labour issues. The colonial state became actively involved with labour issues because of its concern with the supply of labour, beginning with the mobilization of labour for the overseas European colonies and then for railways, plantations and mining within the Indian subcontinent. The most important official texts on labour issues emerged in the form of reports of the numerous Committees and Commissions of Inquiry appointed by the colonial state to look into issues of labour supply, migration, treatment of labour and the functioning of early labour laws in different industries from time to time.[3] The main objective of official policy was, on the one hand, to ensure a steady and adequate supply of suitable labour for the emerging industries and plantations and, on the other, to 'protect' labour. These reports created and reinforced perceptions of certain essential characteristics of 'native' labour which were linked with its rural origins: immobility, 'fickleness', 'inefficiency' and preference for irregular employment.

Growing labour militancy and the development of nationalist politics during the 1920s as well as the onset of depression in 1929 formed the backdrop to the appointment of a Royal Commission on Labour in India which published a multi-volume report in 1930–31. The main focus of the report remained on large industries and plantations though there was a slight gesture towards seasonal and unregulated factories. However rural labour remained completely outside the purview of the Royal Commission's concerns. The report reaffirmed colonial stereotypes of Indian labour, distinguishing workers from their counterparts in the West, by their migratory nature, inherent attachment to the rural habitat, the ubiquitous presence of intermediaries (jobbers, sirdars, maistries and kanganis),[4] both in the processes of recruitment and deployment, and the absence of any tradition of trade unionism. The report thus justified the employers' neglect of minimum welfare provisions and payment of low wages on the grounds of a backward-bending labour supply curve.

Complementing state analysis, the second strand of writing on labour emerged during the reformist phase of Indian nationalism. Members of the contemporary, urban, educated intelligentsia and foreign Christian missionaries articulated their concerns about labour from the late nineteenth century onwards. The British tradition of social reform influenced some of the early Indian reformers like Sasipada Banerji in Bengal and Narayan Meghaji Lokhande in Bombay.[5] A more adversarial position was adopted by the nationalists and Brahmo reformists like Ram Kumar Vidyaratna and Dwarknath Ganguli in Bengal who published a series of articles in nationalist papers like *Sanjibani* and *Bengalee* from Calcutta between 1883 and 1887. They also visited Assam to gather first hand information about the conditions of tea garden labourers. It was on the basis of these investigations that Vidyaratna's *Coolie Kahani* and Ganguli's 'Slave Trade in India' stories appeared in the Calcutta nationalist newspapers.[6]

They were followed by the publication of a book on *Tea Garden Coolies in Assam* in 1894, by the Reverend Charles Dowding, an English missionary. Dowding's volume, a very radical critique by contemporary standards, was a reproduction of a fierce public debate he conducted with the representatives of the tea industry and their supporters. Through their writings, reformers and missionaries scathingly criticized the terrible working and living conditions, low wages, long hours of work, ill treatment in the work place, and the high mortality rates of workers in the Assam tea plantations.[7] However, the early nationalist intelligentsia and the nationalist political parties voiced their concern mostly in support of workers employed in foreign capitalist enterprises. Their attitude towards the issues of workers employed in Indian-owned enterprises was generally ambivalent. Interested primarily in the promotion and protection of indigenous capitalist industries, they were reluctant to take up issues of higher wages and shorter working hours in these enterprises.

The post-First World War years in India, as elsewhere, constituted a period of intense upsurge in working-class activity: Bombay, Calcutta, Ahmedabad, Kanpur, Jamshedpur, Sholapur, Assam and other regions witnessed a series of strike actions. If rising prices and abnormal profiteering spurred strikes in the immediate aftermath of the war, the wage- and cost-cutting rationalization measures introduced with the onset of the great depression in the late 1920s saw another wave of strikes in major industrial centres whose reverberations were felt until late in the 1930s. It was against the background of these events that the condition and history of labour emerged into the public sphere and the realm of state policy. Establishment of the first organized federation of trade unions in 1920 (All India Trade Union Congress), legalization of trade unions in 1926, the appointment of the Royal Commission on Labour and official focus on the depression, generated for the first time academic research interest in labour studies. Works by P.S. Lokanathan, S.G. Panandikar, A.C. Roychowdhury, R.K. Mukherjee and S.M. Akhtar focused on the condition of industrial and plantation workers and their standard of living and welfare.[8] Some important academic publications from outside India appeared during this period, notably by David Buchanan and Margaret Read, which were significant for their focus on the problems associated with India's incomplete transition to capitalism.[9] Supporters of workers' interests and trade unionists like Diwan Chaman Lall, R.K. Das, N.M. Joshi and B. Shiva Rao, produced accounts of colonial labour policies and the emergent labour and trade union movement.[10]

Two paradigms

Studies of labour and the working classes in India became more prominent in the context of the strategies for planned economic development launched in the first decade after independence in the 1950s. Industrialization was to be the preferred route for economic growth and modernization. In so far as labour was recognised as a crucial 'factor of production', its deployment, bargaining practices and conflict behaviour became objects of methodical scrutiny. To the nationalist leadership, industrialization and modernization were the twin interrelated processes that were expected to transform the traditional institutions of Indian society and realize economic growth. This was reflected in Prime Minister Jawaharlal Nehru's vision of modern industries as 'temples' of modern India. In his report to the Avadi (Madras) session of the All India Congress Committee in 1955, Nehru was emphatic: 'the alternative to industrialisation is to remain a backward, underdeveloped, poverty stricken and weak country. We cannot even retain our freedom without industrial growth [...].'[11]

Since the 1950s, two competing paradigms have dominated labour studies in India: one was defined by theories of modernization and the other by Marxism. Despite fundamental differences, the two paradigms shared certain similar assumptions. Both saw the formation of industrial factory labour and its action and behaviour through an optic of transition. In both these frameworks, the newly industrializing countries were perceived as in a stage similar to the early stage of industrialization in advanced countries. While admitting significant national variations, industrialization was assumed to be an inexorable process, marked by a set of universal features that characterized the 'actual course of transition from traditional society towards industrialism [...] an abstraction, a limit approached through historical industrialisation'.[12]

For modernization theorists, a major corollary of this transition in consciousness was the degree of commitment of workers to the industrial way of life. The 'labour commitment' thesis, as it came to be termed, posited that, in the early stages of the industrialization process, workers remained uncommitted to industrialism. This was reflected in the rural and kinship nexus they maintained. A mature industrialism required full commitment of workers through an internalization of work norms and discipline, and a complete severance of their ties with the land. Lack of commitment of labour was considered a serious though not insurmountable barrier to industrialization.[13] Several studies conducted in the 1950s and 1960s set out to test the hypotheses generated by the modernization research programmes, devising indices to measure the degree of workers' commitment to industrialism.[14] Strong rural links, high rates of absenteeism, and weak trade unionism, were seen to indicate that rural migrants were not yet workers fully integrated into the structure of industrial society. By the end of the 1960s, however, many elements of modernization theory and labour commitment were found to be of little use in understanding workers' behaviour and action. Renewed working-class militancy and wild-cat strikes in the 1960s seemed to buck the expectation of a gradual evolution towards responsible unionism.

Morris David Morris's study of the emergence and deployment of the labour force in the Bombay textile mills struck a discordant note in the modernization thesis by suggesting that the standard arguments about the cultural unsuitability of Indian labour for industrial employment had no empirical basis in historical data.[15] If the historical evidence did not support stage theories of modernization, neither did contemporary sociological enquiries. A special study conducted by the National Commission of Labour, set up by the Indian government in 1969, showed that industrial workers in the major industrial cities of India were committed to an industrial way of life uninhibited by ties with their rural past. The National Commission could proclaim with some assurance that the trend towards stabilization of industrial labour had strengthened over the previous twenty years: 'A worker today is far more urban in taste and outlook than his predecessor. The idyllic notion of a "village nexus" has receded to the background.'[16] It may be noted, however, that even though empirically many of the elements of modernization theory were thought to be invalid, the basic framework of modernization, which focused exclusively on the industrial worker in large factories and urban centres, was not questioned. The National Commission on Labour's invocation of the emergence of the fully committed new worker was, as we shall see, rather premature.

The Marxists explained the problems of modern industry in India by referring to colonial constraints which, in their framework, accounted for the partial and disarticulated nature of industrialization. Unlike in advanced capitalist countries, the process of proletarianization in India, they argued, remained disarticulated from industrial growth. The craftsmen displaced by the process of deindustrialization were pushed back into agriculture instead of being absorbed into modern industry. This partial nature of industrialization had a profound effect on working-class formation. Thus, M.N. Roy wrote: 'The normal course of industrial development was obstructed in India. Industry did not grow through the successive phases of handicraft, manufacture, small factory, mechanofacture and then mass production. So the Indian worker has not been trained in industry. He lacks the proletarian tradition.'[17] In 1940, the Marxist theoretician Rajani Palme Dutt examined the formation of the Indian working class in the crucible of colonial economic formation. He visualized the growth of working-class consciousness in the emerging anti-imperialist struggle, focusing mainly on the role of the Communist Party in imparting to the class a revolutionary consciousness. The equation of working-class movement and consciousness with its institutions (trade unions and political party) and its leadership became the hallmark of subsequent detailed investigation on labour in India.[18]

In the post-independence period a series of writings in the 1950s and 1960s by leftwing trade union activists such as Sanat Bose, Indrajit Gupta, J.S. Mathur, V.B. Karnik, G.K. Sharma and others like S.C. Jha, C. Revri and

Sukomal Sen, traced the growth of the labour movement and organization. Their focus was primarily on formal institutional history, on leaders and parties and not on the many conflicting currents and pressures from below which shaped the course of labour organization and politics.[19] In these accounts, the history of labour organization appears as the gradual unfolding of a politically conscious working class. It was difficult to grapple with the complexities of the historical context in India within the limits of such teleological frameworks.

Towards social history: beyond culturalist paradigms

A problem which Marxist histories had to continuously confront was the persistence of consciousness of caste, religion and region among workers. In this situation, class consciousness seemed a perpetually elusive goal. It was always 'emergent', 'elementary', 'embryonic' or 'incipient', gestating in a morass of primordialism. A second, related problem was the continued existence of several forms of labour that were only partially proletarianized. Given such a scenario, a pure class-conscious working class seemed illusory. The reasons for these deviations were sought in the realm of structures (economic and political) and, by extension, in the realm of culture. Thus, the continued rural linkage of the worker, the coexistence of multiple modes of production within the same social formation, the segmentation of the labour market, supposedly accounted for the persistence of pre-modern mentalities and hampered the emergence of a proper proletarian culture.[20] However, the conventional framework of Marxist labour history came to be vigorously debated even as the limits of alternative modernization models were becoming evident in the 1970s.

The present resurgence of interest in labour studies in India can be traced back to certain shifts since the late 1970s. The surge of interest in popular movements culminated, on the one hand, in the writings of what came to be known as the Subaltern Studies group in the early 1980s and, on the other, in a series of independent publications on labour. The dominant concern of the historians of the Subaltern Studies group, with one important exception, was with peasant movements. This was also a period when the influence of ideas drawn from E.P. Thompson's approach to social history became manifest. Two seemingly contradictory trends in writing emerged against this background. A series of writings from the late 1970s focused on the social origins of labour and tried to understand the transformative impact of modern industries. Others critiqued reductionist approaches which characterized modern industry as an agent of change: industrial culture in India in this framework was perceived as essentially pre-modern.

Historians writing social histories of labour probed the social origins of workers and their caste and community background. Among the pioneering works was Ranajit Dasgupta's study of workers in the Calcutta jute mills, their experience of work, discipline and protest. For Dasgupta, as for other Marxist writers of the 1970s and early 1980s, working-class culture was located within a model of transition, which assumed that pre-industrial forms of consciousness – ties of community and religion – would be gradually displaced by mature forms of class consciousness. Dasgupta's impassioned defence of class provided the context for a very lively debate with critics of his reductionist argument.[21]

A critique of reductionist frameworks was powerfully articulated by Dipesh Chakrabarty. Chakrabarty carried on a sharp polemic against the dominant assumptions in labour history in India. Most writings, he argued, even those more sensitive to issues of culture tended, in the end, to reduce culture to certain economic variables.[22] He pressed for an autonomous understanding in which culture was uncoupled from the economic and political determinants external to it: a perspective which looked at culture in its own terms. If the critical 'linguistic turn' of the 1980s in the Anglo-Saxon and European contexts unsettled earlier frameworks, Chakrabarty's radical culturalism disturbed the certainties of conventional Marxist approaches in India and presaged some of the later shifts in the historiography of labour.

In opposition to Marxist contributions that see working-class history in terms of a continuous unfolding of class identities, Chakrabarty's account valorizes certain fixed notions of caste and community identities. Urban life and work in the factory did not have a transforming role – if anything they deepened and intensified the workers' sense of belonging to an ethnic community. In his framework the participation of workers in actions based on wider solidarities cutting across religious and caste divides appears episodic – it has no lasting significance. While Chakrabarty critiques frameworks which reduce culture to economic determinants, he tends to reify culture by seeing identities in terms of fixed cultural meanings.

A series of other writings since the1980s have developed a critique of the teleological assumptions underlining liberal and Marxist historiography; yet they do not identify with the culturalist logic of Chakrabarty's framework. Moving away from a notion which sees culture as pre-given, studies over the last two decades have examined the ways in which it was re-constituted in the urban context. Chandavarkar's study of textile workers in Bombay discussed how the workings of the labour market and patronage networks in the neighbourhood – the nexus between local leaders, dealers in property and credit – were important in forging new ties legitimated through the language of caste, region and religion.[23] Social institutions that were part of everyday life in the neighbourhood – the gymnasium, the chawls (tenements) where workers lived – became sites for new forms of sociability, re-affirming and transforming ties of region, caste and religion.

Other studies over the last two decades enrich and complicate notions of community and identity in the urban industrial context. They point to the fluidity of boundaries between communities, the continuous process of negotiation, realignment and redefinition through which community ties were made. Nandini Gooptu's work on the urban poor in North India demonstrates how particular patterns of exclusion and subordination of the 'labouring poor' in the interwar years created the basis for new networks of solidarity. The urban poor in North Indian cities identified closely with militant forms of self-assertion developed by Hindu revivalist movements in the 1920s and 1930s. Similarly a resurgent Islam drew on the support of Muslim artisans who joined organizations with a powerful religious and egalitarian appeal. But solidarities around these movements were often fragile and fractured.[24]

New alignments in the cities also involved the creation of coalitions of lower-caste groups in their struggles against upper castes: in cities like Kanpur, castes considered ritually 'impure' came together in opposition to Brahmanical norms of purity and pollution.[25] Yet these assertions of community involved processes of appropriation and contestation. In the Kolar goldfields, in South India, for instance, Janaki Nair's work shows how the Adi Dravidas contested Brahmanical distinctions between 'pure' and 'impure'; yet in trying to acquire status and respectability they tended to reaffirm many of these distinctions.[26] These shifts and realignments illustrate how lines of difference between communities were drawn through conflicts and confrontations.

Working-class politics: changing frames

The shifts in historiographical perspectives over the last few decades have raised important issues concerning the nature of working-class politics. The conventional Marxist view was exemplified in Sukomal Sen's 1977 work which narrated a linear growth of trade union organizations and leadership since the colonial period. The study of organization and leadership became synonymous with the study of working-class politics as a whole. This teleological frame was seriously questioned by Chakrabarty. He problematized the conventional equation of trade union leadership with the workers' movement and argued that both the union leadership and the workers were embedded within the overarching 'pre-bourgeois hierarchical culture'. The history of the workers' movement, in his account, was marked by ruptures and breaks and not by steady growth. Religious and primordial ties of workers over-determined class identities and politics in his account. The elements of solidarity that went into the making of strikes were for him no different from those going into communal riots. Chakrabarty's radical revisionism evoked strong debates within academic Marxist history writing.[27] Raj Chandavarkar's work on Bombay textile mills located working-class sectionalism and solidarities in the peculiarities of the labour market in the city. The remarkable fact that Bombay workers could sustain eight lengthy general strikes between 1919 and 1938 was attributed by Chandavarkar not so much to the Communists and their ideologies as to the micro-politics and intersecting networks in the neighbourhood where the colonial state, employers and the Communists competed for influence with each other and *dadas* (local neighbourhood bosses), jobbers and money lenders. The solidarities displayed in general strikes were contingent upon particular political conjunctures rather than representing the results of the unfolding of workers' consciousness.[28]

Moments of upsurge in Ahmedabad, Bombay or Kanpur were momentous times in workers' lives – times which shaped their collective memory and re-configured the social space of the city.[29] In workers' imaginations, Kanpur of the 1930s, for instance, became 'Red Kanpur'. In the present context, when former centres of industry are in decline and memories of collective solidarities and struggles like that of 1928–29 in Bombay or 1938 in Kanpur are virtually effaced, the recovery of such moments by labour historians has special significance. Recent work on Ahmedabad, Bombay and Kanpur using oral accounts of workers provides some insights into what such events meant to them, both in the past and in the transformed present.[30]

While the social history of labour dominated these debates the study of working-class politics did not disappear altogether from Indian labour history. A rich corpus of work by historians has further expanded and redefined the meaning of working-class politics. Sabyasachi Bhattacharya's pioneering essay on the politics of Bombay strikes from 1928 to 1929 critically analyzed colonial state action, mill owners' strategies and the responses of workers and the Communist trade unions, within a finely nuanced theoretical framework which took into account the interplay of structural and ideological determinants.[31] Dilip Simeon's study of labour movement in the coal and steel industries of eastern India analyzed the institutional structures of the labour movement. But it broke new ground in shifting the explanation of the ebb and tide of the movement from leadership initiatives to rank-and-file pressure. Focusing on a particularly volatile period marked by turbulent labour-capital relationships between 1928 and 1938, Simeon sought to comprehend working-class politics in all their complexity by eschewing conventional explanations in terms of the fixed polarities of national/imperial, rural/urban and class/community. By laying out the shifting positions and attitudes of the colonial officials, employers, nationalist politicians, trade union leaders and of an ethnically variegated workforce, Simeon was able to demonstrate the ways in which workers' collective agency, their needs and aspirations, were impressed upon managerial and political practice.[32]

Shubho Basu's work traversed the terrain of the labour movement in the jute mills of Calcutta, territory already made familiar in Chakrabarty's writings, in order to uncover the complexity of conflicts between European-manager-dominated local government and often unruly workers' neighbourhoods. Workers' politics were scarcely confined to the flimsy structures of trade unions but were shaped by collective experience forged daily on shop floors and in neighbourhoods. Religious tensions coexisted with experience of class solidarities in conflict with an overarching employer-state nexus.[33] Nair's study of workers' movements in the former princely state of Mysore, in Kolar gold mines and Bangalore city, similarly examined the contradictory pressures which went into the making of the labour politics in the period in the 1920s and 1930s. Nationalist leadership was impelled to take up workers' issues in Bangalore city under pressure from workers' militancy from below. In the Kolar gold fields, on the other hand, the Congress leadership had to contend with the assertion of Adi Dravida identity forged by the predominantly migrant low-caste workforce. Shashi Bhushan Upadayaya's study of Bombay workers in the late-nineteenth and the early decades of the twentieth centuries looked at the interface between the regional Maratha identity and trans-regional identities of religion, nation and class. Despite the primacy of the Maratha identity to a large majority of workers, he argued that overarching identities – those of religion, nation and class – tended to subsume the local over time.[34]

Common to this recent work is an emphasis on workers' initiative in shaping the course of institutional politics. Periods of workers' militancy described in these writings were not merely episodic but were moments when workers' presence was forcefully inscribed in the public arena. Primordial and class identities are not analyzed in mutual exclusion, with one forming the outer limit of the other as happened in earlier studies, but rather seen to be constituted by, and at the same time constituting, the terrain of conflict. In a broader sense, the labour movement is conceptualized in these studies as defying the constraints imposed upon it by the state and the employers and acquiring the contours of a social movement.

These shifts in historiographical perspectives have raised important issues concerning the place of the political in working-class lives. A move away from linear and universal narratives of labour in recent years has gone along with an engagement with the micro-processes and 'informal' structures through which politics were articulated. Beginning with Chandavarkar's 1981 essay on the working-class neighbourhood in Bombay in the 1920s and 1930s, other writings have looked outside the formal structures of organization in order to understand the political culture of the working class. Chandavarkar scrutinized the close inter-connections between the neighbourhood and the factory, arguing that spaces outside work, such as the gymnasium and the street, were crucial to the generalization of disputes which originated in the workplace. In the postwar context of the 1920s, when repressive measures by the state and mill owners restricted the activities of radical trade unionists, networks forged in the neighbourhood became crucial for mobilization by Communists in Bombay. In order to make strike action effective, Communist trade unionists had to obtain the support of powerful *dadas* and isolate potential blacklegs.[35]

Further writings since the 1980s push forward this critique of conventional narratives of politics, explaining how spaces of everyday work and life were charged with political meaning. Informal, 'invisible' modes through which workers resisted structures of authority and domination and asserted their own interests were important to preserving their notions of dignity.[36] These were not early forms that were gradually displaced by organized modes, but remained integral to the everyday process of work. Nair, Simeon, Joshi and other historians suggest the ways in which the workspace was a contested terrain, an arena where norms were negotiated and redefined. Small gestures of dissent and acts of subversion were just some of the ways in which workers asserted their notions of dignity.[37] These contestatory practices also tell us about the ways in which rules were created and actively redefined through worker practices. In recent times, with the decline of traditional large-scale industries and a proliferation of small workshops, such everyday forms of resistance possess greater significance. Studies of power-loom workers in South India and of diamond workers in Surat, for example, show how practices like the giving of *baki* (advance pay) were often manipulated by workers to secure better terms for themselves.[38]

Gender and labour

Until quite recently there was no serious engagement with questions of gender and women's work in labour history writing in India. At one level, this was because women remained invisible in the pages of history in general, while labour historians, for their part, did little to bring them into visibility for posterity. At another level, it was because labour history in India remained, till very recently, factory-centric. An exclusive focus on the workplace as the site of productive work and workers' activity meant a neglect of sites of work outside the factory, in rural areas and within homes.

A key issue addressed in discussions on women and work in the European context was the issue of the displacement of women from factory industries by the late nineteenth century. This question triggered an animated debate around the emergence of the 'male breadwinner' in working-class families.[39] In India the situation was different, yet many of the issues emerging from the 'breadwinner' debate resonate in discussions on women and work. Samita Sen's study of women in the jute mills of Bengal in the colonial period brings two important matters into focus: the first is the significance of ideological issues in understanding the gendered composition of the labour force; and the second is the connection between rural work and women's lives. She elaborates how ideas of domesticity were appropriated by working-class families, who associated seclusion with a higher social status and tended to withdraw from the labour force.[40] Sen brings out the shared assumptions underlining the masculinist discourse of mill managers and male-dominated unions who legitimized the exclusion of women by valorizing ideals of motherhood and domesticity.

The rural ties of workers have usually been examined in terms of the masculinist assumptions that denote the urban as 'main' and women's earnings as 'supplementary'. The obverse – the contribution of the family in the village, particularly of women, to the reproduction of labour – is rarely recognized. Their contribution was important in sowing, weeding, reaping, winnowing – almost all operations apart from ploughing. The contribution of women within the family was in fact often critical in providing the links connecting the working-class household in the city with the village. Historical research on labour needs to explore these links and focus on women's contribution to the working-class household. Overall, however, Sen's argument about the hegemonic power of ideas of seclusion is problematic. Within this logic, women marginalized from public employment retreat into the home and domesticity. The ways in which women may contest normative ideas or try to exercise their agency, are not taken into account.[41] Boundaries between the domestic and the outside, the inner and outer, are often re-worked: the home itself often becomes an arena of waged work for large numbers of women.

The idea of a 'male breadwinner', never quite an adequate category, is very dubious in today's context. In a scenario where traditional large industries are in decline and there is an expansion of 'informal' work, women's waged work at home is the basis of subsistence for large numbers of urban, working-class families. What we see today in fact points towards a 'feminized' workforce, with women engaged in a range of activities in households and small industrial units.[42] What implications do these changes have for the production of gendered identities, male and female? Recent studies look at the ways in which the everyday culture of work in industrial establishments goes into the making of urban masculinities. Playful banter at the workplace – forms of horseplay and erotic humour – were an affirmation of male selfhood and camaraderie against oppressive structures of authority at the workplace.[43] With the decline of employment in traditional centres of industry and the erosion of spaces from which men derived their sense of masculinity in the past, recent writings argue that there was a crisis of male identities.[44]

The informal sector and the labouring poor

But by far the most significant shift in focus of recent historiography has been in the direction of embracing the concept of workers' history in the informal sector, for so long excluded from the purview of mainstream Marxist and liberal modernization accounts. The growing significance of the informal sector as a distinct category in which to analyze labour relations, especially in the developing world, can be dated to the 1970s. The informal sector, initially identified with urban self-employment, was viewed as the solution to the growing crisis of employment generation through industrialization. The movement of labour from the 'traditional' and agricultural sector to the 'modern' industrial sector was now seen to have included a wayside stop in the urban, informal sector. The dualism of a modern and a traditional sector was replaced by the dualism of a formal and an informal sector. Notably absent from this classification was practically the whole of the rural sector excepting large plantations. The formal sector was where relatively secure, well-paid, skilled and unionized jobs were to be found. The informal sector, in contrast, was characterized by insecure, low-paid and unskilled work and almost all those who worked in it were not unionized. While employment in the formal sector had exhibited a healthy growth through the 1950s and 1960s, by the 1980s the crisis in formal-sector employment was readily apparent. The failure of the year-and-a-half long

Bombay textile strike in 1982, the massive restructuring of the textile mill industry and the shift to power looms highlighted the accelerating process of informalization. Unprecedented economic boom and a high rate of growth in GDP in the 1990s and 2000s were accompanied by a shrinking public sector and stagnant employment in the organized private sector. Almost all of the increase in employment during this period occurred in the informal sector.[45]

The analytical division between 'formal' and 'informal' sectors found expression in Mark Holmstrom's (1976) study where the image of the walled-in citadel of the formal sector surrounded by a vast, unorganized sector was first utilized.[46] Yet the concept of an informal sector and its explicit dualism was simultaneously critiqued by Jan Breman, a sociologist and historian of agrarian servitude. Drawing upon his longitudinal fieldwork in the Southern Gujarat region, which was then embarking on a path of rapid industrialization, Breman pointed out that the vast majority of informal workers were not labouring in urban locations but were to be found in the agrarian sector and non-agrarian rural sites.[47] Neither were labour relations in the informal sector solely characterized by self-employment since a large number of informal sector workers were either fully fledged or thinly disguised wage-earners. And instead of watertight compartmentalization between formal and informal sectors, Breman pointed to the large-scale use of casual and temporary labour within formal sector enterprises and the chains of subcontracting of inputs and labour through which the informal sector was linked to the formal sector. By the 1990s, the concept was appropriated by both economists and sociologists and a spate of studies of workers in the urban, informal sector appeared. However, what was remarkable in this work was the complete absence of a sense of the temporal processes through which the informal sector was constituted. A strong dualism and urban focus remained predominant in these studies.

Jan Breman's research remained an exception to this trend, both in its deep historical sense and meticulous, fieldwork-based observations. In a series of publications in the 1980s and 1990s, Breman had mapped the trajectories of an increasingly mobile labour force, originating in rural India, that fuelled the growth of an informal sector. These workers evocatively termed 'wage hunters and gatherers' and 'Footloose Labour' by Breman, were located at the bottom of the labour pyramid in the construction industry, brick-making, and myriad other occupations in urban and rural India, and rarely ever climbed the wall to secure well-paid jobs in organized industries.[48] At the same time, jobs in the formal sector were being rapidly informalized, as Breman illustrated in a historical account of the Ahmedabad textile mill workers and their expulsion into the informal sector.[49]

Historians have increasingly focused attention on the linkage of informal and formal labour: Chandavarkar and Joshi for instance, in their study of factory labour in Bombay and Kanpur, had pointed to the intimate links between the two. Others like Bhattacharya have argued for the need for a different category – the labouring poor – to indicate the permanently transitional status of workers who moved across the porous boundaries between industrial waged employment, on the one hand, and non-waged homework and self-employment of various kinds on the other. In an address in 1998, Bhattacharya argued that: 'A fuzzy concept like labouring poor, lacking in sharp edges at its boundaries suits the reality of the so-called "transitional" economies [... where] individuals and families are simultaneously located in more than one conventional class category.'[50] While the category of 'labouring poor' has the merit of incorporating forms of labour usually excluded from standard Marxist descriptions of the working class, its usefulness as an analytical category that can substitute for an ideal type 'working class' is an issue historians are still grappling with. Studies of informal labour have highlighted two distinct processes of informalization, from above through a dismantling of the existing formal sector; and from below, through a circulation of seasonal migrant and casual, footloose labour.[51] Recent studies by Barbara Harris-White, Gooptu and Rohini Hensman have made a significant contribution to understanding the role of the state, worker resistance and organization in shaping the worlds of informal labour.[52]

Bondage and unfree labour: old and new

Labour history writing, focused as it was on urban, factory labour, had consistently marginalized rural labour relations. In the 1970s a vigorous controversy on the mode of production in agriculture inconclusively debated the extent to which capitalist relations had penetrated agriculture. A key issue of this debate focused on the 'semi-feudal' labour relations and the existence of 'debt bonded' labour in large parts of rural India.[53] In 1976 the Indian government promulgated a law abolishing bonded labour and other forms of forced labour. This led to the publication of a number of studies documenting debt-bonded labour all over India.[54] Research into the origins of agrarian servitude was initiated, as scholars discussed whether labour bondage was part of 'feudal' relations in agriculture or indicated compatibility with emergent capitalist relations. A related question remained that of the social origins of the bonded labourers; most research showed that historical agrarian servitude in India was specific to certain outcaste and tribal groups in India.[55]

Breman's classic account of labour bondage in South Gujarat located it within the framework of traditional 'patron-client' relations between Anavil Brahmin landlords and their dependent *dubla* tribal labour.[56] The chief merit of Breman's historical sociological account lay in the way it demonstrated that contemporary bondage had been denuded of elements of patronage and was now a purely exploitative labour form. Utsa Patnaik, a leading Marxist economist argued that bondage, in its origin and function, was an instance of feudal relations propped up under colonial rule which persisted under post-colonial dispensations.[57] Sudipto Mundle, on the other hand, utilized Marx's distinction between formal and real subordination of labour. He related labour bondage in South Bihar to capitalist penetration in agriculture and attempts by landowners to hold down wages in the face of a large-scale exodus of workers from the region.[58] These debates on contemporary forms of 'unfree' labour have parallels with new historical studies of forms of labour unfreedom. An area where historical research has been particularly productive is in the exploration of linkages between colonialism and unfree labour. Gyan Prakash's provocative work viewed 'debt bondage' as a construction of 'colonial discourse'. Pre-colonial dependent labour relationships between kamia labourers and their masters, according to Prakash, were transformed by a colonial discourse of freedom which negated 'traditional' slavery yet sanctioned 'bondage' produced by money advances.[59]

This radical view, which denied 'debt bondage' in the pre-colonial period and gave primacy in its construction to colonial discourse, has in turn been contested by several scholars.[60] In recent years a vigorous debate has also been initiated on the characterization of 'unfree' labour in a modern setting, as a system of neo-bondage, distinguishing it from older, traditional systems of bondage.[61] The legal distinction between free and unfree labour has been at the heart of most writings on histories of servitude and freedom. However, recent research on colonial labour laws has problematized the conceptual divide between free and unfree labour. One area of investigation has been around the colonial laws of indenture in plantations inside India and in overseas colonies which immobilized labour after transporting them over long distances.[62] Indenture laws were part of a set of laws instituted during the colonial period which constituted and regulated the labour market. Traditionally, labour history had seen labour law mainly as a post-world-war phenomena and colonial labour policy was construed as one of 'laissez faire'. In stark contrast, recent important studies of labour regulation have constructed a history of state intervention in the labour market from the early colonial period in the form of the Master and Servant laws.[63] These innovative histories have reframed the question of linkage between formal state policy and labour market regulation, on the one hand, and informal modes of regulation based on traditional institutions like that of caste and community, on the other.[64] By constructing a lineage of labour regulation well into the colonial period, it is possible now to throw light on contemporary debates on labour law reforms, flexibilization and informalization which are seen as emerging from the rapid globalization of the Indian economy.

Emerging trends

The historiography of Indian labour has oscillated between conceptualizing the Indian experience as merely an instance of Eurocentric capitalist development and as uniquely indigenous. The renewal of labour history in recent decades has been marked by a definite movement away from this somewhat sterile conceptual straitjacket. The founding of the Association of Indian Labour Historians (AILH) in 1996 was, at least in part, a reflection of this renewal. It is interesting to note that this chapter appears in a volume which celebrates the fiftieth anniversary of the British Society for the Study of Labour History. The formation of the AILH 46 years later evokes the different paths the subject has taken in 'the North' and 'the South'. It also suggests that across the world labour history has a future. Since its inception the Association has sought with some success to provide a forum for intellectual interaction between labour historians from India and from the developed and developing countries, as well as trade unionists and activists of other social movements. The last decade or so has seen similar initiatives in many other countries of the South, marking what Marcel van der Linden has referred to as the 'globalization of labour history'.[65]

What is common to many of these associations is their attempt to break out of old Eurocentric frames and search for other comparisons, other temporalities. The themes on which AILH conferences have centred include questions of 'transition', marginality, mobility, skill and the labour process, law, labour regimes and labour markets, informalization and rural labour. The publication of essays presented at the conferences reflects the major paradigm shifts in the historiography of labour today: the turn towards a focus on the history of labour in the informal sector and the move towards a new, comparative, global history. The first of these publications includes a study of itinerant labour, international migrants, Indian seamen, brick workers, plantation and rural agricultural labour and migrant workers in urban workshops.[66] The second focuses on the experience of convicts, bonded and illegal migrant labour on colonial road construction projects; work in coal mines and on ships; servile labour in Brazil and Portugal as well as in Russia and India; and factory legislation in Britain and India during the nineteenth century. These topics underline the changing concerns of labour historians in India and in other regions today.[67] Interaction between scholars has been complemented by the creation and sharing of materials to promote labour studies. In Delhi, for instance, the AILH was instrumental in setting up a specialized digital repository of documentary, visual and oral resources on labour.[68] These efforts have been important in energizing a new generation of scholars of labour and creating a space for labour studies within academia.

The context in which we see a renewal of labour studies in India today marks a reversal of trends that saw its emergence as a subject of academic concern in post-independence India. Those were years when labour had acquired a public presence, a political voice. Today, when the collective political presence of labour is in decline, the task for labour historians is more difficult and yet more compelling. Writing and recording histories of labour is even more crucial if we are to preserve a public space for labour. It is against this background that scholarly exchanges both global and local, within India and beyond it, assume special significance. They have opened up new possibilities of re-signifying old categories and of extending and enriching the meanings of labour and working-class history.

Notes

1 Sumit Sarkar, 'The Return of Labour to South-Asian History', *Historical Materialism*, 12 (2004), 285–313 (p. 286).

2 For detailed, critical analyses of Indian Labour historiography, see Sabyasachi Bhattacharya, 'Introduction', in *India's Labouring Poor: Historical Studies c. 1600–2000*, ed. by Rana P. Behal and Marcel van der Linden (New Delhi: Foundation Books, 2007), pp. 7–20; Chitra Joshi, 'Histories of Indian Labour: Predicaments and Possibilities', *History Compass*, 6 (2008), 439–54; Prabhu P. Mohapatra, 'Situating the Renewal: Reflections on Labour Studies in India', *Labour and Development*, 5 (1999), 1–30; Sanat Bose, 'Indian Labour and its Historiography in Pre-Independence Period', *Social Scientist*, 143 (1985), 3–10.

3 Prominent among these were the Bengal Labour Commissions of 1868, 1873, 1880, and 1896, the Assam Labour I0nquiry Committees, 1906 and 1921–22, which examined plantation labour; Factory Labour Commissions, 1875, 1891, 1908; Indian Industrial Commission, 1916; Coalfield Committee, 1923; Textile

Labour Inquiry Commission, 1929.

4 These are terms for recruiters and overseers in plantations, mines, jute and cotton mills.

5 Dipesh Chakrabarty, 'Sasipada Banerjee: A Study in the Nature of the First Contact of the Bengali Bhadralok with the Working Class of Bengal', *Indian Historical Review*, 2 (1976), 339–84; Rajnarayan Chandavarkar, *The Origin of Industrial Capitalism in India: Business Strategies and the Working Classes in Bombay, 1900–1940* (Cambridge: Cambridge University Press, 1994), pp. 426–27.

6 Ramkumar Vidyaratna's articles were translated and presented in book form to Lord Ripon, the Viceroy, as a part of a memorandum to champion the cause of labour in Assam tea gardens by the Indian Association. Dwarkanath Ganguli's articles were compiled and published as *Slavery in British Dominion*, (Calcutta: Jijnasa, 1972), pp. vii; Bose, 'Historiography', p. 8.

7 Rev. Charles Dowding, *Tea Garden Coolies in Assam* (Calcutta: Thacker, Spinks, 1894).

8 Palamadai Samu Loknathan, *Industrial Welfare in India* (Madras: University of Madras Economic Studies, no. 3, 1929); A.C. Roy Choudhury, *Report on an Enquiry into the Standard of Living of Jute Mill Workers in Bengal* (Calcutta: Bengal Secretariat Book Depot, 1933); Satrashyaha Gopal Panandikar, *Industrial Labour in India*, (Bombay: Longmans, Green, 1933); Sardar Muhammad Akhtar, *Emigrant Labour for Assam Tea Gardens* (Lahore: The Author, 1939); Radhakamal K. Mukherjee, *The Indian Working Class*, (Bombay: Hind Kitabs, 1945).

9 Daniel H. Buchanan, *The Development of Capitalistic Enterprise in India* (New York: Macmillan, 1934; reprinted London: Cass, 1966); Margaret Read, *The Indian Peasant Uprooted* (London: Longmans, Green, 1931).

10 Diwan Chaman Lall, *Coolie: The Story of Labour and Capital in India* (Lahore: Oriental Publishing House, 1932); Rajani Kanta Das, *Labour Movement in India* (Berlin: W. de Gruyter, 1923); idem, *Plantation Labour in India* (Calcutta: Chatterjee, 1931); idem, *Labour Legislation in India*, (Calcutta: University of Calcutta, 1941); Narayana Malhar Joshi, *The Trade Union Movement in India* (Bombay: Patvardhan, 1927); B. Shiva Rao, *The Industrial Worker in India* (London: Allen and Unwin, 1938).

11 Jawaharlal Nehru cited in Charles A. Myers, *Labour Problems in the Industrialisation of India*, (Cambridge, MA: Harvard University Press, 1958), p. 7.

12 *Labour Commitment and Social Change in Developing Areas*, ed. by Wilbert Ellis Moore and Arnold S. Feldman, (New York: Social Science Research Council, 1960), p. 4.

13 Clark Kerr, John T. Dunlop, Frederick H. Harbison and Charles A. Myers, *Industrialism and Industrial Man: The Problem of Labour and Management in Economic Growth* (London: Heinemann, 1962), pp. 170–74.

14 Oscar A. Ornatti, *Jobs and Workers in India* (Ithaca: Cornell University, 1955); Charles A. Myers, *Labour Problems in the Industrialisation of India* (Cambridge, MA: Harvard University Press, 1958); Morris D. Morris, 'Labour Discipline,

Trade Unions and the State in India', *Journal of Political Economy*, 63 (1955), 293–308; Richard D. Lambert, *Workers, Factories and Social Change in India* (Princeton: Princeton University Press, 1963).

15 Morris David Morris, *The Emergence of an Industrial Labour Force in India: A Study of the Bombay Cotton Mills, 1854–1947* (Bombay: Oxford University Press, 1965).

16 Report of the National Commission on Labour, 1969, p. vii.

17 M.N. Roy, *India in Transition* (Bombay: Nachiketa Publications, 1971), p. 113.

18 Rajani Palme Dutt, *India Today* (London: Gollancz, 1940), ch XII.

19 Sanat Bose, *Capital and Labour in the Indian Tea Industry* (Bombay: All-India Trade Union Congress, 1954); Indrajit Gupta, *Capital and Labour in the Jute Industry* (Bombay: All-India Trade Union Congress, 1953); A.S. Mathur and Jagannath Swarup Mathur, *Trade Union Movement in India* (Allahabad: Chaitanya Publishing, 1957); Vasant B. Karnik, *Indian Trade Unions: A Survey* (Bombay: Labour Education Service, 1960); Giriraj K. Sharma, *Labour Movement In India: Its Past and Present* (Jullunder: University Publishers, 1963); Shiva Chandra Jha, *The Indian Trade Union Movement* (Calcutta: Firma K.L. Mukhopadhyay, 1970); C. Revri, *The Indian Trade Union Movement, 1880–1947* (New Delhi: Orient Longman, 1972); Sukomal Sen, *Working Class of India: History of Emergence and Movement, 1830–1970* (Calcutta: Bagchi, 1977).

20 Ranajit Dasgupta, 'Material Conditions and Behavioural Aspects of Calcutta Working Class 1880–1899', *Occasional Paper*, 22 (Calcutta: Centre for Studies in Social Sciences, 1979); Ira Mitra, 'Growth of Trade Union Consciousness among Jute Mill Workers 1920–1940', *Economic and Political Weekly* (*EPW*), 16 (1981), 1839–48; Dipesh Chakrabarty, 'Class Consciousness and the Indian Working Class: Dilemmas of a Marxist Historiography', *Journal of African and Asian Studies*, 28 (1988), 21–31.

21 See, for example, Dipesh Chakrabarty and Ranajit Das Gupta, 'Some Aspects of Labour History in Bengal in the Nineteenth Century: Two Views', *Occasional Paper*, 40 (Calcutta: Centre for Studies in Social Sciences, 1981).

22 Dipesh Chakrabarty, *Rethinking Working-Class History: Bengal 1890–1940* (Princeton: Princeton University Press, 1988).

23 Rajnarayan Chandavarkar, 'Workers' Politics in the Mill Districts in Bombay between the Wars', *Modern Asian Studies*, 15 (1981), 603–47, and idem, 'From Neighbourhood to Nation', in *One Hundred Years, One Hundred Voices: The Mill Workers of Girangaon: An Oral History*, ed. by Neera Adarkar and Meena Menon (Calcutta: Seagull: 2004), pp. 7–80; Chitra Joshi, 'Bonds of Community, Ties of Religion: Kanpur Textile Workers in the Early Twentieth Century', *Indian Economic and Social History Review*, 22 (1985), 251–80.

24 Nandini Gooptu, *The Politics of the Urban Poor in Early Twentieth-Century India* (Cambridge: Cambridge University Press, 2000), pp. 185–243.

25 Chitra Joshi, *Lost Worlds: Indian Labour and its Forgotten Histories* (Delhi: Permanent Black, 2003), pp. 245–56.

26 Nair points out how the upwardly mobile among them gave up eating beef,

a practice considered 'unclean' by upper castes. Janaki Nair, *Miners and Millhands: Work, Culture and Politics in Princely Mysore* (New Delhi: Sage Publications, 1998), pp. 101–6.

27 Ranajit Dasgupta, 'Indian Working Class and Some Recent Historiographical Issues', *EPW*, 33 (1996), 27–31; Parimal Ghosh, 'Communalism and Colonial Labour: Experience of Calcutta Jute Mill Workers, 1880–1930', *EPW*, 30 (1990), 61–72; Amiya Kumar Bagchi, 'Working Class Consciousness' *EPW*, 30 (1990), 54–60.

28 Rajnarayan Chandavarkar, *Imperial Power and Popular Politics: Class, Resistance and State in India, c.1850–1950* (Cambridge: Cambridge University Press, 1998), ch. 5.

29 It may be useful to draw on recent scholarship on questions of space and memory: see, for example, Kristin Ross, *The Emergence of Social Space: Rimbaud and the Paris Commune* (London: Verso 1988), and idem, *May'68 and its Afterlives* (Chicago: University of Chicago Press, 2002); David Harvey, *Paris: Capital of Modernity* (London: Routledge, 2003).

30 Jan Breman, *The Making and Unmaking of an Industrial Working Class: Sliding Down the Labour Hierarchy, Ahmedabad, India* (Amsterdam: Amsterdam University Press, 2004), pp. 201–31; Adarkar and Menon, *One Hundred Years*; Joshi, *Lost Worlds*, chs 6 and 9.

31 Sabyasachi Bhattacharya, 'Capital and Labour in Bombay City, 1928–29', *EPW*, 16 (1981), 36–44.

32 Dilip Simeon, *The Politics of Labour Under Late Colonialism: Workers, Unions and the State in Chota Nagpur, 1928–39* (Delhi: Manohar, 1995), ch. 2.

33 Shubho Basu, *Does Class Matter? Colonial Capital and Workers' Resistance in Bengal, 1890–1937* (New Delhi: Oxford University Press, 2004).

34 See n. 26. Shashi Bhushan Upadhyaya, '*Existence, Identity and Mobilization: the Cotton Millworkers of Bombay 1890-1919* (New Delhi: Manohar, 2004), pp. 209–11.

35 Chandavarkar, 'Workers' Politics in the Mill Districts'.

36 Writings which decentre the political and look at the informal 'hidden transcripts' of labour have been important in the world of non-Indian labour history for decades: the writings of Alf Ludtke, Jim Scott and Hans Medick to name a few. See, for instance, Alf Ludtke, *The History of Everyday Life: Reconstructing Historical Experiences and Ways of Life* (Princeton: Princeton University Press, 1995) and Jim C. Scott, 'Everyday Forms of Peasant Resistance', *Journal of Peasant Studies*, 13 (1986), 5–35.

37 Nair, *Miners and Millhands*, pp. 45–53, 72–6; Simeon, *Politics of Labour*, pp. 144, 154–55 and 343–45.

38 Geert de Neve, *The Everyday Politics of Labour: Working Lives in India's Informal Economy* (New Delhi: Social Science Press, 2005), pp. 169–203; Miranda Engelshoven, 'Diamonds and Patels: A Report on the Diamond Industry of Surat', in *The Worlds of Indian Industrial Labour*, ed. by Jonathan P. Parry, Jan Breman and Karin Kapadia (New Delhi: Sage Publications, 1999), pp. 353–78.

39 See, for instance, Colin Creighton, 'The Rise of the Male Breadwinner Family:

A Reappraisal', *Comparative Studies in Society and History*, 38 (1996), 145–62; Angélique Jannsens, 'The Rise and Decline of the Male Breadwinner Family? An Overview of the Debate', *International Review of Social History*, 42 (1997), Supplement 5, 'The Rise and Decline of the Male Breadwinner Family', 1–23; Wally Seccombe, 'Patriarchy Stabilized: The Construction of the Male Breadwinner Wage Norm in Nineteenth Century Britain', *Social History*, 11 (1986), 53–76.

40 Samita Sen, *Women and Labour in Colonial India* (Cambridge: Cambridge University Press, 1999), pp. 21–53, 89–141, and idem, 'Gendered Exclusion: Domesticity and Dependence in Bengal', *International Review of Social History*, 42 (1997), Supplement 5, 'The Rise and Decline of the Male Breadwinner Family', 65–86.

41 For an interesting essay which looks at some of the ways in which women exercised their agency in their day to day lives, see Radha Kumar, 'Sex and Punishment among Mill-Workers in Early Twentieth Century Bombay', in *Changing Concepts of Rights and Justice in South Asia*, ed. by Michael R. Anderson and Sumit Guha (New Delhi: Oxford University Press, 2000), pp 179–97; See also Chitra Joshi, 'Notes on the Breadwinner Debate: Gender and Household Strategies in Working-Class Families', *Studies in History*, 28 (2002), 261–74.

42 These changes were grudgingly recognized in governmental policy: see particularly Shram Shakti, *Report of the National Commission on Self-Employed Women and Women in the Informal Sector* (New Delhi: Publication Division, Government of India, 1988).

43 Shankar Ramaswami, 'Masculinity, Respect and the Tragic: Themes of Proletarian Humor in Contemporary Industrial Delhi', in Behal and van der Linden, *India's Labouring Poor*, pp. 203–28.

44 Chitra Joshi, 'Deindustrialisation and the Crisis of Male Identities', *International Review of Social History*, 47 (2002), 159–75.

45 *Report on Conditions of Work and Promotion of Livelihood in the Unorganised Sector* (New Delhi: National Commission for Enterprises in the Unorganised Sector, 2007), p. 4.

46 Mark Holmstrom, *South Indian Factory Workers: Their Life and Their World* (Cambridge: Cambridge University Press, 1976).

47 Jan Breman, 'A Dualistic Labour System? A Critique of the Informal Sector Concept', *EPW*, 11 (1976), 1870–76, 1905–08 and 1933–39.

48 Jan Breman, *Footloose Labour: Working in India's Informal Economy* (Cambridge: Cambridge University Press, 1996), and idem, *Wage Hunters and Gatherers: Search for Work in the Urban and Rural Economy of South Gujarat* (New Delhi: Oxford University Press, 1994).

49 Breman, *Making and Unmaking of an Industrial Working Class.*

50 Sabyasachi Bhattacharya, 'The Labouring Poor and their Notion of Poverty: Late 19th and Early 20th Century Bengal', *Labour and Development*, 3 (1998), 1–23, and idem, 'Introduction', in *Workers in the Informal Sector: Studies in Labour History 1800–2000*, ed. by Sabyasachi Bhattacharya and Jan Lucassen (New Delhi: Macmillan, 2005), p. 4.

51 See Arjan de Haan, 'The Badli System in Industrial Labour Recruitment: Managers' and Workers' Strategies in Calcutta's Jute Industry', in Parry, Breman and Kapadia, *The Worlds of Indian Industrial Labour*, pp. 271–301; Douglas E. Haynes, 'Just Like A Family? Recalling The Relations of Production in the Textile Industries of Surat and Bhiwandi, 1940–60', in ibid., pp. 141–69; Chitra Joshi, 'Hope And Despair: Textile Workers in Kanpur in 1937–38 and the 1990s', in ibid., pp. 171–203; Dilip Simeon, 'Work and Resistance in the Jharia Coalfield', in ibid., pp. 43–75.

52 Barbara Harris-White and Nandini Gooptu, 'Mapping India's World of Unorganized Labour', in *Socialist Register, 2001*, ed. by Leo Panitch and Colin Leys (London: Merlin Press, 2001), pp. 89–118; Rohini Hensman, 'Organizing Against the Odds: Women in India's Informal Sector', in ibid., pp. 249–57. See also Barbara Harris-White, *India Working: Essays on Society and Economy* (Cambridge: Cambridge University Press 2003).

53 The debate was carried out in the pages of *Economic and Political Weekly* and published later as *Agrarian Relations and Accumulation: The Mode of Production Debate in India*, ed. by Utsa Patnaik (Bombay: Oxford University Press, 1990).

54 Marla Sarma, *Bonded Labour in India* (New Delhi: Biblia Impex, 1981); *Report of the National Commission on Rural Labour, Vol. 2: Study Group on Bonded Labour* (New Delhi: Government of India, 1991).

55 Dharma Kumar, *Land and Caste in South India: Agricultural Labour in Madras Presidency in the Nineteenth Century* (Cambridge: Cambridge University Press, 1965).

56 Jan Breman, *Patronage and Exploitation: Changing Agrarian Relations in South Gujarat, India* (Berkley: University of California Press, 1974).

57 Utsa Patnaik, 'Introduction', in *Chains of Servitude: Bondage and Slavery in India*, ed. by Utsa Patnaik and Manjari Dingwani (New Delhi: Sangam Books, 1985), pp. 1–34.

58 Sudipto Mundle, *Backwardness and Bondage: Agrarian Relations in a South Bihar District* (New Delhi: Indian Institute of Public Administration, 1979).

59 Gyan Prakash, *Bonded Histories: Genealogies of Labour Servitude in Colonial India* (Cambridge: Cambridge University Press, 1990).

60 Neeladri Bhattacharya, *Labouring Histories: Agrarian Labour and Colonialism*, Writing Labour History Series (Noida: V.V. Giri National Labour Institute, 2004); Jan Breman, *Labour Bondage in West India: From Past to Present* (New Delhi: Oxford University Press, 2007).

61 Tom Brass, *Towards a Comparative Political Economy of Unfree Labour: Case Studies and Debates* (London: Frank Cass 1999); Jairus Banaji, 'The Fictions of Free Labour: Contract, Coercion and So-Called Unfree Labour', *Historical Materialism*, 11 (2003), 69–95; Surinder S. Jodhka, 'Unfree Labour and Postmodern Myths: Towards a Critical Examination', *Historical Materialism*, 12 (2004), 463–72; J. Mohan Rao, 'Freedom, Property and Bentham: The Debate over Unfree Labour', *Journal of Peasant Studies*, 27 (1999), 97–127.

62 Rana P. Behal and Prabhu P. Mohapatra, '"Tea and Money versus Human Life": The Rise and Fall of the Indenture System in Assam Valley Tea

Plantations', in *Plantations, Proletarians and Peasants in Colonial Asia*, ed. by Valentine Daniel, Henry Bernstein and Tom Brass (London: Frank Cass, 1992), pp. 142–72; Prabhu P. Mohapatra, 'Assam and the West Indies, 1860-1920: Immobilizing Plantation Labour', in *Masters, Servants, and Magistrates in Britain and the Empire, 1562–1955*, ed. by Douglas Hay and Paul Craven (Chapel Hill: University of North Carolina Press, 2004), pp. 455–80.

63 Prabhu P. Mohapatra, 'Regulated Informality: Legal Constructions of Labour Relations in Colonial India, 1814–1926', in Bhattacharya and Lucassen, *Workers*, pp. 65–96; Michael Anderson, ' India, 1858–1930: The Illusion of Free Labour', in Hay and Craven, *Masters, Servants and Magistrates*, pp. 422–54; Ravi Ahuja, 'The Origins of Colonial Labour Policy in Late Eighteenth-Century Madras', *International Review of Social History*, 44 (1999), 159–95; Ian J. Kerr, 'Labour Control and Labour Legislation in Colonial India: A Tale of Two Mid-Nineteenth Century Acts', *South Asia*, 27 (2004), 7–25.

64 Dilip Simeon, 'Calibrated Indifference: Understanding the Structure of Informal Labour in India', in Bhattacharya and Lucassen, *Workers*, pp. 97–120.

65 Marcel van der Linden, 'Labour History: An International Movement', Plenary lecture at the Ninth National Labour History Conference, University of Sydney, 1 July 2005.

66 Behal and van der Linden, *India's Labouring Poor*.

67 *Labour Matters: Towards Global History*, ed. by Prabhu P. Mohapatra and Marcel van der Linden (New Delhi: Tulika, 2009).

68 The archives are freely accessible at www.indialabourarchives.org.

10

Japan

Takao Matsumura, John McIlroy and Alan Campbell

The development of labour and the labour movement in Japan constitutes a distinctive case which has proved engrossing to historians at home and abroad. Unlike the countries of the 'Global North', Japan did not participate in the first wave of industrialization. Unlike many of the nations in the 'South', it was not colonized. It undertook its own path to modernization from the 1860s within the confines of an already established world capitalism and in conjunction with its own form of imperialism. This trajectory ensured that capital and labour possessed characteristics which were singular but not unique. Labour was marked by the actions of a state actively committed to capitalist development and by the world of the peasantry from which it emerged. That capital, the labour movement, trade unions, social democracy as well as communism are far from fixed entities but, as Gramsci suggested, take on different forms in different circumstances, is illustrated by the reaction of workers and the labour movement to the New Order in Japan from the 1930s, the restructuring of capitalism under the American occupation, the growth and militancy of Japanese trade unionism in the 1940s and 1950s, and its decline and domestication in subsequent decades.

The Japanese experience, like that of other countries but sometimes more extremely, demonstrates the tensions and oscillations in labour and labour movements between conflict with capital and accommodation to it, between independence and collaboration, moderation and militancy. In the light of one-sided accounts of harmony between capital and labour, allegedly derived from the national culture and centred on lifelong employment, which gripped the imagination of some intellectuals in the last years of the twentieth century, documenting and explaining the pasts of labour in Japan presents a particular challenge to historians. Like the country's labour history, the historiography is marked by both diverse national-specific and global-general influences.

Because of the earlier climate, it was only in the 1950s that a 'modern' approach to the history of labour took root among Japanese historians. Moreover, the American presence and continuing business, labour and academic links with the USA stimulated the publication of research on Japan by American as well as British, Australian and German scholars, although again this was not exclusive to Japan. Some of the tendencies in both the Japanese and English language literatures will be familiar to historians in other countries as they include the initial employment of institutional approaches focused on labour organization, as well as shifts to history from below, looking at workers themselves, and social history. The historiography of Japanese labour has increasingly reflected international trends. Moreover, globalization has cut both ways: Japanese historians have taken a keen interest in the history of labour in other parts of the world.

This chapter begins with a sketch of the history of Japanese labour from the commencement of industrialization to the 1990s. The second and third sections look at the historiography since the 1950s and survey the literature in Japanese and English. Given language barriers and problems of accessibility which are relevant to most readers, the emphasis is sometimes, although not invariably, on work in English. This chapter has been written as a contribution to the commemoration of the fiftieth anniversary of the foundation of the British Society for the Study of Labour History. The fourth section therefore discusses how the history of British labour has been written in Japan.

I

The industrialization of Japan was perceived as central to national survival and an urgent task of the state. It took off in the last three decades of the nineteenth century after the restoration of the Meiji Emperor in 1868 and the forced opening of the economy to foreign trade. The major industries were textiles, metal and coal extraction, engineering, particularly military munitions, shipbuilding and transport, centred on the development of the railways. The labour force drew on the old artisanate and small groups of skilled workers but the young proletariat came overwhelmingly from agriculture and retained links with the countryside. This was particularly true of the textile industry which relied on young women who often remained part of the rural world and sometimes returned to it on marriage. The evolution of capitalism was moulded by a state determined to catch up with its international competitors, particularly in relation to heavy industry, by the big monopolies and banks, and by its 'late' development. Well into the twentieth century, Japan remained a country of farmers.[1]

To instil discipline into raw workers and counter absenteeism, high turnover and the custom of 'travelling' between jobs, management control in heavy industry was often subcontracted to labour bosses who trained new workers and paid their wages. Some *oyakata* were independent subcontractors; others were more like foremen. In the face of technological developments and continuing difficulties with discipline, companies moved towards the latter model. They prioritized direct control and integrated the labour bosses into more formal structures. Management evolved in the early 1900s as authoritarian, hierarchical and paternalist. Status differentiation between shop-floor, clerical and managerial workers acted as a restraint on rudimentary welfare and training programmes and early attempts to integrate the labour force through philosophies of the enterprise as a harmonious community.[2]

Trade unions encountered a hostile reception from employers and the interventionist state. They were not Japanese. Attempts at organization emerged as economic growth accelerated from the 1890s. Associations developed in the mines and on the railways as well as among groups such as carpenters and printers. All were short lived. Despite promotion by socialist and Christian intellectuals organized in the Association for the Formation of Trade Unions and the Friends of Labour, the early unions were small and usually workplace-based. They were marked by the opposition of employers, an antagonistic state and restrictive legislation, notably the Public Order and Police Provisions Law (1900). They confronted immense problems stemming from the nature of the labour force, the small size of enterprise, the limited scale of industrialization and the absence of any prior regulative impulse among the pre-industrial guilds. The Ironworkers or Metalworkers Union had a base in Tokyo munitions factories. It was formed in 1897 but never enrolled more than 3,000 members and its inability to provide welfare benefits led to its demise within four years.[3]

Nonetheless, Japanese workers demonstrated the ability to mobilize, as witnessed in the strike waves of 1897 and 1907. In the face of police persecution, longer-term solidarity remained a fragile commodity and, despite the appearance of the quickly outlawed Social Democratic Party in 1901, any labour movement remained vestigial.[4] The more liberal atmosphere of the *Taisho* era, which succeeded the Meiji period, saw the creation in 1912 of the *Yuaikai* or Friendly Society at a time when the first wave of trade unionism had spent itself. Initially it aimed to improve the welfare and status of workers. Gradually the *Yuaikai* took on the role of a trade union centre, adopted class-based objectives, and formed union branches in the workplace and regional councils in a number of industries. Facilitated by the more militant attitudes of sections of labour during and after the First World War as well as the more flexible paternalism of some employers, the friendly society orientation of the *Yuaikai's* Christian founder, Bunji Suzuki, gave way to attempts to create industrial unions and collective bargaining arrangements.[5]

Faced with difficulties in attracting textile workers insulated in company compounds and with no experience of trade unionism, and significant impediments to recruiting workers in small workshops, unions targeted more skilled operatives in larger enterprises in engineering factories, steel works, mines, shipyards and chemicals. The state and some of the big monopolies, the *zaibatsu*, viewed these employees as building blocks in the construction of enterprise loyalty. During and after the First World War, some turned towards scientific management and the *yokosuka* system pioneered in the state arsenals and shipyards. This sought to nurture a cadre of white-collar and skilled workers by means of employer control of recruitment and training. Internal labour markets would restrict workers' mobility and crystallize a core of committed employees. Vertical labour markets were based on specialized training, promotion through service and promises of security of employment. In the 1920s such initiatives were small-scale and progress uneven. But employers lodged aspects of this approach in some areas of the commanding heights of industry. The unions were increasingly left to struggle on the margins of their most fruitful territory. They were pushed towards building membership in the smaller enterprises which were more vulnerable to the market, recession and unemployment.[6]

By the 1920s unions recruited no more than 100,000 overwhelmingly manual workers spread across some 200 unions, largely in the Tokyo and Osaka regions. However, many workers who did not pay dues looked to the unions for support and participated in disputes. Wartime inflation and tighter labour markets had bred more aggressive attitudes. The end of hostilities witnessed another strike wave and the transformation between 1919 and 1921 of the *Yuaikai* into the *Sodomei*, the Greater Japan Federation of Labour.[7] The onset of recession and unemployment in the early 1920s limited the *Sodomei*'s attempt to create a labour movement rooted in the favourable habitat of large companies in heavy industry and undermined their efforts in smaller enterprises. Management held off the union threat by coercion and fear of unemployment as well as absorption of conflict through welfare measures, factory councils and consultation, and 'second unions' favourable to company goals, which helped inhibit adversarial collective bargaining.[8]

The strengthening of the social weight of the workers saw the appearance of anarchism and anarcho-syndicalism, and the launch in 1922 of the Japanese Communist Party (JCP). But these developments produced factional struggles within the unions. In 1925 the *Sodomei* split into right, centre and left-leaning federations. The more pragmatic attitude of the state had some consolidating impact on unions. The introduction of universal male suffrage in 1925 increased workers' potential political strength. But the splits in the *Sodomei* were replicated in the formation of competing farmers' and workers' parties. The more liberal times led the government to greater if still limited acceptance of 'responsible' trade unionism, even when organized beyond the enterprise. But across most of Japan's interwar history the state remained authoritarian, at best encouraging moderate organizations but refusing to tolerate anything that smacked of leftism or militancy.[9]

At the start of the 1930s, union membership stood at 400,000 workers, around 8 per cent of the labour force. Unions were small, typically confined to the enterprise and its manual workers, with activity based on workplace councils where any bargaining was in a consultative vein.[10] Employers sustained their determination to restrict trade unionism, to ensure that management and the economic interests of the company became the focus of identification and loyalty, and the economic health of the organization the rationale for wage levels. There was no system of labour law which protected unions and no system of collective bargaining of any formality. The weight of the working class in economy and society remained restricted; the typical factory worker was still a non-unionized worker in a small workshop. The left remained weak: the JCP never had more than a few thousand members and was outlawed from its inception. Against this background, the creation of even such small-scale trade unionism constituted a considerable achievement and Japanese workers demonstrated their combativity by resisting redundancies and organizing against unemployment. In 1930–31, at the heart of the great depression, they mounted a strike wave which exceeded all earlier movements and embraced young, female textile workers.[11]

Attempts at scientific management remained limited. Like all institutions, the unions were influenced by the intensification of nationalist, authoritarian and militarist sentiment from the mid-1930s. It affected their members: many turned to the right. Employers had resisted attempts to prioritize cooperative, 'bread and butter' trade unionism by continued emphasis on the need for one focus of authority, one harmonious enterprise. Realization of the latter was facilitated by accentuation of the dangers of internal conflict. Class struggle at home was a luxury Japan could ill afford if it was to achieve its proper place in the world. Increasing demands for the coordination of all the nation's resources and the 'submersion' of sectionalism bore fruit. The Social Masses Party, created in 1932, united most of the competing union and political factions of labour. Like the union centres it developed social-democratic, nationalist factions as well as a more forthright nationalist grouping.[12]

Organized labour accommodated or supported the subjugation of Manchuria and the invasion of China. There were dreams of transforming the anti-capitalism of sections of the army into 'socialism from above'. The persistent attempts of capital and the state to integrate labour into the national community and eradicate trade unionism culminated in the dissolution of the *Sodomei* in 1940 and the triumph of the Industrial Patriotic Movement and the New Order.[13]

The postwar years saw the resurgence of labour and renewal of the pre-war struggle. The state and capital and those who wanted to create an independent labour movement competed for the allegiance of Japan's workers. The weapons used were material and ideological; initially they favoured the exponents of radical trade unionism. The first period of American occupation saw a push for the democratization of Japanese society by the Supreme Command of the Allied Powers (SCAP). There were moves to break up the old bastions of power, including the big monopolies, land reform and the legalization of trade unions and political parties. There was a conviction that unions could constitute a countervailing, civilizing power in industry. The call for democratization became for many workers, who recalled decades of repression, a demand for democratization of management.[14]

The *Sodomei* was reconstituted as a moderate centre linked to the revived Socialist Party; it competed with the Communist-directed federation, *Sanbetsu Kaigi*, which quickly outflanked it. But there was an independent rank-and-file dynamic and a movement from below and inside the workplace, influenced by the failure of earlier strategies of accommodation. There was a wave of strikes involving both manual and white-collar workers; an amelioration of status distinctions conditioned by rampant inflation and awareness of a common predicament; attempts to establish workers' control over the production process; and political support for the Communists and Socialists. Union membership soared beyond the five million mark, around 40 per cent of the industrial workforce. For the first time, trade unionism covered both manual and white-collar workers; both joined the same enterprise unions. By 1949 trade unionism embraced almost 56 per cent of industrial workers and collective bargaining was expanding.[15]

The movement was curbed by the 'reverse course' of SCAP, heralded by the prohibition of the January 1947 general strike. Change was occasioned by the onset of the Cold War and the communist conquest of China, and intensified by the Korean War. Japan was vital to America's global strategy. The new labour legislation was tightened to ban public sector strikes and controls were placed on collective agreements. A purge of Communists caught many on the left in its net. Seizing the time, the employers organized in the *Nikkeiren* federation mounted an offensive between 1948 and 1950 designed to reverse the gains labour had secured. Repression in the form of victimization of activists and political redundancies was melded with attempts to smother collective bargaining through joint consultation and the sponsoring of enterprise unions in company interests. It was lubricated by the electoral success of the conservative Liberal Democrats. The state and capital amplified and exploited the real differences that existed in the unions. The Americans used the moderate revolt against the JCP leaders of *Sanbetsu Kaigi* to support a new federation, *Sohyo*, including the left of *Sodomei* in the marriage. It did not work. *Sohyo* moved in a militant direction, espoused shop-floor struggle and aligned itself with the left wing of the Socialist Party and the quest for Japanese neutrality.[16]

The contest continued through the 1950s. While the unit of union organization was the enterprise, enterprise unions were often far from cooperative.[17] The *Sohyo* unions pushed for adversarial bargaining and sought an element of control over decisions on hours of work, job allocation and dismissals. They continued to enrol all occupational groups in the workplace and pursued their long-term aspiration to build unions and construct bargaining beyond the enterprise and beyond the rationale of management conceptions of fair wages and reasonable profits. In their turn, management and governments fostered their own version of 'responsible' trade unionism and sought to incorporate unions as facilitators of enterprise efficiency and components in a coalition for productivity. They mobilized moderate leaders and shop floor representatives in a drive to improve competitiveness and performance. The trade-off was improved job security and internal labour markets based on merit and seniority of service for some workers. Where existing unions proved unamenable, management did not hesitate to groom alternative 'second unions'.[18]

A split in *Sohyo* in 1954 and the creation of the more conservative *Zenro*, which recruited in private industry, failed to dent the former's élan. This was reflected in the *Shunto*, the annual spring wage offensives launched from

1955, and *Sohyo's* involvement with student and citizen groups in peace campaigns. However, the Liberal Democrats attempted to influence *Zenro*, marginalize the left and negotiate a 'social contract' on productivity. The American- and state-backed Japan Productivity Centre embraced managers and trade unionists. *Sohyo's* constituent unions in the private sector were worn down in major confrontations, from the battles in the automotive industry in 1953, through the steel strikes in 1957 and 1959, to the lockout in the Miike coal mines in 1960. The remaking of the Japanese labour movement and the subordination of its radicalism was accomplished not only by Japanese capital and the state but also by the active involvement of the Americans. They coordinated the efforts of management to train moderate and breakaway trade unionists and sponsored the 'politics of productivity'.[19]

The year 1960 represented a turning point. The left went into decline after its failure to stop the renewal of the treaty between America and Japan which provided for the continuation of American bases and nuclear weapons in Japan. The ten-month-long dispute at the Miike pits owned by Mitsui Mining began in opposition to lay-offs but developed into an attempt to break the unions in coal and took on aspects of an epochal struggle between capital and labour nationally. The dispute witnessed mass picketing, fighting with police, the emergence of a second union supporting a return to work and the mobilization of support groups across Japan. The miners' defeat encouraged employers and their supporters, and over the next ten years the coverage of trade unionism in private industry diminished.[20]

From 1957 to 1961, days lost through strikes approached the level of the immediate postwar years. Thereafter, the 1960s saw the consolidation in the private sector of the cooperative, business unionism limited to the enterprise, its activities inscribed with economic rationality, which had developed in the pre-war period and which employers had pursued since 1948 through a strategic combination of coercion and social engineering. Through the decade, the moderate unions in the *Domei Kaigi* federation – a merger of *Sodomei* and *Zenro* – supported co-operative collectivism, productivity, 'responsible' wage demands and job flexibility in return for employment security, 'ability pay' and welfare benefits. Inside *Sohyo* the moderates made gains or withdrew to augment the more conservative federation. The left waned, the Socialist Party split and some trade unionists proved susceptible to the Liberal Democrats' attempts to create an industrial constituency. There were still outbursts of militancy in the public sector, where unions remained relatively strong, as in the oil crisis of 1974–75. By then trade union membership encompassed only 34 per cent of the labour force.[21]

Around the globe, the image of Japan as the home of cooperative, enterprise trade unionism, internal labour markets and lifetime employment, a benign system of human resource management which had made an important contribution to the country's prosperity, had come to replace the image of Japan as the perpetrator of Pearl Harbour. Formulaic depiction of Japanese industrial relations in terms of 'the three pillars' – employment for life, wages based on merit and seniority and enterprise unions underpinning corporate loyalty – exaggerated the position, even during the high tide of the economic boom between 1960 and 1980. The system was conventional for male workers in large companies and perceived as desirable more broadly. It covered less than 20 per cent of workers, it largely excluded women and its writ did not run beyond permanent workers or in small enterprises. Rather than stemming organically from Japanese culture, it had been constructed in struggle. Nor did it stave off the prolonged recession from the 1990s which ended the economic miracle.[22]

II

It was only in the unprecedented conditions after the war, with a more open society and academic freedom, that Japanese historians turned towards labour and began to develop a scholarly literature. The initial focus was on understanding the nature and frailty of the early labour movement. Its failings were explained in terms of the opposition of state and employers, the middle-class origin of union leaders and the nature of the workforce, recently rural and in some cases predominantly female. There was a prevailing, often implicit, assumption that development was unilinear, that Britain and/or Germany constituted a model for progress and that Japan's belated entry into the world economy had produced a brittle, 'backward' working class. The leading labour historian of the 1950s was Kazuo Okochi. He had studied in Germany, published his influential *Social Policy in Wartime* in 1940, and kept his post at the elite Tokyo University throughout the war. Okochi was a prolific writer. His pioneering *Reimeiki no nihon rodo undo* (*The Early Japanese Labour Movement*) appeared in 1952. In the context of pervasive suppression of trade unionism, Okochi's 'migrant labour theory' placed interpretive weight on the easy supply of cheap labour to industry, movement of workers from and back to the pre-modern agricultural sector and, crucially, on the links many preserved with it.

The salient aspect of the early Japanese working class, in Okochi's view, was that it was based on migrant workers. This applied to heavy industry and to those employed in textiles for contracted periods, or in building and civil engineering on a seasonal basis. They were often recruited by middlemen and agents, and companies developed connections with particular regions and family networks. In consequence, horizontal labour markets did not develop. The supply of workers remained attached to particular enterprises and workers operated in vertical labour markets. What trade unionism there was, was based on the enterprise and the characteristics of the migrant labour force determined Japanese industrial relations until the Second World War. These characteristics helped preserve pre-capitalist consciousness which harboured acceptance of hierarchical harmony at work, and contributed to the volatility of organization and to fragile enterprise trade unionism.[23]

Other historians had different ideas. They felt that Okochi's thesis was deterministic. It could not explain why organizations such as the Ironworkers' Union at the start of the twentieth century and later the *Yuaikai* and *Sodomei* had emerged and attempted to create, sometimes successfully, occupational and industrial unions. 'Migrant labour theory', Yoshio Otomo argued, was fatalistic. It failed to take account of the diverse experience of Japanese workers. It could not explain the differences between the Meiji and Taisho eras, let alone between pre-1938 and post-1945 trade unionism in Japan.[24] Naomichi Funahashi believed, in similar vein, that Okochi came close to propounding an iron law based on selecting and over-accentuating certain aspects of a complex situation. Okochi's interpretation ignored the changing attitudes of workers and the conscious part they played in building workers' organizations. Trade unionism was not only about 'objective' factors, or rather one such factor – the supply of labour.[25] Wakao Fujita made similar criticisms.[26]

There was no shortage of such theorizing in the years after 1945. The political scientist Masao Maruyama depicted Japanese workers as 'atomized labour'; individualism impeded collective attitudes and collective organization.[27] Marxist writers, who exercised considerable influence in the early postwar period, also looked to the past and to historical schemas to explain what they saw as the teething problems of Japanese labour. Disciples of the *Kozaha*, 'the Lecture School' of which Moritaro Yamada had been the leading light before the war, continued to emphasize the role that feudal features, the agricultural sector and 'the Emperor system' had played in the emergence of an immature proletariat, its inadequacies measured by its distance from its prescribed mission. The landlord system and rack-renting had forced farmers off the land and into the labour market, increasing competition, damping down wages and constraining the development of collective consciousness and strong trade unionism.[28] Another group, the *Ronoha*, 'the Peasant-Worker School', disagreed with Yamada on the necessity for a bourgeois revolution as the first stage of workers' emancipation. In their view, Japan was already a modern capitalist society and only required a socialist revolution not a 'two-stage solution'. These debates between theorists who espoused the JCP, on the one hand, and the social democratic Social Masses Party on the other, continued in the postwar years with the successors of the *Kozaha* and the *Ronoha* now supporting the JCP and the Socialist Party respectively.[29]

By the 1960s there was a switch of emphasis. Okochi now argued, and this was in sharp contrast to his earlier explanation, that before the great depression, at the end of the 1920s, trade unionists had attempted to organize horizontally and recruit members across companies. They had been undermined not only by unemployment but by employer strategies which fostered internal labour markets through the establishment of systems of training, seniority and welfare benefits which committed workers to the enterprise and ensured that trade unionism would be enterprise-based.[30] The 1950s and 1960s produced empirical studies focused on the pre-war development of the Japanese labour movement. Particularly notable was work by Mikio Sumiya, Toru Watanabe, Takao Nishioka, Etsuro Yajima, Ryuji Komatsu and Kanae Iida.[31] The weight of their investigations fell on the attempts by managers in the economic and political conditions of the 1920s to retain, motivate and control labour and utilize the volatility of external labour markets to create internal conditions which would facilitate identification of employees with the fortunes of the firm.

Some historians went back further. In an important series of texts, Yo Nakanishi explored managerial strategy in the Nagasaki Iron Plant before the Meiji Restoration. He reflected on the beginnings of industrialization and examined the labour force in precise detail. Nakanishi detected an absence of craft consciousness and attempts by workers to control entry into employment, while there was little resistance to technological innovation.[32] The Ironworkers' Union also attracted attention. Early work by Okochi and Sumiya had compared it with the British craft unions of the nineteenth century. In one of the first attempts to examine the origins of industrial relations in heavy industry, Tsutomu Hyodo questioned this verdict, as did Makoto Ikeda in his research. These historians pointed to the absence of horizontal craft unionism on the Western model which aspired to regulate entry to the trade and the performance of work, a phenomenon observed earlier by Izutaro Suehiro. The Ironworkers' Union was not comparable with the British 'new model unions'. There was no similar apprenticeship system – although in Japan the labour bosses trained 'apprentices'. A system of mass production had already been introduced into the union's heartland in the Tokyo Artillery Factory before the union gained a foothold and it recruited largely semi-skilled labour.[33] Later analyses related the absence of the regulative impulse in early collectivism to its absence in the pre-industrial Japanese guilds and to meritocratic tendencies in Japanese culture which favoured 'fair' competition among workers.[34]

There were also studies of the *Yuaikai* which demonstrated that workers and their organizations could develop and change and that bodies of philanthropic provenance established by middle-class social reformers possessed of a complacent estimation of capitalism could move towards socialist objectives and collective bargaining.[35] Labour disputes were not neglected. Their reconstruction, rationale and significance was a pre-occupation of Kazuo Nimura. He insisted on the need to transcend analytical narrative. It was important to study workers' attitudes and their relation to trade unionism in particular sectors, as well as their reactions to changes in production processes and labour markets, in order to develop an understanding of the specific characteristics of labour disputes in Japan. He interpreted many of them as motivated by considerations of fairness, equity and the demand for respect as much as by economic issues.[36]

Other research pursued the origins of the Japanese system. In his monograph on the history of labour management between 1868 and 1940 (first published in 1964), Hiroshi Hazama argued that Japan's late industrialization, weak capital accumulation and reliance on imported technology meant that what was distinctive in its development were the values underlying the control of labour. Management was relatively successful in integrating workers' 'groupism', their tendency to see themselves as individual components in a team, with management's 'familism', the projection of the firm as a family with differences which were reconcilable, to create a value system which countered and often overcame elements of adversarial class consciousness.[37]

Hazama suggested how this was achieved. In some, but by no means all, big companies in heavy industry, workers recruited on the basis of suitable educational qualifications were trained on the job, provided with incremental salaries and seniority-based promotions, and rewarded with company housing, medical benefits and, in some cases, lifelong employment. The world of paternalism included company shops, financial advice, personal counselling and sports facilities. These employers encouraged company unions and joint works councils which emphasized joint interests and discussed difficulties in a 'constructive', management-defined way. This system was by no means hegemonic before the war, even in *zaibatsu* enterprises, and it covered a small proportion of workers. Augmented after 1936, it constituted an alternative to independent trade unionism, job control and collective bargaining.[38]

These conclusions, which to some historians smacked of ideal types derived from limited evidence, were borne out by Komatsu's *Kigyobetsu kumiai no seisei* (*The Creation of Enterprise Unions*), published in 1971. Pursuing his research into steelworks and shipyards in the 1920s and 1930s, Komatsu found that employers' strategies impacted on the practice and consciousness of workers. Some accepted the new enterprise unionism. While others remained committed to the labour movement, their loyalties were diluted and they looked increasingly to the company for economic salvation. Moreover, the union federations themselves were inevitably influenced by the environment they operated in and, in comparison with other countries, adversarial class consciousness was restricted.[39] On the basis of these studies, one observer considered:

> [...] enterprise consciousness, at first institutionalised in the policies of industrial paternalism and subsequently institutionalised still further in the Industrial Patriotic Movement after 1938, did as much as police repression to undermine the pre-war Japanese labour movement [...] it could not hold the allegiance of its main core of support, the skilled worker stratum, once the unions were faced with the counter-union movement set up by the government.[40]

By the 1970s research into labour by Japanese historians still represented a recent innovation. It largely involved studies of union organization and the labour movement. But there was some attention to class formation, the development of management, industrial disputes and political parties. Side by side, there had emerged an English language literature. It was related to the close links between America and Japan during the Cold War and the need to enlighten policy makers on the nature of Japanese labour and its evolution. Some of this work, such as Thomas C. Smith's *Political Change and Industrial Development in Japan* (1955), proved to be of enduring importance.[41] Other studies made a valuable contribution, although they were often cast in the chronicle mode. A good example of this genre was the political scientist Robert Scalapino's useful *The Early Japanese Labor Movement*, written in the 1950s although only published in the 1980s, and his *Democracy and the Party Movement in Prewar Japan* (1953).[42] Sometimes the not-so-subtle subtext was to emphasise the importance of Japan's 'indigenous unitary orthodoxies', praise moderates who offered the right mix of conservatism and innovation, but mingle approbation with admonition. Scalapino warned 'those who govern – both in the state and in industry – of the necessity to heed the material and the psychic needs of the worker'.[43]

Similar concerns informed Scalapino's writings on Communism. But his books helped in their synthesis and detail to inform readers in the West of the intricacies of Japanese trade unionism and leftwing politics.[44] The massive tomes of George Totten and his colleagues tracing the history of the socialist parties performed a similar function. They provided painstaking description of policies, organizations, splits and fusions without placing their dense narratives in any comparative perspective or developed theoretical framework.[45] Their dedicated empiricism stood in contrast to its relative absence in some Japanese work of the period. There were also influential writers on more contemporary issues, such as James Abegglen, who produced *Management and the Worker* which in some places questioned the characterization of pre-modern aspects of Japanese management of work as a restraint on progress; Solomon Levine who studied industrial relations and worked with Okochi; and Alice Cook, who wrote about trade unions in the 'non political' fashion, focused on job regulation, which dominated American scholarship of the period.[46]

This work influenced Japanese scholars and occasionally led to collaboration.[47] Very different was the *minshushi*, the 'people's history' that emerged from the 1950s, independent of the infant labour history. Initiated by scholars such as Daikichi Irokawa, Yoshio Yasumaru and Masanao Kano, these histories took as their text the Japan of the village and 'the ordinary farmer'. They pursued history from below and the recovery of everyday life in the countryside rather than the fortunes of trade unionism or the problems of the factory. They studied rural communities, the peasant revolts of the Tokugawa era and the agrarian movements of the 1920s and 1930s. They investigated village institutions, popular consciousness and mentalities, political activism, religion and biography. Whereas earlier scholars had looked to the city and the capitalist enterprise as the modern, the face of the future, 'people's history' was premised on redeeming the majority of the population as real people who were historical actors not 'backward semi-feudal remnants'.[48]

Although these historians used traditional methods and employed documentary sources, as well as ethnography and folklore, their work represented a readjustment which had a political provenance and a political edge. The *minshushi* cultivated an anti-establishment ethos and expressed disillusion with the path Japan had taken in the twentieth century. Modernization theory had led to the disaster of the war; its more sophisticated prosecution under American auspices was far from benign.

Along with many of the Marxist approaches purveyed in postwar Japan, it had failed to valorize the people and its influence on historiography had produced a teleological, schematic and dehumanized history which neglected or objectified real people, their consciousness and their actions. There was some romanticism and resemblances to the Thompsonian social history which became prominent in Britain and North America are striking, although this was a distinctive movement rooted in Japan. Social history in the English language was read in Japan, but Thompson's *magnum opus* was only translated much later.[49]

Its influence can nevertheless be discerned in the turn to recovering the social and cultural aspects of working-class life. By the 1980s history from below, dealing with 'informal workers', 'the underclass' and 'the labouring poor', was being produced by labour historians such as Eiichi Eguchi, Yuji Kato, Kiyoshi Nakagawa and Hirosuke Kawanishi.[50] The social aspects of this approach were represented in the work of Nimura. Some of it bears comparison with the work of Thompson, the historian of the crowd ,George Rudé, and the American exponent of social history from below, Herbert Gutman. Nimura, a professor at Hosei University and a mainstay of the Ohara Institute for Social Research, spent a year researching at the Centre for the Study of Social History at the University of Warwick in England and was influenced by British labour history.

Nimura was sceptical about earlier attempts to explain the formative nature of the Japanese working class and its labour movement, particularly Okochi's migrant labour theory and the latter's subsequent move away from the characteristics of labour to the strategies of capital as the key explanatory factor. A fundamental insight shared with other historians was that labour history could not be reduced to labour economics. A trade union was a purposive human creation with no fixed ends, not simply an instrument for the supply of labour. Earlier work, Nimura felt, had overemphasized the continuity of the experience of the rural past and neglected the way workers' ideas and actions change with circumstances. Some previous studies had constructed a timeless conception of Japanese workers. Other writers, influenced by the *kozaha*, had become absorbed in explaining why workers had not played their assigned part in teleological tales based on experience in very different cultures. Nimura was a critic of Okochi's narrative of pre-modern social relations and Maruyama's version of fragmentation and replaced them with a picture of workers determined to organize rather than determined by their past. The Japanese system of enterprise loyalty, lifelong employment and enterprise unionism was not uniform. While it may have reflected the different forms of consciousness of Japanese and

West European workers, it could not be dated to one fixed point. The task was to trace its protracted, complicated, uneven evolution.[51]

Nimura's major monograph illustrates this approach to labour history. He had begun his study of the Ashio copper mine, which centred on the disturbances there in 1907, much earlier during the 1950s and published an article on the affair as early as 1959.[52] Subsequent essays formed the basis of his book *Ashio bodo no shiteki bunseki*, which was published in Japanese in 1988 and in revised form in English as *The Ashio Riot of 1907* a decade later. Arguably, it remains the most important single work in Japanese labour historiography.[53]

It works on a number of levels. Nimura has always been a master of detail and investigative research who studies legal and police records as well as trade union and corporate documents. These accomplishments are brought to bear in explaining material conditions, technology and the labour process in the copper mines, and in tracing the development of trade unionism and the disputes which made coal and metalliferous mining Japan's most conflict-ridden industries. Assessing the part played by tradition as well as the impact of capitalist rationality, he explores broader debates in Japanese labour history, such as the influence of external societies of supporters of trade unionism in generating grievance and suggesting collective solutions to it, and the significance of the mining brotherhoods, the *tomokodomei*, trade societies which had emerged in the eighteenth century, in stimulating the later unions. In each case his estimation is positive. But he goes beyond developing the historiography of industrial relations and documenting the roles taken by the principal actors – authoritarian management, labour bosses who ran the *hanba* subcontracting system, union activists and higher paid face workers whose piecework wages were under pressure – to evoke not only the intricacies of industrial relations but also the social relations of a company town and the texture of mining culture in early *Taisho* Japan. Nimura takes us a long way towards his objective of capturing the 'subjectivity of the workers themselves – how they lived, worked, thought and felt'.[54]

At the core of the text, recovery of the conscious mobilization which lay at the heart of the riot expands our understanding of the forms that popular protest took in Japan, and enriches the literature pioneered by Rudé, Hobsbawm and Thompson. Nimura demonstrates, using a wealth of sometimes obscure sources, that what was involved was not a spontaneous outburst, the pre-industrial eruption of an immature and 'atomized' working class of the kind analysts such as Maruyama had suggested. The riot reflected a desire and capability to organize. It was a weapon deployed against the employer which contained strong elements of calculation and organization although it reflected limited class consciousness. *The Ashio Riot* signified in a Japanese context that it was possible for labour historians 'to re-create in vivid detail the world of people often called "nameless" and lumped together as a mass'.[55] It provided the basis for a compelling critique of earlier Japanese labour history and a convincing plea for more international comparison.

III

Attempts to establish associations of labour historians have met with limited success in Japan. During the 1950s and 1960s the organizational focus was the Society for the Study of Social Policy (SSSP). Established as long ago as 1897, it was refounded by Okochi and others in 1950 with the objective of fostering research into social welfare, social security, industrial relations and the role of women. By 1960 labour issues had become one of its important concerns and its annual conference that year on the history of the labour movement heard pleas from Nimura, Watanabe and others for an expansion of labour history, more empirical work, higher standards of evidence and more specialized studies of trade unionism, parties and labour movement ideology. In 1957 a Labour History Research Association (*Rodoundoshi Kenkyukai*) had been created. It became active in the late 1950s and 1960s, although it never had more than 100 members, a fraction of those subscribing to the SSSP. The history it favoured was predominantly institutional history: the Association aimed to stimulate interest in the history of the labour movement in Japan and other countries. It encouraged reports on research and helped with the development of archives and the collection of reminiscences. Trade unionists as well as academics participated in its activities. It produced a journal, *Rodoundoshi kenkyu* (*Labour History Review*), which continued until 1980. Thereafter the Association went into decline, in tandem with the labour movement its members studied, and it was wound up in 1995.

The powerhouses of historical investigation continued to be the Institute of Social Research at Tokyo University and the Ohara Institute at Hosei University. Established in 1919 and re-established in 1951, the Ohara Institute possesses a magnificent collection of documentary material which is indispensable to any student of Japanese labour. Its archives include a wide range of primary sources from the papers of the *Kyochokai*, the interwar think-tank on labour issues, to the records of a number of trade unions and the political parties of the left, the Social Masses Party and its successors. The library houses an extensive collection of publications on labour in Japan and abroad, while the Institute publishes bibliographies, a monthly magazine and a series of yearbooks as well as initiating, resourcing and supervising research projects.[56]

A good infrastructure for labour history exists in Japan. But as in other countries the subject was arguably marked by the decline of organized labour and the political left in the 1980s. The institutional approach and the focus on the history of trade unionism were overshadowed. The influence of Marxism diminished and social history became stronger. This was reflected, as we have seen, in histories from below and, particularly, in Nimura's *Ashio Riot* and in new work on coalmining, such as the monographs by Naoki Tanaka and Hiroshi Ichihara. In contrast with the rather stereotyped stories of miners' trade unionism which had hitherto dominated the historiography, these studies transcended the sphere of production and explored the constitution of community among miners.[57] Labour history opened itself to the contexts in which workers and their organizations functioned, embraced wider canvasses and employed oral history. Publications of note included Yasushi Miwa's *Nihon fashizumu to rodo undo* (*Japanese Fascism and the Labour Movement*, 1988), in which labour disputes in the 1930s were reconstructed from oral testimony and Hiroshi Yasuda's 1994 monograph, *Taisho demokurashi shiron* (*The History of Taisho Democracy*).[58] Yasuda, who is a political historian, assessed changes in the class structure and their relevance to the unions during the 1920s, and documented the influence of the state. Refining earlier work, he argued that stratification between workers in large-scale enterprises, medium and small plants and the 'reserve army' of unskilled workers was reflected in a weak and differentiated trade unionism. His book was particularly useful for the way in which it disaggregated the different sectors of the state and rehabilitated the role of the relatively liberalizing Social Bureau of the Home Office in channelling trade unionism in big workplaces towards enterprise unionism and moderation.[59]

Yasuda emphasized the role of unskilled workers in disciplining labour markets and constraining trade unions by reference to the part that Koreans played in Japanese industry. The expansion of the concerns of labour history was exemplified in a move away from male workers in the factories towards a more inclusive emphasis on women and minorities. Already in 1977 Hideo Totsuka had analysed the forced labour of Koreans drafted into the coal mines of Hokkaido using management records.[60] Some of these issues had been taken up by 'the people's historians' in relation to discrimination against Japan's original inhabitants, the Ainu, and the oppressed Burakumin caste.[61] A major contribution in this area was Yutaka Nishinarita's *Zainichi chosenjin no 'sekai' to 'teikoku' kokka* (*The 'World' of Koreans in Japan and the 'Imperial' State*). He followed this with an equally illuminating text on Chinese forced labour in Japan.[62]

The history of working-class women also expanded. The first influential book in this area to appear after 1945 was Kiyoshi Inoue's pioneering *Nihon joseishi* (*The History of Women in Japan*). Within a Marxist perspective, Inoue traced how women suffered under the semi-feudal *Ie* system (legally supported male control of the household, abolished in 1945). In the 1970s and 1980s, Sayoko Yoneda and Haruko Wakita used a similar Marxist framework to develop general histories of Japanese women.[63] In later work, Yuki Sakurai and Noriyo Hayakawa examined the history of feminist movements.[64] The growing significance of women's history in the literature has been underlined by a recent major project which has published important speeches and articles by women activists from the early Meiji era to the Showa period in a twenty-three volume collection; one volume deals exclusively with women workers.[65] If these developments echo trends across the globe, 'the linguistic turn' and varieties of postmodernism, implicated elsewhere with the turn to gender, have had little impact in Japan.

By the 1980s, labour history was a well-established feature of Japanese historiography. This was illustrated by the appearance of general surveys such as Sakuro Omae's *Rodoshi kenkyu* (*The Study of Labour History*) in 1983 and Makoto Ikeda's *Rodoshi no shodanmen* (*Aspects of Labour History*) in 1990.[66] This consolidation failed to revitalize the Labour History Association or stimulate the creation of any alternative organization. A new journal, *Rodoshi kenkyu* (*Studies in Labour History*), was established in 1984. It took greater account of 'the new labour history' and was not limited to the study of the labour movement. But it proved ephemeral. Only five issues were published over seven years. The associational basis for Japanese labour history beyond the universities continues to be the Labour division of the SSSP.

At the same time, the English language literature was taking significant strides and there was more interaction between the two strands of the historiography. In the late 1970s Japanese historians had begun to examine the postwar era and Eiji Takemae's study of the Americans' labour policy during the occupation based on their own records enriched our understanding of the period.[67] A year later, the Australian historian Joe Moore published *Japanese Workers and the Struggle for Power, 1945–1947*. Moore criticized Western scholars for writing unpeopled, technocratic history which celebrated Japan's postwar 'success story' and worshipped the accomplished fact rather than scrutinizing why one path had won out over alternatives through economic, industrial and political struggle:

> What eventually did happen has come to be regarded as what had to happen. The charge of writing history without people has been made in other contexts but has truly been the case here. The flesh and blood of mass firings and joblessness, destitution and hunger, massive strikes and union bashing, class struggle and state repression have been submerged in dry statistics and abstract theory. The revolutionary ferment of the times has not come through and the depth of the postwar crisis of capitalism in Japan has yet to be appreciated.[68]

Moore provided a vivid picture of Japanese workers in these years and raised fundamental problems of continuity and change.[69] Despite the state's harnessing of cooperative enterprise unionism over the decade from 1936 and the experience of collaboration in the war effort, peace brought enthusiasm for independent, militant collectivism. Earlier tendencies would resurface but their triumph was far from inevitable. But Moore's was not some inspirational, leftwing primer. Its arguments were backed by an array of documentary sources from archives in America, Australia and Japan and extensive utilization of Japanese language materials from both union and management sources. Moore illustrated the influx of both blue and white-collar workers into the unions, the origins and conduct of strikes and *seisan kanri*, the movement to bring production under the supervision of workers representatives, through studies of individual workplaces. But he also examined the role of SCAP and the strategies of employers faced with democratization.

His identification with class struggle was creative. There was little reflection on whether what he discerned as the revolutionary impetus of the movement was likely to achieve socialist transformation. A persuasive counterfactual would conceive an alternative outcome in terms of greater liberalization and a historic compromise which granted enhanced participation in production to independent trade unions, accompanied by collective bargaining of greater scope than the settlement which eventually emerged. Despite the brief surge of the JCP, a 'people's democracy' never appeared likely. Moore reminded readers of the creative ingenuity of the Japanese workers after everything they had experienced and the shock they administered to capital. This was an unusual moment. A defeated country lay in chaos, the established order had collapsed, millions were unemployed and hungry. Yet business leaders and political elites were able to recapture the initiative as the presence of the Americans and then the onset of the

Cold War obstructed alternative roads forward.

Moore did not concern himself greatly with the high politics of labour, the intricate internal issues of the revitalized *Sodomei* and the reappearance in industry of the JCP. Such matters constituted an important ingredient in Stephen Large's study of the unions and socialist politics between the wars, which took forward his earlier work on the *Yuaikai*. It constitutes a valuable account of the successes and failures of labour in Japan from the high hopes of 1919 to the unprepossessing realities of 1940. Large had studied at the University of Warwick's Centre for the Study of Social History. But his monograph was substantially a political study, informed by extensive research in the archives of America, Australia and Britain and by comparative insights into labour in Britain and Germany.

Large was approbatory about the course the *Sodomei* set in the 1920s, when its compass was a reformist socialism distanced from the Communist-inspired *Hyogikai* federation, and contributed an innovative essay on the attempt to use newspapers, workers' schools and cooperatives to anchor a labourist sub-culture. In the 1930s, he insisted, choices remained; opportunities were not taken. Large was critical of the caution and conservatism which led the *Sodomei* leaders to accommodate rather than challenge unfavourable trends. He was perhaps over-optimistic: union leaders, custodians of the institutional interests of their organizations were faced with an authoritarian state and a brittle base among workers. It is difficult to discern substantial forces out of which alternatives could have been assembled. Union leaders had choices. They were limited and comparisons with the stronger German labour movement remain instructive, if not pushed too far.[70]

The most significant contribution to the English language literature was made by the American scholar, Andrew Gordon. In his *Evolution of Labour Relations in Japan*, published in 1985, Gordon revisited central preoccupations of the historiography. Drawing on primary Japanese sources, as well as secondary work in both languages, he offered a more specific periodization. Before 1914 he attributed workers' focus on organization in the workplace to the weakness of traditions of craft collectivism rather than to traits inherent in the labour force or to the paternalism of employers. The First World War was a turning point. The challenge from labour leant urgency and substance to employer initiatives aimed at engineering an 'enterprise community'. Management policies were reactive and better characterized by the term 'authoritarian labour control' than 'paternalism'.[71]

In contrast with earlier estimations, Gordon argued that these initiatives predated the 1920s, often seen as the crucible of the Japanese system, but remained rudimentary and restricted. Lifelong employment, recruitment related to educational qualifications and promotion by seniority remained attenuated or absent in heavy industry in the 1920s. What Gordon designated 'imperial fascism', which succeeded 'imperial democracy' from the mid-1930s, substituted the state bureaucracy for organized labour as the main stimulus to management's endeavours. Essentially an overview, the text provided a finely delineated analysis of different aspects of industrial policy in wartime and its impact on labour. Gordon endorsed the earlier emphasis on the significance of the postwar years. He supported the view that Japanese workers attempted to impose a settlement in which job security and progress by seniority would have been complemented, not by business unions, but by independent unions which gave their members a significant say in key decisions, rather than a voice in their implementation. Instead, the defeated struggles of the 1940s and 1950s confirmed the dominance of management and the subordination of the unions and the workers.

The Evolution of Labor Relations sustains precise detail and nuanced interpretation over a century and more than 400 pages. Although its empirical base, which concentrated on five big shipyards and engineering works in the Tokyo-Yokohama industrial belt, premised depth rather than breadth, it constituted an important achievement. Gordon's ensuing monograph, *Imperial Democracy in Prewar Japan* (1991), built on his earlier analysis. It set an examination of the workers' movement in the Nankatsu area of Tokyo, which reassembled the life of the workers from archival documents, neglected labour publications, private correspondence, autobiography and memory, within a reinterpretation of the factors influencing politics between 1905 and 1940. It is an important addition to the social history of Japanese labour. The workers stand at the centre of the text as actors who influenced events and, Gordon believes, state policy, in which domestic considerations were often as important as foreign objectives. Workers took the promise of imperial democracy seriously and fought to realise it in their own lives.[72]

Union organization focused on the workplace not the trade because the workplace provided the superior site for solidarity given the distance of the federations, their frailty and their squabbles. The workplace was where workers acquired skills and began struggles which had as much to do with a desire for recognition, respect and status as with economic necessities. Gordon's optimism is usually justified by the evidence. In the face of tremendous difficulties, organization became a reality in the milieus he reconstructed and the unions reinforced a sense of solidarity. Their path of failure was punctuated by intermittent success. Workers organized strikes. Urban riots were not 'primitive' outbursts of frustration but components of campaigns which expressed political discontent. Japan's rulers had to take account of social conflict and workers' rebelliousness. The impact they had on state policy is more problematic.

The third volume of Gordon's trilogy, *The Wages of Affluence* (1998), sees prosperity for some as related to the low wages of the majority of Japanese workers. It takes us from the excitements of the postwar struggles to the relative calm of the economic miracle. Unlike much of the literature on the Japanese system of labour management, Gordon sensitively historicizes its emergence. He renders its dominance contingent and qualified, by tracing its evolution in the postwar years through the lens of the steel industry. The remaking of capital, labour and the relations between them after the war was, in this account, far from preordained. Gordon rehabilitates the significance of the 'contest for the workplace' waged from 1945 to the early 1960s through a series of chapters headed 'Japan Reborn'; 'Organizing the Steelworkers'; 'Restoring Managerial and State Authority'; 'Forging an Activist Union'; and 'Breaking the Impasse'. By the 1960s, the employers' success had laid the basis for management control of the workplace and corporate hegemony of the Japanese economy. In essays titled 'Fabricating the Politics of Cooperation', 'Mobilizing Total Commitment' and 'Managing Society for Business', Gordon tracks not only the creation of the politics of productivity but the subordination of the unions, the evisceration of broader conceptions of industrial democracy and the impact of change at work on the values of the wider society.[73]

Other important writing appeared in the 1980s and 1990s. Sheldon Garon added to research published in Japanese which addressed the role of labour specialists in the state bureaucracy in the 1920s. He maintained that they purveyed a liberalizing modernism. They were willing to endow moderate unions with a degree of legitimacy, so long as they reflected national objectives. Senior civil servants grappled with the difficulties of maintaining collectivism under state supervision as the 1930s advanced.[74] Another American academic, Michael Lewis, returned to social history and the analysis of riots, particularly the important rice riots of 1918. Like some other writers in this genre, Lewis is stronger on history from below than its impact on high politics. He reconstructs in meticulous detail the ways in which forms of traditional rural protest interacted with urban mobilizations in the *Taisho* period. 'Riots' reflected unrest in the context of wartime expansion of the labour force and declining working conditions, and protest provided a voice for the hitherto voiceless in their rejection of many aspects of modernization. The problem of demonstrating their consequences, of showing, as Lewis concluded, that the rice riots altered the course of Japan's history, remains.[75]

Further notable contributions came from Norma Chalmers who explored the peripheral workforce in postwar Japan;[76] from John Price, who subjected celebration of Japan's industrial relations to a critique based on history, memorable for its essay on the Miike confrontation in 1960 and its compelling assertion that independent trade unionism had not withered in Japanese soil but had been uprooted;[77] and from Michael Weiner, who brought together work on the role of minorities in the workplace which paralleled research being undertaken in Japan.[78] Translation of Japanese texts into English helped flesh out the picture of the past emerging in Japan. Makoto Kumazawa's *Portraits of the Japanese Workplace* recorded the practice rather than the promise of management Japanese-style. Kumazawa depicted Japanese workers as protagonists of self-management by self-induced stress, likened trade unionism to non-unionism and portrayed women workers as providing unpaid household labour as well as underpinning the system by part-time work in insecure, poorly paid jobs which supplied employers with 'numerical flexibility'. By 1990, he emphasized, management had liberated itself almost completely from union regulation, even restraint, and had a free hand in restructuring the workplace.[79] Hirosuke Kawanishi's *The Human Face of Industrial Conflict* collected the reflections on the struggles of the 1940s and 1950s of union participants whose views ranged from the far left to the anti-communist.[80]

The literature on working-class politics is less abundant. The processes of fragmentation and unity, succeeded by factionalism and further fissures, which culminated in the demise of the Social Masses Party, have been chronicled by Large and Totten.[81] Fusions and splits continued in the postwar era. The Japan Socialist Party grouped together the most important pre-war factions of the left, centre and right. Initially successful in garnering votes, it entered coalitions in 1947 and 1948 but split after electoral defeat in the latter year. The 'social democrats' aligned themselves with *Sodomei* and the 'socialists' with *Sohyo* before formal reunification in 1955. Continued factionalism and fractures produced decline in the 1960s before recovery in the late 1980s. The work of Allan Cole and his colleagues remains the most detailed account of these events in English up to the 1960s while Sarah Hyde has charted recent developments.[82]

Beckman and Okubo and Scalapino provide the standard works in English on pre-war Communism. Mahito Tanaka has recently and usefully examined the party in the 1930s.[83] The JCP's record was one of obeisance to the Comintern. Researchers such as Sandra Wilson thought differently but without convincingly revising this conclusion. The opening of the Moscow archives has permitted Japanese historians, notably Tetsuro Kato, to challenge the JCP's official narratives and explore the nature of Russian domination.[84] Perhaps the most reliable guide to later events was the American professor of international relations, Peter Berton. He analysed the party's explosive growth and electoral success between 1945 and 1950, its decline after the Korean War and its consolidation from the 1960s. Distanced from traditional narratives of Communism, the JCP remains a familiar part of Japan's political furniture.[85]

The interest in women's history which had developed in Japan blossomed in Western countries. The image of factory girls as victims had been imprinted on the imagination by Wakizo Hosoi in the 1920s and it endured.[86] Patricia Tsurumi's scholarly study of female textile operatives in Meiji Japan shed new light on their situation. Tsurumi challenged the views of historians such as Okochi, who had attributed the failure of attempts at union before 1914 to the inability of ignorant, submissive young women to challenge their fate, and Hazama, who viewed oppressive conditions as stimulating heightened sexuality.[87] Using official sources, local archives and, particularly effectively, songs written by silk mill workers, Tsurumi exposed a record of rebellion and, as early as the 1880s, strikes over wages but, crucially, over unfair treatment. High turnover of labour inhibited union organizing among the women. More fundamentally, the idea of trade unionism on the Western model was foreign to their thinking. Cultural factors were an impediment to collectivism. But challenge and protest rather than docility and fatalism characterized these women's introduction to the labour market.[88]

Barbara Molony questioned the episodic nature of women's employment and claimed that many women continued to work after marriage to fellow textile operatives. Molony advanced the view that women helped to shape some aspects of Japanese society, including labour-management relations. Oppression did not dictate acceptance of it. Many women were treated as second-class citizens and workers, but capable of purposive action in certain spheres.[89] The complexity of matters is suggested by the collaboration of feminists, in search of protective legislation and improved status, with the imperial fascist regime.[90] Further studies of textile workers, domestic servants and women employed in coal mines have added to our understanding of female labour.[91]

Mikiso Hane gathered together testimony from women radicals and depicted the persecution they suffered in the early twentieth century, while monographs from Britain and America by Patricia McNaughtan and Elyssa Faison re-explored the worlds of factory women.[92] There was extensive address of oppression and victimhood; dependence and independence; employers' attempts to restrain activism and police sexual behaviour; the role of non-Japanese women in industry; and the impact management experiments had on the introduction of lifelong employment arrangements in the postwar period. Mary Brinton and Alice Lam studied the position of women after the war: the latter's claim that the American occupation had brought liberation to Japanese women provoked discussion and rehearsal of women's earlier role in 'riots', strikes, suffrage agitation and union organizing.[93]

This was the subject of Vera Mackie's *Creating Socialist Women in Japan* (1997). Mackie's subjects included activists in women's organizations, leftwing parties and union federations, although she mustered little data on their age, origins, education or marital status. The text was informative on organizing but its main concerns lay with discourse and how women were constituted by male leaders and activists in the labour movement and the state. In the early period women found voice as daughters, wives and mothers, criticizing the state and capital's treatment of a generally perceived male working class. More assertive discourse developed from the pre-1914 period and questioned women's double oppression. It never became dominant in the labour movement, still less in the state. Despite the need for women to aid the military effort, they were still imagined in largely traditional ways and conceived, even by labour activists, as secondary, supportive actors, even as supplicants in need of protection.[94]

IV

Labour history in Japan has developed considerably since the 1950s. It emerged as a history from below which wrestled with issues of class formation and explanations of the shaping of organized labour. In an important sense it was a history of the labour movement, of industrial relations, and of the organized, male, factory worker. It broadened into social history and began to explore workers' lives and culture, women and ethnic minorities. In this it emulated Western historiographies. By the 1990s, a Canadian historian of Japanese labour characterized his own work as 'history from the bottom up', noting:

> This tradition has long been upheld in Japan by scholars [...] who in their voluminous works have stressed the history of workers' struggles. It is only in the past decade, however, that works in English by such scholars as Andrew Gordon, Joe Moore, E.Patrica Tsurumi and Norma Chalmers have revived this more balanced view of labour history and labour-management relations in Japan. They have in their particular ways 'brought workers back in' as Gordon put it.[95]

There have been problems. Only recently have Japanese historians turned to investigate in any depth 'peripheral' workers and 'informal' forms of labour. The two historiographies have tended to operate in relative isolation. Only the English language stream is generally available to non-specialist scholars. This has been repaired to some extent, not least by Andrew Gordon, who has played an exemplary role as author, translator and commentator.[96] Difficulties remain. Much of the literature on organized labour relates to heavy industry and textiles, sometimes to restricted sites within them. There is a need for more extended, deeper and more nuanced comparison. Kazuo Nimura has suggested that American scholars should bring more about the history of the American labour movement to their examination of Japanese labour and the same could apply to historians from other countries.[97]

To take one example, while the absence of a regulative tradition by craft workers was indubitably important in Japan, the workplace as the focus for activity and solidarity was also of tremendous significance in Britain, particularly in periods of union strength such as 1910–21 and from the 1960s to the 1980s. The same is true for other countries. Trade unionism and industrial relations have been significantly decentralized in Britain – and America – as well as Japan. Even among British craft workers, solidarity beyond the workplace could be progressively brittle. A range of comparisons suggest themselves, including the different contours and content of class consciousness in Japan and countries such as Britain, Germany and Italy, not to speak of other countries in Asia; the splits in trade unionism in France, Germany, Italy and Japan; the culture of miners in the different contexts of Asia and Europe; the role women have played in national labour movements; and the position of unorganized and 'informal labour'. In relation to the latter, but overall, comparison of Japan with China and India could prove instructive. Nonetheless, the turn in Japanese labour history to women's history, ethnic divisions and minorities, combined with continued interest in the historical forces which shaped contemporary employment relations – a good example of how the present can inspire interest in the past – promises a future of vibrancy.

Finally, on the occasion of the fiftieth anniversary of the SSLH, it is worth reflecting on the enduring interest in British labour history in Japan. Key works were translated as long ago as the 1920s and their availability has influenced Japanese historians. The Webbs's *History of Trade Unionism* and *Industrial Democracy* appeared in Japanese in 1920 and 1927 respectively; in the postwar years well-known texts by G.D.H. Cole, A.L. Morton and Henry Pelling were translated. The new labour history interested academics and eventually publishing houses. Eric Hobsbawm's *Labouring Men* appeared in Japanese soon after its British publication and a 'collected works' of Royden Harrison in 1972, although translation of Rudé's work and Dorothy Thompson's writings awaited the 1990s and Edward Thompson's *The Making* was only published in Japanese in 2003.[98]

Articles by British scholars were translated by their Japanese counterparts who in addition contributed accounts of British debates for Japanese audiences. Takao Matsumura produced a survey of the controversy between Max Hartwell, Hobsbawm and others on the standard of living during the industrial revolution and Chuuhei Sugiyama and Matsumura translated articles by T.S. Ashton on that subject.[99] Kazuhiko Kondo made Japanese historians aware of Thompson's arguments. Matsumura and Akira Nakayama popularized debates about the role of the labour aristocracy in Britain, as well as writing their own monographs on this subject. Japanese historians were also introduced to the SSLH and the History Workshop Movement.[100]

Enthusiasm was initially fuelled by a desire to learn from more 'advanced' economies and to appropriate and develop theoretical frameworks for researching labour. Until the 1970s, most research on British history in Japan was based on secondary sources. Chushichi Tsuzuki constituted the outstanding exception. He studied for his doctorate under Pelling at Oxford, and the thesis was published as *H.M. Hyndman and British Socialism* (1967). Biographies of Eleanor Marx, Edward Carpenter and Tom Mann followed.[101] The collection edited by Tsuzuki, *Igirisu shakishugi shisoshi* (*The History of British Socialist Thought*) in 1986 included essays by Sidney Pollard, Harrison, Pelling, Matsumura and Masatoshi Miichi. It had a significant impact on Japanese readers.[102] Other researchers concentrated on industrial relations and labour legislation: no less than four books on the Factory Acts in Britain by Japanese authors appeared in the 1960s, including Totsuka's pioneering volume, while Michio Koyama and Mari Osawa published on the Poor Laws.[103]

From the 1980s a younger generation, excited by social history, took an interest in Britain, despite the decline of the labour movement in both Britain and Japan. Japanese historians have researched Chartism, Fenianism, the engineering unions and the Taff Vale judgement.[104] Japanese students have pursued doctoral theses on British topics as varied as provision for the aged in trade unions and friendly societies in the second half of the nineteenth century and unemployment in Britain and Japan in the 1930s.[105] Historians of women have looked *inter alia* at women's trade unionism, women factory inspectors and women in the Second World War.[106]

Labour history in Japan is in a far from perfect state. One of its stronger aspects has been the extent to which historians in these small islands have stretched out to understand the historians and history of other small islands as well as larger nations. The tendency in Japanese history to attempt to transcend insularity is an attractive feature. It deserves to be deepened, extended and emulated, here and elsewhere.

Notes

This chapter and the references below follow Western rather than Japanese convention: the personal name is followed by the family name. We have supplied an English translation of Japanese titles preceded by an oblique (/).

1 Accessible work in English relevant to the pre-war history of Japanese labour includes Stephen S. Large, *The Rise of Labor in Japan: The Yuaikai, 1912–1919* (Tokyo: Sophia University Press, 1972); idem, *Organized Workers and Socialist Politics in Interwar Japan* (Cambridge: Cambridge University Press, 1981); Robert Scalapino, *The Early Japanese Labor Movement: Labor and Politics in a Developing Society* (Berkeley: University of California Press, 1983); Andrew Gordon, *The Evolution of Labor Relations in Japan: Heavy Industry, 1853–1955* (Cambridge, MA: Harvard University Press, 1985); Sheldon Garon, *The State and Labor in Modern Japan* (Berkeley: University of California Press, 1987); E. Patricia Tsurumi, *Factory Girls: Women in the Thread Mills of Meiji Japan* (Princeton: Princeton University Press, 1990); Andrew Gordon, *Labor and Imperial Democracy in Prewar Japan* (Berkeley: University of California Press, 1991).

2 An excellent survey of the period until c.1910 is Kazuo Nimura, 'Japan', in *The Formation of Labour Movements, 1870–1914: An International Perspective,* vol. 2, ed. by Marcel van der Linden and Jürgen Rojahn (Leiden: Brill, 1990), pp. 673–700. Also insightful is Akira Suzuki, 'The History of Labour in Japan in the Twentieth Century: Cycles of Activism and Acceptance', in *Global Labour History: A State of the Art,* ed. by Jan Lucassen (Bern: Peter Lang, 2006), pp. 161–93 (pp. 162–79). See also Hiroshi Hazama, *The History of Labour Management in Japan* (Basingstoke: Macmillan, 1997); and *The Economic Development of Modern Japan, 1869–1945: From the Meiji Restoration to the Second World War,* vol. 2, ed. by Steven Tolliday (Cheltenham: Edward Elgar, 2001), pp. 207–40.

3 Large, *Rise of Labor*; Thomas C. Smith, *Native Sources of Japanese Industrialization* (University of California Press, 1988); Stephen E. Marsland, *The Birth of the Japanese Labor Movement: Takano Fusataro and the Rodo Kumiai Kisekai* (Honolulu: University of Hawaii Press, 1989); Nimura, 'Japan', p. 686; Suzuki, 'History of Labor', pp. 168–9.

4 Kazuo Nimura. *The Ashio Riot of 1907: A Social History of Mining in Japan* (Durham: Duke University Press, 1997; 1st pub. in Japanese, 1988); Gordon, *Labor and Imperial Democracy,* pp. 63–109.

5 Gordon, *Evolution of Labor Relations,* pp. 71–74, 106–10; Large, *Rise of Labor.*

6 Hazama, *History of the Labour Movement,* pp. 109–31; Stephen Large,

'Perspectives on the Failure of the Labour Movement in Pre-War Japan', *Labour History* (Australia), 37 (1979), 15–27. But historians differ about the extent and success of employers' strategies in the 1920s. For a careful discussion see Gordon, *Evolution of Labor Relations*, pp. 211–54.

7 Scalapino, *Early Japanese Labor Movement*, pp. 97–154; Large, *Organized Workers and Socialist Politics*, pp. 24–27; Gordon, *Labor and Imperial Democracy*, pp. 144–75.

8 Gordon, *Labor and Imperial Democracy*, pp. 144–75; Reiko Okayama, 'Japanese Employer Labour Policy: The Heavy Engineering Industry, 1900–1930', in *Managerial Strategies and Industrial Relations: An Historical and Comparative Study*, ed. by Howard Gospel and Craig Littler (London: Heinemann, 1983), pp. 157–70 (pp. 164–68).

9 G.M. Beckmann and Genji Okubo, *The Japanese Communist Party, 1922–1945* (Stanford: Stanford University Press, 1969); George O. Totten, *The Social Democratic Movement in Pre-War Japan* (New Haven: Yale University Press, 1966); Garon, *State and Labor*, p. 51; Gordon, *Evolution of Labor Relations*, pp. 208–11.

10 Gordon, *Labor and Imperial Democracy*, p. 4; Andrew Gordon, *A Modern History of Japan: From Tokugawa Times to the Present* (New York: Oxford University Press, 2003), p. 153.

11 Andrew Gordon, 'The Right to Work in Japan: Labor and the State in the Depression', *Social Research*, 54 (1987), 247–66; Janet Hunter, *Women and the Labour Market in Japan's Industrialising Economy: The Textile Industry before the Pacific War* (London: Routledge Curzon, 2003).

12 Gordon, *Labor and Imperial Democracy*, pp. 310–17; Large, *Organized Workers and Socialist Politics*, pp. 196–230.

13 Ibid.

14 Aspects of the postwar period are covered in Joe Moore, *Japanese Workers and the Struggle for Power, 1945–1947* (Madison: University of Wisconsin Press, 1983); *Workers and Employers in Japan: The Japanese Employment Relations System*, ed. by Kazuo Okochi, Bernard Karsh and Solomon B. Levine (Tokyo: Tokyo University Press, 1973); Charles J. McMillan, *The Japanese Industrial System* (Berlin: De Gruyter, 1984); *Postwar Japan as History*, ed. by Andrew Gordon (Berkeley: University of California Press, 1993); Mary C. Brinton, *Women and the Economic Miracle: Gender and Work in Postwar Japan* (Berkeley: University of California Press, 1993); John Price, *Japan Works: Power and Paradox in Postwar Industrial Relations* (Ithaca: Cornell University Press, 1997); Andrew Gordon, *The Wages of Affluence: Labor and Management in Postwar Japan* (Cambridge, MA: Harvard University Press, 1998); Allan B. Cole, George O. Totten and Cecil H. Uyehara, *Socialist Parties in Postwar Japan* (New Haven: Yale University Press, 1966); and see *The Economic Development of Modern Japan, 1945–1995: From Occupation to the Bubble Economy*, vol. 2, ed. by Steven Tolliday (Cheltenham: Edward Elgar, 2001), pp. 315–486.

15 Gordon, *Modern History*, p. 235; Suzuki, 'History of Labour', pp. 174–75; Moore, *Japanese Workers and the Struggle for Power*, passim.

16 Gordon, *Modern History*, pp. 239–41; Price, *Japan Works*, pp. 72–97; Howard Schonberger, 'America's Cold War in Occupied Japan', *Diplomatic History*, 3

(1979), 249–72.

17 The term 'enterprise union' may be used in different ways. Fundamentally it denotes unions which organize workers within a single plant or company. Most such unions are affiliated to an external federation but control over members' dues, decision-making and selection of officials remains substantially within the enterprise union. In smaller firms and workplaces, there may be less autonomy. Enterprise unions typically recruit manual and white-collar regular employees. See D. Hugh Whittaker, 'Labour Unions and Industrial Relations in Japan: Crumbling Pillar or Forging a "Third Way"', *Industrial Relations Journal*, 24 (1998), 280–94 (pp. 281–82). Today the term carries connotations of collaboration with management to further company objectives and insertion into a pattern of labour-management relations centred on quality circles, lean production, continuous improvement and lifelong employment. In that context, a distinction must be made between enterprise unions before and after World War II, and more specifically before and after the 1950s. Before the war, enterprise unions consisted solely of manual workers and many, by no means all, were independent and militant. Change emerged from the postwar struggles. See Kazuo Nimura, 'Kigyobetsu kumiai no rekishiteki haikei' / 'Enterprise Unionism: The Historical Background', *Kenkyu Shiryo Geppo / Monthly Research Bulletin*, Hosei University, 305 (1984), translated by Terry Boardman and published on line at: http://oohara.mt.tama.hosei.ac.jp/nk/English/eg-enterpriseunion.html, accessed 18 June 2009.

18 Price, *Japan Works*, pp. 122–26; Andrew Gordon, 'The Emergence of a Labor-Management Settlement in Japan, 1945–1960', *International Labor and Working-Class History*, 50 (1996), 133–39 (pp. 134–36); idem, 'Contests for the Workplace', in Gordon, *Postwar Japan as History*, pp. 373–93.

19 Gordon. 'Labor-Management Settlement', pp. 134–35; *The Other Japan: Conflict, Compromise and Resistance since 1945*, ed. by Joe Moore (Armonk: M.E. Sharpe, 1996); Sheldon Garon and Mike Mochizuki, 'Negotiating Social Contracts', in Gordon, *Postwar Japan as History*, pp. 145–66.

20 Price, *Japan Works*, pp. 191–218; Yoichi Hirai, *Mitsui sogi / The Mitsui Dispute* (Kyoto: Minerva-shobo, 2000).

21 Gordon, *Modern History*, pp. 286–88; Garon and Mochizuki, 'Negotiating Social Contracts', pp. 157–163; Suzuki, 'History of Labour', p. 190. By 1990, union density in Japan had declined to around 25 per cent of the labour force (ibid.).

22 Mre benign accounts such as Ronald Dore, *British Factory, Japanese Factory: The Origins of National Diversity in Industrial Relations* (Berkeley: University of California Press, 1973) and Martin Kenney and Richard Florida, *Beyond Mass Production* (Oxford: Oxford University Press, 1993), may be contrasted with Brinton, *Women and the Economic Miracle*, and Price, *Japan Works*. For a critical assessment in Japanese, see *Sengo rodo kumiai undo shi ron / The History of Trade Unionism in the Post-War Period*, ed. by Shinzo Shimizu (Tokyo: Nihonhyoronsha, 1982).

23 Kazuo Okochi, *Reimeiki no nihon rodo undo / The Early Japanese Labour Movement* (Tokyo: Iwanami-shoten, 1952); idem, *Nihon no rodo kumiai / Japanese Trade Unions* (Tokyo: Toyokeizaishinposha, 1954); idem, *Labour in*

Modern Japan (Tokyo: Government Printing Bureau, 1958); Kazuo Nimura, 'The Ashio Riot of 1907: The Traditional Miners' Brotherhood, the Trade Union, the Hamba System and the Company', in *Sozialgeschichte des Bergbau im 19 und 20 Jahrhundert*, ed. by Klaus Tenfelde (Munich: Verlag H. Beck, 1992), pp. 789–808 (pp. 792–94).

24 Yoshio Otomo, Shokichi Endo, Naomichi Funahashi, Wakao Fujita and Kiyoshi Ojima, *Toitsuteki rodo undo no tenbo / Prospects of the Unified Labour Movement* (Tokyo: Rodohoritsujunposha, 1952).

25 Naomitchi Funahashi, *Nihon no rodo kumiai / Japanese Trade Unions* (Tokyo; Toyokeizaishinposha, 1954).

26 Wakao Fujita, '"Kigyobetsu kumiai ron" to sono "hihan" ni tsuite' / 'On Enterprise Unionism and its Critics', *Shakai-seisaku Gakkai Nenpo / Annals of the Society for the Study of Social Policy*, 4 (1956), 9–37.

27 Masao Maruyama, 'Patterns of Individuation and the Case of Japan: A Conceptual Scheme', in *Japanese Attitudes Towards Modernization*, ed. by Marius B. Jansen (Princeton: Princeton University Press, 1965), pp. 489–531.

28 Moritaro Yamada, *Nihon shihonshugi bunseki / The Analysis of Japanese Capitalism* (Tokyo: Iwanami-shoten, 1934). They were referred to as 'the lecture school' because of their multi-volume expositions of 'the two-stages theory'.

29 See for example, Itsuro Sakisaka, *Marukusu keizaigaku no hoho / The Methodology of Marxist Economics* (Tokyo: Iwanami-shoten, 1959); *Nihon no seikatsusuijun / The Standard of Living in Japan*, ed. by Hiromi Arisawa (Tokyo: Tokyo University Press, 1954), both of which were in the tradition of the *Ronoha*; and Shiso Hattori, *Zettaishugi no shitekitenkai / The Historical Development of Absolutism* (Tokyo: Fukumurashuppan, 1974) which represented a continuation of the pre-war *Kozaha*.

30 Kazuo Okochi, 'Kigyobetsu kumiai no rekishiteki kento' / 'A Historical Study of Enterprise Unionism', *Rodo undoshi kenkyu / Labour History Review*, 15 (1959), 1–11; idem, *Roshikankeiron no shiteki hatten / The Historical Development of Labour Management Relations* (Tokyo: Yuhikaku, 1972). See also Ko Takahashi, *Nihonteki roshikankei no kenkyu / Studies in Japanese Labour-Management Relations* (Tokyo: Miraisha, 1965); Nimura, 'Enterprise Unionism'.

31 Mikio Sumiya, *Nihon chin-rodo shiron / The History of Japanese Wage-Labour* (Tokyo: Tokyo University Press, 1955); Toru Watanabe, *Nihon rodo kumiai undoshi / The History of the Japanese Trade Union Movement* (Tokyo: Aoki-shoten, 1954); Mikio Sumiya, 'Sangyohatten to rodo kumiai' / 'The Development of Industry and Trade Unions', in *Sangyo to rodo kumiai / Industry and Trade Unions*, ed. by Mikio Sumiya (Tokyo: Daiamondosha, 1959); Etsuro Yajima, 'Kigyobetsu kumiai no seisei yoin' / 'Factors Generating Enterprise Unions', *Rodo undoshi kenkyu / Labour History Review*, 26 (1961), 1–15; Ryuji Komatsu, 'Senzen ni okeru kigyobetsu rodo kumiai no hassei yoin wo megutte' / 'Factors Influencing Enterprise Unionism in Pre-war Japan', *Mita Gakkai Zasshi / Mita Journal of Economics*, Keio University, 56, 10 (1963), 96–106; Kanae Iida, 'Shoki rodo kumiai soshiki no kokusaiteki hikaku no mondai' / 'International Comparisons of the Formation of Early Trade

Unions', *Mita Gakkai Zasshi / Mita Journal of Economics*, Keio University, 58, 2 (1965), 1–26.

32 Yo Nakanishi, 'Nihon ni okeru jukogyo daikeisei no seisei katei: bakumatsu nagasaki seitetsujo to sono "roshi" kankei' (1), (2), (3) / 'The Birth of Heavy Industry in Japan: The Nagasaki Iron Works, 1857–1867, and its Industrial Relations', parts 1, 2 and 3, *Keizaigaku ronshu / The Journal of Economics*, Tokyo University, 35, 1 (1969), 23–68; 35, 2 (1969), 18–56; 35, 3 (1969), 48–98; idem, *Nihon kindaika no kisokatei: nagasaki zosenjo to sono roshi kankei*, 3 vols / *The Process of Modernization in Japan: Nagasaki Iron Works and its Industrial Relations* (Tokyo: Tokyo University Press, 1982–2003).

33 Makoto Ikeda, *Nihon kikaiko kumiai seiritsu shiron / The Formation of the Ironworkers' Union in Japan* (Tokyo: Nihonhyoronsha, 1970); Tsutomu Hyodo, *Nihon ni okeru roshikankei no tenkai / The Development of Industrial Relations in Japan* (Tokyo: Tokyo University Press, 1971); Izutaro Suehiro, *Nihon rodo kumiai undoshi / Japanese Trade Unionism: Past and Present* (Tokyo: Nihon Rodo Kumiai Undoshi Kankokai, 1950).

34 Nimura, 'Japan', pp. 695–97. Meritocratic attitudes were sometimes contrasted with the 'them and us' solidarity of British workers.

35 Takayoshi Matsuo, *Taisho Demokurashi no kenkyu / The Study of Taisho Democracy* (Tokyo: Aoki-shoten, 1966); Toru Watanabe, 'Yuaikai no soshiki no jittai' / 'How the Yuaikai Really Organized', *Jimbun Gakuho / Journal of Human Science*, Kyoto University, 18 (1963), 1–70.

36 See, for example, Kazuo Nimura, 'Kigyobetsu kumiai no rekishiteki kenkyu' / 'The Historical Background of Enterprise Unions', *Kenkyu Shiryo Geppo / Monthly Research Bulletin*, Hosei University, 305 (1984), 2–22; idem, 'Nihon roshikankei no rekishiteki tokushitsu' / 'The Historical Background of Labour Relations in Japan', *Shakai-seisaku Gakkai Nenpo / Annals of the Society for the Study of Social Policy*, 31 (1987), 77–95 translated by Terry Boardman and published online at: http://oohara.mt.tama.hosei.ac.jp/nk/English/eg-hischarjlr.html, accessed 18 June 2009.

37 Hiroshi Hazama, *Nihon romu kanrishi kenkyu / The History of Labour Management in Japan* (Tokyo: Daiamondosha, 1964). See n. 2.

38 Ibid.

39 Ryuji Komatsu, *Kigyobetsu kumiai no seisei / The Creation of Enterprise Unions* (Tokyo: Ochanomizu-shobo, 1971).

40 Large, 'Perspectives on the Failure of the Labor Movement', p. 25.

41 Thomas C. Smith, *Political Change and Industrial Development in Japan* (Stanford: Stanford University Press, 1955); idem, *Agrarian Origins of Modern Japan* (Stanford: Stanford University Press, 1970), demonstrated the key role of the state in industrialization.

42 Scalapino, *Early Japanese Labor Movement*; idem, *Democracy and the Party Movement in Prewar Japan* (Berkeley: University of California Press, 1953).

43 Scalapino, *Early Japanese Labor Movement*, p. 263.

44 Robert Scalapino, *The Japanese Communist Party, 1920–1966* (Berkeley: University of California Press, 1967); see also Beckmann and Okubo, *Japanese Communist Party*.

45 Totten, *Social Democratic Movement*; Cole et al., *Socialist Parties*.

46 James C. Abegglen, *Management and the Worker: The Japanese Solution* (Glencoe: The Free Press, 1958); Solomon B. Levine, *Industrial Relations in Postwar Japan* (Urbana: University of Illinois Press, 1958); Alice H. Cooke, *An Introduction to Japanese Trade Unionism* (Ithaca: Cornell University Press, 1966). And see a little later, Robert E. Cole, *Japanese Blue Collar: The Changing Tradition* (Berkeley: University of California Press, 1971); Donald R. Thurston, *Teachers and Politics in Japan* (Princeton: Princeton University Press, 1973); Benjamin Duke, *Japan's Militant Teachers: A History of the Left-Wing Teachers' Movement* (Honolulu: University of Hawaii Press, 1973).

47 For example, Okochi, Karsh and Levine, *Workers and Employers in Japan.*

48 A bibliography of writings by the *minshushi* historians is appended to Carol Gluck's excellent survey, 'The People in History: Recent Trends in Japanese Historiography', *Journal of Asian Studies*, 38 (1978), 25–50.

49 See n. 98.

50 Eiichi Eguchi, *Gendai no 'teishotokuso': hinkon kenkyu no hoho*, 3 vols / *The Methodology of Research on 'Poverty'* (Tokyo: Miraisha, 1979–80); Yuji Kato, *Gendai nihon ni okeru fuanteishugyo rodosha*, 2 vols / *The Peripheral Workers* (Tokyo: Ochanomizu-shobo, 1980–82); Kiyoshi Nakagawa, *Nihon no toshi kaso / The Underclass in Japanese Cities* (Tokyo: Keiso-shobo, 1985); Hirosuke Kawanishi, *Sengo nihon no sogi to ningen / Strikes and the People in Post-War Japan* (Tokyo: Nihonhyoronsha, 1986).

51 Nimura's critical views are accessible in his *Ashio Riot of 1907*: see, for example, pp. 4–5, 43–44. See also idem, 'Enterprise Unionism'; idem, 'Nihon roshikankei no rekishiteki tokushitsu' / 'The Historical Background of Labor Relations in Japan'.

52 Kazuo Nimura, 'Ashio bodo no kiso katei: "dekasegigata" ron ni taisuru ichi hihan' / 'On the Objective Conditions of the Ashio Mine Riot, 1907', *Hogaku-Shirin / Review of Law and Political Sciences*, Hosei University, 52, 1 (1959), 30–96.

53 Kazuo Nimura, *Ashio bodo no shiteki bunseki / The Historical Analysis of the Ashio Riot* (Tokyo: Tokyo University Press, 1988); idem, *Ashio Riot of 1907*: see n. 4. The translation eliminated some material in the original and contained a new Introduction, Prologue and Epilogue. An English version of chapter 3, omitted from the translation, is available online at: http://oohara.mt.tama.hosei.ac.jp/nk/English/eg-ashio-3-0.html.

54 Nimura, *Ashio Riot of 1907*, p. 206.

55 Andrew Gordon, 'Editor's Preface', *Ashio Riot*, p. xv.

56 For information on the Institute, see *Keizai to Keizaigaku / Journal of the Faculty of Economics*, Tokyo Metropolitan University, 82 (1997), 31–48; 'History of the Ohara Institute for Social Research', at: http://oohara.mt.tama.hosei.ac.jp/english/history-e.html.

57 Naoki Tanaka, *Kindai nihon tanko rodoshi kenkyu / The History of Labour in Coalmining in Modern Japan* (Tokyo: Sohukan, 1984); Hiroshi Ichihara, *Tanko no rodoshakaishi / A Labour and Social History of Coal Mining* (Tokyo: Tagashuppan, 1997).

58 Yasushi Miwa, *Nihon fashizumu to rodo undo / Japanese Fascism and the Labour Movement* (Tokyo: Azekura-shobo, 1988); Hiroshi Yasuda, *Taisho*

demokurashi shiron / *The History of Taisho Democracy* (Tokyo: Azekura-shobo, 1994).

59 Ibid.

60 Hideo Totsuka, 'Nihon teikokushugi no hokai to "inyu chosenjin" rodosha' / 'The Collapse of Japanese Imperialism and "Imported" Korean Workers', in *Nihon roshikankei shiron* / *The History of Industrial Relations in Japan*, ed. by Mikio Sumiya (Tokyo: Tokyo University Press, 1977), pp. 189–261. See also Kyungshik Pak, *Chosenjin kyoseirenko no kiroku* / *Korean Forced Labour in Japan* (Tokyo: Miraisha, 1965).

61 On the Ainu, see, for example, Susumu Emori, *Ainu minzoku no rekishi* / *The History of the Ainu* (Tokyo: Sohukan, 2007); for the Buraku, see Hiroshi Watanabe, *Mikaiho buraku no keisei to hatten* / *The Formation and Development of Unemancipated Buraku* (Tokyo: Yoshikawakobunkan, 1977).

62 Yutaka Nishinarita, *Zainichi chosenjin no 'sekai' to 'teikoku' kokka* / *The 'World' of Koreans in Japan and the 'Imperial' State* (Tokyo: Tokyo University Press, 1997); idem, *Chugokujin kyoseirenko* / *Chinese Forced Labour in Japan* (Tokyo: Tokyo University Press, 2002); idem, *Kindai nihon rodoshi: rodoryoku hensei no ronri to jissho* / *Labour History of Modern Japan: The Logic and Verification of Labour-force Formation* (Tokyo: Yuhikaku, 2007). See also Toru Sugihara, *Chugokujin kyoseirenko* / *Chinese Forced Labour in Japan* (Tokyo: Iwanami-shoten, 2002).

63 Kiyoshi Inoue, *Nihon joseishi* / *The History of Women in Japan* (Tokyo: Sanichi-shobo, 1949; 2nd edn 1967); Sayoko Yoneda, *Kindai nihon joseishi* / *The History of Women in Modern Japan* (Tokyo: Shinnihonshuppansha, 1972); Haruko Wakita, *Nihon joseishi* / *The History of Women in Japan* (Tokyo: Yoshikawakobunkan, 1987).

64 Yuki Sakurai and Noriyo Hayakawa, *Josei to undo* / *Women and their Movement* (Tokyo: Yoshikawakobunkan, 1998).

65 *Nihon joseishi sosho* / *Collected Documents of Japanese Women's History*, 23 vols, ed. by Shoichiro Kami and Tomoko Yamazaki (Tokyo: Kuresushuppan, 2007–8).

66 Sakuro Omae, *Rodoshi kenkyu* / *The Study of Labour History* (Kyoto: Keibunsha, 1983); Makoto Ikeda, *Rodoshi no shodanmen* / *Aspects of Labour History* (Kyoto: Keibunsha, 1990).

67 Eiji Takemae, *Sengo rodo kaikaku: GHQ rodo seisakushi* / *The Post-War Reform of Labour: America's Policy in Japan* (Tokyo: Tokyo University Press, 1982).

68 Moore, *Japanese Workers and the Struggle for Power*, p. xiv. For debates on the occupation, see Carol Gluck, 'Entangling Illusions: Japanese and American Views of the Occupation', in *New Frontiers in American-East Asian Relations: Essays Presented to Dorothy Borg*, ed. by Warren I. Cohen (New York: Columbia University Press, 1983), pp. 169–236.

69 Much of the English language literature since the 1970s has to be read against the influential work of the British sociologist, Ronald Dore – see n. 22, and idem, *Taking Japan Seriously: A Confucian Perspective on Leading Economic Issues* (Stanford: Stanford University Press, 1987). Dore argued that employers were converted to the Japanese system, which embodied Confucian conceptions of harmony, by the 1920s and were thus able to shape a weak and

fluid trade unionism. After 1945 they reconstructed industrial relations in a welfarist mould, which merited world-wide emulation.

70 Large, *Organized Workers and Socialist Politics.*

71 Gordon, *Evolution of Labor Relations.*

72 Gordon, *Labor and Imperial Democracy.*

73 Gordon, *Wages of Affluence.* See also Gary Dean Allinson, 'The Moderation of Labour in Postwar Japan', *Journal of Japanese Studies*, 1 (1975), 409–36.

74 Garon, *State and Labor in Modern Japan.*

75 Michael Lewis, *Rioters and Citizens: Mass Protest in Imperial Japan* (Berkeley: University of California Press, 1990).

76 Norma J. Chalmers, *Industrial Relations in Japan: The Peripheral Workforce* (London: Routledge, 1989).

77 Price, *Japan Works.*

78 *Japan's Minorities: The Illusion of Homogeneity*, ed. by Michael Weiner (London: Routledge, 1997).

79 Makoto Kumazawa, *Portraits of the Japanese Workplace: Labour Movements, Workers and Managers* (Boulder: Westview Press, 1996).

80 Hirosuke Kawanishi, *The Human Face of Industrial Conflict in Japan* (London: Kegan Paul International, 1999).

81 Large, *Organized Workers and Socialist Politics*; Totten, *Social Democratic Movement.*

82 Cole et al., *Socialist Parties in Postwar Japan*; Sarah Hyde, *The Transformation of the Japanese Left: From Old Socialists to New Democrats* (London: Routledge, 2009).

83 Beckman and Okubo, *Japanese Communist Party*; Scalapino, *Japanese Communist Party*; see also Rodger Swearingen and Paul Langer, *Red Flag in Japan: International Communism in Action, 1919–1951* (Cambridge, MA: Harvard University Press, 1952); Mahito Tanaka, *1930 nendai no nihon kyosanto shiron / The History of the Japanese Communist Party in the 1930s* (Tokyo: Sanichi-shobo, 1994).

84 Sandra Wilson, 'The Comintern and the Japanese Communist Party', in *International Communism and the Communist International, 1919–1943*, ed. by Tim Rees and Andrew Thorpe (Manchester: Manchester University Press, 1998), pp. 285–307; Tetsuro Kato, *Mosukuwa de shukusei sareta nihonjin / The Japanese Purged in Moscow* (Tokyo: Aokishoten, 1994).

85 Peter Berton, 'The Japanese Communist Party and its Transformations', *JPRI Working Paper*, 67 (2000), (Japan Policy Research Institute, University of San Francisco); idem, 'The Chinese and Japanese Communist Parties: Three Decades of Discord and Reconciliation, 1966–1998', *Communist and Post-Communist Studies*, 37 (2004), 361–72; see also Hirotake Koyama, *Sengo nihon kyosantoshi / The Japanese Communist Party in the Post-war Period* (Tokyo: Hagashoten, 1966).

86 Wakizo Hosoi, *Joko Aishi / The Pitiful History of Female Factory Workers* (Tokyo: Kaizosha, 1925).

87 Okochi, *Labour in Modern Japan*, p. 20; Hiroshi Hazama, 'Historical Changes in the Life Style of Industrial Workers', in *Japanese Industrialization and Social Consequences*, ed. by Hugh Patrick (Berkeley: University of California Press,

1976), pp. 21–51 (p. 41).

88 Tsurumi, *Factory Girls.*

89 Barbara Molony, 'Activism amongst Women in the Taisho Cotton Industry', in *Recreating Japanese Women, 1600–1945*, ed. by Gail Lee Bernstein (Berkeley: University of California Press, 1991), pp. 217–38.

90 Yoshiko Miyake, 'Doubling Expectations: Motherhood and Women's Factory Work under State Management in Japan in the 1930s and 1940s', in Bernstein, *Recreating Japanese Women*, pp. 267–95.

91 See the essays in *Japanese Women Working*, ed. by Janet Hunter (London: Routledge, 1993); idem, *Women and the Labour Market in Japan's Industrializing Economy.*

92 *Reflections on the Way to the Gallows: Rebel Women in Prewar Japan*, trans. and ed. by Mikiso Hane (Berkeley: University of California Press, 1988); Helen McNaughtan, *Women, Work and the Japanese Economic Miracle: The Case of the Cotton Textile Industry, 1945–1975* (London: Routledge Curzon, 2005); Elyssa Faison, *Managing Women, Disciplining Labour in Modern Japan* (Berkeley: University of California Press, 2007).

93 Brinton, *Women and the Economic Miracle*; Alice Lam, *Women and Japanese Management: Discrimination and Reform* (London: Routledge, 1992).

94 Vera Mackie, *Creating Socialist Women in Japan: Gender, Labour and Activism, 1900–1957* (Cambridge: Cambridge University Press, 1997).

95 Price, *Japan Works*, p. 35.

96 Particularly in relation to Nimura's *Ashio Riot*, but Gordon has also translated other seminal work such as Kumazawa's *Portraits* (see n. 79) and is an indefatigable reviewer.

97 Kazuo Nimura, review of Stephen E. Marsland, *The Birth of the Japanese Labor Movement*, in *International Review of Social History*, 36 (1991), 440–42 (p. 442).

98 For example, Eric Hobsbawm's *Labouring Men* (1st pub. 1964) was translated into Japanese in 1968 by Mikihisa Suzuki and Yoshio Nagai as *Igirisu rodoshi kenkyu* (Kyoto: Mineruva-shobo, 1968), but Thompson's *The Making of the English Working Class* (1st pub. 1963) only appeared in 2003 as *Ingurando rodosha kaikyu no keisei*, trans. by Hideo Ichihashi and Kenichi Haga (Tokyo: Seikyusha, 2003).

99 Takao Matsumura, 'Igirisu Sangyokakumeiki no seikatsu suijun' / 'The Standard of Living during the Industrial Revolution', *Mita Gakkai Zasshi / Mita Journal of Economics*, Keio University, 63, 12 (1970), 25–37; Chuhei Sugiyama and Takao Matsumura, *Igirisu sangyokakumei to rodosha no jotai / The British Industrial Revolution and the Condition of Workers* (Tokyo: Miraisha, 1972).

100 Kazuhiko Kondo translated Thompson's 'English Trade Unionism and Other Labour Movements before 1790' (1st pub. 1968) as '1790 nen izen no igirisu ni okeru shakai undo', *Shiso*, 663 (1979), 90–105, and his 'Folklore, Anthropology and Social History' (1st pub. 1977), as 'Minzokugaku, jinruigaku, shakaishi', *Shiso*, 757 (1987), 126–51; Takao Matsumura, *The Labour Aristocracy Revisited: The Victorian Flint Glass Makers, 1850–80* (Manchester: Manchester University Press, 1983); idem, 'Igirisu ni okeru rodo-kizoku ronso'/ 'Debates on the Labour Aristocracy in the U.K.', *Nihon rodo kyokai zassi / The Monthly*

Journal of the Japan Institute of Labour, 29, 11 (1987), 34–45; Akira Nakayama, *Igirisu no rodo-kizoku: 19 seiki ni okeru sono kaiso keisei / The British Labour Aristocracy: Its Formation in the Nineteenth Century* (Kyoto: Mineruva-shobo, 1988); Hideo Koga, 'Igirisu ni okeru History Workshop no katsudo' / 'History Workshop in England', *Rekishigakukenkyu / Journal of Historical Studies*, 461 (1978), 28–37; Takao Matsumura, 'Igirisu ni okeru shakaishi kenkyu to marukusushugi' / 'Social History and Marxist History in Britain', *Rekishigakukenkyu / Journal of Historical Studies*, 532 (1984), 15–27.

101 Chushichi Tsuzuki, *H.M. Hyndman and British Socialism* (Oxford: Clarendon Press, 1961); idem, *The Life of Eleanor Marx 1855–1898: A Socialist Tragedy* (Oxford: Clarendon Press, 1967); idem, *Tom Mann, 1856–1941: The Challenges of Labour* (Oxford: Clarendon Press, 1967); idem, *Edward Carpenter 1844–1929: Prophet of Human Fellowship* (Cambridge: Cambridge University Press, 1980).

102 *Igirisu shakaishugi shisoshi / The History of British Socialist Thought*, ed. by Chushichi Tsuzuki (Tokyo: Sanseido, 1986).

103 For example, Hideo Totsuka, *Igirisu kojoho seiritsu shiron / The History of the Factory Acts in Britain* (Tokyo: Miraisha, 1966); Michio Koyama, *Igirisu kyuhinho shiron / The History of the British Poor Law* (Tokyo: Nihonhyoronshinsha, 1962); Mari Osawa, *Igirisu shakaiseisakushi / The History of British Social Policy* (Tokyo: Tokyo University Press, 1986); Norio Anpo, *Igirisu rodosha no hinkon to kyusai: kyuhinho to kojoho / The Relief of Working-Class Poverty: The British Poor Law and Factory Acts*, (Tokyo: Akashi-shoten, 2005).

104 For example, Hiroshi Koga, *Eikoku kikaisangyo roshikankeishi*, 2 vols / *The History of Industrial Relations in the British Engineering Industry* (Tokyo, Ochanomizu-shobo, 1997–98); Hideo Koga, *Chachisuto undo no kenkyu / The Study of Chartism* (Kyoto:Mineruva-shobo, 1975); Takao Matsumura, *Igirisu no tetsudo sogi to saiban: Tafu-veiru hanketsu no rodoshi / A Labour History of the Taff Vale Case* (Kyoto: Mineruva-shobo, 2005).

105 Kazuko Hukazawa, 'Yuai-kumiai to 1908-nen mukyoshutsu roreinenkinho' / 'The Attitudes of Friendly Societies Towards the Old Age Pension Act, 1908', *Hannan Ronshu / Bulletin of Hannan University*, 24, 4 (1989), 1–9.

106 For example, Kei Imai, *Igirisu josei undoshi:feminizumu to josei rodo undo no ketsugo / The History of the British Women's Movement: Feminism and the Labour Movement* (Tokyo: Nihonkeizai-hyoronsha, Tokyo, 1992); and Maki Omori, *Igirisu josei kantoku-shoku no shiteki kenkyu / The History of British Women Factory Inspectors* (Tokyo: Keio University Press, 2001).

11

Labour History Beyond Borders

Marcel van der Linden

The term 'labour history' has a dual meaning. Strictly speaking the concept refers to the history of the labour movement: parties, trade unions, cooperatives, strikes, and related phenomena. More broadly interpreted, the concept also denotes the history of the working classes: the development of labour relations, family life, mentalities, culture. This ambiguity seems characteristic of the term in English. In many other languages labour movement history and working-class history cannot be summed up in a single term.[1] Both 'broad' and 'narrow' labour history have their origins in the North Atlantic region. 'Broad' labour history is older than 'narrow' labour history. Broad labour history could be written as soon as capitalist development had advanced to a certain point and the need arose to situate historically the corresponding social changes in general and the 'social question' in particular. Projects along these lines were undertaken in the aftermath of the European 1848 revolutions, and perhaps even earlier.[2]

'Narrow' labour history began to develop only in the 1870s and 1880s. Political as well as theoretical factors contributed to its rise. Politically, it was significant that labour movements began to be visible on a national scale from the late 1860s onwards. The British Trades Union Congress was established in 1868. Soon other national trade union federations followed: for example, the Canadian Labour Union Congress (1883) and the American Federation of Labor (1886). In Western Europe a major chronological clustering happened in the years 1888–99. In this same period the rise of working-class parties began. The German Social Democracy was the first in the field in 1875. It was followed in most Western European and the North American countries in the subsequent thirty years.

At the same time that these developments made clear to everyone that labour movements had come to stay, a theoretical obstacle was also removed. For most of the nineteenth century the doctrine of the 'wage fund' had possessed broad support among economists and other social scientists. According to this theory there exists a 'natural wage', which collective economic action is incapable of influencing. This standpoint was perhaps best known in the form of the 'iron law of wages' as propagated in the 1860s by the German workers' leader Ferdinand Lassalle, who used it as an argument for political action instead of trade union action. The fact that not only most intellectuals but also substantial groups of workers saw the 'natural wage' theory as plausible was doubtless related to the many defeats with which nineteenth-century strikes often ended, and to the fragility and brief life span of existing labour organizations. In the early 1870s, the wage-fund theory began to lose its credibility. The most significant turning point was an essay by John Stuart Mill in which he broke with the concept.[3] There had, of course, been earlier critics, but until then the impact of their criticisms had been limited. Clearly the time was ripe for this turnaround because within a few years many intellectuals in Europe and North America supported this paradigm shift.[4] Various explanations have been given for this willingness to change standpoint, but evidently the consolidation of the British union movement played a role in it.[5]

This combination of political and theoretical shifts provided sufficient reason for a number of scholars to concern themselves with labour movement history. These labour historians generally belonged to the political left; most of them were socialists or socially conscious liberals or Christians. The work of two economists proved epoch-making: in Europe Lujo von Brentano, who published *On the History and Development of Gilds, and the Origins of Trade Unions* in 1870, and in North America Richard T. Ely, whose *The Labor Movement in America* appeared sixteen years later.[6] From the 1880s onwards, economic historians, who were interested in the evolution of wages and prices, came to the aid of both a 'narrow' and a 'broad' labour history. An early but still much valued work in this field was James E. Thorold Rogers's book on the evolution of wages in England since the thirteenth century.[7] In the late 1880s, the foundations were laid for labour history in all its basic forms.

Eurocentrism and methodological nationalism

In nineteenth-century Europe and North America, the emerging field of labour history was characterized from the beginning by a combination of methodological nationalism and Eurocentrism, a combination which only very recently has become a topic of debate. Methodological nationalism –

not to be confused with *political* nationalism -- links society and the state together, and therefore considers the different nation states as a kind of 'Leibnizean Monads' for historical research. Eurocentrism is the mental ordering of the world from the standpoint of the North Atlantic region: from this perspective, the 'modern' period begins in Europe and North America, and extends step by step to the rest of the world; the temporality of this 'core region' determines the periodization of developments in the rest of the world. Historians reconstructed the history of the working classes and workers' movements in France, Britain and the United States as separate developments. Insofar as they paid attention to the social classes and movements in Latin America, Africa or Asia, these were interpreted according to North-Atlantic schemes.

That is not to say that labour historians did not look beyond national borders. Of course they did, and early on. But the approach nevertheless remained monadologic: the 'civilized' North Atlantic ('Greater European') world was regarded as consisting of peoples who all developed in more or less the same direction, albeit each with a different tempo. One nation was regarded as more advanced than another, and that is why the more backward nations could see their future more or less reflected in the leading nations.

In the course of the twentieth century, attention to reciprocal influences between separate peoples increased, even though those separate peoples remained the fundamental units of analysis. From James Guillaume (1905–10) via G.D.H. Cole (1956) to Julius Braunthal (1961–71),[8] international organizations of the labour movement were interpreted as collaborative ties between workers who represented different countries, associations of patriots with different fatherlands – an interpretation which thrived in the movement itself.[9] And in studies of international labour migration, the migrants were perceived as people who either preserved the culture of their country of origin or assimilated in the culture of the country to which they had emigrated.

Methodological nationalists are the victims of two important intellectual errors. Fundamentally, they naturalize the nation state. By this I mean that they consider the nation state as the basic analytical unit for historical research. Even although they recognize that nation states only flourished in the nineteenth and twentieth centuries, they nevertheless still interpret older history as the *prehistory* of the later nation state and consider cross-border or border-subverting processes as distractions from the 'pure' model. We are therefore dealing with a teleology.

There are three variants of *Eurocentrism* I should mention. The *first* variant is simply *neglect*: attention is only paid to one part of the world; and the author assumes that the history of 'his piece of the world' can be written without considering the rest. This attitude is well expressed by the popular distinction between 'the West' and 'the Rest', mentioned by Samuel Huntington and others. The *second* variant is *prejudice*: the authors do consider global connections, but nevertheless believe that Greater Europe (including North America and Australasia) 'shows the way'. This Eurocentrism is especially evident among modernization theorists.[10] Robert Nisbet characterized this approach to development as follows:

> Mankind is likened to a vast procession, with all, or at least a very large number of peoples made into the members of the procession. [...] Naturally, Western Europe and its specific, historically acquired pattern of economic, political, moral, and religious values was regarded as being at the head, in the vanguard, of the procession. All other peoples, however rich in their own civilization, such as China and India, were regarded as, so to speak, 'steps' in a procession that would some day bring them too into the fulfilment of development that was the sacred West.[11]

The third variant consists of *empirical beliefs*. This is the variant which is most difficult to recognize and combat. We are dealing here with scientific viewpoints which seemingly have been confirmed time and again by research. Empirical Eurocentrists make assertions because they think that all of this is *fact*. They believe, for instance, that trade unions are always most effective if they concentrate on some form of collective bargaining. This, they think, has been proven repeatedly. Historians defending such a view would emphatically deny that they harbour any Eurocentric prejudices; indeed, very few of them actually do hold such prejudices. As the late Jim Blaut wrote: 'Eurocentrism, [...] is a very complex thing. We can banish all the value meanings of the word, all the prejudices, and we still have Eurocentrism as a set of empirical beliefs.'[12] Attacking the first two variants (neglect and prejudice) is relatively straightforward, but the third variant presents a bigger obstacle. Lucien Febvre already formulated it half a century ago: 'Any intellectual category we may forge in the workshops of the mind is able to impose itself with the same force and the same tyranny – and holds even more stubbornly to its existence than the machines made in our factories.'[13]

The new labour history

Within this framework of Eurocentrism and methodological nationalism, substantive historiographical innovation was quite possible. In the 1960s we see the beginnings of the so-called 'new labour history', with E.P. Thompson's *The Making of the English Working Class* as a landmark publication. This great book, by emphasizing culture and consciousness, integrated broad and narrow labour history, once its message was assimilated. In the English-speaking world, Thompson's book was the most important signpost which marked the transition from the so-called 'old labour history' to the new.[14] A broad consensus exists nowadays about the nature of the transition.[15] The old labour history was institutional, focused on the description of organizational developments, political debates, leaders and strikes. It was represented by Sidney and Beatrice Webb, the Wisconsin School of John Commons and others, but also by Marxists like Philip Foner. The new labour history attempted to *contextualize* workers' struggles. As Eric Hobsbawm put it, it accentuated 'the working classes as such [... and] the economic and technical conditions that allowed labour movements to be effective, or which prevented them from being effective'.[16]

The differences between 'old' and 'new' labour history are often exaggerated. In reality the 'old' labour history not infrequently gave attention to 'the working classes as such'. They are visible, for example, in John and Barbara Hammond's magnificent trilogy – *The Village Labourer* (1911), *The Town Labourer* (1917) and *The Skilled Labourer* (1919) – which covered approximately the same period as Thompson's *The Making of the English Working Class.* Even so, it cannot be denied that the new labour history of the 1970s and 1980s introduced a dramatic renewal of the discipline. Not just labour processes and everyday culture, but also gender, ethnicity, race and age finally gained the attention they deserve, along with household structures, sexuality, and informal politics. The new labour history marked a genuine intellectual revolution.

At the same time, however, the new labour history remained imprisoned in the old, limited, perspective. From a global point of view, there is something peculiar about *The Making*, something that probably was not noticed before, but which now, under different circumstances, commands our attention: Thompson reconstructs the process of class formation in England (in the period between 1792 and 1832) as a *self-contained process.* England is, according to his analysis, the logical unit of analysis – while external forces certainly influenced it, these are specifically portrayed as *foreign* influences. Thus, the French Revolution plays an important background role in Thompson's narrative, as a source of inspiration of working-class activities. But developments in the neighbouring countries always remain an 'externality'. Added to this is the fact that Thompson pays no attention in *The Making* to imperial connections. Colonialism, with its increasingly significant influence on the lives of the lower classes through the nineteenth century, is simply disregarded.

Peter Linebaugh and Marcus Rediker have pointed out that the London Corresponding Society (LCS), which plays such an important role in *The Making*, declared itself at its foundation in 1792 in favour of equality, whether 'black or white, high or low, rich or poor'. But in August that same year, the LCS declared: 'FELLOW CITIZENS, Of every rank and every situation in life, Rich, Poor, High or Low, we address you all as our Brethren.' Here, the phrase 'black or white' had disappeared. Linebaugh and Rediker persuasively argue that this sudden change of phrase must be explained with reference to the revolt in Haiti beginning shortly beforehand: 'Race had thus become a tricky and, for many, in England, a threatening subject, one that the leadership of the LCS now preferred to avoid.'[17] Such trans-Atlantic linkages cannot be found in Thompson's writing. Thompson's 'insular' approach is all the more surprising given that politically he was an internationalist, familiar from his childhood days with stories about British India, where his parents had lived for some time.[18] This example suggests that, despite its pathbreaking achievement, *The Making of the English Working Class* demonstrates important continuities between 'old' and 'new' labour history. This continuity is visible in the large majority of publications which tried to overcome the limitations of the old labour history.

Labour history outside the North Atlantic

Gradually, labour historiographies started to develop outside the North Atlantic region. Already in 1898 Mikhail Tugan-Baranovskii had published his history of the Russian factory; path-breaking work was also accomplished by Rajani Kanta Das who in the 1920s wrote a number of books on India and the Indian Diaspora. Another pioneer was Marjorie Ruth Clark, who a little later produced what was probably the first scholarly study of the Mexican labour movement.[19]

In the course of the twentieth century a number of trends emerged. First, labour history spread to the highly developed capitalist countries outside the North Atlantic area: Japan, Australia and New Zealand. In Japan the history of wage labour was neglected for years by 'bourgeois' as well as (the influential) Marxist scholars. The situation began to change in the 1960s, when a school of native historians strove to develop a history from below, a history of 'the ordinary people'. They produced narrative history and tended to romanticize the agrarian under-classes. In Australia, labour history has been flourishing since the 1960s, despite some ups and downs.[20]

Second, labour history burgeoned in states with 'already existing socialism', where it could be written from a Marxist-Leninist viewpoint only. Here labour history served as a science of legitimation, in which, as the Hungarian historian Emil Niederhauser has commented, 'paradoxically only the movement was seen, and the economic and social conditions were ignored or treated only in outline. There was much heroic struggle and many victims, which were not in vain as they produced in the last resort the happy present.'[21] Within this 'real socialist' context, different paths were possible: the Polish-Hungarian variant, in which important scientific innovation was permitted before the Communist collapse of 1989–90; the Russian route, with labour history enjoying an upsurge after 1956 which collapsed and was replaced by dogmatism within a decade; the Chinese road, marked by a crisis in the humanities, and in labour history, prompted by the transformation to capitalism 'from above'.[22] In all these cases, however, historians focused mainly on pre-revolutionary history, thereby avoiding political difficulties.[23] After the regime change of 1989–91 in Eastern Europe, labour history had a hard time, precisely because it was associated with party dictatorship.[24]

Third, and most importantly, there was a growth of labour history on the periphery and semi-periphery. The more countries in 'the South' developed working classes, the more scholarly interest in their activities and pasts increased.[25] Often such studies focused on the 'problems' that labour could cause industrialists and governments. But as soon as self-confidence in the 'Third World' began to grow, the achievements of labour movements attracted more attention. Naturally historians' political leanings could be very different. J. Norman Parmer's thorough *Colonial Labour Policy and Administration* (1960) for instance, which surveyed the rubber plantation industry in Malaya during the last decades before the Second World War, looked at workers through the eyes of entrepreneurs and authorities. Jean Chesneaux's *Le mouvement ouvrier en Chine de 1919 à 1927* (1962) was written from an 'official Communist' standpoint; while Guillermo Lora's *Historia del movimiento obrero boliviana* (1967–70) was a Trotskyist work.[26]

In several 'Southern' countries labour history boomed in the last years of the twentieth century. The development seems to have been most spectacular in Latin America, where, especially in the 1970s, discussion in North America and Europe prompted many historical studies on industrial labour. Interest soon spread from this base to encompass other non-elite groups: peasants, small businesses, indigenous peoples, the 'blacks' and the immigrants. John D. French has summarized this development:

> Those Latin American countries with strong workers' movements have long had a critical mass of labor studies scholarship, most notably Mexico, a world in itself but also Chile and Argentina. After the turbulent 1970s, the field also took off with particular strength and innovativeness in Brazil, Peru, and Ecuador. [...] Scholarship on labor has also shown sustained vigor in Bolivia, Colombia, Venezuela and Uruguay. The study of urban and rural labor has also gained visibility in the modestly-industrialized countries of Central America. In the Hispanic Caribbean, the study of labor has flourished in Puerto Rico while interesting work has been produced on Cuba as well as the Dominican Republic. As for the English-speaking Caribbean countries, still too often ignored, excellent work continues to appear that builds on the classic historical monographs written by Ken Post and Walter Rodney in the 1970s.[27]

The situation is equally remarkable in South Africa. There, too, an upturn in labour and working-class history commenced in the 1970s, albeit with a division between proponents of a 'narrow' (institutional) and a 'broad' (social and cultural) approach: 'Indeed, a bifurcation has developed within South African radical historiography: while labour history focuses on the workplace, industrial relations, and working-class organization, social history considers the fate of the working class and other oppressed groups outside of industrial production.'[28] The reason for this split lies in political developments after 1970. The new trade union movement felt the need to possess a 'personal' historiography, and 'some of the first efforts in labour history were prompted either directly by the needs of the new unions, or were clearly inspired by similar concerns'.[29] Simultaneously, another development was gaining ground: South African historians who had studied abroad, mainly in Great Britain, returned home and fostered a broader-based labour history. A symptom of this was the History Workshop Movement, which was inspired by the works of Raphael Samuel, Thompson and others.[30]

In India, where sections of the political elite are strongly influenced by the British university tradition, interest in labour history began to grow from the late 1960s.[31] Many of the first monographs were strongly traditional, even if some authors relatively early on began to link institutional aspects with the broad stream of social history.[32] A special impulse emanated in the 1980s from the so-called 'Subaltern Studies', of which Ranajit Guha was the main protagonist. This was a very politicized tendency; it concentrated on the history of poor and landless peasants, and produced some influential studies.[33] In the meantime it has lost most of its influence in South Asia but, paradoxically, has become popular amongst scholars in the Americas.[34] Alongside this new development emerged a third current, consisting of young historians interested in labour history, which distanced itself from Subaltern Studies and placed greater emphasis on workers and their families. This third contingent showed comparably more interest in infrastructural problems and also initiated the establishment of an archive for labour history.[35]

Apart from these developments within the global South, historians in Europe, North America and Australia evinced an interest as early as the 1950s in the workers' movement in Africa, Asia and Latin America. This attention, which originally owed a lot to the contexts of the Cold War and decolonization, was politically motivated by anti-Communist sentiment and the accompanying desire to investigate the degree of Communist influence on the working classes in those regions.[36] On the other hand, there were also socialist or Communist historians at that time who were working on the history of semi-colonized countries or of ex-colonies.[37] Somewhat later and under the influence of the international students' movement, young Japanologists, Sinologists and Africa experts became involved in the study of labour history in their specific geographical area of research. Several dissertations and monographs ensued.[38] While Communists and anti-Communists frequently restricted themselves to institutional questions, the followers of the 'New Left' usually preferred to research wider themes.

Second, in some countries which had witnessed the decline in the study of the institutional aspects of labour history, a continuity of sorts followed because scholars moved into neighbouring fields of social history, for example women's studies or research into ethnic groups and immigrants.

Organizations and networks

Since the late 1950s labour historians have been building organizations that further their interests and facilitate communication between them. This collection of essays commemorates fifty years of the British Society for the Study of Labour History. But its emergence was only part of a small wave of similar initiatives. In 1959 the Verein für Geschichte der Arbeiterbewegung (Association for Labour Movement History) was created in Austria. In 1961 the Australian Society for the Study of Labour History was established.[39] Since then, similar organizations have been formed in Canada, the United States, Sweden, Ireland and some other countries.

Outside the North Atlantic region, the real breakthrough, in terms of conferences and associations, is of very recent vintage. After an important early South African effort in 1977 – the History Workshop on labour history of that year – take-off occurred in 1996 with the founding of the Association of Indian Labour Historians, a dynamic organization which not only stages conferences every two years, but also engages in many other activities.[40] In 2000 *Mundos do Trabalho* was established as a network of labour historians within the Brazilian Historical Association.[41] The first conferences were held in Karachi (1999), Seoul (2001), and Yogyakarta (2005). A second South African conference took place in Johannesburg in 2006.[42]

In parallel to these national efforts, contacts between historians of different countries and continents intensified. From the nineteenth century, labour historians had been working together across borders to study the history of the 'Internationals' (First, Socialist and Communist), and how events like the Paris Commune or the Russian Revolution affected developments in many lands.[43] However, a *systematic* type of transnational communication between historians of labour seems to have commenced on a cautious note in the 1960s at the earliest, despite the pioneering work of the *Grünbergs Archiv* (1911–30) or the *International Review for Social History* (1936–40) published by the International Institute of Social History.[44] The exchange of opinion across borders was given institutional status in 1965, when the International Conference of Labour Historians (Internationale Tagung der Historiker der Arbeiterbewegung – ITH) was founded in Austria. The conferences held annually since then in Linz were unique in that historians from East and West met on an equal footing. But even before this singularity became redundant with the collapse of Communism in 1989, the dialogue in Linz had become arid, not least on account of the structural exigency to avoid controversy. Since the early 1990s the organizers have been trying to resolve the ITH's crisis through higher standards of quality.[45]

Symptomatic of the growth in international links was the establishment of the International Association of Labour History Institutions (IALHI) in 1970, or the issue, from 1972, of the USA-based *Newsletter: European Labor and Working-Class History* (since 1976 the journal *International Labor and Working-Class History*).

The rise of global labour history

When labour history spread out over the world, it maintained the Eurocentric and monadological approach. The 'peripheral' historians also focused on mineworkers, dockers or plantation workers and neglected families and households and the work that took place there. They, too, mainly sought out strikes, trade unions and political parties. And, most importantly, they used the development of the North Atlantic as a model that peripheral working classes did 'not yet' match.[46] Gradually, attempts were made to develop a less Eurocentric approach. Path-breaking works included Walter Rodney's histories of the Upper Guinea Coast and of the Guyanese working people (1970 and 1981), Charles van Onselen's *Chibaro* (1976) on mine labour in Southern Rhodesia and the essays collected in Ranajit Das Gupta's *Labour and Working Class in Eastern India* (1994) on plantation workers, miners and textile workers in Assam, Bengal and elsewhere.[47]

Eurocentric monadology was undermined in several parts of the world and from different sides – slowly at first, but more quickly in recent years. An initial cause was the rise of international comparative research, beginning in the North Atlantic region. Naturally, the comparative method was much older, and had already entered the humanities and the social sciences in the nineteenth century. In labour history there had been early examples, sometimes implicitly stated (as in Sombart's famous essay on the question 'Why is there no socialism in the United States?'), but on occasion also explicitly.[48] Since 1970 this type of study has proliferated enormously. But for a while comparative studies did not break with monadology, because they still saw countries as separate 'cases'. The perspective broadened, however, when it became clear that movements sometimes have strongly influenced one another, and that not only 'case studies' but studies of interactions and entanglements were essential.

The rise of labour history in the 'periphery' contributed to the disintegration of Eurocentric monadology. The nation-state was increasingly historicized, and thereby relativized, and Eurocentrism increasingly came under fire. These two subversive tendencies must be clearly distinguished, but they run more or less parallel to each other. Their appearance is linked to a series of changes which occurred since the Second World War, or in some cases started even earlier:

* Decolonization led to researchers in many new independent countries, especially in Africa and Asia, beginning to investigate their own social histories; in this way, labour history acquired not only an increasingly important 'peripheral' component (the number of monads expanded), but it also quickly became clear that peripheral history could not be written without constantly referring to metropolitan history.
* Transcontinental imagined communities developed, such as Pan-Africanism.

* In research about historical migration the insight dawned that the perspective of 'nation to ethnic enclave' misinterpreted the reality of migrant life, because migrants often live transculturally.
* The border cultures which were 'discovered' did not fit in the monadologic schema: for example, creolization.
* The same applied to transnational cycles of protests and strikes.

All these developments, plus the consequences of the contemporary wave of economic de-territorialization (globalization) such as proletarianization in the 'periphery', new forms of workers' protest, new labour movements, and the growing consciousness of worldwide interdependence (One World), seemed to demand a new type of historiography, one which 'overtakes' traditional labour history from North America and Europe by incorporating its findings in a new, globally orientated approach. That is, indeed, an extremely ambitious project which has scarcely begun. Many of the goals of this new departure need elucidation. We are in an exciting transitional situation, in which the discipline is engaged in re-inventing itself. 'Old' and 'new' labour history begin to give way to 'global' labour history.[49]

What does the term 'global labour history' refer to? Everyone can of course attach the meanings they like, but personally I mean the following:

(i) As far as *methodological status* is concerned, I would suggest an 'area of concern' is involved, rather than a theory to which everyone must adhere. We know and should accept the fact that our conceptions of research and our interpretive frameworks can differ. Not only is this pluralism inevitable, it can equally well be intellectually stimulating – provided we are at all times prepared to enter into a serious discussion of our disparate views. Notwithstanding our different points of departure, however, we must also strive to work productively in the same fields of research.

(ii) As regards *themes*, global labour history focuses on transnational and even transcontinental study of labour relations and workers' social movements in the broadest sense of the word. By 'transnational' I mean the placing in a wider context of all historical processes, no matter how geographically 'small', by means of comparison with processes elsewhere, the study of interaction processes, or a combination of the two. The study of labour relations encompasses work that is both free as well as unfree, paid as well as unpaid. Workers' social movements consist of both formal organizations and informal activities. The study of both labour relations and social movements requires that equally serious attention is devoted to 'the other side' (employers, public authorities). The study of labour relations concerns not only the individual worker but also his/her family. Gender relations play an important part within the family, and in labour relations involving individual family members.

(iii) As regards the *period* studied, I think that in global labour history there are in principle no limits in temporal perspective, although I would say that in practice the emphasis is on the study of labour relations and workers' social movements which have evolved along with the growth of the world market from the fourteenth century. Wherever indicated, for instance for comparative purposes, studies going back further in time should by no means be excluded.

This is, indeed, an extremely ambitious project which has just begun. Many of the goals of this new approach remain unclear or need further elucidation.

The need for new foundations

The development of global labour history will have to scale many hurdles in order to flourish. These obstacles include practical problems, such as the fact that in many countries of the Global South well-established institutions which actively build archives are absent.[50] I do not want to dwell on these technical difficulties now. Rather, I want to concentrate on the substantive challenges. Because the greatest obstacle we have is ourselves, with our traditional theories and interpretations. I have mentioned the two most important pitfalls already: methodological nationalism and Eurocentrism.

All core concepts of traditional labour history are primarily based on experiences in the North Atlantic region, and therefore should be critically reconsidered. This applies to the concept of 'labour' itself. In the most important Western languages (English, French, Spanish and Italian), a distinction is often made between 'labour' and 'work', in which 'labour' refers to toil and effort (as in 'women's labour'), while 'work' refers more to creative processes. This binary meaning – to which a philosopher like Hannah Arendt attached far-reaching analytical consequences – simply does not exist in many other languages, and sometimes there is even no single word for 'labour' or 'work', because these concepts abstract from the specific characteristics of separate labour processes.[51] We ought therefore to investigate carefully the extent to which the concepts 'labour' and 'work' are trans-culturally usable, or at the very least, we should define their content much more precisely than we are used to doing. Where does 'labour' begin, and where does it finish? How exactly do we draw the boundary between 'labour' and 'work', or is that boundary less obvious than is often assumed?

The concept of the 'working class' also merits critical survey. It looks like this term was invented in the nineteenth century to identify a group of so-called 'respectable' workers in contrast to slaves and other unfree labourers, the self-employed (the 'petty bourgeoisie') and impoverished outcasts, the lumpen-proletariat. For many reasons, which lack of space does not permit me to elaborate here, this interpretation is simply not appropriate in the Global South. The social groups which in the eyes of old and new labour history are quantitatively not significant exceptions which prove the rule – *are* the rule in large parts of Asia, Africa and Latin America. We will have to devise a new conceptualization which is less oriented to *exclusion* than *inclusion* of various dependent or marginalized groups of workers. We have to recognize that the creation of 'real' wage-workers, which were the centre of attention for Marx, i.e. workers who as free individuals can dispose of their own labour-power as their own commodity, and have no other commodity for sale, constitutes only one way in which capitalism transforms labour power into a commodity.[52] There are many other forms that demand equal attention, such as chattel slavery, indentured labour and sharecropping.[53]

The implication is that the disciplinary boundaries of labour history will have to be overcome, a process that is already taking place. The historiography of chattel slavery, which until recently was generally not taken into account by labour historians, overlaps significantly with global labour history. A similar point can be made about research fields such as the history of indentured labourers, for example, the Indian coolies who were employed in other parts of Asia, as well as in Australia, Fiji, Africa, and the Caribbean.

A broadened approach will allow us to take seriously those 'anomalies' which until now have been neglected, like the slaves for hire that existed in several parts of the world. Take for example the numerous so-called *ganhadores* in North-East Brazil in the mid-nineteenth century. Their masters had ordered these slaves to look for jobs, in towns such as the port of Bahia. The *ganhadores*, according to their historian João Reis:

> moved about freely in the streets looking for work. It was a common, although not general, practice for slaveowners to permit their slaves to live outside the master's home in rented rooms, sometimes with former slaves as their landlords. They only returned to the master's house to 'pay for the week', that is, to pay the weekly (and sometimes daily) sum agreed upon with their masters. They were able to keep whatever exceeded that amount.

In 1857 the *ganhadores* in Salvador struck for a week, using work groups based on ethnic affiliation as the backbone of mobilization.[54]

What this example shows, is that the boundaries of concepts like 'wage labour' and 'chattel slavery' can be extremely fuzzy. It is my contention that labour historians should use this fuzziness as a stimulus for rethinking the concept of the working class. The concept of the 'working class', which originated in nineteenth-century Europe, has been questioned more and more in the past decades. Historians and sociologists point out that the borderlines between 'free' wage labour, self-employment and unfree labour are not clearly defined and that the opposition between urban and rural labour should not be regarded as absolute. First, there are extensive and complicated grey areas full of transitional locations between the 'free' wage labourers and the slaves, the self-employed and the lumpen-proletarians. Second, almost all subaltern workers belong to households that combine several modes of labour. Third, individual subaltern workers can also combine different modes of labour, both synchronically and diachronically. Finally, the distinctions between the different kinds of subaltern workers are not clear-cut.

The implications are far-reaching. Apparently, there is a large class of people within capitalism whose labour power is commodified in various ways. I would like to call this class the *extended or subaltern working class*. Its members make up a very varied group: it includes chattel slaves, sharecroppers, small artisans and wage earners. It is the historic dynamics of this 'multitude' that we should try to understand. We have to consider that in capitalism there *always* existed, and probably will continue to exist, several forms of commodified labour subsisting side by side.

In its long development capitalism utilized many kinds of work relationships, some mainly based on economic compulsion, others with a strong non-economic component. Millions of slaves were brought by force from Africa to the Caribbean, to Brazil and the southern states of the USA. Contract workers from India and China were shipped off to toil in South Africa, Malaysia or South America. 'Free' migrant workers left Europe for the New World, for Australia or the colonies. And today sharecroppers produce an important portion of world agricultural output. These and other work relationships are synchronous, even if there seems to be a secular trend towards 'free wage labour'. Slavery still exists, sharecropping is enjoying a comeback in some regions. Capitalism could and can chose whatever form of commodified labour it thinks fit in a given historical context: one variant seems most profitable today, another tomorrow. If this argument is correct, then it behoves us to conceptualize the wage-earning class as one (important) kind of commodified labour among others. Consequently, so-called 'free' labour cannot be seen as the only form of exploitation suitable for modern capitalism but as one alternative among several.

The question that catches our attention is, of course, what all these different members of the extended working class have in common. Where is the dividing line between them and the other party, the capitalists and employers? Taking the ideas of the French-Greek philosopher Cornelius Castoriadis as a starting point, we could say that all subaltern workers exist in a state of 'instituted heteronomy'. For Castoriadis, instituted heteronomy is the opposite of social autonomy; it manifests itself as 'a mass of conditions of privation and oppression, as a solidified global, material and institutional structure of the economy, of power and of ideology, as induction, mystification, manipulation and violence.' Instituted heteronomy expresses and sanctions 'an antagonistic division of society and, concurrent with this, the power of one determined social category over the whole. [...] In this way, the capitalist economy – production, distribution, market, etc. – is alienating inasmuch as it goes along with the division of society into proletariat and capitalists.'[55]

We can become more specific by following a suggestion by another philosopher of history, G.A. Cohen. He has argued that 'lack of means of production is not as essential to proletarian status as is traditionally maintained. It is better to say that *a proletarian must sell his labour power in order to obtain his means of life.* He may own means of production, but he cannot use them to support himself save by contracting with a capitalist.'[56] Following Marx, Cohen understands the phrase 'must sell his labour power' in this context as economic compulsion, but if we also include physical compulsion, we come close to a clear demarcation. *Every carrier of labour power whose labour power is sold or hired out to another person under economic or non-economic compulsion belongs to the class of subaltern workers, regardless of whether the carrier of labour power is him- or herself selling or hiring it out and, regardless of whether the carrier him- or herself owns means of production.* All aspects of this provisional definition will require further reflection.

Such a reconceptualization and broadening of the notion of the working class will help us to better understand the many forms of resistance that have been used by subaltern workers over time. The classical approach suggests, for example, that strikes are a form of collective action that is associated especially with free wage labourers. But if we look at the ways in which protest is expressed and pressure is exerted by the different groups of subaltern workers (including slaves, the self-employed, the lumpen-proletarians and the 'free' wage labourers), these appear to overlap considerably. In the past, all kinds of subaltern workers went on strike. The sharecropping silver miners in Chihuahua protested as early as the 1730s against the termination of their work contracts by the owners of the mine. They entrenched themselves in the nearby hills. 'There they built a makeshift stone parapet, unfurled a banner proclaiming their defiance, and vowed to storm the villa of San Felipe, kill [the mine owner] San Juan y Santa Cruz, and burn his house to the ground. For the next several weeks they refused to budge from their mountain redoubt, where they passed time by composing and singing songs of protest.'[57] The miners returned only after mediation by a priest sent by the bishop. Slaves regularly went on strike too. Serfs in Russia refused 'to recognize their owner's authority over them'; they stopped working for him and decided 'to go on strike'.[58] On plantations in the British Caribbean in the early nineteenth century there were walkouts by slaves: 'The rebellions in Demerara in 1829 and Jamaica in 1831 both began as versions of the modern work strike, coupled with other acts of defiance, but not with killing. Only when the local militia retaliated with force, assuming that this was another armed uprising, did such an occurrence actually take place.'[59]

A broadened concept of the working class will enable us to rethink the strike phenomenon. By including slaves and indentured labourers, it becomes possible to see that the strike is a very important but also a specific form of collective refusal to work. So-called unfree workers have used other forms of collective refusal that deserve to be integrated in our analysis. We all know of the maroons, the slaves who fled the plantations in North America as well as the Caribbean and South America. But this kind of resistance is not confined to the New World. Already in the ninth century the *Zanj*, slaves of East-African origin working in the salt marshes of South Iraq, left their masters as a group and constructed the city of Al Mukhtara, in a spot chosen for its inaccessibility.[60] And at the mainland coast of Tanganyika in 1873, plantation slaves fled in huge numbers and founded the village of Makorora, 'hidden in a thicket of thorny bushes' and with 'heavy fortifications'.[61] In 1921 coolies on tea plantations in the Chargola Valley in Assam protested when the authorities refused a wage increase. They deserted the plantations en masse: 'They resolved to go back to their home districts, chanting victory cries to Mahatma Gandhi and claiming to have served under his orders.' Soon:

> the entire Chargola valley looked deserted, with two gardens reported to have 'lost' virtually their entire labour force, and on an average,

> most gardens had suffered losses of around thirty to sixty percent. The coolies of Chargola Valley marched right through Karimganj, the subdivisional headquarters, continuing their onward journey either by train or on foot, and also by steamer they made their way back to their home districts.[62]

Against this background, the strikes of so-called free wage-earners constitute just *one* form of collective resistance against the exploitation of commodified labour. And we should also acknowledge that, conversely, free wage labourers have often used methods of struggle which are usually associated with other groups of subaltern workers, such as lynching, rioting, arson, and bombing. By broadening our view on commodified labour under capitalism, we will be better placed to write the history of all those anonymous individuals and families who, as Bertolt Brecht, wrote, 'built Thebes of the seven gates', and so often 'cooked the feast for the victors'.

Teleconnections

While we can reconstruct the great diversity and logics of workers' experiences and actions in this way, the global interconnections between those experiences and actions also demand our attention. Such interconnections were often recognized in the past but they have been neglected equally often by labour historians to the present day.

Rosa Luxemburg devoted attention to them when, in the years immediately preceding the First World War, she worked on an (unfinished) manuscript published posthumously under the title *Introduction to Political Economy*. Early in this study, she engages in a polemic against Karl Bücher, a prominent representative of the Historical School who denied the existence of a world economy.[63] In order to prove the contrary, Luxemburg pointed to the reality of global social, political and economic entanglements. In just a few pages, she illuminated how the mechanization of the British textile industry at the end of the eighteenth century for the most part destroyed manual weaving in Britain, while at the same time it increased the demand for cotton produced by North American slaves. When the transatlantic trade stagnated during the American Civil War between 1861 and 1865, the resulting Lancashire 'cotton famine' entailed not only the pauperization of British workers. It also led to the emigration of workers to Australia, and increased cotton production in Egypt and India. There, the farmers were robbed of their means of subsistence by commercialization, causing, among other things, more famines.[64]

Luxemburg elaborated her example in greater detail. But what is of primary interest here is the fact that she presented a narrative showing the real impact of connections between developments in different continents. She demonstrated how the destinies of North American slaves, British textile workers, small farmers in Egypt and India, and Australian immigrants were bound up with each other. Her story is based on changes within just one commodity chain (cotton), but she is attentive to the wider social causes and implications of those changes. In drawing these out, she provided a wonderful example of what a global history of the subaltern working class *could* look like. Of course, other angles are also conceivable but the focus of global labour history should be, I think, on reconstructing the global interconnections of commodified labour relations and their consequences.

We could also call such connections *teleconnections*, following the example of geologists and climatologists who, since the beginning of the twentieth century, have demonstrated many linkages between regions located at a remote distance from each other.[65] In reality, the immediate interests of workers in one part of the world can have direct repercussions for the immediate interests of workers in another. Such entanglements emerge in all kinds of ways. A valid general theory about them would require much more research and a few examples must suffice here simply to illustrate what is at stake:

* *Labour processes in different locations can be linked via global commodity chains.* Luis Valenzuela, for example, shows how from the 1830s through to the 1860s a very close nexus existed between Chilean copper miners and British copper smelters in Swansea (South Wales): 'Large quantities of Chilean copper and regulus arrived in the Swansea docks to be smelted and refined in the South Wales furnaces. On the other hand, Welsh coal and firebricks as well as other British produce were shipped from South Wales to Chilean ports close to the mines to pay for that copper and, incidentally, stimulated mining and smelting production.'[66]
* *Labour processes are themselves sometimes intrinsically international.* Transport workers such as seamen and longshoremen constitute 'natural' liaisons between regions separated by long distances. Already in the sixteenth and seventeenth centuries, perhaps even earlier, they made logistical connections between subaltern workers in different continents. Seamen 'influenced both the form and the content of plebeian protest by their militant presence in seaport crowds' and 'used their mobility [...] to create links with other working people'.[67] Transport workers have figured prominently in the transcontinental dissemination of forms of collective action, as shown by the diffusion of the model of

the Industrial Workers of the World from the United States to places like Chile, Australia, New Zealand, and South Africa. Moreover, in 1911 they were the first to organize transcontinental collective action, through simultaneous strikes in Britain, the Netherlands, Belgium and on the East Coast of the United States.[68]

* *Migrants can impart their experiences to other workers in the country of settlement* – as Indian workers did in the Caribbean and South-East Asia, British workers did in Australia, Italian workers did in the Americas, and Chinese workers did in the Asian Diaspora. Their presence in the new country may cause segmentation of its labour markets, which might in turn lead to forms of ethnically segregated action. And returning migrants may import back to their countries of origin a repertoire of forms of collective action from their respective countries of temporary residence.[69]
* *The employers' capital likewise realizes transcontinental entanglements.* The staffs of multinational firms are mutually connected via corporate structures – a phenomenon which does not date from the last hundred and fifty years, but is already at least four hundred years old.[70]
* *Consumption by subaltern workers of products produced by subaltern workers elsewhere* is another relationship. The increased use of sugar by workers in Europe in the eighteenth century influenced the activities of slaves in the sugar plantations of the New World. The inverse also seems to apply. For example, Sidney Mintz suggests that sugar made the diet of workers in England more varied and richer, and therefore promoted the industrial revolution.[71]
* *The fate of subaltern workers can be mediated by government agencies.* The introduction of immigration restrictions by nation-states from the last decades of the nineteenth century is probably also bound up with the abolition of slavery, the emancipation of the serfs in Russia and other developments which promoted the mobility of subaltern workers.
* *Last, but not at least, transnational waves of collective action* should be mentioned. In addition to instigating the first Russian Revolution in 1905, the Japanese victory over Russia promoted nationalist and anti-colonial forces throughout Asia, and encouraged workers' collective action in many places.[72] The second Russian Revolution from March 1917 and the Bolshevik seizure of power, inspired an explosive increase of workers' collective action on all continents.[73] The Hungarian uprising of 1956 – influenced by the earlier unrest in Poznan – was a powerful stimulus for labour unrest in Shanghai the following year.[74]

Conclusion

The rise of global labour history means that we will have to integrate the insights of old and new labour history within a new perspective. This perspective will also allow a fresh look at the North Atlantic region, paying serious attention to informal labour relations, debt bondage, and so forth. In that sense labour history may return to its historical point of departure. At the same time, a global approach stimulates research questions that could not even be asked before – for instance the global connections between groups of the extended working class through 'commodity chains', the logic of global class segmentation, or the history 'from below' of multinational corporations.

The Austrian polymath Otto Neurath once wrote that scholars are like sailors,

> who at high sea want to change the shape of their unwieldy ship. For the remodelling of the ship's skeleton and hull they use not only the old construction's boards, but also driftwood. They cannot dock the ship and start afresh. While working, they stay on board of the old construction and weather heavy storms and thundering waves. During the reconstruction they take care that no leak is springing. A new ship grows out of the old, step by step.[75]

This seems to apply to global labour historians as well. But their task is even more daunting. Driftwood doesn't suffice for them; they have to build a new, much bigger and yet manoeuvrable vessel together with the crews of other ships, like the sailors aboard the frigate of slave history.

Notes

1 In German, for example, there exist both *Arbeitergeschichte* and *Arbeiterbewegungsgeschichte*, and in French *histoire du mouvement ouvrier* and *histoire ouvriere.*

2 For overviews, see the introduction to *Class and Other Identities: Gender, Religion and Ethnicity in the Writing of European Labour History*, ed. by Lex Heerma van Voss and Marcel van der Linden (New York and Oxford: Berghahn Books, 2002), pp. 1–39, and Jan Lucassen, 'Writing Global Labour History *c.* 1800–1940: A Historiography of Concepts, Periods and Geographical Scope', in *Global Labour History: A State of the Art*, ed. by Jan Lucassen (Bern: Peter Lang, 2006), pp. 39–89.

3 John Stuart Mill, 'Thornton on Labour and Its Claims' [a review of W.T. Thornton, *On Labour, Its Wrongful Claims and Rightful Dues, Its Actual Present*

and Possible Future (London, 1869)], *Fortnightly Review*, May 1869, reprinted in John Stuart Mill, *Collected Works*, vol. 5, ed. by John M. Robson (Toronto: University of Toronto Press, 1967), pp. 631–68.

4 Although a second round of discussion took place between the mid-1880s and the mid-1890s. Scott Gordon, 'The Wage-Fund Controversy: The Second Round', *History of Political Economy*, 5 (1973), 14–35.

5 For another explanation see T.W. Hutchison, 'The "Marginal Revolution" and the Decline and Fall of English Classical Political Economy', in *The Marginal Revolution in Economics: Interpretation and Evaluation*, ed. by R.D. Collison Black, A.W. Coats and D.W. Goodwin (Durham: Duke University Press, 1973), pp. 176–202 (pp. 194–202).

6 See James J. Sheehan, *The Career of Lujo Brentano: A Study of Liberalism and Reform in Imperial Germany* (Chicago: University of Chicago Press, 1966); E.P. Hennock, 'Lessons from England: Lujo Brentano on British Trade Unionism', *German History*, 11 (1993), 141–60; Benjamin G. Rader, *The Academic Mind and Reform: The Influence of Richard T. Ely in American Life* (Lexington: University of Kentucky Press, 1966).

7 James E. Thorold Rogers, *Six Centuries of Work and Wages* (London: Swan and Sonnenschein, 1884).

8 James Guillaume, *L'Internationale: documents et souvenirs (1864–1878)*, 4 vols (Paris: Société nouvelle de librairie et d'édition, 1905–1910); G.D.H. Cole, *The Second International 1889–1914*, 2 vols (London: Macmillan, 1956); Julius Braunthal, *Geschichte der Internationale*, 3 vols (Hanover: Dietz, 1961–1971).

9 Kevin Callahan, '"Performing Inter-Nationalism" in Stuttgart in 1907: French and German Socialist Nationalism and the Political Culture of an International Socialist Congress', *International Review of Social History*, 45 (2000), 51–87.

10 Leonard Binder, 'The Natural History of Modernization Theory', *Comparative Studies in Society and History*, 28 (1986), 3–33.

11 Robert Nisbet, 'Ethnocentrism and the Comparative Method', in *Essays on Modernization of Underdeveloped Societies*, ed. by A.R. Desai (Bombay: Thacker, 1971), vol. 1, pp. 95–114 (p. 101). Nisbet noted that Eurocentrism (at that time still called Ethnocentrism) is symbolized according to a biological metaphor of growth and development: societies are a bit like plants which emerge from seed and develop into mature organisms. This growth metaphor is based on at least five additional assumptions: 'This meant, in the first place, that change is normally *continuous*. That is, each identifiable condition of a thing, be it a tree, a man, or a culture, is to be understood as having grown out of a preceding condition of that same thing. Second, large changes are to be understood as the *cumulative*, as well as incremental consequence of a host of small changes. Third, social change is characterized by *differentiation*. Precisely as the seed or fertilized germ cell is marked by differentiation and variegation of function and form in its history, so is the human culture or institution similarly marked by this kind of manifestation over time. Fourth, change of a developmental sort is regarded as caused for the most part by some persisting, *uniform* property or set of properties. From the doctrine of uniformity came the belief that social conflict, cooperation, geographic location, race, or any of

the other alleged causes so richly strewn across the pages of social history, are the prime and continuing cause of all development. Fifth, it is clear that in all of these theories of social development a kind of *teleology* is present. Always there is some "end" in view.' The 'end' is conceived 'in purely Western terms.' (Ibid., p. 100.)

12 James Blaut, *The Colonizer's Model of the World* (New York: The Guilford Press, 1993), p. 9.

13 Lucien Febvre, 'How Jules Michelet Invented the Renaissance' (1st pub. 1950), in *A New Kind of History: From the Writings of Febvre*, ed. by Peter Burke (London: Routledge and Kegan Paul, 1973), pp. 258–67 (p. 258).

14 David Brody, 'Reconciling the Old Labor History and the New', *Pacific Historical Review*, 62 (1993), 1–18.

15 The terms 'old' and 'new' labour history seem to have been invented in the USA around 1970: see Thomas A. Krueger, 'American Labor Historiography, Old and New: A Review Essay', *Journal of Social History*, 4 (1971), 277–85. A kind of codification of the distinction can be found in David Brody's article 'The Old Labor History and the New: In Search of an American Working Class', *Labour History*, 20 (1979), 111–26.

16 Eric J. Hobsbawm, *Labouring Men: Studies in the History of Labour* (London: Weidenfeld and Nicolson, 1964), p. 4.

17 Peter Linebaugh and Marcus Rediker, *The Many-Headed Hydra: The Hidden History of the Revolutionary Atlantic* (Boston: Beacon Press, 2000), p. 274.

18 Bryan D. Palmer, *E.P. Thompson: Objections and Oppositions* (London: Verso, 1994), pp. 11–51. See also E.P. Thompson, *Making History: Writings on History and Culture* (New York: The New Press, 1994), pp. 200–25, and Tom Nairn, *The Break-Up of Britain: Crisis and Neo-Nationalism* (2nd edn, London: Verso, 1977), pp. 303–4.

19 Mikhail I. Tugan-Baranovskii, *The Russian Factory in the Nineteenth Century* (Homewood: R.D. Irwin for the American Economic Association, 1970); Rajani Kanta Das, *Factory Labour in India* (Berlin and Leipzig: W. de Gruyter, 1923); idem, *Factory Legislation in India.* With an Introduction by John R. Commons (Berlin and Leipzig: W. de Gruyter, 1923); idem, *The Labour Movement in India* (Berlin and Leipzig: W. de Gruyter, 1923); Marjorie Ruth Clarke, *Organized Labour in Mexico* (1st pub. 1934; New York: Russell and Russell, 1973).

20 Some Japanese developments are described in Carol Gluck, 'The People in History: Recent Trends in Japanese Historiography', *Journal of Asian Studies*, 38 (1978–79), 25–50. Innovation was not restricted to this 'romantic' approach, however; see, for example, Kazuo Nimura, *The Ashio Riot of 1907: A Social History of Mining in Japan*, ed. by Andrew Gordon (Durham: Duke University Press, 1997), and Takao Matsumura, John McIlroy and Alan Campbell, 'Japan', chapter 10 in this volume. On Australian labour history, see Lucy Taksa, 'What's in a Name? Labouring Antipodean History in Oceania', in Lucassen, *Global Labour History*, pp. 335–71, and Greg Patmore, 'Australia', chapter 7 in this volume.

21 Emil Niederhauser, 'Die marxistische Geschichtswissenschaft in Osteuropa',

Österreichische Osthefte, 29 (1987), 147–57 (p. 149).

22 Zenobiusz Kozik gives an English-language survey of the history of Polish workers in 'Research into the History of the Working Class Movement in Poland in the Years 1945–1987', in *La science historique polonaise dans l'historiographie mondiale*, ed. by Marian Leczyk (Wrocław: Wydawnictwo Polskiej Akademii Nauk, 1990), pp. 421–47. See also *Workers, Women, and Social Change in Poland, 1870–1939*, ed. by Anna Zarnowska (Aldershot: Ashgate Variorum, 2004). Hartmut Zwahr single-handedly created a research tradition in the GDR, which, to some extent, was parallel to its Polish counterpart. His ground-breaking work was *Zur Konstituierung des Proletariats als Klasse: Strukturuntersuchungen über das Leipziger Proletariat während der industriellen Revolution* (Berlin: Akademie-Verlag, 1978), on the formation of the working class in Leipzig during the nineteenth century. On developments in China, see Mechtild Leutner, 'Sozialgeschichte in der VR China: Modernisierungsparadigma statt Marxismus?', *Berliner China-Hefte*, 11 (1996), 47–63; and Arif Dirlik, 'Workers, Class, and the Socialist Revolution in Modern China', in Lucassen, *Global Labour History*, pp. 373–95.

23 There was a 'constantly lamented reluctance of Soviet historians to work upon the October Revolution and the years after 1918': Anatole G. Mazour and Herman E. Bateman, 'Recent Conflict in Soviet Historiography', *Journal of Modern History*, 24 (1952), 56–68 (p. 66). From 1956 the Soviet Union underwent a ten-year period of thaw. Subsequently, a new dogmatism gained precedence, which only lost ground from around 1987. See the introduction in Robert W. Davies, *Soviet History in the Gorbachev Revolution* (Basingstoke: Macmillan, 1989). For the period 1956–66, see also Nancy Whittier Heer, *Politics and History in the Soviet Union* (Cambridge, MA: Harvard University Press, 1971). A similar avoidance of post-1917 history could also be seen amongst Communist historians in the North Atlantic region, for example in the British Communist Party Historians' Group which included Eric Hobsbawm, John Saville, and E.P. Thompson.

24 On developments in Russia, see Andrei Sokolov, 'The Drama of the Russian Working Class and New Perspectives for Labour History in Russia', in Lucassen, *Global Labour History*, pp. 397–452.

25 Naturally, there are exceptions to this rule. This is particularly true for some Arabic countries where historiography is in a crisis, due to research being hampered by strict Islamic interpretation and political repression. In a few cases labour history briefly flourished and then almost disappeared again. This was the case in Nigeria, where the historiography developed rapidly from the 1950s but had a strong political orientation and occupied itself primarily with decolonization. The historians' community split in the 1970s between traditionalists and reformers. The reformer wing provided impulses for the study of labour history, but this tendency ended in a cul-de-sac in the 1980s, probably on account of the wretched state of the country. Another symptom of decline was the fact that the *Journal of the Historical Society of Nigeria*, which was founded 1956 and had published a number of labour history pieces, ceased publication in 1985. The study of history in Nigeria, Dibua

noted in 1997, 'is being threatened with extinction': J.I. Dibua, 'The Idol, Its Worshippers, and the Crisis of Relevance of Historical Scholarship in Nigeria', *History in Africa*, 24 (1997), 117–37 (p. 117). See also Toyin Falola's interim report, 'Trends in Nigerian Historiography', *Transafrican Journal of History*, 10 (1981), 96–112; and A.O. Adeoye, 'Understanding the Crisis in Modern Nigerian Historiography', *History in Africa*, 19 (1992), 1–11. For a general survey of African labour history, see Andreas Eckert, 'Geschichte der Arbeit und Arbeitergeschichte in Afrika', *Archiv für Sozialgeschichte*, 39 (1999), 502–30.

26 J. Norman Parmer, *Colonial Labour Policy and Administration: A History of Labour in the Rubber Plantation Industry in Malaya, c. 1910–1941* (Locust Valley, NY: Association for Asian Studies, 1960); Jean Chesneaux, *Le mouvement ouvrier en Chine de 1919 à 1927* (Paris: Mouton, 1962); Guillermo Lora, *Historia del movimiento obrero boliviana*, 3 vols (La Paz: Editorial 'Los Amigos del Libre', 1967–70).

27 John D. French, 'Latin American and International Working Class History on the Brink of the 21st Century: Points of Departure in Comparative Labour Studies', *Development and Society* [Seoul National University], 29, 2 (2000), 137–63 (pp. 138–39). See also idem, 'The Latin American Labor Studies Boom', *International Review of Social History*, 45 (2000), 279–308.

28 Jon Lewis, 'South African Labor History: A Historiographical Assessment', *Radical History Review*, 46–47 (1990), 213–35 (p. 213).

29 Ibid., 218.

30 Belinda Bozzoli, 'Intellectuals, Audiences and Histories: South African Experiences, 1978–88', *Radical History Review*, 46/47 (1990), 237–63; Philip Bonner, 'New Nation, New History: The History Workshop in South Africa, 1977–1994', *Journal of American History*, 81 (1994), 977–85; Alan Cobley, 'Does Social History Have a Future? The Ending of Apartheid and Recent Trends in South African Historiography', *Journal of Southern African Studies*, 27 (2001), 613–25; Martin Legassick, 'The Past and Present of Marxist Historiography in South Africa', *Radical History Review*, 82 (2002), 111–30.

31 On early Indian labour history, see Sanat Bose, 'Indian Labour and Its Historiography in Pre-Independence Period', *Social Scientist*, 143 (1985), 3–10; and Ranajit Das Gupta, 'Indian Working Class and Some Recent Historiographical Issues', *Economic and Political Weekly*, 31–8 (24 February 1996), 27–31. The break-through in the late 1960s is noticeable in the *Proceedings of the Indian History Congress* from 1968 onwards. See also Rana P. Behal, Chitra Joshi and Prabhu P. Mohapatra, 'India', chapter 9 in this volume.

32 Ranajit Das Gupta is perhaps the most important example. Some of his essays are collected in *Labour and Working Class in Eastern India: Studies in Colonial History* (Calcutta: K.P. Bagchi, 1994).

33 Shahid Amin, *Sugarcane and Sugar in Gorakpur: An Inquiry into Peasant Production for Capitalist Enterprise in Colonial India* (Delhi: Oxford University Press, 1984); Dipesh Chakrabarty, *Rethinking Working-Class History: Bengal, 1890–1940* (Princeton: Princeton University Press, 1989); Gyan Prakash,

Bonded Histories: Genealogies of Labour Servitude in Colonial India (Cambridge: Cambridge University Press, 1990).

34 For devastating critiques of Subaltern Studies, see Vinay Bahl, 'Situating and Rethinking Subaltern Studies for Writing Working-Class History', in *History after the Three Worlds: Post-Eurocentric Historiographies*, ed. by Arif Dirlik, Vinay Bahl and Peter Gran (Lanham: Rowman and Littlefield, 2000), pp. 85–124; Vasant Kaiwar, 'Towards Orientalism and Nativism: The Impasse of Subaltern Studies', *Historical Materialism*, 12 (2004), 189–247.

35 Important publications from this circle include Dilip Simeon, *The Politics of Labour under Late Colonialism: Workers, Unions and the State in Chota Nagpur, 1928–1939* (Delhi: Manohar, 1995); Janaki Nair, *Miners and Millhands: Work, Culture and Politics in Princely Mysore* (New Delhi: Sage, 1998); Samita Sen, *Women and Labour in Late Colonial India: The Bengal Jute Industry* (Cambridge: Cambridge University Press, 1999); Rajnarayan Chandavarkar, *The Origins of Industrial Capitalism in India: Business Strategies and the Working Classes in Bombay, 1900–1940* (Cambridge: Cambridge University Press, 1994); idem, *Imperial Power and Popular Politics: Class, Resistance and the State in India, c.1850–1950* (Cambridge: Cambridge University Press, 1998); Chitra Joshi, *Lost Worlds of Indian Labour and its Forgotten Histories* (Delhi: Permanent Black, 2003); *India's Labouring Poor: Historical Studies c.1600–c 2000*, ed. by Rana Behal and Marcel van der Linden (Delhi: Foundation Books, 2007).

36 For example on Latin America: Robert J. Alexander, *Communism in Latin America* (New Brunswick: Rutgers University Press, 1957); idem, *The Communist Party of Venezuela* (Stanford: Hoover Institution Press, 1969); Boris Goldenberg, *Kommunismus in Lateinamerika* (Stuttgart: Kohlhammer, 1971). On South-East Asia: Ruth Thomas McVey, *The Rise of Indonesian Communism* (Ithaca: Cornell University Press, 1965). On Eastern Asia: Robert A. Scalapino, *The Japanese Communist Movement, 1920–1966* (Berkeley: University of California Press, 1967); idem and Chong-Sik Lee, *Communism in Korea* (Berkeley: University of California Press, 1972). As late as 1983, Scalapino published *The Early Japanese Labour Movement: Labour and Politics in a Developing Society* (Berkeley: Center for Japanese Studies, 1983), a study which according to the preface dated December 1982, 'was completed precisely twenty years ago with the exception of the final "summary chapter"'. See also the bibliography in Enrica Colotti-Pischel and Chiara Robertazzi, *L'Internationale Communiste et les problèmes coloniaux 1919–1935* (Paris: Mouton, 1968).

37 For instance in France: Jean Suret-Canale, *L'Afrique noire – l'ère coloniale* (Paris: Editions Sociales, 1964); Chesneaux, *Le mouvement ouvrier chinois de 1919 à 1927*; the English version is *The Chinese Labour Movement, 1919–1927* (Stanford: Stanford University Press, 1968). Chesneaux even developed a schema for western historians of the Chinese working class. See his 'Perspectives des études d'histoire contemporaine chinoise', *Archív Orientální*, 31 (1963), 310–20. For an evaluation of Chesneaux's work, see Dirlik, 'Workers, Class, and the Socialist Revolution'.

38 For instance, Manfred Pohl, *Die Bauernpolitik der Kommunistischen Partei*

Japans, 1922–1928 (Hamburg: Mitteilungen der Gesellschaft für Natur- und Völkerkunde Ostasiens, vol. 62, 1976); Regine Mathias, *Industrialisierung und Lohnarbeit: Der Kohlebergbau in Nord-Kyushu und sein Einfluss auf die Herausbildung einer Lohnarbeiterschaft* (Vienna: Beiträge zur Japanologie, vol. 15, 1978). See also Bill Freund's survey, 'Labour and Labour History in Africa: A Review of the Literature', *African Studies Review*, 27, 2 (1984), 1–58, which discusses not only African but also many European and North American studies.

39 On the Australian society and its journal *Labour History*, see Eric Fry, 'The Labour History Society (ASSLH): A Memoir of its First Twenty Years', *Labour History*, 77 (1999), 83-96, and Greg Patmore, '"The Right Wing Won't Write" – *Labour History* in 1962', *Labour History*, 82 (2002), vii–ix. See also Patmore, 'Australia'.

40 The idea for this association arose during the first conference on Indian labour history, with the title 'South Asian Labour: Local and Global Linkages', held in October 1995 at the International Institute of Social History in Amsterdam (convenors: Prabhu Mohapatra and Marcel van der Linden). The association was founded at a meeting at Jawaharwal Nehru University in New Delhi in December 1996, and has organized bi-annual conferences since 1998. See http://www.indialabourarchives.org/ailh.htm.

41 See http://www.ifch.unicamp.br/mundosdotrabalho/.

42 The convenors of the Karachi workshop were Kamran Asdar Ali (University of Rochester, USA), Karamat Ali (PILER) and Yunas Samad (University of Bradford, UK). See the report: Yunas Samad and Kamran Asdar Ali, 'Labour in Pakistan', *International Labor and Working-Class History*, 58 (2000), 314–17. A report on the Seoul conference was published by the convenor Lim Jie-Hyun, 'From Hard History to Soft History: Cultural Histories of the Korean Working Class', *International Labor and Working-Class History*, 61 (2002), 169–72. The convenors of the Yogyakarta workshop were Jan Elliott (Wollongong University, Australia), Erwiza Erman (LIPI, Yogyakarta, Indonesia) and Ratna Saptari (IISH, Amsterdam, The Netherlands). A report has not been published. The proceedings of the second Johannesburg conference have been published in 'Transnational and Comparative Perspectives on Southern African Labour History', ed. by Philip Bonner, Jonathan Hyslop and Lucien van der Walt, Special Issue of *African Studies*, 66, 2–3 (2007), 137–385. A first conference on Iranian labour history was organized by exiles at the International Institute of Social History in Amsterdam. Convenors were Touraj Atabaki and Marcel van der Linden. See 'Twentieth-Century Iran: History from Below', ed. by Touraj Atabaki and Marcel van der Linden, Special Theme in *International Review of Social History*, 48 (2003), 353–455.

43 The historiography of the Internationals began at the latest with James Guillaume's study of the International Workers' Association, *L'Internationale*. For an overview of the relevant literature until the middle of the 1980s, see: Marcel van der Linden, 'Internationalism in the Labour Movement, 1830–1940: Fragments of a Bibliography', in *Internationalism in the Labour Movement, 1830–1940*, vol. 2, ed. by Frits L. van Holthoon and Marcel van der

Linden (Leiden: Brill, 1988), pp. 624–54.

44 The official name of *Grünbergs Archiv* was *Archiv für die Geschichte des Sozialismus und der Arbeiterbewegung.* The *International Review for Social History* was continued after 1956 as the *International Review of Social History.*

45 Helmut Konrad, 'Die Krise überwunden: Die Linzer Konferenzen der ITH gehen ins vierte Jahrzehnt', *Internationale wissenschaftliche Korrespondenz zur Geschichte der deutschen Arbeiterbewegung,* 30 (1994), 575–78. On the ITH's prehistory, and the central role that Austrian archivist Rudolf Neck (1921–99) played in it, see Herbert Steiner, 'Internationale Tagung der Historiker der Arbeiterbewegung', in *Politik und Gesellschaft im alten und neuen Österreich: Festschrift für Rudolf Neck zum 60. Geburtstag,* vol. 2, ed. by Isabella Ackerl, Walter Hummelberger, and Hans Mommsen (Munich: Oldenbourg, 1981), pp. 351–58. The ITH proceedings were published regularly under the title *International Tagung der Historiker der Arbeiterbewegung.* Well into the 1990s there were scarcely any substantive criteria used in selecting papers for this publication.

46 On the history written outside Europe as the historiography of the '(not) yet', and of 'absences', see Dipesh Chakrabarty, 'Postcoloniality and the Artifice of History: Who Speaks for "Indian" Pasts?', *Representations,* 37 (1992), 1–26. It is interesting to note that the Subaltern Studies project (in which Chakrabarty participated) could not escape this problem. The announcement of the project was worded as follows: 'The central problematic of the historiography of colonial India' was the 'historical failure of the nation to come into its own, a failure due to the inadequacy of the bourgeoisie as well as of the working class to lead it to a decisive victory over colonialism and a bourgeois-democratic revolution of the classic nineteenth-century type.' Ranajit Guha, 'On Some Aspects of the Historiography of Colonial India', in *Selected Subaltern Studies,* ed. by Ranajit Guha and Gayatri Chakravorty Spivak (New York: Oxford University Press, 1988), pp. 37–43 (p. 43). This 'problematic', although couched in Comintern phraseology, is really a Western topos. See also Rajnarayan Chandavarkar, '"The Making of the Working Class": E.P. Thompson and Indian History', *History Workshop Journal,* 43 (1997), 177–96 (p. 182).

47 Walter Rodney, *A History of the Upper Guinea Coast, 1545–1800* (Oxford: Clarendon Press, 1970); idem, *A History of the Guyanese Working People, 1881–1905* (Baltimore: John Hopkins University Press, 1981); Charles van Onselen, *Chibaro: African Mine Labour in Southern Rhodesia* (Johannesburg: Ravan Press, 1976); Gupta, *Labour and Working Class in Eastern India.*

48 Werner Sombart, *Why Is There No Socialism in the United States?* (London: Macmillan, 1976; originally published in German in a series of articles in 1905). The year 1922 seems to have been a miracle year for explicitly comparative labour history. See Hans Bötcher, *Zur revolutionären Gewerkschaftsbewegung in Amerika, Deutschland und England: Eine vergleichende Betrachtung* (Jena: Gustav Fischer, 1922); Edvard Bull, *Den Skandinaviske Arbeiderbevegelse, 1914–1920* (Kristiania: Det Norske Arbeiderparti, 1922); Bo-Gabriel de Montgomery, *British and Continental Labour Politics: The Political Labour Movement and Labour Legislation in Great Britain, France and the*

Scandinavian Countries, 1900–1922 (London: Kegan Paul, Trench, Trubner, 1922). Comparative studies of labour conditions were older than this; see, e.g., Carl Kindermann, *Zur organischen Güterverteilung, II: Die Glasarbeiter Deutschlands und der Vereinigten Staaten von Amerika in ihrer allgemeinen materiellen Lage* (Leipzig: Duncker and Humblot, 1896), on glass workers in Germany and the United States. More extensive bibliographical information on the further development of comparative labour history can be found in 'Multiple Country Surveys of West European Labour History', in Heerma van Voss and van der Linden, *Class and Other Identities*, pp. 186–90, and in Marcel van der Linden, 'A Bibliography of Comparative Labour History', in *Australian Labour and Regional Change: Essays in Honour of R.A. Gollan*, ed. by Jim Hagan and Andrew Wells (Rushcutters Bay, NSW: Halstead Press, 1998), pp. 117–45.

49 Marcel van der Linden, *Workers of the World: Essays toward a Global Labour History* (Leiden: Brill, 2008).

50 That it is possible to build a well-functioning archive with modest financial means is shown by the example of the V.V. Giri National Labour Institute in Noida, India.

51 Hannah Arendt, *The Human Condition* (Chicago: Chicago University Press, 1958).

52 Karl Marx, *Capital*, vol. I, (Harmondsworth: Penguin, 1976), p. 272.

53 A fuller argumentation is given in my book *Workers of the World*, Chapter 2.

54 João José Reis, '"The Revolution of the Ganhadores": Urban Labour, Ethnicity and the African Strike of 1857 in Bahia, Brazil', *Journal of Latin American Studies*, 29 (1997), 355–93.

55 Cornelius Castoriadis, *The Imaginary Institution of Society* (Cambridge: Polity Press, 1987), p. 109.

56 G.A. Cohen, *Karl Marx's Theory of History: A Defence* (Oxford: Clarendon Press, 1978), p. 72.

57 Cheryl English Martin, *Governance and Society in Colonial Mexico: Chihuahua in the Eighteenth Century* (Stanford: Stanford University Press, 1996), p. 51.

58 Peter Kolchin, *Unfree Labour: American Slavery and Russian Serfdom* (Cambridge, MA: Belknap Press, 1987), p. 258.

59 Monica Schuler, 'Akan Slave Rebellions in the British Carribean', in *Caribbean Slave Society and Economy: A Student Reader*, ed. by Hilary Beckles and Verene Shepherd (Kingston and London: Currey, 1991), pp. 373–86 (pp. 382–83).

60 Alexandre Popovic, *La Révolte des esclaves en Iraq au IIIe, Ixe siècle* (Paris: P. Geuthner, 1976); idem, 'Al-Mukhtara', *The Encyclopaedia of Islam. New Edition*, vol. VII (Leiden: Brill, 1993), p. 526; idem, 'Al-Zandj. 2. The Zandj Revolts in Irak', *The Encyclopaedia of Islam. New Edition*, vol. XI (Leiden: Brill, 2002), pp. 445–46. The rebellion was crushed in 883.

61 Jonathan Glassman, 'The Bondsman's New Clothes: The Contradictory Consciousness of Slave Resistance on the Swahili Coast', *Journal of African History*, 32 (1991), 277–312 (p. 308).

62 NitinVarma, 'Chargola Exodus and Collective Action in the Colonial Tea Plantations of Assam', *SEPHISe-magazine* [http://sephisemagazine.org/issues/

vol._3_2.pdf], 2 (January 2007), 34–37 (p. 34).

63 Karl Bücher, *Die Entstehung der Volkswirtschaft: Vorträge und Versuche* (Tübingen: H. Laupp'sche Buchhandlung, 1906), p. 142.

64 Rosa Luxemburg, 'Einführung in die Nationalökonomie,' in Rosa Luxemburg, *Gesammelte Werke*, vol. 5 (Berlin: Dietz, 1985), pp. 524–778 (pp. 557–60).

65 See van der Linden, *Workers of the World*, pp. 373–74.

66 Luis Valenzuela, 'Copper: Chilean Miners – British Smelters in the Mid-Nineteenth Century,' in *World Development: An Introduction*, ed. by Prodromos Panayiotopoulos and Gavin Capps (London and Sterling, VA: Pluto Press, 2001), pp. 173–80 (p. 177).

67 Marcus Rediker, *Between the Devil and the Deep Blue Sea: Merchant Seamen, Pirates, and the Anglo-American Maritime World, 1700–1750* (Cambridge: Cambridge University Press, 1987), p. 294; Linebaugh and Rediker, *The Many-Headed Hydra.*

68 On the IWW model, see Verity Burgman, *Revolutionary Industrial Unionism: The IWW in Australia* (Melbourne: Cambridge University Press, 1996); Erik Olssen, *The Red Feds: Revolutionary Industrial Unionism and the New Zealand Federation of Labour 1908–1914* (Oxford: Oxford University Press, 1988); John Philips, 'The South African Wobblies: The Origin of Industrial Unions in South Africa', *Ufahamu*, 8 (1978), 122–38; Fanny S. Simon, 'Anarchism and Anarcho-Syndicalism in South America,' *Hispanic American Historical Review*, 26 (1946), 38–59; Lucien van der Walt, '"The Industrial Union is the Embryo of the Socialist Commonwealth": The International Socialist League and Revolutionary Syndicalism in South Africa, 1915–1920', *Comparative Studies of South Asia, Africa and the Middle East*, 19 (1999), 5–30. On the 1911 strike see Marcel van der Linden, 'Transport Workers' Strike, Worldwide 1911', in *St. James Encyclopedia of Labor History Worldwide: Major Events in Labor History and Their Impact*, 2 vols, ed. by Neil Schlager (Detroit: Thomson and Gale, 2003), vol. II, pp. 334–36.

69 See, for example, Sandew Hira, *Van Priary tot en met de Kom: De geschiedenis van het verzet in Suriname, 1630-1940* (Rotterdam: Futile, 1982); Chandra Jayawardena, 'Culture and Ethnicity in Guyana and Fiji', *Man*, New Series, 15 (1980), 430–50; Prabhu Mohapatra, 'The Hosay Massacre of 1884: Class and Community among Indian Immigrant Labourers in Trinidad', in *Work and Social Change in Asia: Essays in Honour of Jan Breman*, ed. by Arvind N. Das and Marcel van der Linden (New Delhi: Manohar, 2003), pp. 187–230; Seymour Martin Lipset, 'Radicalism or Reformism: The Sources of Working Class Politics', *American Political Science Review*, 77 (1983), 1–18; Donna Gabaccia, 'The "Yellow Peril" and the "Chinese of Europe": Global Perspectives on Race and Labor, 1815–1930,' in *Migration, Migration History, History*, ed. by Jan Lucassen and Leo Lucassen (Berne: Peter Lang, 1997), pp. 177–96; Touraj Atabaki, 'Disgruntled Guests: Iranian Subaltern on the Margins of the Tsarist Empire', *International Review of Social History*, 48 (2003), 401–26.

70 Jan Lucassen, 'A Multinational and its Labor Force: The Dutch East India Company, 1595–1795', *International Labor and Working-Class History*, 66 (2004), 12–39; Giovanni Arrighi, Kenneth Barr and Shuji Hisaeda,

'The Transformation of Business Enterprise,' in *Chaos and Governance in the Modern World System*, ed. by Giovanni Arrighi and Beverly J. Silver (Minneapolis and London: University of Minnesota Press, 1999), pp. 97–150; *Leviathans: Multinational Corporations and the New Global History*, ed. by Alfred D. Chandler Jr. and Bruce Mazlish (Cambridge: Cambridge University Press, 2005).

71 Sidney W. Mintz, *Sweetness and Power: The Place of Sugar in Modern History* (New York: Penguin, 1986), p. 183.

72 See, for example, Klaus Kreiser, 'Der japanische Sieg über Russland (1905) und sein Echo unter den Muslimen', *Die Welt des Islams*, 21 (1981), 209–39; Nader Sohrabi, 'Historicizing Revolutions: Constitutional Revolutions in the Ottoman Empire, Iran and Russia, 1905–1908', *American Journal of Sociology*, 100 (1994–5), 1383–1447.

73 See, for example, Neil McInnes, 'The Labour Movement,' in *The Impact of the Russian Revolution 1917–1967: The Influence of Bolshevism on the World outside Russia*, ed. by Jane Degras (London: Oxford University Press, 1967), pp. 32–133. The influence might be propagated either indirectly via the mass media or directly. The Iranian migrant workers who regularly came to work in Southern Russia are a case in point. In the early 1920s trade unions expanded faster in the North and Northwest of Iran than in other parts of the country thanks to the 'close proximity to Russia': Habib Ladjevardi, *Labor Unions and Autocracy in Iran* (Syracuse: Syracuse University Press, 1985), p. 8.

74 Elizabeth Perry, 'Shanghai's Strike Wave of 1957', *China Quarterly*, 137 (1994), 1–27 (p. 11).

75 Otto Neurath, 'Grundlagen der Sozialwissenschaften', in idem, *Gesammelte Schriften*, ed. by R. Haller and H. Rutte (Vienna: Hölder-Pichler-Tempsky, 1981), pp. 901–18 (p. 918).

Index